THE JUDICIAL ASSESSMENT OF EXPERT EVIDENCE

THE JUDICIAL ASSESSMENT OF EXPERT EVIDENCE

DÉIRDRE DWYER

CAMBRIDGE
UNIVERSITY PRESS

CAMBRIDGE
UNIVERSITY PRESS

University Printing House, Cambridge CB2 8BS, United Kingdom

One Liberty Plaza, 20th Floor, New York, NY 10006, USA

477 Williamstown Road, Port Melbourne, VIC 3207, Australia

314-321, 3rd Floor, Plot 3, Splendor Forum, Jasola District Centre, New Delhi - 110025, India

79 Anson Road, #06-04/06, Singapore 079906

Cambridge University Press is part of the University of Cambridge.

It furthers the University's mission by disseminating knowledge in the pursuit of education, learning and research at the highest international levels of excellence.

www.cambridge.org
Information on this title: www.cambridge.org/9780521509701

First published 2008

A catalogue record for this publication is available from the British Library

Library of Congress Cataloging in Publication data
Dwyer, Déirdre M. (Déirdre Marie), 1964–
The judicial assessment of expert evidence / Déirdre Dwyer.
p. cm.
Includes bibliographical references and index.
ISBN 978-0-521-50970-1 (hardback)
1. Evidence, Expert – Great Britain. I. Title.
KD7521.D89 2008
347.41′067–dc22 2008034103

ISBN 978-0-521-50970-1 Hardback

For William

CONTENTS

List of figures *page* xii

Preface xiii

Table of legislation xv

Table of cases xxii

Introduction 1

1 General epistemological issues 9

1.1 Introduction 9

1.2 Classical epistemology 14

1.3 Legal epistemology 19

1.3.1 What is 'legal epistemology'? 19

1.3.2 Why is legal epistemology special? 21

1.3.3 Institutional variations affecting legal epistemology 29

1.4 Justifying legal belief 40

1.4.1 Meta-justification: the Rationalist Tradition of evidence scholarship 42

1.4.2 Atomistic reasoning about individuated propositions of evidence 53

1.4.3 Generalizations as inferential glue 60

1.5 The challenge of naturalized epistemology 64

1.5.1 Strategies and shortcomings of social judgment 66

1.5.2 How people process complex specialist information 69

1.6 Conclusion 70

2. Expert evidence as a special case for judicial assessment 74

2.1 Introduction 74

2.2 Questions of fact and opinion 76

2.2.1 The nature of the distinction in English law 78

2.2.2 Operative rationales for the distinction 80

2.2.3 Philosophical difficulties with the distinction 87

2.2.4 Should legal epistemology distinguish facts from opinions? 96
2.3 The court's access to specialist knowledge 97
2.3.1 Substance-blind evidential reasoning 98
2.3.2 Common investigative method 104
2.3.3 Did Hand really present a paradox? 108
2.4 Persistent communities of practice 110
2.5 Epistemological constructivism 113
2.5.1 Definition 114
2.5.2 Epistemological constructivism in modernity 116
2.5.3 Strong epistemological constructivism 118
2.5.4 Autopoietic social systems theory 122
2.6 Conclusion 130

3. Making sense of expert disagreement 133
3.1 Introduction 133
3.2 Legal and expert factual disagreement 135
3.2.1 The need for finality in legal fact finding 135
3.2.2 Reasons for disagreement in expert fact finding 136
3.2.3 Law's perception of scientific knowledge as objective certainty 138
3.3 The selection of generalization sets 139
3.3.1 Scientific realism 140
3.3.2 Logical positivism 141
3.3.3 Scientific constructivism 143
3.4 The application of generalizations to base facts 144
3.4.1 Disagreement in interpretation is accepted 145
3.4.2 Experts do not normally address such questions 145
3.4.3 Courts require special categories to be used 146
3.4.4 Specifics from generals 146
3.5 Types of inferential challenge 147
3.5.1 The condition of a property 149
3.5.2 Quantum of damages in personal injury 149
3.5.3 Causation in personal injury 150
3.5.4 Causation in toxic torts 151
3.5.5 The best interests of the child 155
3.5.6 The standard of care in professional negligence 159
3.6 Expert bias 163
3.6.1 Expert disagreement resulting from bias 163
3.6.2 The manifestations of actual bias 172
3.6.3 Personal and structural bias 176
3.7 Conclusion 178

4. Non-epistemological factors in determining the role of the expert 180

4.1 Introduction 180
4.2 Five approaches to civil expert evidence 184
4.2.1 England and Wales: Civil Procedure Rules 1998 184
4.2.2 United States of America: Federal Rules of Evidence 1975 188
4.2.3 France: Nouveau code de procédure civile 1975 192
4.2.4 Germany: Zivilprozessordnung 1933 195
4.2.5 Italy: Codice di procedura civile 1940 196
4.3 Five non-epistemological factors in expert role definition 197
4.3.1 The social function of civil litigation 198
4.3.2 The role of facts in civil procedure 212
4.3.3 The appropriate conduct of civil litigation 220
4.3.4 The status of experts in society 232
4.3.5 The historical use of experts 234
4.4 Conclusion 236

5. Assessing expert evidence in the English civil courts: the sixteenth to twentieth centuries 238

5.1 Introduction 238
5.2 Tracing the history of civil expert evidence, 1500–1800 240
5.2.1 Source analysis 240
5.2.2 Civil courts before the Judicature Acts 1873 and 1875 244
5.3 Party experts 246
5.3.1 Early uses of party experts 246
5.3.2 The developing complexity of inferential questions 249
5.3.3 Increasing reliance on party expert evidence 253
5.3.4 Developments in the criminal courts in the seventeenth and eighteenth centuries 256
5.3.5 The problem of party expert disagreement 258
5.4 Special juries 261
5.5 Assessors 263
5.5.1 The rise of the Trinity Masters 263
5.5.2 From Trinity Masters to assessors 266
5.6 Court experts 269
5.6.1 Before the nineteenth century 269
5.6.2 Nineteenth-century innovation 271
5.6.3 Twentieth-century disinterest 272
5.7 The Ultimate Issue Rule 274
5.7.1 The rule's nineteenth-century rise 274
5.7.2 The rule's twentieth-century decline 277
5.8 Conclusion 279

6. Assessing expert evidence in the English civil courts today 282
6.1 Introduction 282
6.2 Party experts 284
6.2.1 Selecting party experts 284
6.2.2 Producing full pleadings 294
6.2.3 Challenging expert opinion 294
6.2.4 Delegating fact finding 306
6.3 Single joint experts 307
6.3.1 Selecting single joint experts 307
6.3.2 Producing full pleadings 312
6.3.3 Challenging expert opinion 312
6.3.4 Delegating fact finding 313
6.4 Assessors 315
6.4.1 Selecting assessors 315
6.4.2 Producing full pleadings 321
6.4.3 Challenging expert opinion 323
6.4.4 Delegating fact finding 332
6.5 Conclusion 332

7. The effective management of bias 334
7.1 Introduction 334
7.2 The use of single experts 335
7.3 The presumptive recusal of an expert for bias 338
7.4 The inadmissibility of unreliable expert evidence 341
7.5 Exhortations to an overriding duty to the court 347
7.5.1 The nature of the overriding duty 348
7.5.2 The nature of the overridden obligations 351
7.6 The reform of litigation privilege 352
7.7 Criminal, civil and professional sanctions 358
7.7.1 Criminal sanctions 358
7.7.2 Civil sanctions 360
7.7.3 Disciplinary sanctions 361
7.8 Conclusion 363

Conclusion 366
1 Specialist knowledge and non-specialist courts 367
2 Arranging legal processes to best support accurate fact determination 369
3 The foundational norms of evidence law 370

Appendix 1: Part 35 of the Civil Procedure Rules 1998 374

Appendix 2: Tables of pre-1800 civil cases involving expert evidence 379

Bibliography 388

Index 413

FIGURES

1.1	Corroboration in inferential argument	*page* 56
1.2	Contradiction in inferential argument	56
1.3	Convergence and conflict in inferential argument	57
2.1	Normatively closed systems can exist within society	124
2.2	The incommensurability of normatively closed systems	125

PREFACE

This project began with an interest in two relatively recent developments in expert evidence in the civil courts of England and Wales. The first was the 1997 decision of the House of Lords in the case of *Bolitho* v. *City and Hackney Health Authority*, which appeared to introduce the possibility that a judge sitting at first instance might be able to assess for herself, based on expert evidence, whether a medical professional had been negligent. The second was the extensive reform of the use of expert evidence effected by the Civil Procedure Rules (CPR) 1998. Expert evidence had been one of the two principal areas of concern in the course of Lord Woolf's *Access to Justice* enquiry, the other being uncontrolled discovery. At that time, Lord Justice Judge and several High Court and District judges and masters, interviewed anonymously, were more than generous with their time in discussing these issues from a judicial perspective. More recently, Master Foster has very kindly read a draft of the chapter on experts under the CPR, and provided suggestions, and Senior Costs Judge Hurst has provided advice on the use of costs assessors.

As is perhaps too often the case, what seemed at first blush to be a nicely defined area of enquiry unfolded to reveal a multiplicity of issues. I focussed my attention on two key issues among many: first, 'how can courts, which lack specialist knowledge, assess the evidence of experts?' (a question which seems to be posed more by theorists); secondly, 'how should we best arrange our use of experts to assist the court in addressing issues requiring specialist knowledge?' (a question which seems to be posed more by practitioners). These questions are inextricably bound up together, and in order to answer the one it is necessary to address also the other. They are also non-trivial questions, and addressing them has required investigations into the philosophy of law, epistemology and comparative civil procedure.

It is not possible to thank individually by name all those who have been of assistance, but among those to whom I am indebted are Neil Jones, Patrick Glenn and the late Henrik Zahle. Matilde Betti, David Nelken,

Paolo Biavati and Andrea Tassi provided information and advice on expert evidence in Italy and the use of court experts. I am similarly indebted to Olivier Leclerc and Rafael Encinas de Munagorri for France, and Erica Beecher-Monas for the United States. I should like to give especial thanks to the estate of Boris Anrep, for generously giving permission to use, as the cover illustration for this book, the Boris Anrep mosaic 'Open Mind', from his Modern Virtues at the National Gallery.

Some parts of this book have previously appeared elsewhere. An earlier and shorter version of Chapter 7 was published in 2007 as 'The Effective Management of Bias in Civil Expert Evidence' in volume 26 of the *Civil Justice Quarterly* (pp. 57–78). An earlier version of Section 3.6 appeared in the same volume as 'Causes and Manifestations of Bias in Civil Expert Evidence' (pp. 425–46). Section 6.4 began life in 2006 as 'The Future of Assessors under the CPR', in volume 25 of the same journal (pp. 219–31), but has undergone significant revision. Chapter 5 has been developed out of an article on 'Expert Evidence in the English Civil Courts, 1550–1800', published in 2007 in volume 28 of the *Journal of Legal History* (pp. 93–118).

Above all, this project could never have come to fruition without the assistance, guidance and support of my two mentors in its course, William Twining and Adrian Zuckerman.

The writing of this book has been made possible through the support of the British Academy, in its award to me of a Postdoctoral Fellowship.

Déirdre Dwyer
The British Academy, London
Feast of St John of the Cross, 2007

TABLE OF LEGISLATION

Australia

Federal Court Rules
Ord. 34B 330
Queensland Uniform Civil Procedure Rules
Ch. 11, Pt 5 311

England and Wales

Access to Justice Act 1999
s. 27 169
Asylum and Immigration Tribunal (Procedure) Rules 2005 (SI 2005/230 L.1)
r. 51(1) 30
British North America (Seigniorial Rights) Act 1825 (Imperial) (6 Geo. IV c. 59)
s. 4 242
Chancery Reform Act 1852 (15 & 16 Vict. c. 80)
s. 42 243
Children Act 1989 166
s. 1(1) 156
s. 7 212
s. 25 156
Civil Evidence Act 1972 277
s. 3 32
Civil Evidence Act 1995
s. 1 32
Civil Procedure Act 1997
s. 1(3) 208
Civil Procedure (Amendment No. 2) Rules 2000 316
Civil Procedure Rules 1998 (SI 1998/3132) 4, 188, 198, 207–11, 232, 238, 282–7, 311, 314, 334, 355
Pt 1 187, 282, 283
r. 1.1 26, 32, 170, 185, 208, 227, 282, 285, 292–3

r. 1.2 209
r. 1.3 209, 211, 349
r. 1.4 209
r. 3.1 150
Pt 7 287
r. 9.2 287
r. 26.6 286
26 PD 9.1 286
r. 27.5 286
r. 27.14 286
Pt 28
28 PD 3.9 286
r. 31.14 353
r. 32.1 185, 189, 309
Pt 35 184, 186, 210, 237, 281, 282, 292, 293, 314, 317, 331, 339
r. 35.1 184, 189, 308
r. 35.2 186, 294, 296, 312, 318, 333
r. 35.3 168, 177, 187, 309, 347, 348–51, 353, 360–1
r. 35.4 185, 186, 296, 309, 357
r. 35.5 186, 286, 296, 300, 309
r. 35.6 186, 296, 312, 325
r. 35.7 170, 187, 287, 307, 309, 312, 316, 335
r. 35.8 187, 318
r. 35.9 32, 170, 187, 309
r. 35.10 168, 186, 353, 356–7
r. 35.11 186
r. 35.12 187, 297, 300, 312
r. 35.13 186
r. 35.14 185, 309
r. 35.15 187, 267, 281, 315–19, 323, 325, 327
35 PD 283, 318
35 PD 2.2 307, 310
35 PD 5 311
35 PD 7.4 325
r. 44.3 202
r. 47.26 (repealed) 316
r. 61.12 331
r. 61.13 283, 316, 322, 331
Common Law Procedure Act 1854 271
County Courts Act 1888
s. 103 267, 315

County Courts Act 1984
s. 63 268, 316
Court of Chancery Act 1852 (15 & 16 Vict. c. 80)
s. 42 271
Court of Probate Act 1857 (20 & 21 Vict. c. 77) 235
Courts and Legal Services Act 1990
Pt II 224
s. 58 169, 226
s. 58A 169, 226
Criminal Justice Act 2003 31
s. 321 36
Criminal Procedure (Insanity and Unfitness to Plead) Act 1964
s. 4A 29
Criminal Procedure and Investigations Act 1996
s. 3(1) 355
Criminal Procedure Rules 2005 (SI 2005/384 L.4)
r. 1.1 355
Divorce and Matrimonial Causes Act 1857 (20 & 21 Vict. c. 85) 235
Family Law Reform Act 1969
s. 20 (as amended) 212
Family Proceedings Rules 1991 (SI 1991/1247)
r. 2.22 212
r. 2.61C 212
r. 4.23 354
High Court of Admiralty Act 1859 (22 & 23 Vict. c. 6) 235, 267
Housing Act 1985
s. 604 (as amended) 149
Human Rights Act 1998 188
s. 6 325
Medical Act 1858 111
Merchant Shipping Act 1854 (17 & 18 Vict. c. 104)
s. 434 263
National Insurance (Industrial Injuries) (Determination of Claims and Questions) Regulations 1948 268, 330
Perjury Act 1911
s. 1 358–9
s. 13 358
Pilotage Act 1987 112
Police and Criminal Evidence Act 1984
s. 78 32
Prisoner's Counsel Act 1836 687 Wm. IVc. 114 275
Rules of the Supreme Court 1965 (SI 1965/1776 L.23) 198, 201, 208, 210, 217, 267, 282, 296–7, 304, 348

Ord. 38, rr. 36, 37 210
Ord. 38, r. 38 296
Ord. 40 189, 268, 272, 280, 308–9, 335
Ord. 40, r. 1 273, 309
Ord. 40, r. 2 273
Ord. 55, r. 19 271
Ord. 62 316
Ord. 70, r. 1 201
Supreme Court Act 1981
s. 70(1) 268, 316
s. 70(3) 267, 315
Supreme Court of Judicature Act 1873 (36 & 37 Vict. c. 66) 184, 200, 246, 266, 282
s. 56 266, 315
Supreme Court of Judicature Act 1875 (38 & 39 Vict. c. 77) 184, 200, 235, 246, 266
Workmen's Compensation Act 1925 329
s. 38 268, 330
Sch. 1, para. 5 268, 315

France

Code civil (1804)
art. 10 9, 26, 27, 206, 207, 217, 349
art. 312 215
arts. 1315–69 215
art. 1320 216
arts. 1349–53 215
art. 1349 215
art. 1350 215
arts. 1357–69 216
art. 1363 216
Code de procédure civile (1806) 194–5, 198, 199, 203, 282, 338
Code de procédure pénale (1958)
art. 159 (as amended) 338
Decree no. 2004–1463 of 23 December 2004 193
Law no. 71–498 of 29 June 1971, *Journal Officiel* 30 June 1971 193
Law no. 72–626 of 5 July 1972, *Journal Officiel* 9 July 1972 9
art. 12 206
Law no. 80–538 of 16 July 1980, *Journal Officiel* 17 July 1980 200
Law no. 2000–230 of 13 March 2000, *Journal Officiel* 14 March 2000
art. 1 216
Law no. 2004–130 of 11 February 2004, *Journal Officiel* 12 February 2004 193
Nouveau code de procédure civile (1975) 192–5, 196, 198, 205–7, 282
art. 1 206

art. 4 206
art. 5 206
art. 7 206
art. 11 206, 349
art. 12 206
arts. 14–17 206
art. 133 200
art. 161 197
art. 162 197
art. 188 200
art. 198 200
arts. 200–3 224
arts. 204–31 206
arts. 213–14 207
art. 218 206
arts. 232–84 192
art. 232 192
art. 234 194, 338
art. 238 194
art. 242 193
art. 246 194
arts. 249–55 192
art. 249 192
arts. 256–62 192
art. 256 192
art. 258 192
art. 263–84 192
art. 263 192
art. 274 193
art. 276 197
art. 341 194, 338

Germany

Reichscivilprocessordnung (1877) 203
Zivilprozessordnung (1933) 26, 195–6, 198, 203–4
s. 138 26
s. 139 26, 204, 349
s. 286 196
ss. 402–14 195
s. 402 195
s. 404 195
s. 404(2) 195

s. 404(4) 195
s. 404(7) 195
s. 404a 195
s. 404a(1) 196
s. 406(1) 195
s. 406(5) 195
s. 411(3) 195
s. 412 (1) 196
ss. 445–51 204, 349
s. 452 204, 349

International treaties

EC Treaty
Art. 222 324
European Convention on Human Rights and Fundamental Freedoms 1950
Art. 6 34, 185, 307
Art. 6(1) 194, 292, 295, 317, 318, 323, 325–9, 331, 333, 339
Art. 6(3) 295
International Convention on the Rights of the Child 1998
Art. 3(1) 156

Italy

Codice di procedura civile (1940) 196–7, 198, 204–5, 227
art. 61 196
art. 63 197
art. 70 211
art. 87 197, 349
art. 115 211
arts. 172–9 196
art. 175(1) 205
art. 192 197
art. 195 196
art. 201 197
Codice di procedura civile del regno d'Italia (1865) 196, 203

United States

Constitution of the United States of America (1787) 189
Art. III 37, 223

Federal Rules of Civil Procedure (1938) 188, 227
r. 1 227, 235
r. 11 225
r. 26(a)(2) 189
r. 26(f) 227
Federal Rules of Evidence (1975) 183, 188–91, 218, 343
r. 102 9, 26, 27, 28, 188
Art. III 217
r. 402 188, 191, 342
r. 403 32, 189
Art. VII 189
r. 701 189
r. 702 189
r. 703 189
r. 704 189, 277
r. 705 189
r. 706 189, 190, 335
Uniform Rules of Evidence 1974 183
Art. VII 189

TABLE OF CASES

Australia

Clark *v.* Ryan (1960) 130 CLR 486 95, 277
Ebner *v.* The Official Trustee in Bankruptcy and Clenae Pty Ltd *v.* ANZ Banking Group Ltd [2000] HCA 63 341
F *v.* R (1983) 33 SASR 189 194 162
Genetics Institute Incorporated *v.* Kirin-Amgen Incorporated (No. 2) (1997) 149 ALR 247 330
Goode *v.* Nash (1979) 21 SASR 419 162
Lynch *v.* Lynch (1965) 8 FLR 433 157
R. *v.* Barker (1988) 34 A Crim R 141 95
R. *v.* Bonython (1984) 38 SASR 45 320
Re JRL *ex p.* CJL (1986) 161 CLR 342 330
Rogers *v.* Whitaker [1992] ALJR 47 162

Canada

Anderson *v.* Chasney [1949] 4 DLR 71, aff'd 4 DLR 223 162
Crits *v.* Sylvester [1956] 1 DLR (2d) 502, aff'd [1956] SCR 991 162
Dorion *v.* Roberge [1991] 1 SCR 374 162
Phillips *v.* Ford Motor Co. [1971] 18 DLR (3d) 641 277
R. *v.* Stinchcombe (1991) 68 CCC (3d) 1 355

England and Wales

(1354) YB Trin. 28 Edw. 3 pl. 1 fo. 18b 265
(1354) 28 Edw. 3 Lib. Ass. 5 fo. 145b 265
(1494) YB Hil. 9 Hen. VII 16 pl. 8 269
A *v.* B [2003] EWHC 1376 Fam 175
A *v.* Secretary of State for the Home Department [2004] UKHL 56; [2005] 2 AC 68; [2005] 2 WLR 87; [2005] 3 All ER 169 276

A *v.* Secretary of State Home Department [2004] EWCA Civ 1123; [2005] 1 WLR 414 211
Abbey National Mortgages plc *v.* Key Surveyors Nationwide Ltd [1996] 1 WLR 1534; [1996] 3 All ER 184 (CA) 149, 274, 335
Abinger (Lord) *v.* Ashton (1873) 17 LR Eq 373 169, 260
Adams *v.* Canon (1621) Dyer 53b n 15 78, 85, 91, 252–3, 359
Admiralty Commissioners *v.* Owners of the SS Ausonia (1920) 2 Ll Rep 123 329
Air Canada *v.* Secretary of State for Trade (No. 2) [1983] 2 AC 394; 2 WLR 494; [1983] 1 All ER 910 (HL) 36
Alan Jackson *v.* Marley Davenport Ltd [2004] EWCA Civ 1225; [2004] 1 WLR 2926 353, 356–8
Alsop *v.* Bowtrell (1619) Cro Jac 541; 79 ER 464 (Alsop 1791) 242, 247, 253, 255, 256, 258, 380
Alsop & Stacy pur Trespass de 40l (1619) Palm 9; 81 ER 953 (Alsop 1721) 242, 247, 253, 255, 256, 380
Andrews *v.* Powis (1728) 1 Lee 242; 161 ER 90 247, 385
Armstrong *v.* First York Ltd [2005] EWCA Civ 277; [2005] 1 WLR 2751 314
Arthur J. S. Hall *v.* Simons [2002] 1 AC 615; [2000] 3 WLR 543; [2000] 3 All ER 673 (HL) 298, 361
Associated Provincial Picture Houses *v.* Wednesbury Corporation [1948] 1 KB 223; [1947] 2 All ER 680 (HL) 162
B (Child) [2003] EWCA Civ 1148 175
Badische Anilin und Soda Fabrik *v.* Levinstein (1881) 24 ChD 156 272
Barings plc (In Liquidation) *v.* Coopers & Lybrand (No. 2) [2001] Lloyd's Rep Bank 85 185
Batley *v.* Kynock (No. 3) (1875) LR 20 Eq 632 185
Beck *v.* Ministry of Defence [2003] EWCA Civ 1043; [2005] 1 WLR 2206 356–7
Beckman *v.* Maplesden (1662) Bridg O 60; 124 ER 468 249, 380
Benson *v.* Vernon (1745) 3 Bro PC 626; 1 ER 1539 381
The Beryl [1884] PD 137 268, 329, 331–2
Biguzzi *v.* Rank Leisure [1999] 1 WLR 1926; [1999] 4 All ER 934 (CA) 209
Bittleston *v.* Clark (1755) 2 Lee 229; 161 ER 323 386
Bolam *v.* Friern Hospital Management Committee [1957] 1 WLR 582; [1957] 2 All ER 118 (QB) 112–13, 160–1, 277–8, 291
Bolitho *v.* City and Hackney Health Authority [1993] 4 Med L R 381 (CA); [1997] 4 All ER 771 (HL) 162
Bonnington Castings Ltd *v.* Wardlaw [1956] AC 613; 2 WLR 707; [1956] 1 All ER 615 (HL) 152
Braddyll *v.* Jehen (1755) 2 Lee 193; 161 ER 310 386
Brereton *v.* Cowper (1724) 1 Bro PC 211; 1 ER 521 248, 383
Bristol-Myers Squibb *v.* Baker Norton Pharmaceuticals [2001] EWCA Civ 414 357
Buckley *v.* Rice Thomas (1555) 1 Plowd 118; 75 ER 182 253, 264, 269, 380

Buller *v.* Crips (1703) 6 Modern 29; 87 ER 793 269
Burton *v.* Baynes (1733) Bar N 153; 94 ER 852 381
Bushell's Case (1670) Vaughan 135; 124 ER 1006 78, 84, 186, 252
Cala Homes (South) Ltd *v.* Alfred McAlpine Homes East Ltd [1995] FSR 818 (Ch.) 230–2, 273, 351, 354
Carter *v.* Boehm (1766) 3 Burr 1905; 97 ER 1162 251, 382
Charles Laffitte & Co. Ltd (1875) LR 20 Eq 650 185
Chaurand *v.* Angerstein (1791) Peake 61; 170 ER 79 382
Coate's Case (1772) Lofft 78; 98 ER 542 256
Cooke *v.* Secretary of State for Social Security [2001] EWCA Civ 734, [2002] 3 All ER 279
Coopers Payen Ltd *v.* Southampton Container Terminal Ltd [2003] EWCA Civ 1223 314
Coulson *v.* Disborough [1894] 2 QB 316 268, 312–13, 318
Council of Civil Service Unions *v.* Minister of State for Civil Service [1985] AC 374 (GCHQ) 211
Cropper *v.* Smith (1884) ChD 700 (CA) 202
Cruger *v.* Wilcox (1755) Dickens 269; Ambler 252; 21 ER 272; 27 ER 168 381
Dale *v.* Hall (the Laurel and the Houghton) (1765) Burrell 323; 167 ER 592 265, 387
Daniels *v.* Walker [2000] 1 WLR 1382 (HC) 150, 287–8, 310
Darlow *v.* Late Duke of Wharton (1739) Bar N 258; 94 ER 904 381
De Freitas *v.* O'Brien [1995] 6 Med LR 108 (CA) 161
Deeny *v.* Gooda Walker [1996] Lloyds Reinsurance L Rep 183 (QB) 162
Dimes *v.* Proprietors of Grand Junction Canal (1852) 3 HL Cas 759 167, 340
Directors of the Stockton and Darlington Railway *v.* John Brown (a lunatic) (1860) 9 HLC 246; 11 ER 724 243
DN *v.* Greenwich LBC [2004] EWCA Civ 1659 168
Doe on the Demise of Mudd *v.* Suckermore (1836) 5 A & E 703; 111 ER 1331 266
Dover District Council *v.* Sherred (1997) 29 HLR 864 (CA) 149
DPP *v.* A & B C Chewing Gum [1968] 1 QB 159; [1967] 3 WLR 493; [1967] 2 All ER 504 (HL) 277–8
Ekins *v.* Macklish (1753) Ambler 184; 27 ER 125 381
Enfield London Borough Council *v.* Mahoney [1983] 1 WLR 749; [1983] 2 All ER 901 349
English *v.* Emery Reimbold & Strick [2002] EWCA Civ 605; [2002] 1 WLR 2409; [2002] 3 All ER 385 (CA) 39
ES *v.* Chesterfield North Derbyshire Royal Hospital NHS Trust [2003] EWCA Civ 1284 168, 285, 289, 291–3, 298
Esso Petroleum *v.* Southport Corporation [1956] AC 218; [1956] 2 WLR 81; [1955] 3 All ER 864 269, 317
Evans *v.* Blood (1746) 3 Brown PC 632; 1 ER 1543 383
Everard *v.* Hopkins (1615) 2 Bulst 332; 80 ER 1164 380

Ex p. Bellett (1786) 1 Cox 297; 29 ER 1174 384
Ex p. Ferrers (1730) Mosely 332; 25 ER 423 248, 383
Ex p. Gillam (1795) 2 Ves Jun 587; 30 ER 790 384
Ex p. Mildmay (1795) 3 Ves Jun 2; 30 ER 862 384
Fairchild *v.* Glenhaven Funeral Services Ltd [2002] UKHL 22; [2003] 1 AC 32; [2002] 3 WLR 89; [2002] 3 All ER 305 (HL) 153
Fallows *v.* Randle [1997] 8 Med LR 160 (CA) 161
Faustini de Zugarti *v.* Gazaway B Lamer (1858) 12 Moo PC 331; 14 ER 937 263
Fearon *v.* Bowers (1753) 1 H Bl 364; 126 ER 214 248, 257, 381
Field *v.* Leeds City Council [1999] CPLR 833 (CA) 167, 168, 340
Filmer *v.* Gott (1774) 4 Bro PC 230; 2 ER 156 384
Flannery *v.* Halifax Estate Agencies Ltd [2000] 1 WLR 377 (CA) 157
Folkes *v.* Chadd (1782) 3 Doug 157; 99 ER 589 79, 86, 245, 249–53, 256, 257, 258, 270, 274, 279, 359, 382
Foubert *v.* de Cresseron [1698] Shower PC 194; 1 ER 130 248, 249, 257, 258, 383
Fox *v.* Mackreth (1788) 2 Cox 320; 30 ER 148 384
Gardiner *v.* Johnston (1753) 1 Lee 358; 161 ER 132 385
Giles *v.* Ferrers (1587) Cro Eliz 59; 78 ER 320 269, 380
The Global Mariner *v.* Atlantic Crusader [2005] EWHC 380 (Admlty); [2005] 2 All ER (Comm.) 389 317, 326, 331
Grant *v.* Vaughan (1764) 1 Black W 485; 96 ER 281 262, 381
Graves *v.* Budgel (1737) West T. Hard. 44; 1 Atk 444; 25 ER 812; 26 ER 283 383
H *v.* Lambeth Southwark and Lewisham HA [2001] EWCA Civ 1455 297
Habib Bank Ltd *v.* Jaffer (Gulzar Haider) [2000] CPLR 438 (CA) 209
Hajigeorgiou *v.* Vasiliou [2005] EWCA Civ 236; [2005] 1 WLR 2195 356–8
Hall *v.* British Oil and Cake Mills Ltd (1930) 23 Butterworths Workmen's Compensation Cases 529 329
The Hannibal (1867) 2 A & E 53 266–7, 324
Hedd *v.* Chalenor (1590) Cro Eliz 176; 78 ER 433 269, 380
In the Matter of Dyce Sombre (1849) 1 Mac & G 1207; 41 ER 1207 259
In the Matter of Martha Brown, *ex p.* Newton Wallop (1792) 4 Bro CC 90; 29 ER 794 262, 384
J *v.* C [1970] AC 668 (HL) 156
Jackson *v.* Lever (1792) 3 Bro CC 605; 29 ER 724 384
Jasim *v.* Secretary of State for the Home Department [2006] EWCA Civ 342 218
Jekyll (Lady) *v.* Jekyll (1753) 1 Lee 419; 161 ER 155 385
Johnstone *v.* Sutton (1785) 1 Term Rep. 510; 99 ER 1225 256, 264
Kennard *v.* Ashman (1894) 10 TLR 213 (Ch.) 272
Lane *v.* Willis [1972] 1 WLR 326; [1972] 1 All ER 430 357
Leighton con Moore (1600) Libel file 68, no. 108, 1600–1, in G. Marsden (ed.), *Select Pleas in the Court of Admiralty*, vol. II, *The High Court of Admiralty* (AD 1547–1602) (Selden Soc. 11) (London, 1897), p. lxxv 387

Lethes *v.* Edsforth (1753) 1 Lee 462; 161 ER 171 385
Liverpool Roman Catholic Archdiocese and Trustees Inc. *v.* Goldberg (No. 2), Chancery Division, 2 March 2001 164, 340
Liverpool Roman Catholic Archdiocese and Trustees Inc. *v.* Goldberg (No. 3) [2001] 1 WLR 2337; [2001] 4 All ER 950 (HC) 164, 341
Lloyd *v.* Nevill (1754) 1 Lee 559; 161 ER 206 385
Locabail (UK) Ltd *v.* Bayfield Properties Ltd [2000] QB 451; [2000] 2 WLR 870; [2000] 1 All ER 65 336–7, 341
Loveday *v.* Renton (No. 1) [1989] 1 Med LR 117 (CA) 94, 161
Lucas *v.* Barking Havering and Redbridge Hospitals NHS Trust [2003] EWCA Civ 1102 356
Lushington *v.* Boldero (1819) 6 Madd 149; 56 ER 1048 271
McGhee *v.* National Coal Board [1973] 1 WLR 1; [1972] 3 All ER 1008 (HL) 152
Maddox *v.* Dr M—y (1754), in *British Trials 1660–1900: The Guide to the Microfiche Edition Containing a Full Bibliographical Listing Together with Nine Indexes* (Cambridge: Chadwyck-Healey, 1990), no. 303 248, 381
Magill *v.* Porter [2001] UKHL 67; [2002] 2 AC 357; [2002] 2 WLR 37; [2002] 1 All ER 465 340
The Marquis of Granby (1770) Burrell 323; 167 ER 592 265, 387
Matthews *v.* Tarmac Bricks and Tiles Ltd [1995] CPLR 463 (CA) 185, 300
Meadow *v.* General Medical Council [2006] EWHC 146 (Admin.); [2006] 1 WLR 1452; [2006] 2 All ER 329; [2006] EWCA Civ 1390; [2007] QB 462; [2007] 2 WLR 286; [2007] 1 All ER 1 186, 219, 360, 362, 364
Morgan *v.* Liverpool Corporation [1927] 2 KB 131 (CA) 149
Multiple Claimants *v.* Ministry of Defence [2003] EWHC 1134 (QB) 321
National Justice Compania *v.* Prudential Assurance [1993] 2 Ll Rep 68 (The Ikarian Reefer) (Comm. Ct) 210, 231, 273, 290–1, 347, 348
Nettleship *v.* Weston [1971] 2 QB 691; [1971] 3 WLR 370; [1971] 3 All ER 581 (CA) 159
Nothard *v.* Pepper (1864) 17 CBNS 39; 141 ER 16 263
Nutt *v.* Verney (1790) 4 Tr 121; 100 ER 928 382
O'Connor *v.* A [1971] 1 WLR 1227 157
Owners of the Pelopidas *v.* Owners of the TRSL Concord [1999] 2 All ER (Comm.) 737 (Admlty) 321
Owners of the Ship 'Bow Spring' *v.* Owners of the Ship 'Manzanillo II' [2004] EWCA Civ 1007; [2005] 1 WLR 144; [2004] 4 All ER 899; [2005] 1 All ER (Comm.) 53 188, 317, 325–6, 331
Owners of the SS Australia *v.* Owners of Cargo of SS Nautilus [1927] AC 145 (HL) (The Australia) 320, 332, 337
Oxley *v.* Penwarden [2001] CPLR 1 287–9
Palmer (Thomas, Knight) *v.* Greenwill (Richard) (1613) Bridg J 46; 123 ER 1189 380

Pearce *v.* Ove Arup Partnership Ltd (Copying), Chancery Division, 2 November 2001 111, 361–2, 364
Peet *v.* Mid-Kent Healthcare NHS Trust [2001] EWCA Civ 1703; [2002] 1 WLR 210; [2002] 3 All ER 688 311–13
Penney *v.* East Kent Health Authority [2000] Lloyd's Rep Med 41 (CA) 90, 94
Phillips *v.* Symes (a bankrupt) [2004] EWHC 2329 (Ch.) 360
Pickering *v.* Barkley (1658) Sty 132; 82 ER 587 249, 262, 264, 269, 380
Pike *v.* Hoare (1763) 2 Eden 182; 28 ER 867 384
Popek *v.* National Westminster Bank plc [2002] EWCA Civ 42 312–13
Practice Direction (Criminal Proceedings: Consolidation) [2002] 1 WLR 2870 327
Purdy *v.* Cambran [2000] CPR 67 (CA) 209
The Queen Mary (1947) 80 Ll Rep 609 269, 317
R. *v.* Archer [2002] EWCA Crim 1996 359
R. *v.* Bailey [1961] Crim LR 828 278
R. *v.* Bassi [1985] Crim LR 671 359
R. *v.* Bembridge Old Bailey Sessions Papers, December 1721, 3 255
R. v. Bow Street Metropolitan Stipendiary Magistrate *ex p.* Pinochet Ugarte (No. 2) [2000] 1 AC 119, 145; [1999] 2 WLR 272; [1999] 1 All ER 577 340
R. *v.* Cannings (Angela) [2004] EWCA Crim 1; [2004] 1 WLR 2607 171
R. *v.* Clare [1995] 2 Cr App R 333 (CA) 96
R. *v.* Clark (Sally), Chester Crown Court, 9 November 1999 111, 364
R. *v.* Clark (Sally) (No. 2) [2003] EWCA Crim 1020 (CA) 90, 171, 361–2, 364
R. *v.* Clarke (1787) 1 TR 679; 99 ER 1317 263, 264
R. *v.* Coningsmark (Count) (1682) 9 St Tr 21 270
R. *v.* Connor [2004] UKHL 2; [2004] 1 AC 1118; [2004] 2 WLR 201; [2004] 1 All ER 925 39, 47
R. *v.* Cowper (1699) 13 St Tr 1106 3, 86, 257, 258, 259, 274
R. *v.* Davies [1962] 1 WLR 1111; [1962] 3 All ER 97 (Courts Martial App.) 79
R. *v.* Davies (1974) Cr App R 311 (CA) 358
R. *v.* Deputy Industrial Injuries Commissioner *ex p.* Jones [1962] 2 QB 677; [1962] 2 WLR 1215; [1962] 2 All ER 430 (DC) 268
R. *v.* Esdaile (1858) 1 F&F 213; 175 ER 696 243
R. *v.* Ferrers (Earl) (1760) 9 St Tr 942 275
R. *v.* Gough [1993] AC 646; [1993] 2 WLR 883; [1993] 2 All ER 724 187
R. *v.* Green (1679) 7 St Tr 185 257, 270
R. *v.* HM Coroner for Inner North London District *ex p.* Gregory Linnane (No. 2) (1991) 155 JP 343 (DC) 330, 354
R. *v.* HM Coroner for Surrey *ex p.* Irene Wright, Court of Appeal, 24 October 1996 268, 330
R. *v.* Kai-Whitewind [2005] EWCA Crim 1092; [2005] 2 Cr App R 31; [2006] Crim LR 348 109
R. v. M'Naghten (1843) 10 Cl & F 200; 8 ER 718 259, 275–6

R. v. McIlkenny [1992] 2 All ER 417 355
R. *v.* Maguire [1992] QB 936; (1992) 94 Cr App R 133 (Maguire Seven) 273
R. *v.* Marsham *ex p.* Lawrence [1912] 2 KB 362 268, 327
R. *v.* Matheson [1958] 1 WLR 474 277, 278
R. *v.* Mills [1998] AC 382; [1997] 3 WLR 458; [1997] 3 All ER 780 355
R. *v.* Momodou and Limani [2005] EWCA Crim 177; [2005] 1 WLR 3442; [2005] 2 All ER 571 224
R. *v.* O'Callaghan [1976] VR 676 278
R. *v.* Pembroke (Earl) (1678) 6 St Tr 1337 257, 270
R. *v.* Salisbury (1723) 1 Str 547; 93 ER 691 381
R. *v.* Secretary of State for Home Dept *ex p.* Gangadeen [1998] 1 FLR 162 156
R. *v.* Secretary of State for the Home Department *ex p.* Fayed [2001] Imm AR 134 340
R. *v.* Secretary of State for the Home Dept *ex p.* Gashi [1999] INLR 276 (CA) 354
R. *v.* Secretary of State for Trade and Industry *ex p.* Lonrho plc [1989] 1 WLR 525; [1989] 2 All ER 609 (HL) 276
R. *v.* Sibson Old Bailey Sessions Papers, May 1762, 117 255
R. *v.* Stockwell (1993) 97 Cr App R 260 279
R. *v.* Stretton and McCallion (1988) 86 Cr App R 7 304
R. *v.* Strudwick (1730) 1 Barn KB 402; 94 ER 271 381
R. *v.* Turner [1975] QB 834; 60 Cr App R 80 277, 371
R. *v.* Vezey Old Bailey Sessions Papers, January 1732, 41 86, 255
R. *v.* Wright (1821) Russ & Ry 456; 168 ER 895 253, 259, 275–6
R. *v.* Wyatt [1990] Crim LR 343 304
R. (Factortame) *v.* Secretary of State for Transport, Local Government and the Regions (No. 8) [2002] EWCA Civ 932; [2003] QB 381; [2002] 3 WLR 1104; [2002] 4 All ER 97 169, 225, 226, 340
Rawlinson *v.* Westbrook, Court of Appeal, 26 January 1995 210
Re B [1996] 1 FLR 667 (CA) 158
Re B (Split Hearing) [2001] FLR 334 (CA) 157
Re Carson (1673) 73 SS, No. 36, in D. Yale (ed.), *Lord Nottingham's Chancery Cases*, 2 vols., folios 73 and 79 (London: Selden Society, 1954 and 1961), no. 11. 248
Re Enoch and Zaretsky Bock & Co.'s Arbitration [1910] 1 KB 327 (CA) 284
Re Harbin and Masterman [1896] 1 Ch 351 349
Re The Herald of Free Enterprise, Divisional Court, 18 December 1987 162
Re L (a minor) [1996] 2 WLR 395; [1996] 2 All ER 78 354
Re L (an infant) [1967] 3 WLR 1645; [1968] 1 All ER 20 (F) 188, 212
Re M (a child) (residence order), Court of Appeal, 18 September 2003 158
Re Michael Wilkey, Architects Registration Board, 5 February 2003 111, 361, 364
Re N – B C M [2002] EWCA Civ 1052; [2002] 2 FLR 1059 157
Re Rumney and Wood (1541), in G. Marsden (ed.), *Select Pleas in the Court of Admiralty*, vol. II, pp. 102–4, trans. pp. 213–15 264

Re S (Infants) [1967] 1 WLR 396; [1967] 1 All ER 202 (Ch.) 188, 212
Richardson *v.* Redpath Brown & Co. Ltd [1944] AC 62 (HL) 268, 269, 317, 329–30
Robin Ellis Ltd *v.* Malwright Ltd [1999] CPLR 286 297
Robins *v.* Wolseley (1757) 2 Lee 421; 161 ER 391 386
Rodd *v.* Lewis (1755) 2 Lee 176; 161 ER 304 386
Rondel *v.* Worsley [1967] 1 QB 443; [1966] 3 WLR 950; [1966] 3 All ER 657 (CA); [1969] 1 AC 191; [1967] 1 WLR 142; [1967] 3 WLR 1666; [1967] 3 All ER 993 (HL) 298, 348–50
S (a minor) *v.* Birmingham HA [2001] Lloyd's Rep Med 382 (QB) 287–8, 294
Saul *v.* Saint Andrew's Steam Fishing Company Ltd [1965] 1 Ll Rep 107 (Admlty) (The St Chad) 322
Sayer *v.* Bennet (1784) 1 Cox 107; 29 ER 1084 384
Scammel *v.* Willett (1799) 3 Esp 29; 170 ER 527 382
Severn *v.* Imperial Insurance Co., The Times, 14 April 1820 138, 259
Severn *v.* Olive (1821) 3 Brod & Bing 72; 129 ER 1209 261
Shaw *v.* DPP [1962] AC 220; [1961] 2 WLR 897; [1961] 2 All ER 446; (1961) 45 Cr App R 113 (HL) 278
Sheafe *v.* Row (1757) 2 Lee 415; 161 ER 389 386
Sheldon's Case (1590) 1 Leo 241; 74 ER 220 269, 380
Slater *v.* Baker (1767) 2 Wils KB 359; 95 ER 860 382
Stanton *v.* Callaghan [2000] 1 QB 75; [1999] 2 WLR 745; [1998] 4 All ER 961 (CA) 186, 297–8, 360
Stoker *v.* Hutton (The Friend's Goodwill *v.* The Peggy) (1785) Burrell 328; 167 ER 594 265, 387
Stratton and Stratton *v.* Ford (1755) 2 Lee 216; 161 ER 318 386
Stretch *v.* Wheeler (1754) Bar N 497; 94 ER 1021 381
Taylor *v.* Taylor (1755) 2 Lee 172; 161 ER 303 386
Thorn *v.* Worthing Skating Rink Co. (1877) 6 ChD 415 177, 272
Three Rivers DC *v.* Governor and Company of the Bank of England [2004] UKHL 48; [2005] 1 AC 610; [2004] 3 WLR 1274; [2005] 4 All ER 948 353, 355
Tracy Peerage Case (1843) Cl & Fin 154 228
The Trial of Witches (1665) 6 St Tr 68 270
Turner *v.* Winter (1787) 1 Tr 602; 99 ER 1274 382
Vallejo *v.* Wheeler (1774) 1 Cowp 143; 98 ER 1012 382
Vaughan *v.* Menlove (1837) 3 Bing NC 468; Scott 244 159
Vernon *v.* Bosley (No. 2) [1999] QB 18; [1997] 1 All ER 614 (CA) 44, 166, 172, 304, 354
Vitesse Yacht Charters SI *v.* Spiers [2003] EWHC 2426 (Admlty) 320
Walsh *v.* Misseldine [2000] CPR 74 (CA) 209
Watson *v.* General Medical Council [2005] EWHC 1896 (Admin.) 316, 324, 327
Waugh *v.* British Railways Board [1980] AC 521; [1979] 3 WLR 150; [1979] 2 All ER 1169 355

Welde *v.* Welde (1731) 2 Lee 580; 161 ER 447 247, 248, 385
Whitehouse *v.* Jordan [1980] 1 All ER 650 (CA); [1981] 1 WLR 246 (HL) 172–3, 230, 273, 278, 347, 354
Wilkinson & Wilkinson Section Commissioners of the Navy (c. 1780) 501 nb 117 in J. Oldham, *The Mansfield Manuscripts and the Growth of English Law in the Eighteenth Century* (Chapel Hill NC: North Carolina University Press, 1992), p. 392 382
Williams *v.* General Medical Council [2007] EWHC 2603 (Admin.) 371
Willoughby's Case (1597) Cro Eliz 566; 78 ER 811 262
Woods *v.* Thomas Wilson Sons & Co. Ltd (1915) 8 Butterworths Workmen's Compensation Claims 288 329
Wright *v.* Doe d Tatham (1837) 7 A & E 313, 112 ER 488, aff'd (1838) 5 Cl & F 670; (1838) Bing NC 489 85, 275
X (minors) *v.* Bedfordshire County Council [1995] 2 AC 633; [1995] 3 WLR 152 (HL) 162
XYZ *v.* Schering Health Care [2002] EWHC 1420 (QB) 152, 154–5, 307, 318, 321

European Court of Human Rights

Bönisch *v.* Austria Ser. A No. 92 (1985) 9 EHRR 191 165
Borgers *v.* Belgium (1993) 15 EHRR 92 323, 327
Brandstetter *v.* Austria Ser. A No. 211 (1993) 15 EHRR 378 165
Edwards *v.* UK (1992) 15 EHRR 417 355
Feldbrugge *v.* Netherlands (1986) Ser. A No. 99 (1986) 8 EHRR 425 295
Krčmář *v.* Czech Republic (2001) 31 EHRR 41 323, 326
Kress *v.* France [2001] ECtHR 382 323–4, 326–8
Mantovanelli *v.* France (1997) 24 EHRR 370 193, 295, 323
Orshoven *v.* Belgium (1998) 26 EHRR 55; [1997] ECtHR 3 323–4, 326
Terra Woningen *v.* Netherlands (1996) 24 EHRR 456 307

France

Cour de cassation civ., 1e, 28 March 2000 212
Cour de cassation civ., 1e, 30 May 2000 212

Hong Kong

Edward Wong Finance Co. *v.* Johnson Stokes and Master [1983] 1 AC 296 (PC) 162

Ireland

Birch *v.* Somerville (1852) 2 ICLR (2nd ser.) 253 268, 327
R. *v.* O'Connell (1844) 7 ILR 261 348

Italy

Carlini *v.* Catrigiano, Corte di cassazione 30 January 1960 no. 140 216
Dal Moro *v.* Lucchetta, Corte di cassazione 10 December 1959 216

Malaysia

Chelliah a/l Manickam *v.* Kerajaan Malaysia [1997] 2 AMR 1856 162
Kamalam a/p Raman *v.* Eastern Plantation Agency (Johore) [1996] 4 MLJ 674 162

Northern Ireland

Sherrard *v.* Jacob [1965] NI 151 (HL) 80

Scotland

Davidson *v.* Scottish Ministers [2004] UKHL 34; 2005 1 SC (HL) 7 336–7, 340
Davie *v.* Edinburgh Magistrates 1953 SC 34 276, 278
Glasgow Corporation *v.* Muir [1943] AC 448; [1943] 2 All ER 44; 1943 SC (HL) 3 159
Hunter *v.* Hanley 1955 SC 200 161
McTear *v.* Imperial Tobacco Ltd 2005 2 SC 1 169

Singapore

The Management Corporation Strata Title Plan No. 1075 *v.* RSP Architects Planners and another, High Court, 9 September 1998 162

United States of America

Ambrosini *v.* Labarraque 101 F 3d 129 (1996) 230
Daubert *v.* Merrell Dow Pharmaceuticals 509 US 579; 113 Sup Ct 2786 (1993) (Daubert I) 3, 179, 191–2, 229, 231, 334, 341–7
Daubert *v.* Merrell Dow Pharmaceuticals 43 F 3d 1311 (9th Cir. 1995) (Daubert II) 154
Dowling *v.* L. H. Shattuck, Inc. 91 NH 234; 17 A 2d 529 (1941) 277
Frye *v.* United States 293 F 1013 (DC Cir. 1923) 192, 342–3
General Electric Company *v.* Joiner 522 US 136; 118 Sup Ct 512 (1997) 191, 343
Hertzler *v.* Hertzler 1995 WY 206; 908 P2d 946 164
Kumho Tire *v.* Carmichael 526 US 137; 119 Sup Ct 1167 (1999) 61, 191, 344
Marrogi *v.* Howard 805 S 2d 1118 (LA 2002) 230, 349

People *v.* Wilson 25 Cal 2d 341; 153 P 2d 720 (1944) 277
Re Silicone Gel Breast Implants Products Liability Litigation 793 F Supp 1098 (JPML 1992) (MDL 926) 190
Scott v. Spanjer Bros Inc. 298 F 2d 928 (2nd Cir. 1962) 191
State *v.* Lanza 181 A 2d 390 (1962) 191
United States *v.* Johnson 575 F 2d 1347 (5th Cir. 1978) 95

INTRODUCTION

> Each age has a predilection for a mode of proof. The Christian Middle Ages had a preference for the ordeal and the oath. The *Ancien Régime* developed the document and the confession involving torture. Our age has a predilection for expert evidence. Certainly the confession, testimony, the document or the oath continue to be used, but the means of proof which attracts attention, responds to our expectations, and arouses discussion is expert evidence.[1]

The ability of the courts to assess expert evidence is a cause for concern prevalent in western legal systems today. It seems to cut across the traditional divide between Anglo-American and continental European legal systems. The principal form in which that concern is manifest is discussion of expert bias.[2] Bias is of course something that is not unique to experts; it is quite likely that witnesses will be biased, and it is always possible that a judge will be biased. Different legal systems handle these concerns in different ways: some jurisdictions may exclude the testimony of civil parties, criminal defendants or those in certain relationships to them, others may let the question of witness bias go to weight; judicial bias may be dealt with by recusal, or addressed on appeal. The possibility of bias in the testimony of experts is problematic for the courts in a different way from bias in the testimony of witnesses of fact, and it cannot be addressed, as it can for judges, on appeal, and only rarely through recusal. The leading approach in the United States of America for the last fifteen years has been

[1] E. Jeuland, 'Expertise', in L. Cadiet (ed.), *Dictionnaire de la justice* (Paris: Presses Universitaires de France, 2004), pp. 503–10, pp. 503–4, referencing C. Champaud, 'Société contemporaine et métamorphose de l'expertise judiciaire', in *Mélanges Henry Blaise* (Paris: Economica, 1995), pp. 59–79.

[2] The nature of expert bias is analysed in Chapter 3, in the context of expert disagreement more widely. At this point, it is worth noting that the concept of expert bias is not coterminous with the partisanship that we may encounter with the use of party-appointed experts. Experts, including court experts, may also be biased for a range of reasons arising from predisposition and interest.

to exclude expert evidence that does not pass the *Daubert* test for reliability,[3] so that the jury is not required to evaluate it. But *Daubert* does not escape the problem of assessment; it merely transfers it from being a jury assessment of weight to being a judicial assessment of admissibility. The problems of assessment were succinctly expressed by the American jurist Learned Hand at the start of the last century, discussing the difficulties the courts encounter when two experts disagree with one another in a case: 'But how can the jury judge between two statements each founded upon an experience confessedly foreign in kind to their own? It is just because they are incompetent for such a task that the expert is necessary at all.'[4]

The difficulties faced by the courts in assessing expert evidence are not new. They were recognized, for example, in the summing up of Hatsell B in the 1699 murder trial of *Cowper*, one of the earliest reported English cases in which extensive use was made of expert evidence: 'The doctors and surgeons have talked a great deal to this purpose [on evidence for drowning] . . . but unless you have more skill in anatomy than I, you would not be much edified by it. I acknowledge I never studied anatomy; but I perceive that the doctors do differ in their notions about these things.'[5] The problems of assessment have received increasing attention in recent years, particularly since the early 1980s. Although the assessment of expert evidence itself is fundamentally a question of legal epistemology, the reason why the issue has become highlighted is sociological. Increasing concerns about the use of experts in the legal process mirror to a large extent concerns about the use of experts in political and administrative decision making, and reflect the role of the expert in society generally.[6] This 'rise of the expert' is a symptom of an increasing functional specialization in society that has been apparent since at least the eighteenth century.[7] Society has come increasingly to rely on experts not only to be the most appropriate people to do certain tasks but also to be the most appropriate people to provide us with certain information. This is one

3 *Daubert* v. *Merrell Dow Pharmaceuticals* 509 US 579; 113 Sup Ct 2786 (1993).

4 L. Hand, 'Historical and Practical Considerations Regarding Expert Testimony' (1901) 15 *Harvard Law Review* 40–58, 54.

5 *R.* v. *Cowper* (1699) 13 St Tr 1106, at 1189.

6 M.-C. Meininger (ed.), 'L'administrateur et l'expert' (2002) 103 *Revue Française d'Administration Publique*, 365–527; G. Edmond (ed.), *Expertise in Regulation and Law* (Aldershot: Ashgate, 2004).

7 E.g. R. Porter, *England in the Eighteenth Century*, 2nd edn (Harmondsworth: Penguin, 1990), p. 81. See also N. Luhmann, *Differentiation of Society*, trans. S. Holmes and C. Larmore (New York: Columbia University Press, 1982).

of the reasons why, by the 1990s, many felt the courts to be deluged by expert evidence, with an inordinate number of experts,[8] providing expert opinions of at times questionable value to the courts.[9]

As we increasingly rely on the authority of experts to inform (or even to determine) our practical reasoning in relation to legal fact finding, so the long-standing concerns about the ability of the courts to assess expert evidence come to the fore, and we are forced to address two fundamental questions about the judicial assessment of expert evidence. First, how can a non-specialist court accurately determine facts that require specialist knowledge? As a subsidiary question, if a specialist advises the non-specialist court, how can that court know whether to accept the advice? Secondly, how should we arrange our legal processes best to support our expectations of accurate fact determination, and other procedural goals, arising in whole or in part from expert evidence? The first question is one that affects similarly the use of specialists as advisers by government. The second is one that extends in principle to all areas of judicial fact determination. These fundamental questions are ultimately questions of applied philosophy, rather than of sociology or legal doctrine.

There are two integrating themes that help to define the approach taken in this book to the judicial assessment of expert evidence. The first is the re-integration of legal evidence theory with epistemology. The second is the re-integration of the study of evidence with that of procedure. Legal epistemology, as a branch of applied philosophy, must be concerned as much with the procedural mechanisms by which evidence comes before the court as with the specific evidential rules of admissibility.[10] If we are to

[8] E.g. Lord Woolf, *Access to Justice: Final Report* (London: Her Majesty's Stationery Office, 1996), ch. 13.

[9] E.g. P. Huber, *Galileo's Revenge: Junk Science in the Courtroom* (New York: Basic Books, 1991). In a survey conducted at the turn of the millennium, United States judges said that one of the most frequent problems that they encountered with experts was with them abandoning objectivity and becoming advocates for their side: S. Dobbin, S. Gatowski, J. Richardson, G. Ginsburg, M. Merlino and V. Dahir, 'Applying Daubert: How Well Do Judges Understand Science and Scientific Method?' (2002) 85 *Judicature* 244–7. An empirical survey in Australia in 1997 indicated that the main judicial concern about expert evidence was expert bias: I. Freckleton, P. Reddy and H. Selby, *Australian Judicial Perspectives on Expert Evidence: An Empirical Study* (Melbourne: Australian Institute of Judicial Administration, 1999). The next three concerns were, in decreasing order, failure to prove the basis of expert opinion, failure by advocates to pose questions adequately, and ineffective cross-examination.

[10] On the narrow focus of admissibility rules within the broader context of the evidential process, see D. Dwyer, 'What Does it Mean to be Free? The Concept of Free Proof in the Western European Legal Tradition' (2005) 3 *International Commentary on Evidence* iss. 1,

evaluate how best the courts might assess expert evidence, then we must consider the whole procedural framework within which expert evidence comes before the court. We must also understand better the values and expectations that are embedded into evidential and procedural practices, which sit alongside the straightforward goal of accurate fact determination. Stein has recently suggested that accurate fact determination is in some way prior to the moral values in evidence and procedure: 'Morality picks up what the epistemology leaves off. This motto summarizes the principal thesis of this entire book.'[11] Rather than accept that morality is in some way residual in understanding how the courts approach the assessment of expert evidence, I would suggest that morality sits firmly alongside questions of classical epistemology, particularly in that it shapes the procedural mechanisms through which the expert evidence is developed and presented.[12]

This book seeks to contribute to the development of a general theory of the judicial assessment of expert evidence, and in turn to a general theory of the judicial assessment of all forms of evidence, that might be applicable in any legal system, to any area of law. It does this by developing a special theory that relates to expert evidence in the civil courts in a number of Anglo-American and continental European jurisdictions. In the Anglo-American world, I consider civil expert evidence in England and Wales, as well as in the federal courts of the United States of America, and some aspects of expert practice in Australia. In continental Europe, I consider civil expertise in France, Germany and Italy. The principal focus is on the judicial assessment of expert evidence in English civil procedure, from the earliest recorded cases, at the end of the fifteenth century, to the present day, examining in particular the effect of the Woolf Reforms on the assessment of expert evidence in England, since the Civil Procedure Rules ('CPR') came into force in April 1999.[13] These reforms followed the publication of Lord Woolf's *Access to Justice* report in 1996.[14] Although a number of books have now been published on expert evidence under the Civil Procedure Rules,[15] this is the first theoretical account of how the

art. 6, www.bepress.com/ice/vol3/iss1/art6 (last accessed 1 August 2008). See also W. Twining, 'Some Scepticism About Some Scepticisms', in *Rethinking Evidence: Exploratory Essays*, 2nd edn (Cambridge: Cambridge University Press, 2006), pp. 99–164, pp. 114–16 (first published 1984).

[11] A. Stein, *Foundations of Evidence Law* (Oxford: Oxford University Press, 2005), p. 12.

[12] See also H. Ho, *A Philosophy of Evidence Law: Justice in the Search for Truth* (Oxford: Oxford University Press, 2008).

[13] Civil Procedure Rules 1998 (SI 1998/3132).

[14] Woolf, *Access to Justice.*

[15] E.g. J. Day and L. Le Gat, *Expert Evidence under the CPR: A Compendium of Cases from April 1999 to April 2001* (London: Sweet and Maxwell, 2001); S. Burn, *Successful Use of*

assessment of expert evidence may be affected by the choice of expert role under those rules.

Chapter 1 ('General epistemological issues') provides a necessary theoretical framework, by laying out general epistemological issues relating to the judicial assessment of evidence, within the context of the Rationalist Tradition of evidence scholarship.[16] The chapter begins by defining what we mean by epistemology in its classical sense, relating to how individuals form justified beliefs. In particular, foundationalist and coherentist approaches to epistemological justification are rejected in favour of the foundherentist approach proposed by Haack.[17] This requires that a justified factual determination of a case must be both internally coherent and inferred soundly from evidence (Section 1.2). The concept of 'legal epistemology' is then introduced, and its defining characteristics identified. Within legal epistemology, a wide range of institutional variations are encountered, that arise in particular from fundamental differences between criminal procedure, and from the composition of the court. Issues of composition (Section 1.3) include particularly whether the court is unicameral, considering both questions of law and fact, or bicameral, with separate tribunals of law and fact (usually judge and jury). The chapter then considers how we might evaluate our criteria for determining whether a factual belief is justified. In particular, the possible role of atomistic inferential reasoning and generalizations in such determination is examined (Section 1.4). One of the defining features of sound evidential inference is the combination of facts with generalizations, to produce networks of inferences. In the final section (Section 1.5), some arguments for naturalized epistemology are introduced, and it is proposed that a 'modest naturalism' be adopted, allowing us to benefit from the insights of cognitive psychology into the mechanisms of cognition, without exhausting the requirements of the components of a developed epistemology.

Within this general epistemological framework, Chapter 2 ('Expert evidence as a special case for judicial assessment') examines whether there is anything special about expert evidence that might warrant concerns that the courts have greater difficulty assessing this evidence than other forms of evidence. Three distinguishing features are identified: first,

Expert Witnesses in Civil Disputes (Crayford: Shaw and Sons, 2005); L. Blom-Cooper (ed.), *Experts in the Civil Courts* (Oxford: Oxford University Press, 2006). See also T. Hodgkinson and M. James, *Expert Evidence: Law and Practice* (London: Sweet and Maxwell, 2007).

[16] W. Twining, 'The Rationalist Tradition of Evidence Scholarship', in *Rethinking Evidence*, pp. 35–98.

[17] S. Haack, *Evidence and Inquiry: Towards Reconstruction in Epistemology* (Oxford: Blackwell, 1993).

expert evidence is usually considered to represent statements of opinion rather than fact, and opinions present particular evidential difficulties (Section 2.2); secondly, expert evidence is the product of specialist knowledge unavailable to the courts while non-expert evidence is not similarly distinguished (Section 2.3); thirdly, expert evidence is frequently presented by witnesses who represent persistent communities of practice outside the legal domain (Section 2.4). It is proposed that the court's epistemic competence to assess expert evidence can be justified, at least to a limited extent, on two grounds: first, the fundamental structure of evidential reasoning is substance blind; secondly, expert fact finding is the product of the same common investigative methods as everyday fact finding. Arguments for strong epistemological constructivism, in particular autopoietic systems theory, which have found some favour in legal theories about expert evidence, are examined and refuted in light of this claim for limited epistemic competence (Section 2.5).

Chapters 1 and 2 together provide an argument for the courts possessing limited epistemic competence to assess the validity of expert evidence in general. Chapter 3 ('Making sense of expert disagreement') takes this argument further, to examine in greater detail the specific problem of how the courts are to reach a decision in cases where the expert evidence offers more than one interpretation. It is within this broader framework of expert disagreement that we can situate the phenomenon of expert bias. This chapter is in five parts: first, a discussion of why the legal and expert communities differ in their attitudes towards disagreement (Section 3.2); secondly, a detailed analysis of why experts might disagree, at the level of selecting sets of generalizations (Section 3.3); thirdly, the application of those generalizations to base facts (Section 3.4); fourthly, a consideration of how different types of question addressed in expert evidence lend themselves to different types and degrees of disagreement (Section 3.5); fifthly, a taxonomy of the causes and manifestations of expert bias (Section 3.6). The most valuable free-standing contribution of this chapter to our understanding of expert evidence is perhaps its clarification of how disagreement between experts is to be expected, and of the unreasonableness of lawyers in expecting a 'single right answer' from experts in most if not all cases.

In juxtaposition to the epistemological argument presented in Chapters 1 to 3, Chapter 4 ('Non-epistemological factors in determining the role of the expert') identifies non-epistemological factors that may contribute to determining the role of the expert within a given jurisdiction. This is the analysis of the role of values in procedure and evidence referred to above.

Although Chapters 1 to 3 were illustrated with occasional examples from England, France and the United States of America, they remained essentially jurisdiction-neutral. Chapter 4, in contrast, is jurisdiction-specific. This is because it is only by understanding the specific jurisdictional context within which procedural and evidential rules operate that one can understand properly the role of non-epistemological factors in shaping the functioning of those rules. The chapter therefore introduces the use of expert evidence in five jurisdictions in the western legal tradition: England, the United States federal courts, France, Germany and Italy (Section 4.2). Five non-epistemological factors are then introduced and discussed in relation to these jurisdictions: the social function of civil litigation; the role of facts; the appropriate conduct of litigation; the status of experts in society; the historical use of experts within a jurisdiction (Section 4.3). Chapter 4 is a pivotal point in the book. Up to here, in Chapters 1 to 3, we have considered how the court might assess the expert evidence presented to it. That the focus is civil rather than criminal evidence is largely irrelevant, and jurisdictions provide illustrations rather than determining the substance of the analysis. In Chapters 5 to 7, however, the details of the rules around expert evidence within a jurisdiction become crucial to understanding how that evidence is developed and presented to the court. While Chapters 1 to 3 establish the necessary preliminary point that the courts can assess expert evidence (albeit to a limited extent), Chapters 5 to 7 consider how best to produce and present the evidence.

Chapter 5 ('Assessing expert evidence in the English civil courts: the sixteenth to twentieth centuries') begins the work of examining in detail how epistemological and non-epistemological factors combine to produce a range of expert roles, looking at the case study of English civil procedure. The chapter identifies the historical development of provisions to assist the assessment of expert evidence in the English civil courts from their first mention at the end of the fifteenth century through to the last days of the Rules of the Supreme Court in 1999. In particular, it analyses the historical development of the party expert (Section 5.3), special juries (Section 5.4), the assessor (Section 5.5), and the court expert (Section 5.6), in the context of attempts to address emerging epistemological and non-epistemological issues with expert evidence. The epistemological issues include questions about whether lay fact finders can assess expert evidence, and how to resolve expert disagreement. The non-epistemological issues include broader legal and social developments that may have given rise to the evolving forms that these expert roles have taken. The chapter concludes by considering the rise and fall of the Ultimate Issue Rule in the nineteenth and twentieth centuries, in England and the United States (Section 5.7). This rule can be understood as an attempt to avoid the possibility of de facto delegation of fact finding to an expert, arising from the court's perceived inability to assess the evidence fully, by restricting the nature of the opinion that the expert might provide.

Following on through with the historical momentum built up by Chapter 5, Chapter 6 ('Assessing expert evidence in the English civil courts today') provides the first detailed analysis of the relationship between procedure and the assessment of expert evidence under the CPR. It analyses the selection of experts, varying effects on the ability of the parties to produce full pleadings, opportunities presented to challenge expert opinion, narrowing and possibly resolving differences, and the delegation of decision making, in relation to party experts (Section 6.2), single joint experts (Section 6.3), and assessors (Section 6.4). The purpose of this analysis is to understand how these procedural elements affect the ability of the court to determine accurately the facts of a case, depending on the choice made between the use of party experts, single joint experts and assessors. This analysis allows us to make more nuanced decisions about which expert roles might best be suited to the range of types of expert question identified at the end of Chapter 3.

Finally, Chapter 7 ('The effective management of bias') steps back from the detailed examination of contemporary English civil procedure to consider how best the courts should use procedural techniques to accommodate the epistemological issues presented by the perceived problem of expert bias. This analysis draws on examples from England, the United States and France. In particular, the chapter explores the effectiveness of four measures intended to remove bias: the use of single experts (Section 7.2); the availability, for example in France, of presumptive recusal of an expert for bias (Section 7.3); the gatekeeper function exercised by many United States courts to exclude 'junk science', following the Supreme Court judgment in *Daubert* (Section 7.4); the use of exhortations to experts to observe an overriding duty to the court, as found for example in England in Part 35 of the CPR (Section 7.5). Chapter 7 also considers whether the removal of litigation privilege from the work of experts might reduce expert bias (Section 7.6), and the effectiveness of sanctions (criminal, civil and professional) against experts whose evidence has been found to have been unacceptably biased (Section 7.7).

1

General epistemological issues

1.1 Introduction

> Everyone is bound to cooperate with the judicial authorities with a view to procuring the manifestation of truth.[1]

> These rules shall be construed to secure fairness in administration, elimination of unjustifiable expense and delay, and promotion of growth and development of the law of evidence to the end that the truth may be ascertained and proceedings justly determined.[2]

This book is concerned with how judges seek to the best of their ability to form justified beliefs about the truth where at least some of the evidence on which they must rely is the evidence of experts. It can thus be seen as occupying a space within applied philosophy, in the area of epistemology, as well as within the law relating to evidence and proof. Specifically, it concerns legal rather than classical epistemology. Classical epistemology is concerned with how individuals form knowledge and justified beliefs (Section 1.2). However, in relation to the judicial assessment of expert evidence, this would require that we imagine the judge sitting in splendid isolation, imagining and obtaining whatever information she decides is necessary to decide accurately the facts that lie behind a case. Instead, the judge undertakes her fact-finding work within the context of the legal process, and in particular in the context of the rules and practices of evidence and procedure. Legal epistemology entails fact finding, and belief justification, in a social context.

Legal epistemology tells us how the courts are capable of producing justified true (or, minimally, truth-indicative) beliefs (Section 1.3). These beliefs are produced within the paradigm of the Rationalist Tradition of

[1] France, Code civil 1804, art. 10 (as amended by Law no. 72-626 of 5 July 1972).

[2] United States, Federal Rules of Evidence (1975), r. 102.

evidence scholarship (Section 1.4).[3] Within the Rationalist Tradition, the particular interests of the New Evidence Scholarship with logic, inferences and probability theory form a part of this legal epistemology, but by no means constitute its entirety.[4] The brief preliminary groundwork in applied philosophy undertaken in this chapter is necessary for the development, in Chapter 2, of a special theory for how accurate fact finding by a 'lay' (non-expert) tribunal can incorporate the evidence of experts on a rational basis.[5]

It may be tempting to some readers, particularly perhaps to lawyers, to skip this chapter to get onto 'the stuff about expert evidence' from Chapter 2 onwards, or even to skip that chapter as well, to get onto 'the *legal* stuff about expert evidence'.[6] This would, however, be to ignore one of the two key integrating themes of this book's approach to understanding the judicial assessment of expert evidence, first encountered in this book's Introduction. As well as being concerned with the re-integration of evidence with procedure in developing a legal epistemology, this book is also fundamentally concerned with re-integrating legal evidence theory with classical epistemology. As Laudan has commented, in his recent work on legal epistemology in relation to criminal law, 'The nagging worry was that key parts of *all* these [epistemic] notions (especially proof, relevance, and reliability) were being used in ways that were not only non-standard (or at least among philosophers) but also, apparently, deeply confused.'[7]

3 W. Twining, 'The Rationalist Tradition of Evidence Scholarship,' in *Rethinking Evidence: Exploratory Essays*, 2nd edn (Cambridge: Cambridge University Press, 2006), pp. 35–98.

4 'The New Evidence Scholarship' is the label commonly given to a loosely constituted body of evidence scholarship that attempts to re-integrate legal evidence into a multidisciplinary examination of factual inference and proof, e. g. R. Lempert, 'The New Evidence Scholarship: Analyzing the Process of Proof' (1986) 66 *Boston University Law Review* 439–77; J. Jackson, 'Analysing the New Evidence Scholarship: Towards a New Conception of the Law of Evidence' (1996) 16 *Oxford Journal of Legal Studies* 309–28. Since the early 1980s, the New Evidence Scholarship has widened its interests beyond probabilities and proof to encompass a broader cross–disciplinary revival of interest in evidence and proof in legal contexts.

5 The term 'lay' can mean either 'non-expert' or 'non-lawyer', depending on context. Because of the potential ambiguity, the term is avoided in this book.

6 On how an evidence theorist might respond to a question such as 'What has this got to do with the Evidence course I teach?' see P. Roberts, 'Rethinking the Law of Evidence: A Twenty-First Century Agenda for Teaching and Research', in P. Roberts and M. Redmayne, *Innovations in Evidence and Proof: Integrating Theory, Research and Teaching* (Oxford: Hart, 2007), pp. 19–63, p. 31.

7 L. Laudan, *Truth, Error and Criminal Law – An Essay in Legal Epistemology* (Cambridge: Cambridge University Press, 2006), p. xi (original emphasis).

Since legal philosophy was brought back into the philosophical mainstream from the 1950s, for example by the work of H. L. A. Hart,[8] its main focus has been on the nature of law as a social institution, giving rise to questions such as 'Why should we obey the law?' But another important area of legal philosophy, touched on particularly by the American Legal Realists,[9] is that of adjudication. Within the philosophy of adjudication, most effort has been expended on adjudicating questions of law,[10] with much less attention given to the adjudication of facts.[11] It is time for legal evidence theory to be reintegrated with epistemology. Legal philosophy has unduly ignored fact finding as a core concern,[12] even though 'the legal system is up to its neck in epistemology. It has to be: the truth or falsehood of factual claims is crucial to substantive justice.'[13] There has been a general disregard, for example, for developing a proper understanding of the distinctions between questions of fact and of law, and between questions of fact and of opinion.[14]

Early evidence theorists, such as Gilbert, Wills and Best,[15] focused on attempts to link evidence law to the epistemology of the British empiricists, particularly Locke.[16] From the second half of the nineteenth century, there emerged less ambitious, but perhaps therefore also more successful, attempts, for example by Stephen, Wigmore, Twining and Stein, to

[8] E.g. H. Hart, 'Definition and Theory in Jurisprudence' (1954) 70 *Law Quarterly Review* 37–60; H. Hart, *The Concept of Law*, 2nd edn (Oxford: Oxford University Press, 1994).

[9] E.g. J. Frank, *Law and the Modern Mind* (New York: Tudor, 1930); W. Twining, *Karl Llewellyn and the Realist Movement* (London: Weidenfeld and Nicolson, 1973).

[10] In the post-Hartian legal philosophical landscape, see in particular the work of Ronald Dworkin, e. g. *Taking Rights Seriously* (Cambridge MA: Harvard University Press, 1977), *Justice in Robes* (Cambridge MA: Harvard University Press, 2006). Dworkin's work begins to combine these two philosophical concerns of the nature of law as a social institution and the nature of adjudication.

[11] E.g. W. Twining, 'Taking Facts Seriously', in *Rethinking Evidence*, pp. 14–34.

[12] See W. Twining, 'Evidence and Legal Theory' (1984) 47 *Modern Law Review* 261–83.

[13] S. Haack, 'Crossing My i's and Dotting Some t's: Response to Vern Walker', in C. de Waal (ed.), *Susan Haack: A Lady of Distinctions – The Philosopher Responds to Her Critics* (Amherst NY: Prometheus, 2007), pp. 105–8, p. 107.

[14] See, however, P. Roberts and A. Zuckerman, *Criminal Evidence* (Oxford: Oxford University Press, 2004), pp. 132–46. On the distinction between fact and opinion, see Section 2.2, below.

[15] G. Gilbert, *The Law of Evidence* (London: 1754); W. Wills, *An Essay on the Principles of Circumstantial Evidence* (London: 1838); W. Best, *A Treatise on Presumptions of Law and Fact with the Theory and Rules of Presumptive or Circumstantial Proof in Criminal Cases* (London: Sweet, 1844).

[16] J. Locke, *Essay Concerning Human Understanding* (1690), ed. J. Yolton, 3rd edn (London: Dent, 1993).

link evidence law to a legal theory of proof, distinct from mainstream epistemology.[17] The earliest evidence theorists attempted to get from the mechanics of such common law peculiarities as the best evidence rule and hearsay rule to the epistemological principles in Locke in a single bound. But substantive evidence law, evidence law theory (indeed legal theory generally) and epistemology itself were all in relatively early stages, and so the gap that they sought to traverse was just too wide. Our understanding of epistemology and evidence theory today is considerably more advanced, and so we are now in a much better position to begin to join up the concerns of applied philosophers with the concerns of legal evidence scholars.

Within evidence law, expert evidence is of particular value to this joining-up exercise precisely because it throws up so many difficulties. Because expert evidence involves specialist knowledge, it raises a fundamental question about how, and indeed whether, a non-expert tribunal should attempt to assess such evidence. This is, however, simply an extreme form of a question about how, and indeed whether, a non-expert tribunal should be used to do any legal fact finding, and of a question about how the court should be composed in order to function as a tribunal of fact. Expert evidence also raises two further questions, concerning where the line should be drawn between evidence of fact and evidence of opinion, and whether an expert's evidence (of fact or opinion) is fundamentally any different from a non-expert's similar evidence. These three related questions are aspects of more fundamental questions about what we mean by 'fact' and 'opinion', and about the nature of inferences in fact finding, whether in a legal context or any other. The study of expert evidence thus forces us to confront some of the fundamental questions about the nature of evidence in a legal context, and the role (descriptive and normative) of evidence law, that many other aspects of legal evidence do not.[18] This makes it particularly important that an appropriate foundation in epistemology is laid before one moves on to consider 'the legal stuff about expert evidence'.

[17] E.g. J. Stephen, *The Principles of Judicial Evidence, Being an Introduction to the Indian Evidence Act (I of 1872)* (Calcutta: Thacker Spink & Co., 1872); J. Wigmore, *The Science of Judicial Proof: As Given by Logic, Psychology and General Experience and Illustrated in Judicial Trials*, 3rd edn (Boston: Little, Brown, 1937); Twining, 'Evidence and Legal Theory', 267; A. Stein, *Foundations of Evidence Law* (Oxford: Oxford University Press, 2005); Twining, *Rethinking Evidence.*

[18] The terms 'evidence', 'evidence law' and 'proof' are defined along with 'logic of proof' below in Section 1.3.1.

The body of this chapter is divided into four parts. I begin by presenting the proposed background classical epistemology that will be the foundation for my legal epistemology. This is the foundherentism of Haack,[19] which provides a general theory of how beliefs about facts are warranted and/or justified.[20] Foundherentism is more effective in explaining legal fact finding than the competing theories of foundationalism and coherentism (Section 1.2). Section 1.3 then proposes why legal fact finding should be viewed as a special form of epistemology, related to but distinct from the classical form of epistemology. Some of the special, distinguishing aspects of legal epistemology are elaborated on. This includes a discussion of how the effectiveness of legal epistemology may be affected by choices around the composition of the court as a tribunal of fact, and whether the proceedings are criminal or civil in nature.

Section 1.4 takes us on to a consideration of what we mean when we say that a legal belief about facts is justified. This begins with thinking about justifying our criteria for justification ('meta-justification'). Criteria are introduced based on the Rationalist Tradition of evidence scholarship, described by Twining. Following the optimistic rationalism of the Rationalist Tradition, the role and importance of atomism, generalizations and probabilistic reasoning are introduced. Without some understanding of how it is proposed that these three aspects of the Rationalist Tradition function, it will not be possible to follow the argument for limited epistemic competence developed in Chapter 2. In turn, without the concept of limited epistemic competence, many of the arguments in the rest of the book are in danger of remaining opaque to the reader. The Rationalist Tradition is presented here as a historical fact that helps us to understand how the scholarship and law on evidence and proof have developed to the present day. It is not necessary to accept optimistic rationalism as the paradigm within which the effectiveness of the operation of evidence and proof should be assessed in the present, nor to accept it as the paradigmatic basis of further reform.

[19] A hybrid of the most valuable features of the two main schools of epistemology, foundationalism and coherentism: S. Haack, *Evidence and Inquiry: Towards Reconstruction in Epistemology* (Oxford: Blackwell, 1993).

[20] Epistemology conventionally speaks of 'justification'. Haack distinguishes 'warrant' from 'justification' as follows: 'the warrant of a claim for a person at a time depends on the quality of *the evidence he possesses* at that time, while whether he is justified in believing the claim depends on *the evidence that actually moves him* to give it whatever degree of credence he does': Haack, 'Crossing My i's', p. 105 (original emphasis). For present purposes I am concerned with questions of justification rather than of warrant.

Finally, Section 1.5 addresses one of the main contemporary challenges to classical epistemology and its relative, legal epistemology. This is the development of naturalized epistemology, which concerns the relationship between epistemology and the natural sciences. Of particular relevance here is the suggestion by experiments in psychology that the way in which people form beliefs about the world may not follow the rationalist model on which this chapter (and most of classical epistemology) depends. A threefold argument is presented here against abandoning classical epistemology entirely for naturalized epistemology. First, cognitive biases have been principally observed in operation in artificial, experimental contexts, and there are good reasons to believe that their consequences in practice may be limited. Secondly, the rationalist model is normative and aspirational rather than purely descriptive. Thus, if we identify ways in which people fail to decide facts rationally, then this provides us with an opportunity to develop ways in which to encourage greater rationality, rather than abandoning the norms. Norms can be to some extent counter-factual. The norm that postal workers deliver letters to my letterbox is not destroyed because one errant postal worker (who is subsequently dismissed) decides to hide my letters rather than deliver them for her own personal motives. Thirdly, while psychology may tell us about human beings' capabilities and limitations, it does not define for us key epistemological concepts such as reliability and justification. Rather than rejecting wholesale the claims of either classical or naturalized epistemology, a 'modest naturalism' is accepted here, in which the cognitive sciences have contributory rather than exhaustive relevance to the development of an epistemology.[21]

1.2 Classical epistemology

Any analytical examination of the judicial assessment of expert evidence entails at its foundational level a discussion of epistemology. Epistemology, a branch of applied philosophy, has been usefully defined in its classical form as follows:

> [T]he study of knowledge and justified belief. As the study of knowledge, epistemology is concerned with the following questions: What are the necessary and sufficient conditions of knowledge? What are its sources? What

[21] S. Haack, *Defending Science – Within Reason: Between Scientism and Cynicism* (New York: Prometheus Books, 2003), p. 309; Haack, *Evidence and Inquiry*, p. 118.

> is its structure, and what are its limits? As the study of justified belief, epistemology aims to answer questions such as: How we are to understand the concept of justification? What makes justified beliefs justified? Is justification internal or external to one's own mind? Understood more broadly, epistemology is about issues having to do with the creation and dissemination of knowledge in particular areas of inquiry.[22]

Classical epistemology is principally concerned with questions of individual justified belief and knowledge.

This definition of epistemology begins by referring to 'knowledge and justified belief'. Until 1963, it was common for epistemologists to talk about knowledge and justified true belief together. We could say that a subject *S* knows that a proposition *P* is true if, and only if: (a) *P* is true, (b) *S* believes that *P* is true, and (c) *S* is justified in believing that *P* is true. In 1963, however, Gettier published a short article in which he showed through two counter-examples that justified true belief need not equate with knowledge, since it is possible to have a belief that is both true and justified but which does not constitute knowledge. It is therefore possible to know something but not be justified in believing it.[23] In light of what is now known as the 'Gettier Problem' or 'Gettier Paradox', it is advisable to decide whether one is concerned with epistemology as the study of knowledge or as the study of justified true belief. Since my concern is with the inter-subjective justification of facts based on evidence, I am going to concern myself with justified true belief. Knowledge, if we accept Williamson's persuasive and extended arguments, is in any case prior to evidence and belief,[24] and so we cannot talk about knowledge being justified by evidence.[25] It is important to be clear, for the purposes of legal epistemology, whether we are concerned with knowledge or justified true

[22] M. Steup, 'Epistemology', in E. Zelta (ed.), *The Stanford Encyclopedia of Philosophy (Fall 2006 Edition)*, http://plato.stanford.edu/archives/fall2006/entries/epistemology/ (last accessed 1 August 2008).

[23] E. Gettier, 'Is Justified True Belief Knowledge?' (1963) 23 *Analysis* 121–3. See also T. Williamson, *Knowledge and its Limits* (Oxford: Oxford University Press, 2000), for an extensive argument for why knowledge is fundamentally distinct from belief.

[24] T. Williamson, *Knowledge*, p. 203.

[25] Legal evidence is concerned with bringing the tribunal of fact to a position where it holds a justified true (or truth-indicative) belief. This is not to say that there is no place for the concept of knowledge in legal proof theory. A significant part, possibly all, of the factual matters of which the Anglo-American court will take 'judicial notice' would appear to be classifiable as knowledge: 'Some facts are so notorious or so well established to the knowledge of the court that they may be accepted without further enquiry': H. Malek (ed.), *Phipson on Evidence*, 16th edn (London: Sweet and Maxwell, 2005), p. 53.

belief, because this affects the nature of the epistemological arguments that we employ.[26]

If we accept Gettier's argument that knowledge is distinct from justified true belief (and that is the approach taken in this book), then do we need to concern ourselves with beliefs that are both justified and true, or simply those that are justified? Knowledge could be said to be virtuous, because we have acquired a higher state than simply having a belief that happens to be both justified and true.[27] Justified belief could similarly be said to be virtuous, because we have done something (justification) that enhances the quality of our belief. It may be true, following Gettier's counter-examples, that there is nothing virtuous about a belief that happens to be true, even if it is a justified belief that happens to be true. But there surely is something virtuous about a belief that we hold because we can justify it, and our method of justification is truth-indicative. This need not mean that our method of justification infallibly tells us which beliefs are true, but only that through experience we design and refine our methods with true belief in mind. The ultimate goal of legal fact finding is therefore to reach a set of factual propositions that we can justify as being, minimally, truth-indicative.[28] The value of the process of legal fact finding increases as the likelihood that the propositions concluded are truth-indicative also increases.

So when we say that a belief can be justified, what do we mean? We can identify two main schools within classical epistemology that are concerned with this question, foundationalism and coherentism. The legal epistemology to which we turn in Section 1.3 is grounded in classical epistemology, and so it is important to establish at this stage the classical epistemological basis for saying that a belief is justified. This approach to justification is then carried through into our approach to legal epistemology. Neither foundationalism nor coherentism is fully satisfactory for our purpose of understanding legal fact finding, on the one hand because

[26] D. Dwyer, 'Knowledge, Truth and Justification in Legal Fact Finding' (2007) 1(4) *Reasoner* 5–6, www.kent.ac.uk/secl/philosophy/jw/TheReasoner/vol1/TheReasoner–1(4).pdf (last accessed 1 August 2008), commenting on H. Ho, 'The Epistemic Basis of Legal Fact-finding' (2007) 1(2) *Reasoner* 5–6, www.kent.ac.uk/secl/philosophy/jw/TheReasoner/vol1/TheReasoner–1(2).pdf (last accessed 1 August 2008).

[27] A degree of circularity is allowed in discussions in the area of knowledge and belief: Williamson, *Knowledge*, p. 3. The question of whether knowledge is *actively* acquired is outside the scope of our present discussion.

[28] J. Clendinnen, 'Ratifying Foundherentism', in de Waal (ed.), *Susan Haack*, pp. 73–87; S. Haack, 'The Benefit of Experience: Response to John Clendinnen', in de Waal (ed.), *Susan Haack*, pp. 88–91.

our understanding of the validity of a legal finding of fact involves that it is derived from the facts as presented in evidence, and on the other hand because we tend to expect that a legal finding of fact will present a coherent explanation of events in the case. Instead of these two epistemological approaches, a third, hybrid approach, Haack's 'foundherentism', may provide us with an approach that on the one hand allows for the possibility of legitimate mutual support without circularity, and on the other avoids an infinite regress of reasons with recourse to a privileged class of 'basic' beliefs.[29]

Foundationalism holds that our justified beliefs are based on basic beliefs or experiences, that cannot themselves be justified (they are self-justifying). Foundationalism can thus be rationalist (in its use of basic beliefs, for example by Descartes[30] and Spinoza[31]), or empiricist (in its use of basic experiences, for example by Locke[32]). Proponents of foundationalism say that our beliefs are structured like a building, with a superstructure resting on foundations. Beliefs belonging to the superstructure are non-basic and receive justification from the justified beliefs in the foundation.[33] We could express this as follows: a belief is epistemically justified if and only if (a) it is justified by a basic belief or beliefs, or (b) it is justified by a chain of beliefs that is supported by a basic belief or beliefs, and on which all the others are ultimately based. The merits of foundationalism are that it founds knowledge in our basic experience of reality, and avoids the infinite regression that would result from any belief having to be inferred validly from another belief. Possible limitations are that it must explain the basis on which basic beliefs are self-justifying, and the justificatory relationship between basic beliefs and non-basic beliefs.

The main alternative to foundationalism is coherentism. This seeks to avoid the problem of infinite justificatory regression by saying that a proposition *P* is not justified by reference to an inferential chain of reasoning, but by reference to a complete set of beliefs. There are at least two main challenges to coherentism. The first is that it requires a set of beliefs to be internally coherent, while in practice our incomplete knowledge of a given situation may leave us with areas that remain unresolved. The second is that it does not accommodate a correspondence theory of truth. By this I mean that a coherent theory of justified belief has no provision

29 Haack, *Evidence and Inquiry*; Haack, 'Crossing My i's', p. 105.

30 R. Descartes, *Discours de la Méthode* (Paris: 1637).

31 B. Spinoza, *Ethics* (1677), trans. A. Boyle, ed. G. Parkinson (London: Dent, 1993).

32 Locke, *Essay*. 33 Steup, 'Epistemology'.

for demonstrating that the belief corresponds to reality.[34] The coherentist BonJour, for example, has proposed that, while justified beliefs may in some cases be arrived at by a process of inference, what makes them *justified* beliefs is their connection with a network of beliefs which are coherent with one another.[35]

One solution to the difficulties encountered by foundationalism and coherentism, proposed by Haack, is to create a hybrid, foundherentism. This allows pervasive relations of mutual support among beliefs, like coherentism, but also requires experiential input. At the same time, it allows the relevance of a subject's experience to the justification of empirical beliefs, like foundationalism, but does not require any privileged class of 'basic' beliefs justified by experience alone.[36] This theory is perhaps best illustrated using Haack's own metaphor of the crossword puzzle.[37] When we begin, our understanding of the world is like a blank crossword puzzle. The information that we receive about the world is analogous to the puzzle clues. When we attempt to fill in a word on the puzzle, in part we rely on our attempt to solve the clue on its own terms (a foundationalist approach), but we approach the clue, and we check our proposed result, by reference to the rest of the grid, and particularly the other answers already pencilled in (a coherentist approach). Over time, different answers will be pencilled in with different levels of confidence, and answers may change.[38]

[34] 'Correspond' is used here as a philosophical term of art. 'Narrowly speaking, the correspondence theory of truth is the view that truth is correspondence to a fact – a view that was advocated by Russell and Moore early in the 20th century. But the label is usually applied much more broadly to any view explicitly embracing the idea that truth consists in a relation to reality, i.e., that truth is a relational property involving a characteristic relation (to be specified) to some portion of reality (to be specified).' M. David, 'The Correspondence Theory of Truth', in E. Zalta (ed.), *The Stanford Encyclopedia of Philosophy* (Fall 2005 Edition), http://plato.stanford.edu/archives/fall2005/entries/truth–correspondence/ (last accessed 1 August 2008). However, for reasons discussed in Section 1.3.2.4 below, it may not be necessary (or even desirable) to accept correspondence theory in order to argue for the possibility of justified beliefs about ontological reality.

[35] L. BonJour, *The Structure of Empirical Knowledge* (Cambridge MA: Harvard University Press, 1985), p. 90.

[36] S. Haack, 'Of Chopin and Sycamores: Response to Ryszard Wójcicki', in de Waal (ed.), *Susan Haack*, pp. 69–72, p. 69.

[37] Haack, *Evidence and Inquiry*, pp. 81–9. Compare Haack, *Defending Science*, pp. 57–67 and 93 where Haack notes that a similar analogy had been used by Albert Einstein, unbeknown to her when she first used it: A. Einstein, 'Physics and Reality', in S. Bargmann (ed.), *Ideas and Opinions of Albert Einstein* (New York: Crown Publishers, 1954), p. 295.

[38] V. Walker, 'It's Time to Cross the t's and Dot the i's', in de Waal (ed.), *Susan Haack*, pp. 92–104; Haack, 'Crossing My i's'.

Haack's epistemology links directly to her support of realism in the philosophy of science.[39] We might say that justified true belief is developed in foundherentism in much the same way that a medical practitioner works, through a certain degree of trial and error until she finds something that works, but within boundaries of approaches that are a priori likely to succeed, and not kill the patient. As we work through the puzzle, we are constantly trying to maintain the best possible account of the world that corresponds with our experience of it. 'The characteristic question of the project of ratification is: are these criteria of justification truth-indicative?'[40] Therefore, 'a crossword puzzle exemplifies the possibility of legitimate mutual support without circularity'.[41] Here, as elsewhere in epistemology, I would suggest that we consider a fact to be true to the extent that our belief in that fact is justified as being truth-indicative.

1.3 Legal epistemology

1.3.1 What is 'legal epistemology'?

The term 'legal epistemology' may be an unfamiliar one to most lawyers. Indeed, 'legal epistemology... scarcely exists as a recognized area of inquiry'.[42] Historically, legal theories of evidence and proof separated off from mainstream philosophy, at least in the Anglo-American tradition, around the middle of the nineteenth century. Best could still base a legal evidential work on Locke's epistemology in 1844,[43] and Mill's 1843 *System of Logic* could still extend to encompass inferential reasoning in a legal context. In the second half of that century, however, evidence theorists such as Stephen and Thayer treated legal evidence as a subject *sui generis*.[44] It is important to separate out and define common terms such as 'proof', 'the logic of proof', 'evidence' and 'the law of evidence', to understand their relationship to one another in a legal concept, and to this fresh term 'legal epistemology'. Thankfully, most of these terms have been defined already by Twining, in his essay 'What is the Law of Evidence?',[45] and there appears to be no reason to depart from what seem to be relatively non-controversial definitions for our present purposes.

39 Haack, *Defending Science*, ch. 5.

40 Haack, *Evidence and Inquiry*, p. 203.

41 Haack, 'Crossing My i's', p. 104.

42 Laudan, *Truth, Error and Criminal Law*, p. 3.

43 Best, *Treatise on Presumptions*.

44 E.g. Stephen, *Principles of Judicial Evidence*; J. Thayer, *A Preliminary Treatise on Evidence at Common Law* (Cambridge MA: Harvard University Press, 1898).

45 W. Twining, 'What is the Law of Evidence?' in Twining, *Rethinking Evidence*, pp. 192–236.

'Proof', in a legal context, is 'the establishment of the existence or non-existence of some fact (a *factum probandum* or 'fact in issue') to the satisfaction of the legal tribunal'.[46] The 'logic of proof' is concerned with 'the validity, cogency and appropriateness of arguments as the rational basis for persuasion towards making or justifying a decision or conclusion on a question of fact'.[47] 'Evidence' is a means of proof, consisting of any matter of fact which persuades the mind of the existence or non-existence of another matter of fact.[48] The 'law of evidence' (or 'the rules of evidence') is most difficult to define, but broadly concerns legal constraints on the use of evidence in certain legal contexts.[49]

Laudan has proposed that 'legal epistemology, properly conceived, involves both a) the *descriptive* project of determining which existing rules promote and which thwart truth seeking and b) the *normative* one of proposing changes in existing rules to eliminate or modify those rules that turn out to be serious obstacles to finding the truth'.[50] However, this definition, I would suggest, is unduly restrictive, as it focuses solely on the rules of evidence. While 'the law has no mandamus to logical faculty',[51] practical reasoning in a legal context is shaped in part by the special requirements of legal fact finding.[52] If we take classical epistemology to be concerned with the justification of beliefs, then legal epistemology should, if it is to remain within the philosophical mainstream, be concerned with the creation and justification of beliefs in a legal context, and centrally with the justification of beliefs formed by the court. So beyond Laudan's definition, which focuses on the important question of which rules best promote truth seeking, there needs to be a broader concern with the nature of legal epistemological justification.

If we say that legal epistemology is 'the creation and justification of beliefs in a legal context', then this might appear, at least at first blush, to be not unlike the definition of 'logic of proof', also defined above. So why, if at all, do we need to talk about 'legal epistemology' rather than 'logic of proof'? There are perhaps two reasons. The first is that the phrase 'logic of proof' separates out the legal study of legal evidence from mainstream philosophy. The 'logic of proof' is not a common philosophical

46 Ibid., p. 193. 47 Ibid. 48 Ibid.

49 Ibid, pp. 202–3. Precisely which legal contexts remains open to discussion.

50 Laudan, *Truth, Error and Criminal Law*, p. 3.

51 Thayer, *Preliminary Treatise*, p. 313.

52 E.g. D. Walton, *Legal Argumentation and Evidence* (University Park PA: Pennsylvania State University Press, 2002).

term,[53] and one that, if anything, refers to a subset of the correct concerns of epistemology. Secondly, the phrase implies that proof is produced in a regulated, atomic fashion, in a manner governed by formal logic, and related to mathematics.[54] Thus, for example, an argument for the use of holistic proof (Section 1.4.1) might not fall within the scope of a logic of proof,[55] but would fall within the ambit of legal epistemology. Legal epistemology covers the discussion of the validity of holistic proof and the evidential value of stories on the one hand, and the use of atomistic inferential arguments and the use of probability theory on the other (and within probability theory, whether this should be Pascalian, Baconian, Bayesian or something else).[56]

1.3.2 Why is legal epistemology special?

There are at least four facets of legal fact finding that are distinctive enough to warrant describing legal epistemology as a special form of epistemology, related to but distinct from classical epistemology. These are considered in the subsections below. In summary, the first facet is that while classical epistemology is concerned with how individuals develop justified beliefs, legal epistemology is concerned with the collaborative formation of the same. The second is that the court's justified beliefs affect more than just the conduct of the court, and so represent a special form of practical reasoning. The third is that the courts are subject to rules, which vary from jurisdiction to jurisdiction, about what evidence they can consider, and what significance they may (or in some cases must) attach to certain types of evidence. The fourth facet is the nature of the special relationship between legal process and truth, and the way in which the relationship

[53] The term appears to have been coined by Ferdinand Schiller in 'Scientific Discovery and Logical Proof', in C. Singer (ed.), *Studies in the History and Method of Science*, vol. I (Oxford: Clarendon Press, 1917), pp. 235–89, to distinguish the 'logic of proof' from the 'logic of discovery'.

[54] E.g. D. Schum, *Evidential Foundations of Probabilistic Reasoning* (London: John Wiley, 1994); Walton, *Legal Argumentation*; D. Walton, 'Rules for Reasoning from Knowledge and Lack of Knowledge' (2006) 34 *Philosophia* 355–76.

[55] Although, as we shall see in Section 1.4.1, proponents of an atomistic logic of proof, such as David Schum, do profess also to see a role for holistic arguments.

[56] E.g. J. Cohen, *The Probable and the Provable* (Oxford: Oxford University Press, 1977); Walker, 'It's Time to Cross the t's', p. 98, arguing against the use of single, cardinal values to measure the probative value of evidence. See also N. Taleb, *The Black Swan: the Impact of the Highly Improbable* (London: Penguin, 2007).

between truth and justification may be more carefully defined in a legal context than in most social contexts.

1.3.2.1 Collaborative fact finding

While individuals form justified belief to a large extent on the basis of their own experience, with the testimony of others as secondary means of formation, those arriving at the finding of fact in a legal context almost certainly did not observe the events in question themselves.[57] Rather, the finding of fact is the result of people working together to arrive at a conclusion about what did happen in a particular case. The judge (or the jury) does not work in isolation to identify facts, draw inferences and arrive at conclusions. Rather, she (or they) are presented by others with evidence and theories of how best to interpret that evidence.

Not only is the court assisted in its fact finding, but the court as a tribunal of fact is suddenly presented with a mass of facts, often contradictory, of which it has no prior knowledge, and required to adjudicate. In most everyday situations we come to a factual decision with a background context, and hopefully have had time to reflect upon the facts. As Macpherson wrote in 1871, seeking to justify the need for exclusionary rules of evidence:

> Litigant parties are not permitted to present to the mind of the Court everything which they may think likely to produce conviction. Judges are generally obliged to decide rapidly, and they would be more liable to be misled than persons in private life unless the reception of evidence was subject to some rules which may tend to guard them from error.[58]

While in most collaborative fact-finding exercises we might expect those involved to be working together,[59] in legal fact finding parties are much more likely to seek to deceive, and even attempt to confound one another's efforts. Whereas classical epistemology may be concerned with questions such as whether we should believe our own senses, legal epistemology may be more concerned with questions such as whether we should believe the testimony of others. As Starkie pointed out in 1824, perhaps in response

[57] Indeed, it is likely that a trier of fact with direct prior experience of the case would be recused for predisposition bias.

[58] W. Macpherson, *The New Procedure of the Civil Courts of British India*, 5th edn (London: Lepage & Co., 1871), p. 167.

[59] A. Coady, *Testimony: a Philosophical Study* (Oxford: Oxford University Press, 1992).

to Bentham's 1823 *Traité des preuves judiciaires*,[60] the most obvious difference between legal and classical epistemology is that the evidence on which an individual in everyday transactions might safely rely could not, without the further security of the exclusionary rules of legal evidence, be safely relied on, or even admitted, in judicial investigations. There do not exist in everyday life as many opportunities or temptations to practise deceit as there do in legal investigations.[61]

1.3.2.2 The effect of the finding of fact

Related to the collaborative nature of legal fact finding, legal epistemology is unusual in that the beliefs formed may take effect on a number of people, and possibly on society as a whole, rather than simply on the individual forming the belief, as is common in classical epistemology. If *J* decides that *D* did unlawfully harm *C*, then this is not a piece of information that *C* and *D* receive from *J*, internalize, and that is the end of the matter. It has a wider effect on the lives of *C* and *D* and possibly those around them. The scope of the effect may depend on the nature of the case. One of the peculiarities of legal fact finding is that it does not form binding precedent. The finding of fact does not therefore of itself pre-determine all factually similar cases about to be heard, although it may influence both the parties on whether to settle before trial and the judges on how to decide the case.

The assertion of the court closes the matter in a way that the assertion of the archaeologist, journalist or scientist does not. Once the court has formed its belief, there are only limited circumstances in which that belief can be changed. This is not true, for example, for the scientist. While the courts seek to close issues and prevent them from being re-decided, the scientific community seeks almost always to propose that the findings of one piece of work warrant further investigation. The conclusions of science are always provisional. This is true even in an applied science, such as medicine or engineering. If a doctor or engineer asserts a proposed course of action *P*, and it is then discovered that *P* did not achieve the intended result, we might say, depending on the circumstances, that the doctor or engineer needs to review her decision. We would be less likely

[60] C. Allen, *The Law of Evidence in Victorian England* (Cambridge: Cambridge University Press, 1997), p. 18, on the likelihood that Starkie had read Bentham's work on evidence by 1824.

[61] T. Starkie, *A Practical Treatise on the Law of Evidence and Digest of Proofs in Civil and Criminal Proceedings* (London: Clarke, 1824), p. 18.

to consider *P* to have been 'wrong' or 'a mistake', and would not say that it was 'wrongful', in the way that we might of a legal decision.

Because the assertion of the court closes the matter, there is a need, which is at least psychological and emotional if not actually required in law, that the closure should be on the basis of an account of events that is not only based on the evidence, which is a legal requirement, but also internally coherent. This takes us back to the limitations of the evidence-based beliefs of foundationalism and the internal consistency of coherentism, and to the argument for Haackian foundherentism (Section 1.2). It appears to be only foundherentism that allows us to talk at an epistemological level about the need for there to be a 'theory of the case', that is to say 'a logical statement formulated as an argument supporting one or more conclusions about the case as a whole'.[62]

1.3.2.3 Rules of admissibility and evaluation

The third area in which legal epistemology differs from classical epistemology is in the existence of explicit, socially defined rules for the admissibility and evaluation of evidence. When Bentham attacked the rules of evidence and procedure operating in England at the start of the nineteenth century, one of his arguments was that the rules of evidence and fact finding were unnatural.[63] Common law juries in particular were prevented from receiving and considering information on which they might usually rely in deciding their day-to-day affairs. The courts, said Bentham, should instead be more like family tribunals, with the head of the household calling whatever evidence he deemed relevant, and the parties cooperating in accurate fact finding. Bentham's work was cautiously received among evidence scholars. The principal difficulty, wrote Best in 1849, was that Bentham's 1827 *Rationale of Judicial Evidence* 'embodies several essentially mistaken views relative to the nature of judicial evidence, and which may be traced to overlooking the characteristic features whereby it is distinguished from other kinds of evidence'.[64]

The main 'mistaken view', introduced above, is that it is a characteristic of legal proceedings that parties frequently do not cooperate, and they do

[62] T. Anderson, D. Schum and W. Twining, *Analysis of Evidence*, 2nd edn (Cambridge: Cambridge University Press, 2005), p. 118.

[63] 1823, *Traité des preuves judiciaires* (Paris); 1824, published in English in serial form in the *Law Journal*; 1825, published as a complete work in English; 1827, *Rationale of Judicial Evidence* (London). See also W. Twining, *Theories of Evidence: Bentham and Wigmore* (London: Weidenfeld and Nicolson, 1985), ch. 2.

[64] W. Best, *Principles of the Law of Evidence and Practice as to Proofs in Courts of Common Law* (London: Sweet, 1849), Preface.

not always tell the truth, to an extent that is uncharacteristic of normal social exchange, and particularly of (most) intra-family exchanges. Stein has made the point that, while parties before a Benthamite 'family tribunal' may be prepared to forgo self-interest on the immediate point because of a faith in the overall good of the family, this may not be true of litigants before a court of law. In particular, argues Stein, the relationship between individual and family is not the same as that between individual and state, or (usually) between two people from different families, and so one cannot directly apply the family tribunal argument to questions of judicial evidence.[65]

It is because legal fact finding is so different from everyday fact finding – for example in terms of the number of people involved, the lack of prior knowledge, the propensity to deceive and the potentially wide-ranging effects of any finding of fact – that legal evidence is subject to particular rules on admissibility and evaluation that we do not encounter in everyday fact finding. Different jurisdictions, however, may place differing emphasis on the importance of controlling admissibility and evaluation. In common law jurisdictions, the focus has been more on the rules of admissibility since the eighteenth century,[66] while the Roman-canon tradition developed advanced rules on evaluation, most notably in the requirement that two witnesses were usually required to produce a 'proof', but also in developed rules on presumptions.[67] The Benthamite 'free proof' argument, that the court should be free to receive whatever evidence is relevant, and to assess that evidence in whatever way it sees fit, is ultimately of limited application because it does not take into consideration the number of ways in which the court both is and should be constrained in the evidence it receives and the use it makes of that evidence.[68] Those constraints extend beyond the actions of the court itself, to include also the conduct of fact investigators/collectors and the litigants themselves.

[65] Stein, *Foundations*, pp. 113–15.

[66] T. Gallanis, 'The Rise of Modern Evidence Law' (1999) 84 *Iowa Law Review* 499–560; J. Langbein, *The Origins of the Adversary Criminal Trial* (Oxford: Oxford University Press, 2003), ch. 4.

[67] Compare G. Palazzolo, *Prova legale e pena: la crisi del sistema tra evo medio e moderno* (Naples: Jovene, 1979); J. Langbein, *Torture and the Law of Proof: Europe and England in the* Ancien Régime (Chicago: University of Chicago Press, 1977); R. Helmholz, *The Ius Commune in England* (Oxford: Oxford University Press, 2001), pp. 118ff. On presumptions in common law evidence, see Best, *Treatise on Presumptions.*

[68] Dwyer, 'What Does it Mean to be Free?' D. Menashe and M. Shamash, 'The Narrative Fallacy' (2005) 3 *International Commentary on Evidence* iss. 1, art. 3, www.bepress.com/ice/vol3/iss1/art3 (last accessed 1 August 2008).

1.3.2.4 The special relationship between legal process and truth

The relationship between the legal process and the truth is a special one, which may at first appear paradoxical. On the one hand, the legal process would appear to be concerned fundamentally with the truth. We can see this in the statements of aspiration contained in the French Code civil and United States Federal Rules of Evidence ('FRE') quoted at the beginning of this chapter: 'with a view to procuring the manifestation of truth';[69] 'to the end that the truth may be ascertained and proceedings justly determined'.[70] In England, an aim of determining the truth was only excluded from the English Civil Procedure Rules 1998 ('CPR') because, according to a footnote to the third draft of rule 1.1, 'seeking the truth is so obviously part of the court's role that it does not need to be stated expressly in the Rules'.[71] The Benthamite sentiment that rectitude of decision requires accurate fact determination may therefore seem almost platitudinous.[72] But on the other hand, the manner in which evidence is presented to the court, with the parties each vying to present their version of events, might appear almost inimical to the ascertainment of truth.[73] This observation is perhaps particularly true in Anglo-American jurisdictions, but is not entirely absent from continental European litigation.

This seeming paradox, between the privileging of truth as a virtue in procedural codes and the prioritizing of victory over truth by the parties to litigation, in fact arises from three relatively common misunderstandings of the nature of the relationship between legal process and truth. In summary these are: first, the concept of truth is treated in a philosophically naïve fashion by many legal theorists; secondly, truth is not the only virtue

[69] Code civil, art. 10, quoted above at n. 1. See also X. Lagarde, 'Vérité', in L. Cadiet (ed.), *Dictionnaire de la justice* (Paris: Presses Universitaires de France, 2004), pp. 1324–39.

[70] Federal Rules of Evidence, r. 102, quoted above at n. 2.

[71] A. Zuckerman, *Civil Procedure: Principles of Practice*, 2nd edn (London: Sweet and Maxwell, 2006), p. 7.

[72] The German Zivilprozessordnung 1933 ('ZPO') does not contain a statement that one of the goals of civil proceedings is truth. This may be because, as with the English CPR, such a goal is obvious. ZPO 138, for example, imposes on the parties a duty to tell the truth, while ZPO 139 requires the court to put questions to the parties in order to elicit the truth where the evidence presented is not clear. German judges make extensive use of the fact-finding powers conferred on them: J. Langbein, 'The German Advantage in Civil Procedure' (1985) 52 *University of Chicago Law Review* 823–66.

[73] M. Frankel, 'The Search for Truth: An Umpireal View' (1975) 123 *University of Pennsylvania Law Review* 1031–1059; J. Frank, *Courts on Trial* (Princeton NJ: Princeton University Press, 1950), pp. 80–102; N. Duxbury, 'Jerome Frank and the Legacy of Legal Realism' (1991) 18 *Journal of Law and Society* 175–205, 188–9.

promoted by procedural codes; and thirdly, a procedural arrangement may be truth-conducive at an institutional level, while the conduct of the constituent parties may be truth-adverse.

A detailed philosophical discussion of the nature of truth falls outside the scope of this present work. It is sufficient to make a number of observations, to indicate both that the manifestation or ascertainment of truth is not as straightforward conceptually as the authors of the Code civil or the Federal Rules of Evidence might have believed, and also that this does not lead us inevitably to a post-modernist position where the concept of truth is an illusion. Principally, we must distinguish between ontology (the metaphysics of 'what is') and epistemology (beliefs that we are justified in holding as true). The relationship between what is actually the case and what we believe to be the case is not a straightforward one. In particular, the idea that there is a simple correspondence between statements of true belief and ontological truth is problematic,[74] since it appears to imply the existence of a privileged vocabulary for belief statements, a fixed totality of mind-independent objects, and simple correspondence between them. Instead, the meaning of these terms ('statements of true belief' and 'ontological truth') is unclear.[75] In particular, there may not be a simple linear mapping from signifier to signified. However, correcting metaphysical and epistemological oversimplifications does not require that we succumb to ideas such as 'truth is rhetorical'.[76] The fact that I can give multiple descriptive accounts of Oxford's Pembroke College that are all true means simply that the ontological truth of the college is a complex one. While there may be multiple true epistemological accounts, we can nevertheless distinguish these from untrue accounts (Section 3.3.1). It may be that we can consider a number of epistemological statements to be both valid and true, without losing our commitment to a single ontological truth about that thing. Most valid epistemological statements are based on a degree of uncertainty; there is only a probability that the conclusion reached on the evidence is correct. The best that one can do is to say that the evidence supports the conclusion. One of the distinguishing features of legal epistemology is that there must be a final decision on the

[74] Compare M. Damaška, 'Truth in Adjudication' (1998) 49 *Hastings Law Journal* 289–308, on why a correspondence theory of truth is adequate for legal fact finding purposes, and ontological truth is unnecessary.

[75] S. Haack, 'Innocent Realism in a Pluralistic Universe', in de Waal (ed.), *Susan Haack*, pp. 233–6.

[76] S. Haack, *Manifesto of a Passionate Moderate* (Chicago: University of Chicago Press, 1998); S. Haack, 'Law, Literature, and Bosh', in de Waal (ed.), *Susan Haack*, pp. 259–62.

evidence. This decision requires a finality that is not warranted simply by the evidence before the court. We might therefore say that a legal finding of fact contains a normative element that is not present in straightforward factual conclusions.[77]

The second misunderstanding is that, although it may be true that legal codes may express a high regard for the accurate determination of facts, it is far from clear that truth is the only virtue to which the legal process aspires. If we were to accept that it is the only virtue for process, then our analysis of procedural provisions for the introduction of evidence would be straightforward. For example, Goldman has proposed that true belief is better than either ignorance or error.[78] True belief therefore has fundamental veritistic value, with higher degrees of belief in truth having greater degrees of value. Practices that produce changes in veritistically valuable states have instrumental veritistic value (which Goldman terms 'V–value'). It would be possible and valid for us to evaluate actual and possible social practices in terms of instrumental veritistic value. Similarly, Laudan has proposed that

> [T]here are . . . at least two epistemic demands that we should make of any rule of [criminal] procedure:
>
> a. Rules of Procedure should be designed to optimize the likelihood that the triers of fact . . . receive their information in a way that enables them to draw valid inferences from the evidence about the guilt of the accused . . .
>
> b. Rules of Procedure, taken as a whole, should create a *self-correcting* system of checks so that if serious errors are made along the way, they are likely to be discovered and rectified.[79]

Laudan suggests that 'neither of these suggested meta-rules would seem to be very controversial'. But if we go back to consider FRE r. 102, for example, quoted at the beginning of this chapter, there are two goals, the ascertainment of truth and the just determination of proceedings. These are two goals, truth and justice, that are both to be pursued. There are,

[77] For an extended socio-legal discussion of the differing conceptions of truth in law and science, see D. Nelken, 'The Truth about Law's Truth', in A. Febbrajo and D. Nelken, *European Yearbook in the Sociology of Law 1993* (Milan: Giuffrè, 1994), pp. 87–160. That study identifies that the concept of 'truth' can carry a range of potential meanings. However, although Nelken is no doubt correct that fact finding is value-laden (e.g. pp. 100–1), this is not the same thing as saying, as Nelken appears to suggest, that we cannot disentangle the normative from the factual in our analysis of fact finding.

[78] Goldman, *Knowledge*, ch. 3.

[79] Laudan, *Truth, Error and Criminal Law*, pp. 141–2.

for example, very few circumstances in which the courts are interested in making a finding of fact, without the ascription of any moral judgment to that finding of fact.[80]

The third misunderstanding is the conflation of the interests of the parties with the purpose and operation of the institution taken as a whole. There may be circumstances in which getting two opposing parties to both present their version of the facts of a case means that the court is best informed to be able to make an accurate decision. This is for several reasons: both parties may make better efforts to present a strong case because they are in competition; each party's case is subject to rigorous examination by its opponent; the court is exposed to more than one viable interpretation of the facts of the case. There is little firm empirical evidence on which to base an argument for the respective merits of having two opposing sets of evidence or a single fact finder.[81] However, we should not accept a priori that adversarial fact finding is incompatible with a judicial commitment to the truth. Chapters 5 and 6 explore at some length possible reasons why experts may disagree in their interpretation of events, and the relative merits of single and multiple expert opinions.

1.3.3 Institutional variations affecting legal epistemology

There are two main areas in which legal fact finding exhibits significant internal institutional variation. These institutional variations in turn affect legal epistemology, since they shape the way in which information is received by the finder of fact, and they affect the criteria for ascertaining whether conclusions reached are justified. The first area relates to how the category of substantive law that relates to a specific case may affect the fact-finding exercise (Section 1.3.3.1). The example considered here is the difference between civil and criminal evidence. The second area concerns how the composition of the court may affect its ability to determine facts accurately (Section 1.3.3.2).[82] Arrangements vary between jurisdictions,

[80] A rare example in England being s. 4A of the Criminal Procedure (Insanity and Unfitness to Plead) Act 1964, discussed in D. Dwyer, 'Is a finding that a person deemed unfit to be tried "did the act... charged against him" compatible with Article 6 ECHR?' (2003) 67 *Journal of Criminal Law* 307–10.

[81] M. Damaška, 'Presentation of Evidence and Factfinding Precision' (1975) 123 *University of Pennsylvania Law Review* 1083–106.

[82] I am concerned in this book with fact finding by the courts, and not tribunal or arbitration decisions. The legal rules of evidence developed for civil and criminal process before the courts do not usually apply before tribunals or in arbitration.

and in some cases within jurisdictions, in relation to matters such as whether the court should be unicameral or bicameral (comprising two tribunals, one of law and one of fact), and whether the court should be made up of lawyers, non-lawyers, or subject matter experts. Within the Anglo-American world, this is commonly, and misleadingly, characterized as a straightforward choice between judge-and-jury bicameral courts and judge-only unicameral courts. It is important to understand these variations within legal epistemology, which may be guided by political as well as epistemological factors, because they contribute to defining criteria for what may constitute a justified belief, and may shape the way in which fact-finding processes operate. A procedure conducive to accurate fact determination where expert evidence is presented to a non-expert criminal jury may be correspondingly non-conducive when the same evidence is presented to a panel of experts in a civil case.

1.3.3.1 Differences between criminal and civil fact finding

This first area in which legal fact finding exhibits significant internal institutional variation is relatively straightforward. The fact-finding activity of the criminal courts can be distinguished from that of the civil courts, for at least two reasons.[83] The first is that the effect on the dignity of the person of the decision of a criminal court is more significant than that of a decision by a civil court.[84] The second is that almost all criminal prosecutions in the Anglo-American world, since at least the second half of the eighteenth century,[85] have involved state investigation and prosecution of the individual. There are at least four practical consequences of these two reasons for distinction. These consequences, as much as the underlying reasons, justify the need to consider the assessment of (expert) evidence in the civil courts separately from a similar exercise in the criminal courts. The first practical consequence is that the criminal courts will

[83] The role of non-epistemological factors in determining the design of process and institutional structures is explored in Chapter 4.

[84] Before the UK Asylum and Immigration Tribunal, which does consider matters significantly affecting the dignity of the individual, the legal rules of admissibility do not apply, and the criterion of admissibility is relevance: Asylum and Immigration Tribunal (Procedure) Rules 2005 (SI 2005/230 L. 1), r. 51(1). The effects of UK domestic criminal sanctions may be less serious for the individual than the effects of deportation (which may possibly include torture or execution). An examination of the principled basis (if any) for this distinction is outside the scope of the present work.

[85] Langbein, *Origins*, ch. 3.

be significantly slower than the civil courts to arrive at a decision without certainty.[86] This is most apparent in the differences in the degree of certainty required for an adverse decision in the criminal and civil courts. Criminal courts may only find against the individual when they are close to near certainty. In England this is expressed as certainty of guilt 'beyond reasonable doubt'. In France, it is the requirement that the judge forms a 'conviction intime'. Civil courts do not have the same effect on the dignity of the person, and are supposed to decide disputes between equals. At least in Anglo-American legal systems, the court must decide 'on balance of probabilities' whether the claimant succeeds against the defendant. There is additionally a greater willingness to review a 'guilty' verdict, where new evidence later emerges, than there is to review a civil decision. This is because it is politically less acceptable for a criminal conviction to stand, once it is known to have been wrongful, than it is for a civil judgment to assign liability and remedies wrongly. The former affects the dignity of the individual in a far more profound way. Asymmetrically, new evidence has not traditionally allowed a 'not guilty' verdict to be reviewed, under the double jeopardy rule.[87]

The second practical consequence is a factual asymmetry in criminal cases that does not appear as strongly in civil cases. The asymmetry results from the greater burden of proof in criminal matters, as well as the superior power of the state in such actions, separation of alleged victim from prosecution in criminal actions, and some structural substantive differences between criminal and civil wrongs. When a criminal prosecution succeeds, the defendant is 'guilty' and the victim is believed and the state's decision to prosecute affirmed. When the prosecution fails, the defendant is only 'not guilty' rather than innocent, and there is no legal consequent conclusion that the alleged victim was not in fact a victim, nor that the prosecution was wrong to prosecute. Whether a civil claim succeeds or fails, however, the consequences are broadly the same, although they fall

[86] The mediaeval Roman-canon courts developed processes and evidential rules that respected the dignity of the individual in civil as well as criminal actions, and were consequently slow. The change in civil process may be the result of changes in the commercial courts across Europe in the course of the modern period. Nörr has suggested that this was because 'no more the individual in its entirety is at stake nor the law itself which covers man and his fate. The conflict, instead, turns to demarcated and depersonalized issues': K. Nörr, 'Procedure in Mercantile Matters: Some Comparative Aspects', in V. Piergiovanni, *The Courts and the Development of Commercial Law* (Berlin: Duncker and Humblot, 1987), p. 195.

[87] This rule is no longer absolute in England, following the Criminal Justice Act 2003.

on opposite parties. Because of the use of counter-claims, it is likely that, if the claimant fails against the defendant, then the defendant will succeed in her claim against the claimant.

The third practical consequence is that the civil courts will be more willing to admit evidence of questionable reliability than will the criminal courts, and to decide the question of reliability as a question of weight rather than of admissibility. In England, for example, the ultimate issue and hearsay rules have both been abolished in civil evidence.[88] At the same time, the criminal courts regularly consider an additional ground of inadmissibility: that the evidence, although relevant and reliable, is unduly prejudicial to the defendant.[89] The general effect of this should be that criminal cases will tend to be decided on less evidence than civil cases, with the intention that the more serious consequences of a criminal verdict should only be arrived at by reliance on more reliable evidence.

The fourth practical consequence is that, while the rules of civil procedure assume that the parties are equal, and then make provision for possible inequalities,[90] the rules of criminal procedure assume that the prosecution will be at a considerable advantage, and seek to limit the effect of these inequalities. Expert evidence, for example, is usually provided by the prosecution in North American and European criminal trials. This is for three reasons. First, the prosecution 'owns' the crime scene, controlling its investigation and possession of any evidence taken from it. Secondly, forensic science has little practical application outside the criminal justice system, and most forensic scientists are employed by the state. Thirdly, the state has greater budgetary resources than most defendants for conducting forensic scientific tests. Examples of practical steps taken to reduce this 'inequality of arms' are that the prosecuting counsel in England must act as a 'minister of justice' and exercise restraint in her prosecution, there are greater duties of pre-trial disclosure on the prosecution than there are on the defence, and the defence may be able to exclude evidence because the prosecution has improperly obtained it.[91]

88 Civil Evidence Act 1973, ss. 3(1), 3(2); Civil Evidence Act 1995, s. 1.

89 Police and Criminal Evidence Act 1984, s. 78; Federal Rules of Evidence, r. 403; Roberts and Zuckerman, *Criminal Evidence*, pp. 23, 148, ch. 11.

90 E.g. CPR, r. 1.1(2)(a) requires that the court 'so far as is practicable – ensur[es] that the parties are on an equal footing', while r. 35.9 enables the court to order one party to provide expert information to another party which may otherwise lack that information.

91 E.g. Roberts and Zuckerman, *Criminal Evidence*, ch. 4.

This has been a relatively brief introduction to some of the differences between civil and criminal fact finding, illustrated principally with examples from England. Its purpose has been to show that, in the same way that legal fact finding is a special form of everyday fact finding, so civil and criminal process each have special forms of fact finding falling under the general 'legal' heading. There appears to be a significant focus in criminal fact finding on establishing the truth of a single hypothesis ('D is guilty'), using carefully selected evidence which must reach a high threshold of proof. Although we might say that Anglo-American criminal justice is adversarial, many of the evidential features are shaped around the need to defend the individual against the state. The policy considerations in civil evidence tend to revolve around ensuring that a dispute between two (legally) equal parties is resolved expeditiously and justly.[92] The lower burden of proof reflects a greater preparedness for there to be errors in decision making, in part because the consequences of a wrong civil decision are less significant for the individual than are the consequences of a wrong criminal decision, and in part because civil fact finding is more symmetrical. The policy and practical differences between civil and criminal fact finding in turn justify some consideration of the two areas separately. One illustration that has been given above of the differences between civil and criminal fact finding is the use specifically of expert evidence in the two contexts. It is for this reason that this book is devoted to an examination of the assessment of only civil expert evidence.

1.3.3.2 The composition of the court

The second major area of internal variation within legal fact finding is in the composition of the court. There is scope for considerable variation in composition arrangements, and this variation may reflect the perceived effectiveness of a particular arrangement in supporting the court in arriving at an accurate finding of fact for a particular type of litigation. However, it is also clear that it may reflect political considerations, such as whether the citizen is entitled to be judged by her peers. In England, almost all civil trials (except for malicious prosecution, false imprisonment and

[92] A civil defendant must respond to the allegations against her, or risk default judgment. A criminal defendant, on the other hand, is not required to defend herself, both because there is a much higher evidential burden on the prosecution than on the civil claimant, and because the general rule is that adverse inferences cannot be drawn from a criminal defendant's silence (for exceptions to the 'right to silence', see K. Grevling, 'Restrictions on the Right to Silence – Introduction', in H. Malek (ed.), *Phipson on Evidence* (London: Sweet and Maxwell, 2005), pp. 1039–56.

libel cases) are decided before a judge sitting alone. In the United States, around half of federal trials are decided before a judge sitting alone, and the remainder before a judge and jury.[93] In continental Europe, cases will be heard by one or more judges sitting as a unicameral tribunal. It would be nice to think that we therefore need to consider only three scenarios when evaluating the effectiveness of the different court compositions for civil litigation in terms of accurate fact determination. However, rather than being a simple question of judge-and-jury versus judge-only, the range of options for the composition of the court in fact combines at least six variables, which are rarely explicitly considered. In this section, I shall explore some of the implications of the possible combinations of those variables. There are three benefits to this exercise. First, it helps us to understand better the specific characteristics of the court composition options that we have adopted. Secondly, empirical research intended to assess the merits of one type of tribunal over another needs to take on board that there are multiple variables that need to be controlled.[94] Thirdly, it makes us more aware that the arrangements that we currently have in place are very far from being inevitable, and so we should be prepared to consider varying our current arrangements if this seems a possible route to increasing the fact-finding accuracy of our civil processes. If we discuss only the merits of judge-only versus judge-and-jury trials, then this shows that we have yet to engage fully with the range of possibilities for constituting courts to decide civil or criminal matters.

The first variable is whether the court should be unicameral, deciding questions of law and fact, or bicameral, consisting of separate tribunals of law and fact. The second variable is how many people should be in each tribunal. The third is whether those people should be lawyers or non-lawyers. The fourth is whether the people on the tribunal regularly sit on the tribunal. The fifth is whether those people should be specialists in the factual subject matter in the case or not. The sixth is whether either tribunal should give reasons for its decision; there is little uniformity in

[93] E. Sward, *The Decline of the Civil Jury* (Durham NC: Carolina Academic Press, 2001), p. 13.

[94] E.g. B. Spencer, 'Estimating the Accuracy of Jury Verdicts' (2007) 4 *Journal of Empirical Legal Studies* 305–29 provides useful evidence for how jurors and judges may have come to different decisions in the same cases, but does not consider which variable gave rise to discrepancies between judge and jury decisions in the study, and indeed whether there would have been disagreement if two judges or two panels of juries had been asked to decide the same cases.

this variable in the practice of real-world tribunals. The last two of these variables are not usually considered in any judge/jury debate.

If we simplify the second variable down to a binary choice of 'one' or 'many', assume that there is no need to distinguish between different types of lawyer-judge, and assume that one cannot have mixed tribunals, such as lawyers and specialists sitting together to decide facts, then there are at least 32 possible forms of unicameral court, and 1,024 possible forms of bicameral court.[95] Some of those forms are unlikely to materialize, such as an engineering case in which a panel of non-lawyer engineers decide questions of law while a sole lawyer with no formal engineering knowledge decides all questions of fact, and where neither tribunal gives any explanation for the final verdict, but many of these 1,024 possible court arrangements are viable. This is of course just in relation to trial. One could imagine further combinations for pre-trial case management and post-trial sentencing and costs orders. For each of the six variables, we should consider the fact-finding effectiveness of the options available. This begins to give us some indication of the likely overall fact-finding effectiveness of combinations of variables.

First, what are the relative merits, in terms of accurate fact finding, of the court being unicameral or bicameral? The advantage of a unicameral tribunal is that it is seemingly more natural, and perhaps therefore more effective,[96] for the fact finder to receive all the evidence, and then decide what weight to accord the evidence, or indeed whether to consider it at all. The advantage of a bicameral tribunal is twofold. First, it allows us to use different criteria for selecting what sort of decision maker should sit in each tribunal. Secondly, and this is the converse of the argument for unicameral courts, there are epistemological and political advantages, particularly in the context of legal rather than everyday fact finding, to stopping the tribunal of fact from receiving evidence that is unreliable,

[95] It is just about possible to imagine an arrangement where the trial court had more than two tribunals. For example, there could be a five-part court where one tribunal decided procedural and evidential questions during the trial, a second decided which expert evidence to accept, and a third took the advice of the second and combined it with its own views on the non-expert witnesses and came to a finding of fact, and a fourth took the finding of the third and decided whether this amounted to a finding for the claimant/prosecution or the defendant. The fifth would decide on sentence/remedies. Thankfully, it is difficult to imagine a situation where such a court would come into existence.

[96] It is a limitation of the Benthamite argument for 'natural' fact finding that there is no necessary reason to believe that natural fact finding is always more reliable than artificially constrained fact finding.

prejudicial or improperly obtained. The alternative is for us to require that the judge is aware of evidence as a human being, of which she is judicially unaware in her fact finding.[97]

The second variable concerns how many people should be in each tribunal. It may be the case, for example, that the quality of decision making by a group is greater than the quality of decision making by any individual member of the group. This may be linked to the necessity (in normal circumstances) of reasoned discussion between panel members before a decision is reached.[98] This discussion is likely to ensure both that all involved agree on the nature of the evidence, and that there is reasoned debate about how to derive its significance. An alternative, non-collaborative explanation of how groups arrive at their decision might be that each member of the group reflects by herself on the evidence, and then all vote to see if they have yet formed a consensus, repeating the process in virtual silence until a verdict is reached. This seems, however, to be an unlikely alternative. A related benefit of group rather than individual decision making is that the risk of individual bias is reduced the more decision makers one involves (Section 7.2).

The third variable is whether the tribunal should be made up of lawyers or non-lawyers. The extensive reliance of the English criminal justice system on lay (non-lawyer) magistrates shows that there is no necessary reason why a unicameral court should always consist of lawyers. Non-lawyer magistrates sit in panels of three, with the assistance of a legally qualified clerk. In practice, however, non-lawyer magistrates do not decide legally complex or serious cases. Where a court is to hear a legally complex case, it would be problematic for non-lawyers to preside over a unicameral court or tribunal of law. Conversely, however, there is no conclusive reason why lawyers should not sit in a tribunal of fact.[99] There may at first blush appear to be reasons that relate to lawyers' greater experience of legal evidence, but this in fact falls under our fourth court composition variable. Courts with a non-lawyer tribunal of fact may have a greater ability to achieve accurate fact determination than those with a lawyer tribunal of fact, because the non-lawyer tribunal members bring with them a wider range of experience. This is particularly true where the court is being asked

[97] E.g. *Air Canada* v. *Secretary of State for Trade* (No. 2) [1983] 2 AC 394, at 435.

[98] D. Devine, J. Buddenbaum, S. Houp, D. Stolle and N. Studebaker, 'Deliberation Quality: A Preliminary Examination in Criminal Juries' (2007) 4 *Journal of Empirical Legal Studies* 273–303.

[99] In England, s. 321 of the Criminal Justice Act 2003 now requires that judges serve on juries if called in their capacity as private citizens.

to decide questions of specialist knowledge, involving expert evidence. Most lawyers have a limited scientific education. Against this argument, a random selection of lawyers would have a much higher level of education generally than a random selection of the population as a whole, and there is currently no mechanism for ensuring that jurors with specialist experience appear in relevant specialist cases. Particularly in criminal trials, there may also be constitutional reasons to choose to include non-lawyers in the court's decision-making process, to say whether an individual's behaviour should be classified as criminal. This relates in particular to the selection of the generalizations that the tribunal of fact may use in arriving at its conclusions (Section 1.4.3). These constitutional reasons are independent of the fact-finding effectiveness of the resulting court composition.

The fourth variable relates to the degree of experience of court matters that our tribunal members should have. In the traditional 'judge versus judge-and-jury' debate, it is clear that judges have far greater experience of fact finding in a legal context than do jurors, and so we might expect them to be more practised at receiving large volumes of badly structured, new material, of variable reliability, and making a reasoned decision from it. However, even a cursory examination of this variable indicates that there are far more issues involved in understanding the relative merits of the experienced and the one-off fact finder. First, the English criminal justice system employs lay people to constitute both unicameral tribunals in magistrates' courts and lay juries in the Crown Court. The general experience of the English legal profession is that lay magistrates, who have extensive experience of part-time work in this role, are more likely to convict in criminal trials than are lay juries, who are empanelled only for one trial. There are a number of possible reasons: first, magistrates may have become inured to giving defendants the benefit of the doubt; secondly, magistrates may have developed better fact-finding skills; thirdly, juries usually receive more developed legal arguments and evidence than do magistrates; fourthly, juries may be better fact finders because they consider only questions of fact.

A second reason to believe that experience is a variable that needs to be considered when deciding on the fact-finding effectiveness of different court compositions is that not all judges have equal experience of fact finding, and not all have been selected for any particular skill in this area. An English High Court judge, or a United States Article III federal judge, the most senior levels of appointment in their respective jurisdictions, will have extensive trial experience, and is likely to have been selected towards the end of a distinguished career, for her ability in deciding complex legal and factual issues. An English judge, or a United States federal judge, is appointed as the result of careful consideration by the state. Many United States state judges, however, are directly elected, and may have greater political than legal skills. In continental Europe, most judges belong to a career judiciary, and first instance cases may be heard by a junior appointee in their late twenties, with little trial experience compared with their Anglo-American cousins.

The fifth variable is whether the court should be made up of appropriate technical specialists. This is only really a realistic question in relation to a unicameral court or to the tribunal of fact within a bicameral court. The empanelling of experts onto juries provides a possible means by which to integrate expertise into the legal process. The involvement of specialists in the tribunal of fact has a long history in the Anglo-American tradition, in the form of special juries (Section 5.4). Empanelling tribunals of experts appears to be primarily attractive today to those procedural systems that still rely on non-lawyer juries as the tribunal of fact, particularly the United States of America.[100] In English civil procedure, where the use of the jury has all but come to an end, this is therefore an option of primarily academic rather than immediately practical interest, for example in relation to possible reforms to the conducting of complex criminal trials, such as fraud trials.[101] The practical difficulty with reintroducing special juries is that it may present a drain on the professions involved. For example, where now a medical negligence trial might require two surgeons for a few days each to give expert evidence, if the case were to be heard instead before a special jury of surgeons, we might expect to deprive the country of a panel's worth of surgeons for several weeks.

There are also constitutional and veritistic difficulties. The constitutional difficulty is that if a tribunal of fact is composed of a group of specialists, then if one of the parties is also such a specialist and the other

[100] E.g. L. Hand, 'Historical and Practical Considerations Regarding Expert Testimony' (1901) 15 *Harvard Law Review* 40–58; 'Practice and Potential of the Advisory Jury' (1987) 100 *Harvard Law Review* 1363–81; K. Bertelsen, 'From Specialized Courts to Specialized Juries: Calling For Professional Juries in Complex Civil Litigation' (1998) 3 *Suffolk Journal of Trial and Appellate Advocacy* 1; A. Feigenbaum, 'Special Juries: Deterring Spurious Medical Malpractice Litigation in State Courts' (2003) 24 *Cardozo Law Review* 1361–420; J. Oldham, 'The Origins of the Special Jury' (1983) 50 *University of Chicago Law Review* 137–221; J. Oldham, 'The History of the Special (Struck) Jury in the United States' (1998) 6 *William and Mary Bill of Rights Journal* 623–75; F. Strier, 'The Educated Jury: A Proposal for Complex Litigation' (1997) 47 *DePaul Law Review* 49–83.

[101] R. Auld, *Review of the Criminal Courts of England and Wales* (London: Her Majesty's Stationery Office, 2001), [5.185].

is not (for example in a professional negligence action), then there would be reasonable grounds to suspect potential if not actual bias on the part of the tribunal. Specialist tribunals might therefore only work where both parties belonged to the same group of specialists. The veritistic issue is that, while the specialists may be the most appropriate people to hear those parts of a case that concern their particular specialization, in most cases expert evidence comprises only part of the evidential matrix of the case. There is therefore a significant risk that the specialists will give undue weight to that part of the evidence in which they are themselves experienced.

The sixth variable is whether a tribunal should give reasons for its decision. Under the jurisprudence of Art. 6 of the European Convention on Human Rights, the 'duty to give reasons' is increasingly being seen as a central feature of a fair trial.[102] The duty to give reasons arises both from the requirement that decisions by the tribunals of law and fact should represent the reasoned rather than arbitrary exercise of power, and from the right of those subject to a court's decision to know the basis on which that decision was reached, in order to be able to challenge the decision. Anglo-American juries are forbidden by domestic law from giving reasons for their decisions.[103] It remains untested whether the unreasoned decisions of juries are compatible with Art. 6.[104] A possible basis for allowing unreasoned jury decisions under Art. 6 might be that we can at least be (almost)[105] certain that the jury reached a reasoned decision, although that reasoning is secret. In contrast, where a one-member tribunal gives its decision, we have no guarantee, in the absence of a statement of reasons, that this was not an arbitrary decision.

There is an extensive body of scholarship on the relative effectiveness of the use of judges and juries in relation to accurate fact finding. Most of that scholarship originates in the United States.[106] By identifying that

[102] *English* v. *Emery Reimbold & Strick* [2002] EWCA Civ 605.

[103] *R* v. *Connor* [2004] UKHL 2; [2004] 1 AC 1118; [2004] 2 WLR 201; [2004] 1 All ER 925.

[104] E.g. J. Spencer, 'Inscrutable Verdicts, the Duty to Give Reasons and Article 6 of the European Convention on Human Rights' (2001) 1 *Archbold News* 5–8.

[105] E.g. *Connor*, in which there is evidence that the jury briefly, albeit apparently seriously, considered tossing a coin.

[106] E.g. E. Sunderland, 'The Inefficiency of the American Jury' (1915) 13 *Michigan Law Review* 302–16; J. Miner, 'The Jury Problem' (1946) *Journal of Criminal Law and Criminology* 1–15; H. Erlanger, 'Jury Research in America: its Past and Future' (1970) 4 *Law and Society Review* 345–70; H. Zeisel and S. Diamond, '"Convincing Empirical Evidence" on the Six Member Jury' (1974) 41 *University of Chicago Law Review* 281–95; 'The Case for Special Juries in Complex Civil Litigation' (1980) 89 *Yale Law Journal* 1155–76; A. Rubin, 'Trial

there are at least six variables that relate to decisions about the constitution of the court, with possibly a minimum of 1,056 ways of combining those variables, what I hope to have illustrated is that this literature is for the most part overly narrow in its scope.[107] The scope may allow us to address a question such as 'Should we keep our current judge-and-jury arrangement or should we let our current judges sit alone?' It does not, however, open up the field to begin to consider what combination of variables might be most effective at achieving accurate fact determination,[108] nor how those various combinations combine with non-veritistic criteria for deciding whether a procedural arrangement is appropriate.[109] In turn, the fact-finding effectiveness of the composition arrangement may be affected by the type of litigation in issue, and in particular whether it is civil or criminal.

1.4 Justifying legal belief

We have seen, in Section 1.3, that justified legal belief possesses some distinctive characteristics that relate to the courts as social institutions, and to the courts' use of beliefs about facts in practical reasoning. In this section, I examine the basis on which we justify beliefs about facts, both in terms of a meta-justification known as the Rationalist Tradition (Section 1.4.1) and the elements that arise from that meta-justification, of atomism (Section 1.4.2), generalizations (Section 1.4.3) and probabilistic reasoning.

by Jury in Complex Civil Cases: Voice of Liberty or Verdict of Confusion?' (1982) 462 *Annals of the American Academy of Political and Social Science* 87–103; R. Lempert, 'Civil Juries and Complex Cases: Let's Not Rush to Judgment' (1981) 80 *Michigan Law Review* 68–132; R. Hastie, D. Schkade and J. Payne, 'A Study of Juror and Jury Judgments in Civil Cases: Deciding Liability for Punitive Damages' (1998) 22 *Law and Human Behaviour* 287–314; B. Bornstein, 'The Ecological Validity of Jury Simulations: Is the Jury Still Out?' (1999) 23 *Law and Human Behaviour* 75–91. For an English example, see J. Jackson and S. Doran, 'Judge and Jury: Towards a New Division of Labour in Criminal Trials' 60 *Modern Law Review* 759–78.

107 There are some notable exceptions, which have begun to attempt to deconstruct the judge versus judge-and-jury debate into some of its constituent parts, e. g. M. Damaška, *Evidence Law Adrift* (New Haven CT: Yale University Press, 1997), ch. 2, and, more generally for procedure, M. Damaška, *The Faces of Justice and State Authority: A Comparative Approach to the Legal Process* (New Haven CT: Yale University Press, 1986).

108 Such an exercise would be far from trivial, e. g. Damaška, 'Presentation of Evidence'.

109 Compare the discussion in Chapter 4, as well as Stein, *Foundations*, and Twining, *Rethinking Evidence*, pp. 1–3.

Justification is itself subject to meta-justification. We must be able to justify our criteria for belief justification, in other words show that our justified beliefs approximate to truth, or else we lapse into metaphysics or superstition. For example, in his ethnography of the use of magic among the Azande, a tribe in north central Africa, Evans-Pritchard sought to demonstrate that this usage could be justified on the Azande's own terms.[110] However, the fact that the Azande can justify their practice to themselves does not require that we should necessarily accept that justification. How then do we justify the use of our chosen method of justification? This is perhaps a greater difficulty for legal than for classical epistemology. While classical epistemology may concern itself with the criteria on which an individual chooses to rely in order to be confident that he has got closest to the truth of a matter, legal epistemology needs to establish a common basis on which we as a society (or a group within society) will accept certain criteria in preference to others. Meta-justification is itself subject to justification, and if we seek to justify empirical justification by reference to a form of itself, then our difficulties appear insoluble, and we enter self-referential infinite recursion. The solution, at least for legal (and perhaps other forms of social) epistemology, may be that the ultimate justification comes from outside the justificatory regression, and is based on non-epistemological, political criteria. We have encountered political criteria already, in the context of the distinctions between criminal and civil fact finding (Section 1.3.3.1) and factors that may affect the choice of judges, juries or experts in fact finding (Section 1.3.3.2). The political factors that surround the meta-justification of rationalism are equally profound, and are introduced in Section 1.4.1, and followed through as a thread in the justificatory details of the remainder of Section 1.4.

Politically based meta-justification, such as the Rationalist Tradition, can be seen as being paradigmatic, in a Kuhnian sense, in that assertions made within the paradigm may make little sense to those operating in different paradigms, such as strong forms of naturalized epistemology and post-modernism.[111] To say that the assertions make little sense is not the same as saying that statements in one paradigm are necessarily incommensurable with statements in another paradigm, and this is a discussion to which we return later in Chapter 3. It is not necessary to

[110] E. Evans-Pritchard, *Witchcraft, Oracles and Magic among the Azande* (Oxford: Oxford University Press, 1937).

[111] T. Kuhn, *The Structure of Scientific Revolutions* (Chicago: University of Chicago Press, 1962).

accept the Rationalist Tradition as the paradigm within which evidence law should be developed and understood in order to follow the argument of this book, but it is necessary as a minimum to understand something of what the Rationalist Tradition entails. The optimistic rationality presented in Section 1.4 has been subject to serious challenge by the work of cognitive psychologists on innate, subconscious biases in our decision making, and I move on to consider this in Section 1.5.

1.4.1 Meta-justification: the Rationalist Tradition of evidence scholarship

In his seminal essay on 'The Rationalist Tradition of Evidence Scholarship',[112] Twining proposed that we can observe 'a remarkable homogeneity about the basic assumptions of almost all specialist writings on evidence from Gilbert through Bentham, Thayer and Wigmore to Cross and McCormick'.[113] Twining emphasizes that there is both an analytical and a historical aspect to his account of the Rationalist Tradition.[114] Analytically, it is an attempt to produce an 'ideal type', with which to analyse evidence discourse and doctrine. Historically, it advances the hypothesis that the works of a list of named evidence writers largely conform to the ideal type. It only relates to specialized evidence discourse, noting the historical disjunction from procedural writings, and is based primarily on Bentham's ideas. That Twining has argued that a Rationalist Tradition exists as a historical fact does not entail that he accepts its approach. It is also possible that an alternative model might be produced, which does not take Bentham's ideas as its central point while still exhibiting a similar 'remarkable homogeneity' amongst evidence writers. However, such a model remains to be produced.

[112] Twining, 'The Rationalist Tradition', p. 77. This was based on Twining, *Theories of Evidence*, pp. 1–18. For a critique of Twining's proposed Rationalist Tradition, see K. Graham, '"There'll Always be an England": the Instrumental Ideology of Evidence' (1987) 85 *Michigan Law Review*, 1204–34 (particularly 1207–9, 1227–31), with responses by P. Tillers, 'Prejudice, Politics and Proof' (1988) 86 *Michigan Law Review* 768–75 (particularly 773–4), and W. Twining, 'Hot Air in the Redwoods, A Sequel to the Wind in the Willows' (1988) 86 *Michigan Law Review* 1523–47 (particularly 1528–39, 1544–6).

[113] Gilbert, *Law of Evidence*; Bentham, *Rationale of Judicial Evidence*; Thayer, *Preliminary Treatise*; Wigmore, *Science of Judicial Proof*; J. Wigmore, *A Treatise on the Anglo-American System of Evidence in Trials at Common Law*, rev. edn Tiller (Boston: Little, Brown, 1983); A. Cross, *Evidence* (London: Butterworth, 1958); C. McCormick, *Handbook on the Law of Evidence* (St Paul MN: West, 1954).

[114] Twining, 'Hot Air', 1531.

Twining classifies the majority of these writers as being not only rationalists,[115] but 'optimistic' rationalists, since they tended to believe that the standards of rational adjudication were a feasible aspiration, even if not currently attained.

The assumptions of optimistic rationalism provide us with the default meta-justification for legal fact finding in western legal systems today. The question 'Is this legal belief about facts properly justified?' can be answered in the first instance by asking whether the justification for a belief conforms to Twining's assumptions. We shall begin with Twining's summary of these assumptions, and then move on to consider their own justification.

Twining summarizes these assumptions of rationalist fact finding in the form of two models. The first is of a Rationalist Model of Adjudication. The second represents standard elements in rationalist theories of evidence. Twining concedes that a sharp distinction between the two models is artificial, but not all evidence scholars express clearly what they feel should be in the first model, and there is greater agreement on the content of the second model than of the first.[116] Most debates about evidence have taken place within this rationalist approach. For example, discussion of illegally obtained evidence proceeds on the basis that the value of such evidence to accurate fact finding is of a central importance, and the tightening up of due process is therefore seen as a response to this central concern. We might alternatively conceptualize such 'fruit of the poisoned tree' arguments in terms of the extent to which legal process may deviate from

115 Twining's evidential rationalism is part of a broader English school of rationalism, 'the method and doctrine of those who strive to make reason the supreme regulator of their beliefs, and of their actions; who try to think and speak in terms to which fixed and intelligible senses are attached; who neither assert anything that to their knowledge is inconsistent with admitted truth, nor shrink from accepting the logical consequences of such truth . . . and who similarly desire never to act without a conscious purpose . . . or with means that conflict with their foreseen ends': A. Benn, *The History of English Rationalism in the Nineteenth Century* (London: Longmans, Green & Co., 1906), p. 1. It should be distinguished from the continental rationalist tradition, developed by philosophers such as Leibniz, Descartes and Kant, 'most often characterized as an epistemological position. On this view, to be a rationalist requires at least one of the following: (1) a privileging of reason and intuition over sensation and experience, (2) regarding all or most ideas as innate rather than adventitious, (3) an emphasis on certain rather than merely probable knowledge as the goal of enquiry': T. Lennon and S. Dea, 'Continental Rationalism," in E. Zalta (ed.), *The Stanford Encyclopedia of Philosophy* (Winter 2007 Edition), http://plato.stanford.edu/archives/win2007/ entries/continental–rationalism/ (last accessed 1 August 2008).

116 Twining, 'Rationalist Tradition', p. 79.

fundamental social and procedural values, with the probative value of the evidence as secondary.[117]

Twining's 'Rationalist Model of Adjudication' has twenty-seven elements, divided into Prescriptive and Descriptive, which are reproduced here for ease of reference:

A. Prescriptive
   1. The direct end
   2. of adjective law
   3. is rectitude of decision through correct application
   4. of valid substantive laws
   5. deemed to be consonant with utility (or otherwise good)
   6. and through accurate determination
   7. of the true past facts
   8. material to
   9. precisely specified allegations expressed in categories defined in advance by law, i.e. facts in issue
   10. proved to specified standards of probability or likelihood
   11. on the basis of the careful
   12. and rational
   13. weighing
   14. of evidence
   15. which is both relevant
   16. and reliable
   17. presented (in a form designed to bring out truth and discover untruth)
   18. to supposedly competent
   19. and impartial
   20. decision makers
   21. with adequate safeguards against corruption
   22. and mistake
   23. and adequate provision for review and appeal.

[117] D. Dwyer, 'Closed Evidence, Reasonable Suspicion and Torture' (2005) 9 *Evidence and Proof* 126–31; W. Twining and P. Twining, 'Bentham on Torture' (1973) 24 *Northern Ireland Legal Quarterly* 305–56; Roberts and Zuckerman, *Criminal Evidence*, ch. 4. English civil evidence would appear to have a more ambivalent attitude to improperly obtained evidence than does criminal evidence, e.g. *Vernon* v. *Bosley (No. 2)* [1999] QB 18; [1997] 1 All ER 614, where the Court of Appeal in the Queen's Bench considered evidence from documents that had come anonymously into the possession of one of the parties' solicitors from the Family Division. Only one of the three judges was concerned at the use of evidence obtained in this way.

B. Descriptive
   24. Generally speaking this objective is largely achieved
   25. in a consistent
   26. fair
   27. and predictable manner.

Twining's 'Common Assumptions in Rationalist Theories of Evidence and Proof' has nine, more detailed, elements.

1. Knowledge about particular past events is possible.
2. Establishing the truth about particular past events in issue in a case (the facts in issue) is a necessary condition for achieving justice in adjudication; incorrect results are one form of injustice.
3. The notions of evidence and proof in adjudication are concerned with rational methods of determining questions of fact. In this context, operative distinctions have to be maintained between questions of fact and questions of law, questions of fact and questions of value, and questions of fact and questions of opinion.
4. The establishment of the truth of alleged facts in adjudication is typically a matter of probabilities, falling short of absolute certainty.
5. (a) Judgments about the probabilities of allegations about particular past events can and should be reached from reasoning from relevant evidence presented to the decision maker;
   (b) the characteristic mode of reasoning appropriate to reasoning about probabilities is induction.
6. Judgments about probabilities have, generally speaking, to be based on the available stock of knowledge about the common course of events. This is largely a matter of common sense supplemented by specialized scientific or expert knowledge when it is available.
7. The pursuit of truth (i.e. seeking to maximize accuracy in fact determination) is to be given a high, but not necessarily an overriding, priority in relation to other values, such as security of the state, protection of family relationships, curbing of coercive methods of interrogation.
8. One crucial basis for evaluating 'fact finding' institutions, rules, procedures and techniques is how far they are estimated to maximize accuracy in fact determination but other criteria such as speed, cheapness, procedural fairness, humaneness, public confidence and the avoidance of vexation for participants are also to be taken into account.
9. The primary role of applied forensic psychology and forensic science is to provide guidance about the reliability of different kinds of evidence and to develop methods and devices for increasing such reliability.

Of these criteria, it is questionable whether the seventh and eighth should be correctly included in a definition of rational proof, since they are concerned with modifying a rational fact-finding process in the light of other social requirements, such as duty of the state to act in a lawful fashion,[118] and the physical inviolability of the accused and the convicted. Although this present work broadly concurs with this ideal type of the Rationalist Tradition of evidence scholarship, the main point of departure is over whether an operational distinction has to be maintained between evidence of fact and of opinion. The basis of that dispute is explored in Section 2.2.

The Rationalist Tradition of evidence scholarship, as an ideal type, is proposed by Twining as a historical fact rather than a normative aspiration. However, it seems correct to ask whether we should infer from the general adoption of a rationalist model of legal proof an acceptance by evidence scholars that legal evidence should be rationalist. Further, there seems little reason to dispute a broad congruence between evidence scholarship and evidence practice. But why should we accept that the Rationalist Tradition of evidence scholarship is the best means by which to conduct judicial fact finding? If we were being particularly mischievous, then we might ask why the courts should even seek to engage in judicial fact finding at all.[119] If we begin with the more mischievous question first, it is not as superficial as it may at first seem. We can imagine legal systems in which: (a) the courts invoke a divine decision; (b) the courts take statements from the parties, and resolve conflicting statements on the basis of social status; or (c) the courts will base their decision on compromise between the parties in civil matters, and defendant confession in a criminal matter. Not only can we imagine such situations, but we can observe them either today in non-western legal systems, or in western legal history.[120] We might also imagine

[118] M. Damaška, 'Evidentiary Barriers to Conviction and Two Models of Criminal Procedure' (1973) 121 *University of Pennsylvania Law Review* 506–89; G. Ubertis, *Argomenti di procedura penale* (Milan: Giuffrè, 2002), p. 5.

[119] Whether the courts wish to determine the truth is, strictly, a separate question from whether they have in place effective mechanisms for ascertaining the truth. This frustration with actual mechanisms rather than potential attainment appears to be the origin of Jerome Frank's 'fact scepticism': Twining, 'Some Scepticism About Some Scepticisms', pp. 116–19.

[120] E.g. R. Aigler and I. Yates, 'The Triangle of Culture, Inference and Litigation System' (2003) 2 *Law Probability and Risk* 137–50; M. Damaška, 'Rational and Irrational Proof Revisited' (1997) 5 *Cardozo Journal of International and Comparative Law* 25–39; Langbein, *Torture*; Helmholz, *Ius Commune*, pp. 82–134; F. McAuley, 'Canon Law and the End of the Ordeal'

a legal system in which a dispute is resolved by the rolling of dice,[121] or the tossing of a coin.[122] Such legal systems have never actually existed, but they do provide us with a challenge: if we are to say, as Bentham argued, that rectitude of decision requires accurate fact determination, then we must be able to demonstrate that our chosen method of fact determination provides accurate results more than 50 per cent of the time.

The answer to 'Why bother with judicial fact finding?', or alternatively 'Why decide cases on the basis of something other than judicial fact finding?', turns out not to be straightforward, and allows of more than one answer. First, as McAuley has shown in his masterly study of the end of the ordeal by the Fourth Lateran Council in 1215,[123] the use of such non-rational modes of proof was seen as being a last resort, when judicial fact finding had proved, or would prove, unsuccessful. One of the reasons that the ordeal was effectively ended by the Catholic Church was that more effective procedural mechanisms for fact finding had become available. The use of decisory and compurgatory oaths was similarly a product of a failure of rational fact-finding processes. The decisory oath is available in some continental civil jurisdictions today, such as France and Italy, for use when the parties are unable to present any other evidence. Thirdly, the mediaeval European canon courts and many contemporary Asian courts may be reluctant to engage in judicial fact finding because to do so is to encroach on the dignity of the individual, by concluding that one party is more truthful (and ultimately more right) than the other, and imposing that conclusion. It is only this third answer that provides us with a true alternative to judicial fact finding as the groundwork for correctly deciding a dispute. Although contemporary European civil techniques such as alternative dispute resolution allow for a matter to be resolved without any judicial ascription of blame, it seems that such approaches have developed from motives of efficiency.

So let us return to our first, less mischievous question: why should we accept that the Rationalist Tradition of evidence scholarship is the best means by which to conduct judicial fact finding? This question can be

(2006) 26 *Oxford Journal of Legal Studies* 473–513; R. Rodes, 'The Canon Law as a Legal System – Function, Obligation, and Sanction' (1964) 9 *Natural Law Forum* 45–94.

[121] The practice of Judge Bridlegoose, in François Rabelais' sixteenth-century satirical novel *Gargantua and Pantagruel*.

[122] As in *R* v. *Connor*. [123] McAuley, 'Canon Law'.

addressed at two levels. The first is that developments in legal epistemology, particularly in the areas of atomism, inductive reasoning, generalization and probability are, empirically, conducive to accurate fact determination. The idea that knowledge of the world should be gained and evaluated on the basis of inferences about the world rather than from personal authority and tradition would appear to have begun to develop in European society in the fourteenth century.[124] The concept of facts began to be developed by lawyers, before philosophers and scientists, in the sixteenth century. This is important both for the concept of atomism, and for the operational law/fact distinction within the Rationalist Tradition.[125] The use of generalizations began to be developed in the Roman-canon courts in the form of presumptions, and was well advanced by the late sixteenth century.[126] Probability theory emerged in the middle of the seventeenth century,[127] and was soon applied to legal and moral practical reasoning,[128] alongside the new practice of inductive reasoning in questions about facts.[129] Since induction necessarily lacks the certainty of conclusion that is provided by deduction, Ian Hacking has suggested that a theory of probability was a necessary development to support the use of inductive reasoning.[130]

The philosophical basis for a coherent theory of inferential reasoning as we would understand it today was developed by Locke[131] and Hume[132] between 1670 and 1748. Three core propositions of the work of these empiricist philosophers are of interest here: first, we have no a priori knowledge, and so all our knowledge of the world is gained by induction

[124] U. Eco, *Il nome della rosa*, 47th edn (Milan: Tascabili Bompiani, 2001), pp. 13 and 31. This commitment to reason may, however, have arisen from a 'faith in reason' rather than from the demonstrable success of reason in supporting fact finding.

[125] B. Shapiro, *A Culture of Fact: England 1550–1720* (Ithaca NY: Cornell University Press, 2000).

[126] J. Menochius, *Tractatus de praesumptionibus, conjecturis, signis et indiciis* (Venice: 1590).

[127] I. Hacking, *The Emergence of Probability: A Philosophical Study of Early Ideas About Probability, Induction and Statistical Inference* (Cambridge: Cambridge University Press, 1975).

[128] B. Shapiro, *'Beyond Reasonable Doubt' and 'Probable Cause': Historical Perspectives on the Anglo-American Law of Evidence* (Berkeley CA: University of California Press, 1991).

[129] F. Bacon, *Advancement of Learning* (London: 1605).

[130] Hacking, *Emergence of Probability*, pp. 31–48.

[131] Locke, *Essay*.

[132] D. Hume, *A Treatise of Human Nature* (1740) ed. P. Nidditch, 2nd edn (Oxford: Oxford University Press, 1978); D. Hume, *Enquiries Concerning Human Understanding* (1748), ed. P. Nidditch, 3rd edn (Oxford: Oxford University Press, 1975).

from basic experiences;[133] secondly, these inferences and thus this knowledge are probabilistic;[134] thirdly, we possess a common ability to infer reliably.[135] The effect of this third proposition is to say that all people are in a position to form valid knowledge of the world, and so we should not say a priori that some people will form more reliable probabilistic inferences than others, or that we cannot share the conclusions of our inferences with one another.

Judicial fact finding in the Roman-canon courts of the twelfth and thirteenth centuries had been poorly equipped to handle the complexity of the task. To come to a decision, the court had to have certainty, based on the concept of 'full proof' (of which the main example is the need for two competent witnesses). Where evidence conflicted or was incomplete, and witnesses could not be persuaded to tell the truth (which in turn led to the emergence of and then reliance on judicial torture in the Roman-canon tradition)[136] the fact-finding process came to a halt. The English common law courts effectively side-stepped the problem, of course, by appointing juries whose findings of fact could not be questioned or scrutinized. By the middle of the eighteenth century, a rationalist tool set was in place that would allow for far more sophisticated ways of dealing with factual uncertainty. By the end of the eighteenth century, the revolutionary government in France was confident enough to abolish all the rules of legal proof that had become associated with the *Ancien Régime.*

But like most stories of unrelenting success, the reality is more nuanced and much less straightforward. This is not just a tale of ever more refined inferential tools, to achieve ever more accurate fact finding. The mediaeval Roman-canon approach to evidence was deeply conservative. It would not make a finding unless there was certainty. Thus, the dignity of the court would not be impaired, because it could not be said that the court's decisions were wrongful, and the dignity (and possibly life and property) of the accused were similarly protected. This may have meant that thieves, debtors and adulterers escaped sanction, but it also meant that honest, solvent, chaste people were not wrongly punished or shamed. Similarly, we might all believe that a cleric found kissing a beautiful woman in a secluded part of a house was obviously committing fornication or adultery,[137] but would we be prepared to say that he actually was committing an offence

[133] Locke, *Essay*, II.I.2, IV.I; Hume, *Treatise*, II.13.
[134] Locke, *Essay*, IV.XV; Hume, *Treatise*, VI.47.
[135] Locke, *Essay*, I.IV.23; Hume, *Treatise*, IV.II.33.
[136] Langbein, *Torture.*
[137] Menochius, *De praesumptionibus*, Lib. 5, Praes. 41, no. 19.

and punish him unless he could provide evidence to the contrary?[138] Modern legal theories of evidence and proof are prepared to take a risk that the innocent are sometimes wrongly convicted or made civilly liable, in order to reduce the likelihood that the guilty escape justice.

There is also the question of who has the authority to create a generalization which can be given the status of counting as common sense, and who has the authority to turn a generalization into a presumption and say that the fact will be proven unless the person against whom the presumption operates can disprove it. The approach of the Roman-canon lawyers was to write these presumptions down and classify them. For example, some presumptions automatically proved facts unless rebutted, while others only guided the conscience of the court. The abolition of these legal presumptions under the 1789 Revolution in France formed a key component of the birth of 'free proof'. The (initially citizen) court would now be free to decide on its own generalizations and presumptions. While Napoleon was cleansing the Revolution, he also reintroduced a significant number of presumptions into the Code civil, so that the French legal system is now a mixed system of free proof and legal proof.[139] In England, most generalizations are at the discretion of the tribunal of fact, with some guidance from common law and statute.

So the Rationalist Tradition of evidence scholarship would provide the tribunal of fact with a framework for determining facts, but it does so at a price. The decisions of the court are necessarily based on probabilistic induction rather than on certainties. Rather than protect the court and the defendant against wrongful decisions, a balance must be struck between the rights of the prosecutor/claimant for justice, and the right of the defendant not to be wrongly convicted / found against. That balance differs between criminal and civil justice (Section 1.3.3). The balance between the two parties is struck because of a further balancing act, between the rights of the parties to see their case justly determined, and the needs of society to enforce the law, uphold the sound administration of justice, and allocate proportionate resources to the task. These two

[138] Would our decision change depending on which (if any) of (a) the person finding the pair, (b) the cleric, and (c) the woman, were able to testify?

[139] As is also the case in Italy, where the civil justice system is based extensively on the French: M. Cappelletti and J. Perillo, *Civil Procedure in Italy* (Den Haag: Martinus Nijhoff, 1965), pp. 190–215; Dwyer, 'Free Proof'.

balancing acts appear to represent a fundamentally utilitarian element in the Rationalist Tradition,[140] in that such consequentialism seeks to maximize the efficiency of legal fact finding rather than its fairness. It is possible, however, to apply the Rationalist Tradition model to legal systems that are deontological rather than consequentialist.[141] The principal differences would be less emphasis on utility, and a greater regard for the possibility that probabilistic conclusions may override individual autonomy. There may also be greater emphasis on the shaping of experience by reason.[142]

Having identified that our meta-justification is the Rationalist Tradition of evidence scholarship, let us move to the question of how we form justified beliefs within the context of the Rationalist Tradition. The starting point is to be able to demonstrate that each of our ultimate findings of fact can be clearly shown to be derived from the available evidence.[143] Thus, the final findings of fact can be justified in terms of the evidential matrix of the case. There are four central aspects to the way in which this justification operates. First, it must be possible to deconstruct the final evidential matrix to individuated propositions. By this I mean that it must be possible to identify each individual piece of evidence, atomistically,[144] and demonstrate its relationship to related pieces of evidence in the matrix. Secondly, by 'evidence' I mean all three of the basic experiences that are available in the instant case, the generalizations that guide us on

[140] Compare Stein, *Foundations*, p. 1, for his view that utilitarianism is central to contemporary Anglo-American evidence law.

[141] A. Pundik, 'Statistical Evidence: An Investigation of its Nature and its Usage in the Criminal Context' (2006) *Social Science Research Network*, http://ssrn.com/abstract = 878402 (last accessed 1 August 2008), citing B. Williams, 'Ethics', in A. Grayling (ed.), *Philosophy: A Guide Through the Subject*, 2nd edn, vol. I (Oxford: Oxford University Press, 2000), pp. 545–83, particularly pp. 552–3; and Roberts and Zuckerman, *Criminal Evidence*, pp. 10–16.

[142] Jackson, 'New Evidence Scholarship', 319.

[143] This chapter can be seen as an example of the New Evidence Scholarship (fn. 4, above). However, while one of the main identifying characteristics (but not the only one) of the New Evidence Scholarship has been frequent attention to the role of probability in understanding legal proof, my discussion of probability theories is very much secondary to my primary interest, which is in how expert evidence helps to constitute the overall evidential matrix of a case, and how that matrix can be assessed at least in part in an atomistic fashion.

[144] Strictly, individuated evidential propositions are not atomic, since they are neither indivisible particles in philosophical terms, nor a concept of physics. Individuated evidential propositions can almost always be deconstructed to a finer level of detail.

how to interpret those facts, and the inferences that are derived from combining pieces of evidence.[145] Expert evidence falls into this body of evidence, as a set of inferences that others have drawn, using specialist sets of generalizations applied to basic experiences. This emphasis on the importance of basic experiences takes us back to the foundationalism of Section 1.2, above. Thirdly, the inferential relationship between evidential atoms is probabilistic.[146] Fourthly, the final evidential matrix must make sense not only at an atomic level, but as a coherent whole – that is to say, as a holistic theory of the case.[147] This in turn takes us back to the coherentism. It is because we need to consider both the importance of the basic experiences and their integration into a holistic account that I introduced foundherentism. The practical rationality inherent in legal fact finding makes it necessary that not only must we respect all the basic experiences before us, but we must also be able to make sense of those facts before certain forms of judgment can be given: we cannot find for the claimant, or convict the criminal defendant, if we are left with unconnected, but otherwise well-formed, chains of inferences that do not allow us to come to a conclusion from basic experiences. The inferences must form an integrated evidential matrix for the case, demonstrating clearly how the final findings of fact are arrived at from the available evidence.

In the remainder of this section, I should like to consider in more detail two aspects of this inferential reasoning. Each aspect prepares the ground for further discussion in Chapter 2 of how we can justify the assertion that the tribunal of fact is competent to assess the evidence of experts. The first aspect is the deconstruction of evidence to the level of individuated propositions (Section 1.4.2). Such an atomistic view of evidence allows us to see explicitly laid out all the basic experiences and inferences, and the connections between them, on which the conclusion relies. The second

[145] These generalizations can apply, often unconsciously, at a very early stage in our understanding of basic experiences. For example, whether a person seen running should be described as 'fleeing' may require, in the absence of that person saying that she is fleeing, the application of an appropriate generalization.

[146] Schum, *Evidential Foundations*, p. 195, does give a place to holistic approaches, such as narratives, stories and scenarios.

[147] E.g. R. Burns, *A Theory of the Trial* (Princeton NJ: Princeton University Press, 1999); R. Hastie, *Inside the Juror: The Psychology of Juror Decision Making* (Cambridge: Cambridge University Press, 1993).

aspect is the use of generalizations, the 'inferential glue' that holds all this together, and allows us to make sense of specifics (Section 1.4.3).

1.4.2 Atomistic reasoning about individuated propositions of evidence

Atomistic reasoning involves deconstructing an evidential argument to its base constituent parts, comprising, at the core, base facts, generalizations and inferences. This approach may be particularly attractive to Anglo-American readers because it appears to accord well with an approach to evidence in which each piece of evidence introduced by one party is open to scrutiny and potential challenge by the other parties.[148] Using these constituent parts, it is possible to construct an evidential matrix of the case. The management and interpretation of these matrices is assisted by charting methods (Section 1.4.2.1), and in turn this charting helps to highlight, and possibly resolve, the problem of total inferential drag in inferential arguments (Section 1.4.2.2).

1.4.2.1 The graphical representation of evidential matrices

A textual description of any complex evidential matrix would rapidly become unwieldy and hard to follow. Methods of graphical representation have therefore been developed, particularly in support of research into artificial intelligence, and with the assistance of modern computer software.[149] The first system of argument diagramming to be proposed was developed by Wigmore for representing evidence arguments, in his 1913 *Principles of Judicial Proof* (which became *Science of Judicial Proof* in the 1937 third edition).[150] Wigmore developed his chart method as one aspect of his systematic, and essentially atomistic, theory of proof. The charting method appears to have been largely lost from view by evidence theorists until the end of the twentieth century, and it is now undergoing a mini-renaissance. A modified version has been

[148] Damaška, *Evidence Law Adrift*, p. 50.

[149] F. Bex, H. Prakken, C. Reed and D. Walton, 'Towards a Formal Account of Reasoning about Evidence: Argumentation Schemes and Generalizations' (2003) 11 *Artificial Intelligence and Law* 125–65; G. Rowe and C. Reed, 'Translating Wigmore Diagrams', in *Proceedings of the First International Conference on Computational Models of Argument* (Amsterdam: IOS Press, 2006), pp. 171–82; C. Reed and G. Rowe, 'Translating Toulmin Diagrams: Theory Neutrality in Argument Representation' (2005) 19 *Argumentation* 267–86.

[150] Wigmore, *Science of Judicial Proof.* Other argumentation schemes also exist, e.g. S. Toulmin, *The Uses of Argument* (Cambridge: Cambridge University Press, 1958).

developed by Anderson, Schum and Twining.[151] It has also attracted the attention of computer scientists and philosophers working in the field of artificial intelligence,[152] and of statisticians working on Bayesian networks.[153]

Modified Wigmorean analysis provides a particular heuristic for dealing with complex cases, and allows us to construct, test and reconstruct arguments about questions of fact.[154] It does this by providing a diagrammatic representation of all the relevant evidential propositions (given in a key list), the relations between them, and the 'ultimate *probanda*' in a particular case. The ultimate *probandum* is the major or basic proposition at issue which is to be proved. In criminal cases, for example, an ultimate *probandum* includes all the conditions that the prosecution must prove to be true beyond reasonable doubt, in order to justify a conviction. The chart method structures the analysis at two levels, macroscopic and microscopic. Macroscopically, it structures the analysis of the ultimate and penultimate *probanda*. Microscopically, it structures the precise and detailed analysis of the evidential data for each important phase of the argument. For Anderson and Twining the Chart is useful as a heuristic to develop and analyse an evidential argument. A Wigmore Chart could also be used as a representation of the evidential argument.

There are at least three advantages to using a charting method when articulating an atomistic argument.[155] First, it requires the person doing the analysis to identify and articulate precisely each proposition that she claims is a necessary step in the argument in a case. Secondly, each step in each argument must be specified precisely. Thirdly, it provides a method of marshalling all the relevant and potentially relevant data in a complex case into a single coherent and clear structure in the form of an argument. Wigmore Charts are not context-blind, but are constructed around the

[151] E.g. Schum, *Evidential Foundations*; T. Anderson *et al.*, *Analysis*; A. Palmer, *Proof and the Preparation of Trials* (Sydney: Lawbook, 2003). For an elaboration on 'modified Wigmorean analysis', see W. Twining, 'Argumentation, Stories and Generalizations: A Comment' (2007) 6 *Law Probability and Risk* 169–85.

[152] E.g. Bex *et al.*, 'Formal Account'; F. Bex, S. van den Braak, H. van Oostendorp, H. Prakken, B. Verheij and G. Vreeswijk, 'Sense-making software for crime investigation: how to combine stories and arguments?' (2007) 6 *Law Probability and Risk* 145–68.

[153] E.g. V. Leucari, 'Analysis of Complex Patterns of Evidence in Legal Cases: Wigmore Charts v Bayesian Networks' (2005), www.evidencescience.org/content/leucariA1.pdf (last accessed 1 August 2008).

[154] Anderson *et al.*, *Analysis*, p. 123; Twining, *Theories of Evidence*, pp. 125–35, 179–86.

[155] Anderson *et al.*, *Analysis*, pp. 141–2.

standpoint of the analyst, and require answers to questions such as 'Who am I?', 'At what stage in the process am I?', 'What materials are available for analysis?' and 'What am I trying to do?'[156] They are therefore intended in the first instance to be used to assess the strength of an evidential argument from a particular standpoint, rather than to identify the best hypothesis for the evidence. However, because it is possible to produce a chart that handles two or more rival hypotheses, the chart can be used to decide which hypothesis is best supported by the available factual propositions.

Another possible limitation of charting is that the charts can rapidly become very large and complex for any example that is not trivial. Schum recalls that he once produced a chart with 395 items of evidence that was 18 feet long, while a student of Twining's produced a chart that was 37 feet long.[157] However, raising such criticism may be to confuse a way of learning with a way of thinking. While students are taught to undertake microscopic analysis of all parts of an argument in order to learn the discipline of chart analysis, experienced users only need to do the top (macroscopic level) of the chart, and then produce microscopic analyses for those parts where the factual argument appears to require detailed attention. The use of unduly large charts is therefore usually avoided through the employment of these linked charts.

1.4.2.2 The problem of total inferential drag

One of the analytical strengths of charting is that it makes visible patterns in large, complex networks or matrices of inference-based evidence. For Schum, there are three core recurring combinations of probabilistic argument: 'linear chains',[158] 'corroboration and contradiction', and 'convergence and conflict'.[159] In a linear chain, inferences are catenated together. For reasons that we shall come to in a moment, linear chains have historically been viewed as very problematic for theories of inferential reasoning. The proposed resolution of those difficulties involves an understanding of the other two recurring combinations ('corroboration

[156] Ibid., p. 124.

[157] D. Schum, 'Evidence and Inference About Past Events: An Overview of Six Case Studies', in W. Twining and I. Hampsher–Monk (eds.), *Evidence and Inference in History and Law: Interdisciplinary Dialogues* (Evanston, IL: Northwestern University Press, 2003), p. 29.

[158] Schum, *Evidential Foundations*, ch. 7.

[159] Ibid., ch. 8.

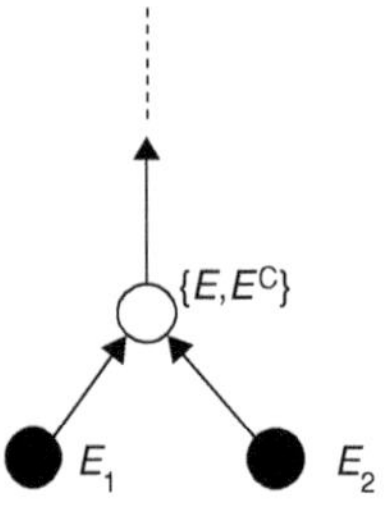

Figure 1.1 Corroboration in inferential argument

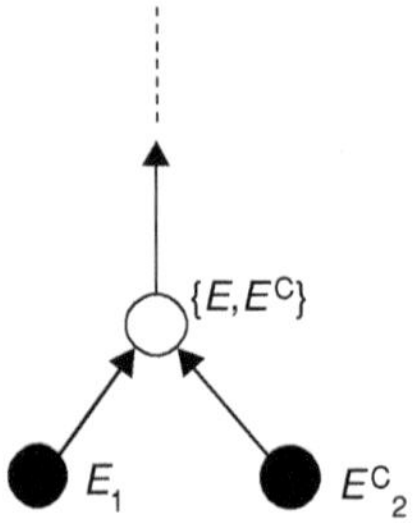

Figure 1.2 Contradiction in inferential argument

and contradiction', and 'convergence and conflict'),[160] and so we shall introduce these first.

Corroboration 'occurs when two witnesses both testify, independently of one another, to the truth of the same proposition'.[161] Figure 1.1 shows two sources, E_1 and E_2, which both report evidence that event E occurred. Mathematically, Schum says, corroboration is almost the same as contradiction[162] and so corroboration and contradiction are paired together here. The structure of contradiction is illustrated in Figure 1.2. One source

160 Schum finds some support for the existence of a difference between corroboration and convergence, through his application of Bayes' theorem: ibid., p. 401. Schum has not been the only evidence theorist to propose the existence of these four patterns (corroboration, contradiction, convergence and conflict) in evidential argument. There has not been agreement among evidence theorists on how exactly these four patterns operate, and how, if at all, they should be distinguished from one another. The mathematician Cohen, for example, believed that 'testimonial corroboration and convergence of circumstances exhibit a common logical structure': Cohen, *Probable and Provable*, p. 93. In other words, the logic in Figures 1.1 and 1.3 is the same. Twining has suggested that, although Wigmore did not address the issue directly, his discussion of his own chart method for evidential argument, and of the role of corroboration, does not suggest that Wigmore saw any logical difference between corroboration and convergence: Twining, *Theories of Evidence*, p. 182.

161 Cohen, *Probable and Provable*, p. 94.

162 Schum, *Evidential Foundations*, p. 393.

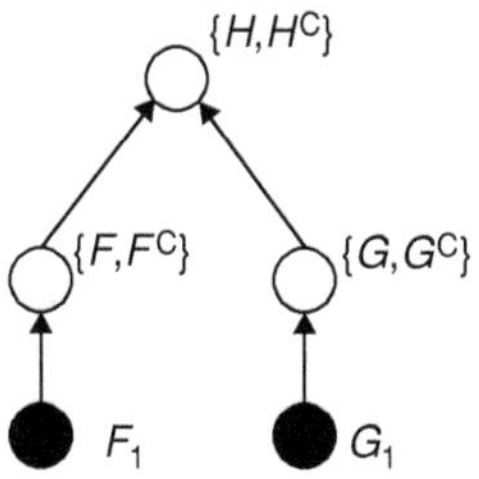

Figure 1.3 Convergence and conflict in inferential argument

(E_1) says that an event (E) occurred and another source ($E^c{}_2$) says that that event did not occur.[163]

Convergence is where '[t]wo items of circumstantial evidence . . . , independently of one another, [support the] probability of the same conclusion'.[164] 'Convergence' is the existence of reports of two or more different events, all of which are said to favour the same hypothesis.[165] The reverse side of this inferential coin is 'conflict'.[166] With conflict, evidence F_1 supports the existence of event F, and G_1 supports the existence of G. F favours hypothesis H occurring, while G favours H not occurring. Both convergence and conflict can be represented using a single diagram, Figure 1.3.

So with the basic structures of inferential argument defined, let us move on to the problem of total inferential drag. Since at least Hume in the eighteenth century, there has been a conceptual difficulty with the notion that conclusions can be derived from inferences built on inferences:

> 'Tis certain, that when an inference is drawn immediately from an object without any intermediate cause or effect, the conviction is much stronger, and the persuasion more lively, than when the imagination is carry'd thro' a long chain of connected arguments, however infallible the connexion of each link may be esteem'd. 'Tis from the original impression, that the vivacity of all the ideas is deriv'd, by means of the customary transition of the imagination; and 'tis evident this vivacity must decay in proportion to the distance, and must lose somewhat in each transition.[167]

Schum has called this perceived phenomenon (whose existence in practice he disputes) 'total inferential drag'.

[163] Ibid., p. 368. [164] Cohen, *Probable and Provable*, p. 94.
[165] Schum, *Evidential Foundations*, p. 401. [166] Ibid., p. 382.
[167] Hume, *Treatise*, III.13.

It is unclear how the probabilities in the inferential chain combine. Using conventional probability theory, the cumulative probability would decay rapidly.[168] In a situation where $E_1 \rightarrow E_2 \rightarrow E_3 \rightarrow P$, the probability that *probandum* P is correct is a direct mathematical product of the probabilities of each of E_1, E_2, E_3. For example, Cohen has argued that in an Anglo-American civil case, where the claimant only needs to prove her case on 'balance of probabilities', $p(E_1)$, $p(E_2)$ and $p(E_3)$ could each be 0.6, so that $p(P) = 0.6 \times 0.6 \times 0.6 = 0.2$. That is, the *probandum* is not proven to the civil requirement of proof. Cohen suggests that this conclusion is counterintuitive, because it would mean that cases with anything other than the most basic inferences would probably fail to meet the burden of proof.

Concern about total inferential drag may constrain Anglo-American legal use of chains of inferences. Schum quotes an unnamed US civil judge in 1942 as saying that there is a strong common law suspicion of 'inference upon inference':

> Inferences alone may, if reasonable, provide a link in a chain of evidence and constitute in that regard substantial evidence. But an inference cannot be piled upon an inference, and then another inference upon that, as such inferences are unreasonable and cannot be considered as substantial evidence. Such a method could be extended indefinitely until there would be no more substance to it than the soup Lincoln talked about that was 'made by boiling the shadow of a pigeon that had been starved to death'.[169]

There appear to be two possible resolutions to this difficulty, one arising from transitivity,[170] and the second from the complexity of almost all evidential matrices. The term 'transitivity' refers to the particular relation between pairs of entities. So, for '>' ('greater than'), if $a > b$, and $b > c$, then $a > c$. Other relations are intransitive. Although a is the father of b, and b is the father of c, it does not follow that a is the father of c. What Schum proposes is that certain probabilistic inferences are transitive. So if a favours b, and b favours c, then a favours c. This can shorten our inference chains considerably. This is an argument that Cohen does not appear to accept, viewing it instead as a re-statement of the 'inference upon inference' problem.[171]

Schum seeks to demonstrate transitivity mathematically, but we may be able to observe it in practice. The existence of transitivity in single

[168] Cohen, *Probable and Provable*, pp. 68–73. [169] Schum, *Evidential Foundations*, p. 112.
[170] Ibid., p. 308. [171] Cohen, *Probable and Provable*, p. 68.

connected chains of reasoning may go some way to explaining a perceived difficulty that Wigmorean Chart analysis can produce very large complex inference networks for problems that we would consider to be relatively straightforward, and can solve relatively quickly. The solution may be that, in practice, we collapse down our inference chains using transitivity. This in turn may not require a substantial exercise in probability calculations. As we shall see in Section 1.5, cognitive psychology suggests that we have access to a large number of techniques, which may not always be reliable, for taking inferential shortcuts. Where Schum would appear to depart from the arguments of cognitive psychology is that, while the former says that we can work out that *a* infers *c*, cognitive psychology says that we use a pre-existing rule of thumb to infer that *a* infers *c*. This would make the use of transitivity itself a probabilistic task.

The second way in which Schum proposes that 'inferential drag' might be avoided in practice is through the complexity of most evidential matrices. Very few inferential arguments are based solely on chains. Complexity is to be expected in the evidential matrices underlying most non-trivial factual conclusions: 'single-stage inductive reasoning is very rare except in contrived abstract examples . . . [H]uman inductive reasoning usually has many stages'.[172] The main recurrent forms and combinations of evidence can be categorized as evidential harmony (corroboration and convergence), evidential dissonance (contradiction and conflict) and evidential redundancy. Redundancy means that there are two or more elements performing the same task, so that if one were removed, the task would still continue. What may therefore happen is that most extended inferential chains do not stand in their own right, but either contribute to evidential harmony by corroborating or converging with other lines of argument (which will reverse the gradual attrition of the probability associated with the inference chain) or else are effectively redundant. In practice, therefore, there may be very few circumstances in which total inferential drag actually affects the evidential matrix as a whole.

When we come to consider the assessment of expert evidence in Chapter 2, there are two crucial issues to consider. The first is how integrating expert evidence into an evidential matrix in this way affects the way in which we perceive such evidence. When we talk of the assessment of expert evidence, it is possible to begin to think of this as a separate task that the tribunal of fact undertakes, unaided by the evidential matrix as

[172] Schum, *Evidential Foundations*, p. 33.

a whole. The second is whether an atomistic analysis of expert evidence is structurally any different from a similar analysis of any other type of evidence, and how that similarity or difference might affect the tribunal's competence to assess expert evidence.

1.4.3 Generalizations as inferential glue

For each inference that we draw in our atomistic evidential matrix, we must be able to state explicitly the basis on which that inference is drawn.[173] That basis is usually a generalization.[174] Generalizations are the 'glue' that holds our arguments together,[175] or the force that allows us to move from one set of facts to another. Two facts cannot combine together on their own to form an inference, without the assistance of a generalization. Even if we were to observe a moving blue billiard ball strike a red billiard ball at rest, and the red billiard ball then move off, the inference that the red billiard ball's movement was caused by contact with the blue billiard ball requires the application of one or more generalizations that we might place under categories concerning 'laws of physics' and 'causation'.[176]

There is no commonly agreed classification of generalizations in evidence jurisprudence. In their text on evidence analysis, first published in 1991, Anderson, Schum and Twining proposed four types of 'general proposition': 'scientific truths', such as the law of gravity; 'common sense generalizations', such as that running away is indicative of guilt; 'commonly held beliefs', such as national or ethnic stereotypes, including prejudices; and 'general background information' about the instant case, such as generalizations about *X*'s habits ('case-specific generalizations').[177] In his 1999 article on generalizations, Anderson proposed a slightly different set, based on source: 'scientific/expert generalizations', based on the

173 Ibid., p. 81.

174 Anderson *et al.*, *Analysis*; W. Twining, 'Narrative and Generalizations in Argumentation about Questions of Fact' (1999) 40 *South Texas Law Review* 351–65; Cohen, *Probable and Provable.*

175 Schum, *Evidential Foundations*, p. 82.

176 We must even apply a generalization about the use of the word 'cause' in this example, since we might choose to insist that an inanimate object cannot 'cause' anything, or that the 'cause' must for some other reason be found earlier in the chain of causation. Compare H. Hart and T. Honoré, *Causation in the Law*, 2nd edn (Oxford: Oxford University Press, 1985). See also Evans-Pritchard, *Witchcraft*, on the question that arises when termites cause a building to collapse: of who sent those termites; and D. Dwyer, 'Is Man the Rational Animal?', BA dissertation, University of Southampton (1996).

177 Anderson *et al.*, *Analysis*, p. 43.

laws of science and research; 'general knowledge', representing generalizations that are so well established that they would probably be admitted through judicial notice rather than evidence; 'experience-based' generalizations, derived from personal experience; 'belief' generalizations, which are gained other than by experience, and may be held in common within a particular community or specific group.[178] While experts base their reasoning on scientific/expert generalizations, which we might expect to have been developed under a rigorous methodology, non-specialists, including lawyers, rely on the other three types of generalization. This is a point to which we shall return at the end of this section, when I discuss how we deal with conflicts either between two sets of expert generalizations or else between one set of expert generalizations and one set of common-sense generalizations, and whether accepting expert generalizations over common sense is to move the legal system from a democratic to a technocratic basis.

The 'common sense' category of Anderson, Schum and Twining is more problematic than their other possible categories, because it is very unclear how such generalizations are derived, or which generalizations will be operating at any place, with any set of people, at any point in time.[179] They constitute an unstructured mass whose contents might include facts, values and received opinion.[180] They are often indeterminate with respect to frequency, level of abstraction, empirical reliability, defeasibility, identity (i.e. which generalization is being employed) and power (i.e. whose generalization). They also provide scope for using emotive language, giving a misleading impression of precision or confidence, or presenting value judgments as if they were empirical facts.[181]

178 T. Anderson, 'On Generalizations I: A Preliminary Exploration' (1999) 40 *South Texas Law Review* 455–81, 458. 'Scientific' and 'expert' are presented separately, but Anderson considers that this might need to be reviewed in light of the Supreme Court's decision in *Kumho Tire* v. *Carmichael* 526 US 137, 119 Sup Ct 1167 (1999) that scientific testimony was not a distinct category of evidence from expert evidence, for the purposes of the *Daubert* admissibility test.

179 On the relationship between common sense and truth, see G. Moore, 'A Defence of Common Sense', in J. Muirhead (ed.), *Contemporary British Philosophy*, 2nd series (London: Allen and Unwin, 1924), pp. 191–223; A. Holmes, 'Moore's Appeal to Common Sense' (1961) 58 *Journal of Philosophy* 197–207.

180 It is unlikely that many generalizations used by fact finders could ever be formulated in words: R. Eggleston, *Evidence, Proof and Probability* (London: Weidenfeld and Nicolson, 1978), p. 145.

181 Twining, 'Narrative and Generalizations', 358.

Cohen, in what may be considered the leading argument on this point, has suggested that juries require only their 'commonplace generalizations' in order to make sense of the factual evidence presented to them.[182] Cohen was keen to argue for the role of the 'person in the street' in determining legal questions of fact, without delegation to experts. However, Cohen's argument rests on a fundamentally cognitive consensualist assumption: that there is broad agreement within society on what the generalizations are that should apply. He argued that 'the main commonplace generalizations themselves are for the most part too essential a part of our culture for there to be any serious disagreement about them'. The most obvious limitation of this approach is that it assumes a monocultural society, but it also assumes that 'commonplace generalizations' apply universally across social or geographic groups within a single culture. It is not demonstrated, however, that this is the case, and intuitively we might think that a young man seen running from a policeman on an East Oxford housing estate might have his actions interpreted, in the absence of any other evidence, in terms different from those that might be applied if the same event occurred in the leafy suburbs of North Oxford. For a theory of a common stock of beliefs to be credible, it must allow for variation within that stock across society, while recognizing that different groups do not have completely distinct sets of generalizations. Belief and common-sense generalizations come from an individual's stock of beliefs, which will have overlap with a common stock of beliefs in society or the individual's group as a whole. This common stock of beliefs manifests itself both in generalizations and in stories, which deal with examples of specific applications of those beliefs.[183]

Menashe and Shamash have made an extremely detailed and useful critique of the use of holistic narrative forms of evidence argumentation.[184] Within what they call 'the narrative fallacy', they would appear to be particularly concerned with the use of 'generalizations based on, or drawn from, the dominant stories of communities'.[185] This is because these generalizations can reflect a range of stereotypes, particularly about minorities, that we might consider to be empirically unjustifiable and socially undesirable. This takes us back to the problem with basing fact

[182] Cohen, *Probable and Provable*, pp. 274–76.

[183] W. Twining, 'The *Ratio Decidendi* of the Parable of the Prodigal Son', in K. O'Donovan and G. Rubin (eds.), *Human Rights and Legal History: Essays in Honour of Brian Simpson* (Oxford: Oxford University Press, 2000), p. 149.

[184] Menashe and Shamash, 'The Narrative Fallacy'.

[185] Ibid.

finding on commonly held beliefs: just because people believe that things are true, does not of itself mean that they are true. The full ramifications of this statement are explored below in the context of cognitive psychology (Section 1.5) but it is important to consider here that many of the beliefs that are commonly held may not have been through any formal process of verification. One of the strengths of the paper is that it reminds us that generalizations can be used for the construction of holistic factual arguments as well as atomistic ones.

There are two difficulties with Menashe and Shamash's argument against generalizations in its full form. The first is that the authors do not distinguish between the many types of generalization that are at work in evidential arguments, but consider all generalizations to be equally dangerous because some are untested or are socially undesirable. The second difficulty is that, although the authors are right to point out that generalizations can be particularly dangerous when used in holistic arguments about facts, they do not consider that generalizations are embedded into the atomistic reasoning that they appear to prefer over holistic reasoning.

Let us return to the distinction between scientific/expert and non-expert generalizations that we encountered above. We have seen that non-expert generalizations are very problematic, and potentially dangerous. Where do non-expert generalizations come from, how much weight should they be given, how should they be applied, and how many people need to subscribe to them before they can be considered to be 'common sense'? With expert generalizations, three more questions emerge. First, what do we do when more than one expert generalization emerges at trial, and we have a conflict of expert generalizations? Presumably the answer to this is that one evaluates the generalizations much as one would evaluate any other piece of evidence.

Secondly, and more problematically, what if an expert generalization conflicts with a non-expert generalization? Particularly where juries are involved, this is a political as much as an epistemological question. If we have brought in juries as a democratic agent, to judge the individual by the standards of her peers, then we may be slow to say that the standards of her peers should be amended on an ad hoc basis to take account of the standards presented by experts. The solution in Anglo-American courts is usually to be found in directions that certain categories of expert evidence are inadmissible because the tribunal of fact (particularly a jury) does not require assistance on things within its everyday experience. The artificiality of the line between what is and is not within a jury's everyday experience is shown by the variations between jurisdictions of what expert evidence is and is not admissible. If we were to solve our second expert generalization problem by simply saying that the court will always receive the advice of experts where it is more reliable by virtue of the scientific method by which it was established, then we encounter a variation of our first problem: that we cannot of course be certain that the expert generalization is correct, and that it will not change every few months or years, while the common-sense generalization remains relatively stable.

The third problem with expert generalizations is that, if we do accept them, then we are effectively delegating fact finding to an arbitrary selection of experts, without appropriate political debate. Our civil and criminal justice systems would then become technocratic.[186] Conversely, if we do not accept expert generalizations on grounds of policy, then we are in danger of creating a legal version of the world which may well tally with common sense, but which departs from scientific consensus. Here is a crucial question, to which there is no straightforward answer: should the courts determine factual issues on the basis of the world as the parties to the dispute understand it to be, or as better-informed experts who are not parties to the dispute understand it to be? The correct answer is probably based on the distinction between subjective and objective responsibility, which in turn depends on the particular part of the substantive law that is in issue. If the defendant's state of mind or intention is important to the determination of the case, then the court's best course of action is probably to consider what common sense should have dictated to the defendant would be the case. However, if the case is to be determined on the basis of an objective set of facts, and intention is irrelevant, then expert generalizations are likely to be more acceptable, even when they run counter to common sense.

1.5 The challenge of naturalized epistemology

These questions around the use of generalizations raise the possibility that fact finding within the Rationalist Tradition is not quite as rational as we may initially have supposed. It is possible that the court will actively disregard relevant, reliable evidence, on expert generalizations, in order to further a non-epistemological, political goal. Of itself that provides us with a challenge, although it is covered by the seventh of Twining's 'Common Assumptions in Rationalist Theories of Evidence and Proof':

[186] Damaška, *Evidence Law Adrift*, pp. 150–2.

'7. The pursuit of truth (i.e. seeking to maximize accuracy in fact determination) is to be given a high, but not necessarily an overriding, priority in relation to other values, such as security of the state, protection of family relationships, curbing of coercive methods of interrogation.' In this section, I suggest a further possible challenge to the rational basis of legal fact finding, which emerges when naturalized epistemology is considered. 'Naturalized', or 'naturalistic', epistemology is a term that covers a range of views concerning the relationship between epistemology and the natural sciences:

> Some advocates of naturalized epistemology emphasize methodological issues, arguing that epistemologists must make use of results from the sciences that study human reasoning in pursuing epistemological questions. The most extreme view along these lines recommends replacing traditional epistemology with the psychological study of how we reason. A more modest view recommends that philosophers make use of results from sciences studying cognition to resolve epistemological issues.[187]

Here, I am concerned with the effect of the findings of cognitive psychology on the rationalist model of probabilistic, inferential, atomistic reasoning introduced earlier, in Section 1.4.[188] I provide an overview rather than a detailed account and analysis, because detailed accounts by cognitive psychologists are readily available elsewhere.[189] The effect of cognitive psychology on epistemology is a large field of research, and the discussion here is focused on the effect of work on decision-making

[187] R. Feldman, 'Naturalized Epistemology', in E. Zalta (ed.), *The Stanford Encyclopedia of Philosophy* (Fall 2006 Edition), http://plato.stanford.edu/archives/fall2006/entries/epistemology-naturalized/ (last accessed 1 August 2008). See also Haack, *Evidence and Inquiry*, p. 118, who has suggested that there are at least five ways in which epistemology could be combined with the cognitive sciences.

[188] Work by cognitive psychologists on how individual decision making differs from group decision making, which may be of relevance to developing the earlier discussion about the composition of the tribunal of fact, is discussed elsewhere, e.g. E. Beecher-Monas, *Evaluating Scientific Evidence: An Interdisciplinary Framework for Intellectual Due Process* (Cambridge: Cambridge University Press, 2006), pp. 27–32. Compare Damaška, *Evidence Law Adrift*, p. 37.

[189] E.g. B. Barnes, D. Bloor and J. Henry, *Scientific Knowledge: a Sociological Analysis* (Chicago: University of Chicago Press, 1996); M. Bishop and J. Trout, *Epistemology and the Psychology of Human Judgment* (Oxford: Oxford University Press, 2004); D. Kahneman, P. Slovic and A. Tversky (eds.), *Judgment under Uncertainty: Heuristics and Biases* (Cambridge: Cambridge University Press, 1982); R. Nisbett and L. Ross, *Human Inference: Strategies and Shortcomings of Social Judgment* (Englewood Cliffs NJ: Prentice Hall, 1980), p. 14; S. Plous, *The Psychology of Judgment and Decision Making* (New York: McGraw Hill, 1993); S. Stich, 'Could Man be an Irrational Animal?' (1985) 64 *Synthèse* 115–35.

biases. Classically minded epistemologists have already produced detailed critiques about why the findings of cognitive psychology do not invalidate classical forms of epistemology (including social epistemology).[190] The view taken here is that the approach of cognitive psychology is valid, in that it identifies cognitive biases that have the potential to affect our reasoning, but its effects have been exaggerated. Further, cognitive psychology does not allow us to dispense with the concerns of classical epistemology, since the former is concerned with human beings' capabilities and limitations, while the latter is concerned with what one does with that information, for example defining key epistemological concepts such as reliability and justification. A 'modest naturalism', adopted here, allows us to benefit from the insights of cognitive psychology into the mechanisms of cognition, without exhausting the requirements of the components of a developed epistemology.[191]

Given that this is a book on the assessment of expert evidence, I have focused on two particular issues within naturalized epistemology that have the potential to affect our rationalist model. The first issue concerns whether people draw inferences on a rational basis, or invoke potentially unreliable shortcuts ('heuristics') (Section 1.5.1). This first issue is of particular importance here because it concerns the question not only of whether tribunal members will be able to draw inferences rationally from expert evidence, but also of whether the experts themselves have drawn inferences reliably from the evidence on which they depend. The second issue concerns how non-experts interpret complex specialist information, and this is of direct relevance to our examination of the assessment of expert evidence.

1.5.1 Strategies and shortcomings of social judgment

Nisbett and Ross, psychology professors at Michigan and Stanford respectively, propose that the range of cognitive biases that have been experimentally identified by psychologists contribute to a range of inferential strategies, which facilitate everyday decision making.[192] These are strategies that non-scientists hold in common with scientists, although scientific method is designed to prevent their use in scientific enquiry:

190 Beecher-Monas, *Evaluating Scientific Evidence*, pp. 20–7; Goldman, *Knowledge*; M. Solomon, 'Scientific Rationality and Human Reasoning' (1992) 59 *Philosophy of Science* 439–55; Haack, *Evidence and Inquiry*, pp. 118ff.

191 Haack, *Defending Science*, p. 309; Haack, *Evidence and Inquiry*, p. 118.

192 Nisbett and Ross, *Human Inference*.

> [S]ome people respond to the material ... with the attitude 'Well, I always knew most people were stupid, and this just proves it'. We hope to show that this comforting attitude is not tenable ... [T]here is no inferential failure that can be demonstrated with untrained undergraduates that cannot also ... be demonstrated in a somewhat more subtle form in the highly trained scientist.[193]

Nisbett and Ross suggest that there are in fact some fundamental distinctions between common-sense ('intuitive') inferential strategies and those developed by science. The 'intuitive scientist' makes use of two broad types of intuitive implements, 'knowledge structures' and 'judgmental heuristics'. Knowledge structures allow us to define and interpret the data of physical and social life quickly and, mostly, accurately.[194] They also define a set of expectations about objects and suggest appropriate responses. Because these structures are themselves produced by induction, they may be relatively poor and inaccurate representations of the real world, and may even at times be dangerously inaccurate.[195] They also vary between individuals.

Judgmental heuristics provide us with cognitive strategies ('rules of thumb') for solving a variety of inferential tasks by taking inferential shortcuts. The three main forms are the representativeness heuristic, the availability heuristic, and weighting. The first of these allows us to reduce many inferential tasks to simple similarity judgments: 'An object is assigned to one conceptual category rather than another according to the extent to which its principal features represent or resemble one category more than another.'[196] However, in many cases 'the extent to which' depends on statistical considerations, including the relative frequency of categories in the population, and people have poor skills at applying these statistical considerations to questions of representativeness. The second form, the availability heuristic, is used when judging frequency, probability and even causality, and is unreliable. Events or objects are deemed to be causally efficacious or frequent depending on whether they are readily 'available' in memory.[197] This heuristic is fallible because of the many

[193] Ibid., p. 14.
[194] Compare G. Gigerenzer, P. Todd and the ABC Research Group, *Simple Heuristics That Make Us Smart* (Oxford: Oxford University Press, 1999).
[195] Nisbett and Ross, *Human Inference*, p. 6. [196] Ibid., p. 7.
[197] Compare N. Harvey and C. Harries, 'Effects of Judges' Forecasting on their Later Combination of Forecasts for the Same Outcome' (2004) 20 *International Journal of Forecasting* 391–409.

irrelevant factors that affect memory availability. The third form of cognitive strategy, weighting, determines how we assign inferential weight to physical and social data. This is determined by the salience and vividness of the data. However, the vividness of data is at best only obliquely related to its true value as evidence.

I would suggest that we can say from this (although this is not a claim made by Nisbett and Ross) that there is a common stock of decision-making shortcuts (including inferential shortcuts) available to all people. This common stock exists in a similar way to a common stock of generalizations (Section 1.4.3). Both of these common stocks contribute to what we might term a 'common-sense' approach to our dealings with the world. This common-sense stock of inferential strategies enables people to bypass the detailed inferential processes that would be required to assess the validity of a detailed specialist argument. This provides us with one means by which people may be able to bypass the need to build and process the complex evidential matrices that the Rationalist Tradition of evidence scholarship suggests that we need to build in order to arrive at justified belief about the facts.

The findings of cognitive psychology do not mean, however, that we are bound to adhere to common-sense reasoning in our investigations and decision making about the world. The refinements that we might associate with 'scientific method', or any other rigorous method of factual investigation, are intended to overcome many of our common-sense assumptions, precisely because experience has indicated the existence of a range of cognitive biases. As people choosing to act as rational agents are made aware of the cognitive biases that they are exhibiting, it should be possible to develop techniques to avoid or control their effect. This takes us back to the recurring problem with reconciling common sense and rationalist reasoning about facts. Common sense exists prior to the individual's contemplation of a subject. If I were to be able to choose which aspects, or which version, of common sense that I adhere to, then it would be difficult to classify it as 'common'. So we have little direct control over the norms and generalizations embodied in common sense, even when they are counter-factual. Some common-sense generalizations may be subject to political change over time, for example through public education programmes, but as individuals we may choose to opt out of common sense for some aspects of our decision making. We may also have practical concerns about being able to say that a particular view is the common-sense view, although, by definition, if these concerns are too great, there is good reason to believe that this is not common sense.

1.5.2 *How people process complex specialist information*

According to Cooper, Bennett and Sukel, psychologists at Princeton, a non-specialist encountering complex specialist information is likely to resort to 'heuristic or peripheral processing'.[198] This means that the observer may rely on how credible the communicator is, whether she used many arguments to bolster her position (irrespective of whether they were good arguments), whether she is attractive, whether she is a bona fide expert about the issues, or whether the observer is in a good or bad mood.

Cooper, Bennett and Sukel conducted an experiment on how United States jurors assessed complex scientific testimony, using fifty-four volunteer participants, and four versions of a video of an imaginary civil case, concerning product liability. The jurors were only shown examination-in-chief of one plaintiff and one defendant expert witness, and their assessment was measured using questionnaires. The jurors were not allowed to discuss the case with one another before completing the questionnaires. The four videos of the case were a combination of either a highly qualified or an adequately qualified plaintiff expert, and simply worded or complex testimony. The defendant's expert witness was in all cases highly qualified and gave complex testimony. The study suggests that when jurors encountered complex testimony, they used the expert's credentials as the basis for their judgments, but when the evidence was presented in more comprehensible language, the advantage of having impressive credentials disappeared.[199]

There are two methodological limitations to the study. The first is that it did not consider the role of cross-examination in informing either the juror's opinion of the credibility of the expert, or her understanding of the evidence presented. This may be a crucial factor in determining the case. The study also did not consider the impact of jury deliberation on these assessments,[200] and so it is not clear what impact this may have on the inferential process. Similar considerations may apply in the case of complex expert evidence, which a deliberative tribunal of fact may, because of the requirement of deliberation, be more likely to analyse using proper inferential reasoning than may a single member tribunal. Nevertheless, there is good reason to be alert to the possibility that

198 J. Cooper, E. Bennett and H. Sukel, 'Complex Scientific Testimony: How Do Jurors Make Decisions?' (1996) 20 *Law and Human Behaviour* 379–94, 381.

199 Ibid., p. 390. 200 Ibid., p. 392.

non-specialist fact finders will process specialist evidence using methods that we would not consider to adhere to the Rationalist Tradition of evidence scholarship. If that concerns us, as I think that it does, then we should give thought to ways in which to encourage rationalist formation of justified beliefs rather than the use of heuristic processing. One of those ways may be to arrange procedural provisions so as to reduce the complexity of the evidence presented.

1.6 Conclusion

This chapter has sought to provide the necessary philosophical framework within which to begin to tackle four epistemological questions that are central to this book: first, can the court assess expert evidence?; secondly, how well can the court do this?; thirdly, what are the mechanisms at the level of practical reasoning and epistemology that allow this assessment to take place?; fourthly, how do procedural arrangements affect the ability to assess? Having regard to the importance of this framework for the remainder of the book, and bearing in mind that this may be unfamiliar territory to many, it is worth recapping on the main points.

Epistemology is taken in this book to mean the study of justified belief rather than the study of knowledge. Knowledge is a distinct state from justified belief. While justified belief depends on evidence, knowledge is prior to evidence.[201] Within a legal context, foundherentism appears to provide a workable theory of justification. This combines the need of legal epistemology for justified beliefs based on evidence with another legal need, that the court's conclusions on the facts in a case form a coherent story, to the extent at least that all the evidence is accounted for by the final decision.

The social characteristics of legal fact finding mean that the processes and criteria for justification differ from those in classical epistemology. For example, truth is the goal of legal fact finding, but there are fundamental difficulties in knowing whether truth has been determined at the time that an individual decision is made. This is in large part because the court's experience of the world in the instant case is mediated by the

[201] In classical epistemology, which is concerned with individual knowledge, we can only consider *E* to be evidence *for* a belief if we first know *E*. In the socially engaged world of legal epistemology, the person offering *E* to the court as evidence is assumed to know *E*. The person adducing evidence in legal epistemology is able to mislead in a way that would not be applicable in classical epistemology.

evidence of the parties. Another example is that legal fact finding is a special form of practical reasoning, in which the court must impose a final and authoritative judgment in the face of often far-from-overwhelming evidence. Legal epistemological certainty may therefore fall short of the criteria for certainty that we might normally expect in classical epistemology. The fact-finding methods of the court are therefore intended to be maximally truth-conducive. This maximization is subject to some non-epistemological factors that result from the social nature of the legal process, such as the need to respect the dignity of the individual in criminal prosecutions.

The theory of meta-justification that is applied in order to determine our theory of justification can be described as the Rationalist Tradition in evidence scholarship. The optimistic rationalism that prevails within the Rationalist Tradition is predicated on the effectiveness of probabilistic inferential reasoning based on a combination of facts and generalizations expressed atomically. It takes into account social constraints on the pure optimization of fact finding in formulating its criteria for justification. The justification for any theory of meta-justification is ultimately political rather than epistemological, and a number of non-rationalist ways of formulating legal epistemology have been introduced in this chapter.

Two elements of our method for justifying legal belief have been explored in this chapter: the deconstruction of evidence to an atomic level, and the use of generalizations. The deconstruction of evidence can be assisted by its graphical representation, for example using Wigmore Charts. This graphical representation can in turn help us to appreciate the structure of complex inferential arguments in a case ('the evidential matrix of the case'). They can also help to resolve some inferential difficulties that we may encounter. For example the problem of 'total inferential drag', which results from the loss of probability that a line of inference incurs as it moves from inferential step to inferential step, may be largely solved by understanding how a single line of inference fits into the overall evidential matrix, and in particular how very few lines are purely linear, but instead frequently involve corroboration or convergence.

Generalizations provide us with inferential glue. They enable us to take a basic experience or inference, and join it into a larger evidential argument through the drawing of conclusions that go beyond the experience/inference itself. The power of generalizations is such that they also give rise to potential dangers in evidential argument. A significant vulnerability with the use of generalizations is an uncertainty in many cases regarding which generalization to apply. This vulnerability can be reduced by looking at how the overall inferential matrix fits together with a particular generalization in place. The principal effect of this in relation to the court's use of expert evidence is that situations may arise in which the common-sense generalizations on which the court usually depends may directly conflict with generalizations proposed by experts, particularly, for example, by social scientists and psychologists. There is no straightforward basis on which to select one set of generalizations over another, since a series of issues are invoked, including the reliability, prevalence and persistence of common-sense and expert generalizations, and whether the democratic remit of the legal process is threatened by technocracy. The preferred approach is to say that, in those limited situations where direct and irreconcilable conflict arises, then common-sense generalizations are to be preferred over expert generalizations, as people are held to account ultimately against the standards of the society in which they live, and people have a right to expect standards to be relatively stable over time, in order to guide their conduct. As expert generalizations become stable, we might reasonably expect them to become incorporated into common sense. The basis for preferring common sense over expert generalizations is particularly applicable where the civil or criminal issue has a strongly subjective component ('What did D believe was the case?'). Where the issue is strongly objective, we might consider resolving the dispute in favour of the expert generalization.

A further challenge to rationalist fact finding comes from the more extreme forms of naturalized epistemology. Empirical research by cognitive psychologists, for example, suggests that people do not always act in a fully rational manner when making decisions, but may instead rely on heuristic shortcuts. These heuristics arise from a series of cognitive biases, which we might in turn consider to be a category of generalization ('situation *x* usually has significance *y*'). Although these heuristics may allow people to conduct practical reasoning effectively in many everyday contexts, they become particularly problematic when applied to complex inferential tasks. This includes both the work of experts in producing their opinions for the court, and the work of the tribunal of fact in assessing complex expert evidence. If left unchecked, the effect of cognitive biases on legal fact finding could be significant. However, the effect can be mitigated through the formulation of fact-finding processes that safeguard against these biases. For example, the emphasis on atomistic inferential reasoning can encourage fact finders to make explicit, at least to themselves, the main generalizations and steps that they are employing. Similarly, a requirement for the tribunal of fact to give reasons, either to other members of a fact-finding panel or in open court, enables others to check that the main elements of the evidential reasoning are rational. Rather than cognitive psychology undermining the fundamentals of rationalist legal fact finding, the principles and methods of this fact finding, as expressed in this chapter, instead allow us to overcome many of our everyday heuristics for this special task of practical reasoning.

2

Expert evidence as a special case for judicial assessment

2.1 Introduction

> The whole object of the expert is to tell the jury, not the facts, as we have seen, but general truths derived from his specialized experience. But how can the jury judge between two statements each founded upon an experience confessedly foreign in kind to their own? It is just because they are incompetent for such a task that the expert is necessary at all ... The truth of either combating proposition lies just in its validity as an inference from a vast mass of experience ... as to the truth of which trained powers of observation are quite essential, the result themselves of a life of technical training. What hope have the jury, or any other layman, of a rational decision between two such conflicting statements each based upon such experience?[1]

The work of the previous chapter has provided us with a general epistemological framework to describe the judicial assessment of evidence. In particular, it has proposed that judicial justified belief should be explained in terms of a Haackian foundherentist model, it has identified features of judicial fact finding that distinguish it as a special form of epistemology, it has presented a meta-justification in the form of Twining's Rationalist Tradition, and it has analysed elements of that meta-justification, particularly atomism and the use of generalizations.

Chapter 1 began to allude to, but deliberately held back from fully engaging with, the question of how expert evidence fitted into this framework. Expert evidence provides us with a good case study to look at the epistemological foundations of legal evidence precisely because it presents particular difficulties. If we can justify the judicial assessment of expert evidence, the argument runs, then we can justify the judicial assessment of

[1] L. Hand, 'Historical and Practical Considerations Regarding Expert Testimony' (1901) 15 *Harvard Law Review* 40–58, 54.

most if not all forms of evidence. That argument makes a major assumption, of course, which is that expert evidence is just a special form of legal evidence, and the judicial assessment of expert evidence is similarly only a special case of the judicial assessment of all legal evidence. If it were instead the case that there is something fundamentally different about expert evidence, then this argument would fail, and expert evidence would become a separate category of proof, perhaps in the same way that judicial notice is a separate category in Anglo-American legal systems.[2]

There are three key features of expert evidence that distinguish it from non-expert evidence. An analysis of these features indicates that expert evidence belongs to the same body of evidence as non-expert evidence, although there are sufficient minor distinguishing characteristics to warrant describing the judicial assessment of expert evidence as a special case of the judicial assessment of evidence generally. The first key feature is that expert evidence is usually considered to represent statements of opinion rather than fact, and opinions present particular evidential difficulties for evidence and proof (Section 2.2). The fact/opinion distinction has been a feature of Anglo-American evidence law since at least the seventeenth century (Section 2.2.1). Once we view legal fact finding in terms of probabilistic inferential reasoning, involving the application of generalizations to basic experiences, the traditional distinction between evidence of fact and evidence of opinion is shown to be one of operational convenience (Section 2.2.2) rather than epistemological substance (Section 2.2.3). There are therefore no fundamental reasons to approach the assessment of facts and of opinions separately (Section 2.2.4).

The second key feature is that expert evidence, unlike non-expert evidence, is the product of specialist knowledge unavailable to the courts. We might expect that the reliability of this specialist knowledge, and of the way in which it is applied to the factual issues in the instant case, cannot properly be assessed by a non-expert tribunal of fact (Section 2.3). However, the structure of evidential arguments at an atomic level is blind to subject matter (Section 2.3.1), and there are no fundamental differences between common-sense and expert approaches to inferential reasoning (Section 2.3.2). In addition, it is a category mistake to address whether the

[2] 'When a court takes judicial notice of a fact . . . it declares that it will find that the fact exists . . . although the existence of the fact has not been established by evidence': C. Tapper, *Cross and Tapper on Evidence*, 11th edn (Oxford: Oxford University Press, 2007), p. 82. Facts may be noticed without or after inquiry.

court can assess expert evidence by asking whether it is able to produce expert evidence (Section 2.3.3).

The final key feature is that expert evidence is frequently presented by witnesses who represent persistent communities of practice outside the legal domain. The court may therefore have to recognise a social aspect to the assessment of expert evidence that does not exist for non-expert evidence (Section 2.4). This social epistemological aspect may constrain the court's ability freely to assess expert evidence. While the court has a competence to assess evidence generally, the court's competence to assess expert evidence specifically is more limited. This limited epistemic competence nevertheless supports the judicial assessment of expert evidence at the level of practical reasoning.

In the penultimate part of this chapter (Section 2.5), I turn to address arguments for strong epistemological constructivism. This is the claim that our factual knowledge of the world is constructed through our social experiences, that knowledge is fragmented into systems (or disciplines or other units), and that it is therefore not possible to identify common ground between two knowledge systems, in order to enable communication between them (Section 2.5.1). Epistemological constructivism is a form of epistemology that has developed in the modern age, for example in the work of Kant and Weber (Section 2.5.2). The strong (incommensurable) form of epistemological constructivism specifies the incommensurability of knowledge systems in society (Section 2.5.3). General difficulties with strong epistemological constructivism in the philosophy of sociology and of science are considered. Finally, the application of autopoietic systems theory to understanding the judicial assessment of expert evidence, which includes a form of strong epistemological constructivism, is evaluated (Section 2.5.4). A proper analysis of the arguments for the incommensurability of 'legal' and 'expert' knowledge, as presented both generally by post-modernists and specifically in autopoietic systems theory, shows them, on examination, to be fundamentally ill founded.

2.2 Questions of fact and opinion

In Twining's list of 'Common Assumptions in Rationalist Theories of Evidence and Proof' (Section 1.4.1), the third assumption includes the maintenance of an operative distinction between facts and opinions. That operative distinction is of central importance to this present chapter because most expert evidence is usually categorized as being expert evidence of opinion, and in turn most academic discussion of the Opinion Rule centres on opinions offered by experts.[3] So there is a significant overlap, although not equivalence, between expert evidence and opinion evidence; one can also have non-expert evidence of opinion, which is mostly inadmissible, and expert evidence of fact.[4] Although not equivalent, expertise and opinion are largely coterminous, at least in Anglo-American evidence law.[5] So in itself this might make us begin to be concerned that expert evidence does not function in the same way as non-expert evidence, at least in the majority of cases, where expert evidence of opinion is contrasted with non-expert evidence of fact. To compound matters, however, Anglo-American law tends to see opinion evidence as being surrounded with sufficient probative issues to make most non-expert opinion inadmissible ('the rule against opinion'). So it is imperative that we understand how evidence of opinion and of fact may differ, in order to identify any specific issues with expert evidence in connection with it usually also being evidence of opinion.

In this section I therefore analyse possible rationales for the operative distinction between facts and opinions (Section 2.2.2), whether it has any philosophical foundation (Section 2.2.3), and whether the distinction should be maintained (Section 2.2.4). A key feature of my conclusion to this analysis is that the classical rationalist distinction between facts and opinions, which has been with us since at least the seventeenth century, does not always assist us in understanding how the courts assess expert evidence. This is because the underlying question, of how inferences have been drawn from basic experiences and generalizations, is structurally the same for questions of both fact and opinion. Therefore when we say 'facts' we are usually referring to a set of propositions which have been inferred through the application of generalizations to other inferences (Section 1.4.2). We may choose to draw the line somewhere and say

[3] E.g. H. Malek (ed.), *Phipson on Evidence*, 16th edn (London: Sweet and Maxwell, 2005), ch. 33.

[4] One of the few texts that recognizes this lack of equivalence in practice rather than mere words is P. Roberts and A. Zuckerman, *Criminal Evidence* (Oxford: Oxford University Press, 2004), in which expert evidence and opinion evidence appear in separate chapters.

[5] In the absence of formal rules of admissibility, civil evidence in continental Europe may not have similar concerns about the nature and function of opinion evidence. For example, in Taruffo's 500-page text on judicial proof, which otherwise appears very similar in layout and subject matter to Anglo-American texts on evidence, there is no discussion of opinion evidence, and seven pages on expert evidence: M. Taruffo, *La prova dei fatti giuridici* (Milan: Giuffrè, 1992), pp. 303–10.

that some of these inferences should be classified as 'brute facts',[6] but the inferential chain properly goes back to basic experiences. What an expert brings to this process is not her opinions per se, since there is no special category of knowledge or justified belief that we can refer to as opinion, but rather specialist advice on the appropriate generalizations to apply to a particular set of facts, and how those generalizations should best be applied, as well as possibly the expert's own conclusion on the application of those generalizations. To talk about evidence of opinion as being quite distinct from evidence of fact may therefore have been a wrong turn in the development of evidence jurisprudence. It creates unnecessary difficulties for us in forming a correct understanding of how the court assesses evidence, and particularly expert evidence.

2.2.1 The nature of the distinction in English law

The Opinion Rule appears to have been established in English law by the seventeenth century, although it had been a long-established principle that a witness testifies to what she has herself seen and heard.[7] By 1621, it was clear that what a witness thought about a case, separate to the facts, was inadmissible: '[I]t is not satisfactory for the witness to say, that he thinks or persuadeth himself, and that for two reasons by Coke: 1st, Because that the Judge is to give an absolute sentence, and therefore ought to have more sure ground than thinking; 2dly, The witness cannot be prosecuted for perjury'.[8] In *Bushell's Case*, almost fifty years later, Vaughan CJ clarified that the drawing of opinions from the facts was in the domain of the tribunal of fact, not of the witnesses: 'A witness swears but to what he hath heard or seen, generally or more largely, to what hath fallen under his senses. But a jury-man swears to what he can infer and conclude from the testimony of such witnesses, by the act and force of his understanding, to be the fact inquired after'.[9]

This distinction is relatively operationally straightforward in relation to ordinary witnesses and, as I suggest below, in tune with contemporary developments in epistemology. However, it was becoming increasingly difficult to apply in relation to those witnesses who were being asked to testify on specialist matters, such as medicine or engineering, and in 1782

6 G. Anscombe, 'On Brute Facts' (1958) 18 *Analysis* 69–72.
7 The principle was in place in English law by at least the fourteenth century.
8 *Adams* v. *Canon* (1621) Dyer 53b n 15 (Coke CJ), in the Star Chamber.
9 *Bushell's Case* (1670) Vaughan 135; 124 ER 1006

Lord Mansfield CJ clarified the matter by ruling the opinions of experts to be admissible:

> In matters of science no other witnesses can be called... I cannot believe that where the question is, whether a defect arises from a natural or an artificial cause, the opinions of men of science are not to be received. Hand-writing is proved every day by opinion; and for false evidence on such questions a man may be indicted for perjury. Many nice questions may arise as to forgery, and as to the impressions of seals ... In such cases I cannot say that the opinion of seal-makers is not to be taken.[10]

Difficulties may also arise where the witness is asked to express what she observed without recourse to an opinion, where that observation can only sensibly be expressed as an opinion. In particular, identification evidence is considered at common law to be evidence of opinion but is admissible of necessity.[11] Similarly, it may be more straightforward for the witness to state the inferences that she has drawn from facts observed than the detailed list of facts. Examples include age, speed, weather and handwriting,[12] or whether a person was drunk.[13] The justification for this is pragmatic, but it does show clearly that the rule has conceptual difficulties:

> Unless opinions, estimates and inferences which men in their daily lives reach without conscious ratiocination as a result of what they perceived with their physical senses were treated in the law of evidence as if they were mere statements of fact, witnesses would find themselves unable to communicate to the judge an accurate impression of the events they were seeking to describe.[14]

By the start of this century, therefore, a straightforward rule that a witness must testify to facts that she directly observed and not to opinions that she has drawn from those facts had become hedged with a number of significant exceptions. Cross and Tapper very helpfully provide us with this definition of the rule which encompasses these exceptions:

> A witness may not give his opinion on matters which the court considers call for the specialist skill or knowledge of an expert unless he is an expert in

[10] *Folkes* v. *Chadd* (1782) 3 Doug 157, at 159; 99 ER 589.

[11] Tapper, *Cross and Tapper*, p. 584. [12] Ibid., p. 567.

[13] *R.* v. *Davies* [1962] 1 WLR 1111; [1962] 3 All ER 97.

[14] Law Reform Committee England and Wales, *Evidence of Opinion and Expert Evidence*, 17th Report, Cmnd 4489 (London: Her Majesty's Stationery Office, 1970), [3], quoted in Tapper, *Cross and Tapper*, p. 525.

> such matters, and he may not give his opinion on other matters if the facts upon which it is based can be stated without reference to it in a manner equally conducive to the ascertainment of the truth.[15]

The rule has not only developed exceptions over its 400-year history, but would appear to have lost some. An early exception to the rule would appear to have been made for statements of opinion resting on 'an inference or conclusion from personally observed data'.[16] That exception would appear to have disappeared for non-expert witnesses by 1848,[17] but it remained the basis on which experts could provide opinions on the facts, even if these touched on the ultimate issue, without recourse to hypothetical questions.[18]

2.2.2 Operative rationales for the distinction

In relation to another rule that particularly relates to expert evidence, the Ultimate Issue Rule (Section 5.7), Jackson has usefully shown the benefit of dissecting the rationales that have accumulated over time for the existence of a rule of evidence.[19] It may well be the case, as with the Ultimate Issue Rule, that no particular evidential benefit is served by having a distinct Opinion Rule. A close examination of the Opinion Rule in this section similarly reveals five overlapping rationales, which are evaluated. By identifying the goals that a rule seeks to further, we can better determine which goals we seek to pursue, and possible areas of overlap, in order to rationalize the rules in a coherent fashion.

2.2.2.1 Finality in fact finding

Firstly, there is an epistemological rationale that, in order for legal findings of fact to be final and authoritative, they must be based on evidence that is certain ('omne sacramentum debet esse de certa scientia').[20] In his philosophical study of the concept of testimony, Tony Coady has

[15] Tapper, *Cross and Tapper*, p. 556; *Sherrard* v. *Jacob* [1965] NI 151 (HL), at 157 (Lord MacDermott).

[16] J. Wigmore, *A Treatise on the Anglo-American System of Evidence in Trials at Common Law* (1923), rev. edn Chadbourn. (Boston: Little, Brown, 1981), vol. VII, p. 5.

[17] J. Taylor, *A Treatise on the Law of Evidence* (London: Maxwell and Son, 1848), p. 940.

[18] Ibid., p. 944.

[19] J. Jackson, 'The Ultimate Issue Rule: One Rule Too Many' [1984] *Criminal Law Review* 75.

[20] 'Every oath ought to be of certain knowledge': E. Coke, *Institutes of the Laws of England*, vol. IV (London: 1644), p. 279. Although the conclusions of the court will usually be probabilistic, our evidence should be certain, e.g. T. Williamson, *Knowledge and its Limits*

suggested that the dominance of an individualistic ideology in the 'post-Renaissance' world was a major factor in the development of the idea that testimony has little or no epistemic importance.[21] Coady suggests that we can see this anti-individualist rhetoric in the work of Descartes and Locke in their arguments that we do not really know things simply because they have been told to us by others in place of personal experience. This inferiority may in part be a response to epistemology before the seventeenth century, in which the authority of a statement depended primarily upon the authority of its maker.[22]

Cartesian scepticism in its purest form extended beyond the testimony of others to reach even the testimony of our senses. Descartes concluded that we cannot even know that our own experience of the world is reliable, since our senses could be unreliable. The only things of which the mind can be certain are the internal properties and functions of the mind itself, starting with the fact that the mind exists:

> I noticed that, while I was trying to think that everything was false, it was necessary that I, who was thinking this, should be something. And observing that this truth 'I am thinking, therefore I exist' ['*cogito ergo sum*'] was so firm and secure that all the more extravagant suppositions of the sceptics were not capable of overthrowing it, I judged that I should not scruple to accept it as the first principle of the philosophy I was seeking.[23]

The work of the seventeenth-century English empiricist Locke not only was a leading – perhaps the leading – contribution to modern epistemology, but also has shaped some of the underlying concepts in modern Anglo-American evidence law. Locke's *Essay Concerning Human Understanding* was developed in the 1670s and 1680s, and published in 1690.[24] The significance of Locke's epistemology for understanding the development of the Opinion Rule is that he made a clear distinction between

(Oxford: Oxford University Press, 2000), ch. 10. 'Certain' is not here simply a synonym for a probability of 1 (pp. 213–15).

21 A. Coady, *Testimony: a Philosophical Study* (Oxford: Oxford University Press, 1992), p. 13. The problems of testimony are related to those of opinion evidence, but nevertheless distinct. It appears to be irrelevant for Coady's argument whether the testimony concerns fact or opinion.

22 I. Hacking, *The Emergence of Probability: A Philosophical Study of Early Ideas About Probability, Induction and Statistical Inference* (Cambridge: Cambridge University Press, 1975).

23 R. Descartes, *Discours de la méthode* (Paris: 1637).

24 J. Locke, *Essay Concerning Human Understanding* (1690), ed. J. Yolton, 3rd edn (London: Dent, 1993).

'knowledge', which was certain, and 'judgment', which was not.[25] The effect of that distinction for evidence jurisprudence is that what the witness says she saw or heard should be treated with a certainty, subject of course to believing the witness, which cannot be accorded to the opinions of the witness. Locke says that 'knowledge' is when we have an actual perception of the agreement or disagreement of any of our 'ideas' with one another.[26] The source of these ideas is sensation, which may be internal (our own existence, and what is passing in our minds) and external (perception of the presence of external objects).[27] This perception of agreement can be either intuitive, when we perceive 'immediately' (that is, without any intervening perceptual medium) by comparison with ideas themselves, or demonstrative when we perceive 'mediately' (that is, through an intervening perceptual medium), by deduction from comparison with intervening ideas which have constant and immutable connection, or sensitive, by being 'aware of things actually present to our senses'.[28] Knowledge therefore includes things that we know through logic and mathematics, and things known by induction. 'Judgment', on the other hand, is the faculty by which our minds take ideas to agree or disagree, facts or propositions to be true or false, by the aid of intervening ideas whose connection with them is either not constant and immutable, or not perceived to be so.[29] Locke attempts to classify types of judgment.[30] It is possible, says Locke, for one person to have knowledge while another has only judgment.[31] This may occur where one person has worked through and understood a mathematical proof while another has merely accepted that it is true.

The detail of Locke's argument suggests that even what we have ourselves seen and heard does not really constitute full knowledge of the world, since the areas in which he proposes that we can have 'knowledge' are almost exclusively mathematical or logical proofs. 'Sensitive' knowledge 'is yet much narrower' than the other types of knowledge. If we want to extend our understanding of the physical world beyond stating that objects exist, to issues such as causation (which is of particular interest to lawyers[32]), we encounter significant problems of epistemology. Locke, an atomist, believed that, in order to achieve a 'necessary knowledge of

[25] Locke's use of the term 'knowledge' pre-dates the modern epistemological distinction between knowledge and justified true belief (Section 1.2).

[26] Ibid., IV.I.2. [27] Ibid., II.1. [28] Ibid., IV.III.1–5. [29] Ibid., IV.XIV.3, IV.XV.1.

[30] Ibid., IV.XVI.6–9. [31] Ibid., IV.XIV.3

[32] E.g. H. Hart and T. Honoré, *Causation in the Law*, 2nd edn (Oxford: Oxford University Press, 1985).

nature', we would have to know both the configuration and motion of atoms, and the way in which the motions of atoms produce ideas of primary and secondary qualities in the observer. Even if we knew the configuration and motion of atoms, which was methodologically possible albeit very unlikely, we still would not know how the atoms achieved their effects. Ultimately, therefore, an unbridgeable epistemological gap separates the 'real world' of atoms from the realm of ideas that constitutes our experience.[33] So, for Locke, scientific knowledge can never be as certain as the 'sensitive' knowledge gained through our immediate senses. Almost the only information about the external world of which we can be certain, other than logical inferences such as that a black thread is not white, is simple sense data. This view reinforces the narrow legal distinction between evidential facts and opinions (Section 2.2.1).

Locke's *Essay* was the philosophical basis of Gilbert's work on evidence, composed in the early eighteenth century. Part of Locke's attractiveness as an empiricist was undoubtedly at least in part because his political philosophy was intellectually fashionable in the late seventeenth and early eighteenth centuries.[34] But Locke also provided lawyers with a theoretical framework within which to explain how we could know things about the world using empirical evidence rather than deductive reasoning, and why knowledge was distinct from judgment. Gilbert, Lord Chief Baron of the Court of Exchequer from 1722 to his death in 1726, began his posthumous 1754 *The Law of Evidence* with an essay on Locke's theory of knowledge. Similarly Best, a barrister and author of a leading evidence text in the mid nineteenth century,[35] wrote an essay in 1844 on presumptions and circumstantial evidence,[36] which considered at length the significance of Locke's work, working both directly with the *Essay Concerning Human Understanding*, and with Bonnier's *Traité théorique et pratique des preuves*,[37] which was heavily influenced by Locke. In Best's account, we move directly from defining knowledge and judgment in philosophical

[33] J. Losee, *Historical Introduction to the Philosophy of Science*, 3rd edn (Oxford: Oxford University Press, 1993), p. 102.

[34] B. Russell, *History of Western Philosophy*, 2nd edn (London: Routledge, 1961), p. 585.

[35] W. Best, *Principles of the Law of Evidence and Practice as to Proofs in Courts of Common Law*, 2nd edn (London: Sweet, 1854).

[36] W. Best, *A Treatise on Presumptions of Law and Fact with the Theory and Rules of Presumptive or Circumstantial Proof in Criminal Cases* (London: Sweet, 1844). The treatise was incorporated into the second edition of Best, *Principles*.

[37] É. Bonnier, *Traité théorique et pratique des preuves en droit civil et en droit criminal*, 2nd edn (Paris: Durand, 1852).

terms, and contrasting them, to defining facts in legal evidential reasoning.[38] We can read Best's text as saying that Locke's 'knowledge' equates with lawyers' 'facts', but that equation is not explicit at that point. Later in the same text, when Best comes to discuss the rule against evidence of opinion, he is prepared to equate facts with knowledge.[39] We might reasonably infer that when Best says 'knowledge' in these two parts of the book, he means the same thing. The main reservation to that inference is that his discussion of Locke comes from his 1844 *Treatise* while his discussion of the Opinion Rule comes from the 1849 first edition of his *Principles*. Authorial intention may have varied between these two source texts. The equation of 'fact' with 'knowledge' would not be entirely straightforward, since Best divides facts into those that are 'physical'[40] and those that are 'psychological'.[41]

2.2.2.2 Constitutional role of the actors

A second rationale is that it is the role of the witness to provide evidence of facts, and of the tribunal of fact to form the necessary opinions from those facts in order to decide the case.[42] When it became clear at the end of the eighteenth century that the opinions of experts would be admissible, a further rule, the Ultimate Issue Rule, was developed, in the early nineteenth century, to ensure that the expert's expressions of opinion did not extend as far as a view on the ultimate issue itself (Section 5.7). We may reasonably suspect that the rule originated out of concern at the epistemic competence of the jury as tribunal of fact. In other words, it is only because we do not expect the jury to be able to assess the evidence of the expert properly that we must be concerned that, if the jury were to be presented with an opinion on the ultimate issue by an expert, then it would accept that opinion as given, rather than forming its own opinion. Thus the expert would de facto decide the case. The tribunal of fact, whether judge or jury, is not, however, entitled to delegate this fact-finding authority. That authority has already been delegated, either historically by the Crown or in a modern context by Parliament, and it is a principle of English administrative law that delegated authority cannot be further delegated by the delegate: *delegatus non delegare potest*. The line of reasoning behind this rule is problematic, because it may be that there is only one conclusion that can be correctly drawn from the facts,

[38] Best, *Principles*, 2nd edn, pp. 2–9. [39] Ibid., p. 587.
[40] Existence of objects or events: ibid., pp. 9–10. [41] Desires, passions, assent: ibid., p. 9.
[42] *Bushell's Case*.

or at least there is only one conclusion that has a very high probability of being correct, and the expert would be able to draw that conclusion. If, however, we prevent the expert from presenting that conclusion, then the inexpert jury may proceed to arrive at a wholly erroneous conclusion.

2.2.2.3 To safeguard other rules of evidence

In his 1854 text on common law evidence, Best proposed that the Opinion Rule should be correctly viewed as serving to safeguard the other rules of evidence: 'The use of witnesses being to inform the tribunal respecting *facts*, their *opinions* are not in general receivable as evidence. This rule is necessary to prevent the other rules of evidence being practically nullified.'[43] Cross and Tapper similarly suggest,[44] citing Thayer,[45] that the rules against opinion and hearsay both originate in the same doctrine that every witness must be able to say that she had seen or heard that to which she deposes. They do not produce direct historical evidence for this proposition, although indirect evidence can be identified. The 1621 case of *Adams* itself concerned whether a witness could testify to facts that he only knew because his father had told them to him. However, the *ratio* was cast more widely than simply the avoidance of hearsay. The case that might be cited as authority for the way in which opinion and hearsay flow through the same evidential channel, *Wright* v. *Doe d Tatham*,[46] turns on a very particular question, of whether opinions should be admitted as evidence that can be inferred from the letters of correspondents who are now dead.

2.2.2.4 To safeguard the tribunal's time

A fourth possible rationale for excluding the admission of opinion evidence would be to say that the tribunal of fact's time would be wasted by listening to people's opinions, when it is able to draw equally valid conclusions from the base facts. This rationale certainly does not provide us with the origins of the rule. First, Coke's *dictum* in *Adams* was concerned with whether a legal decision had a solid epistemological basis, not on whether it was efficiently reached. Secondly, where we have examples of direct witness testimony from the late seventeenth century and

[43] Best, *Principles*, 2nd edn, p. 587. [44] Tapper, *Cross and Tapper*, p. 569.
[45] J. Thayer, *A Preliminary Treatise on Evidence at Common Law* (Cambridge MA: Harvard University Press, 1898), p. 523.
[46] *Wright* v. *Doe d Tatham* (1838) Bing NC 489.

most of the eighteenth century, as in the Old Bailey Sessions Papers[47] and some other criminal cases,[48] witnesses are freely able to express opinions. There appears to have been no question of excluding such evidence as inefficient. Thirdly, when Starkie considered the Opinion Rule in 1824, it was to exclude opinion evidence not from being given, but from being considered by counsel or the jury: counsel cannot cross-examine on witnesses' opinions or conclusions, 'for these are to be made by a jury . . . '[49] Fourthly, when the defendant in *Folkes* v. *Chadd* in 1782 sought to exclude evidence of opinion, it was solely on the basis that it should form no part of the tribunal's deliberations, not that it would waste court time.[50] Finally, the court time that may be taken up in stopping a witness from giving her opinion, getting her to restate her evidence as fact, and directing the jury to ignore the statement of opinion may exceed the time that the witness actually spent giving her opinion. On a related point, counsel's questions to the witness under cross-examination may themselves be an expression of opinion, as well as inviting an opinion.[51]

2.2.2.5 To safeguard the availability of perjury actions

The second reason given by Coke in *Adams*, and one of the arguments considered by Lord Mansfield in *Folkes* against the admissibility of expert opinion, was that a witness could not be prosecuted for perjury for expressing his opinion. This presumably reflects a libertarian point that the individual must be free to hold whatever opinion she chooses, and the State cannot control what a person thinks. Lord Mansfield rejected the argument, pointing out that it was already the case that people were prosecuted for providing false opinions on the identification of handwriting. Whatever the merits of Mansfield's argument with respect to handwriting experts, the view of Coke accords more with that of modern experience. While prosecutions of witnesses for perjury in relation to factual matters are relatively common, there is very little precedent since the time of Mansfield for the prosecution of a witness for perjuring herself in relation to evidence of opinion (Section 7.7.1.1). This is because there are very

[47] Section 5.3.3.2, e.g. *R.* v. *Vezey* Old Bailey Sessions Papers (Jan 1732) 41 (whether death was from a fall or from consumption).
[48] E.g. *R.* v. *Cowper* (1699) 13 St Tr 1106.
[49] T. Starkie, *A Practical Treatise on the Law of Evidence and Digest of Proofs in Civil and Criminal Proceedings* (London: Clarke, 1824), p. 1736.
[50] Best, *Principles*, 2nd edn, p. 587.
[51] A. Keane and S. Seabrooke (eds.), *Evidence*, 6th edn (Oxford: Blackstone, 2001), p. 206.

few circumstances in which it can be shown that an inferred opinion was deliberately false rather than simply erroneous or even negligent.

2.2.3 Philosophical difficulties with the distinction

2.2.3.1 More than one meaning

The primary definition of 'fact' given in *The Oxford English Dictionary* is '[a] thing done or performed: a. in neutral sense: An action, deed, course of conduct'.[52] However, the sense in which lawyers use the word, at least when contrasting it with opinion, is more akin to a subsidiary meaning of the word given in the dictionary: 'Something that has really occurred or is actually the case; something certainly known to be of this character; hence, a particular truth known by actual observation or authentic testimony, as opposed to what is merely inferred, or to a conjecture or fiction; a datum of experience, as distinguished from the conclusions that may be based upon it.'[53] A fact in this sense is more a thing that was done (Latin *factum*) and becomes a thing associated with certainty of knowledge.[54]

The word 'opinion' has at least two uses that are relevant to our present discussion: 'Certainly, experts give the court the benefit of their (and others') experience in the form of conclusions or generalizations from that experience. If this is opinion, it is valuable and often necessary opinion, and differs in several respects from the sort of opinion the courts are understandably anxious to exclude.'[55] On the one hand, we have opinions that reflect a considered weighing-up of available evidence. This is reflected in the primary definition in *The Oxford English Dictionary*: '1 . . . A view held about a particular issue; a judgement formed or a conclusion reached; a belief; a religious or political conviction'.[56] There is a related meaning that is of more specific application to a forensic context: '4. A formal statement by a judge or other competent authority of what he or she judges or advises on a matter; professional advice; as a *legal* (also *medical*) opinion, to get an opinion of counsel, etc.' On the other hand,

[52] J. Simpson and E. Weiner (eds.), *The Oxford English Dictionary*, 2nd edn (Oxford: Oxford University Press, 1989).

[53] Simpson and Weiner (eds.), *Oxford English Dictionary*, 'Fact', def. 4a. Compare Coady, *Testimony*, p. 233.

[54] This transformation may have occurred historically, in legal rather than scientific contexts, in the course of the sixteenth century: B. Shapiro, *A Culture of Fact: England 1550–1720* (Ithaca NY: Cornell University Press, 2000).

[55] Coady, *Testimony*, p. 277.

[56] Simpson and Weiner (eds.), *Oxford English Dictionary*, 'Opinion'.

we have 'opinion' meaning a conclusion that someone draws with little or no regard to the detail of the evidence. This could be brought within the first definition taken from *The Oxford English Dictionary*. Some of the rationales for excluding opinion evidence depend on this second meaning. There is a distinction between 'what I think' and 'what I have concluded through careful reasoning'.

2.2.3.2 Making a clear distinction

The Lockean approach to distinguishing facts from opinions requires the acceptance of a fundamental epistemological distinction between the two. That distinction was almost immediately rejected by subsequent empiricists, particularly Hume and Berkeley, for whom all sense data were bound up in subjective perception. For example, Locke distinguished between primary qualities of objects, which are inseparable from the body, and secondary qualities, which are 'powers to produce various sensations in us by their *primary qualities*'.[57] So, solidity, extension, figure and mobility are inherent to the thing observed, but colours, sounds and tastes are our interpretations. Hume, however, not only took such an argument to be 'universally allowed by modern enquirers', but extended it to suggest that, if secondary qualities are an 'opinion', then so are primary qualities.[58]

The argument that our perception of sense data is fundamentally subjective finds some support in cognitive psychology (Section 1.5). Psychology experiments suggest that our experience and recollection is affected by our prior knowledge of the world. For example, in a study where participants were asked to read a description of a home while taking the viewpoint of either a prospective homebuyer or a burglar, later recall showed that the different perspectives affected what was remembered. In the case of the 'home buyers', a leaky roof was most likely to be remembered, while in the case of the 'burglars', it was a valuable coin collection.[59] In another study, participants who were told about a person's visit to the dentist then falsely recalled hearing some details that typically occur in a dentist's office, such as checking in with the receptionist, looking at a magazine in the waiting room, and so on, even though these were never

[57] Locke, *Essay*, II.VIII.9–10.

[58] D. Hume, *A Treatise of Human Nature* (1740), ed. P. Nidditch, 2nd edn (Oxford: Oxford University Press), XII.II.122. Compare Coady, *Testimony*, p. 59.

[59] R. Anderson and J. Pichert, 'Recall of Previously Unrecallable Information Following a Shift in Perspective' (1978) 17 *Journal of Verbal Learning and Verbal Behavior* 1–12.

explicitly mentioned.[60] These studies do not necessarily show that our understanding of the world is entirely subjective, but it does suggest that how we remember things is subjective.

The role of subjectivity in our understanding of events can also be seen in a well-known example from Collingwood on causation, which highlights the importance of standpoint:

> A car skids while cornering at a certain point, turns turtle, and bursts into flame. From the car driver's point of view, the cause of the accident was cornering too fast, and the lesson is that one must drive more carefully. From the county surveyor's point of view, the cause was a defective road surface, and the lesson is that one must make skid-proof roads. From the motor-manufacturer's point of view, the cause was defective design, and the lesson is that one must place the centre of gravity lower.[61]

The objective reality in this vignette would appear to be that there were multiple causes of the car crash. However, the effect of the standpoint of the different actors is to focus their attention only on that aspect which directly concerns them.

The philosophical rejection of a clear distinction between facts and opinions would appear to have been accepted by evidence lawyers. By the end of the nineteenth century, the rationalist evidence scholar Thayer had concluded that the distinction was arbitrary: 'In a sense all testimony to matter of fact is opinion evidence; i.e. it is a conclusion formed from phenomena and mental impressions. Yet that is not the way that we talk in courts or in common life. Where shall the line be drawn? When does matter of fact first become matter of opinion?'[62] The 1970 Law Reform Committee report on expert evidence similarly noted that:

> In giving the title 'Evidence of Opinion and Expert Evidence' to this, our fourth interim report upon the Law of Evidence in Civil Cases, we do not mean to imply either that there is a hard and fast line to be drawn between evidence of fact and evidence of opinion, or that expert evidence is confined to evidence of opinion. The current rules upon those aspects of the law . . . are derived exclusively from the practice of the courts.[63]

[60] G. Bower, J. Black and T. Turner, 'Scripts in Memory for Texts' (1979) 11 *Cognitive Psychology* 177–220.

[61] R. Collingwood, 'On the So-Called Idea of Causation' (1937–8) 38 *Proceedings of the Aristotelian Society* 85–112.

[62] Thayer, *Preliminary Treatise*, p. 524.

[63] Law Reform Committee, *Evidence of Opinion*, p. 3.

Expert evidence does not allow itself to be classified tidily within the fact/opinion distinction. The problem is that, while part of an expert's evidence consists of opinions that she has drawn from the facts, and another part consists of constituent facts that may have been provided by a non-expert, an expert may also identify and work with facts that are either only observable because of her expertise, or recognized as significant because of her expertise.[64] We might call these facts 'expert facts'. An example of facts that can only be observed by an expert might include the cells on a cervical smear slide.[65] A non-expert would not have the facilities to produce and examine such a slide. An example of the latter is where an expert, through her skill, identifies that certain sense data, which a non-expert might also observe, should be treated as significant and accorded the status of 'facts'. That expert may then further consider that some potential facts are not relevant, and so does not record them. For example, in the English criminal case of *Clark*,[66] a pathologist had decided not to record test results from an infant autopsy because he did not consider them relevant. It was not the pathologist's practice 'to refer to additional results in my post mortem unless they are relevant to the cause of death, as the specimens were referred to another consultant'. This practice was rejected by the Court of Appeal as having an 'obvious' 'inherent danger', since it presumed that the initial expert's selection of relevant facts was correct.[67] It transpired that, to a specialist paediatric pathologist, the results were relevant to the cause of death.

For any evidence-based statement that we may choose to make about the world, therefore, we have been engaged in making a series of inferences. The logician Venn has suggested that there are a potentially infinite number of steps between any two points in a real-world chain of inferences:

> When a 'sequence' is shown to us, that is when there are two groups respectively, of antecedents and consequents, with any appreciable interval between them, however minute this interval may be, we know well enough that if we choose to examine more closely we can subdivide this by the interposition of other so-called links, and so on indefinitely. Nature is continuous, and it depends entirely upon the degree of minuteness to

[64] Roberts and Zuckerman, *Criminal Evidence*, p. 293.
[65] *Penney* v. *East Kent Health Authority* [2000] Lloyd's Rep Med 41 (CA).
[66] *R.* v. *Clark (Sally) (No. 2)* [2003] EWCA Crim 1020. [67] Ibid., at [166]–[167].

> which we decide to work, and upon the existence of appropriate names for the intermediate events, whether or not we impose any of these links.[68]

This view may be to overstate the case, because although we might concede that there are more links in our inferential chain than we can imagine, that is a very long way from saying that this chain has an infinite number of links.

Locke's apparent need to avoid making all statements about the world the product of inferential chains is the development of the realization in the seventeenth century that these inferences were fundamentally probabilistic rather than certain.[69] This creates two difficulties. The first is that no inference can represent a certain causal link, which removes the concept of 'certain knowledge'. The second, which Locke may not have appreciated, is that chains of probabilistic inferences may result in a rapid deterioration in certainty. This concept of 'inferential drag' was introduced and addressed above (Section 1.4.2.2). From that earlier discussion, there are no firm reasons to accept that inferential drag makes complex inferences less certain, as forms of justified true belief, than simple inferences. Indeed, the concept of evidential harmony allows for the possibility that extended inferences may if anything make complex inferences more certain than simple ones.

Does the position that our use of 'fact' and 'opinion' is contextual rather than absolute affect the way in which we view the evaluation of evidence of fact and opinion? In Coke's 1621 *dictum* in *Adams* against the use of opinion evidence, he emphasized that legal decision making must be based on certainty. Similarly, Locke separates sensitive knowledge from inferential judgment. In this context, facts are ontologically separate from opinions, in that while the former are an objective representation of the external world, the latter contain both that objective representation and subjective interpretation. Any inference drawn from opinion is therefore inherently less likely to be correct, because it incorporates an element of inference

68 J. Venn, *Principles of Inductive Logic*, 2nd edn (New York: Chelsea Publishing, 1907), p. 506, quoted in D. Schum, *Evidential Foundations of Probabilistic Reasoning* (London: John Wiley, 1994), p. 34.

69 The probabilistic nature of causation, which has been established since at least Hume in the natural sciences, remains problematic for lawyers: e.g. Hart and Honoré, *Causation*; R. Wright, 'Causation, Responsibility, Risk, Probability, Naked Statistics, and Proof: Pruning the Bramble Bush by Clarifying the Concepts' (1988) 73 *Iowa Law Review* 1001–77; R. Wright, 'Once More into the Bramble Bush: Duty, Causal Contribution and the Extent of Legal Responsibility' (2001) 54 *Vanderbilt Law Review* 1071–132.

from a subjective inference. This becomes particularly significant when the person making the second inference either does not know what part of the opinion is based on the first inference rather than on the (basic experience) fact, or does not understand how that inference was formed.

That distinction in the quality of inferences only exists if we accept that there is an essential rather than pragmatic difference between facts and opinions. If we say that all facts contain some degree of inference, then that distinction potentially disappears. However, if we are saying that the distinction is contextually maintained, then are we still bound to say that evidence of fact cannot be evaluated in the same way as evidence of opinion? I would suggest that the answer is no, because the way in which we use the word does not affect our inferential capabilities to draw conclusions. Rather than trying to maintain, as Locke does, that 'sensitive' facts are true by definition, but inferences are only probabilistic 'judgments', we should instead consider all facts to be essentially probabilistic, albeit that sense data will have an extremely high probability of accuracy.[70]

This does not inevitably mean that the probability of a statement being true decreases as we make more and more inferences. The evidential matrices of cases are complex and so it is possible, at least in principle, for a statement about an event to become more rather than less probable, as that inference chain is bolstered by other, converging inference chains (Section 1.4.2.2). To give a simple example, if A thinks, but is not sure, that she saw a certain car in a certain street at a certain time, and B also thinks, but is not sure, quite independently of A, that she saw the same car in an adjoining street a few minutes later, then our confidence in the statement that the car was in A's street is greater than our confidence in A's statement alone. This is the contrary conclusion to the one that we should draw relying on Locke's idea of knowledge and judgment.

2.2.3.3 The contextual nature of the distinction

When we look at how lawyers use the distinction between facts and opinions, and the rule against opinion evidence, we find that usage depends very much on context. Damaška has rightly pointed out, for example,

[70] Hart and Honoré, *Causation*, p. 406, suggest that Wigmore was wrong to say that causal statements are probabilistic. This assessment is problematic, because Wigmore's point was that cognitively we cannot be certain of a causal connection in looking at the evidence of a case. Whether there was an ontologically certain connection is an irrelevant consideration for evidential purposes.

that 'What lawyers include in their *thema probandi* as "facts" or "events" is actually a jumbled mixture of matters of unequal ontological status with an unequal degree of accessibility to our cognitive apparatus.'[71] By 'unequal ontological status', Damaška means that some 'facts' exist as natural phenomena, while others are produced by social agreements of varying complexity. These different types of fact are not equally accessible to our cognition because they operate in different sorts of ways, both linguistically and cognitively. For example, the statement 'the grocer brought a quarter of potatoes to my house today and left them there' operates in a different way to 'the grocer supplied me with a quarter of potatoes'. The first statement is close to basic experience of sense data, while the second represents the social context within which the delivery of the potatoes occurred. Anscombe has suggested that in such situations we can distinguish between 'brute facts' and 'facts in the context of our institutions',[72] but notes that this distinction is one of convention and convenience rather than being absolute. Searle and MacCormick have made similar proposals,[73] with MacCormick distinguishing 'sheer physical facts' from 'institutional facts'. Institutional facts extend to all facts that we know by reference to a normative framework, including for example the depiction of time: 'I wear on my wrist a disc attached to a strap with a clear surface on one side behind which are visible marks evenly distributed around the perimeter of a white surface.'[74]

We therefore include within 'facts' both the basic sense data and inferences that we draw from those sense data.[75] These can include the social and legal significance of those facts. There is another way of categorizing facts that bears on our present discussion, which relates to the function that the fact serves within judicial decision making. Roberts and Zuckerman, following Hohfeld, have suggested that we distinguish 'evidential facts' from 'constitutive facts'.[76] Constitutive facts are facts to which the

[71] M. Damaška, 'Truth in Adjudication' (1998) 49 *Hastings Law Journal* 289–308; 299.

[72] Anscombe, 'On Brute Facts'.

[73] N. MacCormick, 'Norms, Institutions and Institutional Facts' (1998) 17 *Law and Philosophy* 301–45; J. Searle, *Speech Acts* (Cambridge: Cambridge University Press, 1969).

[74] N. MacCormick, *Institutions of Law: an Essay in Legal Theory* (Oxford: Oxford University Press, 2007), p. 12.

[75] D. Hume, *Enquiries Concerning Human Understanding* (1748), ed. P. Nidditch, 3rd edn (Oxford: Oxford University Press, 1975) IV.I.20. Hume says that all such inferences are examples of relationships of 'cause and effect'.

[76] Roberts and Zuckerman, *Criminal Evidence*, p. 133; W. Hohfeld, *Fundamental Legal Conceptions As Applied to Judicial Reasoning* (New Haven CT: Yale University Press, 1923), p. 34.

law attaches legal consequence, which we might also call, among other things, 'ultimate facts', 'material facts', or 'facts in issue'. Evidential facts are presented to the tribunal for the purpose of establishing a constitutive fact. Evidential facts therefore include opinions, expert and lay. These constitutive facts may include social and moral evaluation of the sense-testimony, such as whether a car driver's driving was 'dangerous', or whether a picture is likely to 'deprave or corrupt'. A constitutive fact will almost certainly represent an opinion.

A statement about the world may be classified by a judge as fact or opinion in order to bring it within, or keep it outside, a legal test. Thus, in the 2000 case of *Penney*, Lord Woolf MR insisted that the interpretation of cervical smear slides by cytology screeners ('cytoscreeners') was a question of fact. If we consider this view within the context of the fact/opinion distinction, it is extremely problematic. Although Woolf considers the disagreements between the experts in great detail, there is no suggestion of disagreement on 'data of experience', to use *The Oxford English Dictionary*'s term. The disagreement is rather on whether the slides should have been interpreted as negative. For example, with the slide known as 'Palmer 2', 'as to which there was a striking conflict' regarding '*what was on* the [slide]',[77] the dispute was actually about the significance of what was seen, and whether the cytoscreener should have referred the slide on to a supervisory checker.[78]

> In relation to Palmer 2 there was a remarkable difference of opinion between the experts. The views differed as to what the cytoscreener should have reported from Professor Cotton's 'urgent referral absolutely mandatory' to negative by Dr Boon and Dr Hughes. Part of the explanation for the striking difference of opinion was that Drs Boon and Hughes attributed the changes which the slide showed as being indicative of or commensurate with inflammation. It was common ground that a screener would (as happened) have identified the relevant cells.

The broader context of Woolf's insistence that this is a question of fact is that he was attempting to apply the distinction in *Loveday* v. *Renton*[79] between issues of fact and issues of what is or is not an appropriate response to facts, which is an issue of law. That distinction does not have a place for distinctions within 'issues of fact' between sense data and inferred fact.

[77] *Penney*, at 49 (my emphasis). [78] Ibid., at 44.
[79] *Loveday* v. *Renton (No. 1)* [1989] 1 Med LR 117.

There is a temptation for the courts to classify witnesses as experts in order to admit evidence that would otherwise be inadmissible as opinion. Where the court maintains that evidence of opinion is admissible only where it is expert evidence, but takes a definition of 'expert' that is narrower than its view of what would constitute admissible opinion, the fact/opinion boundary may be stretched to conceptually unacceptable limits. For example in *R v Barker*,[80] the South Australia Court of Appeal held that a police constable's evidence that, from her 'actual observation and experience', the pipes in the defendant's shop were of a type used for smoking marijuana was a statement of fact and not opinion, and was also not expert evidence. The defendant was charged with selling goods to facilitate the smoking of marijuana. The decision that Constable Raven was not an expert would appear to have arisen from the same line of thinking as that of Menzies and Windeyer JJ in *Clark* v. *Ryan* – another Australian decision – that the witness must gain her expertise from a course of study.[81] That is not, however, the dominant view in Australian evidence practice.[82] Since the constable was not an expert, the defence submitted that any opinion evidence offered would be inadmissible. Rather than review its decision that the constable was not an expert, the court therefore proceeded to hold that her evidence was of fact and not opinion. This is extremely problematic. When the constable says that the pipe in question is of the type used for smoking marijuana, she is moving from making a statement about the pipe as it is to making a statement about the intention of other people in relation to that pipe. The constable's statement is then one that many courts would consider constituted an opinion.[83] We might say that this is a fact because, to a person with experience of marijuana-related utensils, it should be obvious that these pipes are of a sort that is commonly used for smoking marijuana. However, it is not so clear that this is a correct use of the term 'fact'. The officer knows what similar pipes are used for, based on experience in other drug-related incidents, and this requires a judgment on whether these really are similar pipes, and whether there is only one use of such pipes.

80 *R.* v. *Barker* (1988) 34 A Crim R 141, at 143 (*per* King CJ).

81 *Clark* v. *Ryan* (1960) 130 CLR 486, at 591–2. The view was directly opposed by Dixon CJ and McTiernan J, with Fullager J agreeing with both views.

82 I. Freckleton and H. Selby, *Expert Evidence* (Sydney: LBC, 1993), [7.210].

83 In *United States* v. *Johnson* 575 F 2d 1347 (5th Cir. 1978) a defendant agreed with federal authorities to appear as an expert on identifying Colombian marijuana on the basis of his 'experience of being around a great deal and smoking marijuana'.

A similar failure to distinguish expertise from opinion arose in the English case of *Clare*,[84] in which a police officer's testimony on a piece of video footage was admitted as expert opinion, on the basis that he had watched the same CCTV video forty times, sometimes in slow motion, and comparing it with other materials such as colour photographs of suspects. Although the officer's evidence may have been of great assistance to the court, and for that reason probably should have been admissible, there are significant policy reasons for not making the officer an expert, since his status would have been that of an expert ad hoc, whose expertise exists solely for the purpose of supporting the instant litigation.[85]

2.2.4 Should legal epistemology distinguish facts from opinions?

At first glance, it might appear that the operative evidential distinction between facts and opinions is non-problematic. However, once we distinguish between opinions which are little more than idle speculation, or formed on the basis of unclear or inadmissible evidence, opinions formed without 'conscious ratiocination' (to use the words of the Law Reform Committee),[86] and opinions formed on careful reasoning from other admissible evidence, three different sets of issues can be identified. Opinions formed from idle speculation or from no clear evidence can be safely excluded from consideration by the tribunal of fact, since it would allow for decisions based on gossip and speculation, or allow in evidence that would be otherwise inadmissible. The other two forms of opinion are both formed through the making of inferences from sense data, although in the former case these inferences are subconscious. Constitutionally, the drawing of inferences from facts is the function of the tribunal of fact and not of witnesses. Epistemologically, however, it is difficult to talk about very many things as being 'facts' that do not involve some degree of inference. Even Anscombe's concept of 'brute facts' is a pragmatic measure, which we might therefore expect not to function properly in certain circumstances.

We need to identify which inferences by a witness are admissible and which are not. It may be reasonable to say that an opinion can only be considered for admission where the tribunal has access to the facts on which the witness formed the opinion. That access may be actual or

[84] *R.* v. *Clare* [1995] 2 Cr App R 333.

[85] Roberts and Zuckerman, *Criminal Evidence*, p. 309.

[86] Law Reform Committee, *Evidence of Opinion*.

potential, particularly depending on the nature of the evidence. At one extreme, where an opinion is formed from a mass of scientific evidence, it would be impractical to expect that such evidence be prepared for trial and adduced in a bundle. However, it should be possible in principle for the court to obtain that data. At the other extreme, where a witness says that the defendant was drunk, the witness should be able to say on what facts she has formed that opinion. I would also suggest that the tribunal should consider the witness' ability to form reliably the inference that she does, and whether it wishes to allow that inference-making, or restrict the right to draw such an inference to itself. The general basis for allowing such inferences is the rule on expert opinion at common law.

The fact/opinion distinction is also unhelpful in that it rides roughshod over the complexities of the inferential steps that may have led to the formation of a fact or an opinion. First, almost all 'facts' are formed by inference, but are separated from 'opinions' because the degree of inference is considered small. The basis of that consideration is almost never defined. Secondly, however, 'opinion' contains propositions drawn from a wide spectrum of inference, both by witnesses who have themselves witnessed the brute facts, and by witnesses who are depending entirely on the inference-laden accounts of others. Thus, for example, a pathologist who gives a cause of death based on an autopsy which she herself carried out must surely be giving a different sort of opinion from a pathologist who is giving a cause of death based on the autopsy report of another pathologist. I would propose that the tribunal is able to form a more reliable outcome when it is able to consider facts and admissible opinions together, and would have regard instead to the degree of inference that the witness is making, and whether the tribunal is comfortable with the complexity of inferential arguments submitted in individual contexts. An important by-product of this discussion is that we also remove the difficulty that there are certain forms of factual evidence, such as the results of an autopsy, that can only in practice be given by an expert.

2.3 The court's access to specialist knowledge

The second feature of expert evidence that may affect judicial competence to assess it is that it is in most cases the product of a specialist body of knowledge. It is, after all, the specialist nature of expert evidence that appears to have gained it exemption from the Opinion Rule in the first place. A classic statement of this aspect of the difficulties involved in the assessment of expert evidence was presented by Learned Hand in his 1901 essay on expert evidence, a quote from which appears at the beginning of this chapter. But is it true that the use of specialist knowledge in expert evidence effectively places such evidence outside the domain of the general evidential competence of the tribunal of fact? I would suggest that there are at least two grounds to believe that expert evidence, and its judicial assessment, takes the same basic form as non-expert evidence. These two grounds are that the fundamental structure of evidential reasoning is substance-blind (Section 2.3.1) and that expert fact finding is the product of the same common investigative methods as everyday fact finding (Section 2.3.2). In addition, Hand's original paradox may be misplaced, because it fails to take account of the context within which the expert evidence is assessed, both in terms of the assessment as an act of practical reasoning and in terms of the expert evidence as part of the overall evidential matrix of the case (Section 2.3.3).

2.3.1 Substance-blind evidential reasoning

In his *Evidential Foundations of Probabilistic Reasoning*, introduced in Section 1.4.2, David Schum lays the foundations for a substance-blind approach to evidence. There are two specific aspects of his approach that he considers to be 'substance-blind'. The first is that all evidence can be described in terms of its credibility, relevance and inferential force/weight, irrespective of the substance of that evidence.[87] Schum says that he does not intend that the term 'substance-blind', within the context of his theory, be applicable to how one establishes credibility, relevance or inferential force in specific contexts.[88] In other words, there is no substance-blind method for assessing the evidence, but only for describing the heads under which it should be assessed. Schum provides us with some examples of what he means by 'substance or content'. These include business transactions, blood pressure readings, patient reports of anxiety, demographic data, and photographs of a missile supply.[89] Substance-blindness appears therefore to be intended to apply only to the type of evidence being considered, and not to the use being made of that evidence in an argument.

[87] Schum, *Evidential Foundations*, pp. 120, 484.

[88] D. Schum, 'A Reply to the "Schum Challenge" at UCL' (6 September 2005), www.evidencescience.org/content/D.%20Schum%20Reply.doc, pp. 2, 3 (last accessed 1 August 2008).

[89] Schum, *Evidential Foundations*, p. 3.

To this extent, Schum's approach is blind to semantic content rather than syntactic context.

The second aspect of Schum's approach is that the recurring combinations of inferences that occur across all types of complex inference (chains, convergence/conflict, corroboration/contradiction), which we encountered in Section 1.4, provide a structure or logic that exists 'regardless of its substance'.[90] The study of complex inferential reasoning, stripped of the context of its substance or content, therefore allows us to identify substance-blind 'structural similarities'[91] in the inference charts that we produce:

> We usually have some body of evidence whose individual items bear in different ways upon hypotheses of interest. But there is an additional difficulty: Evidence items may bear upon each other in interesting and often complex ways ... Careful analysis of multiple arguments based upon a mass of evidence reveals some remarkably subtle evidential characteristics which, if recognised, can be exploited in the task of drawing conclusions.[92]

Patterns in evidence are particularly visible in large, complex networks of inferences. Substance-blind analysis allows us to make use of cross-disciplinary studies to develop general concepts of inferential reasoning, and then apply these back to our own disciplines. This is because we have developed a semantic-content-neutral syntax for our inferential arguments. The conceptual framework of inferential reasoning has a wide degree of applicability, and concepts can be used across disciplines, although the concepts may be refined in different ways in different disciplines. For example, the concept of relevance may be more sophisticated in linguistics than it is in law.

It would appear that Schum does not intend to claim more than that he has provided an 'approach'[93] or a 'classification' or 'categorization'.[94] However, it is difficult to see how the recurring structural logic that Schum identifies can be seen as simply heuristic rather than reflecting something in the nature of inferential reasoning itself, unless we were to allow that forms of inferential argument exist that cannot be described adequately using Schum's approach. On this basis, I would suggest that we are able to extend the concept of 'substance-blind' to apply to a core of inferential

[90] Ibid. [91] Ibid. [92] Ibid., p. 83.

[93] T. Anderson, D. Schum and W. Twining, *Analysis of Evidence*, 2nd edn (Cambridge: Cambridge University Press, 2005), pp. 71–7.

[94] Schum, *Evidential Foundations*, pp. 1, 3.

reasoning. We would be saying that all inferential reasoning utilizes the same basic syntax. This is still a very long way from suggesting that all disciplines reason through their inferences in the same way, a position from which Schum appears keen to distance himself. A substance-blind approach only allows us to describe how the individual elements have been combined together to form an inferential argument. There are two very real benefits of this approach to understanding how the tribunal of fact is able to make some reasoned assessment of expert evidence.

The first benefit is that, although Schum's approach does not provide us with the tools to decide the credibility, relevance and weight of an atom of evidence in a substance-blind way, the existence of a basic syntax of inferential argument does allow us to follow something of the flow of an inferential argument, albeit without necessarily having the specific vocabulary used for arguments within that substance-context. We may therefore be able to make a reasonable judgment on the syntax of the argument as a whole, although the semantic validity of the argument is something that we would have to assess by other means. This is of course very important for the question of whether non-experts can assess the evidence of an expert. The non-expert may be able, as a minimum, to follow how credibility, relevance and weight of evidential atoms are being utilized in an argument, and how the various lines of inference are combining, without necessarily understanding whether the evidence, and the expert's assessment of the evidence, is semantically correct.

The second benefit is that, since we have a way to describe inferential, atomistic argument using a common syntax that is content-neutral, we are able to combine two arguments that hold at least some evidential content in common. This is true both for arguments that are semantically similar (for example, two civil engineering arguments about a case) and also for arguments that may vary semantically (for example, one argument by a civil engineer and one by a geologist). The fact finder is therefore able to construct a single evidential matrix for the case, and on the basis of this single matrix, to begin to identify candidates for further combinations of evidential atoms. Whether those links can validly be made may be a question that must be referred back to one or more experts. The significance of this is that we are able to move beyond a point where the tribunal receives the evidence of a number of experts, and assesses the evidence of each expert in turn, as a monolithic evidential structure. It takes us instead towards a point where the tribunal is able validly to assess something of the quality of the individual part of an expert's inferential argument, and to benefit from the synergies produced by bringing together a number of experts from different disciplines or different viewpoints within a discipline.

There is a possible significant limitation to the persuasiveness of my claim that a substance-blind approach might enable us to say how the tribunal of fact is competent to assess at least the syntax of an expert's inferential argument. This is that there is a paucity of examples of cross-disciplinary analysis of the structure of inferential argument. I would suggest that there are currently at least two possible sources of material to support my claim. The first is the inter-disciplinary seminar series on evidence held at the Netherlands Institute for Advanced Studies (NIAS) in 1994–5, and the second is the five-year programme on 'Evidence, Inference and Enquiry' at University College London, which ran from 2003 to 2008.

2.3.1.1 The NIAS 1994–1995 Inter-Disciplinary Evidence Seminars

In the academic year 1994–5, NIAS hosted five international groups of scholars, in the fields of history of Dutch political concepts, theatre iconography, magic and religion in ancient Assyria, social dilemmas, and forensic expertise in the Netherlands criminal justice system.[95] To provide focus to a series of informal seminars, set within the theoretical framework of the then recently published *Evidential Foundations of Probabilistic Reasoning*, Twining proposed the following 'deliberately provocative' hypothesis, based on the Schum thesis:

> Notwithstanding differences in (i) the objectives of our particular enquiries, (ii) the nature and extent of available source material, (iii) the cultures of our respective disciplines (including their histories, conventions, states of development, etc.), (iv) national backgrounds, and (v) other contextual factors, all of our projects involve, as part of the enterprise, drawing inferences from evidence to test hypotheses and justify conclusions, and the logic of this kind of enquiry is governed by the same principles.[96]

The outcome of that seminar series, as represented in the resulting 2003 publication,[97] would appear to provide empirical corroboration for the hypothesis. That claim is subject to an important qualification, identified

[95] W. Twining and I. Hampsher-Monk (eds.), *Evidence and Inference in History and Law: Interdisciplinary Dialogues* (Evanston, IL: Northwestern University Press, 2003), p. 3.

[96] D. Schum, 'Evidence and Inference About Past Events: An Overview of Six Case Studies', in Twining and Hampsher-Monk (eds.), *Evidence and Inference*, pp. 9–62.

[97] Twining and Hampsher-Monk (eds.), *Evidence and Inference.*

by the Danish legal theorist Henrik Zahle,[98] which is that the work undertaken in the Netherlands may have been restricted to straightforward cross-disciplinary exchanges. In addition, most of the exchanges were with one discipline, namely history. In order to demonstrate more persuasively that Schum's approach is substance-blind, it would be necessary to show that disciplines with markedly different substances and methodologies adhere to the same 'logic of enquiry'. The hypothesis has so far been tested by comparing legal and historical analyses, but not other practical professions: 'If evidence law and practice are to benefit from experiences in other disciplines, the next step might be to look towards other practical professions, for example clinical psychology, medicine, engineering, business management, or military and political decision making.'[99] In addition, and particularly for the purposes of a theory of expert evidence, it would be beneficial to consider the practical differences in the inferential reasoning of lawyers and of experimental scientists.

One area in which Schum has suggested that the study indicates that the use of evidence is not substance-blind is the way in which different subjects approached the establishment of the three credentials of evidence, namely relevance, credibility and inferential/probative force of evidence.[100] Going beyond Schum's observation on this point, while we may be identifying patterns in the structures of arguments, the values that provide the dynamics for those structures would appear to remain, if not substance-dependent, then at least discipline-dependent.

Another difference in inferential argument between disciplines may be the purpose for which arguments are made. This qualifies the utility of the chart method. Anderson's Wigmorean analysis of Geller's argument for the end of the use of cuneiform suggested that the argument did not entirely support the conclusions presented. After considering whether this means that Wigmorean analysis has found a flaw in his argument, or his argument has found a flaw in Wigmorean analysis (for example, that the argument uses other kinds of logic that the analysis does not recognize), Geller concludes that weaknesses have indeed been identified in the inferential logic in his argument.[101] However, as a piece of ancient historical research, it remains valid, since 'In a field like Assyriology it

[98] H. Zahle, 'William Twining and Iain Hampsher-Monk (eds.) Evidence and Inference in History and Law: Interdisciplinary Dialogues Illinois: Northwestern UP (2003)' (2004) 8 *Evidence and Proof* 211.

[99] Ibid. [100] Schum, *Evidential Foundations*, p. 11.

[101] M. Geller, 'Wigmorean Analysis and the Survival of Cuneiform', in Twining and Hampsher-Monk (eds.), *Evidence and Inference*, pp. 216–30.

is desirable to point out what is possible, if not provable, and to try to identify from where future evidence might be forthcoming.'[102] Geller's argument enters onto weak ground, since it comes close to saying that the logic of evidential argument operates differently in Assyriology from in other subjects, when instead it could be argued that the analysis has highlighted the gaps in the available evidence.

When Anderson produced a Wigmore Chart of Geller's lecture at NIAS on the date of the end of the use of cuneiform, that chart contained 223 propositions and took a month to produce. Admittedly, a large part of that month would appear to have been taken up with a lawyer attempting to understand the background to an Assyriologist's inferences.[103] This raises the important question of whether, if Wigmore's atomistic method is correct, our brains can produce and process very complex inference networks in order to make decisions. There seem to be three possible answers. The first is that our brains are not that powerful, and that for quotidian purposes we make use of extensive inferential shortcuts, of varying reliability. The second possible answer is that Wigmore was wrong in proposing that our inferential reasoning is atomistic. The third is that our brains are capable of producing and processing very complex inference networks but usually we are not conscious of this. It is outside the scope of the current work to evaluate fully the issues raised by these three possibilities.

2.3.1.2 The Leverhulme/ESRC 'Evidence, Inference and Enquiry' research programme

Further testing was undertaken by the multidisciplinary 'Evidence, Inference and Enquiry' research programme, funded by the Leverhulme Trust and the Economic and Social Research Council (ESRC) at University College London, from 2003 to 2008.[104] One of the five 'anticipated outcomes' of that project was 'Identification and improved handling of common features of evidence across disciplines'.[105] The disciplines represented

[102] Ibid., p. 229.

[103] T. Anderson, 'Wigmore Meets "The Last Wedge"', in Twining and Hampsher-Monk (eds.), *Evidence and Inference*, p. 147.

[104] www.evidencescience.org/ (last accessed 1 August 2008). A related project, at the London School of Economics, has considered the cross-disciplinary nature of the concept of 'fact': 'The Nature of Evidence: How Well do Facts Travel?' www.lse.ac.uk/collections/economicHistory/Research/facts/Default.htm (last accessed 1 August 2008).

[105] www.evidencescience.org/info/index.html (last accessed 1 August 2008).

included economics, statistics, psychology, law and ancient history.[106] This project involved a broader range of disciplines, although it still did not address Zahle's point head on, as it did not appear to have constructed inter-disciplinary projects where the disciplines might have been foreseen as particularly prone to incompatibility in their approach to evidence. The project has yet to produce its final conclusions, and so a final evaluation of its success cannot yet be undertaken.

2.3.2 Common investigative method

The second element of my argument for a limited epistemic competence on the part of the tribunal of fact is that the investigative methods that are used in all fields of enquiry for gathering and selecting data from which to draw inferences have a common core. There would therefore appear to be no such thing as a distinctly scientific method. The extent of this claim, made by Haack,[107] is only that scientific method shares the same modes of inferences and procedures of inquiry as everyday empirical inquiry, and not that there is no distinctly scientific method at all. Haack therefore explicitly argues that scientific method is no more than 'a refinement of everyday thinking',[108] and references Peirce's term 'critical common sensism'[109] and Gustav Bergman's phrase 'the long arm of common sense',[110] with the intention of making vivid the idea that scientific enquiry is continuous with ordinary enquiry, and that the evidence with respect to scientific claims is continuous with the evidence with respect to ordinary empirical claims.[111]

106 www.evidencescience.org/people/investigators.asp (last accessed 1 August 2008).

107 E.g. S. Haack, *Defending Science – Within Reason: Between Scientism and Cynicism* (New York: Prometheus Books, 2003), ch. 4; S. Haack, 'Trial and Error: The Supreme Court's Philosophy of Science' (2005) 95 *American Journal of Public Health* S66–S73.

108 A. Einstein, 'Physics and Reality', in S. Bargmann (ed.), *Ideas and Opinions of Albert Einstein* (New York: Crown Publishers, 1954), pp. 290–323, quoted in Haack, *Defending Science*, p. 95.

109 Haack, *Defending Science*, p. 29. Charles Peirce (1839–1914) was an American philosopher and logician.

110 Ibid., p. 95, quoting G. Bergmann, *Philosophy of Science* (Madison WI: Wisconsin University Press, 1957), p. 20. Gustav Bergmann (1906–87) was a member of the Vienna Circle of logical positivists (Section 3.3.2).

111 Common sense for Peirce and Haack is derived from their mild naturalism: 'the results from the sciences of cognition may be relevant to, and may be legitimately used in the resolution of traditional epistemological problems' (S. Haack, *Evidence and Inquiry: Towards Reconstruction in Epictemology* (Oxford: Blackwell, 1993), p. 118). If scientific

This claim for a common investigative method can be divided into five parts. First, 'scientific inquiry is continuous with everyday empirical inquiry – only more so'. Secondly, there exist some 'modes of inferences and procedures of inquiry used by all inquirers' irrespective of discipline. Thirdly, there also exist 'special mathematical, statistical, or inferential techniques, and special instruments, models, etc'. Fourthly, these special techniques are used by various branches of science, but there is not a set of generic 'scientific' techniques, common to all sciences. Fifthly, '[t]he natural sciences are epistemologically distinguished, have achieved their remarkable successes, in part precisely because of the special devices and techniques by means of which they have amplified the methods of everyday empirical enquiry'.[112] This means that when a non-expert hears about an expert's empirical enquiry, that enquiry is based on the same fundamental principles as everyday empirical enquiry, and so the non-expert should be able to identify any fundamental errors, without having to understand all the technical detail of the specialist approach. For example, taking precautions to reduce the risk of unconscious bias in an experiment is something that comes from common investigative method. When non-experts hear evidence from experts, they are therefore already familiar with a significant part of the expert's methodological arsenal. There are no insurmountable difficulties with a non-expert assessing the method of the specialist. The method of the specialist may be more refined, and so may in practice not initially be accessible to the non-expert (even after a three-day 'statistics for non-statisticians' course). However, in principle a non-expert should have no difficulty in assessing the expert's method, because she shares the same fundamental tools.

Haack's claim for common investigative method extends to include the investigative cultures of different disciplines.[113] Scientists are different from attorneys in their approach to investigation. Scientists attempt to discover the truth of a question, and so are obliged to seek out all evidence, assess as impartially as possible, draw conclusions only if warranted, and if necessary seek out further evidence. Attorneys, however, attempt to make a case for the truth of a proposition, and so have a

method is an extension of common-sense method, then common sense arises from our experience of the real world, and not prior to that experience.

112 Haack, *Defending Science*, p. 94.

113 S. Haack, 'Inquiry and Advocacy, Fallibilism and Finality: Culture and Inference in Science and Law' (2003) 2 *Law Probability and Risk* 205–14.

duty to seek out favourable evidence, present it as favourably as possible, play down unfavourable evidence, and look for grounds of exclusion. But scientists and litigation lawyers are not unique in possessing these properties. The investigative approach of scientists is common to all 'professional inquirers', which would also include historians, investigative journalists, legal and literary scholars. Litigation lawyers, on the other hand, can be placed in a class of 'advocates', along with lobbyists and clergy.[114] However, we must not overstate the differences. For example, scientists have personal and financial motivations to do better than their peers, and do not necessarily evaluate evidence in an impersonal detached manner.[115] These investigative roles cannot be freely adopted, but are constrained by broader social expectations. These differences in approach are expressed by Epstein and King in the maxim, 'An attorney who treats a client like a hypothesis would be disbarred; a Ph.D. who advocates a hypothesis like an advocate would be ignored.'[116]

Haack's approach involves many of the same issues as are involved in analysing the role of evidential generalizations. In particular, there is the same issue of the relationship between specialist knowledge and common sense. The investigative method and investigative culture that Haack describes could even possibly be expressed as second-order generalizations, namely generalizations about how generalizations should be applied. Haack sees expert generalizations as existing on the same continuum as common-sense generalizations, and Anderson, Schum and Twining would similarly place generalizations on a continuum of reliability (with perhaps proverbs as the least reliable form of generalization).

An important point of difference may be that there appear to be two distinct uses of the term 'common sense' at work. For Haack, 'common sense' refers to knowledge that we know inherently to be true, without the need for scientific demonstration; 'common' here means something like

[114] Hart and Honoré, *Causation*, and Schum, *Evidential Foundations*, put lawyers and historians into the same class, because they both deal with (1) specifics, (2) events in the past, (3) a range of disjointed evidence. Hart, Honoré and Schum are considering primarily the types of evidence available to lawyers, historians and scientists, while Haack is considering primarily the purposes for which they are using that evidence. This would appear to explain the different groupings at which they arrive.

[115] Haack, 'Inquiry and Advocacy'; H. Collins, 'Scientific Evidence: A Common Sense Approach Is Needed' (1996) 4 *Expert Evidence* 156–8. Compare Section 3.6.1 on the possibility that an expert has an interest in her involvement in a case, or any other work.

[116] L. Epstein and G. King, 'The Rules of Inference' (2002) 69 *University of Chicago Law Review* 1–133, 9.

'everyday', and original and universal. Haack's argument that all scientific method is derived from common-sense method necessarily means that the common-sense method precedes the scientific method, and thus it is original. Since scientific method would appear to hold true in all cultural contexts, then, for it to remain true that scientific method is an 'only more so' form of common-sense reasoning, we must extend at least some elements of common sense to be universal rather than society-specific. For Anderson, Schum and Twining, however, 'common sense' refers to opinions or values that we share as a group; 'common' here means 'shared', and contextually contingent. Under this approach, it is possible for the generalizations involved in scientific method to be quite distinct from those that are prevalent in society generally, although many scientific generalizations, such as the concept of gravity (at least in general terms), are held in common.[117]

Beyond these possible differences in the anticipated relationship between expert and common-sense generalizations, and the meaning of 'common sense' itself, there are a number of possible limitations to Haack's proposal, which make it necessary to say again that the epistemic competence of the tribunal of fact is limited. The first is that, although the general techniques of fact investigation may be the same across disciplines, individual disciplines may have developed refinements to these techniques that make it impossible for a non-specialist to understand whether those techniques are being applied appropriately or correctly. The non-specialist further lacks sufficient knowledge of the semantic content of the investigative challenge to consider possible alternative methodologies. Secondly, reliance on a core of common sense assumes, without clear justification, that specialist methods do make sense in terms of common sense. It is possible, however, that a scientific method may be counterintuitive to common sense. Despite these limitations, Haack's theory does provide us with the means with which to say that a non-expert tribunal of fact would be able to make at least a high-level assessment of whether the investigation undertaken by the expert witnesses made methodological sense.

[117] If by a common-sense definition of 'the law of gravity' we mean something like 'if I drop something gravity pulls it down to the earth', then this would be scientifically incomplete. The statement assumes, for example, that there is not another force holding the object in place (e.g. the object is iron and I am standing under a very large magnet), and that the earth is exerting the greatest gravitational pull. Such points of difference are not insurmountable, but we need to consider the possibility of their presence.

2.3.3 Did Hand really present a paradox?

Drawing on Schum's work on substance-blind complex inferential reasoning, and Haack's work on a common investigative method, and applying them not to general questions about fact finding, for which they were developed, but to specific questions about the competence of the tribunal of fact to assess expert evidence, it appears to be possible to say that the tribunal of fact does possess at least a limited competence to assess expert evidence. That competence is subject to qualification, primarily because the two approaches continue to exhibit actual or potential limitations.

At the same time that the competence of the tribunal is limited, it should also be said that the tribunal is rarely expected to answer questions that would require full epistemic competence in relation to expert evidence. Hand presented us with a paradox that the court called on experts to provide it with the benefits of specialist advice because it lacked the required specialist knowledge, but the court was then required to assess the specialist advice presented.[118] However, this may not be a true paradox at all, for three reasons.

First, the tribunal is only required to decide whether to accept an opinion, and not to produce its own opinion. There are significant qualitative differences between an act of induction (Act 1) and an assessment of the quality of that act (Act 2). Act 1 requires that the person inferring identifies the relevant evidential elements, makes appropriate decisions on the inferences that might be drawn from those elements, and assigns appropriate probabilities and relationships to those inferences. Act 1 is forming an opinion by induction from the facts. If we were to expect the tribunal of fact to undertake Act 1 then we would indeed be caught in the paradox that we are expecting the tribunal to be as expert as the experts before it. Act 2, however, requires only that common inferential reasoning is applied to test the expert reasoning. Act 2 is the assessment of an opinion formed by induction from the facts. Such an act is considerably less epistemically demanding than Act 1, and does not require that the tribunal usurp the role of the expert. It does, however, require two things. The first is that we determine that we are satisfied that the inferential decisions made by the expert are reasonable ones. The second is that, when there are two or more conflicting sets of inferences, we are

[118] Hand, 'Historical and Practical Considerations', 54.

able to form a preference for one over the other, on the basis of either the quality of the inferential reasoning presented, or the degree to which the inferences concur with conclusions that we are reaching by other routes. Hand appears to be suggesting that, because the jury is not competent to do Act 1 (and thus has allowed in expert evidence), it is therefore not competent to do Act 2. The consequence of this is that the tribunal is being presented as lacking the competence to assess the expertise to the standard of another expert producing such an opinion from the same set of facts, when in fact the tribunal is only required to be able to assess whether to accept the expertise.

Secondly, the tribunal is only required to assess expertise to the extent necessary to decide the case before it. It is not therefore necessary to engage in assessments of the validity of general principles of the expert's discipline. The effect of this is that the epistemic demands placed on the tribunal are significantly reduced. In particular, where the tribunal lacks the competence to decide the case on the available evidence, it may fall back on the burden of proof in order to determine the case. Thirdly, the tribunal must consider the expert evidence as part of the overall evidential matrix of the case. There are very few circumstances in which the tribunal is required to make a finding directly on the expert evidence, without the benefit of being able to compare that evidence with other evidential matter.[119] Rather than taking the expert's opinion in isolation, and asking 'do we accept what A says?', or 'do we prefer expert A to expert B?', the individual elements of A's and B's opinion should be considered not only in terms of the coherence of the opinions taken as a whole, but in terms of the other elements and inferences that are being drawn in the overall case. This approach takes advantage of the structural properties of complex inferential arguments that have been identified by Schum. In particular, whether we accept part of an expert's evidence may depend on whether those evidential elements combine with other evidential elements to produce evidential harmony or evidential dissonance. The result of such an approach may be that there are elements in the opinions of both experts A and B that the court finds to be correct when taken as part of the total evidential matrix of the case for these three reasons; the fact that the tribunal of fact possesses only a limited epistemic competence is not of itself a necessary difficulty for the judicial assessment of expert evidence.

[119] E.g. *R.* v. *Kai-Whitewind* [2005] EWCA Crim 1092.

2.4 Persistent communities of practice

The third point of distinction between expert and non-expert evidence is that, in most (but not all) cases, expert evidence is the product of a persistent community of practice within society. This is a subtly different point from saying that expert evidence represents a specialist body of knowledge within society. Some practitioners of specialist knowledge, such as academic research scientists, medical practitioners, architects or engineers, belong to a wider specialist community, which may be formally constituted with clear boundaries of membership (for example as a professional body) or may be informal (for example 'the scientific community'). There may be other specialist knowledge, for example relating to computer security or handwriting analysis, where it is much more difficult to say that the relevant specialists share anything other than a pool of knowledge. There is a third type of specialist knowledge, related to individual rather than pooled knowledge gained from experience.[120] These subtle differences between specialist communities of practice, non-community pools of knowledge, and non-pooled individual expertise have practical consequences for the differences between how courts might approach the assessment of expert and of non-expert evidence.

The court makes its findings of fact for the purposes of practical reasoning, and so must impose sufficient certainty to act often in the face of uncertainty or disagreement from non-expert witnesses and experts. The evidence on which the finding of fact is made is incomplete, and in an adversarial system has been selected by the parties as much as possible,[121] each to put their own case in the best possible light. Non-expert witnesses testify to what they have directly experienced in relation to the instant case, and the boundaries of their testimony are therefore effectively limited. Expert witnesses, on the other hand, are called to bring the benefit of their experience to bear on the facts in issue. That experience may not all have been directly acquired, as the expert may be entitled to rely on pooled

[120] This equates with Bernstein's 'connoisseur testimony': 'A great deal of expert testimony in American courts is based solely on an expert's experience and training, which this Article refers to as connoisseur testimony': D. Bernstein, 'Expert Witnesses, Adversarial Bias, and the (Partial) Failure of the Daubert Revolution' (2007) *George Mason University Law and Economics Research Paper Series* 07–11, http://papers.ssrn.com/sol3/papers.cfm?abstract_id = 963461 (last accessed 1 August 2008).

[121] 'As much as possible' because, although the parties can select witnesses with an idea of what they are going to testify in evidence, there is no guarantee of the evidence that will be given at trial.

knowledge, either within or outside a community of practice. The court may make its finding of fact on the basis of preferring one expert over the other, and the expert has in turn come to the opinion that she considers to be correct, but this entails two stages at which the majority of the pool of knowledge may differ as to the correct finding of fact. Disagreement between experts is, after all, to be expected in most cases (Chapter 3).

So we may have a situation where the decision of the court is at odds with the views of the majority of specialists on a particular subject. The significance of this difference increases as the size and influence of the majority increases. Since experts may themselves be unable to agree, not too much significance might be attached in itself to the existence of a body of experts who think that the court is wrong. But what do we do when there is virtual unanimity that the court has come to the wrong conclusion, perhaps on the advice of a rogue expert? The problem is exacerbated where there is a persistent community of practice that is organized enough to be able to respond formally.[122] In England, many of these communities of practice have been placed on an official footing by statute[123] or royal charter,[124] while others exist as professional membership bodies.[125] At this point a situation may arise where the court system has arrived at a conclusion, binding on the parties, which is not accepted as correct by the official body. At that point the authority of both the court and the official body are potentially in issue. A similar situation may arise where a court concludes that an expert has acted unprofessionally, but the expert's professional body exonerates her.[126] Such a clash of authorities is more likely to happen the greater the degree of organization, and the greater the official status, of the community of practice.

[122] This is not a common occurrence, but perhaps the leading example in England, from a criminal case, is that of the statistical evidence given by Professor Sir Roy Meadow in the case of *R.* v. *Clark (Sally)*, Chester Crown Court, 9 November 1999. The Royal Statistical Society took the very unusual step of issuing a public statement explaining why the expertise was erroneous: Royal Statistical Society 'Royal Statistical Society Concerned by Issues Raised in Sally Clark Case', 23 October 2001, www.rss.org.uk/PDF/RSS%20Statement%20regarding%20statistical%20issues%20in%20the%20Sally%20Clark%20case,%20October%2023rd%202001.pdf (last accessed 1 August 2008).

[123] E.g. the General Medical Council in London exists by virtue of the Medical Act 1858 and subsequent legislation.

[124] E.g. the Royal College of Physicians was established in 1518; the Royal Institute of British Architects was awarded a royal charter in 1837.

[125] E.g. the Institution of Chemical Engineers or the British Computer Society.

[126] *Pearce* v. *Ove Arup Partnership Ltd (Copying)*, Chancery Division, 2 November 2001; *Re Michael Wilkey*, Architects Registration Board, 5 February 2003.

There are procedural and substantive legal devices that can be used to avoid this situation. The most obvious in English law is the rule in *Bolam*: 'A doctor is not guilty of negligence if he has acted in accordance with a practice accepted as proper by a responsible body of medical men skilled in that particular art.'[127] This rule operates at the level of individuals within the community of practice rather than with official bodies, and what it does is prevent a situation arising in which a professional could be found liable in negligence even though there may be others in her field who would say that what she had done was acceptable. The rule is unusual in civil litigation in that it introduces an evidential asymmetry more usually associated with criminal litigation (Section 1.3.3.1). Symmetry would require that the defendant professional could be found liable if the claimant could produce a body of professionals who would say that what the defendant did was *not* acceptable.

An alternative approach might be to incorporate the community of practice directly into the tribunal of fact. Historically this occurred in English courts through the use of special juries in common law courts (Section 5.4), a practice which died out in the nineteenth century, and assessors in the High Court of Admiralty (Section 5.5), a practice which continues to this day. Admiralty's assessors are appointed by Trinity House, on application by the court's Registry, to provide expert advice to the court, particularly in relation to navigation matters. Trinity House was created as a guild of mariners by royal charter in 1514 with a virtual monopoly on pilotage of all vessels passing between the port of London and the open sea, and its Elder Brethren historically served as assessors. Today it is responsible for the lighthouse service in England and Wales; responsibility for pilotage was transferred to Port and Harbour Authorities under the Pilotage Act 1987. Active members of Trinity House no longer serve as assessors, but the corporation appoints suitable persons on the Admiralty Court's behalf (Section 6.4.1).

There are two important differences between the Trinity House approach and the *Bolam* approach to resolving the problem of possible conflicts between the courts and persistent communities of practice. The first is that the Trinity House approach places the experts with the court rather than with the parties.[128] In this, Trinity House assessors are

[127] *Bolam* v. *Friern Hospital Management Committee* [1957] 1 WLR 582, [1957] 2 All ER 118 (QB), at 121.

[128] It is moot whether Admiralty assessors should be seen historically as part of the tribunal of fact (e.g. Section 6.4.3.2).

like special juries. The second is that the expertise that may effectively determine the case is given by the official body for the community of practice in the Trinity House approach, while the *Bolam* approach uses a selection of practitioners. In this, the *Bolam* approach is closer to that of the historical use of special juries, although with special juries the specialists were selected at random rather than because they were likely to agree with one party rather than the other. In either case, there must surely be a concern that where a member of the community of practice is herself one of the parties, and the other party is not a member, then the community representatives will tend to prefer one of their colleagues. Where the community representatives act by virtue of their office, then we might hope that this risk of bias would be reduced. It is nevertheless the case that such methods are unlikely to be perceived as representing a fair trial unless all (or no) parties are members of the community of practice.

Ultimately, whether the courts defer to the external authority or stand against it is a political decision, and one that touches constitutional matters.[129] On the one hand, the inherent jurisdiction of the court gives it an absolute right to determine the cases before it. On the other hand, the sound administration of justice requires that the court does not hand down decisions that are based on beliefs about facts that would not be accepted as justified by those in society who are specialists in such matters, and are recognized as such by society as a whole. Like the question of whether one should employ expert or common sense in applying generalizations to the facts of a case, this is not a problem that allows for a straightforward resolution.

2.5 Epistemological constructivism

So far in this chapter I have analysed three key features of expert evidence that distinguish it from non-expert evidence in order to establish whether expert evidence should be considered as a special case of legal evidence, but nevertheless subject to fundamentally the same methods of assessment, or whether expert evidence forms a distinct category. From this analysis, it would appear that the traditional distinction between expert evidence of opinion and non-expert evidence of fact has been at least overstated, and is possibly erroneous (Section 2.2). It would also appear

[129] E.g. Lord Woolf, 'Are the Courts Excessively Deferential to the Medical Profession' (2001) 9 *Medical Law Review* 1–16.

that the core approach to the justification of beliefs founded on expert evidence is the same as that for non-expert evidence (Section 2.3). The main area of difficulty has been whether the court is in a position to come to a finding of fact in an area of specialist knowledge where there is a persistent community of practice that would come to a different conclusion (Section 2.4). This is *par excellence* a question of social epistemology and of political morality, and falls outside the scope of classical epistemology. Because the justified belief statements of the court conflict with those of the specialist community of practice, which we might normally in society expect to be correct more often than the non-specialists, we have a possible constraint on the preparedness of the court to decide facts in certain situations involving specialist evidence. This is the main area in which the epistemic competence of the court is compromised by its engagement with expert rather than non-expert evidence.

The difficulty presented by Section 2.4 opens up to a further possible difficulty. What would happen if we had approached Section 2.3 by saying that, as knowledge has specialized in modern society, each area of specialization has cut itself off from every other area, and from general societal background beliefs, with the result that knowledge, and rationality with it, has fragmented in modernity? This is the challenge presented by a line of thinking, particularly apparent in post-modernism, that I term 'strong epistemological constructivism'. Under this form of constructivism, the knowledge produced by different specializations within society, and the discourses associated with that specialist knowledge, are incommensurable with one another. The effect of this for the judicial assessment of expert evidence is that a non-expert tribunal can never fully engage with the evidence of an expert, since it can never fully understand the content of that testimony in terms that are meaningful to the legal system. Perhaps the main school of this form of strong epistemological constructivism that appears in the debate surrounding the assessment of expert evidence is autopoietic systems theory, developed by Luhmann. My analysis of autopoietic systems theory suggests that, although it makes some very valuable contributions to evidence jurisprudence, it is not ultimately sustainable in the face of philosophical and empirical objections.

2.5.1 Definition

By 'constructivism', I refer to the sociological theory that our knowledge of the world is constructed through our social experience. The root proposition of the sociology of knowledge is derived from Marx: 'that man's consciousness is determined by his social being'.[130] To facilitate analysis, constructivism can be divided up along two dimensions. Along the first dimension, there is a distinction between 'weak' and 'strong' constructivists. 'Weak' constructivists hold that, although our knowledge is socially situated, there are common knowledge elements between societies, so there are no fundamental problems with communicating between socially constructed knowledge systems. 'Strong' constructivists, on the other hand, hold that it is not possible to identify common ground between two knowledge systems, with which to produce a lexicon of equivalence. The consequence of this would be incommensurability.

Along the second dimension are a number of distinctions between 'epistemological constructivism', which holds that our epistemology of the factual world is socially constructed,[131] and 'value constructivism', which holds that our social values are socially constructed. The epistemological and the normative are separated here because 'of course it doesn't follow from the fact that legal systems are socially constructed . . . that "truth is rhetorical, a mythic moment of rest in a continuous and endless argumentative struggle among different discourses of truth"'.[132] Within 'epistemological constructivism', it is possible to distinguish yet further between the social construction of facts and the social construction of causation. There are conceptually no difficulties with holding that one is a strong value constructivist while being a weak epistemological constructivist. This would mean that one believes that it is possible to agree on statements about the external world with people from another social group, but that statements about values cannot be directly translated.

[130] P. Berger and T. Luckmann, *The Social Construction of Reality* (London: Allen Lane. 1966), p. 17.

[131] An example of weak epistemological fact constructivism would be historical relativism, whose proponents such as James Robinson, Carl Becker and Charles Beard would appear to have accepted the objectivity of 'simple facts', but disputed the objectivity of such historical activities as assigning relevance to facts, and interpreting and arranging facts: W. Twining, 'Some Scepticism About Some Scepticisms', in *Rethinking Evidence: Exploratory Essays*, 2nd edn (Cambridge: Cambridge University Press, 2006), pp. 99–164, pp. 110–16.

[132] S. Haack, 'Law, Literature, and Bosh', in C. de Waal (ed.), *Susan Haack: A Lady of Distinctions – The Philosopher Responds to Her Critics* (Amherst NY: Prometheus, 2007), pp. 259–62, p. 261. See also S. Haack, 'Reflections on Relativism: From Momentous Tautology to Seductive Contradiction', in S. Haack, *Manifesto of a Passionate Moderate* (Chicago: University of Chicago Press, 1998), pp. 149–66.

2.5.2 *Epistemological constructivism in modernity*

While the British Empiricists, such as Locke,[133] Berkeley[134] and Hume,[135] writing between 1671[136] and 1748, were approaching the philosophy of inferential reasoning without concern for whether different groups in society gained their knowledge in different ways, Kant, in his 1788 *Critique of Practical Reason*,[137] was developing the idea that there were self-contained systems in society, each possessing their own faculties of knowledge. In continuing the philosophical tradition of a priori knowledge, Kant allows for the possibility that our knowledge of the world is shaped by pre-existing principles, albeit that, in the case of specialist social functions, those principles must be learned rather than being innate.

Kant defined a system as 'a process according to principles of reason' applied to 'the manifold of any branch of knowledge'.[138] This idea that a system possesses its own distinctive (rational) processes is supported in the later section on 'Critical Examination of the Analytic of Pure Practical Reason', in which Kant argued that what identifies a science is its reasoning and not its subject matter: 'By the critical examination of a science, or a portion of it, which constitutes a system by itself, I understand the inquiry and proof why it must have this and no other systematic form, when we compare it with another system which is based on a similar faculty of knowledge.'[139] Kant is saying here that a 'science' (*Wissenschaft*) is a 'system' characterized by its own process in the way that it is applied to a branch of knowledge. Kant's approach appears to allow us to say that there is such a thing as specialist reasoning within 'faculties of knowledge'. Although Kant's work would appear to support the argument for specialist inferential reasoning, it would be difficult to use it to develop an argument for the incommensurability of different forms of specialist inferential reasoning that we find in the strong epistemological constructivism that was to develop in the second half of the twentieth century. There is no indication in these passages that the system rationalities of each *Wissenschaft* are incommensurable with one another. In addition, Kant's concept of a

[133] Locke, *Essay*.

[134] G. Berkeley, *Principles of Human Knowledge* (1710), ed. R. Woolhouse (London: Penguin, 1988).

[135] Hume, *Treatise*; Hume, *Enquiries*.

[136] Locke, *Essay*, p. xix.

[137] I. Kant, 'Critical Examination of the Analytic of Pure Practical Reason' in I. Kant, *Critique of Practical Reason* (1788), trans. T. Abbott (London: Longmans, Green & Co., 1898); I. Kant, 'Methodology of Pure Practical Reason', in Kant, *Critique of Practical Reason*.

[138] Kant, 'Methodology'.

[139] Kant 'Critical Examination'; Kant, 'Methodology'.

universal *Ratio* would make it probable that any system rationality would incorporate core elements of the universal *Ratio*. The idea that we share core pre-rational principles that cut across different rationalities has also been utilized by the ethicist Gewirth, following Aristotle: pure logic is presupposed by the use of any alternative criteria of rationality.[140]

The theory of specialist reasoning was more fully developed by Weber, just over a century later, who identified compartmentalized formal rationality as a distinguishing characteristic of modernity:

> There is, for example, rationalization of mystical contemplation ... just as much as there are rationalizations of economic life, of technique, of scientific research, of military training, of law and administration. Furthermore, each one of these fields may be rationalized from many different ultimate points of view, and toward many different ultimate ends, and what is rational from one point of view may well be irrational from another. Hence rationalizations of the most varied character have existed in various departments of life in all civilizations.[141]

For Weber, the rationalization of social activity was to be found over time and between cultures, but what distinguished western modernity was the emphasis on formal rather than substantive rationality: 'the specific and peculiar rationalism of western culture'.[142] Weber's rationality was a socially constructed way of being in the world, rather than an instance of a single concept. Weber has no single definition of the word 'rational', but instead uses at least sixteen meanings of the term.[143] It is not that Weber believed that we had a term 'rationality' for which we are trying to find a concept, but rather that we have a phenomenon which we are trying to define more clearly.[144] Rationality for Weber appears to have developed

[140] D. Beyleveld and R. Brownsword, *Human Dignity in Bioethics and Biolaw* (Oxford: Oxford University Press, 2001) 72; D. Dwyer, 'Beyond Autonomy: the Role of Dignity in "Biolaw"' (2003) 23 *Oxford Journal of Legal Studies* 319–31.

[141] M. Weber, *Gesammelte Aufsätze zur Religionssoziologie* (Tübingen: Mohr, 1922), quoted in R. Brubaker, *The Limits of Rationality: An Essay on the Social and Moral Thought of Max Weber* (London: George Allen & Unwin, 1984), p. 8.

[142] Quoted in Brubaker, *Limits of Rationality*, p. 12. Formal rationalism is the philosophical cousin of the legal concept of due process (and, in turn, intellectual due process). Formal rationalism avoids the question of the goal to which practical reason should be aiming, in the same way that due process is not concerned with whether the final outcome of the case is correct, but only with how it was conducted.

[143] *Ibid.*, p. 16.

[144] A. Eisen, 'The Meanings and Confusion of Weberian "Rationality"' (1978) 29 *British Journal of Sociology* 57–70; S. Kalberg, 'Max Weber's Types of Rationality' (1980) 85 *American Journal of Sociology* 1145.

through a number of separate processes, and been made up, depending on context, from a polythetic set of such characteristics as being deliberate, systematic, methodical, rule-governed, calculable, quantitative, exact, predictable, consistent, impersonal, purely instrumental.[145] So Weber provides us with a theory that social functions possess their own rationalities. He does not, however, say that those rationalities are incommensurable with one another.

2.5.3 Strong epistemological constructivism

Strong epistemological constructivism appears to have developed in the philosophies of sociology and science in the 1960s. In the English-speaking world, this development appears to have been strongly influenced by the linguistic philosophy work of the later Wittgenstein on language games.[146]

2.5.3.1 Philosophy of sociology

A leading example of strong epistemological constructivism in the philosophy of sociology can be found in 'Understanding a Primitive Society',[147] by Winch, a Wittgensteinian philosopher. Winch proposed that the best way to avoid misunderstanding any society that seemed seriously different from our own was to try to understand the language game being played by members of that society, rather than apply an objective standard of judgment. Winch's argument results in a form of strong epistemological constructivism that can be expressed as three statements:

1. Since (i) men's perception and understanding of the world is ineradicably theory-dependent, (ii) there is no theory-independent reference for terms like 'the world', 'nature', 'reality' etc., and therefore no theory-independent criterion of truth. Since theories differ, standards of truth differ.
2. The determinants of beliefs are irrelevant to their truth and validity.
3. 'Logical relations between propositions ... depend on social relations between men'.[148] This entails that, for a group G, the truth of its

[145] Brubaker, *Limits of Rationality*, p. 2
[146] L. Wittgenstein, *Philosophical Investigations* (Oxford: Blackwell, 1953).
[147] P. Winch, 'Understanding a Primitive Society' (1964) 1(14) *American Philosophical Quarterly* 307–24, which sought to apply to social anthropology his seminal work on the philosophy of society in his *The Idea of a Social Science* (London: Routledge and Kegan Paul, 1958).
[148] Winch, 'Understanding a Primitive Society'.

members' beliefs and the validity of their reasoning are simply up to them, a function of the norms to which they conform.

Winch's argument has been countered by the sociologist Steven Lukes, who expressed Winch's argument in terms of these three statements.[149] Lukes' first objection to statement 1 is that there is no necessary progression from step (i) to step (ii), as Winch suggests. His second objection to statement 1 is that it does not follow from the existence of different concepts of truth in different contexts that there may not be some such criteria that are invariable because they are universal and fundamental. His objection to statement 2 is that the existence of a causal (relative) social factor for a given belief does not necessarily mean that the truth or validity of the belief is in consequence also relative. The reasons for the belief may be intelligent reasons given people's context.

The effect of statement 3 would be that the validity of a group's reasoning is up to the group. Lukes argues that this cannot be so, for the following reason. Let us suppose a group G. We can then ask, 'Are the truth of their beliefs and the validity of their reasoning simply up to them, a function of the norms to which they conform?' The answer is no. Lukes' first objection to statement 3 is that there must be a common reality required to understand G's language. His second objection is that any group that successfully predicts must presuppose a given reality. His third objection is that G's language must have operable logical rules. If Winch implied that the concept of negation and laws of identity and non-contradiction need not operate, then could we credit G with the possibility of inferring, arguing or even thinking? Assuming that the answer to this hypothetical question is 'no', then G's language must therefore minimally possess criteria of truth (corresponding to a common and independent reality) and logic, which are not and cannot be context-dependent. Winch's proposition is therefore not sustainable.

An argument similar to that of Winch has been presented by Foucault. Foucault uses Borges' example of the Chinese Encyclopaedia, to show how the social construction of reality can 'shatter all the familiar landmarks of our thought', and reveal 'the stark impossibility of thinking *that*'. The passage merits quoting at length because of the prima facie difficulties that it raises for the Rationalist Tradition, and because its detail reveals its ultimate failure as an example:

[149] S. Lukes, 'Relativism in its Place', in M. Hollis and S. Lukes (eds.), *Rationality and Relativism* (Oxford: Blackwell, 1982), pp. 261–305.

> This book first arose out of a passage in Borges ... [which] quotes a 'certain Chinese encyclopaedia' in which it is written that 'animals are divided into: (a) belonging to the Emperor, (b) embalmed, (c) tame, (d) suckling pigs, (e) sirens, (f) fabulous, (g) stray dogs, (h) included in the present classification, (i) frenzied, (j) innumerable, (k) drawn with a very fine camelhair brush, (l) *et cetera,* (m) having just broken the water pitcher, (n) that from a long way off look like flies'. In the wonderment of this taxonomy, the thing we apprehend in one great leap, the thing that, by means of a fable, is demonstrated as the exotic charm of another system of thought, is the limitation of our own, the stark impossibility of thinking *that.*[150]

The Chinese Encyclopaedia would certainly present significant challenges for the meaningful translation of the concepts representing the Chinese Emperor's world view. I say 'would' rather than 'does', however, because in order to make his point, Foucault has had to rely on a fictitious example in order to attempt to demonstrate 'the stark impossibility of thinking *that*'. It is therefore valid to wonder whether any real examples exist that would present commensurability difficulties on such a scale.

The constructivism that linguistic philosophy was bringing to the social sciences in the 1960s can also be seen in the work of Hart on 'the internal aspect' of law in his 1961 *The Concept of Law.*[151] Hart, a member of the Oxford school of linguistic philosophy in the 1950s, argued that the true meaning of law within any given legal system could not be understood by an outsider looking in, but only by somebody who already understood something of the system. Thus, a visitor from Mars might observe only that cars (usually) stop at red lights but not at green lights, but would not understand why. Hart appears to have considered that he had developed the idea of the distinction between internal and external aspects from Winch's 1958 *The Idea of a Social Science,*[152] although there is also some evidence of influence from the sociology of Weber.[153] In support of this influence from Winch one might also cite the similarity of title between

150 M. Foucault, *The Order of Things: An Archaeology of the Human Sciences* (London: Routledge, 1970), p. xv.

151 H. Hart, *The Concept of Law*, 2nd edn (Oxford: Oxford University Press, 1994), pp. 89–91.

152 Winch, *Idea*, pp. 58, 87.

153 Hart owned a copy of M. Rheinstein and E. Shils (eds.), *Max Weber on Law in Economy and Society* (Cambridge MA: Harvard University Press, 1954), in which the relevant pages were heavily annotated. Hart apparently denied to Finnis that Weber had been an influence: N. Lacey, *A Life of H. L. A. Hart: The Nightmare and the Noble Dream* (Oxford: Oxford University Press, 2004), p. 230.

the books of Hart and Winch, and Hart's interest in the philosophy of the later Wittgenstein. Hart's theory of the internal aspect refers, however, solely to normativity, and not facticity. It is therefore unclear how Hart might have applied his theory to evidence jurisprudence.[154]

2.5.3.2 Philosophy of science

In the natural sciences, Kuhn was the leading proponent of a constructivism that might be classified as strong epistemological constructivism. In 1962, Kuhn proposed that periods of 'normal' science were interrupted by rapid periods of change with revolutionary effect: 'Scientific revolutions are here taken to be those non-cumulative developmental episodes in which an older paradigm is replaced in whole or in part by an incompatible new one.'[155] After the revolution, a new paradigm would emerge, the standards of which would be incommensurable with those of the old paradigm. It would be as if one now lived 'in a different world'. As he has been commonly understood, Kuhn appears to have been talking about strong epistemological constructivism. Those who live in the new world cannot measure themselves against anything in the old world.

Members of the predominant school of the philosophy of science, Scientific Realism, have presented a strong counter-argument against this claim for incommensurable social construction of science. They argue that scientific theories are more than social constructs, because they successfully predict how the world will behave in experiments (they 'refer' and 'succeed').[156] The Realist argument is not, however, itself unassailable.[157] The Realist concept of 'success' is vague, and the history of science suggests that there have been theories that have been successful but which, later work has suggested, do not refer.[158] For example, the eighteenth-century chemical atomic theory was remarkably unsuccessful, but is now

[154] One possible indication is that in his joint work with Tony Honoré on *Causation*, Hart appears to accept that law and the physical sciences can simultaneously hold notions of causation that are incommensurable with one another.

[155] T. Kuhn, *The Structure of Scientific Revolutions*, 2nd edn (Chicago: University of Chicago Press, 1970), ch. 9.

[156] R. Boyd, 'On the Current Status of Scientific Realism' (1983) 19 *Erkenntnis* 45–90; L. Laudan, 'A Confutation of Convergent Realism' (1981) 48 *Philosophy of Science* 19–49.

[157] Laudan, 'Confutation'.

[158] Ibid., p. 20, suggests that an approximate definition of 'refer' would be 'there are substances in the world that correspond to the ontologies presumed by our best theories'.

thought to refer. In addition, the success of a theory to 'predict',[159] however that may be determined, does demonstrate that the theory adequately describes an objective reality, but it does not demonstrate that there is a correct way to describe reality. For example, the fact that we can predict that an aeroplane will fly does not mean that our explanation for why it does so is correct. The Realist argument does, nevertheless, strongly suggest that we are able to provide a lexicon of equivalence, based on prediction in experimentation.

2.5.4 Autopoietic social systems theory

2.5.4.1 Application to society and law

Autopoietic systems theory provides a developed argument for incommensurable specialist inferential reasoning. The theory is singled out for attention here because it has been extensively employed by a number of theorists in recent jurisprudential arguments about the relationship between legal and expert systems of knowledge. There is therefore a developed body of literature that can be considered. Autopoietic systems theory should be taken very seriously as a contender against rationalist theories of evidence. Although I conclude this section by rejecting it as a fully persuasive approach to the assessment of expert evidence, I should like to emphasize at the outset that it does raise some very valuable points that might otherwise have been missed under a purely rationalist approach to the question of expert evidence.

Autopoietic systems theory was developed by two Chilean biologists, Varela and Maturana, in 1973, to explain the workings of the biological cell.

> An autopoietic machine is a machine organized (defined as a unity) as a network of processes of production (transformation and destruction) of components which: (i) through their interactions and transformations continuously regenerate and realize the network of processes (relations) that produced them, and (ii) constitute it (the machine) as a concrete unity in space in which they (the components) exist by specifying the topological domain of its realizations of such a network.[160]
>
> The space defined by an autopoietic system is self-contained and cannot be described by using dimensions that define another space. When we refer

[159] I.e., to predict the future of an experiment or similar.

[160] H. Maturana and F. Varela, *Autopoiesis and Cognition: The Realization of the Living* (Dordrecht: Reidel, 1980), p. 78.

> to our interactions with a concrete autopoietic system, however, we project this system on the space of our manipulations and make a description of this projection.[161]

In 1984, the German sociologist Luhmann applied the theory to his existing theory of social systems,[162] which he had developed after studying at Harvard in 1961 with Talcott Parsons, the leading social systems theorist. Autopoietic social systems theory appears to have begun to be applied to the specific case of law as a social system by Luhmann and some of his students, particularly Teubner[163] and also Ziegert, from the late 1980s.[164]

Luhmann and his followers propose that rationality has fragmented in modern society.[165] Communication within society is made up of a number of self-contained systems, an idea that we can trace back at least to Kant. However, in Luhmann's view of modernity, a significant number (if not all) of these systems have become self-referential, and communicate only with themselves about the world. One of the key features that distinguishes autopoietic systems theory from other systems theories is that an autopoietic social system is cognitively open to its environment, but is normatively (or operationally) closed. The consequence of this is that only cognitive environment data can pass into a system. The classical position, that the social system knows nothing of the 'information' that exists within other systems, has been expressed by Luhmann, who argues that, when two autopoietic systems handle the same elements, 'interpenetration' occurs, but '[t]he interpenetrating systems remain environments for each other. This means that the complexity each system makes available is an incomprehensible complexity . . . for the receiving system'.[166] Interpenetrating systems use the same elements, but understand them in their distinct ways. This incomprehensible complexity is a particularly clear expression of incommensurability. The system does, however, exchange

161 Ibid., p. 89.
162 N. Luhmann, *Social Systems* (1984), trans. J. Bednarz Jr (Stanford: Stanford University Press, 1995).
163 G. Teubner (ed.), *Autopoietic Law: A New Approach to Law and Society* (Berlin: Walter de Gruyter, 1988).
164 N. Luhmann, *Law as a Social System* (1993), trans. K. Ziegert (Oxford: Oxford University Press, 2004); G. Teubner, *Law as an Autopoietic System* (Oxford: Blackwell, 1993).
165 N. Luhmann, 'European Rationality', in G. Robinson and J. Rundell (eds.), *Rethinking Imagination: Culture and Creativity* (London: Routledge, 1994), pp. 65–83.
166 Luhmann, *Social Systems*, pp. 213–14.

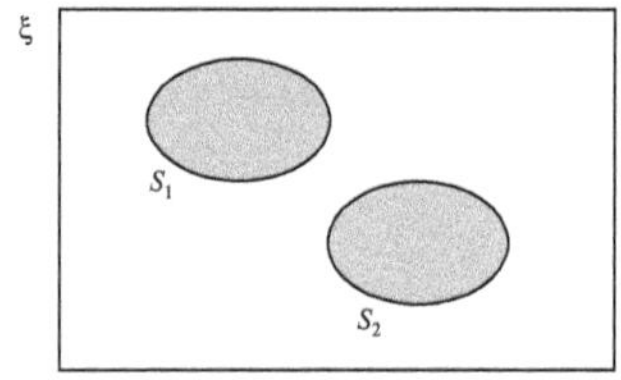

Figure 2.1 Normatively closed systems can exist within society

cognitive communications with its environment of associated activities (Figure 2.1).

2.5.4.2 Application to the judicial assessment of expert evidence

The idea that society can be made up of a number of systems of discourse, which may recognize one another's existence, but which cannot fully engage in one another's discourse, provides an attractive background against which to explore the relationship between social systems, and in particular between law and other systems, such as medicine, science and economics.[167] Because of the developed theory language within autopoietic systems theory relating to specialized, closed systems of discourse, it has proved a popular form of strong constructivism within which to work on general theories of expertise.[168] The majority of the applied studies have concerned normative questions, such as the identification of 'syndromes' and 'best interests' in child litigation,[169] the identification of risk

[167] G. Teubner, '*Altera Pars Audiatur*: Law in a Collision of Discourses', in R. Rawlings (ed.), *Law, Society and Economy: Centenary Essays for the London School of Economics and Political Science 1895–1995* (Oxford: Oxford University Press, 1997), pp. 149–76, p. 150. One potential difficulty with autopoietic systems theory is that it is easier to use monolithic labels such as 'law', 'medicine' and 'science' than it is to define them. If we are to say that these systems are normatively closed, then we are presumably forced to make some very harsh decisions about whether one discipline is really a sub-discipline of another, or a separate discipline. For example, should one include psychiatry within medicine, and do geology and particle physics both sit within science?

[168] E.g. G. Teubner, 'How the Law Thinks: Toward A Constructivist Epistemology Of Law' (1989) 23 *Law and Society Review* 727–58; D. Nelken, 'A Just Measure of Science?' in M. Freeman and H. Reece (eds.), *Science in Court* (Aldershot: Ashgate, 1988), pp. 11–36; J. Paterson, 'Trans–Science, Trans–Law and Proceduralisation' (2003) 12 *Social and Legal Studies* 523–43.

[169] M. King and F. Kaganas, 'The Risks and Dangers of Experts in Court' (1998) 1 *Current Legal Issues* 221–42; M. King, 'An Autopoietic Approach to the Problems Presented by Parental Alienation Syndrome' (2002) 13 *Journal of Forensic Psychiatry* 609–35.

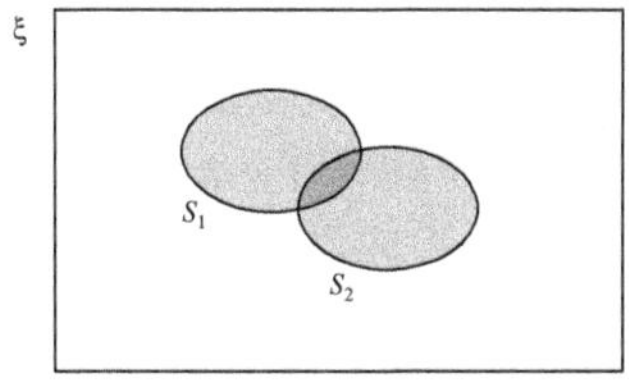

Figure 2.2 The incommensurability of normatively closed systems

in the North Sea oil industry,[170] toxic tort litigation[171] and concepts of reasonableness.[172]

It is the self-containedness of autopoietic social systems that provides the foundation of the problem of the assessment of expert evidence. Since the legal system is normatively and operationally closed, it cannot directly enter into the programmes of another system (such as the medical system). When two systems (S_1, S_2) both seek to describe the same cognitive data ($S_1 \cup S_2$), this intersection produces noise rather than a synergy of communications (Figure 2.2).[173] Interpenetrating systems use the same elements, but understand them in their distinct ways, because of different sets of normative values in S_1 and S_2 that operate within these systems. This gives rise to incommensurability, and to phenomena such as law's difficulties in integrating the norms implicit in expert evidence, in order to evaluate the evidence.[174] These social systems have a self-contained way of perceiving, assessing and acting in relation to the world, because each possesses its own set of normative programmes and coding that describes a complete picture of the world in the system's own terms.[175] The ultimate purpose of law's programmes is to assign to any question / factual nexus the coding of either 'lawful' (*Recht*) or 'unlawful' (*Unrecht*). For this reason alone, law would have fundamental difficulties understanding programmes that produced a different set of codings.

Within the terms of autopoietic social systems theory, it is not strictly possible to speak of how one system's programmes (system-rationality)

170 J. Paterson and G. Teubner, 'Changing Maps: Empirical Legal Autopoiesis' (1998) 7 *Social and Legal Studies* 451–86.

171 A. McConnell, 'Risk and Responsibility: Dealing with Science and Uncertainty in Toxic Torts', Doctor of Laws thesis, European University Institute (2000).

172 M. Hutter and G. Teubner, 'Homo Juridicus and Homo Oeconomicus: Communicate Fictions' in T. Baums, K. Hopt and N. Horn (eds.), *Corporations, Capital Markets and Business in the Law* (Den Haag: Kluwer, 2000), p. 569.

173 Luhmann, *Social Systems*, p. 214.

174 Teubner, 'How the Law Thinks'.

175 Luhmann, *Law as Social System*, ch. 4.

can assess the programmes of another system, because of the axiomatic boundedness of system programmes. Instead the legal system recreates that reasoning within itself through the re-entry of the coding *Recht/Unrecht.*[176] In dealing with expert opinion, the Law therefore 'reconstructs' its own (legal) image of the external system within itself, and disagreements between experts must comply with Law's image of their expertise.

2.5.4.3 Difficulties with applying the theory to expert evidence

Autopoietic social systems theory may initially seem quite attractive to those in search of a theory of expertise, since it provides a fairly robust explanation for why Law encounters difficulty in assessing expert evidence. It runs into both theoretical and empirical difficulties, however.

2.5.4.3.1 Theoretical difficulties The first difficulty is that if, as Luhmann claims, the true function of law in modernity is to stabilize normative expectations over time, then it is difficult to see how this can be achieved if the law has no real interaction with other systems. It may be that the evolution of an autopoietic legal system was a necessary condition for all further social evolution, and this development heralded a new, society-wide importance for law.[177] Law's discourse must be reasonably faithful to the discourse of the specialist system, first because Law requires the cooperation of the specialist system, and secondly because the credibility of Law as a stabilizer of normative expectations over time would be significantly reduced if those observing Law's discourse saw it as detached from the 'reality' of the specialist discourse. The legal system must therefore be capable of reproducing its own conception of the specialist system's rationality in a fashion acceptable to society at large. Within the terms of autopoietic systems theory, the legal system does this through the development of system-specific programmes.

Autopoietic social systems theory, as formulated by Luhmann, therefore begins to run into the theoretical difficulty that, on the one hand, it rests on a form of monadism,[178] while on the other hand it requires some

[176] Teubner, *Law as Autopoietic System*, pp. 24–5.

[177] N. Luhmann, *Differentiation of Society*, trans. S. Holmes and C. Larmore (New York: Columbia University Press, 1982), p. 130.

[178] In Leibniz's 1714 *Monadology*, a monad is an 'individual substance'. The properties of a monad include: (1) it contains every concept consistent with it but no other; (2) it has no parts but the 'accidents' of mental qualities and tendency; (3) there are no causal relations

form of normative communication with other systems. Luhmann's disciples appear to have divided into at least three positions in their attempts to address criticisms of Luhmann's theory. The first position (which I term here 'regressive'), advanced for example by Ziegert, would appear to be that autopoiesis was only a foray into new territory, and that it should be viewed as an extension of Luhmann's earlier work.[179] The second ('conservative') position, advocated for example by King, would appear to be that the criticisms of Luhmann's work arise out of a misunderstanding of what it was that he was trying to say.[180] The third ('progressive') position, led by Teubner, would appear to be to concede that Luhmann's theory needs to be developed: in its emphasis on the creation of self-contained communication systems, autopoietic social systems theory has ignored its 'blind spot', the question of how the interconnection, interference, openness and hetero-reference of these systems can be theoretically reconstructed.[181]

The solution adopted by the progressive autopoietic theorists is to begin to compromise the operational closure of systems. Teubner suggests that, while for Luhmann autopoiesis is an 'inflexible hardness', for him autonomy and autopoiesis are questions of degree.[182] This suggests some degree of normative communication between systems, or between society and the systems. This ability to understand in part the discourse of other systems exists alongside, and beyond, the involvement of all social systems in the general discourse of society. The nature of trans-system rational elements may be defined in the creation of the system. When an autopoietic system of discourse brings itself into being, it brings with it some of the elements of broader social discourse that it made use of before it became normatively and operationally closed. This establishes only the 'ground rules' of social communication (such as negation and non-contradiction), which are not sufficient to reconstruct fully the reasoning discourse of another system, but may be sufficient to identify certain types of flaw in reasoning. The concept of trans-system rationality is antithetical to the theory of

between monads but only between their states; (4) each monad is a microcosmic world-apart which reflects the entire macrocosm. *Monadology* (1714), trans. R. Latta (Oxford: Clarendon Press, 1898).

179 E.g. K. Ziegert, 'The Thick Description of Law: an Introduction to Niklas Luhmann's Theory of Operatively Closed Systems', in R. Banakar and M. Travers (eds.), *An Introduction to Law and Social Theory* (Oxford: Hart, 2002), pp. 55–75.

180 E.g. M. King and C. Thornhill, 'Will the Real Niklas Luhmann Stand Up, Please? A Reply to John Mingers' (2003) 51 *Sociological Review* 276–85.

181 Teubner, 'How the Law Thinks'.

182 Teubner, *Law as Autopoietic System*, p. 27.

Luhmann. It does, however, receive some support in the work of Teubner, who has argued that:

> Although the legal discourse is closed in its self-reproduction and produces its own constructions of reality, it remains always social communication and uses the general social constructions of reality and influences general social communication by its specific world constructions. Any legal act is at the same time – *uno actu* – an event of general social communication. One and the same communicative event, then, is linked with two social discourses, the specialized institutionalized discourse of law and the diffuse and general social communication.[183]

2.5.4.3.2 Empirical difficulties Even if we accept Teubner's modifications, then autopoietic systems theory, although conceptually elegant in some ways, would appear to be unable to sustain itself in the face of empirical data. There are three key difficulties that arise from our experience of law in society. The first, which is most in tune with the claims of autopoietic systems theory, is that our experience of the world is that Law does actually appear empirically to communicate with other disciplines. The second is that below the level of social functions, at the level of the individual, an individual can belong to more than one specialist discipline, and understand more than one body of specialist knowledge. Our experience is that lawyers who do have a formal scientific or medical education[184] are better able to comprehend scientific or medical expert evidence than those who do not. The third is that the normative generalizations that exist within one specialist system may spread over time into other specialist systems, or even into general society. The very concept of 'fact', for example, is one that developed originally in law in the sixteenth century and subsequently spread to the natural sciences and to general society.[185]

In order to accommodate the reality of social cohesion, partial normative communication has had to be allowed by indirect means, and that is antithetical to the very nature of the theory. These are fundamental difficulties that critics of autopoietic systems theory have long recognized. For example, Habermas, who was a critic of Luhmann's work from the

[183] Teubner, 'How the Law Thinks', 745.

[184] I distinguish here a formal scientific education, such as a first degree in the natural sciences, from professional development courses such as 'Scientific Method for Judges' or 'Statistics for Trial Lawyers'.

[185] Shapiro, *Culture of Fact*.

early 1970s, has suggested that Teubner's attempts to soften the normative closure of social systems in order to meet our empirical observations must surely require abandoning fundamental tenets of Luhmann's theory:

> I do not think that this proposal is consistent with the architectonic of systems theory. On the one hand, legal discourse is supposed to be trapped in its self-reproduction . . . , on the other hand, it is supposed to use 'general social communication' so that it can 'influence' general social constructions of reality and in this way influence those of other discursive worlds. It is difficult to reconcile these two statements.[186]

Teubner appears therefore to be conceding that the 'general social construction of reality' is incorporated into the system world view. These rationalities operate as programmes within the communication systems that created and maintain them. However, each autopoietic system was created within an overall social system. In the case of at least some systems, as with the legal system, it is possible that full normative closure only occurred once a non-autopoietic legal system had already come into existence. The building blocks of each autopoietic system are inherited ultimately from the overall social system. That top-level social system must contain, as an autopoietic system, some method of reasoning (rationality) about the world, although this rationality does not determine the validity of all individual and systemic communications. This suggests that autopoietic system rationalities will in fact contain some elements of broader social rationality, although different systems may contain different elements. Most systems would contain core rational elements in the form of logical concepts such as non-contradiction. System rationalities may, however, contain further rules that modify or even nullify these rules. For example, the religious or artistic communication systems may have rules that permit or even encourage contradiction in certain circumstances. This strongly suggests that although autopoietic systems theory supports the existence of specialist inferential reasoning, it does not fully support the claim that these different forms of reasoning are incommensurable.

2.5.4.3.3 Contributions to understanding the social phenomenon of expert evidence The 'regressive' and 'conservative' positions do not provide any adequate explanation for how social systems might understand

[186] J. Habermas, *Between Facts and Norms* (Cambridge: Polity Press, 1997), p. 53.

each other's factual deliberations, for example in the area of expert evidence. They effectively side-step this lack of explanation by saying that these are issues with which autopoietic systems theory is not properly concerned. Instead, as King has shown,[187] the theory can tell us something about how law and other systems co-exist, and form their own understanding of what the other system is saying, without systems ever fully engaging in the self-referential meaning of the other system. This provides us with three valuable insights into law and expert evidence as social phenomena which a purely rationalist theory, or a progressive autopoietic hybrid, might easily lead us to overlook.

First, 'expert opinion evidence' is a purely legal construct. Each of the words 'expert', 'opinion' and 'evidence' has its intended meaning only within the legal system. The information that is deemed admissible and relevant is chosen by the court rather than by the experts. Because law chooses to see the world outside itself in its own terms, it does not comprehend that its view of 'expert evidence' is anything other than the true workings of the other specialist system. Secondly, other systems will have their own, specific concerns about the way that the courts intervene in matters concerning 'expert evidence'. Our problem of the assessment of expert evidence does not exist in this form outside the legal system. The very idea of the court assessing expert opinion evidence is a legal construct. The existence of these multiple perspectives on the same event may become problematic when the legal system and an 'expert' system disagree on whether an expert's conduct in litigation is open to censure. Thirdly, law may construct its own version of how 'the world' (including both social and physical worlds) works, in order to achieve its goal of practical decision making. It is at times more important for it to be seen that justice is done than for it actually to be done. This may require it to impose certainty in a field in which the relevant specialist discipline remains uncertain. It may alternatively require it to impose concepts, such as legal causation, that have no meaning in the systems whose opinion is sought.

2.6 Conclusion

In her valuable contribution to the study of expert evidence, *Evaluating Scientific Evidence*,[188] Beecher-Monas explains in detail how the courts

[187] King, 'Autopoietic Approach', on child syndromes.

[188] E. Beecher-Monas, *Evaluating Scientific Evidence: an Interdisciplinary Framework for Intellectual Due Process* (Cambridge: Cambridge University Press, 2006).

should approach the assessment of various types of expert evidence, such as toxic torts, identification, and future dangerousness, from the perspective of what she terms 'intellectual due process'. I have not taken that route, and have focused instead in this chapter and the preceding one on a specific and necessary preliminary point, of whether the court possesses sufficient epistemic competence to begin to undertake intellectual due process for the assessment of expert evidence. Because Beecher-Monas' focus is elsewhere, she disposes of this question fairly briefly at the start of her first chapter. The detailed analysis of that epistemic competence undertaken in this present chapter has been both necessary and worthwhile.

In this chapter I have sought to demonstrate three things. First, the traditional distinction in evidence jurisprudence between questions of fact and of opinion is ultimately a wrong term in the development of the evidence jurisprudence, although the distinction may have operational value in many contexts (Section 2.2). The direct consequence of removing the distinction is to allow us to consider using one method, namely inferential probabilistic reasoning, that applies to both facts and opinions: 'Insistent application of the principles of analytical thinking helps both insiders and outsiders assess the credibility of evidence.'[189]

Secondly, the non-expert tribunal of fact is epistemically competent to make some assessment of the reasoning of experts, since the way in which experts perform inferential reasoning is fundamentally the same as the approach of non-experts (Section 2.3). This epistemic competence is, however, limited. The limitations are imposed for a number of reasons, but in particular because syntactical similarities between expert and non-expert reasoning do not allow us to extend the competence to differences in the semantic content of the knowledge applied by experts and non-experts, and because cognitive psychology shows us that we often do not, in practice, reason as rationally as we would like to think that we do.

Thirdly, strong constructivist theories, such as Luhmann's autopoietic social systems theory, which would present a significant difficulty for the rationalist theory of evidence assessment presented in Chapters 1 and 2, are not theoretically viable when applied to the assessment of expert evidence (Section 2.5). However, although we have avoided a position where knowledge in society is fragmented into a number of distinct epistemological entities, we do not appear to have avoided the difficulty that there may exist persistent social communities of practice who possess sufficient epistemic authority to be able to challenge the accuracy of a court's

[189] E. Tufte, *Beautiful Evidence* (Cheshire CT: Graphics Press, 2006), p. 9.

finding of fact (Section 2.4). As with the question of whether to use expert or common-sense generalizations in legal fact finding (Section 1.4.3), the question of the extent to which (if at all) the courts should defer to the views of persistent communities of practice in specialist factual matters is a political rather than a philosophical or legal question. There is no straightforward answer, but thankfully this is a question that appears to arise rarely in practice.

3

Making sense of expert disagreement

3.1 Introduction

Chapter 2 provided an argument that the court as tribunal of fact possesses a limited epistemic competence to assess expert evidence. When the court determines the facts of the case before it, it is able to draw a limited set of justified inferences from the evidence presented by experts. It might reasonably be suspected that this is in some sense cheating, because, although there are some concerns about whether the courts can form such justified inferences, the more prevalent concern is whether the court is able to do so when confronted with conflicting expert opinions. This is not cheating, however. The question of epistemic competence has been considered as a necessary preliminary point in Chapter 2, in the same way that Chapter 1 spent necessary time laying down the foundation of the epistemology adopted in my argument, so that in this chapter it is now possible to turn to examining in greater detail the specific problem of how the courts are to decide where the expert evidence in a case offers more than one interpretation.

The body of the chapter is divided into five parts. In Section 3.2, I examine why legal and expert communities differ in their attitudes towards disagreement in drawing inferences from facts. The two main areas for disagreement concern, first, which set of generalizations (which we might call a 'theoretical framework') should be applied to a given set of base facts, and, secondly, how those generalizations should be applied to those base facts. Section 3.3 therefore considers the extent to which philosophers have allowed that disagreements may validly exist at the theoretical level between scientists, one of the main categories of expert. In particular, realist, positivist and constructivist forms of the philosophy of science are examined. Section 3.4 then examines how disagreements may arise in relation to how generalizations are applied to base facts. In Section 3.5, I consider how the different types of question addressed by expert evidence involve a range of inferential challenges, and as such lend themselves to a variety of types and degrees of expert disagreement, at the level of generalizations and in relation to the application of generalizations to base facts.

In the final part of the chapter, I turn to consider the related subject of expert bias, and its relationship to expert disagreement. The term 'expert bias' can be said to cover a number of situations where a reasonable onlooker might conclude that the evidence presented by the expert is not the evidence that a randomly selected expert, acting with equipoise, might reasonably be expected to give. Section 3.6 provides a taxonomy of expert bias, examining possible causes and manifestations of bias, and considering such issues as whether the bias might be considered personal (the expert herself is biased) or structural (the party has selected its expert in a biased fashion), and whether the bias is conscious or unconscious. The taxonomy is illustrated with examples from England, the United States and France. Section 3.6 stands alongside Sections 3.2 to 3.5 but slightly separate from them. On the one hand, not all disagreement is the product of bias, and, on the other hand, experts can be biased without any evidence of disagreement.

By the end of this chapter, it may seem that I have taken the well-known and relatively straightforward phenomenon of 'expert disagreement' (or 'expert bias'), deconstructed it, and left the parts in a pile on the floor. While Chapter 2 confirmed that the courts can draw justified inferences from the evidence of experts, this chapter may seem to fail to do the same for those situations where experts disagree. This is because this chapter does something more sophisticated than simply saying 'yes' or 'no' to the question of whether the courts can decide between divergent expert evidence. It allows us to understand the range of reasons for which the evidence diverges. The court will ultimately fall back on the limited epistemic competence described in Chapter 2, but in many cases it will be possible to reduce or resolve the divergence before undertaking the assessment. The main means by which the court may achieve this is in the shaping of appropriate procedural provisions. In Chapters 5 to 7, I shall consider the relationship between procedural provisions for expert evidence and the court's epistemological competence to assess that evidence. Of particular importance in those chapters is the way in which procedural provisions address expert disagreement. It is only once we have deconstructed the phenomenon of expert disagreement into its constituent elements that we can begin to examine how different procedural techniques can be applied to resolve or accommodate those elements.

3.2 Legal and expert factual disagreement

3.2.1 The need for finality in legal fact finding

The starting point for the legal process is that there must be an end to the matter. Not only must the judgment in the case be final, but any findings of law and fact in relation to that case must be final. In both common law and civilian systems this is expressed through the doctrine of *res judicata.* Once a final judgment has been handed down in a case, subsequent cases that are identical to or substantially the same as the earlier one are barred. The doctrine is cast slightly more widely in common law jurisdictions, in that it also includes collateral estoppel (issue preclusion), which precludes the same facts from being re-litigated under a different cause of action.

If we imagine a case (*C*) of *A* v. *B*, then we can say that this case is decided on the basis of a judicial statement of the law *L* and a finding of fact *F* inferred from evidence *E*. Immediately upon judgment, the losing party may appeal by way of a rehearing of the case on a range of grounds, mostly relating to errors in *L* or in certain circumstances that *F* cannot reasonably have been inferred from *E*. The nature of the appeal process varies between jurisdictions. In the Anglo-American world appeal is by leave of the court, while in continental Europe appeal is usually as of right. Anglo-American appeals are focused upon errors of law, although written evidence, and transcripts of oral evidence, may be referred to. In continental legal systems, where all or most of the evidence is usually presented to the court of first instance in written form in a case file (a *dossier* in France), a full appeal on the facts is relatively straightforward. In Italy, for example, parties are entitled to a full trial of law and fact at first and second instance as of right. The court of second instance can proceed in much the same way as the court of first instance because it has access to the same evidential base *E*, the case file.

Importantly, once the appeal process is ended, then *C* has been decided once and for all on the basis of *F* and *L*. It does not matter if further evidence E_2 emerges, or if another court, even a higher court, comes to a different finding of fact F_2 on a similar set of evidence to *E*, or a different interpretation of the law L_2 is developed.[1] C_2, virtually identical to *C*, could be decided a different way, but the legal effect of the decision in *C* on *A* and *B* does not falter. The legal system allows there to be only one

[1] Perhaps for historical reasons, in the Anglo-American world at least, decisions on the law are binding on subsequent cases in courts of the same or a lower level through the doctrine of *stare decisis*, while decisions on facts are not similarly binding.

set of facts that is legally true in any given case, once the case has been decided, with very limited circumstances in which the formal finding of fact can be changed. Within a legal context, this removal of factual dispute seems almost self-evident, and certainly inevitable. If a doctrine such as *res judicata* did not exist, then we should have to invent it, for without it disputes would be constantly referred back to the courts for re-hearing, like a feud that can never be ended. It would be difficult to imagine a society, at least a complex society, which could operate under such conditions of uncertainty.

However, outside the legal arena factual inferences are constantly subject to review. If historians were only allowed to look at new areas, or new sets of documents, and never to disagree with one another, then our understanding of history would be rudimentary. If research chemists did not revisit existing theories, then industrial chemistry and pharmaceuticals would never develop. We should be concerned if doctors did not ever disagree on how best to treat a patient, and if our doctors did not review how we responded to the treatment they prescribed. There are, in other words, a whole range of situations in everyday life where we expect people to disagree about how best to interpret a set of facts. Where those interpretations result in actions that have ongoing effect (such as many medical treatments, or an emergency relief plan), we would expect responsible review of whether the original interpretation was correct. We live in a world in which we expect people to disagree about the correct interpretation of facts, particularly in situations where the nature of the interpretation, or the facts, is non-trivial.[2] This is a fundamental point to bear in mind when we consider disagreements between experts in the course of litigation.

3.2.2 Reasons for disagreement in expert fact finding

We can identify at least four types of disagreement in the drawing of inferences from base facts to answer some question. First, we might disagree on which base facts are relevant to providing an answer. We can imagine a body of medical practice, for example, in which the phase of the moon or the flight pattern of wild birds determines the correct diagnosis and treatment plan for a patient. We would (presumably) disagree that these

[2] E.g. H. Engelhardt and A. Caplan (eds.), *Scientific Controversies: Case Studies in the Resolution and Closure of Disputes in Science and Technology* (Cambridge: Cambridge University Press, 1987).

are relevant facts in any medical treatment. One of the first rhetorical techniques learnt by the pupil barrister is that the phrase 'the facts of the case are these' should refer neither to a truly neutral statement of facts, nor to an obviously partisan one, but to a version of the facts that appears at first blush to be neutral but which, if adopted by the court in its thinking, would incline the court to one's client's case.

The second area for potential disagreement concerns the set of generalizations (Section 1.4.3) that should be applied to a set of base facts in order to address the question in issue. Depending on the context, we might call such a set of generalizations a theoretical or methodological framework. For example, we might expect an epidemiologist and a pathologist to approach a question such as whether product *P* is carcinogenic using different (albeit possibly overlapping) sets of generalizations, in the form of both theories and methods. For most purposes, I would suggest that the issue of the set of generalizations adopted incorporates the issue of which base facts should be considered relevant, and so they can be considered together.

The third area for potential disagreement concerns which of two competing versions of the base facts is correct. In relation to expert evidence, this is most likely to arise where the base facts are being provided by separate non-expert witnesses of fact (possibly the parties themselves). Where experts are themselves acting as witnesses of fact, then the facts may be capable of experimental replication or are otherwise continuing to be observable. Where this is not the case we would normally expect the expert to be able to provide reliable, probably contemporaneous, notes. If the disagreement cannot be resolved, then it becomes a standard question to be decided by the tribunal of fact. Prior to that decision, the disagreement can be overcome by providing the experts with all versions of the sets of base facts, as hypothetical situations, and their advice sought as if each situation were the case.

The fourth and final point on which experts might disagree is how the selected set of generalizations should be applied to the selected set of base facts. This is a common situation in applied sciences, such as medicine, where the general theory may be relatively stable but the main points of disagreement concern which set of generalizations apply to a specific set of facts, in terms of interpreting the facts and deciding on the course of action. For expert evidence, this situation may be most apparent where experts are used to dealing at the level of generalizations rather than in drawing conclusions in relation to specific cases. An example of this might be the evidence of epidemiologists.

3.2.3 *Law's perception of scientific knowledge as objective certainty*

However, judges have historically expected certainty from experts, particularly scientific experts. This is in large part because, since at least the nineteenth century, the term 'science' has been identified with a project to develop ever more certain and comprehensive objective knowledge about the world. That identification has been promoted by scientists as much as lawyers.[3] The American sociologist Merton has proposed that 'science' as a modern institution can be associated with four normative characteristics: universalism, communism, disinterestedness and organized scepticism.[4] When judges consider scientific evidence, they appear to be expecting conformity with these norms.[5]

These normative statements are, like many normative statements, partly counter-factual. Disagreement between experts not only is inevitable, but forms an essential part of scientific progress. Although we might like to think of many classes of expert, particularly research scientists, as being motivated by a dispassionate interest in the furtherance of human knowledge, the reality is that many experts operate in conditions of fierce competition, motivated by such factors as commercial success, the desire for research funding, and personal reputation. One of the most famous examples of this is Watson's account of the research activity that led to the discovery of DNA.[6] Kitcher has produced a series of models that consider how scientific progress may be made through different patterns of coordination, cooperation and competition between individuals.[7]

It is worth qualifying, however, that, because these norms of scientific research are partly counter-factual, this does not entitle us to conclude that 'science' is in fact a purely social activity that is localized, individualistic, interest-driven and respectful of authority. The Kitcher who models scientific coordination, cooperation and competition is the same man who has argued for the importance of the scientific pursuit of truth, rather

[3] E.g. T. Golan, *Laws of Men and Laws of Nature: The History of Scientific Expert Testimony in England and America* (Cambridge MA: Harvard University Press, 2004).

[4] R. Merton, *The Sociology of Science: Theoretical and Empirical Investigations* (Chicago: University of Chicago Press, 1973), pp. 270–7.

[5] One of the earliest examples of judicial dissatisfaction at expert disagreement is *Severn* v. *Imperial Insurance Co.* The Times, 14 April 1820. For contemporary examples, see G. Edmond, 'After Objectivity: Expert Evidence and Procedural Reform' (2003) 25 *Sydney Law Review* 131–64.

[6] J. Watson, *The Double Helix* (New York: Norton, 1967).

[7] P. Kitcher, *The Advancement of Science: Science without Legend, Objectivity without Illusions* (Oxford: Oxford University Press, 1993), pp. 303–89.

than some Romantic concept of socially constructed knowledge.[8] We are entitled to accept that the means by which we pursue our goals are not perfect, without sacrificing the validity of those goals. Judges may express surprise and disappointment at expert disagreement, but the lesson that we should learn from this is that judges need to be educated in the way in which scientists (or other experts) actually work, rather than concluding that the search for objective expert evidence is a phantasm.[9]

3.3 The selection of generalization sets

One of the central difficulties for the courts in the assessment of expert evidence is that not only is there scope for experts to disagree on how best to draw inferences from the application of discipline-specific generalization sets to sets of base facts (Section 3.4),[10] but in many disciplines it is common to have more than one set of generalizations. These sets may overlap, be distinct or even be contradictory.[11] In itself, this is essentially the core epistemological problem of the justifiable assessment of expert evidence (Chapter 2). If expert *A* says that we should use generalization set G_A, and expert *B* says that we should use generalization set G_B, this is at root no different from non-expert *C* saying that we should use common-sense generalization set G_C. The court must decide which of G_A, G_B and G_C is correctly applied in the instant case, in order to achieve accurate fact determination and thus in turn facilitate rectitude of decision.

This line of argument assumes first that a correct generalization set *G* exists, secondly that it can be identified as being the correct set, and thirdly that it is available to the fact finder in the instant case. Here I should like to sound a note of caution about viewing the first assumption as being self-evident. Although legal decision making, with its requirement for finality

8 P. Kitcher, 'Truth or Consequences?' (1998) 72 *Proceedings and Addresses of the American Philosophical Association* 49–63. Compare A. Goldman, *Knowledge in a Social World* (Oxford: Oxford University Press, 1999), pp. 221–71.

9 Gary Edmond comes close to this counsel of despair in his 'Judicial Representations of Scientific Evidence' (2000) 63 *Modern Law Review* 216–51, e.g. (at 217) 'If *Science* really were homogenous, objective, method driven and determined solely by evidence derived from a [*sic*] natural world' (original emphasis).

10 Alternatively expressed as 'how best to interpret facts within the theoretical framework of their specialist discipline'.

11 E.g. in addressing the phenomena of heredity, what is the relationship between classical genetics, descended from the Mendelian theory of heredity, and molecular genetics, descended from the work of Watson and Crick? P. Kitcher, '1953 and All That: A Tale of Two Sciences' (1984) 93 *Philosophical Review* 335–73, 335.

in the instant case, may be able to say that one of G_A, G_B and G_C is correct for the purposes of deciding the instant case, there is significant disagreement within the philosophy of science about how, and indeed whether, we can say that G_A is valid and G_B is not. We might choose to be pragmatic, and decide that while philosophers and research scientists can afford the luxury of not deciding between G_A and G_B, the courts will nevertheless decide between them. There is an element of *hubris* to this, in allowing a judge to decide a question not only that scientists are unable to agree on between themselves, but that they may feel does not allow of a single right answer. It is because of these concerns about pragmatics and *hubris* that it is worth considering some of the main schools of the philosophy of science, in order to understand what they say about choosing between competing sets of generalizations (theoretical frameworks). Three schools are considered: scientific realism, logical positivism and constructivism, in Sections 3.3.1, 3.3.2 and 3.3.3 respectively.[12]

3.3.1 Scientific realism

Within the philosophy of science, realism has four central theses.[13] First, 'theoretical terms' in scientific theories (i.e. non-observational terms) should be thought of as putatively 'referring'.[14] Secondly, scientific theories, interpreted realistically, are confirmable and in fact are often confirmed as approximately true by ordinary scientific evidence interpreted in accordance with ordinary methodological standards. Thirdly, the historical progress of mature sciences is largely a matter of successively more accurate approximations to the truth. Finally, the reality which scientific theory describes is largely independent of our thoughts or theoretical commitments. Realists say that if two theories exist to explain the same phenomenon then, since experiment and data are theory-neutral

[12] The divisions that can be drawn within the philosophy of science are not firm. E.g., Kitcher would group empiricists and positivists together to the extent that they present essential similar critiques of realism: P. Kitcher, 'Real Realism: The Galilean Strategy' (2001) 110 *Philosophical Review* 151–97. In an earlier version of this chapter, I suggested that, for the purposes of understanding whether we can ever say that one of G_A and G_B is correct, empiricism, positivism and constructivism could all be grouped together as being 'theory–laden' in contrast to 'realist'.

[13] R. Boyd, 'On the Current Status of Scientific Realism' (1983) 19 *Erkenntnis* 45–90, 45.

[14] Laudan suggests that an approximate definition of 'refer' would be 'there are substances in the world that correspond to the ontologies presumed by our best theories': L. Laudan, 'A Confutation of Convergent Realism' (1981) 48 *Philosophy of Science* 19–49, 20.

('pair-wise theory-neutrality'),[15] we can always define a series of experiments that will help us to decide which theory is the more accurate.[16] For present purposes, this assists us in being able to choose one expert as being more correct than the other where two experts disagree.

Haack, a realist, has suggested that her analogy of knowledge as being like a crossword puzzle, created to illustrate foundherentism,[17] is equally applicable to realism.[18] This illustrates how realism, within the philosophy of science, shares many points of similarity with foundherentism, within epistemology. We may currently know, or believe that we know, the answer to each question with varying degrees of 'warrant'.[19] That level of confidence partly depends on our approach to the clue itself, and how each of our answers fits in with the other answers. The more of the grid that is filled in, the more confident we can be that our answers are correct. We may currently have a number of entries pencilled in, and may even have to rub out answers, but the general direction of our work on the puzzle is towards solving it.

3.3.2 Logical positivism

Logical positivism developed in the early twentieth century out of Comtean positivism. It represented a rejection of metaphysical statements, and of the reality of the external world.[20] It made use of the advances in formal deductive logic by philosophers such as Boole, Peirce, Frege and Russell, to conclude that there are only two kinds of meaningful statement: the analytic (including the statements of logic and mathematics) and the empirically verifiable (including the statements of empirical science).[21] The difficulty that was soon identified was that it was not satisfactory to say that theoretical terms are simply abbreviations of congeries of observational terms, and theoretical statements reducible to

[15] Boyd, 'Current Status', 46.

[16] Hacking has suggested that there is a weakness in arguing that, because experimental method works in a realist fashion, this means that realist theories are also correct; I. Hacking, 'Experimentation and Scientific Realism' (1982) 13 *Philosophical Topics* 71–87.

[17] S. Haack, *Evidence and Inquiry: Towards Reconstruction in Epistemology* (Oxford: Blackwell, 1993), pp. 81–9.

[18] S. Haack, *Defending Science – Within Reason: Between Scientism and Cynicism* (New York: Prometheus Books, 2003), pp. 57–67, 93.

[19] Ibid., pp. 57–77.

[20] M. Schlick, 'Positivismus und Realismus' (1932) 3 *Erkenntnis* 1–31.

[21] Haack, *Defending Science*, p. 32.

observational statements by means of correspondence rules. Scientific theories would therefore not be conclusively verifiable.

The two main responses to this difficulty were inductivism and deductivism. The inductivism of Reichenbach, Carnap and Hempel allowed that statements could qualify as empirically meaningful provided that they could be confirmed or probabilified by observational evidence. Popperian deductivism replaced this verifiability as a criterion of meaning with falsifiability as a criterion of the scientific.[22] The weaknesses of both forms of logical positivism arise from their inflexibility in dealing with conceptual innovation, incomplete evidence, and science as a social activity.[23] Where logical positivism touches on our present discussion is that it is not a philosophy that allows us to make definitive theoretical statements about the world.

Under Popperian deductivism, a theory can be corroborated by empirical evidence, but this never confirms its truth. A theory therefore stands only until it can be shown to be false, and experiments should be developed with this test of falsifiability in mind. We could therefore have before us two sets of theoretical statements that are valid because they have not been falsified, and although we might prefer one theory over the other because it is supported by stronger corroborative evidence, this is not, for Popper, a sound epistemological basis on which to say that one theory is more likely to be valid than the other, and it is possible that two theories could exist that are corroborated equally well. Inductivism appears to result in a set of propositions that are logically internally valid but do not necessarily externally refer.[24]

For Hempel, 'what determines the soundness of a hypothesis [is] . . . the way it stands up when tested, i.e. when confronted by relevant observations'.[25] This produces the 'hypothetico-deductive method', in which a hypothesis is tested against evidence in order to deduce the truth of that hypothesis. This provides (relative) confirmation. However, when Hempel later says that the fact that scientific theories conform to empirical evidence 'has no bearing at all on the question of their truth',[26] it would appear that he is moving closer to a Popperian or empiricist

[22] K. Popper, *The Logic of Scientific Discovery* (1934), trans. K. Popper (London: Hutchinson, 1959).

[23] Haack, *Defending Science*, p. 33. [24] Haack, *Defending Science*, p. 40.

[25] C. Hempel, *Aspects of Scientific Explanation* (New York: Free Press, 1965), p. 4.

[26] C. Hempel, 'The Irrelevance of the Concept of Truth for the Critical Appraisal of Scientific Theories' in R. Jeffrey (ed.), *Selected Philosophical Essays [by] Carl G. Hempel* (Cambridge: Cambridge University Press, 1990), pp. 77–78, quoted in Haack, *Defending Science*, p. 40.

position – that ontological truth cannot be known from empirical data. This is still consistent, however, with the idea that confirmation of a theory does not fully equate with its proof.

3.3.3 Scientific constructivism

I use the label 'scientific constructivism' here as an umbrella term to cover particularly the work of two philosophers of science, Kuhn and Quine, who have in common the idea that there can simultaneously exist a number of theoretical explanations for the world that can be equally valid. This argument results from a claim for the underdetermination of theory, that is to say a claim that theories cannot be justified solely in terms of the empirical facts on which they are said to be based.

Scientific constructivism could be said to begin with Kuhn's *The Structure of Scientific Revolutions.*[27] This book 'changed the character of the philosophy of science'.[28] In it Kuhn argued that some changes in scientific theory are not gradual but revolutionary, resulting in a shift in paradigm. That paradigm shift results in a threefold incommensurability: conceptual, observational and methodological.[29] Resolution of revolutions by rational means is impossible, and the decision to accept a radically new theory can only be taken on faith. Similar claims have been made by Feyerabend that different theories share no common statements.[30] The dramatic effect of Kuhn's work has been somewhat meliorated by clarifications from Kuhn in the 1980s and 1990s, which would suggest that Kuhn did not mean to say that those working in different paradigms were unable to understand one another, but only that there was not a simple translation from one theory language to another.[31] Nevertheless, there is no difficulty within a Kuhnian model of scientific knowledge in saying that G_A and G_B are simultaneously true. What does change is that, whereas the 'earlier Kuhn' might have said that the relative merits of G_A and G_B

[27] T. Kuhn, *The Structure of Scientific Revolutions* (Chicago: University of Chicago Press, 1962).

[28] P. Kitcher, 'Implications of Incommensurability' (1982) 2 *Philosophy of Science Association* 689–703, at fn. 1.

[29] Ibid., 690.

[30] E.g. P. Feyerabend, 'Explanation, Reduction and Empiricism', in H. Feigl and G. Maxwell (eds.), *Minnesota Studies in the Philosophy of Science*, vol. III (Minneapolis MN: Minnesota University Press, 1962) pp. 28–97; P. Feyerabend, 'On the "Meaning" of Scientific Terms' (1964) 61 *Journal of Philosophy* 497–509.

[31] Kitcher, 'Implications', 690; Haack, *Defending Science*, p. 44. Contrast P. Kitcher, 'Theories, Theorists and Theoretical Change' (1978) 87 *Philosophical Review* 519–547.

can never be assessed because of problems of incommensurability, the 'later Kuhn' might allow such a dialogue to occur, although the underdetermination of theory might prevent the dialogue from being particularly productive.

Quine takes the underdetermination thesis to argue for the empirical equivalence of theories and the indeterminacy of translation in theory languages.[32] In other words, Quine says that, for any given set of data, it is possible to construct two distinct theories that explain the data equally well. These theories are distinct at the level of the theory-language used to construct them, so it is not possible to discuss the relative merits of the two theories on mutual terms. This argument stands in direct conflict with Boyd's realist argument that, where two conflicting theories exist, it will always be possible to construct a test that will decide between the two theories, relying on pair-wise theory-neutrality of data (Section 3.3.1). While Kuhn's argument is at least partly sociological, and relates to revolutionary developments in experimental knowledge that may be seen as making the older theory no longer as sustainable as the newer theory, Quine's argument is purely epistemological, and there is no suggestion that the one theory might be seen as empirically superior to the other. If Quine's thesis is taken to be correct, then the court would not be entitled, on philosophical grounds, to decide to adopt G_A over G_B.

3.4 The application of generalizations to base facts

Even when the set of generalizations on which expert opinion should be based are agreed between the experts in a case, there may nevertheless arise disagreements between experts on how a given set of base facts is to be interpreted in terms of those generalizations. This relates to both the choice of methodology, and the actual application of that methodology. As with disagreements on the choice of generalizations, disagreement in interpretation may reflect a structural feature of the nature and use of knowledge in the specialist discipline. There may be a number of reasons, not mutually exclusive, for why experts, who are respected practitioners within their own field, are unable to agree on their application of theory to the facts. First, it may be accepted within the discipline that practitioners may disagree in their interpretation of facts. Secondly, the question that the expert is being asked for the purposes of litigation may not be one

[32] W. Quine, 'On Empirically Equivalent Systems of the World' (1975) 9 *Erkenntnis* 313–28.

that she would normally need to address for the purpose of her own work. Thirdly, the courts may require special categories to be used in order for the evidence to be applicable to the relevant legal test. Fourthly, the experts may be accustomed to producing general statements from a mass of specifics, and not interpreting specifics in the context of general statements.

3.4.1 Disagreement in interpretation is accepted

It may be accepted within a discipline that practitioners may disagree in their interpretation of facts. This is likely to arise in applied sciences, such as medicine, where a probabilistic inference network is built up from a large number of observations. Because of the complexities of human biology, different conditions may manifest themselves with similar symptoms, and the same condition may manifest itself in a range of symptoms, so that the selection of relevant facts and the inferences from those facts operates in a state of uncertainty. The result of this is that the practitioner must give a level of confidence to each of her inferences in order to arrive at a conclusion. The allocation of degrees of confidence is at least partly subjective, and where large networks of inferences are produced, small inter-subjective differences in confidence levels for individual inferences may result in different conclusions. In other words, it may be possible to make more than one valid diagnosis from the same set of symptoms, and this is accepted within medical practice. It is then possible, because different patients may react differently to different treatments, for there to be variation between doctors on the 'correct' treatment of a patient. Provided the patient stays alive, the practitioner has the benefit of seeing how the patient's symptoms continue to develop, and how the patient reacts to the treatment plan.

3.4.2 Experts do not normally address such questions

Another possible cause of disagreement is that the question that the expert is being asked for the purposes of litigation may not be one that she would normally need to address for the purpose of her own work. To give a further medical example, an orthopaedic surgeon may examine a weakness in a patient's back for the purpose of deciding on treatment. It may be of relevance to the treatment decision how the weakness was produced, for example whether it was congenital or the result of trauma. Treatment can continue even where the surgeon is unclear on the question of causation, which is of secondary interest to her. Orthopaedics is therefore able to operate without certainty in its method for determining causation in all cases. However, the legal process is concerned primarily with the question of causation, and then only secondarily with the question of treatment. Indeed, provided that the monetary and other costs are roughly equivalent, it would not matter to the defendant in such a case what treatment plan was subsequently followed by the claimant. Causation is central, because it establishes who should pay that money. The interests of law and medicine in the opinion of the orthopaedic surgeon are almost the opposite of one another. In this context, it is quite possible that two eminent orthopaedic surgeons will disagree on the question of causation. The questions that they have addressed in order to become eminent are not the questions in which the court is primarily interested.[33]

3.4.3 Courts require special categories to be used

A variation on the previous reason for disagreement is that many of the questions of expertise are questions that are meaningful only within the legal process. The experts therefore have no experience of addressing these questions except during the course of their work as experts. This situation is less likely to arise in areas, such as forensic psychiatry, where the provision of evidence in court is a significant part of the professional's role.

3.4.4 Specifics from generals

A problem may arise where experts are trained and experienced in producing general statements from a mass of specific data, and not in interpreting specific data in the context of general statements.[34] In the most extreme cases, as in epidemiology, where theories are produced by statistical abstraction from masses of data, it is extremely difficult to reverse the

[33] Similarly, structural engineers have been concerned with ensuring that buildings do not fall down. The study of why particular structures have actually failed is a secondary study. However, unlike the medical example in the text, there are engineers who specialize in the causation of structural failure: e.g. M. Levy and M. Salvadori, *Why Buildings Fall Down: How Structures Fail* (New York: Norton, 1992).

[34] H. Hart and T. Honoré, *Causation in the Law*, 2nd edn (Oxford: Oxford University Press, 1985), pp. 9–10, note that lawyers and historians are interested in particular causation, while the experimental sciences have developed with general rules of causation as their focus.

inferential process, and apply epidemiological statements to specific cases. In particular, experts might fall foul of the 'ecological fallacy', i.e., although an epidemiological group is defined by a set of characteristics considered to produce a clear grouping, an individual in that group may possess other relevant characteristics that are not considered in characterizing the group.

People who are skilled in such disciplines may experience difficulties, which may be surmountable, in applying general propositions back to instant cases. When they appear as experts, they may present to the court as being distinctly inexpert, because they are being asked to do something with their discipline that the discipline's methodology may be ill suited to doing. An examination of the expert's qualifications is likely to focus on her experience of making inferences in order to arrive at a general theory, rather than in application to specifics. The consequence of this is that the expert has no real experience in giving her opinion on what is happening in a specific case. This can be contrasted with some other applied disciplines, such as medicine or engineering, which train their practitioners primarily in the application of the general propositions to instant cases, and only then may train them to conduct research to develop the general propositions.

3.5 Types of inferential challenge

In Sections 3.3 and 3.4, I examined in general terms how disagreements might arise between experts in terms of the choice of generalizations to apply in a given case, and in terms of how those generalizations should be applied to a given set of base facts. In this section, I develop that general discussion by considering in more detail examples of the range of types of inferential challenges facing experts and the tribunal of fact before which they appear. The inferential challenges are not the same for all types of question under consideration. For example, we might expect that the inferences involved in determining the state of a property, whether third-generation combined oral contraceptives cause cardiovascular injuries, or the way in which 'the reasonable specialist' would behave, would be at least partly different from one another. This is because these are very distinct types of question: the specialist description of a current state of affairs, the biological effects of a chemical, and the content of a norm.

The dominant point of view in proof theory would appear to be that expert evidence is epistemologically homogenous, although this view must largely be inferred from the absence of direct consideration of how different types of expert question may give rise to different inferential issues.[35] Mirjan Damaška has suggested that this homogeneity is perceived for the treatment of evidence in general:

> What lawyers include in their *thema probandi* as 'facts' or 'events' is actually a jumbled mixture of matters of unequal ontological status with an unequal degree of accessibility to our cognitive apparatus . . . [A]djudicative fact-finding is not merely a matter of reconstructing historical events. While most facts we seek to establish indeed lie in the past, some exist at the time of inquiry. Still other facts . . . consist of predictions of future occurrences. Second, fact-finding is concerned not only with the empirical question whether something happened, but also with the reasons-seeking question of why something happened. Along yet another dimension, some facts seem easily severable from value judgments . . . Other facts, however, consist of complex social evaluations.[36]

The main inferential issues that are associated with the questions that experts are asked to address can be placed into four groups. First, whether this is a factual or normative question. Secondly, whether we are concerned with general factual principles, such as whether a particular drug increases the chance of a particular illness (theory), or specific events, such as an accident (application). Thirdly, whether the question relates to a past, present or future state of affairs. Fourthly, the degree of inference required (i.e. is this a matter of informed observation and description, or does it require more interpretation, for example determining causation). Members of one or more of these groups of inferential issues are present in the set of inferential issues associated with an expert question. For present purposes, I am only concerned with the properties of the sets of issues, and how they affect the selection of appropriate expert roles.

The expert questions that I consider as examples of question types are: the condition of a property (Section 3.5.1); quantum of damages in personal injury (Section 3.5.2); causation in personal injury (Section 3.5.3); causation in toxic torts (Section 3.5.4); the best interests of the child (Section 3.5.5); the standard of care in professional negligence (Section 3.5.6). These are ranked very approximately in order of increasing complexity of inferential reasoning, with expert inferences making up an

[35] E.g. S. Brewer, 'Scientific Expert Testimony and Intellectual Due Process' (1998) 103 *Yale Law Journal* 1535–681; L. Hand, 'Historical and Practical Considerations Regarding Expert Testimony' (1901) 15 *Harvard Law Review* 40–58; D. Nelken, 'A Just Measure of Science?' in M. Freeman and H. Reece (eds.), *Science in Court* (Aldershot: Ashgate, 1988), pp. 11–36.

[36] M. Damaška, 'Truth in Adjudication' (1998) 49 *Hastings Law Journal* 289–308, 299; M. Damaška, *Evidence Law Adrift* (New Haven CT: Yale University Press, 1997), p. 28.

increasingly large part of the overall inference network. This increasing proportion of expert inference makes the use of common inferential reasoning (Section 1.4) correspondingly more difficult. The questions are illustrated with examples from English case law, with some supporting material from the United States. The questions are, nevertheless, jurisdiction-neutral in their applicability.

3.5.1 The condition of a property

Questions put to experts relating to the condition of a property represent all four of the groups of inferences introduced above. The condition of a property is a factual issue, involving the application of the expert's knowledge to a specific set of facts, relating to the informed observation and description of a current state of affairs. Condition is perhaps the most straightforward type of inference required of an expert. It might arise for example in disputes over property valuation.[37] The expert is required only to describe the property as it is, with the benefit of her experience, and then to match that description against a more generic list. The expert is not required to determine questions such as: how the property has come to be in that state; how long it has been in that state; how the condition may develop. The condition of a property does not therefore appear to be an area of expertise in which there can be much genuine disagreement. The expert may also be required to undertake fairly straightforward inferences in addressing how the situation should be rectified. Rectification provides greater opportunity for disagreement between experts because there is room for difference of opinion both on the state to which the property should be restored, and possibly also on the means by which this should be achieved. In England, the more inferentially advanced question of whether a house is fit for human habitation,[38] is the 'ordinary user' test,[39] and should not be subject to expert determination.[40]

3.5.2 Quantum of damages in personal injury

This is a factual issue of specific application relating to future events. It involves both observation and interpretation. In particular, it relates to the

[37] E.g. *Abbey National Mortgages plc* v. *Key Surveyors Nationwide Ltd* [1996] 1 WLR 1534; [1996] 3 All ER 184 (CA).

[38] Housing Act 1985, s. 604 (as amended).

[39] *Morgan* v. *Liverpool Corporation* [1927] 2 KB 131 (CA).

[40] *Dover District Council* v. *Sherred* (1997) 29 HLR 864 (CA).

nature of a current state of affairs, how it will develop in the future, and what the cost implications of that future state of affairs will be. Prognosis is a strictly medical opinion but calculating the cost involved in meeting that prognosis is open to more general experience. The main difficulty with prognosis is that the claimant's medical condition is still unstable and so there is a wide range of possible developments in her condition. Where the claimant's medical condition is unstable and requires time to settle it is possible in England to conduct separate trials on liability and damages,[41] with damages being established once a prognosis can be given with greater certainty.

The two predictive questions for the expert in calculating personal injury quantum of damages are the future state of health of the claimant and the cost of treatment and lifestyle adjustments that arise as a consequence. These are both questions that allow for a range of opinion, although the former is perhaps a narrower range than the latter. The former is also more heavily dependent on medical experience, while the latter is a mixture of medical and common-sense experience. If the claimant had disability *x*, then what impact would this have on her life, and what steps need to be taken to accommodate this? In the English case of *Daniels*,[42] the expert's opinion was held to be one that was subject to a degree of informed common-sense validation. In that case, the defendant, who had experience of other similar claims, was able to question the size of the compensation proposed by the joint expert, based on the size of awards in similar claims.

3.5.3 Causation in personal injury

A fundamentally different set of questions from those posed for quantum in personal injury arises when we consider causation in the same type of case. This is a factual issue, regarding the interpretation of a specific past event. Questions of causation for the tribunal of fact are whether breach *B* occurred, and whether claimant *C*'s injury *I* occurred as a direct consequence of *B*. That question might be answered in part on the basis of statements by witnesses who saw *B*, and the opinions of experts. Those expert opinions might concern whether, if *B* occurred, an injury such as *I* might result (where causation is in dispute), or whether injury *I* might be caused by a breach such as *B* (where the occurrence of the event is in

[41] R. 3.1(2)(i) of the Civil Procedure Rules 1998 ('CPR').
[42] *Daniels* v. *Walker* [2000] 1 WLR 1382 (HC).

dispute). In either case, the expert is required to take their knowledge and experience of the various possible causes of different types of accident, and apply them to the specific case.

The principal inferential difficulty is likely to be that, in reconstructing a past event from present evidence, injury I could be caused by more than one breach, such as B_1 and B_2, while breach B could give rise to more than one type of injury, I_1 and I_2. It may be that the probabilities of each event causing each type of injury may vary, and that the correct allocation of these probabilities is unclear. The principal concern of medicine is with how one treats I. Whether I_1 was caused by B_1 or B_2 is of only secondary interest, and for clinical purposes whether B_1 is more likely to cause I_1 or I_2 is of only academic interest. It should therefore come as no surprise that medical experts may disagree in addressing such questions. It may be possible, with some types of injury, to instruct experts who are specialists in causation rather than treatment. There is a concern that such specialists may be dedicated to litigation work rather than medical research or practice.[43] It is probable that there would be agreement between most experts on the theoretical framework within which the question of causation should be approached. Any differences of opinion are therefore likely to arise in making inferences from the patient's current condition to what has occurred in the past.

3.5.4 Causation in toxic torts

Toxic torts represent a very different type of inferential reasoning from conventional questions of causation in tort. They are concerned primarily with general scientific principles rather than understanding individual incidents.[44] Most tortious actions require that a claimant prove a physical connection between the defendant's tort and the claimant's damage. The factual issues are therefore that a specific factual scenario occurred, and that causation should be inferred from that scenario. However, in a toxic tort action the primary interest of the claimant is in proving that a substance (or similar) is capable of causing injury in a given state of affairs, and the secondary interest is then in proving that that state of affairs occurred in the claimant's case.

[43] See Edmond, 'Judicial Representations', at 224–9, on Anglo-American judicial concern at expertise that is developed for litigation rather than in the practical sphere outside the litigation context.

[44] Hart and Honoré, *Causation*, ch. 1.

> Toxic torts can be defined as civil actions asserting a demand for recovery of damages that arose from exposure to a chemical substance, emission, or product, where that exposure allegedly caused physical and/or psychological harm. The defining event of a toxic tort is an exposure. The defining consequence is an illness or other adverse human effect, including reproductive problems, which has a nontrivial and non-transitory effect upon persons. Some exposure and some consequence will be found in each case.[45]

The proof of causation occurs not at the level of the individual claimant, but as a general proposition of science: it may be proven to the court's satisfaction, for example, that the third-generation combined oral contraceptive increases the likelihood of members of a group developing cardiovascular injuries.[46] In addition, it may be impossible to prove causation in any given case, but only give a statistical likelihood of causation on the basis of studies of large samples.[47] Epidemiology rather than conventional clinical medicine is therefore central to toxic tort litigation.[48] The burden of proof is 'collapsed'.[49]

In comparison to proving the toxicity of the substance in question for the purposes of litigation, proving a nexus between the claimant and the substance is usually relatively straightforward, as is identifying the defendant legally responsible for that nexus.[50] Where more than one defendant brought the claimant into contact with the substance, liability may depend on whether the resulting injury is based on cumulative exposure over a number of (indeterminate) defendants (as with asbestosis),[51] or whether any one act of exposure could produce the injury, with the degree of

45 J. O'Reilly and C. Buenger, *Toxic Torts Practice Guide*, 2nd edn (Eagan MN: West, 2004), [2.1].

46 *XYZ* v. *Schering Health Care* [2002] EWHC 1420 (QB).

47 Compare J. Weinstein and E. Hershenov, 'The Effect of Equity on Mass Tort Law' [1991] *University of Illinois Law Review* 269–327. The authors argue that equity has relaxed the evidential requirements of tort, in order to ensure that an equitable outcome is achieved.

48 O'Reilly and Buenger, *Toxic Torts*, [4.1].

49 A. McConnell, 'Risk and Responsibility: Dealing with Science and Uncertainty in Toxic Torts', Doctor of Laws thesis, European University Institute (2000) 139–55.

50 In *XYZ*, at [22], of the five issues identified by the parties, the first issue, on scientific causation, was heard first over forty-two days. It was expected that the remaining four issues, which included the existence of a causal nexus for each claimant, would together last about as long.

51 *Bonnington Castings Ltd* v. *Wardlaw* [1956] AC 613; 2 WLR 707; [1956] 1 All ER 615 (HL); *McGhee* v. *National Coal Board* [1973] 1 WLR 1; [1972] 3 All ER 1008 (HL).

injury being independent of the degree of cumulative exposure (as with mesothelioma).[52]

Since the litigation turns upon which scientific theory to adopt in order to explain whether the substance is or is not toxic in the given circumstances, the court is extremely restricted in being able to fall back on considerations such as the wider factual matrix of the case. The inference network that the tribunal must ultimately resolve is filled almost exclusively with specialist rather than non-specialist inferences. Unless the defendant has been reckless in allowing the substance to enter the environment, or the claims are vexatious, it is probable that there are good scientific reasons both to believe that the substance in question is harmless, and to believe that it is toxic. This will therefore almost certainly be an area in which there is fundamental expert disagreement at the level of the choice of generalization set (Section 3.3). Toxic tort litigation can be expensive both to bring and to defend. Therefore, where a case proceeds to trial,[53] without agreement between the two sides on the scientific issues, it is extremely likely that the differences between the two parties either are fundamental in nature, or else represent differing views on how to interpret complex scientific information.

McConnell has suggested that 'such scientific uncertainty about risks associated with allegedly toxic substances blows the myth of factual certainty as a basis of legal intervention'.[54] It is, however, not clear that legal decision making does require factual certainty, in the way that McConnell suggests. The basis of all findings of fact is probabilistic. The main differences between toxic tort litigation and most personal injury work is that the disagreements between experts are more likely to be highly complex and relating to scientific theory rather than interpretation in the instant case, and the way in which causation is established is different. This may increase the perception of uncertainty.

Statistical method involves the formal mathematical collection, analysis and interpretation of large volumes of numerical data. This is in contrast to common inferential reasoning, where the probabilities that we ascribe are primarily intuitive. McConnell provides a detailed explanation of how

[52] *Fairchild* v. *Glenhaven Funeral Services Ltd* [2002] UKHL 22; [2003] 1 AC 32; [2002] 3 WLR 89; [2002] 3 All ER 305 (HL).

[53] In the early 1990s in the United States, in excess of 95 per cent of toxic tort cases ended in settlement or other pre-trial disposition: McConnell, 'Risk', p. 16.

[54] Ibid., p. 1.

statistical assessment of legal proof differs from conventional methods, and how it is applied in English and United States cases.[55] In summary, the risk that a product presents is expressed as a risk ratio: the ratio between the incidence of the disease in the exposed group and the incidence in the unexposed group. Which studies should be used to provide the group sizes for such ratios is the main subject of disagreement between experts. In particular, a study will only be considered significant if the association is statistically significant.

In the United States case of *Daubert II*, the court decided that it would require statistical proof of more than a twofold increase in risk of birth defects from exposure to the anti-morning-sickness drug Bendectin.[56] That increase in relative risk of 2.0 or greater has now become the general requirement in United States toxic tort litigation,[57] and has been accepted by the court and the parties in England.[58] The basis for the use of 2.0 is that the effect of this relatively greater risk is that:

> If factor X increases the risk of condition Y by more than 2 when compared with factor Z it can then be said, of a group of say 100 with both exposure to factor X and the condition, that as a matter of probability more than 50 would not have suffered Y without being exposed to X. If medical science cannot identify the members of the group who would and who would not have suffered Y, it can nevertheless be said of each member that she was more likely than not to have avoided Y had she not been exposed to X.[59]

By convention, scientists require a 95 per cent probability that a finding is not due to chance alone. The risk ratio (e.g. '2.2') represents a mean figure. The actual risk has a 95 per cent probability of lying somewhere between upper and lower limits (e.g. 2.2 ±0.3, which equals a risk somewhere between 1.9 and 2.5) (the 'confidence interval'). The distance between the upper and lower limits (the 'confidence level') is determined by the size of the sample. While understanding the risk ratio and confidence limits for a single study is relatively straightforward, the position for the tribunal of fact becomes more complex when it is presented with a number of studies, where the risk ratio and confidence limits overlap (e.g. a large study suggests a risk of 1.9±0.2 (1.7–2.1), while a smaller study suggests 2.1±0.3 (1.8–2.4)). In the English case of *XYZ*, in which MacKay J conducted (by his own account) an otherwise thorough analysis of the inferential

55 Ibid., pp. 100–37.

56 *Daubert* v. *Merrell Dow Pharmaceuticals* 43 F 3d 1311 (9th Cir. 1995) (*Daubert II*).

57 McConnell, 'Risk', pp. 115, 130.

58 *XYZ*, at [20].

59 Ibid., at [21].

reasoning of the experts before him,[60] the judge nevertheless declined to consider how several risk ratios and confidence levels should be combined.[61] This combination is, however, necessary in order to understand statistically how several studies contributed to an overall risk ratio and confidence level.

Toxic tort actions have two key characteristics that make resolving expert disagreement in them problematic. The first is that, especially for product liability cases, if the case has reached trial, it is almost certain that the position of the experts will be intractable. For a product to have reached the market, the manufacturers will almost certainly have had a high degree of confidence in its safety. In addition, the adverse publicity that will almost certainly result from such litigation would encourage any defendant who did not have confidence in their case to settle early in the litigation. In *XYZ*, for example, the differences between the experts were so irreconcilable that counsel for both sides advised that any attempt at pre-trial discussion was futile, and there was almost no concession by any expert at trial. The second characteristic is that these cases have a very high scientific content, with the overall factual nexus of the case playing a very minor role.

3.5.5 The best interests of the child

Family cases that depend on determining 'the best interests of the child', such as custody or access/contact hearings, depend on normative rather than factual inferences. These norms are applied in the context of the best interests of a particular child. The identification of norms in the legal process is one of the core functions of the tribunal. Where the tribunal is split between law and fact, then – broadly speaking – the tribunal of law determines legal norms as abstract propositions, while the tribunal of fact determines whether legal norms have been breached in the instant case and the nature of any applicable social norms. There are two difficulties: (a) defining what the norm is, and (b) deciding how that norm should be applied in the instant case. It is primarily in the second area that the courts call upon the evidence of experts.

[60] For disagreement on this point, see K. McPherson, 'One Expert's Experience', in L. Blom-Cooper (ed.), *Experts in the Civil Courts* (Oxford: Oxford University Press, 2006), pp. 159–80. McPherson appeared as an expert for the claimants, who were unsuccessful.

[61] *XYZ*, at [41].

The 'best interests' or 'welfare' of the child is a norm of English domestic law[62] (the 'paramountcy principle'[63]) and international law.[64] In a Children Act proceeding, the judge is required to reach a decision which gives paramountcy to the welfare of the particular child. This requires the application of general social norms to the instant case. The principal difficulty is that it is very unclear what society understands to be in the interests of a child's welfare.[65] It is probably the case that judicial interventions equate the welfare of children with the transmission of conventional social norms.[66] Given the uncertainty of what 'welfare' actually means in the context of Family proceedings, the crucial issue becomes in practice not the concept of welfare itself but the choice of decision maker,[67] so that 'What is or is not in the children's interests depends largely on who is asking the question.'[68]

In considering how best to apply the welfare norm in the instant case, the judge may request and rely on expert reports, in particular from social workers and from psychiatrists. Expert evidence is extensively used in Family proceedings.[69] We might therefore be tempted to say that modern society has spread the authority for imposing its norms about the rearing of children across a number of disciplines.[70] This would be true to the extent that different institutions within society, such as the family, the courts, education authorities, health authorities and social services, have the authority to apply their own interpretation of what constitutes a child's welfare and best interests to that child within their own areas of activity.

62 Children Act 1989, s. 1(1). It is not a principle of universal application, however. For example, it does not apply to decisions on secure accommodation (s. 25 of the Children Act 1989) or to immigration decisions (*R.* v. *Secretary of State for Home Dept* ex p. *Gangadeen* [1998] 1 FLR 162).

63 *J* v. *C* [1970] AC 668 (HL).

64 International Convention on the Rights of the Child 1998, Art. 3(1).

65 For an introduction to the extensive literature on this point, see R. van Krieken, 'The "Best Interests of the Child" and Parental Separation: on the "Civilizing of Parents"' (2005) 68 *Modern Law Review* 25–48, and S. Sclater and C. Piper, 'Social Exclusion and the Welfare of the Child' (2001) 28 *Journal of Law and Society* 409–29.

66 J. Eekelaar, 'The Emergence of Children's Rights' (1986) 6 *Oxford Journal of Legal Studies* 161–82.

67 R. Mnookin, 'Child Custody Adjudication: Judicial Functions in the Face of Indeterminacy' (1975) 39 *Law and Contemporary Problems* 226–93.

68 A. Bainham, *Children: The Modern Law*, 2nd edn (Bristol: Jordan Publishing, 1998), p. 35.

69 J. Brophy P. Bates, L. Brown, S. Cohen and P. Radcliffe, *Expert Evidence in Child Protection Litigation – Where Do We Go From Here?* (London: The Stationery Office, 1999), p. 11 suggested its use in 80 per cent of cases.

70 N. Rose and M. Valverde, 'Governed by Law?' (1998) 7 *Social and Legal Studies* 541–53.

There has certainly been a shift from the position in the 1970s, when the courts were very reluctant to allow psychiatric evidence in child cases: 'In my view, the evidence of a psychiatrist usually has little place in a contested custody application.'[71]

However, the English courts do not appear to have delegated fully their duty to determine the child's welfare. In *Re N – B C M*,[72] the Court of Appeal held that the trial judge, in explaining his rejection of the expert evidence on welfare and placement, had not erred in failing to give reasons, or adequate reasons, for departure from the opinion of the expert. Counsel cited a *dictum* of Otton LJ that '[t]he judge was not entitled to reject the non-contradicted medical findings and opinion and to conclude that this opinion was either unreasonable or irresponsible'.[73] Alternatively, counsel suggested that the court should follow *Flannery* v. *Halifax Estate Agencies*:

> The extent of the duty, or rather the reach of what is required to fulfil it, depends on the subject matter. Where there is a straightforward factual dispute whose resolution depends simply on which witness is telling the truth about events which he claims to recall, is likely to be enough for the judge (having, no doubt, summarised the evidence) to indicate simply that he believes X rather than Y; indeed there may be nothing else to say. But where the dispute involves something in the nature of an intellectual challenge, with reasons and analysis advanced on either side, the judge must enter into the issues canvassed before him and explain why he prefers one case over the other. This is likely to apply particularly in litigation where as here there is disputed expert evidence; but it is not necessarily limited to such cases.[74]

This submission was rejected by Thorpe LJ on the basis that both *dicta* clearly applied to expert evidence of a 'much more specific character, particularly evidence of medical experts as to physical injuries'.[75] What is central to this case is that it demonstrates different types of issues to which different types of expertise give rise. Expert evidence on issues of placement, management and welfare are very different in character from medical or similar evidence, since the former involves balancing risks

[71] *Lynch* v. *Lynch* (1965) 8 FLR 433, at 433 (Begg J). Similar views were expressed in *O'Connor* v. *A* [1971] 1 WLR 1227, at 1230 (Lord Reid).
[72] *Re N – B C M* [2002] EWCA Civ 1052; [2002] 2 FLR 1059.
[73] *Re B (Split Hearing)* [2001] FLR 334 (CA), at 341.
[74] *Flannery* v. *Halifax Estate Agencies Ld* [2000] 1 WLR 377 (CA) (Henry LJ).
[75] *Re N – B C M*, at [56].

against advantages. The correct test for the assessment of such evidence, said Thorpe LJ, comes from a *dictum* of Butler-Sloss LJ:

> Family judges deal with increasingly difficult child cases and are much assisted in their decision-making process by professionals from other disciplines: medical, wider mental health and social work among others. The courts pay particular attention to the valuable contribution from paediatricians and child psychiatrists as well as others, but it is important to remember that the decision is that of the judge and not of the professional expert. Judges are well accustomed to assessing the conflicting evidence of experts.[76]

The principal difference between the types of evidence obtained in a medical or surveying case, and that presented in care proceedings, is that the former types are concerned with opinions on the correct factual inferences to draw from past or present facts ('causation' or 'state of affairs'), while the latter is concerned with value judgments on how best to act in relation to the present child, taking into account both the known facts about that child and her environment, and expectations of what constitutes 'best interests' or 'welfare'. The court is competent to make these value judgments because this is a role allocated to it in society, to determine factual and value-laden disputes. In doing this, the judge makes use of her own stock of common-sense judgments, probably honed by experience of working in Family cases. The experts are competent to make value judgments because their own disciplines have amassed experience, including evidence-based theories, on how certain factors are likely to result in certain outcomes. The judge's decision prevails primarily because this is a legal decision, rather than one made within the specialist's own discipline. Yates has suggested, however, that we should also have regard to the fact that the judge will have access to a wider range of evidence than will the expert.[77]

Hence, in *Re M (a child) (residence order)*,[78] the judge received a number of reports from C's social worker and child psychologist, in harmony with reports from the guardian and local authority, expressing clear reservations at the notion of returning C to her father, F. F and his new partner, L, already had six children and C had special needs disabilities. It was held by the Court of Appeal that the judge had accurately stated the extent of C's needs, and had concluded that the correct question was not whether

[76] *Re B* [1996] 1 FLR 667 (CA), at 674.

[77] C. Yates, 'Doctoring the Evidence: Medical Evidence in Child Custody Cases in Australia' (1986) 5 *Civil Justice Quarterly* 144, 148.

[78] *Re M (a child) (residence order)*, Court of Appeal, 18 September 2003.

someone else could provide better care for C, but whether F and L could provide appropriate care. The trial judge had given due reflection to this question. The case is relevant here because it illustrates that, although the experts are well placed to comment on C's care requirements, the question of where C is best placed is a question of social value, which is best determined by the judge.

3.5.6 The standard of care in professional negligence

The standard of care in professional negligence raises inferential issues that are general rather than specific. In most circumstances, the claimant in an action for negligence is entitled to expect that the defendant will have acted to the same standard as the 'reasonable man' would have done.[79] This standard is to be determined by the tribunal of fact, on the basis of its common-sense knowledge. This is an objective test, in that the claimant does not expect the standard of care to vary depending upon the idiosyncratic characteristics of the defendant at that moment.[80] While what the average person does could in principle be demonstrated empirically, for example through surveys, the 'reasonable man' is a purely legal construct.[81] This construct is informed both by precedent and by the personal views of appropriate conduct held by the tribunal: 'What to one judge may seem far fetched may seem to another both natural and probable.'[82]

However, where the defendant is exercising a specialist skill, the court will seek expert opinion on what the standard of care should be. How do we determine that standard? There are broadly two options: first, the court could set its own standard, based on what it feels society is entitled to expect from a person with that skill; or secondly, the court could use the standard set by the relevant profession itself. Neither of these options provides an entirely satisfactory solution.

If we take the first option, then the court is quite likely to set a standard higher or lower than that exercised by responsible practitioners. If the legal standard is set lower than the professional standard then the consequences will be indirect. An individual can practise below the threshold of

[79] *Vaughan* v. *Menlove* (1837) 3 Bing NC 468; Scott 244.

[80] *Nettleship* v. *Weston* [1971] 2 QB 691; [1971] 3 WLR 370; [1971] 3 All ER 581 (CA).

[81] M. Hutter and G. Teubner, 'Homo Juridicus and Homo Oeconomicus: Communicate Fictions', in T. Baums, K. Hopt and N. Horn (eds.), *Corporations, Capital Markets and Business in the Law* (Den Haag: Kluwer, 2000), p. 569.

[82] *Glasgow Corporation* v. *Muir* [1943] AC 448; [1943] 2 All ER 44; 1943 SC (HL), 3 at [1943] AC 457 (Lord Macmillan).

acceptability of her professional body or of her peers, and possibly receive disciplinary sanctions in that arena, but remain untouched at law. The eventual consequence of that might be the lowering of standards in the profession. If, on the other hand, the legal standard is set higher, then a direct conflict will be produced between the profession and the courts. Practitioners may be in good standing with their professional body but receive civil penalties for their practice. These penalties may in turn affect their ability to continue work, either directly, through loss of business, or indirectly, through loss of insurance cover. Outside the profession, the public will be presented with situations where professional conduct could be simultaneously unlawful and professionally acceptable. This conflict can be resolved in one of two ways: the courts could change their standard, or the profession could change its standard. This potentially could become a question of which institution has the most authority in society. The question of the correct legal standard of care in professional negligence is not one that can be addressed simply as a nice question of legal reasoning. It is one that would also have wide-ranging social consequences.

If we instead take the option that the court could use the standard set by the relevant profession itself, then we risk creating a situation in which the profession sets its own legal standard of conduct. It also gives professional bodies total control over the regulation of the professional conduct of their members, outside of the law. Unless the professional body is prepared to provide a representative to advise the court on acceptable practice in every instance, and the court agrees, then the task of advising the court falls to individuals within that profession. The very real danger then arises that members of a profession might close ranks in order to protect their own. If it is a question of fact whether a defendant's conduct was acceptable within her profession or discipline, then she need only produce sufficient fellow members who say that this practice is acceptable for her to defeat the claim. This potentially gives the case to the defendant, since the claimant is then unable to prove that the defendant's conduct was unacceptable by professional standards. Since the politically safe move for the courts in the face of expert conflict on the standard of care is to decline to comment, defendants in professional negligence actions are placed in a very strong position.

This second option is the one that has been adopted by the English courts following *Bolam*.[83] The test provided by that case for the standard

[83] *Bolam* v. *Friern Hospital Management Committee* [1957] 1 WLR 582; [1957] 2 All ER 118 (QB).

of care should be divided into two parts, which I call '*Bolam One*' and '*Bolam Two*'. *Bolam One* concerns how the tribunal of fact is to determine the standard of care for a specialist, where there is no dispute between specialists. It requires that the defendant meet '[T]he standard of the ordinary skilled man exercising and professing to have that special skill . . . It is sufficient if he exercises the ordinary skill of an ordinary competent man exercising that particular art.'[84] *Bolam Two* concerns how the tribunal of fact is to determine that standard when there exists a divergence of opinions among the specialists: 'A doctor is not guilty of negligence if he has acted in accordance with a practice accepted as proper by a responsible body of medical men skilled in that particular art.'[85] The *Bolam* tests apply only to questions of norms requiring expert opinion, and not to questions of fact.[86]

The risk inherent in the *Bolam* approach is that, in allowing a profession to define for itself what is an acceptable standard, the courts would both de facto and de iure delegate a key part of the decision making in a professional negligence case to the profession itself. Given the natural tendency in any community to close ranks against the outside to protect one of its own, it becomes extremely difficult for somebody who has been harmed, negligently or maliciously, by a member of the group to prove that the conduct was culpable by the standards of that group, since the group will define the standards by which the case will be heard. Under *Bolam Two*, a defendant need find only a few supportive colleagues, perhaps as few as two,[87] to mount an almost absolute defence.

It might seem obvious to say that the solution to this problem is to compromise: the court will receive expert advice on the appropriate standard of care, but will then determine that standard for itself. Ultimately, however, the question remains of whether the standard of care in professional negligence is that of the (normative) 'reasonable' member of that profession or of the (factual) 'typical' member. Extra-curially, Lord Woolf CJ has suggested that the judiciary may have been unduly deferential to the medical profession in the past, but that this would now change.[88]

[84] Ibid., at 121. [85] Ibid., at 121 paraphrasing *Hunter* v. *Hanley* 1955 SC 200.

[86] *Loveday* v. *Renton (No. 1)* [1989] 1 Med LR 117 (QB), at 182 (Stuart–Smith J); *Fallows* v. *Randle* [1997] 8 Med LR 160 (Stuart–Smith LJ).

[87] *De Freitas* v. *O'Brien* [1995] 6 Med LR 108 (CA).

[88] Lord Woolf, 'Are the Courts Excessively Deferential to the Medical Profession' (2001) 9 *Medical Law Review* 1–16.

Similar opinions have been expressed elsewhere in the Commonwealth,[89] and by the Privy Council,[90] which have declined to accept that a professionally accepted practice is reasonable in law solely as a consequence of that practice.

In *Bolitho*, Lord Browne-Wilkinson sought to clarify that the various terms, such as 'responsible', 'reasonable' and 'respectable', which had been used to describe whether the defendant's body of opinion should be accepted, all represented the same thing. They 'all show that the court has to be satisfied that the exponents of the body of opinion relied on can demonstrate that such opinion has a logical basis'.[91] Strictly, then, *Bolam Two* does provide an objective safeguard against the de facto autonomy of the professions. Although it is possible to show that a professional practice was unreasonable, what is the threshold for this unreasonableness? It would appear that the claimant must therefore be prepared to prove that the defendant's conduct was such that no reasonable doctor would have acted the same.[92] This in effect introduces *Wednesbury* Unreasonableness into negligence law,[93] despite the objection of Lord Browne-Wilkinson in *X (minors)*.[94] The difficulty with *Wednesbury* for our current purpose is the high evidential burden, 'overwhelming proof',[95] that it places on any claimant. There are very few examples where the court has declined to accept expert evidence of acceptable professional practice,[96] and these have been where the practice in question had little technical content, and its unreasonableness was considered a matter of common sense.

89 For Australia, see *Goode* v. *Nash* (1979) 21 SASR 419; *F* v. *R* (1983) 33 SASR 189, at 194; *Rogers* v. *Whitaker* [1992] ALJR 47. For Canada, see *Anderson* v. *Chasney* [1949] 4 DLR 71, aff'd 4 DLR 223; *Crits* v. *Sylvester* [1956] 1 DLR (2nd) 502, aff'd [1956] SCR 991; *Dorion* v. *Roberge* [1991] 1 SCR 374. For Malaysia, see *Chelliah a/l Manickam* v. *Kerajaan Malaysia* [1997] 2 AMR 1856; *Kamalam a/p Raman* v. *Eastern Plantation Agency (Johore)* [1996] 4 MLJ 674. For Singapore, see *The Management Corporation Strata Title Plan No. 1075* v. *RSP Architects Planners and another* High Court, 9 September 1998.

90 *Edward Wong Finance Co.* v. *Johnson Stokes and Master* [1983] 1 AC 296 (PC).

91 *Bolitho* v. *City and Hackney Health Authority* [1997] 4 All ER 771 (HL), at 777.

92 *Bolitho* v. *City and Hackney Health Authority* [1993] 4 Med L R 381 (CA) (Dillon LJ).

93 *Associated Provincial Picture Houses* v. *Wednesbury Corporation* [1948] 1 KB 223 at 233; [1947] 2 All ER 680 (HL): '[I]t may still be possible to say that, although the local authority have kept within the four corners of the matters which they ought to consider, they have nevertheless come to a conclusion so unreasonable that no reasonable authority could ever have come to it' (Lord Greene MR).

94 *X (minors)* v. *Bedfordshire County Council* [1995] 2 AC 633; [1995] 3 WLR 152 (HL), at 170.

95 *Associated Provincial Picture Houses.*

96 *Re The Herald of Free Enterprise*, Divisional Court, 18 December 1987; *Deeny* v. *Gooda Walker* [1996] Lloyds Reinsurance L Rep 183, at 207 (QB), on spiral underwriting at Lloyd's. Both cases were decided by Phillips J (later Master of the Rolls).

3.6 Expert bias

In this chapter so far I have been concerned with relatively high-level questions about the nature of expert disagreement: why courts, unusually within society, are intolerant of disagreements in the interpretation of a specific set of facts (Section 3.2); why, at least philosophically, we might expect experts to disagree about the sets of generalizations that they apply in a case (Section 3.3); why experts may genuinely disagree in how they apply those generalizations to a specific set of base facts (Section 3.4); how different types of question in litigation may give rise to different types and degrees of expert disagreement (Section 3.5).

This section turns to consider in much more detail the relationship between expert disagreement and civil litigation. Such disagreement is commonly perceived as a failing on the part of the experts or the lawyers who call them – as a manifestation of bias on the part of the expert.[97] Specifically, I identify, as a taxonomy, the possible causes (Section 3.6.1) and manifestations (Section 3.6.2) of expert disagreement in the context of litigation, illustrated with examples from England, the United States and France. Where expert disagreement is the result of bias, it may reasonably be viewed as constituting a threat to the sound administration of justice. It is therefore necessary to be clear, in a particular context, whether one considers an expert's disagreement to be the product of bias or not. In particular, it is necessary to be clear whether the disagreement represents personal bias or is a structural product of litigation (Section 3.6.3). Such structural bias may occur, for example, where the parties present only the impartially provided expert evidence that supports their case. If we confuse the phenomena of disagreement and bias, and do not understand the causes of each, then we risk confused analysis, and proposing ill-suited remedies.

3.6.1 Expert disagreement resulting from bias

There are three categories of interest that can be said to cause disagreement between experts: personal interest (Section 3.6.1.1), financial interest (Section 3.6.1.2) and intellectual interest (Section 3.6.1.3). These three categories of interest may exist externally to the instant litigation (which I term here 'predisposition'), or arise in direct relation to the litigation (which I term 'involvement'). The various forms of cause are considered in this subsection.

[97] P. Huber, *Galileo's Revenge: Junk Science in the Courtroom* (New York: Basic Books, 1991). See also examples of judicial opinions presented in Edmond, 'After Objectivity'.

3.6.1.1 Personal interest

An expert's personal interest may arise as either a predisposition (Section 3.6.1.1.1) or as involvement in the case (Section 3.6.1.1.2).

3.6.1.1.1 Personal predisposition Personal predisposition is where the formation of the expert's opinion is affected by personal factors that arise outside the instant litigation. Examples of this are moral opinions, personal relationships, membership of the same body as one of the parties, and other professional relationships. There are few clear examples of moral opinions affecting expert evidence in case law. One such example, from the United States of America, is the Wyoming state Family case of *Hertzler* v. *Hertzler*,[98] in which the main expert at trial, Mr Rhodes, who believed that two children had been sexually abused by their mother and her lesbian partner, was appointed by the father only after first establishing that Mr Rhodes had 'anti-gay bias'.[99] Under cross-examination Mr Rhodes conceded that his recommendation that the children should have no contact with their mother was a moral decision. This type of issue may be limited to those cases where the expert is required in effect to make a judgment based at least in part on personal values, such as in Child Law.

The issue of a pre-existing personal relationship arose in the English case of *Liverpool Roman Catholic Archdiocese and Trustees Inc.* v. *Goldberg*.[100] In that case, David Goldberg QC, a tax law specialist, sought to call a long-standing colleague, Mr Flesch, as an expert on professional practice. In a pre-trial review, Neuberger J ruled that as a matter of law and fact Mr Flesch's expert evidence was admissible, but that the issue of bias 'may well provide fertile cross-examination ground'. Neuberger J therefore felt that 'the judge deciding the case may discount Mr Flesch's evidence altogether on this ground, or at least view it with very considerable care'.[101] The importance of the pre-existing relationship should, according to Neuberger J, be treated as a question of fact rather than of

98 *Hertzler* v. *Hertzler* 1995 WY 206; 908 P2d 946.

99 S. Becker, 'Child Sexual Abuse Allegations Against a Lesbian or Gay Parent in a Custody or Visitation Dispute: Battling the Overt and Insidious Bias of Experts and Judges' (1996) 74 *Denver University Law Review* 75–158. In her article Becker declares an interest, in that she represented the mother in the case, Pamela Hertzler.

100 *Liverpool Roman Catholic Archdiocese and Trustees Inc.* v. *Goldberg (No. 2)*, Chancery Division, 2 March 2001; *Liverpool Roman Catholic Archdiocese and Trustees Inc.* v. *Goldberg (No. 3)* [2001] 1 WLR 2337; [2001] 4 All ER 950 (HC).

101 *Liverpool RC Archdiocese (No. 2)*.

law. The trial judge, Evans-Lombe J, subsequently reviewed the report produced by Mr Flesch.[102] In that report Flesch had written that, 'I should say that my personal sympathies are engaged to a greater degree than would probably be normal with an expert witness.' Evans-Lombe J therefore held the evidence to be inadmissible 'on grounds of public policy that justice must be seen to be done as well as done'. Where it is demonstrated that there exists a relationship between the proposed expert and the party calling him, which a reasonable observer might think was capable of affecting the views of the expert so as to make him unduly favourable, his evidence should not be admitted, however unbiased the conclusions of the expert might probably be. The question is one of fact, namely the extent and nature of the relationship between the proposed witness and the party.

Pre-disposition may also arise where the expert is associated with one of the parties by virtue of membership of an organization, such as a professional or public body. This is most likely to arise where an assessor or expert has been appointed by the court, or where a party from body *A* has appointed an expert who is also from body *A*. A party would not knowingly appoint an expert who might be predisposed towards the opposing party in this way. This situation may, however, occur where court experts are used. An extreme example occurred in the criminal case of *Bönisch* v. *Austria*,[103] where the Austrian Bundesanstalt für Lebensmitteluntersuchung ('Federal Food Control Institute') not only instigated the prosecution of Mr Bönisch, but then also served as a court expert.[104] In the later case of *Brandstetter*, the European Court has clarified that the scenario in *Bönisch* was extreme, and there must be justifiable concerns regarding apparent bias before the expert should be disqualified.[105] There is extensive, although far from straightforward, English case law on whether tribunal members are biased by virtue of their membership of a body appearing before them.[106] The guiding principle in English law, as before the European Court, would appear to be that the existence of such institutional bias should be treated as a question of fact.

An expert may have additional professional relationships with their client, which began prior to the instant litigation. That relationship may not be contractual. The most likely example of this is where a party is being treated by a medical practitioner who is also appearing as an expert

[102] *Liverpool RC Archdiocese (No. 3)*.

[103] *Bönisch* v. *Austria* Ser. A No. 92 (1985) 9 EHRR 191. [104] *Bönisch*, at [33].

[105] *Brandstetter* v. *Austria* Ser. A No. 211 (1993) 15 EHRR 378.

[106] P. Craig, *Administrative Law*, 5th edn (London: Sweet and Maxwell, 2003), pp. 459–61.

in her case. A potential danger here is that a medical expert may see their testimony as a way of achieving their clinical aims.[107]

3.6.1.1.2 Personal involvement The close association of the expert with a case may give rise to sympathy with the instructing party which may in turn give rise to conscious or unconscious adaptation of the expert's opinion: 'Human nature being what it is, there is a tendency to want the side that hired you to win the contest.'[108] This may be particularly true where the subject is an emotive one, such as the recovery of damages in personal injury or medical negligence litigation, or where the expert also has a role in the treatment of the patient. In such cases, the expert may be able to justify bias to herself ethically, as success for the claimant will have considerable personal benefits for the claimant.

In the English case of *Vernon* v. *Bosley (No. 2)*, in which the two claimants' experts were shown to have acceded to a solicitors' request for reports to be adapted, two mitigating circumstances were identified by Thorpe LJ. First, they had an extensive relationship with their patient and had been 'sucked into' the personal injury litigation, with deleterious effects on their objectivity as experts. Similar concerns had been expressed by the trial judge, Sedley J, about the defendant's experts. Secondly, neither was fully aware of his duties as an expert in Children Act proceedings.[109]

3.6.1.2 Financial interest

Financial interest, like personal interest, may arise from predisposition (Section 3.6.1.2.1)) or involvement (3.6.1.2.2).

3.6.1.2.1 Financial predisposition There are at least three forms of potential financial predisposition for an expert: where the expert has a shareholding or similar interest in one of the parties, where the expert is an employee of one of the parties, and where the expert wishes to build a career as an expert. Examples of cases in which the expert is a shareholder in one of the parties instructing her would appear to be uncommon. This

[107] E.g. M. King, 'An Autopoietic Approach to the Problems Presented by Parental Alienation Syndrome' (2002) 13 *Journal of Forensic Psychiatry* 609–35.

[108] T. Bingham, 'Hired Gun Takes a Bullet' (2005) 5 *Building* 50.

[109] *Vernon* v. *Bosley (No. 2)* [1999] QB 18; [1997] 1 All ER 614, at 649. The implication of this second circumstance would appear to be that, while Thorpe LJ found such instructions and resulting partisan reports to be quite unacceptable in Children Act proceedings before the Family court, he might not have such concerns about such conduct before the Queen's Bench or Chancery courts.

is likely to be because a party would be ill advised to instruct an expert whom it knew was a shareholder and an expert would be ill advised to accept such an instruction. In cases where a judge has been found to be a shareholder in one of the parties, that judge has been automatically recused.[110] Although such automatic recusal would appear only to apply where it is the judge who holds a financial interest,[111] it is likely that significant prejudicial weight would be given to an expert's testimony where that expert similarly held a pecuniary interest.

Conscious expert disagreement may arise where the expert is employed by the party on an ongoing basis, beyond the scope of the immediate litigation. What we should expect to see is that the courts will treat such relationships as being at least as likely to give rise to bias as those in which the expert has simply been paid, since the expert both has a duty to her employer and may not wish to endanger her employment. That employment may be endangered directly through actual or constructive dismissal,[112] or indirectly because the continuity of the business may depend on the expertise provided.

The question of whether an 'in-house' expert could be 'impartial and independent' had already arisen in the consultation following the publication of Lord Woolf's *Interim Report* in 1995,[113] but was not directly addressed in the 1996 *Final Report.*[114] The question arose again before Lord Woolf MR in *Field* v. *Leeds City Council*,[115] where the council wished to call one of its employees as an expert. Lord Woolf held that the correct course of action was not simply to reject the request that the employee provide expert evidence, but rather to indicate that, on the information provided, the judge could not assent to him as a witness. The council would then be able to attempt to satisfy the court that its employee had full knowledge of what was required of an expert giving evidence before the court, and that he was fully familiar with the need for objectivity. Such awareness could be evidenced, for example, by a training course. Once

110 *Dimes* v. *Proprietors of Grand Junction Canal* (1852) 3 HL Cas 759, at 793–4.

111 *R.* v. *Gough* [1993] AC 646, at 661; [1993] 2 WLR 883; [1993] 2 All ER 724.

112 A situation does not yet appear to have arisen in which an employment tribunal has considered that a person was wrongfully dismissed because she appeared as an expert for her employer.

113 Lord Woolf, *Access to Justice: Interim Report* (London: Her Majesty's Stationery Office, 1995).

114 Lord Woolf, *Access to Justice: Final Report* (London: Her Majesty's Stationery Office, 1996), at [13.38]–[13.40].

115 *Field* v. *Leeds City Council* [1999] CPLR 833.

admitted as evidence, the expert's employment would go to the question of weight. This approach has been developed further by the Court of Appeal in *ES* and *DN*.[116] In both cases, professional defendants have been permitted to give expert advice on whether their own conduct was negligent, on the basis that expert interest goes to cogency rather than admissibility.

Lord Woolf's decision in *Field* turns on the court being satisfied that the expert is able to fulfil her overriding duty to the court. It may, however, be overly optimistic in its belief that, if the employee expert is able to demonstrate that she is aware of her overriding duty, and is prepared to state her compliance with that duty in any report under CPR r. 35.10, then the court should be happy to admit the evidence. The employee may be placed in an ethically compromised position, since she has both a contractual duty to further the interests of her employer and a contractual duty to act as an expert within the law, when reasonably asked to do so by her employer. We might hope that the employer and employee would see that the best interests of the employer are served by the employee acting lawfully as an expert. Any term that required that the employee act illegally, for example by breaching the overriding duty of the expert to the court under CPR r. 35.3, would surely be void for illegality.

Where the specialist wishes to develop her work as an expert as an ongoing source of income, it may be in her interests to gain a reputation as an expert who assists her instructing party to the greatest possible extent. The expert may also choose to specialize, for example as either a claimant's or a defendant's expert: 'The legal system's preference for proven winners encourages such repeat witnessing, although it substantially narrows the range of expertise that finds its way to court.'[117] The expert therefore has a predisposition interest in assisting her client in winning whatever case she becomes engaged in.

3.6.1.2.2 Financial involvement The most likely form of financial involvement is where the expert's payment depends, directly or indirectly, on the outcome of the case. There is a common assumption that payment will induce a 'natural bias to do something serviceable for those

[116] *ES* v. *Chesterfield North Derbyshire Royal Hospital NHS Trust* [2003] EWCA Civ 1284; *DN* v. *Greenwich LBC* [2004] EWCA Civ 1659.

[117] S. Jasanoff, *Science at the Bar: Law, Science and Technology in America* (Cambridge MA: Harvard University Press, 1995), pp. 46–7.

who employ you and adequately remunerate you'.[118] Payment for taking on the role of an expert in the litigation context is almost inevitable, and there is little that can be done to avoid it.[119] Although we might have an alternative arrangement where the state pays for the instruction of experts, in the same way that it may do for the instruction of solicitors and counsel under Legal Aid for the poorest litigants, such an arrangement would be counter to the current trend of scaling down Legal Aid expenditure. Potentially this places us in a position where we are saying that all party experts will disagree with one another in favour of their parties, simply by virtue of their being paid by their instructing party. If this is true, then we must accept that the only way that we might begin to remove such artificial disagreement is to remove party experts. Alternatively, we might accept artificial disagreement as a price worth paying for the use of party experts.

Where the expert is not only paid to provide her opinion, but depends for her payment on the success of the litigation, then not only is there an increased likelihood that the expert will be consciously biased, but the effect of that bias is likely to be more significant. Prior to 1990, champerty (making payment conditional on success) as well as the related activity of maintenance (funding of litigation by a third party with no interest in that litigation) had been contrary at common law to the interests of the administration of justice. In consequence, contracts relying on maintenance or champerty were unenforceable at law, and prior to 1967 they were also both crimes and torts.[120] Since 1990, however, the Lord Chancellor has permitted solicitors and barristers to enter into civil action under conditional fee agreements (CFAs).[121] Under a CFA, payment to the service provider is based on the normal professional rate ('conditional normal fee agreement') or the normal fee plus a success uplift ('conditional uplift agreement') if their instructing party is successful. Parliament permitted CFAs only between litigants and solicitors and barristers.[122]

[118] *Abinger (Lord)* v. *Ashton* (1873) 17 LR Eq 373 (Lord Jessell MR).

[119] In *McTear* v. *Imperial Tobacco Ltd* 2005 2 SC 1, the fact that the claimant's experts acted without payment raised concerns about possible bias. The experts were clearly acting out of sympathy with the claimant's cause.

[120] *R. (Factortame)* v. *Secretary of State for Transport, Local Government and the Regions (No. 8)* [2002] EWCA Civ 932; [2003] QB 381; [2002] 3 WLR 1104; [2002] 4 All ER 97, at [31].

[121] See A. Zuckerman, *Civil Procedure: Principles of Practice*, 2nd edn (London: Sweet and Maxwell, 2006), [26.142]–[26.190], for an overview of CFAs.

[122] Courts and Legal Services Act 1990 ss. 58 and 58A, as amended by Access to Justice Act 1999 s. 27, provided the Lord Chancellor with the necessary powers to introduce statutory instruments relating to conditional fee agreements.

There is no provision for others professionally involved in the support of litigation, such as litigation services provided by non-lawyers and experts.

Because of the increased risk that the expert's overriding duty to the court might be compromised, the Protocol for the Instruction of Experts prohibits both conditional and contingency fee agreements.[123] In the absence of expert CFAs, where the litigant has entered into a CFA with her solicitor because she cannot pay in advance, or would not be able to pay at all if she lost, situations may arise where either the solicitor must bear the cost of disbursements to experts, or the litigant cannot have access to an expert. Solicitors may be unwilling to pay disbursements under a CFA because, unlike with the solicitors' own fees, these represent expenditure of assets rather than loss of revenue.

The English civil courts have a duty to ensure 'as far as is practicable' that all parties to a dispute are 'on an equal footing',[124] with equal opportunity to present evidence, including expertise. Through its wide discretionary case management powers, including control over costs, the court does in principle have the opportunity to direct that one party pays for another's experts. It is more likely, however, to direct that one party pays for a single expert to be jointly instructed,[125] or simply shares its expert's report with the other party.[126] The extent to which the court would intervene on this unequal footing is likely to depend on factors that would include the size of the discrepancy in resources, the effect of inability to access expertise on the litigant's case, and the prima facie merits of the case. However, there appear to be no reported cases in which such a situation has yet arisen. Two norms of civil justice, both relatively new, appear to come into conflict in this situation. On the one side, all but the poorest individuals in society are expected to fund their own litigation, including the use of experts where appropriate, with CFAs being the default option in money claims for those without sufficient reserve funds. On the other side, experts are increasingly expected to be neutral, and involvement in CFAs would compromise at least the perception of neutrality.

[123] Civil Justice Council, *Protocol for the Instruction of Experts to Give Evidence in Civil Claims* (London: 2005), [7.6]. Although permissible in the United States, professional ethical concerns do exist: B. Sales and D. Shuman, *Experts in Court: Reconciling Law, Science, and Professional Knowledge* (Washington DC: American Psychological Association, 2005), p. 139.

[124] CPR r. 1.1(2)(a). [125] CPR r. 35.7 [126] CPR r. 35.9.

3.6.1.3 Intellectual interest

The third form of interest, in the form of intellectual predisposition, may arise in areas where there is genuine scope for disagreement. The expert may believe that a particular set of facts should be interpreted using a particular method or within the context of a particular theory, and the expert's standing, either as an expert or within her own speciality, may be positively or adversely affected depending on the outcome of a case. Thus, if I am a leading authority that an injury of type *I* is caused by event *E*, then every time that a court concludes that an *I* was caused by an *E*, my standing in my profession and as an expert is increased. Conversely, if courts were to conclude that *I* was not caused by *E*, then this would be likely to affect my standing adversely. Intellectual predisposition is likely here also to have financial repercussions, and so it would be in both my intellectual and financial interests to encourage the court to find that *E* causes *I*.

Intellectual predisposition is significant in adversarial litigation because it means that a litigant should be able to identify an expert who can be reasonably expected to give a favourable opinion. Separately, intellectual predisposition is significant where a single joint expert or court expert is appointed, since there is no counter-expert to offset any predisposition on the part of the one expert. The problem of intellectual predisposition or involvement is most likely to arise where an expert has been engaged who is eminent among her peers. In terms of predisposition, this is because the expert's eminence is likely to rest upon a particular view of how such cases should be interpreted. In terms of involvement, an eminent expert is particularly likely to benefit from, or be harmed by, the outcome of a case in which she testifies. For example, when the Crown engaged Professor Sir Roy Meadow as an expert in several multiple infant murder cases at the end of the last century,[127] it did so not only in the knowledge that a substantial part of Meadow's career had been built on the identification of a particular form of physical abuse ('Munchausen's Syndrome by Proxy'), but almost certainly in the expectation that he would apply a line of reasoning known as 'Meadow's Law': 'One sudden infant death is a tragedy, two is suspicious and three is murder unless proved otherwise.'[128] If we were to say that a party should not employ an expert because he has a personal interest of

[127] E.g. *R.* v. *Clark (Sally)* [2003] EWCA Crim 1020; *R.* v. *Cannings* (Angela) [2004] EWCA Crim 1; [2004] 1 WLR 2607.

[128] R. Meadow (ed.), *The ABC of Child Abuse*, 3rd edn (London: BMJ Publishing, 1997), p. 29.

this nature in a case, then we run the danger of effectively saying that a whole section of experts, who are most likely to be leaders in their field, are to be excluded from acting as experts.

3.6.2 *The manifestations of actual bias*

Although the potential causes of bias may exist in relation to an expert in a case, it does not necessarily follow that there is actual bias. Actual bias may manifest itself in one of two ways: consciously (Section 3.6.2.1) or unconsciously (Section 3.6.2.2).[129] We may reasonably consider that greater ethical responsibility attaches to conscious bias, since it requires the party actively to amend the opinion that they might otherwise have reached. However, ethical considerations may also attach to unconscious bias, since some of the forms of unconscious bias can be avoided or made less likely through the taking of responsible steps. We may therefore wish to consider whether or how we should view differently experts who have exhibited conscious bias, from those who have recklessly or consciously not taken methodological steps that would have reduced the risk of unconscious bias.

3.6.2.1 Conscious bias

By 'conscious bias', I mean a situation where the expert chooses to adapt her opinion in order to favour one of the parties. The most common reason for conscious expert bias would appear to be that the expert sees this as being part of her duty towards her party, for which she is financially well remunerated.[130] There are a few examples of experts producing or adjusting reports in direct response to intervention by their party's lawyers. For example, in *Vernon* v. *Bosley (No. 2)*, the Court of Appeal reviewed its draft judgment on damages awarded to the plaintiff in a personal injury action before the Queen's Bench, after documents were anonymously provided to the defendant's counsel, which included correspondence indicating that the plaintiff's experts had, at the plaintiff's solicitor's request, produced reports in related Family proceedings tailored to support the litigation requirements of the plaintiff. Similarly, in *Whitehouse* v. *Jordan*,[131] it was

129 Alternatively, we might speak of 'hot' and 'cold' biases, where hot biases stem from desires, motivations, interests or emotions, and cold biases reside in purely cognitive, intellectual processes: Goldman, *Knowledge*, p. 230.

130 J. Langbein, 'The German Advantage in Civil Procedure' (1985) 52 *University of Chicago Law Review* 823–66, at 835.

131 *Whitehouse* v. *Jordan* [1981] 1 WLR 246 (HL), at 256.

found that an expert report had been 'settled' (amended) by counsel.[132] Because draft expert reports produced with an eye to litigation are usually protected by litigation privilege, we are rarely able to see how an expert's report has changed in the course of preparation for disclosure.

3.6.2.2 Unconscious bias

3.6.2.2.1 The effect of cognitive heuristic biases on expert fact finding Experimental work by cognitive psychologists such as Nisbett and Ross,[133] and Kahneman, Slovic and Tversky,[134] suggests that human reasoning does not even approximate to normative guidelines of logic, probability and confirmation theory, either in method or in results. Subjects weight salient and available information more heavily in their decision making than rationalist theories indicate that they should. Salience factors include concreteness (the detail with which things are described, even if irrelevant detail), proximity, emotional interest and perceptual biases. Availability factors include biases in exposure and attention to data, and biases in memory retrieval. Because of the representativeness heuristic, subjects assume that similar events have similar causes, without regard to base rates of the scientific relevance of similarities. The heuristics of salience and availability give rise to the phenomenon of confirmation bias (belief perseverance), in which individuals are more likely to accept information that confirms beliefs that they already hold.[135] This is partly because memory retrieval and perceptual attention operate in such a way that the evidence for beliefs already held is more available and salient, and therefore is weighted more heavily, than the evidence against them.[136]

Should we assume experts, particularly scientists, to be subject to such cognitive biases? The answer in summary would appear to be that scientific method is designed to reduce, although not remove, the effect of many of these heuristics. This is one of the senses in which we might accept

132 *Whitehouse* v. *Jordan* [1980] 1 All ER 650 (CA), at 654.

133 R. Nisbett and L. Ross, *Human Inference: Strategies and Shortcomings of Social Judgment* (Englewood Cliffs NJ: Prentice Hall, 1980).

134 D. Kahneman, P. Slovic and A. Tversky (eds.), *Judgment under Uncertainty: Heuristics and Biases* (Cambridge: Cambridge University Press, 1982).

135 One effect of this is that scientists, who do not have time to check the results of all published scientific research, may concentrate their efforts on checking those results that would go against their current beliefs. Similarly, judges and barristers may not spend much time considering whether the current law is correctly understood when it supports their argument or conclusion.

136 M. Solomon, 'Scientific Rationality and Human Reasoning' (1992) 59 *Philosophy of Science* 439–55, 439–40.

Haack saying that scientific investigative method is the same as everyday investigative method 'only more so' (Section 2.3.2). For example scientific reasoning makes greater use of statistics than does everyday reasoning, and scientists tend to make decisions more in teams than people do in everyday life, and teamwork provides opportunities for correction of some errors (and opportunities for creating others).[137]

At the level of scientific communities, these biases may cancel one another out, but the disagreement between scientists that they artificially produce may provide a stimulus to rigorous scientific investigation and the development of knowledge: 'When the community is characterized by diversity, we benefit from having our hypotheses subjected to a wide range of criticism. Despite the fact that each individual scientist may be partial, collectively the scientific community is able to reach a consensus about which view is epistemically superior.'[138] When we come, in Chapters 5 to 7, to consider the recurring theme of the relative merits of single and multiple experts, it will be worth remembering that, within the philosophy of science, there is a respectable body of opinion that would hold that a group of experts will form a less biased opinion than an individual expert.

It is nevertheless worth spending a little time considering three ways in which these heuristic biases may affect scientific fact finding. The first two, the 'interpreter effect' (Section 3.6.2.2.2) and 'observer effect' (3.6.2.2.3), are both types of behaviour observed in the conducting of scientific experiments, where the experimenter comes to err in favour of her hypothesis when conducting experiments.[139] The third, the 'fallacy of verification' (3.6.2.2.4), is where one sets up only those experiments that favour confirming the hypothesis.

3.6.2.2.2 Interpreter effect The interpreter effect occurs where experimenters approach an experiment with the belief that their hypothesis will be borne out by their experiment. As a result of this expectation they tend

[137] Ibid., at 442. It is worth considering whether legal fact finding by juries or panels of judges is similarly less susceptible to cognitive heuristic errors than when a judge sits alone.

[138] K. Brad Wray, 'Science, Biases, and the Threat of Global Pessimism' (2001) 68 *Philosophy of Science* S467–S478, at S476. Compare Solomon, 'Scientific Rationality'; Kitcher, *Advancement of Science;* M. Solomon, *Social Empiricism* (Cambridge MA: MIT Press, 2001).

[139] A. Zuckerman, 'Miscarriage of Justice – A Root Treatment' [1992] *Criminal Law Review* 323–45, at 331, citing R. Rosenthal, 'Interpersonal Expectations: Effects of the Experimenter's Hypothesis', in R. Rosenthal and R. Rosnow (eds.), *Artifact in Behavioral Research* (New York: Academic Press, 1969), pp. 181–277, pp. 181–84.

to make mistakes in interpretation that favour their hypothesis, and tend to overlook interpretations unfavourable to their hypothesis. For example, in *B (Child)* the court considered whether, at the request of the fathers of the two children involved, it should order that the children be immunized with the Measles-Mumps-Rubella (MMR) vaccine, against the wishes of the children's mothers.[140] The trial judge, Sumner J, supported by the Court of Appeal, was highly critical of the expertise of Dr Donegan, a general practitioner and homeopath. He held that she had allowed her deeply held feelings on the subject of immunization to overrule the duty owed to the court to give objective evidence: 'Dr Donegan's report was based on no independent research, and most of the published papers cited by her in support of her views turned out either to support the contrary position or at least to give no support to her own.'[141]

The same effect may be operating in the work of expert fingerprint examiners. A psychology experiment by Dror and Charlton suggests that the identifications made by fingerprint examiners are prone to cognitive error, and that one of the main causes of that error is the availability of contextual information.[142] Where experts are provided with contextual information, and are asked to disregard it in making their identification, the experiment indicated that the contextual material was still taken into account. This would suggest that the examiners were making the identifications that contextual factors were directing them to expect to make.

3.6.2.2.3 Observer effect The observer effect is where belief in one's hypothesis leads to errors in observing and recording the results of experiments. A leading example is the homeopathic research of a team of scientists, led by Benveniste, who claimed to have obtained results whereby water that once contained a certain substance, and that then had that substance removed, continued to behave as if the substance were present.[143] Beneviste's team concluded that the water retained a 'memory' of that substance. The scientific journal *Nature* dispatched a team, which included a stage magician, to observe the conduct of the experiments. The team

[140] *B (Child)* [2003] EWCA Civ 1148, upholding *A* v. *B* [2003] EWHC 1376 Fam.

[141] *B (Child)*, at [6].

[142] I. Dror and D. Charlton, 'Why Experts Make Errors' (2006) 56 *Journal of Forensic Identification* 600–16; I. Dror, D. Charlton and A. Peron, 'Contextual Information Renders Experts Vulnerable to Making Erroneous Identifications' (2006) 156 *Forensic Science International* 74–8.

[143] J. Maddox, J. Randi and W. Stewart, '"High–Dilution" Experiments a Delusion' (1998) 334 (6180) *Nature* 287.

found that the results arose from basic mistakes in observation and calculations of data. The relevant experiments had been conducted entirely by one member of Benveniste's team, Elisabeth Davenas, who had a special interest in homeopathy. The *Nature* team concluded that she had examined very small samples of data on each occasion, and had discarded data that she felt to be insignificant. The observer effect differs from the Interpreter Effect in that in the former the fact finder excludes data that do not confirm her theory (she may, for example, find reasons for why those particular data should be considered poor-quality), while in the latter the fact finder excludes explanations for those data that do not confirm her original expectation.

3.6.2.2.4 The fallacy of verification The fallacy of verification arises where the experimenter designs experiments with the purpose of showing that the hypothesis is true. In a legal context an expert might, for example, conduct a series of experiments that show that the defendant's car could have caused the damage to the claimant's wall. The difficulty with this approach, raised by Popper in his proposal for an alternative approach based on falsification, is that it does not demonstrate that another hypothesis could not equally be the case.[144] This fallacy is likely to be encountered in criminal and intelligence investigations,[145] where officers actively seek out evidence that confirms their hypothesis, rather than also looking for evidence that might refute it.

3.6.3 Personal and structural bias

The third factor to consider in describing the phenomena of bias is whether the bias that we perceive is personal (i.e. it resides with the expert) or structural (i.e. it is only apparent within the structural context of a given litigation model). Personal bias is where the individual expert is presenting an opinion that is affected by an interest that she holds, whether personal, financial or intellectual. Structural bias is a fundamentally different phenomenon, where the expert is presenting an opinion that is free from any interest, but which clearly supports the version of the facts presented by her instructing party, to an extent which a reasonable onlooker

[144] Popper, *Logic.*

[145] Compare J. Jackson, 'The Effect of Legal Culture and Proof in Decisions to Prosecute' (2004) 3 *Law Probability and Risk* 109–31, 124–5; A. Zuckerman, 'Coercion and the Judicial Ascertainment of Truth' (1989) 23 *Israel Law Review* 357–74, 363–9.

might conclude is greater than would arise if the expert were neutral. This structural bias occurs where the party is free to appoint whichever expert she chooses.[146] The party can consult as many experts as she chooses or can afford, until she finds one who fully supports her case, free from any interest. Because of the protection provided by litigation privilege, the court will not become aware of the number of experts consulted. This phenomenon is known as 'expert shopping', and has been practised in England since at least the middle of the nineteenth century.[147]

There are two forms of expert shopping, which in practice overlap. In the first, the party obtains a series of expert opinions until she receives one that is favourable to her case. The fact that the party has obtained a number of expert opinions other than those presented in evidence is shielded from the court and the other parties by litigation privilege. In the second form, the party goes to the expert already knowing from the expert's reputation that she will support the party's case. There are two main advantages to the parties in expert shopping. The first is that the party is able to obtain the expert opinion that best supports their case. The second is that the party is able to use an expert who genuinely holds the opinion that she presents, rather than adapting the opinion to meet the requirements of the party. This means that the expert can maintain her opinion with integrity at pre-trial meetings between experts and under cross-examination, and in full compliance with any overriding duty to the court that may arise, for example, under r. 35.3 of the CPR.

We might expect that over time such experts would become known to judges. Although it would be difficult to rule their evidence inadmissible, it could be subject to rigorous cross-examination by counsel and

[146] We should be careful not to confuse personal and structural bias, to produce an argument along the lines of 'because we know that scientists are affected by personal cognitive biases anyway, we should not worry that the adversarial process also imposes biases'. Compare M. Redmayne, *Expert Evidence and Criminal Justice* (Oxford: Oxford University Press, 2001), p. 202, who addresses the question 'If bias affects all scientific opinion, is there any point in worrying about the biases produced by adversary expertise?'

[147] *Thorn v. Worthing Skating Rink Co.* (1877) 6 ChD 415. Redmayne, *Expert Evidence*, pp. 201–2, suggests that the effect of expert shopping is to take expert opinions from the tails of a 'bell curve' distribution of the possible range of expert opinions. While this analogy is useful as an initial illustration of the problem of expert shopping, it unfortunately becomes problematic when we consider exactly whose distribution we are examining. When we say that there is a range of expert opinion, we do not usually mean a range in the same way that we might say that there is a range of claim values or ages of judges.

examination by the judge. However, judges may be reluctant to take this approach, as it is not clear that the Court of Appeal would recognize a judge's opinion that an expert is biased on the basis of experience over a series of cases, rather than in relation to the current case. Instead, and somewhat ironically, the judge might have to recuse herself from hearing a case where such an expert was to give evidence, unless evidence is available of a previous case in which the expert's evidence was rejected.

The fact that a party only adduces expertise that supports her case does not necessarily mean that she has selected her opinions to be favourable to her. It may alternatively mean that the party has continued with the action because she has received genuinely favourable opinions, and that if unfavourable opinions had been received she would have settled before trial.

3.7 Conclusion

This chapter has addressed three related questions: why does it matter to judicial fact finders that experts disagree, why do experts disagree, and what do we mean when we say that experts are biased? At root, the problem of deciding between divergent expert evidence should be epistemologically the same as that of assessing congruent expert evidence: 'How do I know that I am drawing justified inferences from the evidence of this expert?', which in turn raises the question of how I can know that the expert's inferences are themselves justified. But of course in practice the court will have few qualms about accepting the evidence of a single expert, without the need for a detailed assessment of that evidence.[148] As the dissection of the concepts of disagreement and bias in this chapter illustrate, to remove competing expert evidence does not of itself remove the problems of expert disagreement and bias. It may simply remove the issues from the sight of the tribunal, and provide false certainty. It is even possible that, under the categories of bias introduced in Section 3.6, all of the experts who might be called to testify should be classified correctly as biased.

This takes us to an epistemological issue with expert evidence that does not lend itself to simple resolution, but which will recur in the remainder of this book. Almost all experts in the civil courts are specialists who,

[148] Under what circumstances a non-expert tribunal of fact can be said to be able to reject validly the opinion of a single expert is a recurring chestnut in English and continental European jurisprudence.

when not involved in litigation, are engaged in communities of practice. The knowledge that an expert possesses is therefore the product of social epistemology: the knowledge is to some extent justified by virtue of being accepted by the community. By extension, but in a weaker sense, we might say that if there is a range of opinions accepted by the expert community, then the courts should be more inclined to favour the opinion that is most widely accepted. We should also like to believe that it is also the product of a veritistic epistemology: the belief is justified because it is true.[149] It is possible to imagine situations in which an expert presents evidence to a court that it concludes to be true, but which is not accepted by any of her peers as justified. First, as a question of principle, should the court follow the evidence that it believes to be true, or the evidence that is accepted by the expert community to be true? Secondly, as a question of practice, how does the court establish that the lone expert's voice is the true one? These may seem to be rather nice questions, of interest only to legal philosophers and epistemologists. But in Chapter 4, and again in Chapter 7, we encounter the 1993 decision of the United States Supreme Court in the case of *Daubert* – which dominates expert evidence practice and scholarship in the United States – and one of the fundamental issues that lies beneath the surface of *Daubert* is whether the assessment of expert evidence is fundamentally a question of epistemology or of politics.

Chapters 1 to 3 have taken us through developing an answer to the question of how a non-specialist court can accurately determine facts that require specialist knowledge. In summary, expert evidence is a special form of evidence generally, and presents some particular difficulties for judicial assessment. Chapters 5 to 7 consider the question of how we should arrange our legal processes to support best our expectations of accurate fact determination, and other procedural goals. Chapter 4 links the first question, of epistemic competence, to this second question, of procedural arrangement, and begins to address the second question by considering the non-epistemological factors that may affect our approach to designing procedural provisions for expert evidence.

[149] Goldman, *Knowledge*, pp. 4–5.

4

Non-epistemological factors in determining the role of the expert

4.1 Introduction

An explanatory theory of evidence generally, or expert evidence specifically, might be concerned solely with identifying arrangements that are optimal for accurate fact determination.[1] However, evidential arrangements are inextricably linked to non-epistemological questions about the political, moral and cultural values that ought to be promoted through the procedural activity of fact finding.[2] In Chapters 1 to 3, I explored the extent to which it can validly be said that the non-expert tribunal of fact is epistemologically competent to assess the evidence of experts. I proposed a basis for such competence, based on a common set of evidential techniques. Any account of how the court descriptively does, or normatively should, approach the assessment of expert evidence should be given in the context of this theory of limited epistemic competence. It is both a necessary preliminary point, to demonstrate that the court is able to assess expert evidence, and an analytical framework within which to think about the fact-finding effectiveness of various approaches to presenting and assessing expert evidence.

Alongside this epistemological account runs an understanding of the non-epistemological factors that contribute to defining expectations of the role of the expert, held by those involved in the litigation process.[3] These factors may shape both the normative procedural provisions for

1 Alternatively, evidence law should be optimized for error avoidance: A. Stein, *Foundations of Evidence Law* (Oxford: Oxford University Press, 2005).

2 E.g. H. Ho, *A Philosophy of Evidence Law: Justice in the Search for Truth* (Oxford: Oxford University Press, 2008); L. Laudan, *Truth, Error and Criminal Law – An Essay in Legal Epistemology* (Cambridge: Cambridge University Press, 2006); Stein, *Foundations.*

3 Most previous work on the role of political, moral and cultural values in evidence and procedure has been in relation to criminal rather than civil justice, e.g. J. Jackson, 'The Effect of Legal Culture and Proof in Decisions to Prosecute' (2004) 3 *Law Probability and Risk* 109–31; M. Damaška, 'Evidentiary Barriers to Conviction and Two Models of Criminal Procedure: A Comparative Study' (1973) 121 *University of Pennsylvania Law Review* 506–89.

the way in which experts are to be used, and the way in which parties and the experts themselves act within the context of those provisions. They help us to define the procedural and evidential system within which the litigation is being conducted. I do not mean to suggest that epistemology is not central to understanding the perceived problems with expertise, as Edmond and Mercer have done,[4] and that we should look instead at another explanation for the problems. For Edmond and Mercer, this is a sociological explanation. Rather, I am proposing that epistemology alone will not provide us with an understanding of, and possible solutions to, these perceived problems. Epistemology may, for example, take us to a point where we advise that certain expert roles would be better suited to a specific subject matter than other roles, but that final selection is made on the basis of non-epistemological factors that assist in determining which expert roles are appropriate.

Although we may be able to assess in the abstract the merits and demerits of any given procedural arrangement for expert evidence in relation to the court's likely ability to assess that evidence accurately, this does not tell us how well that procedural arrangement is likely to operate in a particular procedural system. There are some superficial similarities between this argument and one presented in comparative law, particularly by Legrand, that the operations of legal systems, in both substantive and procedural law, are so culturally embedded that it is not possible to transplant an element of one legal system into another legal system, and similarly that legal systems cannot be forced to converge, for example at the insistence of legislators.[5] This stands in contrast to a relatively well-established view that, as legal systems develop, they are constantly borrowing concepts or approaches from other legal systems.[6]

But Legrand's argument can only be taken so far. Empirically we know that legal systems do borrow from other legal systems. It also seems relatively non-contentious that, when an element of a legal system is borrowed, that element is quite likely to take on a form and a life of its

[4] G. Edmond and D. Mercer, 'Experts and Expertise in Legal and Regulatory Settings', in G. Edmond (ed.), *Expertise in Regulation and Law* (Aldershot: Ashgate, 2004), pp. 1–31, p. 9.

[5] E.g. P. Legrand, 'European Legal Systems are not Converging' (1996) 45 *International and Comparative Law Quarterly* 52–81; P. Legrand, 'The Impossibility of Legal Transplants' (1997) 4 *Maastricht Journal of European and Comparative Law* 111–24.

[6] E.g. A. Watson, *Legal Transplants*, 2nd edn (Athens GA: Georgia University Press, 1993). See also W. Twining, 'Social Science and Diffusion of Law' (2005) 32 *Journal of Law and Society* 203–40; P. Glenn, *Legal Traditions of the World*, 3rd edn (Oxford: Oxford University Press, 2007).

own in the new system.[7] One thinks, for example, of the way in which Italy introduced adversarial elements into its criminal process.[8] These were not adversarial elements conceived in the abstract, as they might appear in a text on procedural theory, but were directly shaped by reference to the Anglo-American tradition. At least anecdotally, the policy makers would appear to have drawn most of their knowledge of adversarial criminal process from Hollywood movies rather than from a detailed study of comparative law.

However, to focus on transplants or imports from foreign legal systems is to look in the wrong direction in understanding change in a legal system. It encourages us to think of legal change as exogenous, something that ultimately is done to a legal system rather than by that system, in that the essence or true nature of the change is something that can only be found outside the system. We should instead think of importation as one of the ways in which legal systems develop endogenously. Our focus should be not on the source of the idea, but rather on how that idea shapes and positions itself within the existing legal system to which it is introduced.

This is a discussion about how one effects legal change, whatever the provenance of the new elements.[9] We cannot simply compare two approaches to an element of procedure, such as the relative merits of using court-appointed and party-appointed experts, without considering the wider procedural, cultural and political context within which that element will be used.[10] It is not enough to suggest that legal procedure

[7] E.g. A. Watson, 'Legal Transplants and European Private Law' (2000) 4 *Electronic Journal of Comparative Law*, www.ejcl.org/44/art44–2.html (last accessed 14 December 2007).

[8] E. Grande, 'Italian Criminal Justice: Borrowing and Resistance' (2000) 48 *American Journal of Comparative Law* 227–59.

[9] E.g. D. Dwyer, 'Changing Approaches to Expert Evidence in England and Italy' (2002) 1 *International Commentary on Evidence* iss. 2, art. 4, www.bepress.com/ice/vol1/iss2/art4 (last accessed 1 August 2008); J. Resnik, 'Changing Practices, Changing Rules: Judicial and Congressional Rule Making on Civil Juries, Civil Justice and Civil Judging' (1997) 49 *Alabama Law Review* 133–219.

[10] E.g. O. Chase, 'Legal Processes and National Culture' (1997) 5 *Cardozo Journal of International and Comparative Law* 1–24, which attempts to counter John Langbein's suggestion (in 'The German Advantage in Civil Procedure' (1985) 52 *University of Chicago Law Review* 823–66) that United States procedure should be more like its German counterpart with an argument that German civil procedure works with German culture, which is particularly risk-averse, but not with American culture, which is not risk-averse. For Langbein's response, see 'Cultural Chauvinism in Comparative Law' (1997) 5 *Cardozo Journal of International and Comparative Law* 41-50. See also J. Jackson, 'Playing the Culture Card in Cross-Jurisdictional Transplants' (1997) 5 *Cardozo Journal of International and Comparative Law* 51–67; D. Nelken and J. Feest (eds.), *Adapting Legal Cultures* (Oxford: Hart, 2001).

is inherently conservative, that 'habit grooves sensibilities'.[11] In England in the 1990s, for example, the suggestion that party experts should be replaced with court experts was rejected in civil and criminal contexts,[12] but single joint experts appear to have been introduced with relatively few difficulties into low-value civil cases.[13] What is needed is a more thorough analysis of the cultural factors that may determine how a procedural element operates within a procedural context. That analysis is undertaken in this chapter, in examining how the roles of experts are defined within their procedural context.

There are at least five types of non-epistemological factor that contribute to defining the expert's role in civil evidence (Section 4.3). The factors need not operate individually alongside rational fact determination in defining the expert's role, but could come as a bundle, with several operating together. The factors are: the social function of civil litigation; the role of facts in civil procedure; the appropriate conduct of civil litigation; the status of experts in society; the historical use of experts. These factors are explored in the context of five civil procedural systems, which are introduced in Section 4.2.

The English and United States federal civil procedural systems have been selected for study because they represent the two most significant contemporary forms of a common law approach to civil expert evidence.[14] These two systems appear to have begun to develop their approach to expert evidence along increasingly diverging paths from some time in the first half of the twentieth century. Alongside the English, the French and German civil systems represent the main civil procedural forms in Western Europe. Both are strongly influenced by the Roman-canon tradition.

[11] M. Damaška, *Evidence Law Adrift* (New Haven CT: Yale University Press, 1997), p. 119.

[12] E.g. C. Oddie, *Science and the Administration of Justice* (London: Justice, 1991); M. Howard, 'The Neutral Expert: A Plausible Threat to Justice' [1991] *Criminal Law Review* 98–105; Lord Woolf, *Access to Justice: Final Report* (London: Her Majesty's Stationery Office, 1996), [13.5].

[13] At an initial case management hearing, following submissions, the judge will give directions on whether the parties may appoint experts separately or whether they should agree a single joint expert between them. Where the court accepts that multiple areas of expertise may be in issue, it is possible that a single joint expert will be directed for each area of expertise. The appointment of single joint experts is examined in Section 6.3.

[14] Although evidence law in the United States has its origins in the common law, it is now extensively codified. At a federal level, Congress enacted the Federal Rules of Evidence ('FRE') in 1975, while many states have adopted the Uniform Rules of Evidence ('URE'), originally promulgated in 1974. The Uniform Rules attempt to achieve uniformity of the law of evidence between all states, as well as providing large-scale unity between state rules of evidence and the FRE.

Although both France and Germany make use of court experts in civil proceedings, they do so with very different attitudes to the function of civil litigation and the relationship between the court and the facts of the case. The Italian civil system has been selected because it represents a hybrid of French and German theories of the purpose of civil procedure, and because it combines the use of both court and party experts.

4.2 Five approaches to civil expert evidence

This section introduces the provisions for expert evidence in the five civil procedural systems mentioned in the introduction to this chapter: England and Wales, the United States federal courts, France, Germany and Italy. This introduction is intended to be descriptive of current provisions. Attempts to explain those provisions, for example in terms of history or fundamental objectives of the procedural system, will be carried over into Section 4.3. This is because the explanatory analysis is better carried out from a comparative perspective, after the five jurisdictions have been introduced.

4.2.1 England and Wales: Civil Procedure Rules 1998

The current regime for expert evidence in the English civil process was introduced in April 1999 by Pt 35 of the Civil Procedure Rules 1998 ('CPR').[15] The CPR replace the Rules of the Supreme Court ('RSC'), first introduced following the introduction of the Judicature Acts 1873 and 1875.[16] CPR Pt 35, which is reproduced in the Appendix, should be read alongside a number of other normative documents, particularly the Part 35 Practice Direction, the 2005 Protocol on experts,[17] the appropriate Pre-Action Protocols, and case law.

The fifteen rules of Part 35 (forty-five rules if one includes the sub-rules) might usefully be placed into six functional groups. First, CPR 35.1 asserts the ultimate authority of the court in matters of expert evidence.

[15] It is a peculiarity of English and United States civil procedure that its provisions are drafted by lawyers, particularly members of the judiciary, and issued with the authority of secondary legislation, while in continental Europe procedural codes are the work of primary legislators.

[16] Supreme Court of Judicature Act 1873 (36 & 37 Vict. c. 66); Supreme Court of Judicature Act 1875 (38 & 39 Vict. c. 77).

[17] Civil Justice Council, *Protocol for the Instruction of Experts to Give Evidence in Civil Claims* (London: 2005).

The rule echoes CPR 1.1 and CPR 32.1,[18] in that it limits the use of experts to that which is 'reasonably required to resolve the proceedings'. This is elaborated on in CPR 35.4 ('Power to restrict expert evidence'), which is a form of admissibility rule, based on the relevance of the evidence, and is presumably intended to curb what was perceived as the excessive use of experts in English civil litigation in the 1990s.[19] CPR 35.14 allows the expert to approach the court directly for directions, and this reduces the ability of the parties to manipulate the evidence of experts once appointed.

The court will actively manage cases as part of 'enabling the court to deal with cases justly', and the court may direct the parties as to what evidence to produce, and exclude otherwise admissible evidence. The effect of this is that, even where expert evidence might, in conventional evidence law terms, be admissible, the court may exclude it as not helping to determine the issues.[20] This is in effect a form of relevance test for admissibility. In addition, the court might consider that, although strictly relevant to determining the issue, the use of such expertise would not farther the Overriding Objective. This is most likely to be on grounds of proportionality. Separate to the possible risk that a decision to exclude expert evidence on grounds other than relevance might, depending on the case as a whole, breach Art. 6(1) of the European Convention on Human Rights, there is a real danger that, where expert evidence has been confined to one or two specialities, an expert might be encouraged to step outside her expertise, and to give opinion on matters on which she is not competent.[21]

There is also a terminology change, with 'expert witness' being replaced by 'expert'.[22] It may have been intended by those drafting the CPR that,

[18] CPR Pt 32 concerns evidence generally. Rule 32.1 provides that '(1) The court may control the evidence by giving directions as to – (a) the issues on which it requires evidence; (b) the nature of the evidence which it requires to decide those issues; (c) the way in which the evidence is to be placed before the court. (2) The court may use its power under this rule to exclude evidence that would otherwise be admissible. (3) The court may limit cross-examination.'

[19] E.g. *Matthews* v. *Tarmac Bricks and Tiles Ltd* [1995] CPLR 463 (CA) (Lord Woolf MR). This case was the first appeal on a procedural point under the CPR. See also Section 4.3.3.2.

[20] *Barings plc (In Liquidation)* v. *Coopers & Lybrand (No. 2)* [2001] Lloyd's Rep Bank 85.

[21] Lord Justice (Sir Mark) Waller, I Scott, Sir Henry Brooke *et al.* (eds.), *Civil Procedure*, 2 vols. (London: Sweet and Maxwell, 2007) (*The White Book*), [35.4.1].

[22] It may be that not too much weight should be placed on this change. The term 'expert witness' appears to have been introduced into English civil procedure by the RSC, with the earliest usage in case law dating from 1875, e.g. *Batley* v. *Kynock (No. 3)* (1875) LR 20 Eq 632, and *Charles Laffitte & Co. Ltd* (1875) LR 20 Eq 650. But as we will see

by removing the 'witness' label, a greater conceptual distance would be placed between 'experts'[23] and 'witnesses'.[24] However, experts retain the legal status of a witness, for example continuing to enjoy immunity from civil suit for their conduct as a witness.[25]

The second function is to split CPR Pt 35 into two halves (CPR rr. 35.2–14 and CPR r. 35.15), and to restrict the effect of CPR rr. 35.2–14 to those experts whom the court has agreed can prepare evidence for proceedings. This is important because it means that the parties can still appoint other experts, often called 'shadow experts', who are effectively invisible to the court and to their opponents, and whose costs cannot be recovered. The existence of shadow experts becomes important when we consider such questions as whether a party is in a position to make informed decisions where the number of experts has been restricted. It also means that, when we consider references to experts in English civil procedure, we must distinguish whether the experts have been appointed under CPR r. 35.2. For example, the references to experts in the Pre-Action Protocols cannot, by definition, be references to CPR r. 35.2 experts because the necessary case management decisions have not been taken.

The third function is to define the use of the expert's written report (CPR rr. 35.4, 35.5, 35.6, 35.10, 35.11 and 35.13). This is a key development under the CPR, as it indicates that a significant part of the evidence in a case may be submitted in writing to the court rather than being given orally at trial. The expert report is an important feature of the CPR. It is one of the key ways in which the CPR's approach to expert evidence should be distinguished from the classical Anglo-American focus on the presentation of oral evidence at trial. The CPR seek to discourage the use of experts at trial, and to focus attention on the exchange of expert evidence and narrowing of issues before trial. Rule 35.6 provides for a party to put written questions to an opponent's expert, requiring a written response.

(Section 5.1), the word 'expert' itself hardly has an established legal lineage, only appearing in the English case reports from the 1850s.

23 'The proof from the Attestation of Persons on their Personal Knowledge, we may properly . . . call proof by Experts': G. Gilbert, *The Law of Evidence*, ed. C. Lofft, 4th edn (Dublin: 1795).

24 'A witness swears but to what he hath heard or seen, generally or more largely, to what hath fallen under his senses': *Bushell's Case* (1670) Vaughan 135; 124 ER 1006.

25 *Stanton* v. *Callaghan* [2000] 1 QB 75; [1999] 2 WLR 745; *Meadow* v. *General Medical Council* [2006] EWHC 146 (Admin.); D. Dwyer, 'Legal Remedies for the Negligent Expert' (2008) 12 *Evidence and Proof* 93–115.

Where a civil case does reach trial, it will almost always be heard by a judge sitting without a jury.[26]

The fourth function is to regulate the use of party experts. CPR r. 35.3 introduces the concept that the expert (and in context this particularly means the party expert) has an overriding duty to the court.[27] CPR r. 35.12 allows the court to order pre-trial discussions between experts instructed by opposing sides, in order to narrow issues (Section 6.2.3.1.2). CPR r. 35.9, regarding the sharing of information between parties, harks back to CPR r. 1. Since a principle of civil procedure is that the dispute is fought between equals, where one party has access to a resource that the other does not – here information – then the court may require that that resource be shared. These provisions are also strictly applicable to single joint experts, although with little practical effect.

The fifth function is to regulate the use of single joint experts (CPR rr. 35.7 and 35.8). The decision to appoint a single joint expert may be made by the parties or by the court. The selection of which expert to appoint is almost always made by agreement between the parties. Single joint experts are instructed by both parties, but are not necessarily jointly instructed; by joint instruction I mean an arrangement under which the instructions are agreed between the parties before being issued. Single joint experts are usually found in middle-value cases, which are assigned by the court to 'Fast Track' case management. These cases are considered to be relatively straightforward, and as a guide have a value between £5,000 and £15,000 (Section 6.2.1.1.2).

The sixth function is to regulate the use of assessors (CPR r. 35.15). Unlike single joint experts, assessors are appointed by the court, to provide advice in whatever manner the court deems appropriate. Assessors are used almost exclusively in Admiralty and Patents proceedings. It is customary in the Admiralty Court to receive expertise from assessors, who are appointed by Trinity House at the request of the Court.[28] This usage and that of assessors in the Patents proceedings were the only areas in

[26] Libel, malicious prosecution and wrongful imprisonment are now the main categories of civil case that may be heard by a jury in England and Wales.

[27] The concept of the overriding duty conveys the spirit in which the role of the expert should be understood, and appears to have been largely successful. Master Leslie, for example, has commented that '[I]t seems that the legal profession and the courts now accept and recognise the impartiality of expert witnesses much more readily': J. Leslie, 'From Bear Garden to Swan Lake' *Counsel* (August 2005) 22–3, 23. It is more difficult to define that duty precisely, however (Section 7.5).

[28] The practice of the Admiralty Court is developed further in Section 6.4.

which the Law Reform Committee in 1970 was prepared to accept the use of court experts rather than party expert witnesses.[29] Because the court has access to the opinions of assessors, the additional use of experts by the parties is discouraged as not providing any more assistance to the court than is available. Assessors sit with the judge(s) in open court. Historically, they have also advised the judge in her private deliberations. This in effect made her a non-voting member of the tribunal. However, as a result of the CPR and the Human Rights Act 1998, there would appear to be a move towards treating the assessor as a court expert, and excluding her from private deliberations.[30]

The CPR are applied in two of the three Divisions of the High Court: Queen's Bench and Chancery. The third Division, Family, has adopted its own practice in relation to experts since at least the 1960s. At that point Family judges began to instruct the Official Solicitor, an officer of the court who may act as guardian *ad litem* of a child, to instruct an expert on behalf of the court.[31] More recently, the Family Court has been a keen adopter of single joint experts.

4.2.2 United States of America: Federal Rules of Evidence 1975

Discussion of civil procedural practice in the United States is complicated by the existence of the multiple jurisdictions of the federal, state and tribal courts. Most of the discussion of American civil procedure in this book is therefore restricted to the practice of the federal courts. The use of evidence, including expert evidence, is governed in the United States federal courts by the FRE. The FRE are arranged into eleven Articles, comprising a total of sixty-seven rules. For civil litigation, the FRE should be read in the context of the Federal Rules of Civil Procedure 1938 ('FRCP'). Like the CPR, the FRE begins with a rule, FRE r. 102, on 'purpose and construction'. This rule provides that: 'These rules shall be construed to secure fairness in administration, elimination of unjustifiable expense and delay, and promotion of growth and development of the law of evidence to the end that the truth may be ascertained and proceedings justly determined.' FRE r. 402 provides that all relevant evidence is admissible, unless

[29] Law Reform Committee England and Wales, *Evidence of Opinion and Expert Evidence*, 17th Report, Cmnd 4489 (London: Her Majesty's Stationery Office, 1970).

[30] *Owners of the Ship 'Bow Spring'* v. *Owners of the Ship 'Manzanillo II'* [2004] EWCA Civ 1007; [2005] 1 WLR 144; [2004] 4 All ER 899.

[31] E.g. *Re S (Infants)* [1967] 1 WLR 396; [1967] 1 All ER 202 (Ch.); *Re L (an infant)* [1967] 3 WLR 1645; [1968] 1 All ER 20 (F).

excepted by the Constitution, congressional legislation, the FRE or the Supreme Court. FRE r. 403 allows the court to balance the probative value of relevant evidence (including expert evidence) against factors such as the danger of the evidence being unduly prejudicial or involving undue delay, and to exclude evidence as appropriate. The substance of the provision would therefore appear to be similar to that of CPR rr. 32.1 and 35.1 in England, discussed in the previous sub-section.

Expert evidence is dealt with specifically under FRE Art. VII.[32] In civil cases, this article is supplemented by FRCP r. 26(a)(2), which requires the disclosure of the names of experts and the expert report. FRE rr. 701 and 702 identify the types of opinion evidence that may be given by a non-expert and an expert witness, respectively. While FRE r. 701 limits the subject of the non-expert opinion testimony to the witness's perception, FRE r. 702 permits expert opinion testimony as long as it is based upon sufficient facts or data, and is the product of reliable principles and methods, applied reliably to the facts of the case. Under FRE r. 703, the expert's opinion may be based on facts that are otherwise inadmissible 'if of a type reasonably relied upon by experts in the particular field in forming opinions or inferences upon the subject'. FRE r. 704 allows expert opinions on the ultimate issue, except in relation to mental state evidence constituting an element of the crime or defence. FRE r. 705 allows that an opinion may be given without stating the facts on which the opinion is based, although the facts may be elicited through cross-examination.

FRE r. 706 provides for the appointment of court experts, on the motion of either the court or the parties. The expert may be selected by the court, or by the parties together. Unlike a CPR single joint expert, it is expressly provided for that an FRE court expert may be cross-examined by both sides. Like its contemporary English counterpart at the time of its introduction in the 1970s, Ord. 40 of the Rules of the Supreme Court, FRE r. 706 has met with significant disinterest in practice.[33] A likely cause of this disinterest is the traditional division of Anglo-American process into pre-trial and trial phases, with party domination of the pre-trial phase. Until recently, American and English judges have had little engagement

[32] The structure of Art. VII in the FRE is mirrored by the structure of Art. VII in the URE.

[33] J. Basten, 'The Court Expert in Civil Trials – A Comparative Appraisal' (1977) 41 *Modern Law Review* 174–91, 181; P. Johnston, 'Court Appointed Scientific Expert Witnesses: Unfettering Expertise' (1987) 2 *Berkeley Technology Law Journal*, www.law.berkeley.edu/journals/btlj/articles/vol2/johnston.pdf (last accessed 14 December 2007); H. Erichson, 'Mass Tort Litigation and Inquisitorial Justice' (1999) 87 *Georgetown Law Journal* 1983–2024, 1987.

with the case in its pre-trial phase, which is when the parties assemble their evidence and arguments. By the time the case enters the trial phase, therefore, and the trial judge might consider appointing an FRE r. 706 expert, the parties will already have completed the task of assembling expert reports.[34] As American judges become more involved in pre-trial case management, there may be greater opportunities for them to appoint court experts.

One high-profile area of use of FRE r. 706 to date has been in the appointment of panels of experts in the 1990s in litigation relating to silicone breast implants.[35] In 1996, Pointer J, who had been in charge of all several thousand silicone breast implant cases before the federal courts, invoked FRE r. 706 to convene a 'National Science Panel', consisting of an immunologist, an epidemiologist, a toxicologist and a rheumatologist.[36] The panel selected around 200 studies from an available 2,000, published and unpublished. After two years, at a cost of $800,000, the panel concluded in December 1998 that the available evidence did not warrant the claim that silicone breast implants caused the diseases claimed. Similarly, Jones J, responsible for hearing 70 breast implant cases in the United States District Court for the District of Oregon, appointed his own scientific panel.[37]

Before FRE r. 706 was introduced in the 1970s, the use of court experts was effectively barred by a rule common in all state jurisdictions (except New Jersey) that the judge could not comment on the evidence.[38] This rule was considered to preclude a judicial decision to appoint a court expert. There are examples of limited use of court experts in New Jersey and the federal courts from the 1950s, where the court has acted because it felt that the parties had failed to provide satisfactory expert evidence. In 1952, the Supreme Court for the County of New York introduced a court-appointed (and state-funded) physician scheme for assessment in personal injury cases. Basten argues this was very successful and popular with many litigants because it provided a straightforward, low-cost method of

[34] Langbein, 'German Advantage', 845.

[35] S. Haack, *Defending Science – Within Reason: Between Scientism and Cynicism* (New York: Prometheus Books, 2003); Erichson, 'Mass Tort', 1983. See also M. Angell, *Science on Trial: The Clash of Medical Evidence and the Law in the Breast Implant Case* (New York: Norton, 1996).

[36] *Re Silicone Gel Breast Implants Products Liability Litigation* 793 F Supp 1098 (JPML 1992) (MDL 926).

[37] Haack, *Defending Science*, p. 248. These scientific panels are an interesting phenomenon, in that they go beyond the use of court experts seemingly envisaged by FRE 706.

[38] Basten, 'The Court Expert', 177.

obtaining the expert advice that the defendant needed in order to decide whether to settle a claim.[39] In the New Jersey case of *State* v. *Lanza*,[40] a court expert was appointed because the parties' expert evidence regarding the quantity, quality and value of the nursery stock in issue was 'shocking in disparity'. The appointment was upheld on appeal. In *Scott* v. *Spanjer Bros Inc.*,[41] the federal court sought to appoint a single neuro-physician acceptable to both parties in a personal injury case relating to a child. The parties were able to agree on three experts, none of whom was available, and so the court appointed an expert who was available, but who was not acceptable to the defendant. The court's decision, upheld on appeal, was based on its 'very important duty to protect an infant's rights'.

Since 1993, the approach of the federal courts to expert evidence has been strongly shaped by the decision of the United States Supreme Court in *Daubert*,[42] and subsequent clarifications by that court in *Joiner*[43] and *Kumho Tire*.[44] In *Daubert*, the Supreme Court held that, while FRE r. 402 allowed the court to admit evidence, including expert evidence, that was relevant, the test for relevance implied also a test of reliability. While there was no 'definitive checklist or test' for reliability, the court did suggest that four relevant factors were testability, peer review or publication, the known or potential rate of error, and widespread acceptance. It was therefore a question of law for the judge whether the expertise was the product of an acceptable scientific method. The validity of the conclusions arrived at through that method were then a question of fact for the jury. In the 1997 case of *Joiner*, the Supreme Court clarified on appeal that the trial judge had not abused his discretion by ruling on admissibility on the basis of conclusions rather than methodology, using the test in *Daubert*, since 'conclusions and methodology are not entirely distinct from each other'.[45] The *Daubert* principles were extended to all expert evidence, not just scientific expert evidence, by the Supreme Court in *Kumho Tire* in 1999.[46]

[39] Ibid., 180–1. [40] *State* v. *Lanza* 181 A 2d 390 (1962) (NJ).

[41] *Scott* v. *Spanjer Bros Inc* 298 F 2d 928 (2nd Cir. 1962).

[42] *Daubert* v. *Merrell Dow Pharmaceuticals* 509 US 579; 113 Sup Ct 2786 (1993) (*Daubert I*).

[43] *General Electric Company* v. *Joiner* 522 US 136; 118 Sup Ct 512 (1997).

[44] *Kumho Tire* v. *Carmichael* 526 US 137; 119 Sup Ct 1167 (1999).

[45] The decision in *Joiner* does not sit comfortably with the rationale for *Daubert*: Haack, *Defending Science*, p. 246.

[46] P. Oh, 'The Proper Test for Assessing the Admissibility of Nonscientific Expert Testimony Under Federal Rule of Evidence 702' (1997) 45 *Cleveland State Law Review* 437–67; D. Mogck, 'Are We There Yet? Refining the Test for Expert Testimony Through *Daubert, Kumho Tire* and Proposed Federal Rule of Evidence 702' (2000) 33 *Connecticut Law Review* 303–36. P. Roberts, 'Tyres with a "Y": An English Perspective on Kumho Tire and its Implications

The *Daubert* approach to assessing the admissibility of expert evidence has replaced the earlier *Frye* test in the federal courts and the majority of state courts. In *Frye*, the federal court of the District of Columbia had ruled, in a criminal case, that 'novel scientific testimony' is admissible only if it is 'sufficiently established to have gained general acceptance in the particular field to which it belongs'.[47] Although the paradigm in which *Daubert* operates is the jury trial, it is worth noting that very few civil (or criminal) cases reach trial in the United States, and not all of those that do reach trial are decided by a jury (Section 4.3.3.1.2). The difficulty with the *Frye* test is that it is, on the one hand, too liberal, in that it often allows experts to determine the quality of their colleague's expertise, while, on the other hand, it is too restrictive, in that general acceptance may not reflect reliability.

4.2.3 France: Nouveau code de procédure civile 1975

The French Nouveau code de procédure civile of 1975 ('NCPC') makes provision for the judge to instruct a *technicien*, who may be a moral or natural person, to clarify (*éclairer*) a question of fact (arts. 232–84). This *instruction* may be by means of a *constatation*, a *consultation* or an *expertise* (art. 232). In a *constatation* ('observation') (art. 249–255), the *constatant* ('observer') simply reports back to the court on the fact she has been asked to observe (such as the existence of adultery), although the *constatant* may not hear from witnesses. She cannot give any advice on any legal or factual consequences of her observation (art. 249). This task may be undertaken by a *huissier* ('bailiff').[48] In a *consultation* (arts. 256–62), the *technicien* is appointed to address a purely technical question that does not require complex investigation (art. 256). The result of a *consultation* will normally be presented orally, unless the judge directs otherwise (art. 258).[49] An *expertise* (arts. 263–84) is used where a *constatation* or a *consultation* would not be adequate (art. 263). One or more *experts* can be appointed. The French system appears, therefore, to classify its experts by the degree of inference that each is required to make.

for the Admissibility of Expert Evidence' (1999) 1 *International Commentary on Evidence* iss. 2, art. 5, www.bepress.com/ice/vol1/iss2/art5 (last accessed 14 December 2007).

47 *Frye* v. *United States* 293 F 1013 (DC Cir. 1923) 1014.

48 J. Beardsley, 'Proof of Fact in French Civil Procedure' (1986) 34 *American Journal of Comparative Law* 459–86, 468.

49 On the differences between a *constatation* and a *consultation*, see L. Cadiet and E. Jeuland, *Droit judiciaire privé*, 5th edn (Paris: Litec, 2006), p. 394.

The Cours d'appel and the Cour de cassation each maintain a list of experts, from whom judges may make a selection.[50] The list system is modern in origin, and appears to have been a response to increasing concerns in the middle of the twentieth century over the quality of experts, particularly in criminal cases where miscarriages of justice arose.[51] In practice, judges tend to develop a preference for particular experts.[52] For example, a systematic examination of psychiatric and medico-psychological expertises in France over a ten-year period has revealed the existence of magistrate–expert pairs that constitute '*tandems synergiques*'.[53] This relationship of trust might be seen as increasing the likelihood that the judge will defer to the expert's decision. However, this deference may in fact be because the expert has come to the conclusion for which the judge had hoped. The fact that the decision to appoint an expert rests with the judge may mean in practice that judges seek expert opinions to gain confirmation of their own hypotheses rather than information.[54] One consequence of this judicial selection is the possibility that there comes to exist a judicial construction of science.[55]

A French civil *expertise* very much resembles a mini-trial, with the *expert* making investigations and receiving oral testimony (NCPC art. 242).[56] The case of *Mantovanelli*, reviewed before the European Court of Human Rights, provides an example, accessible in English, of how a French civil *expertise* is conducted.[57] Although the judicial role should not be delegated to *techniciens*, in practice there is a significant risk of

50 Lists are created and maintained by virtue of law no. 71–498 of 29 June 1971, significantly amended by law no. 2004–130 of 11 February 2004, and decree no. 2004–1463 of 23 December 2004. R. Encinas de Munagorri, 'La communauté scientifique est-elle un ordre juridique?' [1998] *Revue trimestrielle de droit civil* 247–83; O. Leclerc, 'Les réformes du droit de l'expertise' (2006) 71 *Experts* 12.

51 J. Spencer, 'Court Experts and Expert Witnesses: Have We a Lesson to Learn from the French?' (1992) 45 *Current Legal Problems* 213–36, 225–6.

52 E.g. Cadiet and Jeuland, *Droit judiciaire privé*, p. 396.

53 D. Bourcier and M. De Bonis, *Les paradoxes de l'expertise: savoir ou juger?* (Paris: Institut Synthélab, 1999), p. 17.

54 Ibid., p. 54.

55 O. Leclerc, *Le juge et l'expert: contribution à l'étude des rapports entre le droit et la science* (Paris: LDGJ, 2005).

56 This includes respecting the principle of *contradiction*, although experts do not have appropriate relevant training to conduct an investigation in line with procedural principles, and the French judge is not required to be present at the *expertise* (NCPC art. 274). See E. Jeuland, 'Expertise', in L. Cadiet (ed.), *Dictionnaire de la justice* (Paris: Presses Universitaires de France, 2004), pp. 503–10, p. 508; C. Ngwasiri, 'Some Problems of Expertise in French Civil Procedure' (1989) 8 *Civil Justice Quarterly* 168–83.

57 *Mantovanelli* v. *France* (1997) 24 EHRR 370, at [17–25].

delegation of fact finding to the *expert*.[58] *Experts*, like a common law jury, are often asked questions of fact that are difficult to disentangle from questions of law.[59] For example, when an *expert* is asked by the court to determine *responsabilité*, this means both factual 'responsibility' and legal 'liability'.[60] There is therefore also a risk of de facto delegation of legal decision making to experts.

As in Anglo-American procedure, French courts are not required to accept the expert's opinion (art. 246), since 'dictum expertorum nusquam transit in rem judicatam' ('the statement of experts never passes (directly) into a legal decision').[61] The courts are entitled to reach a conclusion contrary to that of the expert's professional opinion, but rarely do so.[62] But the status of the expert's opinion in France is, on closer examination, different from its status in England. Experts are not only appointed by the court, but are considered as officers of the court (*auxiliaires du juge*) rather than as evidential sources. Whether this makes an expert more akin to a witness or a member of the tribunal is a debate that has been ongoing in French law since at least the seventeenth century.[63] The state of that debate may be seen as a key determinant in whether the court is inclined, at least in practice, to defer to the opinion of the expert. Under the 1806 Code de procédure civile, *techniciens* were to be treated as witnesses of fact for the purposes of recusal.[64] However, under the new code, a *technicien* can be recused on the same grounds as those for a judge (NCPC arts. 234, 341), and the investigations of an *expert* must adhere to the rules of procedural fairness. In relation to this obligation, Jacquin has suggested that the term 'tribunal' in Art. 6(1) of the European Convention on Human Rights should be interpreted in a broad sense, to include *techniciens* appointed by the tribunal.[65] At the same time, the findings of an expert are separate from those of the tribunal, to the extent that an expert's opinion may be appealed separately from the opinion of the tribunal.[66] Thus, at present, the *expert* as *auxiliaire du juge* would appear to have some form of quasi-judicial

58 E.g. Jeuland, 'Expertise', p. 504.

59 Beardsley, 'Proof of Fact', 482. This is contrary to NCPC art. 238. 60 Ibid., 483.

61 B. De La Roche-Flavin, *Arrests notables du parlement de Toulouse*, ed. N. Caranove (Toulouse: 1745), p. 458.

62 M.-L. Rassat, 'Forensic Expertise and the Law of Evidence in France', in J. Nijboer, C. Callen and N. Kwak (eds.), *Forensic Expertise and the Law of Evidence* (Amsterdam: Royal Netherlands Academy of Arts and Sciences 1993), p. 54, p. 62.

63 Leclerc, *Juge et expert*. 64 Ibid.

65 A. Jacquin, 'L'impartialité objective de l'expert judiciaire et sa récusation' 31 *Gazette du Palais* (1 February 2003) 3–8, 4.

66 Cadiet and Jeuland, *Droit judiciaire privé*, p. 397.

status rather than being a member of the tribunal proper. The difference in status between the 1806 and 1975 codes suggests that the current quasi-judicial status of the expert is a relatively recent development in France.

4.2.4 Germany: Zivilprozessordnung 1933

German civil procedure is defined by the Zivilprozessordnung 1933 ('ZPO'). Experts are provided for under ZPO ss. 402–14, and the code distinguishes between non-specialist witnesses of fact and court experts.[67] An expert is not a witness, but provides a separate form of evidence. To the extent that the rules pertaining to court experts do not provide specific regulations, however, the rules about non-expert witnesses are partly applicable (s. 402). The court selects the expert (s. 404), usually from a prepared list. Where the judge departs from the list, she must give priority to those experts who are officially designated for a specific field of expertise (s. 404(2)). The court can also ask the parties to suggest an expert, and the court is bound to appoint an expert on whom both parties agree (s. 404(4)). Where the parties have not agreed on the expert, a party may seek to recuse the expert, where there are grounds to believe that she is not neutral (s. 406(1)). The grounds of recusal of an expert are similar to those for a judge, and a refusal by the court of a request to recuse an expert can be appealed (s. 406(5)). Other than recusal, the court's decision on which expert to appoint cannot be reviewed without appealing the entire case (s. 404(7)): 'German procedure makes liberal provision for adversary participation in the system of selection, instruction and examination of neutral experts.'[68]

The court then instructs the expert on which issues should be examined, and the extent of contact with the parties (s. 404a). All instructions to the expert must be disclosed to the parties. Although many experts submit a written report, they may still be required to testify at trial, where they will be examined by the judge (s. 411(3)), and then by the parties. As German procedure does not allow for leading questions by examining advocates, this questioning takes the form of 'polite questions' rather than Anglo-American cross-examination.[69] The judge may appoint a new

[67] See, generally, S. Timmerbeil, 'The Role of Expert Witnesses in German and US Civil Litigation' (2003) 9 *Annual Survey of International and Comparative Law* 163–87; Langbein, 'German Advantage'.

[68] Langbein, 'German Advantage', 775.

[69] Timmerbeil, 'Role of Expert Witnesses', 175.

expert where she is not convinced of the expert's conclusions (s. 412(1)). This includes situations where 'a litigant can persuade the court that an expert's report has been sloppy or partial, that it rests upon a view of the field that is not generally shared, or that the question referred to the expert is exceptionally difficult, the court will commission further expertise'.[70]

The court in all cases has discretion as to whether or not to follow the view of the court expert (s. 286). The court must provide a reasoned opinion on why it believes that the expert has the necessary scientific knowledge and why it follows the expert's opinion or not. Under no circumstances should fact-finding authority be delegated to the expert (s. 404a(1)). The expert is not required to mention scientific methods other than the one that she followed. Although the parties are free to appoint their own experts, these experts cannot testify.

4.2.5 Italy: Codice di procedura civile 1940

Most of the general rules on the role of a *consulente tecnico d'ufficio* ('court-appointed technical adviser') in Italian civil procedure under the Codice di procedure civile 1940 ('CPC') are similar to or the same as those in French civil procedure. This may be because, following Unification, the Italian Code of 1865 based civil justice extensively on the French model.[71] In addition, both the French and Italian state codes were directly descended from the Roman-canon tradition. One or more *consulenti* may be appointed (CPC art. 61) by the *giudice istruttore* ('examining judge'), 'normally' from a court list (arts. 172–9).[72] Where the expert examines witnesses without the examining judge being present, she submits a *relazione* (written report). Where the expert has sat with the *giudice istruttore*, her opinion is entered in the *processo verbale* (official record) (CPC 195).

However, there are two significant differences today between the Italian CPC of 1940 and the French NCPC of 1975 in relation to the appointment of experts. The first is that the CPC does not make the same distinctions for the *consulente tecnico* that are present in the French code between the roles of *techniciens* in a *constatation*, a *consultation* and an *expertise*. The second difference is that the Italian code allows the parties to appoint

[70] Langbein, 'German Advantage', 840.

[71] H. Hammelmann, 'Rules of Evidence Under the New Italian Civil Codes' (1947) 29 *Journal of Comparative Legislation and International Law* 39–46, 40.

[72] The *giudice istruttore* is delegated the task of gathering evidence and preparing the final hearing by the *tribunale*. However, the increasing volume of cases in Italy means that the *giudice istruttore* may in effect be the only judge in the case.

their own *consulenti* (art. 201), which they usually do.[73] In the same way that the court's *consulente* is an assistant to the court rather than an evidentiary source, so the party's *consulente* is an assistant, in the same way as an *avvocato* (art. 87). The *consulente* has contractual obligations to her instructing party, but no duty to the court. The party *consulente* is questioned by the court *consulente* rather than by the judge. The introduction of party experts under the CPC presumably reflects a concern that the parties have insufficient control over a significant part of the factual material before the tribunal. In Italy, where court *consulenti* can also be recused on the same grounds as a judge (arts. 63, 192), party *consulenti* have the status not of witnesses but of assistants to the party, in the same way as an advocate. This would suggest that Italian court experts should also not be seen as a form of witness. Perhaps more so in Italy than in France, evaluation of expert opinion is guided by two somewhat contradictory maxims inherited from canon law, which reflect the paradox inherent in the judicial use of expertise: *iudex peritus peritorum* ('the judge is the expert of the experts'), and *peritis in arte credendum* ('experts are to be believed on their skill').[74]

4.3 Five non-epistemological factors in expert role definition

With the benefit of this brief introduction to the civil procedure relating to expert evidence in these five jurisdictions, I explore in this section the possible role of five non-epistemological factors that may affect the way in which the courts and the parties in a particular jurisdiction define their expectations of an expert's role in litigation, and how selections may be made between multiple party roles. The five factors are the social function of civil litigation, the role of facts, the appropriate conduct of litigation, the status of experts in society, and the historical use of experts. The first and fourth of these factors might be considered broadly sociological, while the second and third call for a more legal analysis. Each is dealt with in turn under its own heading.

[73] It is possible for the parties to French civil proceedings to appoint their own *conseillers techniques*, using the general provisions of NCPC art. 161. Such a specialist may then be present at the *expertise*, and formulate any observation she may find necessary (art. 162). If such observations have been raised, the *expert* is bound to give them a specific answer (art. 276). However, the NCPC does not make express, formal reference to the use of *conseillers techniques*, and their degree of prevalence in civil practice is unclear.

[74] J. Martin de Agar, 'Giudice e perito', paper presented at the 29th Congresso Nazionale di Diritto Canonico, Vatican City, 1998.

4.3.1 The social function of civil litigation

Civil litigation is a social activity, and as such we can see it as serving two roles: first, it reflects, directly or indirectly, wider values and expectations of conduct in society; secondly, it helps to shape or reinforce those values (that is to say, it is instrumental). I say 'indirectly' because some legal systems would often appear to present exhortations to conduct that is 'necessarily opposed to many normal social and business practices'.[75] Mirjan Damaška, a leading proponent of an instrumental theory of adjective law,[76] has suggested that the form of procedure adopted reflects a combination of the state's conception of the goal of the legal process (policy-implementing or conflict-solving) and its organization of legal authority (hierarchical or coordinate). Litigation is therefore itself instrumental in reinforcing a normative expectation of the correct roles of citizen and State.[77] This goes beyond simple accuracy of fact determination, since, 'All adjudication – no matter what its purpose – lies in the domain of social activity where truth values cannot be maximized because they are not the only ones that count.'[78]

In this section, I provide examples of three models of the state in modern civil procedure: the liberal state (the French CPC of 1806 and the English Rules of the Supreme Court of 1883, amended most recently 1965), the welfare state (the French NCPC of 1975, the Italian CPC of 1940, and the German ZPO of 1933) and the managerial state (the English CPR 1998). I also consider the special nature of family proceedings. The relevance to expert evidence is that we might reasonably expect the role of the expert to be aligned with the social function of civil litigation.

4.3.1.1 The liberal state

The dominant model for the social function of civil procedure in Western Europe and North America during the nineteenth century and much of the twentieth century has been *laissez-faire* liberalism.[79] Civil litigation has been seen as a manifestation of a private dispute between two private

[75] D. Nelken, 'Law and Disorder: A Letter from Italy' (1992) 8 *Socio-Legal Newsletter* 6.

[76] M. Damaška, *The Faces of Justice and State Authority: A Comparative Approach to the Legal Process* (New Haven CT: Yale University Press, 1986).

[77] For a civil example, see Chase, 'Legal Processes'.

[78] Damaška, *Evidence Law Adrift*, p. 121.

[79] M. Ferrarese, 'An Entrepreneurial Conception of the Law? The American Model Through Italian Eyes', in D. Nelken, *Comparing Legal Cultures* (Aldershot: Ashgate, 1997), pp. 157–81.

parties,[80] and the State has only a minimal role in resolving that dispute.[81] The current interest in 'alternative dispute resolution', for example, implies that civil litigation should be seen as a form of dispute resolution between private parties, and indeed as only one of the forms available to them.[82]

4.3.1.1.1 France: Code de procédure civile 1806 The Roman-canon ideal that the judge had a duty to pursue justice lessened its grip in nineteenth-century Europe, with the development of the concept of individual autonomy.[83] Under adversarial proceedings,[84] only litigants may institute proceedings, whose subject matter and evidence the litigants determine, and which they may terminate prior to judgment. In early twentieth-century France, for example, the French civil judge acted largely in the role of an umpire. This is expressed in a passage by the French proceduralists Aubry and Rau, which 'is frequently quoted as a kind of *summum* on the subject':[85]

> [The judge] is to decide the claims that the parties submit to him, and, consequently, to decide these claims as they are submitted to him. It is not his task to seek out himself the facts, documents or [other written] evidence, which may support or weaken those claims. Any initiative on his part in this respect violates the fundamental rule that no fact may be invoked against a party except insofar as it has been submitted to him in advance and he has had an opportunity to challenge it . . . But there is yet more to be said against the initiative of the judge in matters of proof. The position of each of the parties is closely linked to the evidence upon which he intends to rely; it is the evidence which gives to the claim its character, its dimensions and its limits.[86]

[80] Where one of the parties to a civil dispute is the state, then, in continental legal systems, the litigation is covered by a separate procedural structure, relating to public law.

[81] This is not necessarily a product entirely of nineteenth-century liberalism. Under canon law, not only were the parties encouraged to seek conciliation rather than judgment, but conciliation was possible even once judgment had been handed down: R. Helmholz, *Canon Law and the Law of England* (London: Hambledon Press, 1987), pp. 36–7.

[82] J. Jolowicz, *On Civil Procedure* (Cambridge: Cambridge University Press, 2000), p. 3. See also W. Twining, 'Alternative to What? Theories of Litigation, Procedure and Dispute Settlement in Anglo-American Jurisprudence: Some Neglected Classics' (1993) 56 *Modern Law Review* 380–92.

[83] Damaška, *Faces of Justice*, p. 110.

[84] For a discussion of the meaning of 'adversarial' in relation to civil procedure, and the sense in which it is used in this chapter, see Section 4.3.3.1.

[85] Beardsley, 'Proof of Fact', 460.

[86] C. Aubry and C. Rau, *Cours de droit civil français*, 5th edn (Paris: Billard, 1922), p. 74.

Civil procedure in France has traditionally been seen as a means by which private parties seek to resolve a dispute, with minimal assistance from the State. Because it is a private dispute, whose limits are set by the parties, the court is reluctant to investigate facts of its own motion, in case this would result in the boundaries of the litigation being extended. This attitude affects the mechanisms by which the French courts might pursue the truth. For example, the civil courts are reluctant to exercise their inherent powers to order the attendance of witnesses, since they are not parties to the dispute.[87]

The courts are also slow to order the disclosure of a document, unless the requesting party can demonstrate both its existence and relevance (NCPC art. 133).[88] Since the role of the court is to adjudicate between the private parties who have come before it, the courts do not see it as their role to assist the parties in their dispute: 'The parties will produce the documents necessary to the resolution of their dispute. If they are unable to do so, that is unfortunate, but the willingness of the courts to decide the matter on the basis of what they can produce is enough for the preservation of public order.'[89] The Anglo-American practice of discovery is antithetical to French notions of the correct role of the civil court: the court is to resolve an existing dispute on the basis of already available evidence, not enable the pursuit or development of a dispute by obtaining new evidence. As a result, the investigative discovery of documents is illegal.[90] Civil parties also have the right not to give evidence against themselves: *nemo tenetur edere contra se* ('no one is obliged to testify against herself').[91] Parties do not take an oath, although non-parties do, since the factual statements of parties do not constitute evidential material in the same way that the statements of third parties do. When the parties make statements to the court, there is no requirement that the statements be made to the court in public (NCPC art. 188). These statements 'enlighten' the judge, but cannot resolve issues of fact.[92]

4.3.1.1.2 England and Wales: the Rules of the Supreme Court English civil litigation in the nineteenth century and most of the twentieth century was governed by *laissez-faire* liberalism. Until the Supreme Court of Judicature Acts 1873 and 1875, commonly referred to simply as 'the Judicature

[87] Beardsley, 'Proof of Fact', 462. [88] Ibid., 474. [89] Ibid., 464.
[90] Law No. 80–538 of 16 July 1980, *Journal Officiel* 17 July 1980.
[91] The same principle has not made much headway in French criminal law.
[92] See also NCPC art. 198.

Acts', English civil litigation had fallen within the jurisdiction of a number of courts, whose origins were in common law (King's Bench, Exchequer and Common Pleas), equity (predominantly Chancery, with Exchequer exercising some equitable jurisdiction) and civil law (the High Court of Admiralty and a number of ecclesiastical courts). By the nineteenth century, it was recognized that complex and rigid rules of procedure, across a multiplicity of courts with overlapping jurisdiction, were the main focus of courts and litigants, rather than the merits of the case.[93] Odgers has suggested that, by the time of the Judicature Acts, 'half the actions were decided not on their real merits, but on questions of form and pleading'.[94] The Judicature Acts unified and simplified the jurisdiction of these civil courts, and the RSC were subsequently introduced in 1883.[95] The RSC sought to rectify a situation in which a plaintiff who brought an action under the wrong form of action could be non-suited, even though her case had substantive merit.[96]

The effect of this focus on procedural formalities was that parties were able to use procedural technicalities as a weapon in litigation, rather than addressing the substantive merits of the case. For example, repeated interlocutory applications to resolve procedural irregularities could be used to attempt to trip up one's opponent, or to exhaust her financially,[97] and parties could delay in complying with procedural requirements. A defining characteristic of the RSC was that doing justice on the merits of the case was more important than enforcing compliance with the rules or court orders.[98] Bowen LJ, for example, commented in 1884 that:

> [T]he object of the Courts is to decide the rights of parties, and not to punish them for mistakes they make in the conduct of their cases by deciding otherwise than in accordance with their rights . . . I know of no kind of error or mistake which, if not fraudulent or intended to overreach, the

93 A. Zuckerman, *Civil Procedure: Principles of Practice*, 2nd edn (London: Sweet and Maxwell, 2006), pp. 27–9. A well-known fictional example is Charles Dickens' Chancery suit of *Jarndyce and Jarndyce*, in his 1852–3 *Bleak House*.

94 W. Odgers, 'Changes in Procedure and the Law of Evidence', in *A Century of Law Reform* (London: Macmillan, 1901), pp. 203–40, p. 203.

95 See J. Jacob, *The Fabric of English Civil Justice* (London: Stevens, 1987), pp. 246–50.

96 Odgers, 'Changes in Procedure', p. 212.

97 This was again observed to be the case just over a century later, when Lord Woolf considered the reform of the civil justice system in his *Access to Justice: Final Report*, [7.23].

98 Zuckerman, *Civil Procedure*, pp. 30–1. RSC Ord. 70 r. 1.

> Court ought not to correct, if it can be done without injustice to the other party.[99]

In one sense, the RSC did not change the approach to civil litigation that had gone before. While the RSC ended the practice of parties moving between courts, at least in part to create expense and delay that might wear down their opponents, it did not address an underlying difficulty, that the parties not only had the right to determine which legal and factual issues would be put before the court, and the evidence that would support those issues, but also had dominant control over the procedures that would be used to address those issues, and the timescales. It therefore continued to be the case that the civil courts provided a backdrop against which the parties could argue out their disputes before an authoritative third party. With this adversarial culture in place, it was almost inevitable that parties and their legal teams would find ways in which the new procedural culture of the RSC could be turned to each party's advantage. The consequence was that, rather than attempting to use the rigidity of the old systems to delay or defeat claims on points of procedure, the parties turned instead to using the flexibility of the new system to wage wars of attrition against their opponents. Although one may argue that every procedural rule is in principle capable of being manipulated for strategic advantage, this is only possible if the manipulation is permitted by the judge as referee of the contest. Since the courts had bound themselves not to intervene in the conduct of litigation, and to tolerate breaches of the rules, parties could create delay by deliberate minor infringements of the rules.[100]

Where the Judicature Acts and RSC did introduce significant change was that the liberal approach to civil litigation was now expressly intended, rather than perhaps being perceived as an accident of history. One of the benefits of codification may be seen as the provision of a clearer canvas on which those who write and those who judicially interpret the rules can lay out how they see the rules as operating. The RSC were clearly intended to make it easier for parties to conduct their private disputes before the courts. The relaxation of procedural formalities drew a clear line beyond which the judiciary could not tread in their involvement in the running of a case. In the long term, the way in which procedural systems operate may not be the way in which their creators intended. Not only do we have

99 *Cropper* v. *Smith* (1884) ChD 700, 710–11 (CA).

100 The enhanced case management powers available under the CPR have effectively ended such delays, which are now likely to be penalized in costs, under CPR r. 44.3(4)(a) and 44.3(5).

the example of how the RSC merely created new opportunities for parties to engage in delaying tactics in litigation, but also the relaxation of the rules of pleading, and the introduction of judge-only ('bench') civil trials, had the effect that the judiciary were intended to play a greater role in fact finding.

4.3.1.2 The welfare state

The work of Klein, and in particular his 1893 draft of the Austrian Zivilprozessordnung,[101] had a significant impact on procedural reform in Europe in the course of the twentieth century. Klein argued that legal disputes should be perceived as negative social phenomena. His proposals for the reform of civil procedure were therefore focused on developing a procedure that would make it possible to deal with this social phenomenon in an expedient and efficient way. His proposed measures included restricting procedural objections, simplifying the regulations on jurisdiction, limiting trials where possible to a single oral hearing, shortening time limits and preventing party adjournments. The central aspect of his proposals was a massive strengthening of the powers of the judge, especially by giving him control over the substantive aspects of litigation and also the power to direct the formal course of proceedings.

4.3.1.2.1 Germany: Zivilprozessordnung 1933 In the course of the eighteenth and nineteenth centuries, the German states had begun the codification of their respective civil systems, so that, by the time of Unification in 1871, the 'pure' procedure of the old *gemeines Recht*, itself born out of Roman-canon law, had already disappeared all over Germany.[102] The Reichscivilprocessordnung 1877, [103] like the codes in France and Italy,[104] was based on strong liberal principles, under which the parties had total power to manage their case and to determine and specify the contents, course and duration of the proceedings. These liberal

[101] P. Oberhammer and T. Domej, 'Germany, Switzerland and Austria (ca. 1800–2005)', in C. van Rhee (ed.), *European Traditions in Civil Procedure* (Antwerp: Intersentia, 2005), pp. 103–28, p. 121.

[102] Ibid., p. 107.

[103] P. Gottwald, 'Simplified Civil Procedure in West Germany' (1983) 31 *American Journal of Comparative Law* 687–701, at 687.

[104] Code de procédure civile 1806 in France; Codice di procedura civile del regno d'Italia 1865.

principles were replaced in Germany in 1933 by the Zivilprozessordnung, which presented a model of judicial procedure as a 'public welfare institution'.[105]

The German ZPO of 1933 was strongly influenced by developments in Austrian procedural theory. The ZPO also imposed on the parties a duty to tell the truth in their pleadings. Where the parties are required to make a statement to the court on the facts, this is not usually under oath (ZPO ss. 445–51). However, 'if the result of the un-sworn statement of a party is not sufficient to convince the court of the truth or untruth of the fact which can be proven', then the party can be required to give a statement under oath (s. 452). There is also a duty on the court to clarify issues of fact and law (s. 139), and not to take into account allegations known to be untrue.[106] Although the court may obtain evidence *ex officio*, it may not consider that evidence unless it is adopted by one of the parties in its submissions.[107] However, the court may probe the quality of the evidence, and appoint an expert to make investigations: 'In other words, the court may look for the truth beyond the confines of the evidence offered by the parties.'[108] German judges make extensive use of the fact-finding powers confided in them.[109] The use of German court experts can be seen as tying in with this interest in defining the truth. German judges are constrained to the factual issues to investigate, as are German experts. Experts therefore do not undertake a free-ranging enquiry, and there are in practice strong political controls over the choice of expert.

4.3.1.2.2 Italy: Codice di procedura civile 1940 Although the civil procedural codes of the nineteenth century Italian states and the early unified Kingdom of Italy were based extensively on the French Code civil, by the fascist era Italian procedural theory was heavily influenced by the German welfare state model. The CPC of 1940 merged existing *laissez-faire* ideas about civil procedure with the newer idea of civil procedure as an activity of the welfare state. The drafting of the CPC was heavily influenced by the work of Giuseppe Chiovenda, 'the father of modern civil

105 Gottwald, 'Simplified Civil Procedure', 688–9.
106 A. Freckmann and T. Wegerich, *The German Legal System* (London: Sweet and Maxwell, 1999), p. 142.
107 Gottwald, 'Simplified Civil Procedure', 692.
108 H. Kötz, 'Civil Litigation and Public Interest' (1982) 1 *Civil Justice Quarterly* 237, 239.
109 Langbein, 'German Advantage'.

procedure in Italy'.[110] He elaborated a system of civil procedure based on German procedural concepts. Chiovenda argued that the administration of justice is the proper function of the modern state. Civil justice is more than just arbitration, by virtue of the presence of a public body. Civil litigation reinforces social (or at least state) values by being policy-implementing. The state reserves to itself the right to apply the law to concrete cases, but the exercise of this right pre-supposes that the state believes that it has correctly ascertained the facts.[111] The state therefore has a duty and a right to engage in accurate fact finding, as part of its right to apply the law. The decision is binding as an act of public will, independently of the intrinsic truth of the case and the agreement of the parties. Therefore, the state cannot allow itself to be drawn blindly into proceedings in which it has no basis on which to be confident that the law is being applied to the correct facts.

Chiovenda's aspirations are not fully realized in the CPC. It is true that Italian civil procedure has inherited from the Germans a general duty to establish the truth. For example, the *giudice istruttore* has 'all powers necessary for the prompt and fair unfolding of the proceeding' (CPC art. 175(1)). Strong powers to direct proceedings and to find the truth[112] are not, however, fully utilized: '[T]his general provision has not been interpreted to invest the judge with sufficiently broad discretionary powers to make it of great practical importance.'[113] Alongside this seeming reluctance by the Corte di cassazione to encourage the lower courts to interpret the code in a way compatible with the CPC art. 175(1) objective, the code also fails to impose a duty on Italian parties to tell the truth. We might see the Italian civil provision for both court and party experts in a single civil case as an expression of some uncertainty about how liberal and welfare concepts should be combined.

4.3.1.2.3 France: Nouveau code de procédure civile of 1975 The Nouveau code de procédure civile of 1975 is the product of a period of reform

[110] S. Chiarloni, 'Civil Justice and its Paradoxes: An Italian Perspective', in A. Zuckerman, S. Chiarloni and P. Gottwald, *Civil Justice in Crisis: Comparative Perspectives of Civil Procedure* (Oxford: Oxford University Press, 1999) pp. 263–90, p. 265.

[111] G. Chiovenda, *Principii di diritto processuale civile: le azioni, il processo di cognizione*, 3rd edn (Naples: Eugenio Jovene, 1965), p. 65.

[112] Chiarloni, 'Civil Justice', p. 266.

[113] M. Cappelletti and J. Perillo, *Civil Procedure in Italy* (The Hague: Martinus Nijhoff, 1965), pp. 174–5.

that lasted from 1963 to 1981.[114] It is founded on 'guiding procedural principles', contained in its first chapter, comprising twenty-four articles in ten sections. Cadiet has suggested that the new code is 'essentially a work of composition', attempting to combine France's liberal procedural tradition with a future direction towards greater judicial management.[115] French civil procedure continues to be adversarial, in the sense that only the parties may institute proceedings, which they may terminate prior to judgment (NCPC art. 1). The parties also have the right to determine the subject matter of the case (art. 4), and the judge must rule only on the points in issue introduced by the parties (art. 5), and on the facts relating to those issues (art. 7). However, the parties may not limit the legal points that the judge may consider (art. 12), and the judge is entitled to call and question, of his own motion, 'any person whose hearing he deems useful for the manifestation of truth' (art. 218) as part of the *enquête* ('investigation') (arts. 204–31).[116] Under the principle of *contradiction* ('adversarial process') (arts. 14–17), the parties have the right to respond to issues of fact and law adverse to their case, but the judge is not limited only to the evidence and legal arguments that the parties choose to present.

The French civil reforms of the 1970s introduced provisions to increase the commitment of the court and the parties to accurate fact determination. Code civil ('CC') art. 10 (as amended in 1972)[117] provides that: 'Everyone is bound to cooperate with the judicial authorities with a view to procuring the manifestation of truth. He who, in the absence of a legitimate motive, fails to respect this obligation when he has been legally required to do so, may be forced to comply by penalty or civil fine, and this without prejudice to damages'. NCPC art. 11 supports this by requiring that:

> Parties shall be held to assist in the implementation of directions, save that the judge may draw such conclusions from the abstention or refusal of a party in relation to the same. Where a party is withholding an item of evidence, the judge may, on the application of the other party, order him to produce the same, where necessary under pain of a civil penalty. He may, on

[114] L. Cadiet, 'The New French Code of Civil Procedure (1975)', in C. van Rhee (ed.), *European Traditions in Civil Procedure* (Antwerp: Intersentia, 2005), pp. 49–68, p. 50; Cour de cassation, *Le nouveau code de procédure civile: vingt ans après* (Paris: La Documentation Française, 1998).

[115] Cadiet, 'New French Code', pp. 58–9.

[116] On the origins of the *enquête* in civil procedure, see R. Millar (ed.), *A History of Continental Civil Procedure* (London: J. Murray, 1928), pp. 681 and 723.

[117] Law no. 72–626 of 5 July 1972, art. 12, *Journal Officiel* 9 July 1972.

> application by one of the parties, request or order, where necessary under the same penalty, the production of all exhibits in the possession of third parties where there are no legitimate impediments to producing them.

This new emphasis did not represent a radical departure from adversarial principles, however. The primary focus of these new duties is on the parties to assist the court, not on the judge to direct the parties. The parties produce the evidence, and must persuade the court of the pertinence of the proposed testimony. Evidence is received directly by the judge, with the witness speaking largely discursively (arts. 213–14), and there is no cross-examination. The judge asks the *avocats* at the end of her questioning if there are any other questions. Despite the introduction of CC art. 10, it continues to be the case that the discovery is an exception rather than a norm in French civil procedure.[118]

4.3.1.3 The managerial State

Within the welfare state, civil disputes are seen as being a pathology within a smoothly functioning society. The courts therefore have a mandate to resolve the disputes, for the good not only of the parties but of society as a whole. To that end, civil justice might be treated like a health service, in which the state pays for, or subsidizes, treatment at the point of delivery. However, irrespective of whether the state is resolving disputes for the good of the parties (a liberal model) or of society (a welfare model), such a service consumes resources. As the volume and complexity of civil litigation increases over time, states must increasingly be conscious of the public resources, in terms of time and money, that are invested in civil litigation. Unnecessary delay in litigation affects the efficient functioning of the everyday lives of the parties, and it affects the same functioning in the court service. The managerial state takes control of its expenditure of these resources, and reconsiders how costs are distributed.

A leading example of the development of managerial civil justice can be seen in England at the end of the twentieth century, through a threefold development. First, the Lord Chancellor's Department amended the civil court fee system, so that litigants were in principle responsible for all the courts' costs in handling litigation. Secondly, the state's financial assistance that had been available to certain categories of litigant was significantly reduced (Section 3.6.1.2.2). Thirdly, the CPR granted the courts extensive

[118] Beardsley, 'Proof of Fact', 462.

powers of case management, including control over the progress of a case, timetabling, resources and costs.[119]

The introduction in England and Wales of the CPR in April 1999 saw a clear change in the stated purpose of English civil procedure. This in turn affected the way in which experts are used and perceived. It continues to be the case that English civil procedure under the CPR, as under the RSC, is perceived primarily as being intended to resolve private disputes between parties. However, the CPR have qualified the idea that the courts should be a state-funded dispute resolution service, by requiring that the judge have regard to the finite resources both of the litigants themselves and of the State. This in turn required that the judiciary be given much greater powers of case management, including greater discretionary power.

The change under the CPR was the result of Lord Woolf's conclusion, in his 1996 *Access to Justice: Final Report*, that the problems of cost and delay facing the civil justice system in the 1990s were the direct products of a formalistic approach to litigation, in which litigants controlled the course of litigation and manipulated the wording of the RSC in order to use the court system as a weapon in the dispute rather than as part of the solution. Woolf recommended that the key to resolving this abuse of process was to give greater control over civil actions to the judiciary, in the form of greater case management responsibilities and powers.[120] These rules represent a significant development in English civil procedure culture. While the initiation of litigation and definition of its scope is still determined by the parties, the conduct of litigation is now primarily controlled by the court (CPR r. 1.1(1)).

CPR r. 1.1 introduces a 'three-dimensional concept of justice' that requires the court to consider the imperatives of ascertaining the truth, proportionality and timely dispute resolution.[121] It therefore discourages a legalistic approach to the interpretation of the CPR. It passes control over the litigation process from the litigants to the courts, and ensures

[119] In recent years, French judges have similarly been granted greater powers to manage cases, e.g. J.-C. Magendie, *Célérité et qualité de la justice: la gestion du temps dans le procès. Rapport au Garde des Sceaux, ministre de la Justice* (Paris: La Documentation française, 2004).

[120] Woolf, *Access to Justice: Final Report*, [3.1].

[121] Zuckerman, *Civil Procedure*, pp. 3–6. The CPR are secondary legislation, which have force by virtue of the Civil Procedure Act 1997. Section 1(3) of that Act charges the Rules Committee to 'make Civil Procedure Rules . . . with a view to securing that the civil justice system is accessible, fair and efficient'.

that the spirit of the rules prevails over the exact letter. Decisions under the CPR can only be understood properly by reference to the Overriding Objective. The court further has a duty both 'to give effect to the overriding objective . . . ' (CPR r. 1.2) and to 'further the overriding duty by actively managing cases' (CPR r. 1.4). For their part, 'the parties are required to help the court to further the overriding objective' (CPR r. 1.3). If the parties are to comply with this duty, then they must of their own initiative forgo a large part of their ability to manipulate procedural rules to their advantage. Failure to comply with this duty may result in retrospective penalties, primarily in costs, at a later stage in the litigation. Unlike the French procedural reforms of the 1970s, the CPR do not expressly commit the court or parties to the pursuit of truth. It would appear that it was felt by the CPR's authors to be 'so obviously part of the court's role that it does not need to be stated expressly in the Rules'.[122] The issue is correctly framed as being not whether the court has a commitment to truth, but rather where truth fits into its overall hierarchy of goals.

Woolf himself appears to have believed that the CPR, and in particular the Overriding Objective, represented a total break with the traditions of the RSC. For example, in *Biguzzi* v. *Rank Leisure*, Lord Woolf, presiding in the Court of Appeal, held that 'The whole purpose of making the CPR a self-contained code was to send the message which now generally applies. Earlier authorities are no longer generally of any relevance once the CPR applies.'[123] Lord Woolf may be overstating his case, however, for two reasons. The first is that to apply Lord Woolf's advice would be to go against the spirit of the Overriding Objective, in incurring unnecessary costs in re-establishing principles of procedure that, pragmatically, remain largely untouched from the RSC. The Court of Appeal subsequently qualified, in relation to this, that the underlying thought processes of previous decisions should not be thrown completely overboard.[124] But even if it is true that the old precedents do still apply, the basis on which we recognize their validity as precedents, our 'rule of recognition',[125] has changed. Rather than simply say that the old precedents remain valid because the wording of the rules and principles has remained 'undisturbed', the basis on which we should retain them is new: it would be contrary to the

122 Zuckerman, *Civil Procedure*, p. 7.
123 *Biguzzi* v. *Rank Leisure* [1999] 1 WLR 1926; [1999] 4 All ER 934 (CA).
124 *Purdy* v. *Cambran* [2000] CPR 67 (CA); *Habib Bank Ltd* v. *Jaffer (Gulzar Haider)* [2000] CPLR 438 (CA); *Walsh* v. *Misseldine* [2000] CPR 74 (CA).
125 H. Hart, *The Concept of Law*, 2nd edn (Oxford: Oxford University Press, 1994), p. 57.

imperative of proportionality for the old precedents to be lost, because it would require that the court expend effort re-implementing elements of a procedural framework that were perceived to function adequately under the RSC.

The second difficulty with Lord Woolf's view is that some of the changes contained in the CPR were already beginning to be implemented in the final years of the RSC. Concerns about the excessive use of experts in civil litigation were already being raised in the early 1990s.[126] In addition, the right of the parties to rely on an unlimited number of experts was limited by RSC Ord. 38 rr. 36, 37 in the 1990s,[127] and experiments with the use of single (court-appointed) experts began in 1996 (Section 5.6.3). In relation to the use of expert evidence, the CPR may be seen as an evolutionary development rather than a revolution.

The CPR seek to provide more efficient use of state resources, and more predictable and controlled use of party resources, through more active case management. This is, however, at the expense of elements of the principle of adversarialism within the Anglo-American tradition, including party control of evidence. Whereas the RSC provided an adversarial forum in which the parties were able to produce whatever (relevant) evidence best supported their case, irrespective of the impact on the cost or length of litigation, the CPR now require that the party persuade the court that the cost required to adduce that evidence is warranted by the benefit that it will provide (a utilitarian argument). Under the RSC, it was not only in the interests of the parties to produce as many expert witnesses as they could afford, in the hope that this would help persuade the tribunal of fact that this was the most appropriate expert opinion, but also in a party's interest to produce as many, and as lengthy, expert reports as possible, and examine as many expert witnesses as possible at trial, in the hope that this would wear down her opponents financially. The 'unnecessary' use of expert witnesses can in this way be very effective in civil litigation, in terms of winning a case, although not necessarily in terms of ascertaining the truth.

The significant change in the use of experts under CPR Pt 35, and the nature of the expert roles, is a direct reflection of the much broader change in the culture of English civil procedure. Following the

[126] E.g. *National Justice Compania* v. *Prudential Assurance* [1993] 2 Ll Rep 68 (*The Ikarian Reefer*) (Comm. Ct).

[127] Introduced following criticism by Staughton LJ in *Rawlinson* v. *Westbrook*, Court of Appeal, 26 January 1995.

principle of proportionality in the Overriding Objective, experts are only to be used in litigation to the extent that a judge can be persuaded is necessary, based on both the value of the case and its complexity. In the majority of cases, it is therefore probable that only one expert will be appointed in total in each area of required expertise. Thus, the single joint expert is a logical extension of the principle of proportionality.[128] Where party experts are to be used, their overriding duty is now to the court rather than to the party that instructs them. This change in duty at least in part reflects change in ethos embodied in the new requirement on the parties 'to help the court to further the overriding objective' (CPR r. 1.3).

4.3.1.4 The special nature of Family proceedings

Family disputes are one area in which states appear reluctant to leave the conduct of civil litigation solely to the parties. Damaška has suggested that it is a feature of the European legal tradition for Family (and related) civil proceedings to be dealt with differently from other types of civil proceeding, with the state taking a more active interest in Family matters.[129] The state sees itself as being automatically joined to such actions as *parens patriae*. For example, Italian civil procedure since 1940 has allowed for state intervention in certain proceedings, such as divorce, by the *pubblico ministero* ('the public prosecutor').[130] The *pubblico ministero*'s submissions are not purely evidential, and may also form the basis of a decision (CPC arts. 70, 115).

In England, proceedings in the Family Division of the High Court, unlike in the Chancery and Queen's Bench Divisions, have made extensive use of court experts since the late 1960s. At that point Family judges began to instruct the Official Solicitor, an officer of the court who may act as guardian *ad litem* of a child, to instruct an expert on behalf of the

[128] The introduction of proportionality into decisions in civil case management under the CPR broadly coincides with the emergence of proportionality as a free-standing ground of judicial review: contrast *Council of Civil Service Unions* v. *Minister of State for Civil Service* [1985] AC 374 ('*GCHQ*') 411 ('possible adoption in the future') with *A* v. *Secretary of State Home Department* [2004] EWCA Civ 1123; [2005] 1 WLR 414, at [234] ('which the common law has made its own'). Woolf is himself an administrative lawyer: e.g. Lord Woolf, J. Jowell and A. Le Sueur (eds.), *De Smith, Woolf and Jowell's Judicial Review of Administrative Action*, 5th edn (London: Sweet and Maxwell, 1995).

[129] Damaška, *Evidence Law Adrift*, p. 104 fn. 64.

[130] The use of the *pubblico ministero* in civil proceedings was one of the features introduced by the fascist-era CPC.

court.[131] Basten provides two convincing reasons for why this development occurred in the Family Court and not elsewhere.[132] First, the Family Court did not stand as a neutral onlooker to a dispute, as was the case in Chancery or the Queen's Bench. Instead, it had a legal duty as *parens patriae* to have regard for the best interests of the child, separate from those of the parties (Section 3.5.5). Secondly, the Family Court had the practical ability, through the Official Solicitor, to identify and instruct suitable experts.[133] Court experts are today used in child law matters, certain types of nullity, and paternity cases.[134] Since 1999, parties to ancillary relief proceedings[135] have been encouraged to make use of single joint experts.[136] In France, the *enquête* ('oral enquiry') is common practice only in Family cases,[137] where the courts have a particular interest in establishing the truth independently of the parties. The usual right of a French civil judge to refuse a party's request to appoint an expert, when the judge thinks she is sufficiently informed, is constrained in relation to certain matters in Family law, beginning with questions of parentage.[138]

4.3.2 The role of facts in civil procedure

4.3.2.1 The 'fact avoidance' hypothesis

Tied up in the discussion about the function of civil litigation in society is a question about the extent to which the court should engage in the discovery of the truth. Although the Benthamite model of fair procedure

[131] E.g. *Re S (Infants)*; *Re L (an infant)*. In any civil proceedings, the Official Solicitor 'may at any time be called on by a judge to carry out an investigation and to assist the court to see that justice is done between the parties'. However, the Family courts make particular use of her to act as guardian *ad litem*.

[132] Basten, 'The Court Expert', 177.

[133] The difficulty of appointing court experts may be the main obstacle to their appointment in the United States: S. Gross, 'Expert Evidence' (1991) 6 *Wisconsin Law Review* 1113–232, 1191.

[134] Law Reform Committee, *Evidence of Opinion*; Jolowicz, *On Civil Procedure*, p. 229; Children Act 1989 s. 7; Family Proceedings Rules 1991 ('FPR') r. 2.22; Family Law Reform Act 1969 s. 20 (as amended).

[135] These deal with the financial and property aspects of divorce.

[136] FPR r. 2.61C.

[137] Beardsley, 'Proof of Facts', 478.

[138] Where the mother of a child seeks a legal declaration of the paternity of a child, the court must appoint an expert unless there is a legitimate reason not to do so: Cour de cassation civ., 1e, 28 March 2000; Cour de cassation civ., 1e, 30 May 2000. This ruling has been extended to other aspects of Family law. The default position is otherwise that a judge may always refuse to appoint an expert when she thinks she is sufficiently informed.

requires rectitude of decision, which in turn rests on accurate fact determination,[139] there appears to be a general recognition that the pursuit of truth by the state cannot be unbridled. A theory of the role of the state in civil as well as criminal justice requires the balancing of a number of rights and duties, in which rights to the truth and possible duties to establish the truth must be weighed against other interests necessary to the safeguarding of a free society.[140] The question of the extent and nature of the court's interest in the truth in civil process is therefore addressed primarily by a consideration of the court's general role in civil litigation.

Within that general discussion, there is, however, also a more specialized question, about the extent to which the courts will engage with the facticity of a case. In particular, the American attorney Beardsley has suggested that French courts practice systematic 'fact avoidance'.[141] A similar view was taken by Capelletti and Perillo, who wrote that '[a]s a rule, Italian lawyers [i.e. not just judges] do not "waste" their time digging into the facts of the case'.[142] This is not the place to conduct a detailed comparative analysis of the relative merits of fact-finding mechanisms and cultures in the English, American, French, German and Italian civil systems. Some very preliminary attempts at such an exercise were made by Mirjan Damaška in the 1970s, looking at the relative merits of 'adversarial' and 'inquisitorial' criminal systems.[143] I wish merely for present purposes to consider some of the points made by the American attorney Beardsley in levelling the charge of 'fact avoidance', and suggest that, although it is a valid point that Franco-Italian courts, and trial lawyers, are less interested in facts than their Anglo-American colleagues, the differences between Franco-Italian and Anglo-American approaches to evidence are best understood more in terms of variations in emphasis and style, than as significant differences in approach. The German civil courts show a commitment to investigating the truth of parties' factual allegations that excludes them from this charge.

This brief analysis is worthwhile in the current context because Beardsley's argument includes the contention that the use of single experts by the French courts represents an example of 'fact avoidance', through systematic de facto, if not actually de iure, delegation of complex fact

[139] W. Twining, *Theories of Evidence: Bentham and Wigmore* (London: Weidenfeld and Nicolson, 1985), pp. 47–8.

[140] Damaška, 'Evidentiary Barriers'. [141] Beardsley, 'Proof of Facts'.

[142] Cappelletti and Perillo, *Civil Procedure in Italy*, p. 182.

[143] M. Damaška, 'Presentation of Evidence and Factfinding Precision' (1975) 123 *University of Pennsylvania Law Review* 1083–106.

finding to specialists outside the tribunal of fact. In addition to proposing that Beardsley has overstated his case, and that most of his proposed 'fact avoidance' features in French civil procedure can also be identified in Anglo-American civil procedure, I should also like to propose possible reasons for the differences.

4.3.2.2 'Fact avoidance' or 'fact aversion'?

There are four main areas in which Beardsley contrasts 'fact avoidance' by the French courts with a willingness to engage in facts by American courts: first, an emphasis on written over *viva voce* evidence; secondly, the use of legal proof devices such as presumptions and oaths rather than full reliance on free proof; thirdly, the reluctance of the French courts to engage in the disclosure of documents; fourthly, the use of single court experts by the French courts, and an aversion to such practice by the American courts. Because of similarities between the French and Italian systems on the one hand, and the American and English on the other, Beardsley's argument is usefully assessed in terms of a wider comparison between Franco-Italian and Anglo-American civil procedural systems.

'Orality' is a defining feature of French civil procedure, at least since the 1789 Revolution. However, this term applies to the orality of legal argument rather than the orality of evidence. Oral testimony is collected before trial, and recorded in written form by the *juge de la mise én etat* ('pre-trial judge') to form part of the *dossier*.[144] The *dossier* contains all the case material before the court, and is passed on to a higher tribunal on appeal. Although this use of the *dossier* to record testimony does in part reflect 'the traditional distrust of oral evidence'[145] in favour of written forms of evidence, it could be countered in opposition that Anglo-American civil procedure has traditionally over-emphasized the importance of oral testimony at trial, even when examination-in-chief and cross-examination often elicit no further information than was available from the written witness statements exchanged before trial. This over-emphasis on oral

[144] In Germany at least, the judge will summarize the testimony, and the parties' lawyers are then free to suggest improvements in the wording: J. Langbein, 'Trashing the German Advantage' (1988) 82 *Northwestern University Law Review* 763–84, 772. See also B. Kaplan, A. von Mehren and R. Schaefer, 'Phases of German Civil Procedure I' (1958) 71 *Harvard Law Review* 1193–268.

[145] Beardsley, 'Proof of Facts', 459.

testimony in English civil procedure has been moderated by the CPR, particularly in low-value cases, and particularly in relation to the evidence of experts. Two additional advantages of the *dossier* over the contemporaneous trial transcript are, first, that it allows the trial court to consider the content of witness testimony at its leisure, and, secondly, that it allows for a full review of the evidence by an appellate court, on a similar basis to that of the initial assessment by the court of first instance. Where evidence is given orally at trial, appellate courts may be reluctant to review evidence in full, since they do not have access to all the information available to the court of first instance.

The second aspect of the Franco-Italian approach to evidence that might be considered to display 'fact avoidance' is the use of presumptions and oaths to resolve conflicts, or inadequacies, of evidence. French (and Italian) civil procedure are based on a mixed system of proof, combining free proof with legal proof.[146] Although continental European evidence may be based on the twin principles of *liberté des preuves* ('freedom of proof') and *liberté d'appréciation* ('freedom to assess, appreciate and evaluate evidence'),[147] so that 'all data which can prove a relevant fact are admissible in evidence',[148] in practice the court chooses to constrain its own freedom.[149]

In the CC, the main section on obligations appears in the third section (CC arts. 1349–53) of the chapter relating to obligations (arts. 1315–69), although presumptions do not only belong to the realm of the law of obligations. Presumptions can also be created by statute (art. 1350). They are 'the consequences that a statute or the court draws from a known fact to an unknown fact' (art. 1349). A classic example of a presumption in French civil law is that 'a child conceived during a marriage has the husband for his father" (art. 312). In addition, the CC provides some indications of the weight to be given to certain pieces of evidence. For example, 'An instrument, either authentic, or under private signature, is evidence between the parties, even of what is expressed only in declaratory

[146] Cappelletti and Perillo, *Civil Procedure in Italy*, pp. 190–215; D. Dwyer, 'What Does it Mean to be Free? The Concept of Free Proof in the Western European Legal Tradition' (2005) 3 *International Commentary on Evidence* iss. 1, art. 6, www.bepress. com/ice/vol3/iss1/art6 (last accessed 1 August 2008).

[147] P. Margot, 'The Role of the Forensic Scientist in an Inquisitorial System of Justice' (1998) 38 *Science and Justice* 71–3, 71.

[148] Rassat, 'Forensic Expertise', p. 55.

[149] On constraints on freedom of proof in continental criminal law, see W. Twining, 'Freedom of Proof and the Reform of Criminal Evidence' (1997) 31 *Israel Law Review* 439–63.

terms, provided the declaration has a direct connection with the operative part. Declarations irrelevant to the operative part may only be used as a commencement of proof' (art. 1320).[150]

The *serment décisoire* ('decisory oath') operates by allowing one of the parties, who would otherwise be unable to testify under oath, to take a solemn oath that a particular set of contended facts is true (art. 1357–69). Such an oath is irrefutable by other means: 'Where an oath tendered or tendered back has been taken, the opponent is not admitted to prove the falsity of it' (art. 1363). Decisory oaths, although available in France, are rarely invoked.[151]

For Beardsley, presumptions are 'the most telling demonstration of fact avoidance in the Civil Code provisions on proof'.[152] He would present the effect of the two techniques of presumptions and oaths as being to reduce the number of situations in which the court is required to decide between conflicting pieces of evidence. This would, however, be to present the situation unfairly. Oaths and presumptions have developed in the western legal tradition primarily to handle situations where the court has felt that reliable factual evidence has come to an end, but that the interests of justice would not best be served by ending deliberations. Presumptions exist in French criminal as well as civil evidence. They are used, for example, 'when the crime is relatively serious or difficult to establish, for example, in cases of crime against state security, customs laws, pimping or drug dealing'.[153] Presumptions in particular do not in most cases avoid decisions between facts, but they instead attempt to stretch the available facts as far they will responsibly go. Where facts conflict, the French and Italian courts have the assistance of both *présomptions du fait de l'homme* (presumptions made by the judge, which we might term 'common-sense generalizations': Section 1.4.3) in evaluating the evidence,[154] and *présomptions légales* (specifically legal norms about how such facts should be interpreted).

As well as providing a formalized means of applying generalizations, and stretching evidence in a controlled way, presumptions may also be used to further particular values. One example already given would be the French presumption of paternity, which promotes the primacy and

[150] Law no. 2000–230 of 13 March 2000, *Journal Officiel* 14 March 2000, art. 1.

[151] Beardsley, 'Proof of Facts', 472. [152] Ibid., 472.

[153] Rassat, 'Forensic Expertise'.

[154] The court must give reasons for how it has evaluated this evidence, and cannot make arbitrary decisions: Carlini v. Catrigiano, Corte di cassazione 30 January 1960 no. 140; Dal Moro v. Lucchetta, Corte di cassazione 10 December 1959.

stability of the married family unit, at the likely expense of accurate fact determination. Another would be the presumption of innocence, which places a (generally socially agreed) higher value on protecting the innocent than on punishing the guilty. Presumptions are not alien to Anglo-American fact finding, although this is the implication of Beardsley's case. They are present, for example, in the form of the burden of proof, and the presumption of innocence in criminal trials.[155] In England, the presumption of advancement, in equity, requires that in a situation where *A* buys a property, but transfers its title to *B*, then in the absence of evidence to the contrary, the court must conclude that *A* has created a resulting trust, with *B* as trustee and *A* as beneficiary. This presumption is reversed when *A* is the father of *B*, or there is a similar relationship, in which circumstance the transfer will be presumed to be a gift. Although we might think, from an Anglo-American perspective, that the French place undue emphasis on obligations and presumptions, it would be unreasonable to highlight this approach as constituting 'fact avoidance', since the Anglo-American tradition employs similar techniques.

The third area, the reluctance to use disclosure,[156] raises a seeming paradox, that on the one hand the French courts have a greater interest in determining the truth than Anglo-American courts, but on the other hand it is the Anglo-American courts that are more willing to use the powerful tool of disclosure to allow the parties to bring to trial the evidence that will better allow the truth to be discovered. Like many seeming paradoxes, this is a false dilemma, because the duty to get to the truth is a creature of French criminal rather than civil procedure, and liberal civil procedure only became subject to a nominal duty to pursue truth in the 1970s art. 10 of the Code civil. Under the traditionally *laissez-faire* approach to French civil evidence, the burden is on the parties to come to the court with the evidence required to prove their case, which is seen as a private dispute on which the state adjudicates. For the court to allow disclosure, either against the opposing party or against a party not joined to the litigation, would be to step outside the boundaries of this paradigm. The paradox therefore disappears when one understands that civil litigation has traditionally been perceived as having a different social function in France from that in the Anglo-American world.

[155] H. Malek (ed.), *Phipson on Evidence*, 16th edn (London: Sweet and Maxwell, 2005), ch. 6. See also FRE Art. III 'Presumptions in Civil Actions and Proceedings'.

[156] The older Chancery term 'discovery', used under the RSC, continues to be used in the United States of America.

The fourth and final area of possible fact avoidance is the readiness with which the French and Italian civil courts will delegate complex fact finding de facto (albeit not de iure) to a non-legal specialist, the French *expert* or Italian *consulente tecnico d'ufficio*. The use of a single court expert might be seen as constituting fact avoidance in two ways. The first is that having only one expert reduces the likelihood that the judge will choose to, or be able to, assess properly the expert's evidence, in the absence of an alternative expert view.[157] The second is that judges may be tempted to appoint experts whose opinions they believe, from past experience, are likely to support the view that the judge has herself already begun to form. There is empirical evidence from France to support both concerns.[158] In Italy, the combination of court and party experts modifies this situation, but judges still tend to put much more faith in the opinion of a court expert than that of a party expert. The use of court experts is well established in French civil and criminal procedure. However, restricting the number of experts to one is a relatively modern development, apparently driven by the desire to reduce costs.

Provisions for court experts exist under the United States FRE, although they have rarely been used, and the English civil courts have made extensive use of single experts, albeit appointed and instructed jointly by the parties, since 1999. As with the other three areas of concern drawn from Beardsley, upon closer examination what might at first have appeared as fact avoidance might be better characterized as fact aversion.

4.3.2.3 Possible reasons for fact aversion

It is worth considering two possible reasons for why a tribunal of fact might be averse to engaging in complex fact finding: a social reluctance to find adversely, and a disregard for facts in the perception of what is properly legal. The first possible reason is that the tribunal's reluctance may reflect broader cultural and social concerns about adverse fact finding. In particular, by preferring the testimony of *A* over *B*, one may be suggesting that *B* is at least wrong, and possibly lying, in a culture in which such a determination may cause loss of face, with serious social and emotional consequences for *B*. This is encountered, for example, in some South-East

157 Even when a single expert is used, it is common ground between French and English judges that the judge is free to reject the expert's opinion, e.g. *Jasim* v. *Secretary of State for the Home Department* [2006] EWCA Civ 342.

158 Bourcier and De Bonis, *Les paradoxes*.

Asian countries,[159] though there is no obvious evidence of its prevalence in modern western countries. As one of its non-epistemological concerns, the court may have a social desire not to decide between the truth statements of *A* and *B*, because to conclude that *A* has told the truth would mean that *B* has lied, and to be considered to have lied has significant social and moral consequences. The court may therefore go to efforts to avoid a statement in which facts are in issue between *A* and *B*. We might say that the risk of loss of face should be an incentive to *B* to speak only the truth, but we must bear in mind that courts are not infallible in their fact finding. For policy reasons, the courts may be slow to place potential witnesses in a position where their testimony may be affected by the fear of subsequent consequences of testifying.[160] In the western European legal tradition, where evidence is given under oath, the force of that oath was originally intended to be that perjury would have consequences before a divine as well as a terrestrial court. For a court to find against the testimony of a sworn witness may therefore be to place the witness in the category of one whom the court believes has endangered her mortal soul. However, it is unclear how, if at all, the evidential finding of a terrestrial court was historically considered to have affected the likelihood of divine retribution on a perjured witness. In the absence of such information, we should not give too much weight to the perjury argument in considering possible reasons for fact aversion among modern courts.

The second possible reason for fact aversion is that French and Italian legal education focuses so much on norms at the expense of facts that continental lawyers do not consider facts to be a full part of their legal world. It is probably fair comment that an Anglo-American legal education gives disproportionately little coverage to the analysis of facts,[161] but nevertheless Anglo-American law students are raised on a steady diet of case law, in which they must pay at least some attention to how common law principles have been developed, and statutory principles interpreted, in the light of 'the facts of the case'. There is more than a grain of truth in the notion that, while French or Italian law students learn articles of

[159] R. Aigler and I. Yates, 'The Triangle of Culture, Inference and Litigation System' (2003) 2 *Law Probability and Risk* 137–50. See also M. Damaška, 'Rational and Irrational Proof Revisited' (1997) 5 *Cardozo Journal of International and Comparative Law* 25–39; M. Damaška, 'Truth in Adjudication' (1998) 49 *Hastings Law Journal* 289–308; M. Damaška, 'Epistemology and Legal Regulation of Proof' (2003) 2 *Law Probability and Risk* 117–30.

[160] E.g. *Meadow* v. *General Medical Council* [2006] EWCA Civ 1390.

[161] W. Twining, 'Taking Facts Seriously', in *Rethinking Evidence: Exploratory Essays*, 2nd edn (Cambridge: Cambridge University Press, 2006), pp. 14–34.

codes as the sources of the law, English law students learn stories. Those stories are rich in facts, albeit facts selected to suit the eventual principle.

Franco-Italian courts do not appear to see the analysis of facts as being a proper legal function at all. The Italian proceduralist Michele Taruffo has commented on the conceptual difficulty that Italian lawyers appear to have in thinking of judges as engaging in problems using common sense, experience and science rather than legal norms.[162] Similarly, in the analysis of expert evidence, Sériaux has suggested that although both law and science produce pictures of the world, only the picture produced by science is one grounded in epistemology, while the legal picture is grounded in authority.[163] When French or Italian statutes and courts say 'fact' they seem to have in mind something close to 'ultimate fact' in common law parlance, that which makes us apply legal rule *X* rather than *Y*.[164] There is virtually no attention to intermediate facts. This may in part be the result of a legal education which is focused on legal principles rather than facts of cases when at university, and then entry directly into the judiciary, without spending time as a lawyer, dealing with the factual detail of cases for a client.

4.3.3 The appropriate conduct of civil litigation

The third possible non-epistemological factor in determining the role of the expert is the nature of what is deemed appropriate conduct in litigation, on the part of the expert, and the party and advocates who instruct her. This factor applies only to the role of party experts. Where parties or their legal representatives are expected to act with little or no restraint in their dealings with one another, for example becoming overtly pugnacious or confrontational before and at trial, we might expect this to have some effect on whether experts present themselves openly as advocates for the party calling them. In contrast, where advocates present themselves as servants of the court and of justice, and the parties exercise restraint, we might expect that experts will act in a more detached and objective fashion. Since France and Germany do not employ party experts, discussion in this section is limited to the effects on the conduct of party

[162] M. Taruffo, 'Senso comune, esperienza e scienza nel ragionamento del giudice', in *Sui confini: scritti sulla giustizia civile* (Bologna: Il Mulino, 2002) pp. 121–55, pp. 121–2.

[163] A. Sériaux, 'Pouvoir scientifique, savoir juridique' (1991) 13 *Droits* 61–6.

[164] E.g. M. Taruffo, *La prova dei fatti giuridici* (Milan: Giuffrè, 1992), p. 67.

experts in England, the United States of America and Italy. The primary focus is on litigation in the English and United States federal courts.

4.3.3.1 The appropriate conduct of litigation lawyers

The paradigm of the conduct of litigation in both Anglo-American and continental European civil jurisdictions is adversarial. This is a term that requires careful definition, because it is open to ambiguity and misinterpretation: 'Many lawyers debate procedural change and compare actual systems by invoking "the adversarial system" while remaining reluctant to define its pure form. As a result, such discussion often proceeds in the hazy atmosphere of half sense, as in the predicament of one trying to express the finely shaded nuances of cappuccino with only vague notions about coffee and milk.'[165]

By 'adversarial' in a civil context I mean a procedural system in which litigants initiate proceedings and define both the legal issue and the facts on which the issue will be determined. Before a passive tribunal, the litigants will then direct the course of litigation and the adduction of evidence. A litigant has the right to respond to any legal or factual point made by their opponent, by an evidentiary source or by the tribunal. The litigants may at any time terminate the case before the tribunal's decision is given. I do not take 'adversarial', in a procedural context, to be a synonym for 'pugnacious'. Terms like 'confrontational' or 'contentious', like 'adversarial', carry an unfortunate degree of semantic ambiguity. All adversarial litigation is 'confrontational' to the extent that the parties have the right to confront in open court those who make charges against them.[166] 'Contentious' is similarly a term of art that refers to litigation which is contested by another party.

Within this adversarial paradigm, the Anglo-American civil process tradition has a number of additional characteristics, of which the main ones are as follows. After the initial filing of claim and defence, the parties reserve the presentation of their legal and factual case until trial, which is conducted orally in open court. Witnesses, including expert witnesses, provide testimony orally, and are first questioned by the party which calls them to testify ('examination-in-chief') and then by the opposing party ('cross-examination'). Examination-in-chief is characterized by

[165] Damaška, *Evidence Law Adrift*, p. 97.

[166] As well as this general use, 'the right to confrontation' is a specific right of the defendant in Anglo-American criminal process, to confront the person bringing the charge against them.

open questions, to allow the witness to speak in their own words, with the hope that the testimony will support the case of the party calling the witness. Cross-examination is focused on trying to clarify points of evidence, with the primary intention of assisting the case of the opposing party. There is limited opportunity for the tribunal of fact to ask questions of the witness. The passive tribunal has, within modern historical times, often been bicameral. The tribunal of fact (the jury) should have no prior knowledge of the facts of the case, and no knowledge of the law. The tribunal of law (the judge) can limit the evidence that may lawfully be presented to the tribunal of fact, can direct the jurors on any legal constraints on how they may assess the evidence, and otherwise controls the conduct of the parties. Although the rules of procedure are relatively straightforward, the rules of evidence in Anglo-American courts, which are limited almost exclusively to questions of admissibility, have been increasingly complex since the eighteenth century.

I would therefore depart from a commonly held view that French civil procedure is not adversarial because the parties do not fully control the evidence.[167] Instead, I would suggest that Anglo-American civil procedure possesses an additional characteristic, beyond the core adversarialism that we see in both Anglo-American and continental European practice. In turn, the Anglo-American civil process tradition, while homogeneous when taken with a measure of spatial and temporal abstraction, becomes much more heterogeneous when we examine the detail, for example the difference between English and United States federal litigation. Three areas are of particular relevance to understanding the conduct of litigation as it affects the role of the expert: first, the role of the trial in civil litigation; secondly, the use of unified and bicameral tribunals; thirdly, the pugnacity of civil litigation.

4.3.3.1.1 The role of the trial in civil litigation The first area of relevance is that the trial is no longer the dominant focus in English or United States federal civil litigation. Pre-trial case management is of increasing importance in both English and United States federal civil litigation,[168] and, particularly in the United States, civil cases are very likely to be

[167] E.g. Jolowicz, *On Civil Procedure*, pp. 176–7.

[168] English judicial case management began to develop in the 1990s. For a discussion of the rise of the managerial judge in the United States federal courts, see Resnik, 'Changing Practices' and J. Resnik, 'Trial as Error, Jurisdiction as Injury: Transforming the Meaning of Article III' (2000) 113 *Harvard Law Review* 924–1037.

discontinued by the parties or the judge before trial.[169] In 1941, only 11.7 per cent of federal cases reached trial, while by 1995 that number had fallen to 3.2 per cent.[170] American courts make extensive use of pre-trial conferences, to identify the facts that will be in issue in trial and determine to a large extent the course of the trial, while English courts have in the main been content to issue directions, which are often of a standard form.[171]

4.3.3.1.2 Unified and bicameral tribunals The tribunal of fact is today rarely bicameral in England, with tribunals now consisting almost always of a judge sitting alone, and only half of United States federal civil trials are heard before a bicameral tribunal.[172] Advocates may be inclined to use different techniques when seeking to persuade judges and juries of the merits of their arguments. We might expect, for example, that an advocate before a judge-only trial would rely less on rhetoric and more on detailed analytical factual and legal argument.

It is worth noting that the term 'judge' here has slightly different meanings in different jurisdictions.[173] English judges are experienced lawyers, who have mostly already had successful careers as barristers, although it is now possible for a solicitor to become a judge. Although United States federal judges, appointed under Article III of the Constitution, are drawn from the ranks of experienced attorneys,[174] if we include the state judiciaries, then approximately 90 per cent of judges, being almost all state judges, are directly elected.[175] In continental Europe, by way of important contrast, the judiciary is a graduate-entry career, and it is not uncommon for lawyers to move between the judiciary and academia. Unlike in the Anglo-American world, continental judges are unlikely to have significant

[169] Discontinuance can be for a number of reasons, in particular that the litigation was commenced as a negotiating tactic by one of the parties, with no intention of proceeding to trial, or that the parties came to an agreed settlement.

[170] E. Sward, *The Decline of the Civil Jury* (Durham NC: Carolina Academic Press, 2001), p. 13; see also M. Galanter, 'The Vanishing Trial: An Examination of Trials and Related Matters in Federal and State Courts' (2004) 1 *Journal of Empirical Legal Studies* 459–570.

[171] Jolowicz, *On Civil Procedure*, pp. 41–2.

[172] In 1995, 55.4 per cent: Sward, *Decline*, p. 13.

[173] P. Atiyah and R. Summers, *Form and Substance in Anglo-American Law* (Oxford: Oxford University Press, 1987), ch. 6.

[174] Resnik, 'Trial as Error'.

[175] R. Posner, *Law and Legal Theory in England and America* (Oxford: Oxford University Press, 1996), p. 30. Langbein, 'German Advantage', has suggested that many American state appointments are overtly political in nature.

experience in private legal practice. When we consider therefore both the relationship of judges to the conduct of the parties and the expertise, and the way in which judges approach the assessment of expert evidence, we should bear in mind that, particularly depending on the jurisdiction, judges come to the bench with a very wide range of experiences.[176]

4.3.3.1.3 The pugnacity of civil litigation The conduct of litigation in the United States would appear to be far more pugnacious than in England.[177] At least five reasons can be suggested for this difference: the differing roles of the lawyers, the differing ways of funding litigation, the differing proximities of working relationship between judge and trial lawyer in the two countries, the different tribunals before which the lawyers appear, and the different formal procedural norms governing the conduct of litigation. The first possible reason for the differing degrees of pugnacity is that there are much sharper divisions in England than in the United States between the people involved in pre-trial and trial activity. In England, solicitors have the right to conduct litigation,[178] and are likely to attend pre-trial instruction hearings before Masters (judicial officers specialized in case management). One of the most important functions of the solicitor is to marshal evidence for trial, including taking sworn statements from witnesses. For trial, the case is then likely to be handed to a barrister. The barrister should not usually meet the witnesses before trial,[179] and must not under any circumstance 'coach' a witness, including an expert witness, in the case-specific questions that they might be asked or possible approaches to answering such questions.[180] In the United States, attorneys usually take a case from initial client interview through to conclusion, although specialist trial attorneys do exist. There are no constraints on the attorney meeting witnesses or preparing them in how to answer questions

[176] Although very few judges have received a scientific or technical education before entering law.

[177] Jolowicz, *On Civil Procedure*, p. 52.

[178] The right to issue a writ to start legal proceedings and to do any of the other work necessary to prepare or continue with legal proceedings, other than appearing in court: Courts and Legal Service Act 1990, Pt II.

[179] In France, *avocats* cannot communicate with non-party witnesses before the taking of evidence. Therefore, *attestations*, which are written documents, similar to affidavits, in which the witness could state her relationship to the parties and what she saw or knew, must be obtained by the parties (NCPC arts. 200–3).

[180] *R.* v. *Momodou and Limani* [2005] EWCA Crim 177; 2005] 1 WLR 3442; [2005] 2 All ER 571; P. Cooper, 'Training', in L. Blom-Cooper (ed.), *Experts in the Civil Courts* (Oxford: Oxford University Press, 2006), pp. 149–57.

(although they may not tell the witness what to say).[181] The client's advocate at trial has therefore been much more involved in the development of the case, including the assembly of evidence, in the United States than in England. The barrister's role is not only to act as an advocate for a case assembled for a party by their solicitor, but, Posner has suggested, we might take it further to suggest that barristers act almost as junior judges.[182] In particular, English barristers provide judges with advice on the law, and they are expected to eschew unmeritorious claims.[183]

The second possible reason is linked to the first. Contingency fee arrangements are prevalent in the United States for personal injury claims. This means that the attorney is paid only if her client wins, and she takes a percentage of the amount awarded. In England and Wales, either the solicitor and barrister are paid for work done, by the client or the government's Legal Aid scheme, irrespective of the outcome of the case, or else payment of a previously agreed fee (rather than a percentage) becomes due in the event of success. Prior to 1990, champerty (making payment conditional on success) as well as the related activity of maintenance (funding of litigation by a third party with no interest in that litigation) had been contrary at common law to the interests of the administration of justice. In consequence, contracts relying on maintenance or champerty were unenforceable at law, and prior to 1967 they were also both crimes and torts.[184] Since 1990, however, the Lord Chancellor has permitted solicitors and barristers to enter into civil action under conditional fee agreements ('CFAs').[185] Under a CFA, payment to the service provider is based on

[181] Atiyah and Summers, *Form and Substance*, ch. 6. In case preparation, English solicitors construct witness statements, from the information the witness provides, to best support the case. With the exchange of these statements before trial, they have increasingly taken on the role of a form of written advocacy. It is not inevitable that the attorney must meet witnesses. F. Carter, 'Court Order Violations, Witness Coaching, and Obstructing Access to Witnesses: An Examination of the Unethical Attorney Conduct that Nearly Derailed the Moussaoui Trial' (2007) 20 *Georgetown Journal of Legal Ethics* 463–74.

[182] Posner, *Law*, pp. 23–4.

[183] Although under the 'cab rank rule', a barrister cannot decline a case, one of the first acts of a barrister on taking on a 'brief' is to provide an 'opinion' on the merits of the case. One of the key functions of the opinion is to advise the client, and her solicitor, of the merits of the case, including likelihood of success. In the United States, FRCP r. 11 prohibits attorneys from filing unmeritorious claims, and provides the judge with discretion to sanction attorneys who do.

[184] *R. (Factortame)* v. *Secretary of State for Transport, Local Government and the Regions (No. 8)* [2002] EWCA Civ 932; [2003] QB 381; [2002] 3 WLR 1104; [2002] 4 All ER 97, at [31].

[185] See Zuckerman, *Civil Procedure*, pp. 1053–71, for an overview of CFAs.

the normal professional rate ('conditional normal fee agreement'), or the normal fee plus a success uplift ('conditional uplift agreement') if their instructing party is successful. Parliament permitted CFAs between litigants and solicitors and barristers.[186] In *Factortame (No. 8)* which concerned costs for litigation support services in the *Factortame* litigation, the Court of Appeal allowed that, although contingency fee agreements in general continued to give cause for concern, in certain circumstances such agreements might be in the interests of the sound administration of justice: 'One must today look at the facts of the particular case and consider whether those facts suggest that the agreement in question might tempt the allegedly champertous maintainer for his personal gain, to inflame the damages, to suppress evidence, to suborn witnesses or otherwise to undermine the ends of justice.'[187] Under any 'no win no fee' arrangement, whether on a conditional or contingency fee basis, there is surely an incentive on the lawyer to push for the success of their client's case. This may even be at the expense of professional ethics or legal constraints. Where the size of the fee depends on the size of the final award, there may be a further incentive to exaggerate the party's entitlement to damages. We might reasonably expect that this encourages more pugnacious litigation.

The third possible reason, also linked to the first, is that, because of the relatively small number of judges and barristers, a barrister is more likely to appear often before the same judge than is her American equivalent in most states. The consequences of this may be that the barrister's conduct is more likely to be moderated than that of an attorney. A barrister who expects to appear before, and so have a good working relationship with, a judge on an ongoing basis is unlikely to wish to antagonize her, or to appear to be observing rules of procedure only to the letter. Similarly, a barrister's prospects of promotion to the rank of Queen's Counsel, or to one of the grades of judiciary, continue to rest extensively on judicial opinion. These constraints may operate to a lesser extent with attorneys, since they spend less of their time in court. In a country where the career paths of advocates and judges are separate, and there is not a separation between pre-trial and trial lawyers, such as in Italy, then we might expect to see fewer constraints on the conduct of attorneys. However, in Italy, legal practice tends to centre more around local urban tribunals, and so,

186 Courts and Legal Services Act 1990, ss. 58 and 58A, as amended by Administration of Justice Act 1999, s. 27, provided the Lord Chancellor with the necessary powers to introduce statutory instruments relating to conditional fee agreements.

187 *Factortame (No. 8)*, at [36].

as in England, we might expect the same advocates to encounter the same judges on a regular basis.

The fourth possible reason for the more pugnacious nature of United States civil litigation is that jury trial is still common in America, albeit in only around half of federal cases.[188] It may be felt that the skills needed to persuade a jury of the merits, legal and factual, of a case are different from those required to persuade a judge. A jury, for example, might be persuaded by a stumbling or seemingly self-contradicting witness, or expert, under cross-examination that the testimony should be given little weight, while a trial-experienced judge might be expected to understand more the tricks of advocacy that can be used in cross-examination.

The fifth and final possible reason is that the procedural codes in the different jurisdictions, and rules of professional conduct, impose different expectations of behaviour on the party's lawyers. Both the English Civil Procedure Rules (CPR r. 1.1) and the Federal Rules of Civil Procedure (FRCP r. 1) begin with a principle of construction, incorporating elements of overall justice, speed and cost. The CPR extend this principle (their 'Overriding Objective') to the parties, who must cooperate with the court in its furtherance, while the FRCP appear to restrict this injunction to the court in its direction of proceedings. As a result of CPR r. 1, the adversarial nature of English civil procedure has been significantly reduced, both normatively and in practice: 'To the surprise of many, the response of lawyers has been wholly favourable. The adversarial advocate has given way to lawyers taking a far more co-operative stance than anyone has ever suspected would be possible.'[189] Neither the United States FRCP nor the Italian CPC impose on the parties similarly clear duties, actively enforced by the courts, to cooperate.[190]

4.3.3.2 The appropriate conduct of party experts

There would appear to be a broad correlation between the norms of conduct of litigation lawyers and those of the experts whom they employ. The most obvious area in which these party expert conduct norms operate is in relation to partisanship or bias. A detailed taxonomy of the causes

[188] Sward, *Decline*, p. 13.

[189] R. Turner, 'A New Approach to Civil Litigation', paper given at the Royal Courts of Justice, 24 June 2002. However, Master Turner was one of the architects of the CPR reforms, and so perhaps his views on its success may have been coloured by his involvement.

[190] FRCP 26(f) does impose on the parties a duty to cooperate in relation to disclosure.

and manifestations of expert bias was developed at the end of the previous chapter (Section 3.6). That taxonomy sought to be independent of jurisdiction and legal culture, although examples from primarily English and United States jurisdictions were used as illustrations. In this section, I should like to consider the question of expert bias from a different angle: how it is perceived by those in the legal system in which it occurs. The most obvious point to be made is that bias on the part of an expert is not necessarily seen as an inherently bad thing.

Judicial complaints about expert partisanship date back to the first half of the nineteenth century in England. By 1843, the view was expressed in the House of Lords in the *Tracy Peerage Case* that '[S]killed witnesses come with such a bias on their minds to support the case in which they are embarked that hardly any weight should be given to their evidence'.[191] In 1947, Hammelmann considered the view in the *Tracy Peerage Case* to be still applicable in his day. He contrasted it, however, with the situation in the United States where experts were additionally prized for their skill as advocates in the witness box: 'Private experts can be found who will set themselves up as true advocates of the party calling them, and whose fees depend not only on their professional eminence, but also upon their rhetorical gifts'.[192]

Since the late 1970s, there has been a growth in judicial concern about expert bias. In the United States it has been complained that experts would say whatever they were paid to say,[193] that parties would only employ experts who offered this service,[194] and that experts would even invent scientific methods to produce results that supported their client's case ('junk science').[195] Two clarifications need to be made about this depiction of the practice of experts in the United States courts. Both come out of the paucity of objective empirical studies of the phenomenon of expert bias.

The first clarification is that, since most of the discussion of expert partisanship is anecdotal, and takes place outside an analytical framework with which to classify properly what we mean when we talk about 'biased'

[191] *Tracy Peerage Case* (1843) Cl & Fin 154, at 191. The use of the term 'skilled witnesses' here predates the English adoption of the term 'expert' (Section 5.2.1).

[192] H. Hammelmann, 'Expert Evidence' (1947) 11 *Modern Law Review* 32–9.

[193] Langbein, 'German Advantage'.

[194] S. Moss, 'Opinion for Sale: Confessions of an Expert Witness' *Legal Affairs* March/April 2003.

[195] P. Huber, *Galileo's Revenge: Junk Science in the Courtroom* (New York: Basic Books, 1991).

or 'partisan' experts, the extent and degree of partisanship is uncertain.[196] There are at least two motivations for ascribing partisanship to an opponent's expert. The first is that the American trial process requires that the credibility of the expert's testimony needs to be proved afresh for each trial, and both parties will seek to prove not only the credibility of their own experts but also the untrustworthiness of the opponent's expert.[197] The second is that there may be political pressures to discredit certain types of expertise, in order to reduce the success of certain types of litigation. For example, Edmond and Mercer have persuasively argued that heightened concern over 'junk science' in United States civil actions in the early 1990s, culminating in *Daubert*, can be seen as an attempt by large corporations, particularly in the pharmaceutical industry, to weaken significantly toxic tort actions being brought against them.[198] Although it is tempting to wave aside concerns about an absence of objective empirical evidence for expert bias, on the grounds that we all know that such bias exists, it is a point of very important methodological concern that our evidence for bias as a phenomenon is almost entirely subjective and anecdotal.[199]

The second clarification is that practice may differ between jurisdictions within the United States, but it is not clear to what extent this is the case. The *Daubert* decision might be taken as an indication that the federal courts see expert partisanship, extending to the creation of 'junk science' for the purpose of litigation, as a real threat to the administration of

[196] This is a subject that receives little attention from legal academics in the United States. E.g. D. Bernstein, 'Expert Witnesses, Adversarial Bias, and the (Partial) Failure of the Daubert Revolution' (2007) *George Mason University Law and Economics Research Paper Series* 07–11, http://papers.ssrn.com/sol3/papers.cfm?abstract_id=963461 (last accessed 1 August 2008).

[197] S. Jasanoff, *Science at the Bar: Law, Science and Technology in America* (Cambridge MA: Harvard University Press, 1995). See also D. Walton, *Legal Argumentation and Evidence* (University Park, PA: Pennsylvania State University Press, 2002), pp. 178, 239, on the importance of an expert as someone who makes an impression on the jury.

[198] G. Edmond and D. Mercer, '*Daubert* and the Exclusionary Ethos: The Convergence of *Corporate* and *Judicial* Attitudes Towards the Admissibility of Expert Evidence in Tort Litigation' (2004) 26 *Law and Policy* 231–57; Edmond and Mercer, 'Experts and Expertise', pp. 4–5; G. Edmond and D. Mercer, 'The Invisible Branch: The Authority of Science Studies in Expert Evidence Jurisprudence', in G. Edmond (ed.), *Expertise in Regulation and Law* (Aldershot: Ashgate, 2004), pp. 197–291, pp. 225–6; K. Chesebro, 'Galileo's Retort: Peter Huber's Junk Scholarship' (1993) 42 *American University Law Review* 1637–726.

[199] For a more detailed analysis of the way in which we tend to treat as established fact the perceptions of a (significant) minority in relation to expert bias, see G. Edmond, 'After Objectivity: Expert Evidence and Procedural Reform' (2003) 25 *Sydney Law Review* 131–64.

justice. The federal court in *Ambrosini* v. *Labarraque*[200] was alert to the need to distinguish between those experts who were 'hired guns', and those who were not. This view does not appear to extend to all state courts. In Louisiana, for example, the state Supreme Court has suggested that there is no inconsistency between an expert presenting truthful testimony and doing so in the best interests of her client: 'Properly viewed, however, the roles of "hired gun" and servant of the court are not necessarily incompatible. In reality, the expert retained for litigation is hired to present truthful and competent testimony that puts his client's position in the best possible light.'[201] The advice of Sales and Shuman, in their discussion of primarily mental health experts in the federal system, suggests the degree of partisanship may vary between experts, rather than being almost uniform: '[E]xperts may have difficulty balancing these roles because of the seductiveness of the litigant, the litigant's case, or the lawyer who asks for assistance, or because they see their role as advocate for the client rather than for scientific and professional knowledge.'[202] A text such as Matson's *Effective Expert Witnessing*, a manual written for experts, has ten pages on 'effective winning strategies' and no discussion of ethics.[203]

In England, an underlying concern about expert partisanship, mentioned by Hammelmann in 1947, began to surface in the civil courts in the 1990s.[204] We can measure the speed of its ascent by reference to an article written in 1990 by Goodall, an eminent architect, a Fellow of the Chartered Institute of Arbitrators and a Fellow of the Academy of Experts, in which he had set out, among other things, the appropriate approach an expert should adopt when preparing a report for use in litigation.[205] He made it clear that, since the legal system 'makes no pretence of determining the truth but seeks only to weigh the persuasive effect of arguments deployed by one adversary or the other', it is 'within the rules of our particular game' to produce reports in which material is played down

[200] *Ambrosini* v. *Labarraque* 101 F 3d 129 (1996).

[201] *Marrogi* v. *Howard* 805 S 2 d 1118 (LA 2002), at [50].

[202] B. Sales and D. Shuman, *Experts in Court: Reconciling Law, Science, and Professional Knowledge* (Washington DC: American Psychological Association, 2005), p. 139.

[203] J. Matson, *Effective Expert Witnessing*, 3rd edn (Boca Raton FL: CRC Press, 1999), pp. 17–26.

[204] The first notable contemporary criticism of an expert for consciously adapting their report to suit her party's case occurred in the medical negligence case of *Whitehouse* v. *Jordan* [1980] 1 All ER 65 (CA), [1981] 1 WLR 246 (HL), which had been litigated in the 1970s.

[205] F. Goodall, 'The Expert Witness: Partisan with a Conscience' (1990) 56 *Journal of the Chartered Institute of Arbitrators*, quoted in *Cala Homes (South) Ltd* v. *Alfred McAlpine Homes East Ltd* [1995] FSR 818 (Ch.), at 841–4.

or omitted in order to present a particular impression. He likened being an expert to playing the three-card trick, and said that no blame should attach to the expert if the rustic chose to play. This article would appear to have passed without legal notice until the case of *Cala Homes* in 1995. Goodall appeared in that trial as an expert witness, and confirmed at the start of cross-examination that he had followed his own 1990 advice in producing his report for that case. This approach was strongly criticized by the trial judge. That an experienced and respected expert can advocate a professional position in 1990 that is judicially unacceptable by 1995 might reasonably lead us to conclude that there have been some fairly specific developments in the intervening period. What might these have been?

There are four candidate causes, which may of course operate side by side. The first is that, in 1993, in *The Ikarian Reefer*, Cresswell J expressed concern at the conduct of the expert witnesses before him, and laid down the duties of an expert witness at common law, which, seemingly for the first time, emphasized that the expert had a duty to the court as well as to their party. These principles received considerable attention in the legal and expert witness press. We could ask in turn why this particular case arose this particular judge's ire, and the answer would appear to be relatively straightforward, that this was a particularly lengthy and expensive case, in which the misuse of expert witnesses had been particularly excessive, and in which the judge had already sought before and during trial to prevent such misuse.

The second candidate is that the late 1980s and early 1990s had seen a series of convictions, mainly for terrorist offences, overturned because it was discovered that the expert evidence relied on at trial had been defective. This gave rise to significant discussion about whether the English criminal process could rely on party experts.[206] This discussion might reasonably have affected views of expert partisanship in the civil courts. The third candidate is the decision of the United States Supreme Court in *Daubert* in 1993, which may have raised the profile of the issues surrounding expert bias in the English judicial mind. The fourth candidate cause is that, by the early 1990s, both in England and in the United States, scientific and other specialist evidence was becoming so important to the administration of justice that the courts could no longer afford to tolerate

[206] Oddie, *Science*; Howard, 'The Neutral Expert'; J. Spencer, 'The Neutral Expert: An Implausible Bogey' [1991] *Criminal Law Review* 106–10; Spencer, 'Court Experts'.

partisanship on the part of the experts. It is not clear, however, why the courts would have reached this conclusion at this point in time.

The judge in *Cala Homes*, Laddie J, was not alone in deciding that expert partisanship was now unacceptable. In the *Counsel* in 1992, an editorial expressed grave concern about the state of expert evidence: 'Expert witnesses used to be genuinely independent experts. Men of outstanding eminence in their field. Today they are in practice hired guns: there is a new breed of litigation hangers on, whose main expertise is to craft reports which will conceal anything that might be to the disadvantage of their clients.'[207] This editorial statement is problematic, because it is unclear what period of time the editor had in mind when writing 'used to be'. As mentioned above, there has been common judicial concern for over 150 years that experts are not 'genuinely independent'. It was, nevertheless, a common view in the mid 1990s that the use of experts in civil litigation had to be constrained. When Lord Woolf began his enquiry into civil justice at that time, he was critical of this use of experts as 'adversarial weapons'.[208] The resulting CPR ('the Woolf Reforms') made a number of changes to the role of the expert, discussed in more detail in Section 4.2.1, and Chapters 6 and 7. Anecdotally, the effect of these reforms has been to reduce significantly the extent and degree of expert partisanship, although, as with the conduct of experts in the United States, it is not possible to present objective empirical evidence for this.

In Italy, where party experts are used alongside court experts in civil litigation, there would appear to be no formal expectation that the party expert will act neutrally. Indeed, the provisions for party experts appear in the same section as the provisions for advocates. Perhaps partly for this reason, the Italian courts generally give little weight to party expert opinions. However, anecdotally, party experts conduct themselves in a relatively neutral fashion. Their incentive to do so is the desire to come to the attention of the court as a suitable person to be appointed as a court expert in a future case, since considerable professional and social status attach to working as a court expert.

4.3.4 The status of experts in society

The fourth possible factor that contributes to determining the role of the expert in litigation is the way in which experts are perceived in society. For

[207] 'Editorial' *Counsel* November/December 1994.
[208] Woolf, *Access to Justice: Final Report*, [13.16].

example, van Kampen has suggested that the almost universal acceptance of court expert opinions by the criminal courts in the Netherlands reflects a broader social deference to the opinions of specialists in that country.[209] Similarly, societies where there is a long history of state organization and sponsorship of the activities of specialist disciplines, such as France, might be more likely to engage court experts than societies where specialists have been seen, since at least the eighteenth century, as acting in an individual capacity.

The French state has a long tradition of funding and controlling professional and other specialist bodies,[210] and, in the same vein, the office of court expert is a long-established one, being capable of inheritance under the *Ancien Régime*.[211] In contrast, experts in England and the United States have historically acted in an individual capacity. This is reflective of the way in which technologists and scientists emerged in English society more generally: 'Whereas technologists on the Continent generally formed a state salariat or held military rank, in England most were self-employed entrepreneurs of expertise.'[212]

Specialists in French, German and Italian society have a status above that of their colleagues in England. In addition, court experts have a particular status among their peers. The office of court expert, in both criminal and civil procedure, is seen as an honourable one.[213] Not only individuals but institutions can appear on expert lists in some jurisdictions, such as Germany.[214] Conversely, therefore, where party experts are allowed, as in Italian civil proceedings and occasionally in French criminal proceedings, the party expert is viewed with suspicion. If the proper expression of civic service for a technical specialist is to be a court expert, then to be serving as a party expert implicitly suggests that one is either not good enough to be a court expert, or else motivated by financial rather than civic gain.

209 P. van Kampen, *Expert Evidence Compared: Rules and Practices in the Dutch and American Criminal Justice System* (Antwerp: Intersentia Rechtswetenschappen, 1998).

210 R. Porter, *England in the Eighteenth Century*, 2nd edn (Harmondsworth: Penguin, 1990).

211 Leclerc, *Juge et expert.*

212 Porter, *England in the Eighteenth Century*, p. 81.

213 M. Bardet-Giraudon, 'The Place of the Expert in the French Legal System', in J. Spencer, G. Nicholson, R. Flin and R. Bull (eds.), *Children's Evidence in Legal Proceedings. An International Perspective* (Cambridge: Cambridge Law Faculty, 1990), pp. 68–70, p. 69.

214 There is some parallel here with the use of Trinity House as a source of expertise in Admiralty matters in England.

4.3.5 The historical use of experts

The final factor under consideration is that the definition of the role of the expert may be at least in part a product of history.[215] Within the English High Court, there are two notable exceptions to the dominance of party experts. The first is that the Court of Admiralty has never departed from its use of assessors, accompanied by a virtual exclusion of party experts (Section 4.2.1). The second is that the Family Division has encouraged the use of single experts since at least the 1960s (Section 4.3.1.4). Accompanying the noteworthiness of these exceptions, the Admiralty and Family courts share civilian origins. It is therefore worth considering whether the current use of experts reflects these historical origins. A more detailed analysis of the historical development of experts in these courts is undertaken in Chapter 5.

The Family Court has its origins in the ecclesiastical courts, and the basis of English ecclesiastical law is canon law, rather than common law.[216] As an example of how this affects the court's approach to proof, family proceedings in the early nineteenth century required two witnesses for proof of a fact, as in a continental European court. An exception was where the matter was one cognizable at common law which arose incidentally in Family proceedings, such as where the revocation of a will was pleaded, in which case common law rules applied.[217] The Court of Admiralty, whose origins date from at least the middle of the fourteenth century, was a firmly civilian court by the middle of the sixteenth century.[218] Civilian practice may have been adopted because international law and the law of our European neighbours were civilian.

From 1664, the ecclesiastical courts in London (the Prerogative Court of Canterbury, the Court of Arches, and the Consistory Court of the Bishop of London) and the Court of Admiralty held session in the Hall

[215] I refer to 'history' rather than to 'tradition' because, although 'tradition' does carry with it the sense that the values of history have come through into the present (compare Glenn, *Legal Traditions*), it also carries with it the sense that what is of value is determined, and possibly amplified and extended, by the needs of the present: E. Hobsbawm and T. Ranger (eds.), *The Invention of Tradition* (Cambridge: Cambridge University Press, 1983).

[216] E.g. N. Cox, 'The Influence of the Common Law on the Decline of the Ecclesiastical Courts of the Church of England' (2001) 3 *Rutgers Journal of Law and Religion*, www.camlaw.rutgers.edu/publications/law-religion/articles/RJLR_3_1_3.pdf (last accessed 1 August 2008).

[217] S. Phillips, *A Treatise on the Law of Evidence*, 2nd edn (London: Strahan, 1815), p. 110.

[218] W. Senior, *Doctors' Commons and the Old Court of Admiralty* (London: Longmans, Green & Co., 1922), pp. 14–16.

of the College of Advocates, in Doctors' Commons, although the College had existed since the beginning of the sixteenth century.[219] In both the ecclesiastical and Admiralty courts, the Crown was represented by the Procurator General ('the Queen's Proctor') and Advocate General.[220] The jurisdiction of the ecclesiastical courts in Family and Probate matters was transferred in 1857 to the Divorce Court and Court of Probate, respectively.[221] Barristers and solicitors were admitted to the Admiralty Court in 1859, and proceedings were transferred to Westminster in 1860.[222] The last civilian judge of the Admiralty Court, Sir Robert Phillimore, resigned in 1883 when the Court moved to the Royal Courts of Justice in the Strand, and he was replaced by a Common Lawyer, Sir Charles Butt.[223] When the Judicature Act of 1875 combined the civil courts into one, Probate, Divorce and Admiralty were all brought together within one Division. They were only separated out in 1971, when Family formed its own Division, and Probate and Admiralty joined the Queen's Bench.[224]

Despite these close historical links between Family and Admiralty, and the initial similarity in their preference for single experts, the two courts appear to have developed their use of experts separately. While Admiralty's use of assessors can be traced back to the eighteenth century, the earliest reported Family cases involving expert evidence suggest the use of party-instructed experts, with single experts seemingly being a late nineteenth-century development. It nevertheless remains arguable that the continued use of assessors in Admiralty is a historical survival, rather than reflecting any specific contemporary factors. This survival may have been possible because of the largely self-contained nature of the Court of Admiralty, which has historically consisted of only one judge, hearing cases submitted by a small number of barristers specializing in Admiralty matters. Howard has suggested that it is possible to use court experts in Admiralty, but not in other courts, because of the degree of specialization of the lawyers involved.[225] Howard's argument is unconvincing for

219 E. Roscoe, *The High Court of Admiralty: The Last Phase* (London: Kelly Law Book, 1927), pp. 3–4.

220 The Queen's Proctor also acts for the Crown in international law matters.

221 Court of Probate Act 1857 (20 & 21 Vict. c. 77), Divorce and Matrimonial Causes Act 1857 (20 & 21 Vict. c. 85).

222 High Court of Admiralty Act 1859 (22 & 23 Vict. c. 6).

223 Roscoe, *High Court of Admiralty*, p. 6.

224 In the United States, Admiralty continues to constitute one of three distinct types of civil law, the others being Common Law and Equity: FRCP r. 1.

225 Howard, 'Neutral Expert'.

its original purpose: to justify Admiralty practice while arguing against extending it to other courts. It does, however, provide a possible explanation for why the Admiralty court has felt itself able to continue without the assistance of party experts.

4.4 Conclusion

This chapter began life as an attempt to answer a pair of questions that kept being asked, by others and myself, when I first began to look at the assessment of expert evidence. These might be loosely formulated as 'Why distinguish between civil and criminal evidence?' and 'Why don't we adopt the French / German / another model of court experts?' There are some obvious answers. For the first question, we might get 'because criminal evidence is concerned with forensic science' or 'because criminal evidence is different / more specialised / much more a creature of statute'. For the second question, we may have 'because ours is an adversarial and not an inquisitorial system' and 'because the court expert system is much less efficient at getting at the truth'. Sadly, obvious answers are rarely incisive (so why is criminal evidence different / more specialized / much more a creature of statute?) and may even be ill informed (continental civil procedure is not inquisitorial, and it is questionable whether the investigating judge is particularly committed to investigating).

So what are the more sophisticated answers, which this chapter may help us to give? The first thing that we can say is that the provisions for expert evidence in any given jurisdiction are rarely, if ever, determined by someone (or a committee) sitting down and asking, in the abstract, how expert evidence should be presented to the tribunal of fact in order best to achieve accurate fact determination. The provisions for expert evidence fit into a complex procedural framework. This framework provides an operational system, in that the parts are designed to interlock, so that one cannot change one part without regard to the effective functioning of the others. It is also a normative framework, in that the way in which the procedural system works is intended to further some political/ethical goal of society. That goal of civil procedure may be, for example, individual autonomy, social cohesion, or fiscal prudence within society as a whole. If we turn to criminal procedure, the policy issues tend to revolve much more around the balancing of the rights of the defendant with those of society, and of the victim, and around ideas of how the resources of the state should best be utilized, without unduly affecting the rights of individuals. Civil and criminal procedure, and within those frameworks civil and criminal expert evidence, are directed to quite different policy objectives, which run alongside the rationalist goals of rectitude of decision and accurate fact determination. Alongside such big themes, there are subsidiary issues, such as how experts function and are viewed in society outside the litigation context, and the role of history in shaping current expectations.

One could not simply change one procedural arrangement for another. To introduce a full, French-style court expert system into English civil justice, for example, would require far wider-reaching changes than simply adding a line into Pt 35 of the CPR. That is not to go to the other extreme and argue, alongside Legrand, that such a transplant could not work because the idea of a court expert system is so culturally embedded that it simply would not make sense in an English context. Those who responded to proposals for court experts in the 1990s that such a solution would be unworkable in England were presenting an argument that was far more emotional than rational. Party experts fit into the overall way in which litigation has historically been undertaken in England, and it would not only be unsettling if they were not there but it would raise understandable anxieties that the checks and balances that have been carefully developed over decades (if not documented and properly understood) around the use of party experts would be lost in the switch to court experts.

In the next two chapters, I examine how the current arrangement in England of party experts, single joint experts and assessors has come into existence, and how well that arrangement works in practice. This includes the tracing of the development of these roles, and the aborted role of the court experts (Chapter 5) and a detailed understanding of how these expert roles interact with their procedural environments (Chapter 6). As part of the historical analysis, I address suggestions that the historical mode of expertise in the English civil courts is the court expert, and that the party expert is a development of the late eighteenth / early nineteenth century.

5

Assessing expert evidence in the English civil courts: the sixteenth to twentieth centuries

5.1 Introduction

This chapter is the first of a pair which examine in detail how epistemological and non-epistemological factors combine to produce a range of expert roles, taking English civil procedure as a case study. In this chapter, I examine the historical development of provisions intended to assist the assessment of expert evidence in the English civil courts. My time frame is from the end of the fifteenth century, when civil cases involving expert evidence are first recorded, through to the last days of the Rules of the Supreme Court at the very end of the twentieth century. The relationship between the Civil Procedure Rules 1998 and the effective assessment of expert evidence are the subject of Chapter 6, the second chapter in this pairing.

Some might approach this as an optional chapter within the book as a whole. What, after all, can legal history tell us about modern-day evidence law? This is both a normative question (what should legal history be entitled to tell us?) and an evidential question (how much do we know about the history of evidence law for it to be able to tell us anything useful?).[1] The history of civil expert evidence is relevant to the modern-day question of its assessment in two ways. The first is that, by understanding the traditions of procedural and evidential thought and practice that have led us to where we are today, we might have a better understanding of relevant non-epistemological factors, such as are described in Chapter 4. This is because 'habit grooves sensibilities'.[2] Whether a contemporary practice is optimal for the assessment of expert evidence is a different question from whether it is a practice with which we are comfortable, and

[1] Compare P. Tillers, 'The Authority of History for the Modern Law of Proof and Evidence' Blog Tillers on Evidence and Inference, 4 November 2003, http://tillerstillers.blogspot.com/2003/11/authority-of-history-for-modern-law-of.htm (last accessed 1 August 2008) for a reasoned though sceptical view.

[2] M. Damaška, *Evidence Law Adrift* (New Haven CT: Yale University Press, 1997), p. 119.

which fits into a broader set of expectations. We must be aware of our sensibilities in our analysis. The second way in which history is relevant to current practice is that we should not presume that the difficulties that we encounter today are novel. History may provide us with examples of other attempts to address similar challenges.

The principal sections of the chapter examine the development of four expert roles: party experts (Section 5.3), special juries (Section 5.4), assessors (Section 5.5) and court experts (Section 5.6). In Section 5.7, I examine how the development of expert roles relates to developing concerns about delegation of fact finding (Section 5.7.2). The chapter begins, however, on a methodological point. The history of expert evidence is relatively well known for the criminal courts,[3] and there is work on the history of civil expert evidence in the nineteenth century.[4] However, our understanding of civil expert evidence before 1800 is very poorly developed. In Section 5.2, I therefore outline the methodology that I adopted to identify civil expert evidence cases reported before 1800, and present the results of that research.[5]

Two points of historical interest can be drawn out from the analysis in this chapter. The first is that expert evidence as we might understand it today is a relatively late evidential concept in England, which does not properly emerge until the end of the eighteenth century, with the term 'expert' itself not coming into legal usage until the second half of the nineteenth century. The second is that, contrary to a commonly presented version of the history of expert evidence,[6] the party expert would appear to have been the dominant expert role in civil litigation since at least the

[3] E.g. T. Forbes, *Surgeons at the Bailey: English Forensic Medicine to 1878* (New Haven CT: Yale University Press,1985); S. Landsman, 'One Hundred Years of Rectitude: Medical Witnesses at the Old Bailey, 1717–1817' (1998) 16 *Law and History Review* 445–94; J. Mnookin, 'Scripting Expertise: The History of Handwriting Identification Evidence and the Judicial Construction of Expertise' (2001) 87 *Virginia Law Review* 1723–1845; T. Ward, 'Experts, Juries and Witch-Hunts: From Fitzjames Stephen to Angela Cannings' (2004) 31 *Journal of Law and Society* 369–86; T. Ward, 'Observers, Advisers, or Authorities? Experts, Juries and Criminal Responsibility in Historical Perspective' (2001) 12 *Journal of Forensic Psychiatry* 105–22.

[4] E.g. T. Golan, 'The History of Scientific Expert Testimony in the English Courtroom' (1999) 12 *Science in Context* 7–34; T. Golan, *Laws of Men and Laws of Nature: The History of Scientific Expert Testimony in England and America* (Cambridge MA: Harvard University Press, 2004).

[5] See also D. Dwyer, 'Expert Evidence in the English Civil Courts, 1550–1800' (2007) 28 *Journal of Legal History* 93–118.

[6] E.g. Landsman, 'One Hundred Years'; J. Thayer, *Select Cases on Evidence at the Common Law*, 2nd edn (Cambridge MA: Charles W. Fever, 1900), p. 666.

middle of the sixteenth century, while the court expert is really only a fleeting experiment at the end of the nineteenth century.

5.2 Tracing the history of civil expert evidence, 1500–1800

This chapter is based in large part on reported pre-1800 civil cases relating to the use of expert evidence. Those wishing to study the history of civil evidence face two challenges. The first is that there is not a substantial body of material equivalent to that provided by the *Old Bailey Sessions Papers*[7] to those studying criminal evidence and procedure.[8] In Section 5.2.1, I outline the methodology employed to obtain the cases relied on in the remainder of the chapter. The second challenge is that, prior to the Judicature Acts of 1873 and 1875, civil justice in England was administered by a number of courts, with overlapping jurisdictions, and their own substantive and adjective law. Section 5.2.2 provides a very brief overview of that arrangement.

5.2.1 Source analysis

The principal source relied on for this research was the *English Reports.*[9] These are a re-print of previously printed reports. In addition, a number of other sources were examined. These included contemporary texts on court practice in the Admiralty and ecclesiastical courts,[10] modern editions of the case notebooks of Lord Mansfield and Lord Nottingham,[11] and other reports in Admiralty, Chancery and at common law.[12]

7 The papers are now available online: www.oldbaileyonline.org (last accessed 1 August 2008).

8 J. Langbein, *The Origins of the Adversary Criminal Trial* (Oxford: Oxford University Press, 2003); Landsman, 'One Hundred Years'; Forbes, *Surgeons.*

9 Published between 1900 and 1932, the 178 volumes of the *English Reports* contain published sets of reports of cases covering the period 1220 to 1865. By far the majority of cases in the *English Reports* are from civil rather than criminal trials.

10 H. Consett, *Practice of the Spiritual or Ecclesiastical Courts* (London: Basset, 1685); J. Hall, *The Practice and Jurisdiction of the Court of Admiralty* (1809) (Ann Arbor MI: Scholars' Facsimiles & Reprints, 2004); J. Prichard and D. Yale (eds.), *Hale and Fleetwood on Admiralty Jurisdiction*, folio 108 (London: Selden Society, 1992).

11 J. Oldham, *The Mansfield Manuscripts and the Growth of English Law in the Eighteenth Century* (Chapel Hill NC: North Carolina University Press, 1992); D. Yale (ed.), *Lord Nottingham's Chancery Cases*, 2 vols., folios 73 and 79 (London: Selden Society, 1954 and 1961).

12 W. Bryson, *Cases Concerning Equity and the Courts of Equity 1550–1660*, 2 vols., folios 117 and 118 (London: Selden Society, 2000 and 2001); *British Trials 1660–1900: The*

The *English Reports* were published with a substantial but far from comprehensive index, and a significant advance in the historical analysis of these cases was made with the publication of the *English Reports* on two CD-ROMs in the 1990s.[13] Since 2005, the reports have been available on the Internet.[14] The word-searching facility for the *English Reports*, both on CD-ROM and via the Internet, is not perfect.[15] It appears to have been undertaken using optical character recognition software, and the often poor quality of the scanned image being processed and the variability in the fonts used in the reports have both presented challenges for the software in accurately indexing the text. Even if the researcher identifies all the correct search terms, therefore, it is likely that not every instance in the reports will be identified. The other sources, which remain in a paper-based format, were searched using their published indexes. Oldham's 2002 comparison of CD-ROM searches with paper index searches in relation to special jury cases in the *English Reports* would suggest that using paper indexes, or even scanning each page by eye, will return fewer results than an electronic search.

There are four difficulties with using reports of cases as sources for historical developments. The first is that we do not know the basis on which an individual reporter decided whether to report a case, and the basis is likely to have varied between reporters. The reporters of cases prior to 1865 cannot be thought of as in any way providing uniformly representative coverage of decided cases. Cases were most likely to be reported because they raised important points of law. The reports may therefore be an unreliable source of information about everyday practices, particularly when they were not central to the legal point being discussed. The second difficulty is that different reporters might have given different amounts of coverage to procedural details in their selection and reporting of cases. For example, Lee appears to be the only reporter of ecclesiastical trials to record the use of experts (see Table A.3 in Appendix 2). The

Guide to the Microfiche Edition Containing a Full Bibliographical Listing Together with Nine Indexes (Cambridge: Chadwyck-Healey, 1990); G. Marsden (ed.), *Select Pleas in the Court of Admiralty (1547–1602)*, 2 vols., folios 6 and 11 (London: Selden Society, 1892 and 1897).

13 T. Gallanis, 'Legal History with 21st Century Tools: the *English Reports* on CD-ROM and *Bracton* on the Web' (1999) 20 *Journal of Legal History* 109; J. Oldham, 'Jury Research in the English Reports in CD-ROM', in J. Cairns and G. McLeod (eds.), *The Dearest Birthright of the People of England: The Jury in the History of the Common Law* (Oxford: Hart, 2002), pp. 131–53.

14 www.justis.com (last accessed 1 August 2008). This service is currently available on a subscription basis.

15 Oldham, 'Jury Research', pp. 152–3.

third difficulty is that the decision whether to publish a set of reports, and possibly whether to exclude cases from a set for publication, was a commercial one, separate from the reporter's original basis for choosing which cases to report.[16] The fourth difficulty is that law reporting for the period 1550–1800 was of variable quality over time. Baker has suggested that many of the reports republished in the *English Reports* before 1660 present 'considerable textual problems',[17] while reports between 1650 and 1750 'were mostly of an inferior nature . . . Some of them were so bad that judges forbade their citation.'[18]

A difficulty that is specific to this exercise is that there was no legal term for what we now call an 'expert' or 'expert witness' until some time after 1790.[19] This means that searching in reports for the use of experts is not straightforward. The development of the etymology of 'expert' as a legal term is outside the scope of this research,[20] but a brief introduction can be provided. The term appears first to be used in legal English in 1795, when Capel Lofft wrote in his edition of Gilbert's *Law of Evidence* that 'The proof from the Attestation of Persons on their Personal Knowledge, we may properly, with the French lawyers, call proof by Experts.'[21] The *Oxford English Dictionary* cites section 4 of the British North America (Seigniorial Rights) Act 1825[22] as the first use of the term to mean a

[16] Only a minority of Tudor and Stuart reports were printed. The legal profession relied instead on manuscript records of current cases: J. Baker, *An Introduction to English Legal History*, 4th edn (London: Butterworths, 2002), p. 182.

[17] Ibid., p. 182. The leading civil case for expert evidence for the first half of the seventeenth century is *Alsop*, decided in 1619 but not reported in print until 1721, with a more comprehensive report in 1791: *Alsop & Stacy pur Trespass de 401* (1619) Palm 9; 81 ER 953 (*Alsop 1721*); *Alsop* v. *Bowtrell* (1619) Croke Jac 541; 79 ER 464 (*Alsop 1791*).

[18] Baker, *Introduction*, pp. 183–4.

[19] The absence of a term does not necessarily mean that the concept was also absent. However, until the rules on expert opinion evidence developed in the second half of the eighteenth century, it seems probable that the different professions and disciplines were seen as presenting distinct types of specialist advice, rather than being specific examples of a general legal category which we now call experts.

[20] On the etymology of the French *expert*, see O. Leclerc, *Le juge et l'expert: contribution à l'étude des rapports entre le droit et la science* (Paris: LDGJ, 2005).

[21] G. Gilbert, *The Law of Evidence*, ed. C. Lofft, 4th edn (Dublin: 1795). By 'personal knowledge', Lofft is referring to knowledge that the witness possesses, separate from what was seen or heard in the instant case. According to Leclerc, *Juge et expert*, *expert* was not used as a legal noun in France until the end of the eighteenth century. The word as an adjective was also used to refer to a person of practical skill rather than special knowledge until around the same time.

[22] 6 Geo. IV c. 59, 1825 (Imperial).

specialist in a legal context.[23] However, the legal system of Lower Canada was based on French law, and so we cannot be sure that 'expert' is not being used here as a term of art. It is not used in the *English Reports* as an indigenous term until 1858, when it appears in scare quotes. In *R* v. *Esdaile*,[24] Lord Campbell CJ said during the hearing that 'The proper way of putting the question is to ask the witness, as an "expert", whether mines are convertible securities.' The witness had been called 'to show that the investment of money in landed property was not a legitimate part of the business of banking'.[25] Two years later, in the Chancery case of *Directors of the Stockton and Darlington Railway* v. *John Brown (a lunatic)*,[26] before the House of Lords, counsel submitted that 'the court is not bound by the report of the expert'. The case was on appeal to the House of Lords from the Lord Justices of Appeal in Chancery sitting in Lunacy. The Lords Justices had appointed an engineer as a court expert with the consent of both parties, to inquire whether it was necessary for the defendant railway company to take a particular part of the plaintiff's land.[27] By 1863, Stephen could write extra-curially that 'No one expects an expert . . . to be quite candid',[28] apparently expecting his reader to understand 'expert' as a standard legal term.

In the absence of a technical legal term for an expert, our starting point for identifying what we would now call experts has to be to decide what these types of people might be called, and then to search for their use as an evidential source in the reports. The formulation of such a list of people inherently limits the scope of the results. It cannot therefore be claimed that this method provides a comprehensive list of the use of expert evidence prior to the introduction of the term 'expert', but only that it represents the most comprehensive attempt to date. The following terms were searched for, including variants of spelling and plurals: apothecary; assessor; chemist; elder brethren; engineer; expert; grammarian; jury of

[23] '[W]hich price, indemnity, or consideration, in case the parties concerned therein shall differ respecting the same, shall be ascertained and fixed by experts, to be in that behalf nominated and appointed, according to the due course of law in the said province of Lower Canada'.

[24] *R.* v. *Esdaile* (1858) 1 F&F 213 at 230; 175 ER 696 at 705.

[25] Ibid., at 229.

[26] *Directors of the Stockton and Darlington Railway* v. *John Brown (a lunatic)* (1860) 9 HLC 246; 11 ER 724

[27] 15 & 16 Vict. c. 80, s. 42.

[28] J. Stephen, *A General View of the Criminal Law of England* (London: McMillan, 1863), pp. 189–90.

merchants; man of science; man of skill; merchant; midwife; physician; shipwright; surgeon; surveyor; Trinity House; Trinity Master. These 'key words' were identified from leading cases known prior to the search, such as *Folkes*[29] and *Buckley* v. *Rice Thomas*,[30] and from research on experts in criminal litigation.[31] The civil cases in which the terms appeared are listed in Appendix 2 categorized by the type of court in which they were heard.

In addition, manuscript material may also exist that throws light on the origins of expert evidence in the civil courts, for example in the records of the Courts of Chancery and Admiralty in the National Archives. There are also unpublished notebooks, such as those of Sir Dudley Ryder,[32] and contemporary newspaper accounts.[33] These materials have not been searched,[34] and this would represent a significant undertaking beyond the scope of this volume. Without such a search of materials, of course, the conclusions drawn here necessarily remain provisional.

5.2.2 Civil courts before the Judicature Acts 1873 and 1875

The study of civil procedure between the sixteenth and nineteenth centuries is complicated by the multiplicity of courts and legal systems operating in this period. The main jurisdictions were common law (King's Bench, Common Pleas and Exchequer), equity (Chancery) and civil law (ecclesiastical and Admiralty). No doubt in part because the types of factual issues to be decided varied according to the nature of the case, there is significant variation between the courts in this period, and over time, as to the substance of expertise required, in terms of both subject matter and the inferences involved. A very brief introduction to the jurisdictions is presented here. This is sufficient to understand the discussion of developments in expert evidence law that follow, although it fails to do justice to the complexity of either synchronic detail or diachronic variation.

[29] *Folkes* v. *Chadd* (1782) 3 Doug 152; 99 ER 589.

[30] *Buckley* v. *Rice Thomas* (1555) 1 Plowd 118; 75 ER 182.

[31] E.g. Landsman, 'One Hundred Years'; Forbes, *Surgeons.*

[32] J. Langbein, 'Shaping the Eighteenth-Century Criminal Trial: A View from the Ryder Sources' (1983) 50 *University of Chicago Law Review* 1–136.

[33] For an example of newspapers as sources of legal history, see G. van Cleve, 'Somerset's Case and its Antecedents in Imperial Perspective' (2006) 24 *Law and History Review* 601–46; Golan, *Laws of Men.*

[34] One eighteenth-century newspaper source available in electronic format, the *Gentleman's Magazine*, www.bodley.ox.ac.uk/ilej/ (last accessed 1 August 2008), has been searched but appears to contain no mention of relevant cases.

Actions at common law were available before the King's Bench, Common Pleas and Exchequer (the last of these also having an equitable jurisdiction for most of the period under consideration). Common law trial courts consisted of a bicameral tribunal of judge and jury. Each of the three courts comprised four judges, and where a point of law arose before a court, its judges would sit *in banco*. On particularly significant points of law, the Twelve Judges would sit together.

The proceedings of the Court of Chancery were broadly Roman-canon in character.[35] Parties made submissions to the Lord Chancellor, with the evidence of witnesses being given as depositions in writing. Chancery appears never to have deviated in theory from the principle that witnesses are examined by officers of the court rather than by the parties or their agents.[36] Parties in Chancery did not have access to cross-examination as a tool in providing evidence. Perhaps at least in part because of this, and reliance on the civilian system of proof, contentious questions of fact were commonly referred to a common law jury, 'to inform the conscience of equity'.[37]

The ecclesiastical courts had jurisdiction not only over ecclesiastical matters, but also over family matters, including probate. With the Reformation, the teaching of canon law had been ended in England, and the need for legal practitioners in the church's courts was met by civilian lawyers. Parties were represented by civilian advocates, rather than common law serjeants or barristers. These were university-educated doctors of civil law, who operated out of the Hall of the College of Advocates ('Doctors' Commons'), which had existed since the sixteenth century.[38] From 1664 Doctors' Commons was located near St Paul's Cathedral.[39]

[35] M. Macnair, *The Law of Proof in Early Modern Equity* (Berlin: Duncker and Humblot, 1999), pp. 25–40.

[36] Ibid., p. 173.

[37] *Folkes* is an example of a case brought in Chancery that went before a common law jury for the determination of a particular fact, namely whether the embankment was responsible for the silting of the harbour.

[38] G. Squibb, *Doctors' Commons* (Oxford: Oxford University Press, 1977), pp. 1–22, has proposed the 1490s, and R. Helmholz, *The Oxford History of the Laws of England*, vol. I: *The Canon Law and Ecclesiastical Jurisdiction from 597 to the 1640s* (Oxford: Oxford University Press, 2004), p. 227, has suggested that the institution or a predecessor was in place by 1469, to receive a bequest of twenty-eight law books.

[39] E. Roscoe, *The High Court of Admiralty: The Last Phase* (London: Kelly Law Book, 1927); W. Senior, *Doctors' Commons and the Old Court of Admiralty* (London: Longmans, Green & Co., 1922), pp. 3–4.

The High Court of Admiralty had a strong civilian character to its adjective rules, although it did not directly apply the *Corpus Juris Civilis* in its substantive law. This civilian character no doubt reflected the international nature of its cases, since international law was civilian.[40] Proceedings were conducted in Latin until 1733, with the exception of the years of the Commonwealth,[41] and the court was served by advocates, based at Doctors' Commons.

This multiplicity of jurisdictions was finally rationalized by the Supreme Court of Judicature Acts of 1873 and 1875. These consolidated the superior courts into the Supreme Court, comprising the High Court and the Court of Appeal.[42] The High Court in turn had three divisions of Queen's Bench,[43] Chancery and Probate, Divorce and Admiralty.[44]

5.3 Party experts

5.3.1 Early uses of party experts

The earliest recorded use of party-instructed experts comes from the ecclesiastical courts, where by the 1570s use was being made of artificers in dilapidation suits to provide estimates of the extent of repair needed. A Precedent Book of *c.* 1575 and a Formulary of *c.* 1630 refer to such inspections, which were to result in written reports.[45] The 1685 *Practice of the Spiritual or Ecclesiastical Courts* notes that there must be two witnesses of each craft, in order to make a sufficient proof for the civilian court.[46] In the *English Reports*, our evidence for the use of experts in the ecclesiastical courts is limited to *Lee's Ecclesiastical Judgments*, and these are the earliest published ecclesiastical cases in the *English Reports*, dating

40 Roscoe, *High Court of Admiralty.*

41 'Extracts from the Record of the High Court of Admiralty and Court of the Judges Delegates' Burrell 231; 167 ER 549. The common law courts proceeded on the basis of a strange mixture of legal French and Latin, with some English. Only in equity were proceedings entirely in English.

42 The Judicature Act 1873 came into force in November 1875.

43 The consolidation of the common law courts into one was not immediate. Common Pleas and Exchequer Divisions continued to exist until 1880, to avoid the compulsory retirement or demotion of the former Chief Justice of the Common Pleas and the Chief Baron.

44 This consolidation has still not resulted in total integration, with each Division being allocated its own judges, and still largely being served by its own barristers: A. Samuels, 'A Unified Civil Court' (2006) 25 *Civil Justice Quarterly* 250–60.

45 Precedent Book (*c.* 1575) NNRO PCD/2/3, fo. 19; Formulary (*c.* 1630) DRO, Chanter MS, 724 fos., 64v–65.

46 Consett, *Practice*, ch. X, s. I.3, 363–4.

to the 1750s. Here, the cases concern family rather than ecclesiastical matters. Although most of the reported cases in *Lee* involving experts were heard between 1753 and 1757, there are two exceptions from a quarter of a century earlier.[47] One indication that the use of experts in family matters at this time was relatively immature is that in the 1731 case of *Welde* v. *Welde*, a surgeon called by Mrs Welde to testify that her husband was impotent because of a growth proceeded to testify that the growth had been successfully removed, and the condition cured. This use of party expert witnesses whose probable answers have not been established by instructing counsel prior to examination is also a feature of criminal trials at around this time.[48]

At common law, party experts first appear in reported cases in the early seventeenth century. In *Alsop* v. *Bowtrell* in 1619, expert evidence was given by physician party witnesses on the length of human gestation, but it would appear that the witnesses had been called primarily as witnesses of fact.[49] The 1791 report of the case then records that 'The Court held here, that it might well be as the physicians had affirmed . . . and so the Court delivered to the jury, that the said Elizabeth . . . might well be the daughter of the said Edmund'.[50] 'Held' implies more than a jury direction, but the repeated use of 'might' suggests that this may represent a ruling on admissibility, that the physicians' evidence should be considered by the jury.

There is then a substantial gap in reported common law expert cases until the 1750s. That gap might make us question whether *Alsop* really did involve the use of party experts, but comparison with the (common law) criminal courts from the mid seventeenth century to the mid eighteenth century (Section 5.3.4) suggests that there is no reason not to infer that

47 *Andrews* v. *Powis* (1728) 1 Lee 242; 161 ER 90; *Welde* v. *Welde* (1731) 2 Lee 580; 161 ER 447.

48 Landsman, 'One Hundred Years', 476.

49 '[The alleged facts] being proved, and this misusage, by five women of good credit, and two doctors of physic, Sir William Baddy and Doctor Munford, and one Chamberlaine (who was a physician, and in nature of a midwife) . . . upon their oath, they affirming that the child came in time convenient to be the daughter of the party who died'. *Alsop 1791*, at 541.

50 *Alsop 1791*, at 542. In contrast, *Alsop 1721* does not record this decision by the Court. It is also not clear in the 1721 report that the physicians were sworn witnesses, and the text suggests more submission than testimony: 'et fuit argue per Doctor Pady, et Doctor Mounford phisitians, & Paddie affirme, et Mounford agree a ceo, que le pluis natural temps del birth est le 10. jour del 10. moies apres conception'. The 1791 report indicates that the doctors gave evidence along with five women ('and this being proved') under oath.

party experts were being used in the civil courts at this time. In 1753, in *Fearon* v. *Bowers*, '[m]erchants were examined on both sides' to establish whether the endorsement of a bill of lading vested the property.[51] As with *Welde*, these witnesses do not appear to have been carefully selected to support their party's case, as they agreed on the point in issue on which their expertise had been sought.[52] The following year, in *Maddox* v. *Dr M—y*, a jury received in evidence the opinions of several physicians and man-midwives, in a case which concerned whether the defendant had discharged his duties properly as a 'man-midwife'.[53]

The first reported use of any form of expert advice in Chancery is relatively late, in the 1698 case of *Foubert* v. *de Cresseron*.[54] That case was heard before the House of Lords on appeal, and concerned the correct construction of a phrase in a will that had been written in French. The report provides us with a number of details about the way in which advice on construction was sought, both at first instance and on appeal. These details indicate that evidence on the interpretation of a foreign or specialist term had not previously been brought in Chancery, although its use was established in the common law courts.[55] The specialist advice was provided by the parties, on the instruction of the court, and there was argument by counsel on what sort of person would be suitable to provide this evidence in Chancery. It seems likely that this was the first time that specialist advice on any subject had been admitted.[56]

After *Foubert*, there are no further identified cases involving experts in Chancery until 1724, when a party in *Brereton* v. *Cowper* introduced evidence from a surveyor on the value of a property.[57] In *ex p. Ferrers* in 1730, evidence was admitted from a physician and a surgeon on insanity. The experts who appeared in reported equity cases from the 1730s were almost exclusively medical practitioners who were attending to the person whose

[51] *Fearon* v. *Bowers* (1753) 1 H Bl 364; 126 ER 214.

[52] It is possible that the point was too clear for argument, but that in turn would raise the question of why the parties had bothered to call the experts.

[53] *British Trials*, no. 303. The jury was a special jury, but it is not clear whether this was a jury of experts or some other form of special jury.

[54] *Foubert* v. *de Cresseron* [1698] Shower PC 194; 1 ER 130.

[55] Merchants, Trinity Masters, 'Grammarians, Criticks, Chymists and Artificers' 'upon words belonging to, and used in their respective professions': *Foubert*, at 197.

[56] As an example of evidence of absence, in *Re Carson* (1673) 73 SS, No. 36, in Yale (ed.), *Lord Nottingham's Chancery Cases*, no. 11, the court decided the question of insanity without expert advice. Such evidence was being received by 1730: *ex p. Ferrers* (1730) Mosely 332; 25 ER 423.

[57] *Brereton* v. *Cowper* (1724) 1 Bro PC 211; 1 ER 521.

physical or mental health was in question. All the experts were instructed by one of the parties rather than by the court. The expert evidence admitted in Chancery was only of two types: the correct construction of a word, first identified in *Foubert*, and 'state of affairs' evidence, such as whether a person was physically or mentally unwell, which appears to have begun to be admitted in the eighteenth century. This choice of expert evidence largely reflects, of course, the types of factual issues that arose in Chancery.

5.3.2 The developing complexity of inferential questions

The eighteenth century witnessed two significant changes in the court's use of expert evidence. The first related to the developing complexity of the inferential questions that experts were asked to address, considered in this section. The second related to the increased reliance on experts, considered in the following section (Section 5.3.3). The types of question that formed the substance of expert evidence expanded and developed in complexity over time. In the sixteenth century, the reports suggest that the specialist questions asked were of the type 'What does this foreign word mean?', and the experts called were, in consequence, grammarians. In the seventeenth century, two further types of question were added: 'What do experts believe to be the nature of things?' (such as length of gestation)[58] and 'What is the practice of experts?' (such as whether pirates are considered 'perils of the sea', or the use of standard measures).[59] These questions of practice continue to be put to merchants, whether as advisers or as special jurors, in the eighteenth century. From the 1730s we start to see cases in which surgeons, apothecaries or physicians are asked to testify as to the physical or mental health of an individual. This was an advance in the types of inference involved, because experts were now being asked to apply their knowledge to an individual rather than simply to describe the general state of affairs. It remained, however, a statement of how things were in the present, rather than estimation of how they had been in the past or would be in the future. This inferential breakthrough occurred with *Folkes*, where the expert witness testifies to a question about causation.

The 1782 case of *Folkes* v. *Chadd* is usually taken as the leading case on the admissibility of expert opinion evidence. The case concerned whether

[58] *Alsop 1791.*

[59] *Pickering* v. *Barkley* (1658) Sty 132; 82 ER 587, and *Beckman* v. *Maplesden* (1662) Bridg O 60; 124 ER 468, both decided in the middle of the century.

the construction of an embankment on the land of Sir Martin Folkes Bart, to prevent the sea from flooding his meadows, was responsible for the silting up of Wells Harbour in Norfolk. The harbour trustees cut the embankment, and the question for the jury was whether the cutting was justified because of the damage done to the harbour by the embankment. The case report indicates that the admissibility of expert evidence on matters of opinion on behalf of the plaintiff was a key issue in the case. At the first *nisi prius* trial, Folkes called a civil engineer, Robert Mylne FRS, to testify as to his 'opinion' on the cause of the silting, and to 'show that, in his judgment, the bank was not the occasion of it'. The jury found for Folkes, and the harbour trustees sought and were granted a new trial on the basis that they were surprised. 'Surprise' was a routine procedural gambit, and we cannot infer automatically that the evidence was genuinely unexpected, nor that it was unexpected because it was the opinion evidence of an engineer. Indeed, the parties were directed to exchange engineers' reports before the second trial, which would suggest that the harbour trustees had not expressed a legal difficulty with this type of evidence. At the second trial, Folkes produced two new pieces of evidence: that other harbours on the same coast were also silting up, and the opinion of a second civil engineer, Smeaton, on the cause of the silting.[60] The harbour trustees objected to the evidence, both since it introduced a multiplicity of facts and because the jury's verdict must be based on fact and not opinion. Gould J accepted the objection, and Folkes sought a new trial on the basis that the evidence had been improperly rejected. The case was then heard before the whole court, Lord Mansfield CJ delivering the opinion of the court. It was held that a civil engineer's opinion, 'formed on facts, was very proper evidence' since '[i]n matters of science, no other witnesses can be called'.

To a modern reader, these proceedings have an air of unreality about them, because expert evidence on matters of opinion had been admitted into civil and criminal proceedings for several centuries by 1782. Indeed Lord Mansfield suggested in his judgment that expert evidence on matters of opinion was admitted all the time. But, unlike the 'surprised' objection

[60] What is not apparent to a casual reader of the report is that Folkes was calling in evidence two of the country's leading authorities in a relatively new field. Smeaton was the first to use the term 'civil engineer' in England, and in 1771 formed the Society of Civil Engineers. Mylne was elected vice-president of the Society of Civil Engineers in 1772. T. Allibone, 'The Club of the Royal College of Physicians, the Smeatonian Society of Civil Engineers and their Relationship to the Royal Society Club' (1967) 22 *Notes and Records of the Royal Society of London* 186–92.

after the first trial, the objection to the opinion evidence at the second trial may not have been formulaic. It certainly appears to be an argument accepted by Gould J.[61] Although the authority is not cited in the *Folkes* report, counsel may have had in mind *Carter* v. *Boehm* in 1766,[62] in which Lord Mansfield had held that no weight should have been given to the opinion of a broker who had negotiated the insurance policy whose validity was in issue:

> Lastly – Great stress was laid upon the opinion of the broker. But we all think the jury ought not to pay the least regard to it. It is mere opinion which is not evidence. It is opinion after an event. It is opinion without the least foundation from any previous precedent or usage. It is an opinion which, if rightly formed, could only be drawn from the same premises from which the Court and jury were to determine the cause: and therefore it is improper and irrelevant in the mouth of a witness.[63]

Evidence historians have disagreed as to what the novel issue in *Folkes* actually was. None of the explanations presented to date is wholly satisfactory in light of other evidence. In 1900, Thayer proposed that the case was significant because it saw the introduction of an expert testifying directly to the jury.[64] Landsman has similarly argued that, 'In this case, Mansfield placed the court's seal of approval on the whole adversarial apparatus including contending experts, hypothetical questions, and jury evaluation.'[65] These are not wholly satisfactory explanations, since contending party expert witnesses had appeared before a common law jury by at least 1753. Wigmore thought that the significance of the case was that it permitted the admission of the opinions of experts who 'personally knew nothing about the circumstances of the particular case'.[66] This is similarly unsatisfactory since Mr Smeaton, whose evidence was in question, had made a detailed factual study of the subject of the case.[67]

[61] Strictly, it is not clear from the report whether Gould J rejected Smeaton's evidence, or the evidence on multiple harbours, or both. However, most of the judgment of the court delivered by Lord Mansfield concerned expert evidence, so it seems reasonable to conclude that this was the main issue at *nisi prius*.

[62] *Carter* v. *Boehm* (1766) 3 Burr 1905; 97 ER 1162. [63] Ibid., at 1918.

[64] Thayer, *Select Cases*, p. 666.

[65] S. Landsman, 'Of Witches, Madmen, and Products Liability: An Historical Survey of the Use of Expert Testimony' (1995) 13 *Behavioral Sciences and the Law* 131–57, at 141.

[66] J. Wigmore, *A Treatise on the Anglo-American System of Evidence in Trials at Common Law* (1923), rev. edn Tiller (Boston: Little, Brown, 1983) vol. IV p. 105.

[67] T. Golan 'Scientific Expert Testimony in Anglo-American Courts, 1782–1923', Ph.D. thesis, University of California at Berkeley (1997), 14.

Golan has suggested that Lord Mansfield may have allowed the use of party expert witnesses on the basis of the current use of court experts because he did not appreciate how their use would differ from that of the court experts to which he was accustomed.[68] The difficulty with accepting this explanation is that it relies on supposing a lack of foresight by one of the greatest English judicial minds of the eighteenth century, with no evidence to support the supposition.

An understanding of the changing roles of experts at this time provides us with a more robust explanation for the significance of *Folkes*: this was the first case in which a party-instructed witness had provided expert evidence on matters of opinion to a common law jury in a civil matter, where the opinion required the expert witness to have drawn inferences that went beyond describing the current state of affairs with the benefit of a particular skill. The case therefore broke down the conventional distinction that witnesses testified as to what they had seen and heard, while juries formed opinions on those facts, which in turn formed the basis of their verdicts. In *Folkes*, the expert witness gives his opinion on a question about causation.

It is true, as Lord Mansfield said in *Folkes*, that a question such as 'Is this seal genuine?' requires an 'opinion' in the sense that the expert is asked to apply their personal knowledge to a set of facts, rather than testifying directly to a brute fact that they have seen or heard. But this is not the same sort of 'opinion' as one on causation, because a causation opinion requires one to reconstruct a past event on the basis of external evidence. This latter sort of opinion is much closer to the sort of opinion that the jury is asked to form as tribunal of fact. It therefore breaches two well-established principles dating from at least the seventeenth century. The first, expressed in the leading seventeenth-century case on the role of the jury, *Bushell*, is that witnesses testify to facts, and jurors form opinions on facts.[69] The second principle is that decisions must be based on facts. In the 1621 Star Chamber case of *Adams* v. *Canon*,[70] Coke gave three reasons for the inadmissibility of evidence of opinion: first, the judge must give sentence on the basis of 'more sure ground than thinking', in other words the sentence must be based on facts; secondly, a witness cannot be prosecuted for perjury for merely giving an opinion; thirdly, judges must give judgment on what has been alleged and proven. This third reason represents the civilian doctrine that a judge must decide

[68] Ibid., 14. [69] *Bushell's Case* (1670) Vaughan 135; 124 ER 1006.
[70] *Adams* v. *Canon* (1621) Dyer 53b n 15.

secundum allegata et probata ('according to what has been alleged and proved') by the parties.[71]

The discussion here is, of course, moving between different forms of 'opinion', relating to different types of inference. The opinion of a seal-maker on seals is a skilled description or interpretation of a state of affairs. The opinion of a civil engineer on the cause of silting is a matter of much more complex interpretation, about past events. The opinion of an underwriter on insurance practices was about what should have been the case, with little factual basis. This is perhaps the type of opinion that Coke had in mind in *Adams* v. *Canon*. The opinion of a jury is the controvertible but necessarily final set of inferences drawn after careful consideration from evidence. The civil engineer's opinion on causation is very like a jury's opinion on causation, and not like the 'state of affairs' evidence that had gone before judges and juries in previous decades. Lord Mansfield's conclusion is pragmatic: if we were to say that an expert opinion on causation usurped the proper role of the jury, and so was inadmissible, then we would be expecting juries to form opinions on insufficient evidence. In turn, of course, it gives rise to concerns about whether the expert is de facto deciding the ultimate issue,[72] which is outside the scope of this chapter.

5.3.3 Increasing reliance on party expert evidence

The second significant change in expert usage in the eighteenth century was in the degree to which the court relied on the opinions of experts. In the 1550s, the court appears to have taken expert advice because it informed decision making, as in *Buckley* v. *Rice Thomas*. Specialists were obviously good people to ask, but it seems likely from the 1791 report of *Alsop* (1619) that a jury was not bound by the expert's opinion. By the 1780s, however, certain questions were considered to be in effect answerable only by an expert. The changes identified in the courts' use of expert evidence between 1550 and 1800 are broadly reflective of society's increasing reliance on specialists, particularly in the eighteenth century. There are two elements of that social change that are relevant here: the growth of specialist occupations and professions, particularly in the eighteenth century, and the development of the belief that certain matters could only properly be advised on by these specialists.

[71] Macnair, *Law of Proof*, p. 46.

[72] *R.* v. *Wright* (1821) Russell & Ry 456; 168 ER 895.

5.3.3.1 The growth of specialist occupations and professions

The growth of specialist occupations and professions in eighteenth-century England has been well documented by social historians:

> As the century wore on, new occupations found niches for themselves between the plutocrat and the humble shopkeeper . . . The male obstetrician was a new specialist . . . More people also carved out careers as technical specialists. Agricultural experts . . . guidebook writers and handbook compilers earned livings by the pen. Surveyors, technicians, civil engineers, instrument-makers, cartographers, millwrights, turnpike-builders . . . swelled in number as the economy demanded greater technical expertise.[73]

This development should not be seen merely as an epiphenomenon of modern economic growth. The development of the tertiary (service) sector in England, particularly from the eighteenth century, indicates sufficient individual or state resources to pay for these services, but how those resources were expended was a non-economic decision.[74] These specialists, particularly the 'learned professions' of medicine, the clergy and the law, had an economic interest in fostering the idea that they had sole access to a specialist set of knowledge. The new specialist disciplines of the eighteenth century largely replaced the specialities that had been embodied in, and protected by, the guilds and mysteries (cohesive occupational groups) of the Middle Ages. These guilds appear to have declined sharply between 1690 and 1770, with the mercers' and drapers' guilds declining at the start of this period, and the service guilds (including surgeon-barbers) at the end.[75] The evidence of Trinity Masters is an example of how the courts before the eighteenth century made use of guild-based specialists. The artisans who advised the ecclesiastical courts on building matters would similarly have been guild members, although there is no indication that the artisans were called because they were members of a particular guild, as was the case with Trinity Masters.

[73] R. Porter, *England in the Eighteenth Century*, 2nd edn (Harmondsworth: Penguin, 1990), p. 81.

[74] P. Corfield, *Power and the Professions in Britain 1700–1850* (London: Routledge, 1995), p. 23.

[75] R. O'Day, *The Professions in Early Modern England 1450–1800* (Harlow: Longman, 2000), p. 23.

5.3.3.2 The need for specialist advice

The second element was the development of the belief that certain matters could only properly be advised on by specialists. There had been an increasing awareness of epistemological issues in England in the seventeenth century, which Barbara Shapiro has suggested was in large part due to questions having to be asked about the basis on which practical decisions could be made, following the end of Church authority in everyday life with the Reformation.[76] These practical questions existed alongside philosophical ones.[77] This epistemological concern increased in the eighteenth century, with the increasingly rapid growth of knowledge and specialization. In *Alsop* in 1619, it appears that the court was not sure how much weight the jury should be allowed to give to expert evidence on the length of human gestation. We know from the *Old Bailey Sessions Papers* that, up until the 1760s, it was common for non-expert witnesses to give their opinions in court on questions that we might now consider to fall firmly within the domain of an expert, such as cause of death.[78] Rather than being a peculiarity of criminal evidence, the idea that non-specialists were competent to express medical opinions was a feature of eighteenth-century English society in general: 'Every man of sense at forty [fallaciously thinks he] knows what is good for his constitution.'[79] Just before this period, however, from 1640 to 1660, there had been a reaction against the nascent learned professions, with the argument that they wrongly sought to make the laity believe that the professions possessed expertise and authority that was out of the reach of ordinary people.[80] Although there is no direct evidence, it may be that the paucity

[76] B. Shapiro, *'Beyond Reasonable Doubt' and 'Probable Cause': Historical Perspectives on the Anglo-American Law of Evidence* (Berkeley CA: California University Press, 1991).

[77] Sir Francis Bacon's 1605 *Advancement of Learning* (London); Galileo Galilei's 1632 *Dialogo sopra i due massimi sistemi del mondo* (Florence: Giovanni Battista Landini, 1632); John Locke's *Essay Concerning Human Understanding* (*c.* 1690), ed. J. Yolton, 3rd edn (London: Dent, 1993), commenced in 1671. The Royal Society was founded in 1662, following the Restoration of the Monarchy in 1660.

[78] E.g. *R.* v. *Bembridge* Old Bailey Sessions Papers, December 1721, 3 (death resulted from inflammation of the lungs caused by heavy drinking); *R.* v. *Vezey* Old Bailey Sessions Papers, January 1732, 41 (whether death was from a fall or from consumption); *R.* v. *Sibson* Old Bailey Sessions Papers, May 1762, 117 (whether death was from poisoning or consumption). This might alternatively be viewed as a laxness on the part of the Court in excluding evidence of opinion.

[79] Thomas Beddoes (1760–1808), quoted in Landsman, 'One Hundred Years', 485 fn 177. Beddoes was educated at Pembroke College, Oxford, and was a prominent physician and philosopher.

[80] O'Day, *Professions*, p. 15.

of evidence for the use of experts for most of the seventeenth century, after *Alsop* v. *Bowtrell* in 1619, reflects reluctance to base jury decisions on expert evidence.

After the 1760s, there was a clear inclination to hear certain types of opinion only from expert witnesses.[81] In 1772, Lord Mansfield CJ commented in a misdemeanour case that the question of insanity could only be determined by 'an able physician' who has viewed the party for the purpose of determining admission to a 'mad-house'.[82] By 1782, in *Folkes* v. *Chadd*, Lord Mansfield held that 'in matters of science the reasonings of men of science can only be answered by men of science'. In 1785, Lord Thurlow LC held that a non-expert jury was not competent to second-judge the decision of a naval court martial, since it concerned terminology and life outside the experience of non-expert jurors. He noted *obiter* that where special provision has not been made for other types of specialist evidence, such as by a surgeon on the cause of death or a naval man on a naval insurance claim, then 'A jury must necessarily be presumed but imperfectly qualified to try questions which depend upon knowledge they cannot be supposed to possess, but the law has not appointed any tribunal more competent to the purpose.'[83] By 1821, the perceived limited epistemic competence of the tribunal of fact in expert matters provides the theoretical basis for the development of the Ultimate Issue Rule (Section 5.7).

5.3.4 Developments in the criminal courts in the seventeenth and eighteenth centuries

When the quality of the reports as a source for procedural history was being discussed (Section 5.2), the particularly poor quality of reports between the middle of the seventeenth century and the middle of the eighteenth century was highlighted. It is therefore possible that the paucity of civil cases involving expert evidence before the early eighteenth century is a function of the source material rather than a true reflection of historical events. One piece of evidence that this might indeed be the case can be extracted from accounts of criminal trials in the last quarter of the seventeenth century.

[81] Landsman, 'One Hundred Years', 455. [82] *Coate's Case* (1772) Lofft 78, 79; 98 ER 542.
[83] *Johnstone* v. *Sutton* (1785) 1 Term Rep. 510; 99 ER 1225.

Reports of criminal trials in the seventeenth and eighteenth centuries suggest that party expert witnesses were appearing before a jury in criminal cases earlier than in any form of civil proceeding. The first appearance of party-instructed expert witnesses that I have been able to identify in Chancery was in the 1698 case of *Foubert*, and at common law was in the 1753 case of *Fearon*. In contrast, party expert witnesses were already being used in the criminal courts by 1678.[84] In addition, while opinions on causation were not put to a civil jury until 1782, such opinions were already being expressed to a criminal jury in relation to causes of death by 1678. When the barrister Spencer Cowper defended himself against a murder charge in 1699,[85] he made extremely sophisticated use of party expert witnesses, which suggests familiarity with the use of such witnesses.

The significantly earlier use of party expert witnesses in criminal trials than in civil trials raises a potential difficulty with the proposition that party expert witnesses were not testifying to common law juries on questions of causation until the 1780s. It would seem unlikely that the constitutional role of the jury to form opinions on the basis of facts presented in evidence could be at risk in 1782 in a civil matter but had not been at risk in the late seventeenth century in a criminal matter. One solution to this difficulty might be that medical questions of causation were not treated as being questions of opinion in the same way that opinions on engineering or insurance matters might be. We are unable to test this theory directly against the case law, since almost all expert evidence in criminal cases in the seventeenth and eighteenth centuries was medical in nature. Another solution might be that, when party expert opinion evidence had begun to be admitted in criminal cases, in or prior to the 1670s, challenges to evidence had usually gone to weight rather than to admissibility.[86] When expert evidence relevant to civil questions had begun to be admitted, a century later, it was more common to test the admissibility of evidence. Thus the question arose in *Folkes* because this was an early example of such evidence being used in civil proceedings, at a time when it had become common to challenge admissibility. It is likely, however, that if such evidence had been introduced earlier, it would have not have been challenged.

A third explanation might be to say that party expert witnesses were being used in civil cases in or before the 1670s, although this usage is not

[84] *R.* v. *Pembroke (Earl)* (1678) 6 St Tr 1337; *R.* v. *Green* (1679) 7 St Tr 185.

[85] *R.* v. *Cowper* (1699) 13 St Tr 1106.

[86] Langbein, *Origins*, pp. 248–9.

visible in the sources examined for this chapter. One possible exception is *Alsop*, in which the expert evidence did not touch on the facts of the instant case.[87] The possibility of earlier civil usage is supported by the sophisticated use of party experts in the criminal case of *Cowper*. Given that counsel did not normally appear in felony cases, for prosecution or defence, where did counsel on both sides learn to conduct a trial of such length and complexity? This is similar to a question that Langbein asks, regarding how the criminal bar already possessed sufficient skills to defend felony defendants, when the judges first allowed their use in the eighteenth century.[88] The two most likely answers are that these are skills developed in misdemeanour cases, where counsel were already permitted, or else in the civil courts. Langbein proposes the first option, suggesting that counsel, particularly young barristers, practised their skills in the misdemeanour courts. The difficulty with that explanation is that there is no evidence that misdemeanour cases were conducted at the level of sophistication apparent in *Cowper*. Civil litigation, however, was highly developed by the end of the seventeenth century, and the only significant obstacle to saying that counsel in *Cowper* were applying civil trial skills to a criminal trial is that there is no firm evidence of party expert witnesses appearing before a civil common law jury at this time. We have seen that party expert witnesses appeared in Chancery in *Foubert* in 1698, and the absence of evidence for contemporary use should not be taken as conclusive evidence of absence. It is therefore proposed that civil litigation was employing party expert witnesses in some form by the end of the seventeenth century, although probably not involving the level of inference employed in *Folkes*.

5.3.5 The problem of party expert disagreement

From the perspective of the nineteenth century, the sixteenth to eighteenth centuries must have seemed a golden age of expert evidence, free from the difficulties and complexities that were to come.[89] For most of the period under consideration, the conventions of medical and scientific gentlemanly discourse strongly discouraged direct disagreement.[90] This dispute

87 *Alsop 1791.* 88 Langbein, *Origins.*

89 E.g. C. Jones, *Expert Witnesses: Science, Medicine, and the Practice of Law* (Oxford: Oxford University Press, 1994), chs. 4–6; Golan, *Laws of Men*; F. Freemon, 'The Origin of the Medical Expert Witness: the Insanity of Edward Oxford' (2001) 22 *Journal of Legal Medicine* 349–73.

90 Landsman, 'One Hundred Years', 486–9; S. Shapin, *A Social History of Truth: Civility and Science in Seventeenth Century England* (Chicago: University of Chicago Press, 1994).

avoidance was supported by the predominance of court experts and special juries, which restricted the opportunity for disagreement between experts and when party experts had appeared against one another, there was usually ample opportunity to find common ground.[91] In the course of the eighteenth century, however, there was an increasing willingness on the part of specialists to disagree publicly, including in court.

By the 1820s, party expert witnesses had begun to disagree directly with one another. Apart from the difficulties caused for the accurate determination of facts (Chapter 3), the sight of open scientific disagreement in the courtroom sat uncomfortably with the Victorian idea of a society based on scientific progress, and judges were expressing serious concern that experts were being used as weapons of combat rather than sources of information, 'drawn up, not on one side, and for the maintenance of the same truths, but, as it were, in martial and hostile array against each other'.[92] By the middle of the nineteenth century, it appears to have been generally accepted among lawyers that much of the evidence of experts was unreliable by virtue of its partisan nature.[93] At the same time, the realization that the evidence of experts was essential in some cases on questions such as causation, rather than merely of assistance, raised fears, expressed most loudly in criminal matters, that the role of the tribunal of fact would be usurped.[94] These are problems that remain, and do not permit a simple resolution.[95] Judges in the nineteenth century appear to have explained expert disagreement in one of two ways. The more charitable explanation was that the opinions of experts were of little value, since experts were prone to producing a range of possible opinions. In the 1849 case of *Dyce Sombre*,[96] Lord Cottenham LC received evidence that the

Shapiro has questioned whether Shapin's equation of gentlemanly discourse with the new scientific discourse is valid, although Shapiro's concern is more with whether assertions of fact are more likely to be believed if their maker is a gentleman: B. Shapiro, *A Culture of Fact: England 1550–1720* (Ithaca NY: Cornell University Press, 2000), pp. 25 and 118.

91 A notable exception is the criminal case of *Cowper*, where defence and prosecution witnesses vigorously disagreed. That stand-off may in large part be explicable by the social differences that existed between the local medical witnesses, called by the prosecution, and the eminent London medical witnesses, called by the defence.

92 *Severn* v. *Imperial Insurance Co.*, The Times, 14 April 1820.

93 E.g. *In the Matter of Dyce Sombre* (1849) 1 Mac & G 1207; 41 ER 1207; W. Best, *Principles of the Law of Evidence and Practice as to Proofs in Courts of Common Law*, 2nd edn (London: Sweet, 1854), p. 593; J. Taylor, *A Treatise on the Law of Evidence* (London: Maxwell & Son, 1848), p. 55; Stephen, *General View*, pp. 189–90.

94 *R.* v. *Wright*; *R.* v. *M'Naghten* (1843) 10 Cl & F 200; 8 ER 718.

95 Damaška, *Evidence Law Adrift*, pp. 144–7. Golan, 'Scientific Expert Testimony', 157. See also Golan, *Laws of Men*, ch. 2.

96 *In the Matter of Dyce Sombre.*

applicant had commissioned a Dr M. in Paris for £10,000, conditional on his securing favourable expert opinions in London to secure a petition to supersede a commission of lunacy. This would in turn grant Dyce Sombre full control over his financial affairs, worth £500,000. While declining to give any weight to the opinions of the experts because of the way in which they had been obtained, Lord Cottenham would also not suggest that the experts had deliberately shaped their opinions to meet the needs of their pay masters:

> I beg that I may not be understood in what I have said . . . as imputing to any of the physicians who signed the letter to me any intention to deceive me, or to suggest that they respectively do not honestly and sincerely entertain the opinions they have expressed . . . [B]ut I have seen enough of professional opinions to be aware that in matters of doubt upon which the best constructed and best informed minds may differ, there is no difficulty in procuring professional opinions upon either side.[97]

That approach may have been motivated at least in part by a desire to avoid criticizing eminent medical men directly. Elsewhere, however, judges and commentators suggested the motives were more mercenary. There was an expectation by the Victorian courts of a 'natural bias to do something serviceable for those who employ you and adequately remunerate you'.[98] 'No one', Sir James Fitzjames Stephen, Chief Justice, wrote extra-curially in 1863, 'expects an expert, except in the rarest possible cases, to be quite candid. Most of them are all but avowedly advocates who speak for the side which calls them.'[99] In 1854, Best, a London barrister, was similarly unreserved in his comment on expert disagreement, which he ascribed as being in large part due to a lack of honesty:

> Now, after making every allowance for the natural bias which witnesses usually feel in favour of causes in which they are embarked, and giving a wide latitude for *bonâ fide* opinions, however unfounded or fantastical, which persons may form on subjects necessarily much depending on conjecture, there can be no doubt that much testimony is daily received in our courts as 'scientific evidence' to which it is almost profanity to apply the term; as being revolting to common sense, and wholly inconsistent with the commonest honesty on the part of those by whom it is given.[100]

[97] Ibid., at [128].
[98] *Abinger (Lord)* v. *Ashton* (1873) 17 L Rep Eq 373 (Jessell MR).
[99] Stephen, *General* View, pp. 189–90.
[100] Best, *Principles*, 2nd edn, 1854, p. 593. See also Taylor, *Treatise*, p. 55.

Concerns about bias were exacerbated by the increasingly common practice of paying experts for their services. Many of the experts of the eighteenth century and before had been gentlemen, who were therefore likely not to have received payment for their services. There are some qualifications to that statement, since surgeons would not have been socially barred from receiving payment as they were not gentlemen. Questions of class aside, Landsman has used comparison with United States practice at that time to suggest that medical witnesses may not have been paid until well into the nineteenth century.[101] There is no direct evidence of payment or non-payment in case reports, such as the *Old Bailey Sessions Papers*.

Expert payments were not recoverable in costs until at least the 1820s. By 1821, it was established that compensation for loss of time for medical men who appeared as experts was allowable in costs.[102] It was not possible to recover costs for the expenses of other scientific or professional men, either for their time in court or for preparing their evidence. It was conceded by the defence in *Severn* v. *Olive* that it was not clear why there should be an exception for medical men, but nevertheless there was a principle that the party bearing costs should not pay to develop an expert's skill or knowledge. From the case as reported, including its head note, the distinction does not appear to be based on knowledge derived from professional education versus knowledge from practical experience, as Golan has suggested.[103] The experts of the nineteenth century increasingly relied on their work for their income, however, and scientific research was poorly remunerated at this time.[104] As continues to be the case today, there were clear financial advantages to appearing as an expert witness, and expert witnesses who were likely to be favourable were more likely to be re-employed by litigants than those who approached the question before them impartially.

5.4 Special juries

The term "special jury" covers a range of phenomena: a jury of individuals of higher class than usual; a jury of experts; a 'struck' jury, that is to say one formed by a special procedure allowing parties to strike names from

[101] Landsman, 'One Hundred Years', 461, citing J. Mohr, *Doctors and the Law: Medical Jurisprudence in Nineteenth-Century America* (Oxford: Oxford University Press, 1993).

[102] *Severn* v. *Olive* (1821) 3 Brod & Bing 72; 129 ER 1209.

[103] Golan, 'Scientific Expert Testimony', 94–6. [104] Golan, 'History', 23–4.

an unusually large panel of prospective jurors.[105] The origins of the special jury are unclear.[106] The mediaeval jury would appear to have taken a range of forms, including juries made up of matrons for determining whether a pregnancy was genuine (the writ of '*de ventre inspiciendo*'[107]), members of a particular trade for trade-related cases, or a jury *de medietate linguae* (of mixed tongue), where a foreigner was one of the parties.[108] Although juries of merchants appear to have been used from at least 1303,[109] the first reported cases do not appear until the 1640s.[110] Thayer notes that, by the second half of the fourteenth century, there existed London juries of cooks and fishmongers, to try those accused of selling bad food, and a 'jury of merchants' is recorded in the Kings Bench in 1645.[111]

By the eighteenth century, 'the term "special jury" appeared in the case reports without explanation or definition, suggesting a concept that was widely understood'.[112] Of 600 special jury trials conducted by Lord Mansfield in the eighteenth century, Oldham found that only around 27 per cent were purely commercial and 31 per cent were non-commercial. In addition to special juries of merchants, juries of matrons were empanelled as part of the writ of *de ventre inspiciendo*. The special jury could be used directly to decide a case,[113] or else, it would appear, the verdict of the special jury could be provided as advice to the judges in the main trial, as in *Pickering v. Barkley*, where 'a certificate of merchants was read in court'.[114]

Special juries continued to be used into the nineteenth century,[115] but proved to be an evolutionary dead end for the provision of expertise to the civil courts. This was for at least three reasons. The first was that it became

[105] J. Oldham, 'The Origins of the Special Jury' (1983) 50 *University of Chicago Law Review* 137–221, 138.

[106] N. Howlin, 'Special Juries: A Solution to the Expert Witness' (2004) *Irish Student Law Review* 19–47, 33.

[107] The performance of this writ is described in *Willoughby's Case* (1597) Cro Eliz 566; 78 ER 811. The practice of the writ may not have been static over time. Whereas, in 1597, twelve knights were required to observe twelve women (of unspecified type) who inspected the woman subject to the writ, by 1792, a jury of midwives was required: *In the Matter of Martha Brown, ex p. Newton Wallop* (1792) 4 Bro CC 90; 29 ER 794.

[108] Oldham, 'Origins', 167–73. [109] Ibid., 173. [110] Ibid.

[111] J. Thayer, *A Preliminary Treatise on Evidence at Common Law* (Cambridge MA: Harvard University Press, 1898), p. 94.

[112] Oldham, 'Origins', 137.

[113] E.g. *Grant* v. *Vaughan* (1755) 1 Black W 485; 96 ER 281.

[114] *Pickering*. It is clear from *Willoughby's Case* that a certificate was the form in which the special jury's report was brought back to the main proceedings.

[115] Oldham, 'Origins'; Oldham, 'Jury Research'.

increasingly difficult to assemble a jury of merchants resident in the City of London.[116] The second was the demise of jury use in general in civil trials. There appears to be no appetite to introduce special juries where the alternative would be trial by a judge sitting alone, and ongoing, periodic discussion of special juries is restricted to contexts in which non-expert juries continue to be used, such as the English criminal courts[117] and the United States courts.[118] The third reason was that special juries were only able to provide specialists in commercial matters, while the increasingly problematic factual questions before the courts were primarily scientific or medical in nature. The particular strength of a special jury was its understanding of how the commercial world operated, not its ability to handle complex evidence.

5.5 Assessors

5.5.1 The rise of the Trinity Masters

Admiralty was the only court in which providers of expert evidence served by virtue of an office. These were the Master and Elder Brethren of Trinity House.[119] The origin of this practice is unclear. Trinity House was established by a royal charter of Henry VIII in 1514 as a guild of mariners, with a virtual monopoly on pilotage of all vessels passing between the port of London and the open sea.[120] There is no reference in that charter

[116] M. Lobban, 'The Strange Life of the English Civil Jury, 1837–1914', in J. Cairns and G. McLeod (eds.), *The Dearest Birthright of the People of England: The Jury in the History of the Common Law* (Oxford: Hart, 2002), pp. 173–215, pp. 199–203.

[117] R. Auld, *Review of the Criminal Courts of England and Wales* (London: Her Majesty's Stationery Office, 2001), ch. 5.

[118] E.g. 'Practice and Potential of the Advisory Jury' (1987) 100 *Harvard Law Review* 1363–81; K. Bertelsen, 'From Specialized Courts to Specialized Juries: Calling for Professional Juries in Complex Civil Litigation' (1998) 3 *Suffolk Journal of Trial and Appellate Advocacy* 1; A. Feigenbaum, 'Special Juries: Deterring Spurious Medical Malpractice Litigation in State Courts' (2003) 24 *Cardozo Law Review* 1361–420.

[119] The charters of the guild indicate a classical structure of Master, Elder Brethren and Younger Brethren. The eighteenth-century case law, however, seems to use the terms 'Masters' and 'Elder Brethren' interchangeably, even within the same case report. The term 'nautical assessor', common from the second half of the nineteenth century to the present day, does not appear in the reports until *Faustini de Zugarti* v. *Gazaway B Lamer* (1858) 12 Moo PC 331; 14 ER 937. *Nothard* v. *Pepper* (1864) 17 CBNS 39, 141 ER 16, suggests that the term was used on the authority of the Merchant Shipping Act (1854) 17 & 18 Vict c. 104, s. 434.

[120] A. Ruddock, 'The Trinity House at Deptford in the Sixteenth Century' (1950) 65 *English Historical Review* 458–76, at 464; *R.* v. *Clarke* (1787) 1 TR 679, at 679; 99 ER 1317, at 1317.

to a legal function. The earliest case that I have been able to identify in which Trinity House provides assessors is in 1541.[121] In *Buckley* v. *Rice Thomas* in 1555,[122] Saunders J gave examples from the civil and criminal courts of the receipt of specialist advice but did not mention the use of Trinity Masters. This might be taken to indicate that the practice was not widespread. Ruddock similarly does not mention this legal function in his account of Trinity House in the sixteenth century. Charles II's charter of 1666 again does not refer to this function, but in the common law trial of *Pickering* v. *Barkley* in 1658, the Trinity Master is named as an authoritative, though not definitive, source of information about nautical usage. It appears to have been around this time that the courts' use of Trinity House as a source of expert evidence began, because when the 1685 charter of James II exempted Trinity House members from legal services such as jury service, this expressly did not extend to those duties where members were 'compellable by reason of their tenures'.[123] Those duties may not necessarily have been to attend as assessors at trial, however, since Steckley notes that collision cases in the seventeenth century could be assigned by the Admiralty Court to arbitration by appointed experts.[124] In the 1768 Chancery case of *Johnstone* v. *Sutton*, Lord Thurlow mentioned that the use of Trinity House as a source of expert evidence was authorized by Parliament, but unfortunately did not mention the relevant Act. Going back before *Buckley* in 1555, there is a paucity of information generally about the Admiralty Court in the fifteenth century, but the little information that we have suggests that juries of merchants and mariners were used.[125]

I have been able to identify only a handful of Admiralty cases decided before 1800 in which Trinity Masters were used.[126] These reports suggest that contentious factual issues were decided by two Trinity Masters. Where the Masters could not agree, one or more further brothers would be

[121] *Re Rumney and Wood* (1541), in Marsden (ed.), *Select Pleas in the Court of Admiralty*, pp. 102–4, trans. pp. 213–15; A. Dickey, 'The Province and Function of Assessors in English Courts' 33 *Modern Law Review* (1970) 494–507.

[122] *Buckley* v. *Rice Thomas* (1555) 1 Plowd 118; 75 ER 182.

[123] *Clarke*, at 681.

[124] G. Steckley, 'Collisions, Prohibitions, and the Admiralty Court in Seventeenth-Century London' (2003) 21 *Law and History Review* 41–67 at fn. 69; G. Steckley, 'Merchants and the Admiralty Court During the English Revolution' (1978) 22 *American Journal of Legal History* 137–75.

[125] Prichard and Yale (eds.), *Hale and Fleetwood*, vol. I, p. liii.

[126] Although Trinity House is made up of one Master and a number of Brethren, the Elder Brethren who assist the courts as assessors are often referred to by lawyers as 'Trinity Masters'.

consulted.[127] For example, in the 1765 case of *Dale*, the reporter notes, possibly quoting another commentary on the case, that:

> The Trinity Masters declared their opinion concerning the situation and position of the ships at the time of the damage in question, and of their behaviour relative to the accident, and, having differed in their judgment, the judge, by consent of the parties, gave leave to the assessors to consult a third Brother, and make their report by the next Court, with the other Trinity Master.[128]

In *Dale*, the decision of the Trinity Masters is referred to as a 'judgment' and an 'opinion', with the latter term also being used in *The Marquis of Granby* in 1770.[129] The report of *The Marquis of Granby* suggests that the judge directed the trial, while the Trinity Masters decided the facts. In *Stoker* v. *Hutton*,[130] on appeal to the High Court of Delegates,[131] the report quotes from a later entry in the Delegates' Assignation Book for 11 May 1789, referring back to this case, that:

> The Judges having consulted with counsel on both sides, did by and with their consent refer the merits and the whole cause to the two Trinity Masters present . . . they taking to their assistance such other Trinity Masters . . . as by the Trinity Board should be directed to attend, for them to report their opinion to the Court whether the sentence appealed from ought to be sustained, altered or modified, or wholly reversed; and directed the registrar to write to the Trinity Board requesting that a third Trinity Master might attend the other two upon the reference.

This entry suggests that it was open to the court and to the parties to delegate not only the finding of fact, but the deciding of the whole appeal, to the Trinity Masters.

The mode of expert evidence employed in Admiralty proceedings was unlike that in the other civil courts. The use of a court-appointed officer,

[127] This may be a product of the civilian proof model. Consett, *Practice*, ch. X, s. I.3, pp. 363–4, has indicated that, for there to be a full proof in the ecclesiastical courts, there had to be two such expert witnesses. The use of two experts also appears in perhaps the first recorded criminal case involving expert evidence, before the King's Bench in 1354 in the Year Book account: YB Trin 28 Edw. III pl. 1 fo. 18b (1354). The *Liber Assisorum* account of the same case does not quantify: 28 Edw. III Lib. Ass. 5 fo. 145b.

[128] *Dale* v. *Hall* (1765) Burrell 323; 167 ER 592.

[129] *The Marquis of Granby* (1770) Burrell 323; 167 ER 592.

[130] *Stoker* v. *Hutton* (1785) Burrell 328; 167 ER 594.

[131] The court of appeal from the archbishops' courts and the High Court of Admiralty until 1833.

drawn from membership of a court-sanctioned institution, who is, or is almost, part of the tribunal, makes Admiralty practice more akin to that of the continental civilian courts at this time.[132] There are two reservations to saying that Admiralty practice was distinctive solely because it was a civilian court. The first is that the ecclesiastical courts, which were served by the same College of Advocates, made use of party expert witnesses from at least 1575 (above, Section 5.3), and there is no evidence of court-appointed experts. That may be because of a difference in subject matter, or the absence of a suitable pool of experts akin to Trinity House. The second reservation arises from an absence of contemporary comparisons by common lawyers between French *experts* – whose usage was being referred to at least by the 1790s – and Trinity Masters.[133] Alongside a civilian-origins explanation for the distinctive use of the nautical assessor, it is possible that the Trinity Masters emerged as a type of special jury. This idea is supported by the suggestion in the reports that, although a judge presided over the trial, evidence was handed to the Trinity Masters at the end for a finding of fact.[134] Continental experts do not appear to have been delegated to in this fashion. In addition, the advice of the Masters is termed 'opinion' or 'judgment'. The true nature of the Trinity Masters' role in the eighteenth century must therefore remain unclear.

5.5.2 From Trinity Masters to assessors

The use of Trinity Masters in Admiralty underwent a number of significant changes in the second half of the nineteenth century. The first reform was to restrict discussions between court and Trinity Masters about the evidence until all the evidence had been given. It would appear that, up until 1867, the nautical assessors consulted with the judge in open court. However, in *The Hannibal*, the practice was introduced that, '[F]or the future in causes of collision and salvage, heard before the Trinity Masters,

132 For an introduction to the role of medical experts in continental criminal proceedings from the sixteenth to eighteenth centuries, see C. Crawford, 'Legalizing Medicine: Early Modern Legal Systems and the Growth of Medico-legal Knowledge', in M. Clark and C. Crawford, *Legal Medicine in History* (Cambridge: Cambridge University Press, 1994), pp. 89–116.

133 E.g. Gilbert, *Law of Evidence*, 4th edn; *Doe on the Demise of Mudd* v. *Suckermore* (1836) 5 A & E 703, at 710; 111 ER 1331; Best, *Principles*, on the French use of three *experts* for handwriting identification.

134 Prichard and Yale (eds.), *Hale and Fleetwood*, pp. xxxi and xxxiii, identify the use of a jury of mariners and merchants in a flooding case of 1384, and an appeal in 1410 on the basis that the Admiralty judge's jury had not been composed of merchants or mariners.

[the judge] should not sum up the evidence; but that the Court and Trinity Masters would retire and, on their return, the judgment of the Court would be given'.[135] This change may have followed on from the introduction of common lawyers into the High Court of Admiralty in 1859.[136]

The second reform was the fusion of the superior courts into one Supreme Court by the Judicature Acts of 1873 and 1875. The Judicature Acts replaced the specific use of Trinity Masters with a general practice of assessors and special referees. Section 56 of the 1873 Act provided that:

> Subject to any Rules of Court and to such right as may now exist to have particular cases submitted to the verdict of a jury, any question arising in any cause or matter (other than a criminal proceeding by the Crown) before the High Court of Justice or before the Court of Appeal, may be referred by the Court or by any Divisional Court or Judge before whom such cause or matter may be pending, for inquiry and report to any official or special Referee, and the report of any such Referee may be adopted wholly or partially by the Court, and may (if so adopted) be enforced as a judgment by the Court. The High Court or the Court of Appeal may also, in any such cause or matter as aforesaid in which it may think it expedient so to do, call in the aid of one or more assessors specially qualified, and try and hear such cause or matter wholly or partially with the assistance of such assessors. The remuneration, if any, to be paid to such special Referees or assessors shall be determined by the Court.

The role of the assessor introduced by the RSC achieved two goals. First, it provided a means by which Admiralty practice could be assimilated into the standardized procedural format of the new Supreme Court. Secondly, it extended access to such experts to courts hearing all types of actions. This was a potential means by which to meet objections that courts, whether a judge sitting alone or with a jury, could not reasonably be expected to understand technical evidence presented. General access to assessors was subsequently extended to County Court actions,[137] and assessors were also introduced into the Patent courts.[138] This general approach to assessors remained unchanged throughout the history of the RSC.[139] However, as

135 *The Hannibal* (1867) 2 A & E 53, at 56.

136 In 1859 common law barristers were granted rights of audience, in 1860 the court was transferred to Westminster Hall: (1857) 22 & 23 Vict. c. 6. A common lawyer was appointed Admiralty judge in 1883: Roscoe, *High Court of Admiralty*, p. 6.

137 County Courts Act 1888, s. 103.

138 As 'scientific advisers', under s. 70(3) of the Supreme Court Act 1981, and CPR r 35.15.

139 Dickey, 'Province and Function'.

with the introduction of court experts under RSC Ord. 40, there was little common adoption of the practice of assessors. Section 70(1) of the Supreme Court Act 1981 limits the role of the assessor to 'assistance' to the court to 'hear and dispose' of a case. Section 63 of the County Courts Act 1984 says that an assessor may 'sit with the judge'.[140]

Parliament also began to direct that assessors sit on specialist tribunals,[141] and in such situations Parliament may also provide that the court has access to a separate court-appointed expert. Examples of this occur in the form of the medical referee for the purposes of the Workmen's Compensation Act 1925,[142] and the National Insurance (Industrial Injuries) (Determination of Claims and Questions) Regulations 1948.[143]

From at least 1867 until the introduction of the CPR, an assessor, whether acting in a normal civil capacity or under a particular statutory form of proceeding, was not an evidentiary source.[144] By 1884, nautical assessors were held to be part of a mixed tribunal, albeit they 'take no part in the judgment whatever; they are not responsible for it, and have nothing to do with it'.[145] In consequence, assessors are not sworn,[146] and they may not be cross-examined by the parties.[147] The advice that the assessor may provide can extend from the factual clarification of the evidence of other experts through to comments bearing directly on the ultimate issue (Section 5.7), unlike other types of expert. The former type

[140] A reasonable case might be made that it would be ultra vires for a court to direct an assessor to 'take such part in the proceedings' other than as has been provided for by the Supreme Court Act 1981 or the County Courts Act 1984 as appropriate.

[141] E.g. Workmen's Compensation Act 1925, Sch 1, para 5.

[142] Workmen's Compensation Act 1925, s.38.

[143] R. v. *Deputy Industrial Injuries Commissioner ex p. Jones* [1962] 2 QB 677; [1962] 2 WLR 1215; [1962] 2 All ER 430 (DC).

[144] *Richardson* v. *Redpath Brown & Co Ltd* [1944] AC 62 (HL). This also applies to coroners' courts: *R.* v. *HM Coroner for Surrey* ex p. *Irene Wright*, Court of Appeal, 24 October 1996.

[145] *The Beryl* [1884] PD 137, at 141.

[146] If assessors are classed as an evidentiary source, then the effect of the unsworn nature of their testimony would presumably be that the trial should be considered a nullity and any judgment based on it should be set aside: P. Murphy, *Evidence*, 9th edn (Oxford: Oxford University Press, 2005), p. 501, citing *R.* v. *Marsham* ex p. *Lawrence* [1912] KB 362 and *Birch* v. *Somerville* (1852) 2 ICLR (2nd ser.) 253.

[147] Lord Justice (Sir Mark) Waller, I. Scott, Sir H. Brooke *et al.* (eds.), *Civil Procedure*, 2 vols. (London: Sweet and Maxwell, 2007) (The *White Book*), 35.15.4. The *White Book* appears to imply that while an assessor cannot be cross-examined, an expert witness appointed by the court could be. Aside from the point that in practice the English civil courts do not appoint expert witnesses, it is not clear that a court-appointed expert could be cross–examined, following the rule in *Coulson v Disborough* [1894] 2 QB 316 on the examination of witnesses called by the court generally.

of advice would appear to be what non-Admiralty judges have had in mind when discussing the role of the assessor,[148] but advice of the latter form is common in Admiralty. For example, in *The Queen Mary*, the Court of Appeal received assessor advice on the normative question of whether the *Queen Mary* should have given way to a cruiser acting as an anti-aircraft defence ship.[149]

5.6 Court experts

5.6.1 Before the nineteenth century

Despite Thayer's claim that the 'old way' was for experts to act as 'helpers of the court',[150] there are very few references to the use of experts as court advisers, inside or outside the court room, before the nineteenth century. The first recorded consultation of an expert in a civil case involved a court-instructed adviser to the court, and dates from at least the very end of the fifteenth century, when grammarians were consulted by the court on the correct construction of Latin texts.[151] This consultation could be formal or informal, and there would appear to have been few rules on the selection of these advisers. In *Pickering* v. *Barkley* in 1658, the court consulted the Master of Trinity House, the head of the mariners' guild, on whether mariners considered pirates to be 'perils of the sea'.[152] During a trial in 1703, Holt CJ approached two merchants out of court for advice, during the course of a trial.[153] The available evidence suggests an occasional reference to specialists by the court, rather than an institutionalized use.

The relationship between court and party experts in the civil courts is more complex than that presented by Landsman in his account of expert evidence in the criminal courts.[154] As part of his overall theory of an 'Adversarial Revolution',[155] Landsman presents a picture in which the use

148 E.g. *Esso Petroleum* v. *Southport Corporation* [1956] AC 218; [1956] 2 WLR 81; [1955] 3 All ER 864; *Richardson*.

149 *The Queen Mary* (1947) 80 Ll Rep 609, at 631.

150 Thayer, *Select Cases*, p. 666.

151 In *Buckley*, Staunford J (at 122) and Saunders J (at 125) both refer to a 1494 case (YB Hil. 9 Hen. VII 16 pl. 8) in which masters of grammar were consulted on the Latin word for 'fine'. On the use of grammarians, see also *Giles* v. *Ferrers* (1587) Cro Eliz. 55; *Hedd* v. *Chalenor* (1590) Cro Eliz. 176; 78 ER 433; *Sheldon's Case* (1590) 1 Leo 241; 74 ER 229.

152 This case makes Lord Mansfield's use of assessors in the King's Bench less remarkable: Oldham, *Mansfield Manuscripts*, p. 395 fn. 5.

153 *Buller* v. *Crips* (1703) 6 Modern 29; 87 ER 793.

154 Landsman, 'Of Witches'; Landsman, 'One Hundred Years'.

155 S. Landsman, 'The Rise of the Contentious Spirit: Adversary Procedure in Eighteenth Century England' (1990) 75 *Cornell Law Review*, 497–609. See also Golan, 'History', 9;

of experts in criminal trials moved from court experts in 1665,[156] to party experts by the 1730s. Leaving aside historical difficulties such as *R.* v. *Pembroke* in 1678, *R.* v. *Green* in 1679 and *R.* v. *Coningsmark* in 1682,[157] which affect the validity of the claim for an adversarial revolution in expert evidence in criminal cases, it is clear that there was no straightforward revolution in expert evidence in civil cases. Party experts appear in the King's Bench by 1619, forty-six years after the first recorded use of party experts in the ecclesiastical courts in 1575. Looking at alternatives to party experts, the first identified report of the use of Trinity Masters was in 1541, but the use of special juries has not been identified until 1645. There are very few references to the use of experts as court advisers, inside or outside the court room, although common law judges were still consulting with experts out of court in 1703, and it would appear from *Folkes* in 1782 that Lord Mansfield may previously have consulted Smeaton as an informal court adviser.

In examining the developing modes of expert evidence, we must bear in mind the mechanisms by which experts were instructed. While the French had a developed judicial bureaucracy, and experts were office holders,[158] the English did not possess a similar system. The High Court of Admiralty was unusual, because it could call on the services of Trinity House. The Lord Chancellor in Chancery, and the Twelve Judges at Common Law, had no effective mechanism, and no resources, for the appointment of court experts. In civil cases, a judge could always ask friends outside court for their advice. In criminal cases, the judge had no sight of any case papers before trial, and because criminal cases were tried within one day, the judge could not consult while the trial was in progress. Where party experts had not been instructed, the best that the criminal court might be able to do would be to call experts from the public gallery.[159] The demise of the court adviser may therefore have been related to the desire of parties and their counsel increasingly to control the admission of evidence.[160] The

Langbein, *Origins*, p. 2. Although never explicitly stated, Landsman's use of historical evidence indicates that his theory relates solely to criminal process.

156 *The Trial of Witches* (1665) 6 St Tr 68. Landsman, 'of Witches', 136; Landsman, 'One Hundred Years', 447.

157 *R.* v. *Coningsmark (Count)* (1682) 9 St Tr 21.

158 Leclerc, *Juge et expert.*

159 *Trial of Witches.*

160 Similarly, a rule of law developed in the earlier eighteenth century that juries should not use their own knowledge, and this in turn enabled the further development of rules controlling the admission of evidence: e.g. J. Mitnick, 'From Neighbor-Witness to Judge of Proofs: the Transformation of the English Civil Juror' (1988) 32 *American Journal of Legal History* 201–35.

corollary to this was that judges were increasingly unwilling to intervene in the selection of evidence for a case.

5.6.2 Nineteenth-century innovation

While the nineteenth century is in many ways the heyday of the English *laissez-faire* model of civil procedure, the increasing concerns that were being raised about the effects of expert partisanship on the sound administration of justice led to significant interest in court experts in the second half of the nineteenth century. In his 1854 edition of *Principles of the Law of Evidence*, Best considered the French practice of court-appointed experts. He suggested that, although the English courts are generally reluctant to appoint their own witnesses, it may be to the court's advantage to appoint its own experts, in addition 'of course' to party experts. A similar view was being expressed by scientists outside the courtroom in the 1850s,[161] and there were associated reforms in common law and Chancery procedure at this time. First, the Court of Chancery Act 1852 allowed a judge in chambers to seek the assistance of specialists.[162] Beuscher has suggested that the 1852 Act incorporated an existing power,[163] although its existence is not clear from the authority of *Lushington* v. *Boldero* that he cites.[164] This may be the power to which Sir Page-Wood, Vice-Chancellor, was referring when he said in 1860 that 'in many cases he had availed himself of the privilege which was accorded to judges of the Chancery Court, of calling in disinterested witnesses in matters of opinion'.[165] Secondly, the Common Law Procedure Act 1854 allowed the court to compel the parties to resolve the matter in arbitration before a Referee.[166]

In a report of 29 July 1864, the Patent Law Commissioners advised that the current mode of trying patents cases was unsatisfactory, and recommended that instead a judge should sit with scientific assessors selected by himself and without a jury, unless both parties agreed otherwise. This model was viewed favourably by the Judicature Commissioners in 1869,

161 L. Blom-Cooper, 'Historical Background', in L. Blom-Cooper (ed.), *Experts in the Civil Courts* (Oxford: Oxford University Press, 2006), pp. 1–15, p. 7.

162 Court of Chancery Act 1852, 15 & 16 Vict. c. 80, s. 42, carried over into RSC Ord. 55, r. 19.

163 J. Beuscher, 'The Use of Experts by the Courts' (1941) 54 *Harvard Law Review* 1105–27, 1118.

164 *Lushington* v. *Boldero* (1819) 6 Madd 149; 56 ER 1048.

165 Blom-Cooper, 'Historical Background', p. 8

166 Judicature Commission, *First Report of the Commissioners* (London: Her Majesty's Stationery Office, 1869), p. 12.

who recommended that the court should have the case management discretion to direct that a case be heard by judge, jury or referee, with the appointment of Official Referees,[167] and that Patent practice should be extended to 'any cases involving questions of a scientific or technical character'.[168]

Sections 56 and 57 of the Judicature Act 1873 subsequently allowed for the appointment of court experts, although, in 1877, Sir George Jessell MR said in the case of *Thorn* that he had 'hitherto abstained from exercising the power which, no doubt, the Court has of selecting an expert to give evidence before the Court'.[169] Some courts at first instance did make use of court experts, for example in a Patents case in 1881,[170] and in an 1894 case in which the evidence of the parties' surveyor experts was so divergent as to be of no assistance to the court.[171] In the first edition of his *Law of Evidence* in 1892, Phipson wrote that 'It must be remembered that, in addition to the scientific evidence adduced by the parties, the Court may always, for its own guidance and information, except in cases of Crown prosecution, order independent reports to be made or experiments to be tried by experts of its own selection, and may act on such reports.'[172]

The court experts of the Judicature Acts were appointed by the courts. This, as Jessell pointed out in *Thorn*, required the court to identify an appropriate expert prior to instruction. This was something that late Victorian courts were not resourced to do, and perhaps for this reason court experts were not extensively instructed. The use of court experts also offended against the principles of adversarial justice, in that it took away from the parties the right to determine the evidence.

5.6.3 Twentieth-century disinterest

An amendment to the Rules of the Supreme Court in 1934 went some way to addressing the conflict between adversarial principles and the court appointment of experts. Order 40 empowered the judge to appoint an expert 'on the application of any party'. That provision was almost certainly intended to facilitate the use of a common law power by providing

[167] Ibid., p. 12. [168] Ibid., p. 14.
[169] *Thorn* v. *Worthing Skating Rink Co.* (1877) 6 ChD 415, at 418.
[170] *Badische Anilin und Soda Fabrik* v. *Levinstein* (1881) 24 ChD 156.
[171] *Kennard* v. *Ashman* (1894) 10 TLR 213 (Ch.).
[172] S. Phipson, *The Law of Evidence*, 1st edn (London: Stevens, 1892).

the procedure for the instruction of such an expert.[173] However, its wording made clear the dominance of adversarial thought on the introduction of evidence in English civil law. Order 40 r. 1 required that at least one of the parties applied to the court for a court expert (other than a medical expert) to be appointed. Until the mid 1990s, Ord. 40 r. 1 was only applied where all parties consented and, in consequence, was hardly ever used. Ord. 40 r. 2, which dealt with medical experts, appears never to have been used at all. Other than a passing suggestion by Hammelmann, following the Second World War, that many of the difficulties in the assessment of expert evidence might be overcome by adopting the French practice of court experts,[174] there would appear to have been no significant interest in the use of court experts in England until the late 1960s, when some use was made of court experts in the Family courts (Section 4.3.1.4).

Interest in court experts resurfaced again in the 1990s, in both the civil and criminal courts. The civil courts had been increasingly concerned since the 1980s that party expert witnesses were providing partisan rather than impartial advice to the court.[175] In the criminal courts, the early 1990s saw the discovery of a series of miscarriages of justice, in which the misuse of expert evidence by the prosecution had played a central part.[176] This gave rise to serious discussion of the possible advantages of adopting a court expert system. The response of the judiciary in the 1990s was to seek to clarify the duties of a party expert witness at common law,[177] but also to reconsider the use of court experts. Despite some academic legal interest in a continental model of court experts,[178] this interest was fiercely resisted by legal practitioners,[179] who saw court experts as infringing on the fundamental right of the accused to present the best possible defence. A report commissioned by Justice into the use of scientific evidence in

173 J. Basten, 'The Court Expert in Civil Trials – A Comparative Appraisal' (1977) 41 *Modern Law Review* 174–91, 177.

174 H. Hammelmann, 'Expert Evidence' (1947) 11 *Modern Law Review* 32–9.

175 *Whitehouse* v. *Jordan* [1980] 1 All ER 650 (CA); [1981] 1 WLR 246 (HL); *National Justice Compania* v. *Prudential Assurance* [1993] 2 Ll Rep 68 (*The Ikarian Reefer*) (Comm. Ct); 'Editorial' *Counsel* November/December 1994; *Cala Homes (South) Ltd* v. *Alfred McAlpine Homes East Ltd* [1995] FSR 818 (Ch.).

176 E.g. *R.* v. *Maguire* [1992] QB 93b; [1992] 94 Cr App R 133 (*Maguire Seven*).

177 *The Ikarian Reefer*, at 81–2.

178 J. Spencer, 'Court Experts and Expert Witnesses: Have We a Lesson to Learn from the French?' (1992) 45 *Current Legal Problems* 213–36; J. Spencer, 'The Neutral Expert: An Implausible Bogey' [1991] *Criminal Law Review* 106–10.

179 M. Howard, 'The Neutral Expert: A Plausible Threat to Justice' [1991] *Criminal Law Review* 98–105.

the criminal courts concluded in favour of retaining a system of separate party expert witnesses,[180] although there had been some initial indications that the report would favour moving to a court expert system. In *Abbey National Mortgages plc* v. *Key Surveyors Ltd*,[181] the court instructed a court expert in a valuation matter, despite the objection of one of the parties. That case management decision was upheld in the Court of Appeal.

5.7 The Ultimate Issue Rule

5.7.1 The rule's nineteenth-century rise

The general question of whether a non-expert fact finder is competent to assess the evidence of an expert is one that tended to come up in relation to expert disagreement. For example in the 1699 criminal case of *Cowper*, in which extensive use was made of party experts, the trial judge, Hatsell B, was able freely to admit in his summing up that he did not understand the medical evidence, and doubted that the jury did either: 'The doctors and surgeons have talked a great deal to this purpose [on evidence for drowning] . . . but unless you have more skill in anatomy than I, you would not be much edified by it. I acknowledge I never studied anatomy; but I perceive that the doctors do differ in their notions about these things.'[182]

It may seem curious to us now that Hatsell did not seem to think that the jury's inability to engage rationally with the experts' evidence would particularly affect the validity of their verdict. This may simply be because evidential jurisprudence had yet to reach the stage where certain types of question could only be answered by an expert and, as in *Folkes* v. *Chadd*, the jury could no longer simply ignore the expert's opinion.

By the nineteenth century, it appears to have been generally accepted that juries were not particularly well suited to accurate fact finding, although other valid constitutional reasons might exist for their continuance.[183] The juries' lack of epistemic competence in relation to expert evidence may therefore have been seen as part of a broader malaise. The problem that appears to have vexed nineteenth-century jurists more is that, because juries did not properly understand expert evidence, they might not only accept an erroneous finding of fact, but go beyond this

[180] C. Oddie, *Science and the Administration of Justice* (London: Justice, 1991).

[181] *Abbey National Mortgages plc* v. *Key Surveyors Nationwide Ltd* [1996] 1 WLR 1534; [1996] 3 All ER 184 (CA).

[182] *R.* v *Cowper*, at 1189.

[183] E.g. Lobban, 'Strange Life', pp. 199–203.

to give an erroneous verdict, where the expert's evidence went beyond simple inferences about the facts to trespass onto the ultimate issue before the court, such as whether the defendant was insane, or had committed murder.

In *R.* v. *Wright*, which involved a defence of insanity, the Twelve Judges of the common law courts agreed that medical witnesses could testify as to 'whether the appearances proved by other witnesses were symptoms of insanity' but not whether the non-expert evidence showed the particular defendant to be insane. The rule was affirmed in *Wright* v. *Doe d Tatham* in 1837.[184] The effect of the rule was to make it impossible for juries to delegate their verdict-giving authority de facto to experts, consciously or unconsciously, although it remained possible for juries to delegate fact finding on subsidiary issues to the expert. The rule may already have been in operation by 1760, when the House of Lords had refused Earl Ferrers permission to ask his expert witness whether behaviours he had exhibited 'are symptoms of lunacy'.[185] Under the Ultimate Issue Rule, therefore, 'experts give evidence and do not decide the issue'.[186]

The limitations of the rule were demonstrated in the high-profile case of *R.* v. *M'Naghten.* The defendant had attempted to assassinate the Prime Minister, Sir Robert Peel, but instead shot and killed his secretary. At trial, he pleaded a defence of insanity. This was one of the first high-profile cases following the enactment of the Prisoner's Counsel Act 1836, which had enshrined as a right in statute the developing practice of full representation by an advocate at trial. In his opening speech, M'Naghten's barrister, Cockburn, reminded the jury that they should not 'surrender [their] minds and understanding to the opinion, of any set of men'. However, Cockburn then drew the jurors' attention to the growth of an intellectual division of labour: the jurors had their own jobs to attend to and could not devote time to a systematic study of madness. In this way, he effectively side-stepped the Ultimate Issue Rule as it was then understood. Cockburn intended to call nine expert witnesses, but after the seventh expert was called, Tindall CJ invited the jury to acquit M'Naghten on the grounds of insanity.[187] There was considerable concern at the outcome

184 *Wright* v. *Doe d Tatham* (1837) 7 A & E 313, 112 ER 488, aff'd (1838) 5 Cl & F 670; (1838) Bing NC 489.

185 *R.* v. *Ferrers (Earl)* (1760) 9 St Tr 942.

186 H. Malek (ed.), *Phipson on Evidence*, 16th edn (London: Sweet and Maxwell, 2005), [33.12].

187 Ward, 'Observers, Advisers, or Authorities', 111.

since, according to Lord Campbell, 'The impression in the public mind, was, that if a certain number of medical witnesses . . . had come into court and said that the prisoner was insane when he committed the act, the trial was to be stopped'.[188] The Twelve Judges, including Tindall, subsequently provided the House of Lords with answers to a series of questions on insanity. These answers gave a strict interpretation of the common law 'knowledge of right and wrong' test, and are retained today as the M'Naghten Rules.

M'Naghten represented a high-profile public airing of concerns that had been expressed judicially since at least *Wright*. If the jury is not able to engage on a rational basis with the evidence provided by the experts, then it may accept that evidence at face value, as having been given by a reputable specialist. This raises the concern that the tribunal of fact (whether judge or jury) either does,[189] or perhaps should,[190] delegate or abdicate the fact-finding process to experts, although these experts lack a democratic mandate.[191] Delegation offends the constitutional principle *delegatus non potest delegare*.[192] Abdication similarly offends principles of sound administration.[193] An expert could provide an opinion on the facts of the case, provided that opinion did not determine the ultimate issue. The purpose of the rule was to remove the pre-rational nature of trial by expert witness, and require that the court engage in rational assessment of that expert evidence, since, 'the parties have invoked the decision of a judicial tribunal and not an oracular pronouncement by an expert'.[194]

188 Ibid.

189 W. Twining, 'Civilians Don't Try: A Comment on Mirjan Damaška's "Rational and Irrational Proof Revisited"' (1997) 5 *Cardozo Journal of International and Comparative Law* 69–78; M. Damaška, 'Rational and Irrational Proof Revisited' (1997) 5 *Cardozo Journal of International and Comparative Law* 25–39.

190 L. Hand, 'Historical and Practical Considerations Regarding Expert Testimony' (1901) 15 *Harvard Law Review* 40–58; Auld, *Review*, [5.185].

191 On the democratic mandate of the judiciary, see the comments by Lord Bingham in *A* v. *Secretary of State for the Home Department* [2004] UKHL 56; [2005] 2 AC 68; [2005] 2 WLR 87; [2005] 3 All ER 169, rejecting the Attorney-General's submission that the courts should defer to the government and Parliament, which held a democratic mandate.

192 A power must be exercised by the person in whom it is vested, and cannot be delegated: P. Craig, *Administrative Law*, 5th edn (London: Sweet and Maxwell, 2003), pp. 522–3.

193 M. Fordham, *Judicial Review Handbook*, 4th edn (Oxford: Hart, 2004), [50.2]; *R.* v. *Secretary of State for Trade and Industry* ex p. *Lonrho plc* [1989] 1 WLR 525, at 538; [1989] 2 All ER 609 (HL).

194 *Davie* v. *Edinburgh Magistrates* 1953 SC 34.

5.7.2 *The rule's twentieth-century decline*

Despite its constitutional significance, the ascendancy of the rule was short-lived, and it soon fell into decline in both England and the United States. Wigmore, for example, thought that it was 'a mere bit of empty rhetoric',[195] and the rule began to be disregarded in the United States civil courts in the 1940s. For example, in *Dowling* v. *L. H. Shattuck, Inc.*,[196] expert evidence was permitted on the proper method of shoring a ditch, while in *People* v. *Wilson*,[197] expert opinion was admitted on whether an abortion was necessary to save the life of a patient. The rule was finally abolished in 1975 by Federal Rule of Evidence 704. In England, the decline began in the civil courts in the 1950s,[198] and the Civil Evidence Act 1972 abolished the rule.

Technically, the rule remains in criminal law, although in 1968 Lord Parker noted that '[A]lthough technically the final question "Do you think he was suffering from diminished responsibility?" is strictly inadmissible, it is allowed time and again without objection'.[199] Jackson has argued that, rather than representing a single exclusionary principle, three separate rationales can be distinguished, and that each of these rationales can be more effectively achieved through other rules of evidence.[200] The first rationale is to prevent the expert from usurping the role of the advocate, but the case law for this rationale involves situations where the expert gave an opinion on ultimate causation without making clear the facts on which this opinion was based.[201] This rationale can therefore be enforced through the Opinion Rule, requiring an expert to state the facts on which his opinion is based.[202] The second rationale is to prevent the expert from usurping the task of the tribunal of fact in fact finding. In *Turner*, the accused was not permitted to call a psychiatrist to support his plea that he had killed his girlfriend in a fit of rage caused by her confession of infidelity,

195 J. Wigmore, *A Treatise on the Anglo-American System of Evidence in Trials at Common Law* (1923), rev. edn Chadbown (Boston: Little, Brown, 1981), vol. VII, [1920]–[1921].

196 *Dowling* v. *L. H. Shattuck, Inc.* 91 NH 234; 17 A 2d 529 (1941).

197 *People* v. *Wilson* 25 Cal 2d 341; 153 P 2d 720 (1944).

198 E.g. *Bolam* v. *Friern Hospital Management Committee* [1957] 1 WLR 582, [1957] 2 All ER 118 (QB), on medical negligence; *R.* v. *Matheson* [1958] 1 WLR 474, on psychiatric evidence on diminished responsibility, in which the Court of Appeal held that the jury must accept medical evidence on this matter where it was unchallenged.

199 *DPP* v. *A & B C Chewing Gum* [1968] 1 QB 159; [1967] 3 WLR 493; [1967] 2 All ER 504.

200 J. Jackson, 'The Ultimate Issue Rule: One Rule Too Many' [1984] *Criminal Law Review* 75.

201 *Clark* v. *Ryan* (1960) 103 CLR 486; *Phillips* v. *Ford Motor Co.* [1971] 18 DLR (3d) 641.

202 *R.* v. *Turner* [1975] QB 834; 60 Cr App R 80.

since, if psychiatrists could testify to the veracity of the accused, then this would replace the role of the tribunal of fact. The orthodox view is that the expert is only to assist the tribunal of fact,[203] although there have been directions that jurors should accept expert testimony where the evidence is of a kind that only an expert could provide and is unchallenged by any other expert evidence.[204] Only in these last cases is the expert usurping the role of the jury, although in such cases the jury is still at liberty to choose to ignore the evidence.[205] The third rationale is to prevent the expert from usurping the task of fact-classification. It prevents the expert from determining whether the fact found can be classified within the terms of the ultimate issues. Jackson sees this as being of particular relevance in the area of psychiatric experts, where legal conceptions such as 'mental responsibility' have no direct psychiatric equivalent. Jackson would exclude opinion evidence where the witness is not qualified to give such an opinion, under the existing Opinion Rule. This is especially true of opinions requiring moral evaluation. For example in *A & B C Chewing Gum*, expert psychiatrists were permitted to give evidence on the effect of the battle cards on children, but not on whether the cards would deprave and corrupt. Similarly in *Shaw*,[206] Lord Morris held that 'current standards' in society are in the keeping of jurors. An exception would appear to be that professionals may give conclusive opinion on negligence, following the test laid down in *Bolam* and approved by the House of Lords in *Whitehouse* v. *Jordan*.

What Jackson's analysis demonstrates is that there is no strictly doctrinal justification for the Ultimate Issue Rule. Instead, the rule is a response to a perceived emerging problem: that the expert is able to give an opinion which the court can only nominally assess. A modern example is given in *R.* v. *O'Callaghan* [1976], where it was held that:

> Even where such testimony [on the ultimate issue] is received, the trier of fact, judge or jury, retains the power of decision. This is so, even when the decision turns in a matter on which the tribunal would be unable to understand the evidence without the assistance of experts. Thus, expert testimony is essential for the purpose of identifying the patterns and characteristics of a set of fingerprints but it remains for the jury to decide whether the two sets of fingerprints are identical.

203 *Davie* v. *Edinburgh Magistrates*; *R.* v. *O'Callaghan* [1976] VR 676.

204 *R.* v. *Matheson*; *R.* v. *Bailey* [1961] Crim LR 828.

205 Such a jury decision runs the risk of being overturned at appeal.

206 *Shaw* v. *DPP* [1962] AC 220, at 292; [1961] 2 WLR 897; [1961] 2 All ER 446; (1961) 45 Cr App R 113 (HL).

In such a case, it is difficult to imagine how a tribunal of fact, presented with two sets of prints that they are told by an expert are identical, could be expected to come to a reasoned decision that the prints were not identical. To this extent, the view expressed by Lord Taylor CJ in *Stockwell*,[207] and echoed by Roberts and Zuckerman,[208] does not properly address the paradox that the tribunal of fact must reason through to its own conclusion, but it may have no options before it between which it can reasonably decide. This is particularly problematic where the tribunal of fact is presented with only one expert point of view.

5.8 Conclusion

A peculiar feature of the history of expert evidence in the English civil courts is that it was not until the 1780s, for example in the case of *Folkes*, that people began to discuss whether the courts should recognize a particular category of evidence, which was necessary to determine certain types of factual question but which could only be given on the basis of specialist knowledge. The witnesses who gave such evidence would speak of the inferences that they were able to draw from the application of personal knowledge to base facts. Such evidence mostly fell within the category already recognized as 'opinion evidence', but it was not possible to exclude such evidence for the reasons normally given for excluding opinions. The available civil and criminal case law would not allow us to say that the evidence of such specialists was not seen as being the same as the evidence of non-expert witnesses prior to 1782, but it does suggest that the evidence was not seen as falling into its own category.

Even once the general concept of expert evidence was accepted, lawyers were slow to group the people who gave such evidence into a single category. Capel Lofft did suggest adopting the French term *expert* in 1795, but we have seen that the term appears only finally to have been adopted in the 1850s or 1860s. Before then, expert evidence appears to have been divided up according to the nature of the specialist discipline involved, so that we might speak of the evidence of physicians, engineers or chemists, for example. Occasionally a term such as 'men of skill', or Mansfield's 'men of science', might be used. The date at which the term 'expert' appears in its modern usage is not just of idle etymological interest, because it is in the 1850s and 1860s that we see a burst of interest in the idea of

207 *R.* v. *Stockwell* (1993) 97 Cr App R 260, at 265–6 (CA).

208 P. Roberts and A. Zuckerman, *Criminal Evidence* (Oxford: Oxford University Press, 2004), p. 321.

some form of specialist adviser, who might act as court expert, assessor or referee. Interest in court experts is still around in the 1890s, but there are very few examples of court experts actually being instructed. If we look at the details of the proposed and actual procedural reforms from the 1850s to the 1870s, the idea that the court could appoint a court expert, instead of, or as well as, party experts, was of secondary interest. What reformers appear to have been interested in was an expert who would be directly associated with the tribunal of fact, so that, for example, the assessor would sit with the judge, or the expert referee would sit alone, instead of a judge. The problem of whether non-expert juries were really competent to assess complex facts could be solved by judges sitting alone or, and this idea was fashionable in the 1850s–1860s, the judge sitting with one or more experts, rather than a jury panel.[209]

This desire to replace the jury with experts as fact finders is surprising when we consider the lengths to which the courts went to prevent experts from testifying on the ultimate issue, lest this result in *de facto* delegation of fact finding to the jury (Section 5.7). The difference in approach may be because of different attitudes by the courts and by the legislators, which Allen has suggested can be seen more widely in English evidence reform in the nineteenth century.[210] An alternative explanation is that, while the courts were prepared to accept de iure delegation of fact finding, established by the constitutionally proper means of primary legislation, they would not accept de facto delegation. The evidence for the use of court experts at the end of the nineteenth century and the beginning of the twentieth is thin, and so it is difficult to move beyond informed speculation.

What is clear is that, by the 1930s, policy makers were interested in the court expert as we might use the term today: an expert role like that of the party expert but instructed by the court instead. RSC Ord. 40 was a failed attempt to implement such an expert role. The disinterest associated with Ord. 40 appears to result from the failure of the provision to strike a balance between the court's desire for impartial expert opinion, and the parties' right and desire to present the evidence that best supports their case. Woolf tried and failed to rekindle interest in *Access to Justice*, and the CPR's single joint expert presents a modified form of the Ord. 40

[209] On the decline of the jury at around this time, see Lobban, 'Strange Life', and R. Jackson, 'The Incidence of Jury Trial during the Past Century' (1937) 1 *Modern Law Review* 132–44.

[210] C. Allen, *The Law of Evidence in Victorian England* (Cambridge: Cambridge University Press, 1997), p. 14.

expert, with greater party involvement. If we include then the informal 'court expert advisor' role of the eighteenth century and before, then we can see that the English civil courts have experimented with a number of ways of bringing expert evidence within the control of the court, either to reduce partisanship, or to overcome difficulties in non-experts assessing conflicting party expert evidence. In the following chapter, I examine the relative merits of party expert and single joint experts as they have been implemented by Pt 35 of the CPR, and consider whether the modified assessor role introduced by CPR r. 35.15 represents an attempt to re-introduce the expert-*cum*-tribunal-member role of the second half of the nineteenth century.

6

Assessing expert evidence in the English civil courts today

6.1 Introduction

The previous chapter took us from the end of the fifteenth century through to the end of the twentieth century in considering the judicial assessment of expert evidence in the English civil courts. This journey looked at the range of expert roles that have existed historically in the civil courts (party expert witnesses, special juries, assessors and court experts), both under the several jurisdictions that existed prior to the Judicature Act 1873 (common law, equitable and civilian), and subsequently under the fused jurisdiction of the Supreme Court, whose procedure was governed by the Rules of the Supreme Court ('RSC'). Our journey ended in 1998, on the eve of the introduction of the Civil Procedure Rules 1998 ('CPR'), which came into force in April 1999.[1] This chapter analyses the operational veritistic value of the expert roles provided for under Pt 35 of the CPR (party experts, single joint experts and assessors).

The CPR are intended to be 'a new procedural code with the overriding objective of enabling the court to deal with cases justly' (CPR r. 1.1). Implicit in this statement are five elements of the paradigmatic shift that was intended to distinguish the CPR from the RSC. First, it is 'new', and this implies a break with the RSC rather than a progression. Secondly, 'code' is a legal term of art, that carries with it a sense of self-containment and completeness that is not equally true of 'rules'. Thirdly, this code, like the French Nouveau code de procédure civile ('NCPC') 1975, but unlike the *Code de procédure civile* ('CPC') 1806, is driven by a set of core principles.[2] Here they are expressed as the Overriding Objective (CPR Pt 1), which

[1] SI 1998/3132, made pursuant to s. 1 of the Civil Procedure Act 1997. The CPR applies to proceedings in the Queen's Bench and Chancery Divisions of the High Court and County Courts, but does not apply to proceedings in the Family Division.

[2] L. Cadiet, 'The New French Code of Civil Procedure (1975)', in C. van Rhee, *European Traditions in Civil Procedure* (Antwerp: Intersentia, 2005), pp. 49–68, pp. 56–9.

is summed up in the final word of the clause, 'justly'.[3] To understand the life of the code, one must first understand the principles that drive it. Everything within the CPR must be understood within the context of the Overriding Objective. Fourthly, it is the court, and not the parties, which is the focus of civil litigation. This signals the shift away from purely *laissez-faire*, adversarial litigation towards a more managerial model of civil justice. Fifthly, the code is concerned with 'cases' and not just the instant case. Thus, the court must balance its resources between the needs of all litigants across all actions. The rationale for this paradigm shift, and its effect on the culture of English civil procedure, and in particular on attitudes towards expert evidence, formed part of the subject of Chapter 4 (particularly Sections 4.2.1, 4.3.1.3, 4.3.3).

This chapter analyses for each expert role in turn the procedural provisions for the selection of experts, variations in the ability of the parties to produce full pleadings when such experts are employed, opportunities presented to the parties to challenge expert opinion and possibly narrow issues, and the delegation of fact finding. This analysis provides us with two things. First, it is a detailed case study of how procedural context can affect the judicial assessment of expert evidence. Secondly, it is the first analysis of how the selection of expert roles under the CPR might affect accurate fact determination, and as such it may be of assistance to both practitioners and law reformers. This chapter proceeds on the (deliberately naïve) assumption that we are dealing with impartial expert evidence, produced with the intention of enabling the court to get to the truth. The question of how we manage bias on the part of experts, and the parties who instruct them, is addressed in the next, final chapter. Part 35, which is reproduced in Appendix I, comprises fifteen rules (forty-five if one counts sub-rules). It is supplemented by a Practice Direction, the *Protocol for the Instruction of Experts to Give Evidence in Civil Claims*, a series of guides for specific Divisions and specialist courts,[4] and the provisions on Track management (Section 6.2.1.1).

[3] The CPR presents a 'three-dimensional model of justice', under which the court must balance deciding cases within a reasonable time, using no more than proportionate resources, and doing justice on the merits of the case: A. Zuckerman, *Civil Procedure: Principles of Practice*, 2nd edn (London: Sweet and Maxwell 2006), [1.7]–[1.14].

[4] For directions specific to the Chancery and Queen's Bench Divisions, see also the *Chancery Guide* (revised November 2005) [4.6]–[4.19], and the *Queen's Bench Guide* (revised January 2007) s. 7.9, both reproduced in Lord Justice (Sir Mark) Waller, I. Scott, Sir H. Brooke *et al.* (eds.), *Civil Procedure*, 2 vols. (London: Sweet and Maxwell, 2007) (The *White Book*). For directions specific to specialist courts, the *Admiralty and Commercial Courts Guide* (revised December 2006) s. H.2, the *Technology and Construction Court Guide* (revised October 2005) s. 13, and CPR r. 61.13 on Admiralty assessors.

6.2 Party experts

6.2.1 Selecting party experts

In the nineteenth and twentieth centuries, the party expert witness was the dominant expert role in the Anglo-American courts. As an integral part of a party's adversarial right to identify and introduce evidence favourable to her case,[5] the party was entitled to produce those expert witnesses whom she felt best supported her case. The CPR makes a number of significant changes in relation to the traditional adversarial use of experts, which we have already encountered above in Section 4.2. In particular, the party expert is to act under an overriding duty to the court, and should seek to identify genuine common ground with opposing party experts.

There are three issues regarding the selection of party experts that touch on the ability of the court to assess expert evidence. The first is whether the court should direct the parties to appoint party experts or a single joint expert. The second issue concerns the number of experts instructed by the party. These two issues are discussed in Sub-sections 6.2.1.1 and 6.2.1.2 below. The third issue is the extent to which parties are able to select party experts on the basis of their expectation that a particular expert has provided (or is likely to provide) a favourable opinion. The epistemological background to this phenomenon, known as 'expert shopping', was introduced in Section 3.6.3, and its possible management under the CPR is considered in Section 7.6. It is therefore not examined further here.

6.2.1.1 Deciding between party and single joint experts

Although the CPR leave the selection of expert roles ultimately as an area for judicial discretion in case management, it is possible to identify general guidelines for the basis on which this discretion will usually be exercised. These guidelines can be derived from Lord Woolf's *Access to Justice* Reports,[6] the CPR themselves, related Practice Directions, case law, extra-curial judicial guidelines, and guidelines issued by practitioner

[5] M. Damaška, *Evidence Law Adrift* (New Haven CT: Yale University Press, 1997), p. 74; I. Dennis, *The Law of Evidence*, 2nd edn (London: Sweet and Maxwell, 2002), p. 431. 'A judge has nothing to do with the getting up of a case' and cannot call a witness in civil litigation except with the consent of the parties: *Re Enoch and Zaretsky Bock & Co.'s Arbitration* [1910] 1 KB 327 (CA), at 332 (Fletcher Moulton LJ).

[6] Lord Woolf, *Access to Justice: Interim Report* (London: Her Majesty's Stationery Office, 1995); Lord Woolf, *Access to Justice: Final Report* (London: Her Majesty's Stationery Office, 1996).

bodies. These sources are considered here in turn. The sources suggest that Woolf originally envisaged a proportionality test as the criterion for expert role selection, which weighed the cost of expert evidence against the value of the case, with a presumption that a single joint expert will be appointed. Over time, there appears to have been a shift towards weighing the cost of expert evidence against the complexity of the issues and the degree to which there is a significant range of opinions.

6.2.1.1.1 The *Access to Justice* reports The *Access to Justice* reports are the main *travaux préparatoires* for the CPR. In particular, the use of the *Final Report* as an authoritative source for interpreting the intention behind the CPR was approved by Brooke LJ in *ES* v. *Chesterfield North Derbyshire Royal Hospital NHS Trust*.[7] In addition, as part of the implementation of the CPR, Lord Woolf presided over early appeals on the major points of the new code, in order to promote decisions in accordance with the intended spirit of the code.[8] It is therefore important to consider his views when interpreting the intention of the drafters of the CPR.[9]

In his *Interim Report*, Lord Woolf proposed that the selection of the expert role should depend primarily on 'expedition and economy'.[10] This was developed considerably in the *Final Report*, which presented five indicators for role selection in order to produce a 'just result': first, the size of case, although Woolf did not define what he meant by 'size' in this context; secondly, its complexity; thirdly, the strength of party disagreement; fourthly, the existence of tenable expert disagreement; fifthly, whether the boundaries of knowledge are being extended.[11] We should probably take Lord Woolf to be using 'just' in the same sense as it is used when the Overriding Objective refers to 'dealing with cases justly' (CPR r. 1.1). It is not clear from the *Final Report* whether the expansion in the criteria reflects a fundamental change in emphasis, or whether the additional criteria should only be applied to an anticipated minority of cases where 'expedition and economy' would not be sufficient criteria for dealing with the case justly. However, subsequent judicial writings, both curial and

[7] *ES* v. *Chesterfield North Derbyshire Royal Hospital NHS Trust* [2003] EWCA Civ 1284.

[8] D. Dwyer, 'Changing Approaches to Expert Evidence in England and Italy' (2002) 1 *International Commentary on Evidence* iss. 2, art. 4, www.bepress.com/ice/vol1/iss2/art4 (last accessed 1 August 2008).

[9] It should be borne in mind that the intentions of the drafters of a procedural code are not always followed through into practice by those who use it.

[10] Woolf, *Access to Justice: Interim Report*, [23].

[11] Woolf, *Access to Justice: Final Report*, [13.19].

extra-curial, suggest that these should be taken as a new set of criteria, although Woolf would have preferred to maintain the focus on expediency and economy.

6.2.1.1.2 The CPR and Practice Directions The CPR appears to indicate that the primary basis on which expert role selection should be made is the Track to which a case is allocated. Three Tracks are available under the CPR. The Small Claims Track is available for cases with a value below £5,000 (CPR r. 26.6(5)). The Fast Track is intended for cases of (relatively) low value (£5,000 to £15,000), which are expected to be resolved promptly (within thirty weeks) and straightforwardly (expected to be listed for a single day) (CPR r. 26.6(6)).[12] The Multi-Track is for all other cases, in other words those that are of high value or are not straightforward (CPR r. 26.6(7)).

The CPR make little direct provision for the use of experts in Small Claims cases.[13] However, as CPR r. 27.14(3)(d) limits the amount of costs recoverable by the successful party for the use of an expert to £200 per expert, the use of experts is 'considerably curtailed'.[14] The Practice Direction for CPR Pt 28, regarding the Fast Track, indicates that the court will direct that a single joint expert be instructed 'unless there is good reason not to do so' (CPR Pt 28 PD 3.9(4)),[15] and where party experts are instructed, their use at trial will be limited to 'one expert per party in relation to any expert field; and... expert evidence in two expert fields' (CPR r. 26.6(5)(b)). However, experts will not be directed to appear at trial in Fast Track cases 'unless it is necessary to do so in the interests of justice' (CPR r. 35.5(2)). Equivalent guidelines do not exist for the Multi-Track, which is to be used for all other cases. The selection of expert roles in Multi-Track cases is largely determined by case law (below).

Since the directions and guidance provided by the CPR on expert role selection are largely determined by the procedural Track to which the case has been allocated, and Track allocation is largely a question of cost, we might be tempted to say that the CPR therefore places cost ahead of

[12] The expectation that the case might realistically be heard in a single day should be put in the context that cases under the CPR appear to take significantly less time than similar cases under the RSC: The *White Book*, [26.6.6]. For case management purposes, a 'day' is approximately five hours long: CPR Pt 26 PD 9.1(2)(a).

[13] 'No expert may give evidence, whether written or oral, at a hearing without the permission of the court': CPR r. 27.5.

[14] The *White Book*, [27.5.1].

[15] See also Woolf, *Access to Justice: Final Report*, [13.12].

ascertaining the truth. The veritistic value of a procedural provision would therefore be an irrelevant consideration. However, this would be to focus unduly on the value aspect of Track allocation. Instead, we might say that if the parties expect that a case can be resolved straightforwardly (listed for a single day), then they themselves do not believe that there is scope for genuine expert disagreement. If they did, then they would request a longer hearing.

6.2.1.1.3 Case law Given that there is only limited use of experts in Small Claims cases, and there is a strong presumption in favour of single joint experts in Fast Track cases, the main Track in which case management decisions need to be made regarding role selection is the Multi-Track. In addition to the lack of guidance from the CPR, the higher value of these cases may explain a greater willingness on the part of the parties to instruct party experts, and justify the cost of appealing adverse case management decisions on this point. Three Multi-Track cases appear to have provided conflicting guidance on the selection of expert roles in the early years of the CPR. In *Daniels*,[16] which concerned quantum of damages in a personal injury case, Lord Woolf held that the preferred course of action, even where the amount in question was substantial, was for the parties to instruct a single joint expert first and only then to consider whether there was a need to appoint separate party experts. An alternative approach was taken by the Court of Appeal in *S (a minor)*,[17] and in *Oxley*.[18] *S (a minor)* concerned causation in medical negligence, and it was agreed that the case was extremely complex, and of very high value. In that case, Curtis J held, on appeal, that in the early stages of such litigation it was preferable for each party to have its own experts in order to ensure that a full case is presented in pleadings.[19] The court may later decide that litigation should continue with only a single expert. In *Oxley*, which concerned liability in medical negligence, the Court of Appeal considered that the correct reading of CPR r. 35.7 is that there is no presumption in favour of the appointment of a single joint expert.[20] The object of the rules, Mantell LJ held, is simply to do away with multiple experts where the nature of the issue does not justify it. The instant case was one in which causation

[16] *Daniels* v. *Walker* [2000] 1 WLR 1382 (HC)

[17] *S (a minor)* v. *Birmingham HA* [2001] Lloyd's Rep Med 382 (QB).

[18] *Oxley* v. *Penwarden* [2001] CPLR 1.

[19] In particular, Particulars of Claims (CPR Pt 7) and Responses (CPR r. 9.2).

[20] CPR r. 35.7: '(1) . . . [T]he court may direct that the evidence on that issue is to be given by one expert only'.

would turn on expert evidence, and if there were more than one school of thought, then selection of an expert from one particular school would effectively decide an essential question. It was therefore inevitable that the parties would find the greatest difficulty agreeing on the appointment of a single expert.

The correct basis for distinguishing *Daniels* from *S* and *Oxley* would appear to be that the cases are using experts in fundamentally different ways. *Daniels* concerned expertise on quantum of damages, while *Oxley* concerned expertise on causation. These different expert questions raise fundamentally very different inferential issues (Sections 3.5.2 and 3.5.3). In particular, questions of quantum of damages represent estimates of future costs that are very open to negotiation between experts. They are therefore an area in which it is more likely that the opinions of experts can be placed along a continuum of varying cost. Questions of causation are more likely to give rise to irreconcilable divergence of views between two or more experts than are questions of quantum of damages.

There is a pragmatic advantage to instructing party experts from the outset in causation cases. By the time the parties approach the court for approval to appoint experts, they will probably already have sought the advice of specialists or will be aware of the broad specialist issues, and of whether two or more schools of thought exist in relation to a particular matter. In such cases, it would surely be a waste of the resources of both court and party to appoint a single joint expert when the parties can already advise the court that they will almost certainly not agree to the single joint expert's report. That explanation does not, however, address the principled points made in *Oxley* that causation and professional negligence are complex, and so warrant the use of party experts, and that the parties are entitled to the fullest information to present proper Claims and Responses.

The question of whether to appoint a single joint expert or separate party experts can be broken down into two component questions: first, should experts be appointed by the parties jointly or separately; secondly, should there be one expert or multiple experts. The identification of these component questions in turn takes us to the question of which principle underlies the provision of a choice between single joint experts and separate party experts. There appear to be four likely candidates: first, that by seeking consensus in the appointment of an expert, the likelihood of partisanship will be removed or significantly reduced; secondly, that reducing the number of experts reduces the costs of litigation; thirdly, that single experts are appropriate where there is little scope for genuine expert disagreement (where 'little' might be proportionate to the value of the case), while multiple experts are appropriate where there is significant scope, or the subject matter is otherwise similarly complex; fourthly, that the party's adversarial entitlement to present the evidence that best supports its case increases, the greater the value of the case. Thus, conceptually, the point in *Oxley* might be addressed by appointing several joint experts to address one subject area, if we were to conclude that consensus in appointing experts and the need for multiple experts in factually complex cases are the two driving principles behind expert role selection.

6.2.1.1.4 Extra-curial judicial guidelines Guidelines issued by the judiciary on the interpretation of the CPR have no legal force but provide a good indication of the way in which senior judges might be thinking about, and would like their colleagues to think about, certain issues. The advice of Senior Master Turner in the *Queen's Bench Guide* is that single experts are 'usually' appropriate where the expert is being asked to relate a matter of 'expert fact' rather than opinion, and 'often' appropriate in determining quantum of damages.[21] Party experts 'will' be appropriate 'where liability will turn upon expert evidence'. The particular example that Master Turner provides of such cases is professional negligence. This is for two reasons. The first is 'in order that the court becomes acquainted with a range of views existing upon the question'. The second is that the court can only benefit from cross-examination if party experts are appointed. The complexity of questions of standard of care in professional negligence cases was also recognized by the Court of Appeal in *ES*.

The *White Book*, which has extensive judicial input, suggests that 'the court is likely to direct that the evidence on a particular issue is to be given by a single joint expert where it appears to the court, on the information then available, that the issue falls within a substantially established area of knowledge and where it is not necessary for the court to sample a range of opinion'.[22]

6.2.1.1.5 Practitioner guidelines The *Pre-Action Protocol for the Resolution of Clinical Disputes*, issued by the Clinical Disputes Forum in 1999, states that 'Decisions on whether experts might be instructed

[21] [7.9.5], The *White Book*, 1B–49. See also the *Technology and Construction Court Guide* [13.3], ibid., 2C–110.

[22] The *White Book*, [35.7.1].

jointly . . . should rest with the parties and their advisers. Sharing expert evidence may be appropriate on issues relating to the value of the claim. However, this protocol does not attempt to be prescriptive on issues in relation to expert evidence.' This statement is of particular interest because the Clinical Disputes Pre-Action Protocol is one of the earliest guidance documents produced under the CPR, which took effect from the date of the CPR's introduction. It might therefore be seen as expressing the considered view, of those involved in interpreting the CPR at the beginning, that there would not be a judicial presumption towards single joint experts in Multi-Track cases, and indeed that judges would usually defer to the wishes of the parties.

6.2.1.2 The number of party experts

While the number of witnesses of fact is usually limited, the number of potential expert witnesses is effectively unlimited, provided the party has sufficient funds to instruct them.[23] Inflation in the use of party experts can therefore occur. This was perceived to be happening in the 1990s,[24] and contributed to Lord Woolf seeing expert evidence as one of the 'major generators of unnecessary cost' in civil procedure.[25] The leading supporting authority for Lord Woolf's propositions is the commercial shipping case of *The Ikarian Reefer.*[26] In that case, the court had to decide whether a ship had been deliberately set on fire by its crew on the instruction of its owners and whether the defendant insurance company should therefore pay the amount insured. The pre-trial and trial judges went to great lengths to control the use of expert witnesses. For example, because of the number and complexity of the technical issues, HHJ Hirst had issued pre-trial instructions permitting no more than eight party expert witnesses to be called by each side, subject to exchange of reports six months before trial and supplementary reports one month before trial. Despite regular reviews with counsel and further directions during trial by Cresswell J, the use of expert evidence at the trial was, in that judge's opinion, often unnecessary. For example, one expert witness spent several days

[23] This applies in the vast majority of cases. Although we can imagine scenarios, such as football matches, where the number of witnesses of fact can be measured in thousands, in most cases the number is unlikely to reach triple figures.

[24] Woolf, *Access to Justice: Interim Report*, [23.17].

[25] Woolf, *Access to Justice: Final Report*, [13.1].

[26] *National Justice Compania* v. *Prudential Assurance* [1993] 2 Ll Rep 68 (*The Ikarian Reefer*) (Comm. Ct).

giving testimony on the heating of a valve mechanism. However, that evidence was not then referred to in counsel's closing submissions, suggesting to Cresswell J that it was not in fact relevant to the case being presented.[27]

Such expert inflation is particularly likely to happen where it is believed that the number of experts testifying affects the weight of the testimony. The danger of this approach is that, where the first party relies on several expert witnesses, but the second party relies on only one, it may seem that the second party was only able to locate one supportive expert and, therefore, erroneously, that its position represents the views of a minority of specialists. Because, as has been noted, the number of witnesses of fact is for practical purposes finite, there is some merit in the argument that the relative number of witnesses fielded by the parties reflects the relative likelihood of factual veracity. A similar form of this argument may apply to character witnesses, who are witnesses of opinion rather than of fact. However, there is almost no relationship between the veracity of a case and the number of experts a party can produce, except perhaps where the experts are drawn from a very small field of practice. The number of experts instructed by a party can simply be a function of the financial resources of the party.

This possible advantage to the party with more experts was considered by the Court of Appeal in *ES*.[28] The case concerned whether the claimant's cerebral palsy was the result of the negligence of two senior obstetricians employed by the defendant Trust. The claimant, citing the principle of 'equality of arms', was concerned that the defendant would present not only an expert on the question of negligence, but also the two defendants as witnesses of fact, who would effectively present expert opinion on whether their own conduct was *Bolam* negligent (Section 3.5.6). The defendant would therefore have the benefit of presenting three expert opinions before the court while the claimant would present only one. The Court of Appeal agreed that one expert might therefore appear to the trial

[27] Cresswell J's use of this expert as an example of the unnecessary use of experts may be misleading, as it is possible that, under examination, it became apparent that reliance on the expert's evidence might weaken the party's case.

[28] In practice, the number of cases in which more than one expert in each discipline will be permitted is very small. An example of when one party may be allowed more experts in a particular field than his opponent arises in matters of quantum, where one party's experts can each only deal with condition and prognosis for a limited period of time, whilst the other party's expert can deal with the whole of the relevant period.

judge to be a single voice with a 'bee in his bonnet',[29] and that the parties would therefore not be on an even footing (CPR r. 1.1(2)(a)). Brooke LJ, giving the leading judgment, considered that a 'real purpose'[30] was served by allowing a second expert in this case, 'and that real purpose is the achievement of justice in accordance with the overriding objective on the particular facts of the present case'.[31] In particular, having regard to CPR r. 1.1(2)(c), the case involved a large amount of money (at £1.5m it stood at the top end of non-commercial cases), it was important both to the claimant and her family and to the medical staff whose standard of care was being impugned, and the issues, which concerned professional negligence,[32] were complex.

The approach taken by Brooke LJ to addressing the question of whether a second expert might be permissible merits attention because of his use of both *Access to Justice* and the Overriding Objective, in a situation where CPR Pt 35 itself is silent, and case law at that point in time had little to say. As the *White Book* rightly points out, judges should be slow to fall back on the Overriding Objective as a free-standing set of basic norms. This is because, in the absence of specific procedural context, practicalities and precedent, there is a real danger that reliance on the Overriding Objective will give rise to 'palm tree justice'.[33] Brooke LJ says that it is the proposed 'real purpose' criterion in *Access to Justice* for allowing more than one expert in any one specialty that triggers this reliance on the Overriding Objective. This, of course, begs the question of the extent to which, or indeed whether, *Access to Justice* has normative value. That Lord Woolf proposed a criterion does not necessarily mean that it is carried through implicitly into the correct construction of the CPR.

The default position, Brooke LJ suggests, is that, for reasons of efficiency, there should normally only be one expert. But the appellant's argument was that we should depart from this, because the respondent effectively has three experts while the appellant has only one, and this breaches the principle of equality of arms that arises both under CPR r. 1.1(2)(a)) and potentially under Art. 6(1) of the European Convention on Human Rights. What the appellant appears to have asked is that the court weigh the efficiency argument against two other arguments, namely equality of arms,

[29] *ES*, at [24] (Brooke LJ). [30] Woolf, *Access to Justice: Final Report*, [13.11].

[31] *ES*, at [26] (Brooke LJ). Strictly, the Court of Appeal only varied an order of Master Ungley, so that a master might at a future point permit a second expert to be appointed.

[32] This decision should therefore not be simply extended to cases where experts disagreed on factual questions such as causation. *ES*, at [34] (Holman J).

[33] The *White Book*, [1.3.2].

and the provision of an additional perspective.[34] Brooke LJ simplifies this to the weighing of efficiency against equality. The relationship between efficiency and equality of arms, as with the relationship between efficiency and accuracy, is a paradox at the heart of the CPR, and one which falls outside the scope of the current work.[35] It is effectively side-stepped by Brooke LJ in *ES*, not necessarily consciously, when he argues that, as there is a presumption in favour of efficiency, we must therefore find an additional reason (his 'real purpose') to come down on the side of equality of arms. That reason Brooke LJ finds elsewhere in the Overriding Objective, in CPR r. 1.1(2)(c) which provides criteria for applying a proportionality test, and equality of arms is found to outweigh efficiency in this case. Bundled into this proportionality decision are questions about the value of the case, the rights of the parties to an accurate – as opposed to an expedient – determination, and the complexity of the issues on which expert evidence would be received. Under this proportionality heading, therefore, fall a number of possible principles that might be used properly to determine whether to permit multiple experts. But this whole line of reasoning arises only because, at the heart of CPR Pt 35, there is uncertainty about the reasons for having both single joint experts and party experts available. Brooke LJ was forced to fall back on the Overriding Objective because there were no established criteria in place. It would have been more satisfactory if a set of guiding principles for deciding on expert roles were to be provided.

The appellant is in effect arguing that the court will rely on simply adding up the number of experts. This argument ignores three points. The first is that the number of experts who could be called is in most cases effectively unlimited. Since the parties are able to call only those experts who support their case, the parties are limited as to the number of supporting experts that they could call only by the size of their purse. The second is that it would be obvious at trial that the only reason that the defendant is able to produce three experts is that two of them are the alleged tortfeasors. This fact would go to the question of weight. The third is that it also assumes that the trial judge would not involve herself with understanding and evaluating the basis of the experts' opinions, which is contrary to a theory of rational proof.

[34] *ES*, at 39 (Kennedy LJ).

[35] J. Jacob, *Civil Justice in the Age of Human Rights* (Aldershot: Ashgate, 2007), does consider this paradox.

6.2.2 *Producing full pleadings*

In the case of *S (a minor)*, Curtis J suggested that one advantage of parties having access to their own experts would be to encourage the production of full pleadings. At first glance, it might appear that an argument based on the quality of pleadings is reinforcing the use of experts to support adversarial conduct. However, a well-thought-out Particulars of Claim should encourage the production of a similarly well-thought-out Response, with various combinations of Admission, Defence and Counter-Claim, so that the parties are aware at the outset of the action, if they had not become aware in pre-action communications, of the precise issues in dispute. This should facilitate the narrowing of issues at the earliest opportunity so that only the relevant issues are addressed in pre-trial exchanges and at trial. This is presumably the reasoning behind Curtis J's decision.

Curtis J's suggestion is, however, slightly misleading because his ruling concerns the appointment of a CPR r. 35.2 expert, in other words one who can prepare evidence to adduce at trial. It is not necessary for an expert to be appointed under CPR r. 35.2 for her to advise a party in relation to pleading. This advice could equally be given by a shadow expert, since CPR r. 35.2 concerns only evidence to be presented to the court by the expert, and not advice by the expert to a party. Unpublished empirical work by the Law School at Nottingham Trent University suggests that 'the use of joint or agreed experts is working well but there are concerns that the cost of this approach might not save a great deal, or even be more expensive, as compared to instructing separate experts. Additionally, there is evidence that in commercial litigation parties are employing shadow experts to second-guess agreed or joint experts.'[36] The drawback of using a shadow expert is that her costs cannot be recovered. A shadow expert is therefore likely to be used where the claim is of a high value, or the party has access to 'in-house' expertise.

6.2.3 *Challenging expert opinion*

A fundamental principle of due process in the continental and Anglo-American legal traditions is the right to respond to and challenge one's opponent's case. This is the continental right of *contradiction*,[37] which is

[36] J. Peysner, 'Controlling Costs' (2003) 153 (7090) *New Law Journal* 1147–8.

[37] Damaška, *Evidence Law Adrift*, p. 81.

expressed in the Anglo-American and continental maxim *audi alteram partem* ('hear the other side'): 'For example, the right to a defence can be conceived exclusively as a guarantee for the accused, or also (and really primarily) as an aspect of adversarialism [*contraddittorio*] which one wishes to be observed in the course of the procedure as an expression of that dialectic method considered essential in the search for every truth concerning factual statements'.[38]

The right to an adversarial trial (*une procédure contradictoire*) is a fundamental principle of due process in the continental and Anglo-American legal traditions: the right to respond to and challenge a case adverse to one's own.[39] In relation to evidence law, the right to an adversarial trial, which arises from the Art. 6(1) jurisprudence of the European Court, should be distinguished from the Art. 6(3) right to examine or have examined opposing witnesses, which is restricted to criminal trials.

Mantovanelli is the leading Convention case on the right to an adversarial trial in relation to expert evidence. The case concerned an attempt by civil claimants (Mr and Mrs Mantovanelli) to have the decision of a court expert set aside in the French Administrative Court, and a new expert appointed, because the expert had failed to inform the claimants of the dates of his investigation, and had consulted papers to which the claimants did not have access. Because the expert's report would de facto, though not de iure, determine the outcome of the original action (relating to the death of the claimants' daughter following routine minor surgery), the claimants asserted that they had been denied the right to comment effectively on the expertise, which constituted the main piece of evidence in the case. This in turn denied them the right to adversarial process. The court held that any comment that might be made to the court on the expertise must represent 'a real opportunity to comment effectively'. However, the use of single experts, even if court-appointed, does not of itself breach Art. 6(1).

The extent to which each of the expert roles that we are considering permits the parties to address or challenge the opinions expressed by the expert varies markedly between roles. Where party experts are used, English civil procedure provides opportunities for the party to challenge an opponent's expert's opinion before and at trial. The various situations in which this may occur are examined below.

[38] G. Ubertis, *Argomenti di procedura penale* (Milan: Giuffrè, 2002), p. 5.

[39] Damaška, *Evidence Law Adrift*, p. 81; *Feldbrugge* v. *Netherlands* (1986) Ser. A No. 99 (1986) 8 EHRR 425.

6.2.3.1 Before trial

6.2.3.1.1 Exchange of written reports The presumption of CPR r. 35.5(1) is that expert evidence will be given in a written report rather than orally. This report will be disclosed before trial, at a time specified in the case management directions. Once the use of an expert has been approved by the court (CPR r. 35.4(1)), and a party expert's written report has been disclosed to the other party,[40] the other party may usually (r. 35.6(2)(c)) put one set of written questions to the expert within twenty-eight days, for the purpose solely of clarifying the report (r. 35.6(1),(2)). The expert's answer to those questions will be appended to her report (r. 35.6(3)). If the expert fails to respond to a question, then the court has discretion not to allow the party to rely on that expert's evidence, or not to recover costs (r. 35.6(4)).

This exchange of reports, and subsequent exchange of questions, provides the party experts with an opportunity to question, through their instructing parties, the opinions and conclusions of opposing experts. It may also provide the expert with the opportunity to reflect upon her own position, and possibly amend her report. The limitation on the number of times (usually one) that a party can submit questions to an expert prevents this written exchange from becoming a proper debate between the experts. CPR r. 35.6 specifies that it is the party that puts the question to the opponents' CPR r. 35.2 expert. Implicit in this is the party's ability to rely on shadow experts as well as CPR r. 35.2 experts. Although experts' reports had been increasingly exchanged under RSC Order 38 r. 38, even where the parties were opposed to it, in practice it had rarely resulted in any extensive agreement between the parties.[41]

6.2.3.1.2 Expert discussions RSC Order 38 r. 38 gave the court the power to order experts to meet 'without prejudice' and seek to agree or narrow the issues.[42] However, these meetings, like written reports, were seen by the parties either as an opportunity to show the strength of their case to force their opponents to settle, or else as a necessary court-imposed formality. The British Academy of Experts, an expert witness

[40] Pre-trial exchange of expert reports only began under the RSC in the early 1980s: R. Jacob, 'Court Appointed Experts v Party Experts: Which is Better?' (2004) 23 *Civil Justice Quarterly* 400–7.

[41] P. Bowden, P. Croall and R. Parker, *The Woolf Reforms in Practice: Freshfields Assess the Changing Landscape* (London: Butterworths, 1999), p. 89.

[42] J. Jacob, 'Meetings of Experts Without Prejudice' (1986) 5 *Civil Justice Quarterly* 279.

trade association, made a submission to the *Access to Justice* inquiry in which it made it 'abundantly clear' that meetings of experts were often unproductive because experts were frequently instructed prior to the meetings not to agree anything. Despite the judge's direction, the decision as to what to agree was treated as a matter not for the experts but for the lawyers.[43]

The CPR has made significant changes to the occurrence and workings of party expert meetings. The first is that meetings have become the norm rather than a court-imposed exception. Party experts are to meet at the earliest opportunity to identify those areas in which their opinions disagree and 'where possible' reach agreement (CPR r. 35.12(1)). The court may instruct the experts to discuss specific issues (r. 35.12(2)). The court may request a report from a court-directed meeting identifying issues on which there is agreement and the reasons for any remaining disagreement (r. 35.12(3)). The court may direct that the experts meet without lawyers present, although the lawyers may set an agenda and a recording may be made of the meeting.[44] There is currently no provision for these meetings to be chaired by a neutral party.[45] Both the discussion itself and any report to the court are protected by litigation privilege: 'the content of the discussion between the experts shall not be referred to at trial unless the parties agree' (r. 35.12(4)) (Section 7.6). An agreement between the party experts does not bind the parties in litigation (r. 35.12(5)).[46]

Experts present at discussions potentially have a conflict of interest. Their client's entry into litigation may have been in partial or total reliance on the expert's advice. If that expert were then to conclude, having discussed the matter further with a peer who is instructed for the other side, that her opinion should be modified, it would in theory be open to the instructing party to claim against the expert for negligent misstatement. A situation such as this arose in *Stanton* v. *Callaghan*, which was heard under the RSC.[47] There, the Court of Appeal held the expert witness could not be sued for negligence because he changed his original opinion following a meeting with the opponent's expert. The precise reason for that immunity remained in dispute between the members of the court, but overall the Court was in agreement that it was not in the overarching

[43] Woolf, *Access to Justice: Interim Report*, [23.9].

[44] *H* v. *Lambeth Southwark and Lewisham Health Authority* [2001] EWCA Civ 1455.

[45] Ibid., at [28]. [46] *Robin Ellis Ltd* v. *Malwright Ltd* [1999] CPLR 286.

[47] *Stanton* v. *Callaghan* [2000] QB 75; [1999] 2 WLR 745; [1998] 4 All ER 961 (CA), discussed in I. Scott, 'Immunity from Suit of Expert Witnesses' (1998) 17 *Civil Justice Quarterly* 349–53.

interests of the administration of justice for there to be any disincentive against an expert coming to a valid agreement in discussion with opposing experts.[48]

Analogies were drawn in *Stanton* with the immunity from civil suit of both witnesses and advocates,[49] with the preference appearing to be for comparing the role of experts with that of advocates. Since *Stanton*, however, the immunity of advocates has been clarified by the House of Lords to extend only to work done during the trial, and to pre-trial work intimately connected with the conduct of the case in court.[50] Would *Stanton* now survive a challenge in the courts? I would suggest that the answer is at least a qualified 'yes', in that the CPR's model for expert evidence requires not only that experts have a general overriding duty to the court, but specifically that experts should identify genuine common ground wherever possible. Although we might say, in the abstract, that an expert, like an advocate, should be liable for her negligent advice outside the heat of the courtroom because there is no clear public policy ground to grant immunity, this should be weighed against the clear difficulties that will arise when an expert realizes in the course of litigation that she wishes to change her opinion, for non-negligent reasons, but is alive to the possibility that to inform her client of her change of opinion might result in an action in negligence. There would be strong incentives for the expert to conceal her agreement in her own interests, but contrary to the interests of justice. While we continue to believe that in the vast majority of cases the advice of an expert is non-negligent, I would suggest that we continue to maintain expert immunity from civil suit, at least in relation to expert agreement.[51]

The purpose of this expert discussion is presumably for the experts involved to discuss the facts that they consider central and how they have arrived at their conclusions. This is free from pressure from instructing parties, and protected by privilege from the concern that what they say will be admissible as evidence. The experts may recognize that they have

[48] Circumstances may exist where the negligence of the expert in providing her original opinion is such that it overrides immunity from suit on public policy grounds: *White Book*, [35.12.4].

[49] Following *Rondel* v. *Worsley* [1969] 1 AC 191; [1967] 1 WLR 142; [1967] 3 WLR 1666; [1967] 3 All ER 993 (HL).

[50] *Arthur J.S. Hall* v. *Simons* [2002] 1 AC 615; [2000] 3 WLR 543; [2000] 3 All ER 673 (HL).

[51] Compare the opinion of Lord Hobhouse, *ES* at [188]: 'Since the question of public policy is based not upon some higher moral imperative but upon a pragmatic assessment of what is justifiable in our society, that assessment may change as circumstances change.'

given undue or insufficient weight to certain facts, or that they have been too confident that one interpretation is correct rather than another. The objective of these discussions should be distinguished from pre-trial negotiation between the parties themselves. In negotiation, the parties are encouraged to weigh up their litigation objectives against risks, and seek areas for compromise on their respective objectives, in order to be sure to achieve some of their objectives rather than risk achieving none. The negotiated compromise is not in the area of inferential reasoning, and so is not analogous to expert discussions. It would be inappropriate for experts to agree, solely for the sake of coming to an agreement, if that were to mean that one or both were to compromise on factual inferences that they hold to themselves still to be valid.

Davies, a Judge of Appeal in Queensland, has suggested extra-curially that the disadvantage of such meetings between experts is that they do not take place until too late in the litigation process, when the experts have already taken a polarized position on behalf of their instructing party.[52] They do, however, have the advantage that experts may discover that their differences of opinion result from differences in instruction on the facts.[53] Jacob LJ has, however, argued, similarly extra-curially, that these meetings are useful, particularly in the case of accounting evidence: 'Perhaps because [experts'] reports often condescend to unnecessary detail. Meetings certainly get rid of quibbles – and are apt to achieve some resolution of bigger points.'[54]

The benefit of these written and oral exchanges prior to trial is that not only are the party and her expert aware of the position that the opposing party would take if the case were to reach trial, but there is opportunity for the experts to try to come to agreement on the correct set of inferences to draw. Where the court might otherwise find difficulty in deciding between two opposing experts, a situation where the experts who initially disagreed now come to an agreement increases the likelihood of rectitude of decision in the case. Because the experts agree, it does not mean that their position is certainly correct, as they could now both be wrong, but it does increase the likelihood that they are correct. Where parties are able to agree a statement of fact, the court will not normally then investigate the veracity of that statement.[55] This is similarly true in continental civil

[52] G. Davies, 'Court Appointed Experts' (2004) 23 *Civil Justice Quarterly* 367–85.

[53] G. Davies, 'Recent Australian Developments: A Response to Peter Heerey' (2004) 23 *Civil Justice Quarterly* 396–99 at fn. 3.

[54] Jacob, 'Court Appointed Experts', fn. 25.

[55] Damaška, *Evidence Law Adrift*, p. 104.

systems: *pactum legem vincit et amor judicium* ('agreement prevails over law, and love over the court's judgment').[56]

6.2.3.2 At trial

CPR r. 35.5 seeks to keep experts from trial if possible. This is for at least four reasons. First, the oral examination of experts may add significantly to the length and cost of the trial. Secondly, the listing of the trial is affected by the availability of experts.[57] Thirdly, each party has already had the opportunity to put written questions to opposing experts. Fourthly, the experts have already met and identified those areas in which they might amend their opinions in light of hearing the other experts explain how they arrived at their opinions. Where experts do appear at trial to give oral evidence, this will therefore usually be because there are irreconcilable differences between the experts which the parties do not believe could be resolved simply by reference to the written reports. Expertise at trial is therefore likely to present the most marked differences between party experts since, where the potential for agreement existed, that potential has mostly already been realized.[58] Since these are differences on which the experts do not agree, they are likely to represent irreconcilable differences within the experts' discipline. These present particular challenges for the tribunal of fact (Section 3.3).

6.2.3.2.1 Cross-examination The approach taken at trial to the examination of experts is the same as for the examination of witnesses of fact. Counsel for the party calling the expert will conduct examination-in-chief,[59] and then other parties may cross-examine the expert. The two-fold purpose of cross-examination is 'to elicit information concerning the facts in issue or relevant to the issue that is favourable to the party on whose behalf the cross-examination is conducted', and 'to cast doubt upon the accuracy of the evidence-in-chief given against such party'.[60] In

[56] Ibid., p. 114.

[57] Following *Matthews* v. *Tarmac Bricks*, however, the court will be more active than it had been under the RSC in exploring whether expert availability can be adjusted in order to fit in with available court listing slots.

[58] Although the experts may have reached an agreement which the parties do not adopt: CPR r. 35.12(5). M. Damaška, 'Truth in Adjudication' (1998) 49 *Hastings Law Journal* 289–308, 306, similarly notes that the search for truth in the criminal trial appears complicated and arduous because only contested cases reach trial.

[59] An expert report will 'generally' stand as evidence in chief: The *White Book* [35.5.6].

[60] C. Tapper, *Cross and Tapper on Evidence*, 11th edn (Oxford: Oxford University Press, 2007), p. 336.

relation to experts, the use of written reports means that the first purpose is of minor importance. The opposing party is given the opportunity to demonstrate to the court that the opinion of the expert does not properly accommodate all the relevant facts. The main advantage for the tribunal of fact is that it is able to see the expert challenged in detail on her argument. For Bentham, England had developed, in the practice of oral examination and counter-interrogation, 'the perfect mode' of extracting testimonial evidence.[61] In particular, he believed that cross-examination would provide a more rational safeguard against the introduction of perjured testimony than the exclusionary rules of evidence which Bentham sought to have abolished.[62] Wigmore similarly believed that, despite 'the abuses, the mishandlings, and the puerilities which are so often associated with cross-examination', it is 'beyond any doubt the greatest legal engine ever invented for the discovery of truth'.[63] It is generally true that proponents of cross-examination extol its virtues with hyperbole: 'The right to cross-examine is enveloped in clouds of eulogy, almost apotheosised for its role in truth discovery.'[64] Not all proponents are so quick to eulogize. In relation to eliciting the truth in matters of expertise, Jacob LJ has also supported the effectiveness of cross-examination of party experts, while also noting its cost:

> I do not think one can escape from the fact that testing evidence – expert or fact – is the best way humans have devised for trying to get at the truth. When conducted on a fully funded basis by skilled properly instructed cross-examiners you will get as close as can be done. But the cost (both in time, of individuals and in getting to a hearing, and in money) is immense. So I think it impractical and unconstructive to insist on this procedure for all cases – compromises have to be made.[65]

We might wish to say that cross-examination represents a dialectic method of fact finding. However, we should be careful of the sense in which we intend to use the term 'dialectic'. For classical philosophy, the dialectic method consists of arriving at truth through a series of questions and answers. It was made famous by Socrates in fifth-century-BC Athens,

[61] W. Twining, *Theories of Evidence: Bentham and Wigmore* (London: Weidenfeld and Nicolson, 1985), p. 31.
[62] Ibid., p. 45.
[63] J. Wigmore, *A Treatise on the Anglo-American System of Evidence in Trials at Common Law* (1923), rev. edn Tiller (Boston: Little, Brown, 1983), vol. V 32, s. 1367.
[64] Damaška, *Evidence Law Adrift*, p. 79.
[65] Jacob, 'Court Appointed Experts', 407.

although not necessarily invented by him.[66] In the nineteenth century, the dialectic method becomes associated with Hegel and Marx. In the Hegelian dialectic, one moves from a thesis and contradictory antithesis to a synthesis that combines and resolves these contradictions. The determination of truth for the purposes of resolving a dispute should not though be allowed to rest on compromise in the same way that may be appropriate for normative or political disputes. Cross-examination is therefore dialectic, in the sense that, through a series of connected questions and answers, one can establish the coherence of a factual position. It is not dialectic in the sense that counsel and expert are able to identify how to accommodate the contradictions between their parties' starting positions. Similarly, developments in argumentation theory are not directly applicable to theories of legal fact determination.[67]

Since cross-examination is directed principally at identifying inconsistencies and contradictions between and within testimonies, it is perhaps not surprising that its critics focus on its disorienting and stress-inducing aspects. Jolowicz, for example, has described it as a tool to 'discover and reveal untruth'.[68] There are four major points of criticism.[69] First, compared to other methods of eliciting testimony, cross-examination produces a large number of errors, including greater caution, without any increase in completeness. Questions are not open-ended to enable witnesses to give their own testimony, but rather frequently take the witness along a narrowly defined path in small steps with no opportunity for deviation. Secondly, distortion can be produced by putting leading questions to witnesses about peripheral matters, and confusion can be created by asking unconnected questions. Leading questions in cross-examination provide 'innuendo that can swell in the hands of skilful cross-examiners like notes ballooning out of an oboe'.[70] Thirdly, cross-examination is designed to put the witness in a state of stress, especially when in the course of testing the witness' sincerity. Counsel is, for example, permitted to suggest that the

66 B. Russell, *History of Western Philosophy*, 2nd edn (London: Routledge, 1961), p. 109. Russell suggests that it was invented by Zeno of Elea (495? – 435? BC), a student of Parmenides.

67 E.g. R. Alexy, *A Theory of Legal Argumentation: The Theory of Rational Discourse as Theory of Legal Justification* (Oxford: Oxford University Press, 1989).

68 J. Jolowicz, 'Adversarial and Inquisitorial Models of Civil Procedure' (2003) 52 *International and Comparative Law Quarterly* 281–95, 283.

69 The first three are taken from J. Spencer and J. Flin, *The Evidence of Children – The Law and the Psychology*, 2nd edn (London: Blackstone, 1993), p. 270.

70 Damaška, *Evidence Law Adrift*, p. 97.

witness is lying. The tribunal may be tempted to assess how well an expert provides oral responses on often complex technical points to a non-expert enquirer in a pressured environment. While it may be true that the tribunal of fact should draw inferences of unreliability from witnesses of fact who are slow or uncertain to answer questions, or who appear to change their position, this may not be the case when assessing the testimony of experts. To answer a question of fact, relying solely on memory, may itself be difficult when the wording of a question is unclear, the answer requires thought or there is pressure to answer. This difficulty has been exploited by counsel since the development of cross-examination in the eighteenth century.[71] Since confused testimony is unlikely to be deemed reliable by the tribunal of fact, it may be in the interests of counsel to induce confusion in the witness. The fourth point of criticism is that cross-examination emphasizes differences and disagreements between experts: 'It skews the picture of science that is presented to the legal fact finder and creates an impression of conflict even where little or no disagreement exists in practice.'[72] This point should be qualified though, by saying that, if there was no disagreement in practice, then in current English civil procedure it is very unlikely that the two experts would be called in evidence. Critics might suggest that the idea that counsel seek to attain the truth through cross-examination is either romantic or disingenuous. Counsel's true purpose is to persuade the judge of their client's case:

> But in engaging in trial, by examination-in-chief, if any, and cross-examination, it is not the purpose of the lawyers to assist the judge in understanding and resolving the question. Rather it is to persuade the judge that their client's 'truth' is the correct one. So the process is, in an objective sense, a wasteful one. Moreover, when opposing experts are called there is inevitably duplication, much of it unnecessary. The result is, therefore, a great expenditure of time and cost, most of it for a purpose inconsistent with the just resolution of the question.[73]

Wigmore argued that such criticisms were directed at abuses of cross-examination, and not at cross-examination itself: 'But this abuse of its power is able to be remedied by proper control.'[74] The degree to which

[71] J. Langbein, *The Origins of the Adversary Criminal Trial* (Oxford: Oxford University Press, 2003), p. 270.

[72] S. Jasanoff, 'What Judges Should Know About the Sociology of Science' (1992) 32 *Jurimetrics* 345–59, 353.

[73] Davies, 'Court Appointed Experts', 371.

[74] Wigmore, *Treatise*, rev. edn vol. V 32, s. Tiller 1367.

cross-examination is aggressive is determined by the prevailing culture of the court room, and the presiding judge. The English judge has a residual discretion to regulate the proceedings before her, and may curb excessive cross-examination,[75] especially if the witness becomes ill or distressed.[76] There is markedly conflicting evidence on the extent to which the cross-examination of experts in England and the United States of America was aggressive in the 1990s. On the one side, Jones has suggested that English experts in civil cases were no longer being aggressively cross-examined in the final years of the RSC, and that such an examination would be considered 'infra dig.' by barristers.[77] Her evidence for those propositions was the opinions of barristers rather than experts. Similarly, Howard QC claimed in the early 1990s that it was a myth that the adversarial system in general and the adversarial examination of witnesses in particular distort the evidence of experts.[78]

On the other side is the evidence of the experts themselves, and in particular the fact that much that is written in the way of guidance for potential expert witnesses[79] assumes that cross-examination does attempt to undermine experts in the witness box.[80] An extreme example comes from a text for American experts, written by an environmental engineer. Although this should be read in the context of a more aggressive culture of cross-examination prevalent in the United States (Section 4.3.3.1.3), it nevertheless conveys the expert's perception of the lawyer's attempt to identify inconsistencies:

> How does it feel to be boiled in your own blood? That is one of the many emotions I have felt during the cross examination of the expert witness. The opposing attorney has the opportunity to question the validity of your

[75] See *Vernon* v. *Bosley (No. 2)* [1999] QB 18; [1997] 1 All ER 614 (CA), which was decided under the RSC, and CPR r. 32.3, which provides that 'The court may limit cross-examination.'

[76] *R.* v. *Stretton and McCallion* (1988) 86 Cr App R 7; *R.* v. *Wyatt* [1990] Crim LR 343.

[77] I.e. *infra dignitatem* ('beneath their dignity'): C. Jones, *Expert Witnesses: Science, Medicine, and the Practice of Law* (Oxford: Oxford University Press, 1994), p. 149. In criminal litigation, expert witnesses have been observed to be more respectfully treated than other witnesses: P. Rock, 'Witnesses and Space in a Crown Court' (2001) 31 *British Journal of Criminology* 266–79, 268.

[78] M. Howard, 'The Neutral Expert: A Plausible Threat to Justice' [1991] *Criminal Law Review* 98–105.

[79] E.g. D. Carson, *Professionals and the Courts – A Handbook for Expert Witnesses* (Birmingham: Venture Press, 1990).

[80] J. Spencer, 'The Neutral Expert: An Implausible Bogey' [1991] *Criminal Law Review* 106–10, 107.

> opinions expressed during direct examination. He will also question the veracity of the witness – you. It is the opportunity the opposing attorney has been waiting for. The strategy is to impeach your testimony and destroy your credibility. He wants to make you sound unbelievable to the jury. The attorney has spent much of his professional life training to discredit you in cross examination.[81]

Examination of experts will help to elucidate three things for the court. These are: first, whether the expert is impartial; secondly, whether she has exercised due diligence; and thirdly, by what inferential process the expert has arrived at her conclusions. The purpose of examination-in-chief is to seek to persuade the tribunal of fact that this is the most impartial and conscientious of expert witnesses, whose every stage in her reasoning is considered and robust. The opinion of this expert is to be given the greatest possible weight. The purpose of cross-examination, however decorously conducted, is to suggest that the expert has an interest in the outcome of the case, whether direct or indirect, that she has not given the case the consideration that it warrants, or that her reasoning is open to serious question. This is a witness who, whatever her status in her own field, does not have a valuable contribution to make to the case.

6.2.3.2.2 Hot tubbing An alternative to conventional examination is 'hot tubbing', developed in Australia in 1976 in what is now the Australian Competition Tribunal.[82] After all the non-expert evidence on both sides has been given, the experts for all parties are sworn in and sit in the witness box or at a suitably large table which is treated notionally as the witness box. A day or so previously, each expert will have filed a brief summary of her position in the light of all the evidence so far. The plaintiff's expert will give a brief oral exposition, and then the defendant's expert will ask the plaintiff's expert questions directly without the intervention of counsel. Then the process is reversed. Finally, each expert gives a brief summary. Once the experts have completed their colloquium, counsel is free to cross-examine and re-examine in the conventional way.[83] There are four advantages to this method. First, the experts give evidence at a time when the critical issues have been refined and the area of real dispute narrowed to the bare minimum. Secondly, the judge sees the opposing

[81] J. Matson, *Effective Expert Witnessing*, 3rd edn (Boca Raton FL: CRC Press, 1999), p. 96.

[82] The practice is not unique to Australia. In Swiss arbitration proceedings, for example, both sides' experts are brought in together, to be questioned both at the same time.

[83] P. Heerey, 'Recent Australian Developments' (2004) 23 *Civil Justice Quarterly* 386–95, 390.

experts together and does not have to compare a witness giving evidence now with the half-remembered evidence of another expert given perhaps some weeks previously and based on assumptions which may have been destroyed or substantially qualified in the meantime. Thirdly, the physical removal of the witness from her party's camp into the proximity of a (usually) respected professional colleague tends to reduce the level of partisanship. Fourthly, the procedure can save a lot of hearing time.[84]

Davies has suggested, however, that this practice has not been followed in the state courts of Australia because it is relatively expensive and produces less effective results than exchanging expert reports and holding expert discussions.[85] There is no reason in principle why pre-trial exchange of reports and discussions should not be used alongside trial hot tubbing. There may be a concern that, if the experts have, in good faith, been unable to reach agreement by this point, then they are unlikely to arrive at a consensus at trial. However, after the initial expert colloquium, hot tubbing does then provide the benefit of cross-examination by counsel, which may help elucidate matters, including by encouraging experts to clarify the extent to which they agree or disagree with one another. In addition, the experts hold their discussions in front of the court. Pre-trial meetings and hot tubbing should not represent a straight duplication of effort, since hot tubbing would only occur where the pre-trial meetings have failed to bear fruit.

6.2.4 Delegating fact finding

There has been a concern since at least the early nineteenth century that the use of experts may result in de facto, even if not de iure, delegation of fact finding from the tribunal of fact to the expert. This delegation may occur because the tribunal of law is unclear whether the tribunal of fact, judge or jury, will be competent to decide whether to accept expert opinion or to decide between conflicting expert opinions. It may also arise because the tribunal defers to the social standing of the discipline in question (Section 2.4). The courts have been particularly reluctant to admit expertise that would infringe on the primary competence of the tribunal of fact to judge the actions of individuals against social and legal norms. This resulted in the development of the Ultimate Issue Rule, discussed in Section 5.7. The rule is no longer operational in English civil evidence law.

[84] Ibid., 391. [85] Davies, 'Recent Australian Developments', 398.

This delegation of fact-finding authority is constitutionally dangerous. In English law, this delegation is without prerogative or statutory authority, and therefore offends the public law maxim *delegatus non delegare potest* ('a person to whom authority is delegated cannot further delegate that authority to another'). Under Art. 6 of the European Convention, a court trying a dispute has no power to delegate its judicial role of deciding the case to another person.[86] The risk of this delegation occurring is lowest when the expert role employed is that of the party expert, since the tribunal is required to decide between experts rather than simply deferring to an expert opinion. Within the context of party expert use under the CPR, there are at least two epistemological advantages to the court receiving evidence from party experts. The first advantage is that the court is able to receive more than one expert point of view. This is particularly important where there exists a range of opinions. Although an expert is required in her written report to advise the court if there is a range of opinions on the matter in issue (CPR r. 35 PD 2.2(6)), it might be difficult to see how someone who is attached to one point of view, for whatever reason, could advise dispassionately on other points of view, which she has already rejected. This rejection may be quite vehement.[87] The second advantage is that experts may be challenged to think through their opinions more thoroughly if they are aware that what they say will be open to challenge by their peers. This provides a form of peer review of the expert's opinion.

6.3 Single joint experts

6.3.1 Selecting single joint experts

The single joint expert is a creature of CPR r. 35.7(1), and is a central feature of the Woolf Reforms. It appears to have no direct precedent within or outside the Anglo-American civil procedure family, and arose as a compromise between Lord Woolf's desire to introduce court experts[88] and strong opposition from solicitors and barristers to such an introduction. In *Access to Justice*, Lord Woolf saw the excessive and partisan use of expert witnesses as one of the greatest areas for concern in the civil justice system, since it resulted in unnecessary delays, trial lengths and expense.

86 *Terra Woningen* v. *Netherlands* (1996) 24 EHRR 456.
87 E.g. *XYZ* v. *Schering Health Care* [2002] EWHC 1420 (QB).
88 Woolf, *Access to Justice: Interim Report*, [23.19].

His proposals for changing the way in which experts are used could be grouped broadly under four headings. First, there should be a reduction in the overall use of experts.[89] Secondly, where separate party experts have been instructed, the primary duty of these experts is to inform the court, not to support the case of the instructing party.[90] Thirdly, there should be greater use of court experts in the style of RSC Ord. 40.[91] Fourthly, the use of assessors should be extended out from the Admiralty and Patents courts, to provide technical assistance to judges and possibly to chair meetings of separate party experts.[92] The *Interim Report* indicated an intention to make greater use of court experts.[93]

Woolf encountered three major concerns about the proposal to adopt continental-style court experts. First, the expert and not the judge would decide the case. Secondly, there would be increased cost in addition to the parties' own experts. Thirdly, court experts would be unable to handle situations where there was more than one acceptable view.[94] Lord Woolf saw this as reluctance on the part of practitioners 'to give up their adversarial weapons',[95] and was at pains to reassure his opponents that the adversarial safeguards would remain:

> It needs to be understood that a neutral expert, under the system I am proposing, would still function within a broadly adversarial framework. Wherever possible, the expert would be chosen by agreement between the parties, not imposed by the court. Whether appointed by the parties or by the court, he or she would act on instructions from the parties. The appointment of a neutral expert would not necessarily deprive the parties of the right to cross-examine, or even to call their own experts in addition to the neutral expert if that were justified by the scale of the case. Anyone who gives expert evidence must know that he or she is at risk of being subjected to adversarial procedures, including vigorous cross-examination. This is an essential safeguard to ensure the quality and reliability of evidence.[96]

However, Lord Woolf made it clear in his *Final Report* that 'given the strength of opposition to my proposals, it would not be realistic to expect a significant shift towards single experts in the short term'.[97] The first two proposed reforms (restricted use of experts, overriding duty of experts to the court) were implemented by the CPR in April 1999 (CPR rr. 35.1,

[89] Woolf, *Access to Justice: Final Report*, [13.11]–[13.15]. [90] Ibid., [13.25]–[13.37].
[91] Ibid., [13.16]–[13.24]. [92] Ibid., [13.58]–[13.60].
[93] Woolf, *Access to Justice: Interim Report*, [23.20]–[23.23].
[94] Woolf, *Access to Justice: Final Report*, [13.12]. [95] Ibid., [13.16]. [96] Ibid., [13.17].
[97] Ibid., [13.20].

35.4, 35.5; CPR r. 35.3). The third reform (court experts) was, at least at first blush, implemented in a significantly amended form, as 'single joint experts' (r. 35.7). The fourth reform (assessors) is discussed below in Section 6.4.

At first blush it would seem that the court expert provision of RSC Ord. 40 was removed, and replaced with a new, party-focused 'single joint expert' under CPR r. 35.7. The change in role is, however, relatively minor, and seems to have allowed the courts to make far greater use of single joint experts after April 1999 than was ever the case with court experts. The main difference between a CPR single joint expert and an RSC court expert is that the instructions to appoint the former may be given of the court's own initiative. In both cases, the parties will agree an expert wherever possible (CPR r. 35.7(3); RSC Ord. 40.1(2)). Under the CPR, the parties will instruct the single joint expert, unless the expert approaches the court for instructions. An RSC court expert may be instructed by the court from the outset, but only where the parties are unable to agree instructions (RSC Ord. 40.1(3)). The change effected by CPR r. 35.7 is therefore less in the substance of the expert's role, and more in the extent and manner of the court's use of it.

Under the CPR it is no longer possible for the court to appoint its own expert. However, the court does have the power to direct the issues on which it requires evidence, the nature of the evidence it requires, and the way in which the evidence is to be placed before the court (CPR r. 32.1). Since the court has the power to direct that it wishes to receive expert opinion, it is technically possible that the 'instructing party' may not actually 'wish' to submit expert evidence under CPR r. 35.7(1). The court is also entitled to direct that a single joint expert be appointed and, where the parties cannot agree on whom that expert should be, the court may appoint that expert itself (CPR r. 35.7(3)). The court has therefore in practice appointed its own expert. In addition, the expert's overriding duty is to the court rather than to an instructing party (r. 35.3). The court can direct that the expert produce a report (r. 35.9), and the expert can at any time request directions from the court (r. 35.14(1)). Since December 2001, the expert has been required to give all parties advance notice of such a request (r. 35.14(2)). This is a very important clarification to CPR r. 35.14, because it effectively removes the ability of the expert to gain access to the case management judge unless she is 'robust and determined'.[98] The

[98] The *White Book*, [35.14.1]. It is arguably an important point of principle that the parties must be aware of how their case is being directed by the court.

court therefore has potentially wide powers over the activities of an expert within a case, although it would be acting ultra vires if it were to create a free-standing 'court expert'. One effect of these measures is to provide a challenge to the adversarial principle that parties select which evidence to adduce in order best to support their case.

The advantage of a system where the single joint expert is chosen by the parties is that the court is freed from the difficulty of deciding between experts who are in profound disagreement. Where this disagreement has been largely engineered by the contentious nature of the process of instructing party experts, then this absence of disagreement is of obvious assistance to the tribunal of fact. Even where there are a range of opinions, the expert should advise the court of the nature of that range (CPR Pt 35 PD 2.2(6)) and her reasons for reaching the conclusion that she does.

In *Daniels* v. *Walker*, Lord Woolf appears to say that the court will not know whether the specific question before it is one that allows for such a divergent range of opinion that it would be better addressed by party experts rather than a single joint expert. Although it might appear, at first blush, to be simpler and cheaper to start with a single joint expert and then decide on the basis of that expert's advice whether this is a matter better suited to party experts, the disadvantage of this approach is that it does not provide clear criteria for then deciding whether to proceed from a single joint expert to party experts. There are at least two separate grounds for proceeding in this manner. The first is that a party may disagree that the expert's opinion is the correct one. The second is that the expert may say that there is a range of responsible opinions, and either she or the parties is not happy that she will be able to provide adequate advice to the court on all of them. The first ground is akin to 'expert shopping' (Section 7.6) in that parties will have a natural inclination to seek a second opinion where the first was not favourable. The second ground is a valid one from a veritistic perspective. The court must therefore determine the extent to which this divergence of opinion should be considered. However, the court, having only limited experience of the specialist material, is unsure of the extent to which disagreement is genuine. Empirical research in France on the appointment of experts suggests that judges would not make the same decisions as experts on whether there is genuine scope for expert disagreement in a range of hypothetical cases.[99] This raises the

[99] D. Bourcier and M. De Bonis, *Les paradoxes de l'expertise: savoir ou juger?* (Paris: Institut Synthélab, 1999), pp. 45–58.

possibility that the gates would be prematurely closed to the admission of such expertise. The courts should therefore err in favour of admitting multiple experts.

Rather than this being simply a choice between single joint or party experts, there is also a third option of creating multiple joint experts. The advantage of multiple joint experts over single joint experts in this situation is that they can provide full advice on the different options, including possible weaknesses of each other's options. The advantage over party experts is that they are jointly instructed and will not meet with individual parties without the consent of all parties.[100] However, the CPR have limited provisions for the instruction of multiple single joint experts. Where more than one subject matter is being addressed by a number of single joint experts, CPR Pt 35 PD 5 directs that a lead expert should be appointed to compile a joint report. This is intended to consolidate the expert material to be considered by the court. This approach is problematic, however, because the lead expert may not agree with the opinions of the other experts whose work he is effectively editing, it may not be possible to produce a coherent report from divergent expert opinions, and there is a residual danger that the expert will trespass on an area outside her expertise. Perhaps because of these three difficulties, this provision is little used in practice.[101]

Conversely, the use of multiple experts to address a single issue is not a scenario that Woolf and the drafters of the CPR appear to have envisaged, and no provisions are made for the practice. This approach would lose the cost efficiency benefits of employing a joint expert, but might increase the veritistic value of the expertise. In principle, however, if the court is concerned that there may exist more than one body of opinion with which it should be acquainted, it should be able to instruct more than one expert. Such an ability to instruct more than one expert was recommended, for example, by the Litigation Reform Commission of Queensland, chaired by Davies JA, in its 1993 proposed draft set of rules for the appointment of a court expert, or panel of experts, in that state.[102] That proposal paid relatively little regard, however, to the possible cost implications of the instruction of multiple experts.

[100] *Peet* v. *Mid-Kent Healthcare NHS Trust* [2001] EWCA Civ 1703; [2002] 1 WLR 210; [2002] 3 All ER 688.

[101] The *White Book*, [35.7.2].

[102] Davies 'Court Appointed Experts', 373. Provisions for court experts came into force on 2 July 2004 in the *Queensland Uniform Civil Procedure Rules*, Ch. 11, Pt 5 ('Expert Evidence').

6.3.2 Producing full pleadings

In *Peet* v. *Mid-Kent Healthcare NHS Trust*, the claimants sought to meet with the single joint expert in order to test the strength of their claim. It was held, however, that, where a single joint expert has been appointed, this is likely to prevent the parties from meeting with the expert separately to explore the merits of the case, without the written consent of all parties. The effect of this may be that, where a single joint expert is in place and the party cannot afford a shadow expert, the parties are never fully confident that they are aware of the merits that they are seeking to present. Although the issue did not arise in *Peet*, a situation could arise where one or both of the parties produces pleadings that are not as well formed as might have been the case if there had been access to a party expert.

6.3.3 Challenging expert opinion

As with the production of pleadings, the use of single joint experts reduces the ability of the parties to challenge effectively the opinion of an expert, either before or at trial. Parties may put questions to a single joint expert under CPR r. 35.6 as they would to an opposing r. 35.2 party expert, and they may be assisted by a shadow expert in compiling those questions. In *Peet*, it was established that this would be the default means by which a party could test the single joint expert's opinion. However, a CPR r. 35.12 expert discussion can only take place between r. 35.2 experts. A discussion cannot take place between a r. 35.7 single joint expert and a party's 35.2 expert or shadow expert. The veritistic limitation of this is that, while a party expert is invited to consider her opinion in the light of detailed discussion, and alternative arguments by another expert, and her opinion may be refined by this process, the single joint expert must produce her opinion in procedural isolation. This may adversely affect the quality of the final opinion submitted to the court.

The courts' current thinking on the possibility of cross-examining a single joint expert would appear to be, following Lord Woolf CJ in *Peet*, that, where a single joint expert has been instructed, then there should be no need 'in the normal way' for cross-examination, since no need has been identified before trial for evidence to be produced other than the report of the single joint expert.[103] The presumption against cross-examination

[103] *Peet*, at [28].

also appears in the Academy of Experts' *Code of Guidance*.[104] A difficulty arises, however, when, as in the case of *Popek*, one of the parties does not accept the opinion of the single joint expert, but the court refuses to grant permission for the appointment of a party expert because the application is made too close to trial.[105] In such a situation, the dissenting party is still prevented from cross-examining the expert with whose opinion she disagrees. Lord Woolf's ruling in *Peet* would appear to contradict his expectation in his *Final Report* that: 'The appointment of a neutral expert would not necessarily deprive the parties of the right to cross-examine' (see p. 308 above).[106]

The position at common law, following *Coulson* in 1894,[107] is that a court witness in civil proceedings is not open to cross-examination without the permission of the judge, and that permission is likely to be restricted to cross-examination on testimony adverse to the requesting party. What the rules in *Coulson* and *Peet* appear to have in common is that, since neither party called the witness for examination-in-chief, the opposing parties do not have the right to cross-examine. For single joint experts, all questioning should have been conducted before trial, or else party experts should have been appointed, while, for court experts, examination will be conducted by the judge. To cross-examine after judicial examination might be to suggest that the judge's examination had been incomplete or partisan. Where the rule in *Coulson* departs from that in *Peet* and *Popek* is that, where an adverse statement is made by a court witness, the affected parties would almost certainly be entitled to cross-examine. Cross-examination in *Coulson* would appear to have been blocked because, on the facts, 'the only reason for cross-examining him must have been a wish to prejudice the jury'.[108]

6.3.4 *Delegating fact finding*

It is settled law that the court is not bound generally to accept the evidence of an expert.[109] However, there appears to be a degree of judicial uncertainty concerning whether the court should accept the opinion of a single

[104] Academy of Experts, *Code of Guidance for Experts and Those Instructing Them*, 2nd edn (London: Academy of Experts, 2001), [19.9].
[105] *Popek* v. *National Westminster Bank plc* [2002] EWCA Civ 42.
[106] Woolf, *Access to Justice: Final Report*, [13.17].
[107] *Coulson* v. *Disborough* [1894] 2 QB 316.
[108] *Coulson*, at 318 (Lord Escher MR).
[109] H. Malek (ed.), *Phipson on Evidence*, 16th edn (London: Sweet and Maxwell, 2005), [33.50].

joint expert admitted under the CPR. The main danger of delegation that arises when a single joint expert is used is that the tribunal has no other option on which to rely, and no alternative expert view against which to compare the evidence. The effect may be that in some cases 'there is a risk that the joint expert may in effect become the judge of the issues on which he reports',[110] since the court will have no real basis on which to accept or reject the expert's conclusion.

In *Coopers Payen Ltd*,[111] the Court of Appeal held that the evidence of a single joint expert should only be disregarded in very rare circumstances. In *Armstrong*,[112] however, the Court of Appeal distanced itself from that view. In that case the claimants' car had been struck by a bus, and the claimants said that the impact had forced them from their seats. The single joint expert, a forensic motor vehicle engineer, said that there had been only a minor impact that could not have ejected the claimants as they said. The Court of Appeal upheld the decision of the judge to prefer the evidence of fact of the claimants to the expert since matters are to be determined not by trial by expert but by trial by judge. Where there is conflicting evidence the judge is entitled to determine which she finds more credible. The judge was not required to explain how the expert evidence was wrong. This raises an important point, discussed in Section 2.3.3, that the expert's evidence forms only one part of the evidential matrix of a case. There is no intrinsic reason why expert evidence should be given greater weight than any other evidence, or be viewed in isolation from the other available evidence.

Similarly, there is a real danger that, once a single joint expert has been appointed, neither the court nor the parties will be in an informed position to determine whether the advice of the expert is within the mainstream or should be accepted. Where the parties wish to obtain guidance on the validity of the opinion of a single joint expert, they are free to seek the advice of a shadow expert, outside the gaze of the court. The court does not have a similar freedom, and it would be constrained to appoint and instruct an expert, probably an assessor, within the framework of CPR Pt 35. This need not be a straight duplication of effort and hence costs, since the scrutinizing expert would only be required to check the opinion of the single joint expert, and not to duplicate her work. However, the appointment of a scrutinizing expert in addition to a single joint expert

110 Zuckerman, *Civil Procedure*, [20.54].

111 *Coopers Payen Ltd* v. *Southampton Container Terminal Ltd* [2003] EWCA Civ 1223.

112 *Armstrong* v. *First York Ltd* [2005] EWCA Civ 277; [2005] 1 WLR 2751 (Brooke LJ).

might raise questions about why the court directed that a single joint expert be appointed at all, and it would certainly raise a question about whether the opinion of the single joint expert carried as much weight as if a scrutinizing expert had not been appointed.[113]

6.4 Assessors

6.4.1 Selecting assessors

Assessors have been used in the civilian Court of Admiralty since at least the second half of the eighteenth century (Section 5.5). One or more nautical assessors, drawn from the Elder Brethren of Trinity House,[114] have sat with the Admiralty judge[115] in certain cases regarding navigation issues, especially collisions. The role of the assessor was made available to all types of civil case when the Admiralty Court was brought within the framework of the new High Court by the Judicature Act 1873.[116] This was subsequently extended to county court actions.[117] Assessors are also used in the Patent courts,[118] and Parliament may direct that assessors sit on specialist tribunals.[119]

6.4.1.1 What is the role of an assessor?

In his *Access to Justice Interim Report*, Lord Woolf suggested that the use of assessors be extended, for example to attending non-Admiralty trials, and to presiding over pre-trial meetings of separate experts.[120] In the *Final Report*, following 'some resistance', largely on the grounds that an assessor would usurp the role of the judge, Woolf clarified that an assessor would act in complex technical cases to 'educate' the judge. Under the CPR, the

[113] In Italy, where civil litigation may involve both a court expert and party experts in the same case, court experts are viewed as being of higher status, and their opinions carry greater weight (Section 4.3.4).

[114] In 1992 Trinity House was restructured, and the Elder Brethren became full-time paid directors of the Lighthouse Service. They were therefore no longer available to serve as assessors, and so Trinity House now instead provides Younger Brethren and Members of the Board of Assistants to fill this role: Captain Malcolm Edge (Deputy Master of Trinity House), letter to Clarke J (Admiralty and Commercial Registry) (9 November 1993).

[115] Also in the Court of Appeal and House of Lords in Admiralty matters from the nineteenth century.

[116] Judicature Act 1873, s. 56. [117] County Courts Act 1888, s. 103.

[118] As 'scientific advisers', under s. 70(3) of the Supreme Court Act 1981, and CPR r. 35.15: The *White Book*, 2F [40].

[119] E.g. Workmen's Compensation Act 1925, Sch. 1, para. 5.

[120] Woolf, *Access to Justice: Interim Report*, [23.24].

proposed extension of the use of assessors was implemented, in that new mechanisms were put in place (CPR rr. 35.15, 61.13), but the full extent of these mechanisms has not been utilized by the judiciary, and the scope of assessors has not extended beyond Admiralty and Patents actions,[121] and costs appeals.[122]

We have seen that the change effected by CPR r. 35.7 in introducing the single joint expert was a change less in the substance of the expert's role and more in the extent and manner of the court's use of it. A cursory examination of r. 35.15 might be similarly misleading. Although Lord Woolf appeared to retreat in his *Final Report* from his initial enthusiasm for broadening the role of assessors in his *Interim Report*, his retreat was more on the extent to which assessors would be used initially, rather than on the substance of the role. CPR r. 35.15 in fact implements two significant changes to the role of the assessor. The effect of these changes is arguably to transform the assessor's role into something akin to that of a court expert. The first change is that an assessor shall now 'take such part in the proceedings as the court may direct' (r. 35.15(3)). This goes beyond the underlying statutory provisions for assessors. The Supreme Court Act 1981, s. 70(1), limits the role of the assessor to 'assistance' to the court to 'hear and dispose' of a case. The County Courts Act 1984, s. 63, says that an assessor may 'sit with the judge'.[123] There is also no longer a requirement that an assessor may only be appointed in a case being heard in the county court where appointment has been requested by one of the parties. The second significant change is that an assessor

[121] Medical assessors are not, for example, used in medical cases in the civil courts, although medical assessors do sit with the Fitness to Practise Panel of the General Medical Council in the United Kingdom: *Watson* v. *General Medical Council* [2005] EWHC 1896 (Admin.).

[122] The use of assessors in costs appeals is not considered in this book. Costs assessors may be costs judges or practising solicitors or barristers; their expertise consists in greater experience of current litigation costs than may be possessed by the judge or judges hearing the appeal. The use of costs assessors began under RSC Ord. 62, which made specific provision for the appointment of assessors to sit in costs appeals. When the CPR were introduced the old rule was repeated, as CPR r. 47.26, but when the Civil Procedure Rule Committee came to look at the provision in more detail it was decided that it was not needed, since CPR r. 35.15 provided the appropriate procedure. CPR r. 47.26 was therefore repealed by the Civil Procedure (Amendment No. 2) Rules 2000. As a matter of practice, in appeals emanating from the Supreme Court Costs Office, every appeal is passed to the Senior Costs Judge to decide whether he is of the view that assessors are required. If assessors are required then two are appointed, one a practising barrister or solicitor, and the other a Costs Judge. There is no rule making this a requirement, but the previous practice under the RSC has been retained.

[123] The *White Book*, [35.15.1].

may now be asked to prepare a report, which may be used as evidence by the parties (CPR r. 35.15(3), (4)).[124] The significance of this development is discussed below (Section 6.4.3, on challenging evidence).

Under the CPR, the assessor now therefore has a potentially very wide range of functions, that do not all sit comfortably alongside one another. An assessor is potentially able to be instructed to take such part in the proceedings as the court may direct, including the preparation of an expert report before trial, possibly chairing meetings between experts, sitting with the judge during trial, and retiring with the judge to decide the case. The advice that the assessor may provide can extend from the factual clarification of the evidence of other experts through to comments bearing directly on the ultimate issue. The former type of advice would appear to be what non-Admiralty judges have had in mind when discussing the role of the assessor,[125] but advice of the latter form is common in Admiralty. For example, in *The Queen Mary*, the Court of Appeal received assessor advice on the normative question of whether the *Queen Mary* should have given way to a cruiser acting as an anti-aircraft defence ship.[126] Similarly, in *The Global Mariner*, the assessors provided advice on what 'a prudent mariner' 'would' have aimed for, and what the correct anchoring selection 'unquestionably' was.[127] In Admiralty, the modern practice is for such questions to be formally put and replied to, usually in writing. This is a very different role from that of the judicial assistant envisaged in *Access to Justice*. The scope of the role of the nautical assessor is such that the Court of Appeal has raised concerns that the practice as it existed until 2004 may not be compatible with Art. 6(1) of the European Convention.[128] The issue of compatibility is discussed in Section 6.4.3.

[124] The word 'evidence' does not appear in CPR r. 35.15(4)(b). It is difficult however, to see in what sense a party might be said to 'use' a report at trial except as evidence. For a similar conclusion, see L. Blom-Cooper, 'Experts and Assessors: Past, Present and Future' (2002) 21 *Civil Justice Quarterly* 341–456, 352. There is no indication in CPR Pt 35, or in its Practice Direction, of what might be in such a report. In particular, it is unclear whether the assessor would be asked to produce a background general report such as 'known causes of engine failure', or a case-specific report such as 'likely causes of engine failure in the instant case'.

[125] E.g. *Esso Petroleum* v. *Southport Corporation* [1956] AC 218; [1956] 2 WLR 81; [1955] 3 All ER 864; *Richardson* v. *Redpath Brown & Co. Ltd* [1944] AC 62 (HL).

[126] *The Queen Mary* (1947) 80 Ll Rep 609, at 631.

[127] *The Global Mariner* v. *Atlantic Crusader* [2005] EWHC 380 (Admlty); [2005] 2 All ER (Comm.) 389, at [66] and [68].

[128] *Owners of the Ship 'Bow Spring'* v. *Owners of the Ship 'Manzanillo II'* [2004] EWCA Civ 1007; [2005] 1 WLR 144; [2004] 4 All ER 899; [2005] 1 All ER (Comm.) 53, at [61].

In light of these changes, four distinct roles can be identified for assessors within the current scope of CPR r. 35.15: tribunal member, court expert, court officer and scientific adviser. 'Assessor as tribunal member' is the role already undertaken by assessors in Admiralty. The tribunal-member-assessor sits with the judge during and after trial, and provides non-binding opinions on questions of fact, causation and responsibility, based on the facts presented by the parties. The 'assessor as court expert' would, like a CPR r. 35.2 expert, conduct investigations, including possibly interviews and examinations, in order to arrive at an opinion on the facts, which can be presented to the court as evidence. It is probable that such an assessor would be open to cross-examination in the same limited circumstances as a court witness, and potentially by both parties.[129] The 'assessor as court officer' might be expected to act for the court in specialist matters, such as chairing pre-trial meetings of experts.[130] Such an assessor might also produce reports on background information for the court. The 'assessor as scientific adviser' would seek to clarify technical points of evidence for the judge, and might suggest to her possible areas for further questioning in relation to a CPR r. 35.2 expert's opinion. This appears to be the type of assessor Mackay J had in mind in *XYZ* v. *Schering Health Care* when considering expert evidence involving algebra.[131]

The separation out of the four assessor roles (tribunal member, court expert, court officer and scientific adviser) should be implemented by appropriate amendments to CPR Pt 35 and its Practice Direction. Of the four roles, the court expert should be classified as a single expert, under CPR r. 35.8, rather than as a CPR r. 35.15 assessor. There would be two advantages to the creation of these four distinct roles. The first would be that judges might be more inclined to consider appointing an assessor where the boundaries of that assessor's role were more clearly drawn. Parties would similarly be able to give more reasoned consideration to how to respond to such an appointment. At present, assessors are considered to be the reserve of Admiralty and Patents proceedings, and to be particularly suited to the work of those courts, but not transportable elsewhere. The second advantage would be that it would become more straightforward to consider how the use of assessors might be made compatible with Art. 6(1) of the European Convention. The issues raised by Art. 6(1) in relation to the use of assessors are considered in Section 6.4.3. At the same time,

[129] *Coulson.*

[130] The CPR does not make provision for such meetings to be chaired by a third party.

[131] *XYZ* v. *Schering Health Care*, at [148]–[149].

the open-ended provision of CPR r. 35.15.3, that an assessor may do such things as the court directs, should be removed.

6.4.1.2 Approaches to appointment

There are two main difficulties with appointing specialists as assessors, relating to the court's identification of possible assessors, and the possible unwillingness of specialists to serve as assessors. First, the court has very limited experience of appointing experts, or mechanisms for doing this. In France, the Cour de cassation and the Cours d'appel produce lists of approved experts revised on an annual basis.[132] An expert gains entry to the list by application.[133] A judge is not required to appoint as an expert only someone who appears on that list. Although most tribunals have a *bureau du contrôle des expertises*, this is concerned with administration rather than quality assurance of the experts used,[134] and there is little research into the quality of court experts' work.[135] The experts are therefore themselves the main source of a judge's idea of whether a particular opinion is a mainstream one within the discipline.

If the English courts were to begin to appoint court experts, then a formal mechanism would need to be developed for their selection. Based on the continental model, one option would be for the creation of official court lists. This might be a modification of Auld LJ's proposal, in his review of the criminal justice system, for a single regulatory professional body for experts.[136] This body would replace the work of the current expert bodies, the Academy of Experts, Council for the Registration of Forensic Practitioners, Expert Witness Institute, Forensic Science Society and Society of Expert Witnesses. The limitation of the court official list method is that it is only as good as the quality controls on it. Practical questions are raised of how an expert gets onto a list, and how she might be removed from that list, but these are not insoluble.

Since there is a direct relationship between the court and the expert, there is a strong possibility that a long-term relationship of trust might develop between expert and judge. This has been noted in France where

[132] Bourcier and de Bonis, *Les paradoxes*, p. 17.

[133] M. Bardet-Giraudon, 'The Place of the Expert in the French Legal System', in J. Spencer, G. Nicholson, R. Flin and R. Bull (eds.), *Children's Evidence in Legal Proceedings. An International Perspective* (Cambridge: Cambridge Law Faculty, 1990), pp. 68–70, p. 68.

[134] Bourcier and de Bonis, *Les paradoxes*, p. 33. [135] Ibid., p. 34.

[136] R. Auld, *Review of the Criminal Courts of England and Wales* (London: Her Majesty's Stationery Office, 2001), [11.131].

individual judges often appoint the same expert time and again.[137] We might then expect a judge to appoint the same expert in cases on the same subject matter, and in turn to defer increasingly to the expert's opinion, as experience has shown it to be one to which the judge has previously deferred with acceptable results. The potential danger to the administration of justice here is that judicial scrutiny of expert opinion diminishes over time. This is problematic where that expert has an intellectual pre-disposition to interpreting facts in accordance with a particular theory (Section 3.6.1.3). Pre-disposition by a single expert or assessor may have a greater adverse effect on accurate fact determination than conscious adaptation by separate party experts.

An alternative would be to look at the long-established practice of the Admiralty Court in its appointment of assessors. Trinity House itself determines which assessors to send to any given case. Of thirty-two applications for assessors made by the Registry to Trinity House between 1998 and 2003, only two required specific expertise.[138] All bar three of the applications were for cases involving a collision.[139] There is, however, no requirement that the assessors have specific experience of collisions.[140]

The practice of the Admiralty Court suggests that it would probably be acceptable for the court to appoint an assessor on the basis not of her personal expertise, but of her membership of a body whose members are in general expected to have relevant expertise (Section 2.4). This represents a marked difference from the common law rules on the admission and evaluation of expert evidence, which are based on the court's own evaluation of the proposed expert's expertise.[141] The advantages of relying on membership of a specialist body are threefold: first, the identification of an appropriately qualified assessor becomes relatively straightforward; secondly, the court avoids the creation and maintenance of court lists;

[137] Bourcier and de Bonis, *Les paradoxes*, pp. 17 and 45.

[138] *Owners of the Vessel 'Rafael'* v. *Owners of The Demise, Charterers of the Vessel 'Germania IV'* (trial listed for 5 July 2004: 'expertise with yachts'), *Vitesse Yacht Charters SI* v. *Spiers* [2003] EWHC 2426 (Admlty) (trial listed for 1 October 2003: 'experience in the field of navigation and seamanship').

[139] The exceptions were: *Vitesse Yacht Charters* ('breach of contract'); *Santos* v. *The Owners of the Ship 'Baltic Carrier'* (listed for 21 October 2002: 'personal injury'); *Owners of the MT 'Sun Trader'* v. *Tidewater Marine International Inc.* (listed for 2 December 2002: 'breach of agreement').

[140] *Owners of the SS Australia* v. *Owners of Cargo of SS Nautilus* [1927] AC 145 (HL) ('The Australia').

[141] Tapper, *Cross and Tapper*, p. 572; *R.* v. *Bonython* (1984) 38 SASR 45.

thirdly, the court can approach the body rather than a number of individuals to identify an available assessor. The difficulty with any method of appointing a court expert or assessor is that the court is likely to seek to identify an expert from mainstream thought within a particular speciality. This approach is problematic where there is more than one valid school of thought within a speciality.

It would be necessary to identify specialists prepared to sit on such a mixed tribunal. If a specialist could be freed from their main work to do litigation work, then it is probable that a good specialist would be able to earn more working as a party expert than as an assessor. The courts would then be relying on either a sense of public duty, or else the specialist being able to gain professional advantage from sitting as an assessor. The successful use of assessors in the Admiralty Court may depend on trials there lasting for relatively short periods of time, and so the amount of time required of the specialist is very short. In Admiralty cases listed between 1998 and 2003, none was listed for more than ten days.[142] By way of comparison, two Queen's Bench cases heard in 2002 that made extensive use of expert evidence, *XYZ* v. *Schering Health Care*,[143] on product liability for the third-generation combined pill, and *Multiple Claimants* v. *Ministry of Defence*,[144] on liability for failure to prevent psychiatric injury following combat, lasted for ten weeks (with forty-two days of actual hearings) and thirty-six weeks, respectively. The judges involved then required a further seven weeks and twenty-seven weeks, respectively, to produce their judgments. We might hope that, with a mixed tribunal, hearings and deliberations would proceed more quickly, but we would nevertheless be expecting a considerable amount of a specialist's time.[145]

6.4.2 Producing full pleadings

Admiralty practice has traditionally discouraged the use of party experts where there is an assessor, and their utility has been judicially questioned:

[142] *Pelopidas* v. *Concord* was listed for ten days, to commence 12 July 1999, but the trial in fact lasted for six days: [1999] 2 All ER (Comm.) 737 (Admlty).

[143] *XYZ* v. *Schering Healthcare*, at [22].

[144] *Multiple Claimants* v. *Ministry of Defence* [2003] EWHC 1134 (QB).

[145] In criminal litigation, the trials that present the most difficulties to jurors because of their complexity and technical material are complex financial ones. These are trials that typically last for months or years, and it is unlikely that finance specialists would be willing or able to take time off from their work to serve on such tribunals.

> I have had the evidence of one expert, called by the defendants, Mr. Robinson. I accept his evidence as to the general practice among trawlers in the sort of conditions I have described. I am not, however, prepared to accept his final conclusion as to the balancing of the risks involved, even if I could be sure that I understood it. I intend no disrespect to him when I say that I doubt the value of expert evidence when the Court has the advantage of a Nautical Assessor.[146]

CPR r. 61.13 similarly provides that traditional Admiralty practice will continue in that, where a nautical assessor has been appointed, party experts will not normally be permitted by the court.

Party experts may, however, be appointed to prepare the arguments under current Admiralty practice.[147] Howard, an opponent of court experts, has suggested that the significance of this use of court experts should be read in the specific context of the Admiralty Court, where judges and counsel are themselves usually specialists, and have some understanding of navigation matters. The court does not therefore have the same need of a second expert opinion to ensure the reliability of the first opinion. Howard makes this suggestion in the context of a broader argument against the introduction of court experts into English criminal law. The long-standing use of assessors in Admiralty cases is a potential weakness to Howard's argument,[148] and so he appears to seek to play down their significance by arguing that, in this particular type of case, the parties are not disadvantaged and the ultimate issue is not handed to a court expert, because Admiralty counsel and judges are particularly knowledgeable on their subject matter. Howard's argument has two main weaknesses. The first is that Admiralty is not the only area of law with specialist judges and counsel, and so his argument could be extended, for example, to taxation, Family and medical negligence cases. The second is that Admiralty litigants do not engage with the assessor, and so they have limited opportunity to exhibit their specialist knowledge. If the litigants require access to a shadow expert to give advice outside court then this is not prohibited in Admiralty cases. The use of assessors and virtual absence of party experts in Admiralty cases is unlikely therefore to be affected, as Howard has suggested, by the presence of specialist counsel.

[146] *Saul* v. *Saint Andrew's Steam Fishing Company Ltd* [1965] 1 Ll Rep 107 (Admlty) (*The St Chad*), at 109 (Sir Jocelyn Simon P).

[147] Howard, 'The Neutral Expert', 104 at n. 19.

[148] The more recent use of assessors in Patents cases also weakens Howard's case, although to a lesser extent, as this is not a practice that has the authority of long-standing use.

6.4.3 Challenging expert opinion

Traditional English civil court practice regarding the use of assessors gives rise to three potential difficulties with the ability of the parties to challenge the expert opinion of an assessor. The first, which is relatively straightforward, is that, where the court appoints an assessor but does not permit the parties to appoint their own experts, the parties may lack sufficient expertise to challenge a statement by the assessor. The issues surrounding this point are substantially the same as those surrounding the ability of the parties to produce full pleadings, discussed in the previous sub-section. The second potential difficulty is that the parties may have little or no opportunity to challenge the opinion effectively, and the third is that, once the assessor has expressed an adverse opinion and the party has responded, the assessor may then retire with the court to further present her point of view.

It is clear from the jurisprudence of the European Court of Human Rights, discussed below, that the second and third potential difficulties, if they were to materialize, would be likely to constitute a violation of Art. 6(1) of the Convention.[149] When the CPR were being drafted, the potential Art. 6(1) difficulties raised by CPR r. 35.15 should have been apparent from the European Court of Human Right's recent judgments in *Mantovanelli* v. *France*,[150] *Borgers* v. *Belgium*[151] and *Orshoven* v. *Belgium*.[152] However, it is only with *Krčmář* v. *Czech Republic*[153] and *Kress* v. *France*[154] that the full difficulties of assessor practice become apparent. These cases concern a range of practices, in criminal, civil and administrative courts, where an officer of either the executive or the court makes a legal submission to the court at its final hearing, once the parties have finished their final submissions. Following the final hearing, judicial officers may then retire with the court to consider its verdict.

149 Sir Louis Blom-Cooper QC, chairman of the Expert Witness Institute, has suggested that the *Code of Guidance on Expert Evidence*, issued by the Working Party set up by the Head of Civil Justice, which Blom-Cooper chaired, omitted any guidance on CPR r. 35.15 'presumably because the Working Party entertained doubts about the constitutionality of the assessor system': Blom-Cooper, 'Experts and Assessors', 353.

150 *Mantovanelli* v. *France* (1997) 24 EHRR 370.

151 *Borgers* v. *Belgium* (1993) 15 EHRR 92.

152 *Orshoven* v. *Belgium* (1998) 26 EHRR 55; [1997] ECtHR 3.

153 *Krčmář* v. *Czech Republic* (2001) 31 EHRR 41, at [40].

154 *Kress v France* [2001] ECtHR 382.

6.4.3.1 Challenging the assessor's opinion

Up until 1867, nautical assessors would appear to have consulted with the judge in open court. However, in that year, in *The Hannibal*, the practice was introduced that, 'for the future in causes of collision and salvage, heard before the Trinity Masters, [the judge] should not sum up the evidence; but . . . the Court and Trinity Masters would retire and, on their return, the judgment of the Court would be given'.[155] It would appear that, until the introduction of the CPR in 1999, a nautical assessor did not express her opinion during the trial. This made it impossible for parties to challenge the views of an assessor, because they would often not know what they were.

A less extreme situation was considered by the European Court of Human Rights in the case of *Orshoven*, which concerned a practice, common in continental European criminal jurisdictions, where a state lawyer addresses the court with her reasoned opinion on the merits of the case, after the parties have concluded their submissions, and before the court begins its deliberations. The European Court of Human Rights has held that this practice violates a party's Convention rights where that party does not have adequate notice of the opinion or opportunity to respond adequately to the points raised in this opinion.

Although these cases have all concerned a private individual and a state body, the European Court has expressly stated that there is no suggestion that the state official providing the opinion could be considered to be on the same side as the prosecution or other government litigant, irrespective of whether the official is formally a member of the executive or the judiciary.[156] In the 2001 case of *Kress* v. *France*, the European Court considered this practice for the first time in the context of a civil court (the French Administrative court). The court noted that: '[T]he concept of a fair trial also means in principle the opportunity for the parties to a trial to have knowledge of and comment on all evidence adduced or observations filed, even by an independent member of the national legal service, with a view to influencing the court's decision'.[157] On this basis, the court found that there had been no breach of Art. 6(1) as regards compliance with the principle that proceedings should be adversarial. Although the

[155] *The Hannibal* (1867) 2 A & E 53, at 56. See also the recent practice of the General Medical Council's Fitness to Practise Panel in *Watson* v. *General Medical Council.*

[156] E.g. *Orshoven* v. *Belgium*, at [38]. A similar role is undertaken by the Advocate General before the European Court of Justice, under Art. 222 of the EC Treaty.

[157] *Kress* v. *France*, at [74].

Government Commissioner speaks last in an Administrative law hearing, the parties have the opportunity beforehand to ask what the general tenor of his submission will be and to submit a memorandum in reply to those submissions for the tribunal's deliberations. If the Commissioner raises orally a ground not raised by the parties, then the case would be adjourned to enable the parties to present argument on the point. The recent historical position regarding assessors in English civil courts has of course been more extreme, in that the parties might not even have known the view of the assessors until the court gave, or was about to give, its judgment.

CPR r. 35.15(3) allows one situation in which the parties will know at least some of the opinions of the assessors. It allows the court to ask the assessor to produce a pre-trial report 'on any matter at issue in the proceedings', which she is to distribute to the parties. Part 35 PD 7.4, which concerns the distribution of the report to the parties, indicates, however, that 'the assessor will not give oral evidence or be open to cross-examination or questioning'. The parties may seemingly therefore know the content of the report, and can make submissions on it to the court, but cannot ask questions of the assessor in the same way that they can ask questions of an expert (CPR r. 35.6). Blom-Cooper is almost certainly being overly optimistic when he suggests that 'If the [party] submissions raised questions which ought properly to be directed towards the assessors for any answers, the court would no doubt enable this to be done.'[158] He is, however, surely correct to suggest that:

> The tentative view is that the assessor's report, consisting of written evidence not subject to questioning, but no doubt highly influential in the court's adjudication on the expert issue, falls foul of Article 6. The fact that, unlike the pre-1999 practice, the parties see the assessor's report (if there is one, at the court's discretion) and may comment on it, does not suffice, in my view, to escape the precept of Article 6. Parties are entitled to be heard on all important issues, including a challenge direct to the expert witness.[159]

CPR r. 35.15 would appear to have been drafted without proper regard to the United Kingdom's obligations under Art. 6(1) of the European Convention, and the consequent obligations of the English courts under s. 6 of the Human Rights Act 1998.

In 2004, the Court of Appeal considered *obiter* in the case of *The Bow Spring* that current assessor practice would not be compatible with the

[158] Blom-Cooper, 'Experts and Assessors', 353. [159] Ibid., 353.

United Kingdom's obligations under Art. 6(1).[160] The court's concern was that counsel should have the opportunity to make submissions on the assessors' answers, in order to comply with the right to adversarial process, arising under Art. 6(1). The Court of Appeal cited *Krčmář*[161] as evidence for the principle that the parties should have the opportunity to know, and comment on, all evidence adduced or observations filed with a view to influencing the court's decision. In *The Global Mariner*, the Admiralty Court has accordingly amended its practice, as follows:

> (i) The range of topics on which advice might be sought from the Assessors should be canvassed with counsel by, latest, the stage of final submissions.
> (ii) Ordinarily, the questions asked of the Assessors by the Judge should not stray outside the range previously discussed with counsel...
> (iii) The questions ultimately put by the Judge, together with the answers given by the Assessors, should be disclosed to counsel before any draft judgment is handed down.
> (iv) Counsel should thereafter be given the opportunity to make submissions to the Judge, as to whether the advice given by the Assessors should be followed. Ordinarily, any such submissions should be in writing...
> (v) Generally speaking, the interests of proportionality and finality will make it unnecessary to repeat the procedure after the Judge and the Assessors have had the opportunity of considering the parties' submissions and any suggested further or revised questions.[162]

English practice in Admiralty now differs from that considered by the European Court (and found to be Art. 6(1) compliant), in that in Admiralty the judge and assessors retire before the assessors' opinions are given and party submissions on these are received, and then the judge and assessors retire again. There are some slight similarities here with the practice of the French Conseil d'état, where the Government Commissioner (an independent judicial officer) attends the deliberations of the judicial tribunal before the final hearing.[163] At this stage, however, one should be slow to conclude that Admiralty is returning to its civilian roots, and hearing a case in stages rather than at a single trial.

The *Orshoven/Kress* line of authority concerns legal submissions rather than the submissions of an expert regarding questions of fact. The principle applicable to the use of assessors is that, where an adverse legal

[160] *The Bow Spring*, at [61].
[161] *Krčmář* v. *Czech Republic*, at [40].
[162] *The Global Mariner*, at [14].
[163] *Kress*, at [43].

submission is made, following the parties' own submissions, then the affected party should have the opportunity to respond. This does not mean that the affected party necessarily has the right to cross-examine, or to re-open formal final submissions, but only that the party should have the right to comment. The right to respond to legal submissions would appear to be a sufficient safeguard to the adversarial rights of the parties to satisfy Art. 6(1). However, as Stanley Brunton J noted in *Watson* v. *General Medical Council*, when comparing the role of a justices' legal adviser[164] with that of a medical assessor, 'A legal adviser to justices advises only on questions of law, and the decisions of the justices may be appealed on issues of law. A medical examiner advises on factual issues, and there is no appeal against a panel's decision on issues of fact.'[165]

Stanley Brunton concluded that this not only made it all the more important that the assessor's advice be given openly, and that the parties be able to respond, but further that, where the advice is controversial, the parties should be able to submit their own experts' responses. I would further suggest that, depending on the nature of the advice, the parties should be given the right to cross-examine the assessors, given the difficulties inherent in appealing decisions of fact. The advice of a medical assessor in Fitness to Practise proceedings is closely defined, but, as has been seen above, a CPR r. 35.15 assessor might potentially fulfil a range of roles. This may in turn raise an evidential issue that, since assessors have not conventionally been viewed as evidential sources, they are not sworn as witnesses.[166] It may therefore become necessary for assessors to be sworn, at least for the giving of cross-examination.[167]

6.4.3.2 Assessor retiring with the court

In addition to the question of whether the parties had adequate opportunity to respond to the final submissions of a state or judicial officer, the European Court of Human Rights further considered in the criminal case of *Borgers* v. *Belgium*, and the medical negligence case of *Kress* v. *France*, the practice of that officer then withdrawing with the tribunal to

[164] *Practice Direction (Criminal Proceedings: Consolidation)* [2002] 1 WLR 2870, at [55.7].

[165] *Watson v. General Medical Council*, at [57].

[166] They do not appear to take any oath as a member of the tribunal either, as a judge or juror would have to do.

[167] If assessors are classed as an evidentiary source, then the effect of the unsworn nature of their testimony would presumably be that the trial should be considered a nullity and any judgment based on it should be set aside: P. Murphy, *Evidence*, 9th edn (Oxford: Oxford University Press, 2000), p. 471, citing *R.* v. *Marsham* ex p. *Lawrence* [1912] 2KB 362 and *Birch v Somerville* (1852) 2 ICLR (2nd ser.) 253.

consider its decision, after giving an opinion on the merits of the case presented. In *Kress*, the French government emphasized that the Government Commissioner advised the tribunal in its deliberations, because she had the greatest knowledge of the contents of the *dossier* (judicial case file), but that she played no part in the final decision. If the Commissioner had merely studied the *dossier*, but not made a submission in open court on the merits of the case, then it is probable that no Art. 6(1) issues would have arisen in relation to this case. However, because the Commissioner had expressed an opinion adverse to one of the parties, and then retired with the tribunal, the European Court was of the opinion that the parties were entitled to conclude that they had been denied access to an independent tribunal. The European Court also did not accept that the Commissioner was in fact truly a member of the tribunal, since he had no right to vote, and 'as a judge cannot abstain from voting unless he stands down'.[168]

The European Court in *Kress* did not engage fully with the question of why there was an appearance of bias. The reason, as the judgment is written, would appear to be that the Commissioner gave his opinion in open court before the tribunal's secret deliberations began. That, however, would suggest that if the Commissioner had formed his opinion, but did not disclose it until the beginning of the secret deliberations, then there would be no indication of bias. Indeed, the French government in its submission to the European Court argued that the giving of the opinion was much praised by legal practitioners and academics, as contributing to the openness of the judicial process. The correct reason, however, is likely to be that the appearance of bias arises because the Commissioner has come to the final hearing with his mind already made up, before final submissions are received from the parties. Although his submission is oral, and so in principle might be adjusted in light of final party submissions, one of the reasons that the European Court found the use of the Commissioner to be Art. 6(1) compliant was that the parties were able to establish from the Commissioner in advance the tenor of his intended submission. It is at least possible, therefore, that Art. 6(1) compliance might be retained if the Commissioner were to refrain from disclosing his opinion until the tribunal meets behind closed doors, and the Commissioner were to be a full voting member of the tribunal.

If we relate this principle to the English use of assessors, then the similarity with the French Government Commissioner is that an assessor, at

[168] *Kress*, at [79].

least in Admiralty, assists the court in its deliberations, but has no say in the final decision.[169] Could one argue, as the French government did in relation to the Commissioner, that an assessor is a full member of the tribunal? I would suggest that the argument for English assessors is, if anything, weaker than that for French Commissioners, since it is no longer clear that an assessor is a member of the tribunal rather than an evidential source. It would appear that current practice regarding nautical assessors still constitutes a prima facie breach of Art. 6(1) of the European Convention.

Under the RSC, and contemporary statutory provisions for assessors, it was settled law that an assessor, whether acting in a normal civil capacity or under a particular statutory form of proceeding, was not an evidentiary source, and almost certainly constituted part of the tribunal. Historically, therefore, challenges to an assessor's opinion have been limited by the assessor's status as a non-voting member of the tribunal. In 1884, Brett MR expressed the view that assessors were part of a mixed tribunal, although they 'take no part in the judgment whatever; they are not responsible for it, and have nothing to do with it'.[170] The *White Book* is similarly unequivocal that 'The assessor has a judicial role, he is not an expert witness appointed by the court.'[171] If assessors are to be viewed correctly as part of the tribunal rather than as a form of witness, then they should be seen as a non-voting member of a unified tribunal, rather than as a form of special jury answering specific questions of fact, because the advice of an assessor is not binding on the judge, in the same way that the response of a civil jury would be.[172]

In *Richardson* v. *Redpath Brown & Co. Ltd*, heard in 1944 under Workmen's Compensation Act 1925 proceedings, the House of Lords held that the correct role of an assessor was to help the judge to follow and understand specialist evidence, and to suggest questions that the judge might ask a witness to test his views or make plain his meaning.[173] The assessor should not be treated as an unsworn witness able to give to the judge, publicly or privately, evidence which, even if revealed to the parties, could not be challenged by cross-examination. Scrutton LJ in *Hall* v. *British Oil and Cake Mills Ltd* had therefore been wrong to suggest that the advice of an assessor was evidence.[174] Parliament had made separate provision

[169] *The Beryl* [1884] PD 137, at 141. [170] Ibid. [171] The *White Book*, [35.15.4].

[172] E.g. *Admiralty Commissioners* v. *Owners of the SS Ausonia* (1920) 2 Ll Rep 123, at 124.

[173] *Richardson* v. *Redpath Brown*, at 70, following *Woods* v. *Thomas Wilson Sons & Co. Ltd* (1915) 8 Butterworths Workmen's Compensation Claims 288, at 299 and 311.

[174] *Hall* v. *British Oil and Cake Mills Ltd* (1930) 23 Butterworths Workmen's Compensation Cases 529, at 533.

for a court expert, in the form of the medical referee.[175] Parliament similarly distinguished between court experts and assessors in relation to the National Insurance (Industrial Injuries) (Determination of Claims and Questions) Regulations 1948.[176] It is worth noting, however, that neither the House of Lords in *Redpath* nor the 1948 Regulations explicitly consider an assessor to form part of the tribunal. So by the 1940s there may have been a move away from the late nineteenth-century view that assessors were tribunal members. The focus instead became on assessors performing a separate role from that of expert witnesses.

The distinction between assessor and expert witness has also been emphasized by the High Court, and upheld in the Court of Appeal, in relation to the practice of coroner's courts. In *R.* v. *HM Coroner for Surrey* ex p. *Irene Wright*,[177] the Court of Appeal considered whether the Surrey Coroner had been correct in law to appoint an assessor in an inquest into the death of the applicant's son, and if so whether he had been correct to permit the assessor to testify as an expert witness. Hearing an application for judicial review, Tucker J held that the Coroner had fallen into error in allowing the assessor to testify as an expert witness, since: 'There is a danger that it might appear (whether justifiably or not) that the evidence of such a witness might attract the special confidence of the coroner, and might carry greater weight than would otherwise be the case. It is better that the roles of the assessor and expert witness should be kept separate.' However, the judge was not persuaded that this error had made a material difference to the verdict. The decision was upheld on further appeal to the Court of Appeal.

An alternative approach might be to view assessors as court officials. This approach was previously accepted by the Full Court of the Federal Court in Australia.[178] Where an assessor had been appointed by the trial judge, without the agreement of the parties, the judge was free to consult with that assessor in the same way that she would be with an associate or research assistant.[179] The federal court has subsequently sought to restrict this power to the appointment of assessors under statute. Outside of statutory provisions for assessors, it has introduced Order 34B, which

175 Workmen's Compensation Act 1925, s. 38.

176 *R.* v. *Deputy Industrial Injuries Commissioner* ex p. *Jones* [1962] 2 QB 677; [1962] 2 WLR 1215; [1962] 2 All ER 430 (DC).

177 *R.* v. *HM Coroner for Surrey* ex p. *Irene Wright*, Court of Appeal, 24 October 1996.

178 Heerey, 'Recent Australian Developments', 389; *Genetics Institute Incorporated* v. *Kirin-Amgen Incorporated (No. 2)* (1997) 149 ALR 247.

179 *Re JRL* ex p. *CJL* (1986) 161 CLR 342, at 351.

replaces assessors with expert assistants. These can only be appointed with the consent of the parties, and can only communicate with the judge by means of written report, which is also to be provided to the parties. These expert assistants would appear to be closer to filling the role of a court expert than would a traditional assessor.

From at least the second half of the nineteenth century until 2005, there appears therefore to have been judicial consensus that assessors are not expert witnesses, and while some judges have viewed them as members of the tribunal, no English judge appears to have directly said that they are not. However, in the 2005 case of *The Bow Spring*, Clarke LJ, in the judgment of the court, noted in relation to Art. 6(1) compliance that, 'Where the court has evidence from an expert who has not been called as a witness by either party – and CPR r. 61.12 makes it clear that nautical assessors are such experts – the principle needs to be adapted to the procedure.'[180] Of particular significance to us here are the words 'and CPR r. 61.12 makes it clear that nautical assessors are such experts'. This statement is *per incuriam*, both for its misinterpretation of the CPR, and for its failure to deal with relevant precedents. Aside from the issue that CPR r. 61.12 actually concerns stays of proceedings, and Clark LJ surely meant CPR r. 61.13, that rule actually states that 'The court may sit with assessors when hearing / (a) collision claims; or / (b) other claims involving issues of navigation or seamanship, and / the parties will not be permitted to call expert witnesses unless the court orders otherwise.' It does not suggest that assessors are expert witnesses. Further, the title of CPR Pt 35, 'Experts and Assessors', strongly suggests that assessors are a different creature from experts. In relation to precedent, Clarke LJ does not deal with relevant precedents, such as *The Beryl*, which indicate that assessors are part of the tribunal, or with the established practice that assessors are not sworn as witnesses.

For these reasons, it is far from clear in English law whether an assessor can correctly be viewed as a member of the tribunal. If she is not, then her presence and involvement with the judge or judges in their deliberations is a prima facie breach of Art. 6(1), in light of current jurisprudence. It is not sufficient to say that, following *The Global Mariner*, the court returns to inform the parties of the assessors' advice and to receive submissions on that advice because, following those submissions, the judge(s) and

[180] The *Bow Spring*, at [59].

assessor(s) then retire for further deliberations, and it is not expected that there will usually be opportunity for further submissions.

6.4.4 Delegating fact finding

As with experts, it is established that the court is not required to defer to the opinion of the assessor, since, 'After all, experience at sea is not everything. Assessors are not chosen for their personal conversance with collisions, and an experienced judge or counsel may boast that he has, in a sense, been in hundreds of collisions while the assessors have hardly seen tens.'[181] Many judges may, however, feel effectively bound. For example, Brett MR was of the opinion that 'it would be impertinent in a judge not to consider as almost binding upon him the opinion of the nautical gentlemen who, having ten times his own skill, are called in to assist him'.[182] The difference in approach between *The Australia* and *The Beryl*, which were heard only a quarter of a century apart, may be explicable in terms of the former reflecting a Law Lord's view on the experience of the Admiralty judge, while the latter reflects the view of a non-Admiralty judge receiving assessor evidence on an Admiralty matter on appeal. This would correspond with Howard's view (above) that the judge and counsel of the Admiralty Court are themselves a form of expert by virtue of their specialist experience in this niche area of litigation.

6.5 Conclusion

With the exception of the use of assessors in the High Court of Admiralty, the party expert has been the dominant mode of expertise in the English civil courts since records began. The CPR have sought to effect two significant changes to that arrangement: the court will encourage or direct the parties to agree on a single joint expert wherever possible (and possibility depends on complexity as well as cost), and the court is free to appoint its own expert, under the historically more comfortable guise of an 'assessor', to undertake a range of tasks. Although there continues to be little statistical information on the use of single joint experts, this new expert role appears to have been widely adopted, albeit under the ongoing supervision of active case management. The full extent of the use of shadow experts, outside the gaze of CPR Pt 35, is unclear, in

[181] *The Australia.* [182] *The Beryl*, at 141.

the absence of firm empirical evidence, but anecdotally their use is significant, particularly in higher-value cases. The use of assessors, however, does not appear to have spread far beyond Admiralty and Patents actions. Where party experts have continued to be appointed under CPR r. 35.2, there appears to have been a marked shift away from the increasingly open partisanship of the 1990s towards more restrained, balanced behaviour by parties and experts. The current balance between the use of single joint experts and party experts appears to be reasonably well struck, with an increasing emphasis on having regard to the epistemological difficulties as well as the costs in issue. As party expertise becomes less partisan, we may see a greater willingness by the court to instruct party experts again.

There remain some significant definitional issues about the nature of the role of the single joint expert and the assessor. It is unclear whether the ultimate purpose of the single joint expert is to minimize cost or to reduce partisanship. It is similarly unclear whether an assessor is ultimately a tribunal member, court expert, court officer or scientific adviser. Understanding the principle that underlies these roles is important when we seek to understand how the role is to be used or adapted on a principled basis in novel situations, such as the possibility of an Art. 6(1) challenge to the current provisions for assessors. In addition, any assessment of the success of the CPR's three expert roles is difficult while it remains unclear what the basis has been for creating these three roles and not others. The existence of four sub-roles under the heading of 'assessor' suggests that no clear basis was established. If, as seems possible, the purpose of the single joint expert role is to remove expert bias by eliminating partisanship, then the veritistic effectiveness of this approach must be open to challenge, since expert bias may arise for reasons other than partisanship. Approaches to managing expert bias are the subject of the next, final chapter.

7

The effective management of bias

7.1 Introduction

Chapter 6 examined the relationship between the civil procedure provisions for expert evidence, using the Civil Procedure Rules ('CPR') as a case study, and the court's ability to assess that evidence effectively. Particular attention was paid to the relative merits of the range of expert roles available (party expert, single joint expert, assessor), and to the way in which procedure can be used to assist the court in narrowing the issues between the parties' experts. In this final chapter I turn to consider how procedural provisions might in particular be used to overcome the problem of expert bias, and how the broader procedural framework may constrain available options.

The effectiveness of six possible approaches to discouraging or preventing bias is examined, drawing on current practice in England, the United States of America and France. First, the use of single experts, currently in the form of court experts (in practice) in France and (more in theory) in the United States federal courts, and in the form of single joint experts in England (Section 7.2). Secondly, the French practice of the presumptive recusal of an expert for bias (Section 7.3). Thirdly, the United States practice, following *Daubert*,[1] of excluding certain expert evidence from consideration by the tribunal of fact, on the legal ground that such evidence is unreliable, therefore is not relevant, and therefore is inadmissible (Section 7.4). Fourthly, the English practice of exhorting experts to remember that they have an overriding duty to the court, above any duty they may have to the parties or to others (Section 7.5). Fifthly, the possibility of making more information about the litigation work of party experts available to other parties and to the court, through reform of litigation privilege in England (Section 7.6). Finally, the availability of professional, civil and criminal sanctions against experts who have produced biased or otherwise false expert evidence (Section 7.7).

[1] *Daubert* v. *Merrell Dow Pharmaceuticals* 509 US 579; 113 Sup Ct 2786 (1993) (*Daubert I*).

The total elimination of bias in expert evidence is not considered here for two reasons. 'Bias' is a multi-faceted concept, and what we mean by 'expert bias' depends on the context in which we use the term. The elimination of a particular form of bias may be incompatible with the role that is expected of the expert. The second reason is that it may be evidentially all but impossible to identify expert bias in normal circumstances, for example where our definition is based on the expert's state of mind, and the question is whether the expert has given her honest opinion. The intended benefits of this exercise are to assist policy making and judicial decisions in relation to expert bias in actual cases, and to identify those artefacts of bias that are unlikely to be addressed by these practical measures, and therefore should be accepted as inherent – at least for the present – in a given form of expertise.

7.2 The use of single experts

As introduced in Chapter 4, single court experts are the dominant expert role in the French civil courts. In the federal courts of the United States, court experts may be appointed under r. 706 of the Federal Rules of Evidence ('FRE') although the preference appears to be for the appointment of panels of court experts. Since 1999, single joint experts have been extensively used in low-value civil claims in the English civil courts under CPR r. 35.7,[2] although the previous court expert provisions of Ord. 40 of the Rules of the Supreme Court ('RSC') were almost never used.[3]

The argument for the use of neutral experts as a solution to the problem of expert bias is that, since expert bias currently arises from favouring the case of the instructing party, then by removing the instructing party from the equation bias will also be removed. Although at first blush this argument is compelling in its simplicity, on further consideration it is fundamentally limited. The use of single experts can be seen as a way of removing structural forms of bias, and many of the forms of personal bias associated with interest in the outcome of the case. However, it has little effect in removing other forms of personal bias, particularly bias arising from predisposition.

Structural and personal interest biases are to some extent countered by the adversarial system, since all parties are able to produce experts

[2] S. Burn and B. Thompson, 'Single Joint Expert', in L. Blom-Cooper (ed.), *Experts in the Civil Courts* (Oxford: Oxford University Press, 2006), pp. 57–75, p. 58.

[3] *Abbey National Mortgages plc* v. *Key Surveyors Nationwide Ltd* [1996] 1 WLR 1534; [1996] 3 All ER 184 (CA).

in support of their case and there is therefore the opportunity for the informed challenging of any one expert's opinion. Where only one expert is appointed then, not only does the court retain the risk that it will be exposed to the full range of predisposition biases, but there is much less information with which the court can decide whether such biases are present.

We might say, as Goldman suggests,[4] that the unpredictability in expert opinions that might arise from having a single expert is no different from the unpredictability in law that already accompanies the appointment of a single judge. If my patent infringement case is listed to be heard before a judge who has never found for a claimant in any of the twenty similar actions that she has heard on the bench, and who always defended such actions when at the bar, then my heart may sink and I may move to settle, but I cannot recuse that judge for bias. Similarly, following Goldman's argument, I should not be entitled to object if a particular court expert is appointed, even though that expert has never given an opinion favourable to a claimant, but twenty favourable to defendants. Goldman's argument is correct up to a point in that we must accept that the decision maker will bring her own personality to the decision-making process, although the House of Lords in *Davidson*[5] noted that one must distinguish between a predisposition where the judge has previously closed her mind to other possibilities, and one where the judge remains open to persuasion in the instant case. In the case of *Timmins* v. *Gormley*, which formed part of the *Locabail* appeal,[6] the Court of Appeal felt that there was a real danger of bias in a personal injury case, where the presiding Recorder had previously strongly criticized in the trade press the behaviour of insurance companies in such cases.

> Rarely, if ever, in the absence of injudicious or intemperate behaviour, can a judge's previous activity as such give rise to an appearance of bias. Over time, of course, judges acquire a track record, and experienced advocates may be able to predict with more or less accuracy how a particular judge is likely to react to a given problem. Since judges are not automata this is inevitable, and presenting a case in the way most likely to appeal to a particular tribunal is a skill of the accomplished advocate. But adherence to an opinion expressed judicially in an earlier case does not of itself denote

[4] A. Goldman, *Knowledge in a Social World* (Oxford: Oxford University Press, 1999), p. 310.

[5] *Davidson* v. *Scottish Ministers* [2004] UKHL 34; 2005 1 SC (HL) 7, at [11].

[6] *Locabail (UK) Ltd* v. *Bayfield Properties Ltd* [2000] QB 451; [2000] 2 WLR 870; [2000] 1 All ER 65, at [71]–[89].

> a lack of open mindedness; and there are few experienced judges who have not, on fresh argument applied to new facts in a later case, revised an opinion expressed in an earlier.[7]

It is likely, however, that *Timmins* will be found to turn largely on its facts, and that extra-curial writing by judges in learned journals is unlikely to attract similar censure.

There are three difficulties with Goldman's argument. The first, as Ward points out, is that if our example judge gives her twenty-first judgment for the defendant, then I have reasonable opportunity for appeal to a higher court, where there exists more than one viable legal opinion on the matter. There is, however, no appeal against the opinion of a court expert, as it is evidence rather than a decision on the ultimate issue.[8] My only option would therefore be to recuse the expert. There is no precedent for this course of action in English law, since an expert is not usually considered to be a judicial or quasi-judicial figure, and it would be associated with similar difficulties of proof to those encountered with recusing a judge. In addition, a party that seeks, but fails, to disqualify an expert, as with a judge, will still then be the subject of that expert's opinion in the case. The second difficulty with Goldman's argument is that, while there are clear legal rules of recognition for judges, with an identifiable process by which one becomes a judge, there is no equivalent process for an expert. The third difficulty is that, while a judge is required to give a reasoned decision on the law in her judgment, which can be scrutinized by the lawyers on all sides, the (by definition) specialized nature of the expert's opinion may make it difficult for the parties to be sure whether they have been the subject of an acceptable variation in opinion, or of a 'rogue' opinion.

Ward suggests that a better analogy that Goldman might have used would be the unpredictability of juries.[9] However, the crucial difference between a court expert and a panel of jurors is that the number of jurors who have been randomly selected might be expected to reduce significantly the chance of a markedly unrepresentative decision being made. If we were to accommodate the idea that a number of randomly selected individuals is more reliable than a single such individual, then this would

[7] *Davidson* v. *Scottish Ministers*, at [11].

[8] Although courts of first instance and appeal may both use assessors, this does not represent an appellate hierarchy of assessors: *Owners of the SS Australia* v. *Owners of Cargo of SS Nautilus* [1927] AC 145 (HL) (*The Australia*).

[9] T. Ward, 'Experts, Juries and Witch-Hunts: From Fitzjames Stephen to Angela Cannings' (2004) 31 *Journal of Law and Society* 369–86, 375.

lead us to appoint more than one court expert. This would inevitably affect costs.[10]

7.3 The presumptive recusal of an expert for bias

Judicial recusal for interest proceeds from the maxim *nemo judex in causa sua* ('no one may be a judge in her own case'). Such recusal is a long-established practice in the Roman-canon legal tradition,[11] although the common law did not recognize judicial recusal until the nineteenth century.[12] Under modern French civil procedural law, a *technicien* (including an *expert*) may be recused for bias on the same grounds as a judge.[13] These grounds mainly fall under the same heads of financial, personal and familial interest as are to be found in the work of the mediaeval canon lawyers. To apply the grounds of judicial recusal to an expert is an innovation in French law. Under the 1806 code, *techniciens* were to be treated as witnesses of fact for the purposes of recusal.[14]

The rationale for this development would appear to be that, if we assign fact investigation to an expert as an officer of the court de iure, and we are also in most cases assigning an aspect of fact determination to the same expert de facto, then we should recognize the expert as a member of the tribunal of fact, although we may be entitled to insist that she is a tribunal member who has no final say in, or responsibility for, the court's determination of fact in the case. Although this may go against the principles that the expert has no legal authority to determine any aspect of the case, and that the tribunal of fact has no legal basis for delegating its responsibilities, we are in danger of failing to invoke legal safeguards for

[10] Hence French criminal judges rarely exercise their power to appoint more than one court expert under Code de procédure pénale 1958, art. 159 (as amended): M. Bardet-Giraudon, 'The Place of the Expert in the French Legal System', in J. Spencer, G. Nicholson, R. Flin and R. Bull (eds.), *Children's Evidence in Legal Proceedings. An International Perspective* (Cambridge: Cambridge Law Faculty, 1990), pp. 68–70, p. 69.

[11] From the thirteenth century, canon lawyers began to develop the right to challenge and remove ordinary judges and judge delegates for interest, prejudice or unfitness for office: R. Helmholz, *Canon Law and the Law of England* (London: Hambledon Press, 1987), pp. 21 and 35. Civilian lawyers allowed recusal of a judge delegate for the mere suspicion of bias, but not the recusal of an ordinary judge: p. 34.

[12] Ibid., p. 21.

[13] Nouveau code de procédure civile ('NCPC') arts. 234, 341. Such recusals have occurred: A. Jacquin, 'L'impartialité objective de l'expert judiciaire et sa récusation' 31 *Gazette du Palais* (1 February 2003) 3–8, 5.

[14] O. Leclerc, *Le juge et l'expert: contribution à l'étude des rapports entre le droit et la science* (Paris: LDGJ, 2005).

the sake of protecting the principle that experts do not decide cases.[15] If we allow the expert to be at least de facto a member of the tribunal of fact, then it seems appropriate to allow the parties the protection of rights of recusal that apply to other members of that tribunal. The French have of course taken the issue one stage further, because it is not simply the case that an expert can be recused, but that she can be recused on the same grounds as a full judge. This implies that the expert is so like a judge that the parties should have protection from potential abuse of her power as if she were a judge. Other legal consequences flow on from this approach. For example, Jacquin has proposed that that the term 'tribunal' in Art. 6(1) of the European Convention on Human Rights should be interpreted in a broad sense, to include *techniciens* appointed by the tribunal.[16] This would provide litigants (and criminal defendants) with the same rights in relation to a court expert as they currently enjoy under the Convention against the courts themselves.

It is more moot whether a single expert appointed with the agreement of the parties, such as the English single joint expert, should be similarly considered to be a tribunal member. I would suggest that, because the single joint expert may only be classed as a Pt 35 expert by virtue of court direction, because once appointed it is difficult for the parties to de-instruct a single joint expert, and because a single joint expert can obtain independent direction from the court, the single joint expert should be considered more a court expert than a party expert. As such, there should be opportunity for the parties to recuse a single joint expert. However, since the parties usually agreed to the instruction of the single joint expert in the first place, there are likely to be few situations in which valid grounds for recusal would arise. Recusal is more likely to be an issue in the unusual situation where the judge has imposed a single joint expert on parties who have been unable to agree. Recusal may also arise in relation to the appointment of assessors.

The most appropriate grounds of recusal in English law would be those developed in administrative law in relation to tribunal bias. In English administrative law, bias can be treated under one of three heads: presumed, apparent and actual.[17] Presumed bias arises when the tribunal member has a pecuniary or proprietary interest in the outcome of the case, or shares

[15] Whether experts should decide cases is a separate policy issue, outside the scope of this work.

[16] Jacquin, 'L'impartialité', 4.

[17] E.g. M. Fordham, *Judicial Review Handbook*, 4th edn (Oxford: Hart, 2004), p. 1044.

the same cause as one of the parties.[18] This may include close links with an organization that is joined to the action.[19] The advantage of the rule in *Dimes* is that the applicant party is not required to demonstrate that the tribunal member has actually exhibited bias.[20] As with actual (but not apparent) bias, the parties cannot waive the disqualification of the tribunal member, because disqualification serves the broader public interest rather than the narrow rights of the litigants.[21] Recusal for presumed bias has the evidential advantage that the party raising the matter is required only to produce evidence that a particular state of affairs exists, such as that the judge has a financial interest. However, while financial interest may be a mortal sin on the part of the tribunal, it is almost a necessary part of the expert's involvement in the case. We could say that some forms of interest result in automatic disqualification, such as a conditional or contingency fee agreement, employment by the party, or a shareholding, although the approach of the English courts would appear to be more relaxed.[22]

The test for apparent bias is now whether, having regard to the relevant circumstances, as ascertained by the court, the fair-minded and informed observer, having considered the facts, would conclude that there was a real possibility that the tribunal was biased.[23] The boundaries between the tests for presumed and apparent bias are unclear, both conceptually[24] and increasingly in case law:[25] 'Although the tests are described differently, their application . . . is likely in practice to lead to results which are so similar as to be indistinguishable'.[26] In some other jurisdictions there is only the one test for disqualification for bias, but there is no agreement on whether that test should be for presumed[27] or apparent

[18] *R.* v. *Bow Street Metropolitan Stipendiary Magistrate* ex p. *Pinochet Ugarte (No. 2)* [2000] 1 AC 119, 145; [1999] 2 WLR 272; [1999] 1 All ER 577 (Lord Hutton).

[19] Ibid.

[20] *Dimes* v. *Proprietors of Grand Junction Canal* (1852) 3 HL Cas 759, at 793.

[21] *R.* v. *Secretary of State for the Home Department* ex p. *Fayed* [2001] Imm AR 134, at [86].

[22] *R. (Factortame)* v. *Secretary of State for Transport, Local Government and the Regions (No. 8)* [2002] EWCA Civ 932; [2003] QB 381; [2002] 3 WLR 1104; [2002] 4 All ER 97; *Field v. Leeds City Council* [1999] CPLR 833 (CA); *Liverpool Roman Catholic Archdiocese and Trustees Inc.* v. *Goldberg (No. 2)*, Chancery Division, 2 March 2001.

[23] *Magill* v. *Porter* [2001] UKHL 67; [2002] 2 AC 357; [2002] 2 WLR 37; [2002] 1 All ER 465, at [102].

[24] A. Zuckerman, *Civil Procedure: Principles of Practice*, 2nd edn (London: Sweet and Maxwell, 2006), p. 84.

[25] *Davidson* v. *Scottish Ministers*, at [6].

[26] *Pinochet (No. 2)*, at 142.

[27] NCPC art. 341 gives eight causes for *recusement*, which refer to pre-existing situations, which is the approach taken for presumed bias, rather than to the expert's conduct.

bias.[28] The shortage of cases relating to actual bias of any sort may reflect both its rarity and the evidential difficulties of demonstrating it.[29]

Practically, presumed, apparent or actual bias is unlikely to become evident until litigation is under way, and possibly at trial itself. Actual bias on the part of the tribunal cannot be accommodated by the decision-making process, but the extent of the bias is limited to the trial or other hearing. It is therefore necessary to commence a fresh trial, but this does not require that litigation be commenced again from the beginning. In contrast, where an expert is found to be biased, the tribunal may consider that it is able to accommodate this in its inferential reasoning. To disqualify the expert would mean repeating a significant part of trial preparation, and near-intractable questions might arise of whether a party would have settled at an earlier stage, thus avoiding consequent costs, if a different expert opinion had been available originally. The consequences of disqualifying a judge are therefore markedly different from those of disqualifying an expert. Disqualification of an expert may only be practicable when it is at a relatively early stage in proceedings that the expert exhibits actual bias.[30] Parties should be alert to the possibility that they may wish to seek the recusal of a particular expert. If they do decide to seek recusal, it is preferable to do so before the expert has been formally instructed, so as to reduce delay and cost.

7.4 The inadmissibility of unreliable expert evidence

The recusal of an expert for bias may be an appropriate solution where the expert exercises a judicial or quasi-judicial function. Where there is reason to believe that it would be contrary to the interests of justice to consider evidence from a particular expert, because of the effect of bias on the reliability of that evidence, but the expert is considered to be an agent of one of the parties rather than of the court, then an alternative to recusal needs to be identified that allows the court to exclude the offending evidence while continuing to recognize the right of the parties to instruct their own experts. This is the approach taken by the United States Supreme Court in the leading case of *Daubert*.[31]

[28] Australia, as with most other Commonwealth countries, has a test for apparent bias but not presumed bias: *Ebner* v. *The Official Trustee in Bankruptcy and Clenae Pty Ltd* v. *ANZ Banking Group Ltd* [2000] HCA 63.

[29] In particular, a judge cannot be questioned on her decisions: *Locabail* v. *Bayfield*, at 472.

[30] *Liverpool RC Archdiocese (No. 2)*.

[31] See Section. 4.2.2 for the context in which *Daubert* was decided.

In that case, the court held that, as is the case for all types of evidence, expert evidence is only admissible under FRE r. 402 if it is relevant, and implicit in the concept of relevance is reliability. While there was no definitive checklist or test for reliability, the court suggested that four relevant factors were: (1) testability, (2) peer review or publication, (3) the known or potential rate of error, and (4) widespread acceptance. The *Daubert* approach to assessing the admissibility of expert evidence has replaced the earlier *Frye* test in the federal courts and the majority of state courts. In *Frye*, the Federal Court of the District of Columbia ruled, in a criminal case, that 'novel scientific testimony' is admissible only if it is 'sufficiently established to have gained general acceptance in the particular field to which it belongs'.[32]

Like the issue of recusal, evidential admissibility is a question of law rather than fact. The effect of that in a unified tribunal is largely academic, because the court *qua* tribunal of law must receive and assess the evidence in order to decide its admissibility, and so is likely to have that evidence in mind de facto, albeit not de iure, when it later determines the facts *qua* tribunal of fact. It is probably at least in part for this reason that courts that are descended from the Roman-canon tradition, which historically have been unified courts, have paid little regard to the rules of admissibility. The practical effect of the distinction only really arises before a bicameral court, where the judge may rule on admissibility in the absence of the jury. The jury can then determine the facts of the case free from undue influence from evidence that was not in the event admitted. This justification for the division often overlaps with a second justification: that jurors, not being used to the everyday assessment of adversarial evidence, or the complexity of expert evidence, should be protected from evidence that might be extraneous or unnecessarily misleading.

As a high-level statement of principle, the decision in *Daubert* is straightforward and relatively non-contentious: if we want to give a group of people a complex set of facts to consider and decide between, then we will be assisting them, and hopefully assisting a more accurate decision, if we do not give them material that we think is likely to be unreliable. It is worth bearing this in mind as one enters the forest of *Daubert*-related literature.[33] The need for *Daubert* appears to have arisen in the early 1990s

[32] *Frye* v. *United States* 293 F 1013 (DC Cir. 1923), at 1014.

[33] Not only is the volume of *Daubert*-related literature so extensive that one could probably dedicate a career to '*Daubert* studies', but it is one of the few legal decisions in the world to have its own website (www.daubertontheweb.com) and t-shirts (www.cafepress.com/daubertontheweb) (last accessed 1 August 2008).

for three related reasons. The first was that the highly pugnacious nature of United States litigation, particularly civil litigation (Section 4.3.3), means that lawyers and experts are highly prone to partisanship. The second was that an earlier rule of expert evidence admissibility, *Frye*, which was designed to address the first reason, was considered to be threatened by the liberal admissibility rules of the 1970s FRE. The third was heightened public concern regarding the phenomenon of 'junk science', particularly in relation to toxic tort cases (Section 4.3.3).

There are at least four main areas in which the test in *Daubert* is problematic in its detail: first, as a philosophy of scientific method; secondly, its failure to recognize the range of expertise presented under the single category of 'expert evidence'; thirdly, its inherent bias towards defendants; fourthly, ambiguity as to whether the test is ultimately epistemological or political. The *Daubert* factors are a product of the litigation that gave rise to them, in that they are designed to address the reliability of the evidence of research scientists in an area of science where there is controversy.

The first problem for *Daubert* is that it requires judges to second-judge experts on whether the methods that they are employing are properly 'scientific', and as such reliable.[34] The relevant factors here are: testability; peer review or publication; the known or potential rate of error; widespread acceptance. On a practical level, this requires a degree of scientific literacy on the part of judges that it is unreasonable to expect. On a philosophical level, it is unclear that the four *Daubert* factors would actually be accepted by all (or sufficient) scientists as indicating reliable scientific method. For example, some branches of science, such as fingerprint evidence and ballistics, are not academic research sciences, and so receive little peer review or publication.[35] Similarly, error rates exist only in some experimental sciences. Further, it is unclear that either of the terms 'scientific' and 'method' is meaningful within the philosophy of science. By 1997, the Supreme Court decided that its distinction between methodology and conclusions was too problematic for federal judges to maintain, and so in *Joiner* it held that methodology and conclusions are largely the same thing.[36]

The second problem is that a test for the reliability of scientific evidence is poorly suited to assessing the reliability of non-scientific expert

[34] E.g. S. Haack, *Defending Science – Within Reason: Between Scientism and Cynicism* (New York: Prometheus Books, 2003), pp. 223–64.

[35] See also E. Beecher-Monas, *Evaluating Scientific Evidence: An Interdisciplinary Framework for Intellectual Due Process* (Cambridge: Cambridge University Press, 2006).

[36] *General Electric Company* v. *Joiner* 522 US 136; 118 Sup Ct 512 (1997).

evidence. This was exacerbated by the Supreme Court's decision in 1999 to extend *Daubert* to apply to non-scientific expert testimony.[37] David Bernstein has helpfully identified two categories of evidence, speculative causation evidence and 'connoisseur' testimony,[38] where the reliability test goes too far in excluding evidence that one might reasonably consider reliable. At the same time, Bernstein suggests that the *Daubert* test does not do enough to remove partisanship from forensic science.

The third problem is that *Daubert* unfairly favours defendants in at least two types of case. In the first type, where both claimant and defendant are relying on expert evidence to decide a case, because the non-expert evidence is equally balanced or otherwise inconclusive, it is in the interests of the defendant to have the expert evidence ruled inadmissible, since the burden of proof will then fall back on the claimant and the claim will fail. In the second type of case, the defendant has acted in reliance on scientific orthodoxy, and the claimant would need to challenge that orthodoxy in order to succeed. The classical example of this type of case is a toxic tort action.[39] We would hope that the defendant undertook appropriate assessment of the safety of their activity or product prior to commencement or production, and that appropriate assessment will have relied on orthodox science. Assuming that the defendant acted in good faith, and was not subject to cognitive error in reviewing the results of the assessment, then scientific orthodoxy will defend the actions of the defendant. It is possible that there is disagreement within the scientific orthodoxy (or that such disagreement has developed since the original assessment). But, absent that orthodox disagreement, the claimant is likely to have to rely on novel or otherwise non-orthodox expert evidence in order to proceed with her claim. Thus, the *Daubert* test particularly favours

[37] *Kumho Tire* v. *Carmichael* 526 US 137; 119 Sup Ct 1167 (1999).

[38] Bernstein's 'connoisseur' is one who has acquired expertise through practical experience. D. Bernstein, 'Expert Witnesses, Adversarial Bias, and the (Partial) Failure of the Daubert Revolution' (2007) *George Mason University Law and Economics Research Paper Series* 07–11, http://papers.ssrn.com/sol3/papers.cfm?abstract_id=963461 (last accessed 1 August 2008).

[39] G. Edmond and D. Mercer, '*Daubert* and the Exclusionary Ethos: The Convergence of *Corporate* and *Judicial* Attitudes Towards the Admissibility of Expert Evidence in Tort Litigation' (2004) 26 *Law and Policy* 231–57, 231; G. Edmond, and D. Mercer 'Experts and Expertise in Legal and Regulatory Settings', in G. Edmond (ed.), *Expertise in Regulation and Law* (Aldershot: Ashgate, 2004), pp. 1–31, pp. 4–5; G. Edmond and D. Mercer, 'The Invisible Branch: The *Authority* of Science Studies in Expert Evidence Jurisprudence', in G. Edmond (ed.), *Expertise in Regulation and Law* (Aldershot: Ashgate, 2004), pp. 197–291, pp. 225–6.

toxic tort defendants, in the absence of evidence that the defendant had been negligent or reckless in the conducting of safety assessments.

The fourth problem is that *Daubert* presents a mixture of epistemology and politics. By this I mean that *Daubert*'s criteria for establishing justified belief relate to the extent to which that belief is accepted by a community, rather than whether the belief is true. If we go back to the four *Daubert* factors (testability; peer review or publication; the known or potential rate of error; widespread acceptance), the first and third of these are veritistic – that is, they relate to whether a methodology is accurate, or conclusions are true. The second and fourth are social, in that they are concerned with whether others in the scientific community[40] accept the expert's method. The concern about consensus as a test for admissibility is that it means that the court will accept or reject expert evidence on the basis not of whether it believes it to be true but of whether it is accepted by others in the field. Truth may therefore be blocked by false orthodoxy. We might call this a 'Copernicus effect', after the rejection of the work of the sixteenth-century Polish astronomer and mathematician Copernicus by his contemporaries. Lakatos suggested that to deem certain lines of research and theory as 'pseudoscience' was an ethical and political rather than pure philosophical problem:

> The problem of demarcation between science and pseudoscience has grave implications also for the institutionalization of criticism. Copernicus's theory was banned by the Catholic Church in 1616 because it was said to be pseudoscientific. It was taken off the index in 1820 because by that time the Church deemed that facts had proved it and therefore it became scientific. The Central Committee of the Soviet Communist Party in 1949 declared Mendelian genetics pseudoscientific and had its advocates, like Academician Vavilov, killed in concentration camps; after Vavilov's murder Mendelian genetics was rehabilitated; but the Party's right to decide what is science and publishable and what is pseudoscience and punishable was upheld . . . All these judgments were inevitably based on some sort of demarcation criterion. And this is why the problem of demarcation between science and pseudoscience is not a pseudo-problem of armchair philosophers: it has grave ethical and political implications.[41]

[40] This presupposes an agreed definition of 'scientific community', and the actual existence of such a community.

[41] I. Lakatos, 'Science and Pseudoscience' Lecture, broadcast 30 June 1973, as Programme 11 of The Open University Arts Course A303, 'Problems of Philosophy', www.lse.ac.uk/collections/lakatos/scienceAndPseudoscience.htm (last accessed 1 August 2008).

When Lakatos talks of 'grave ethical and political implications', he would appear to take it as a given that it is ethically and politically desirable to pursue truth and the development of human knowledge.[42] Is this true for courtroom fact finding? I distinguished in Section 3.2 between scientific and legal interests in truth in fact finding, and the analysis there may be of assistance here. If a court needs to decide the case of *A* v. *B*, should it prefer the evidence E_A of *A*'s expert, which is based on scientific well-respected theories and methods, or the evidence E_B of *B*'s expert, which breaks with orthodoxy but which appears to the court to be particularly convincing in the instant case? Does it matter whether E_B is cautiously welcomed by the scientific community, treated with suspicion or even ignored?

My initial reaction is to say that I would prefer it to be the case that, if the court were convinced that E_B is correct, then the court should adopt E_B. It is worth exploring this initial reaction. This may be because I prefer the David against the Goliath, and if I were told that not only E_B but *B* herself was a 'David' then my preference for E_B would only be increased. But what if *B* was actually a multinational corporation, while *A* was a vulnerable, impecunious party? I suspect that E_B would be transformed in my mind from being the product of a maverick genius scientist, to being a mercenary charlatan in the pay of *B*, and I should be outraged that *A*, even with the might of scientific orthodoxy on her side, might be denied justice.

Perhaps we can justify *Daubert* in terms not of accurate fact determination, but of risk allocation.[43] However attractive E_B might be, modern science is littered with the remains of methodological advances that seemed too good to be true, because they were just that, too good to be true. Although we might like to believe that the risk is reduced by peer acceptance, as *Daubert* suggests, there is the peer acceptance that recognizes that new ground may be being broken, and the peer acceptance that an approach or theory is established and reliable. *Daubert* is (or should be) only really concerned with the latter. Many of the methodological advances that were too good to be true aroused significant positive interest in the scientific community at the time. In recent times, one need think only of erroneous reports of successful cold fusion[44] and fraudulent

[42] See also P. Kitcher, 'Truth or Consequences?' (1998) 72 *Proceedings and Addresses of the American Philosophical Association* 49–63.

[43] A. Stein, *Foundations of Evidence Law* (Oxford: Oxford University Press, 2005).

[44] Energy Research Advisory Board to the United States Department of Energy, *Cold Fusion Research* (Washington DC: 1999) DOE/S–0073 DE90 005611.

reports of human cloning.[45] It is therefore (perhaps regrettably) the case that the courts should err in favour of established expertise over innovative expertise. That does not necessarily mean that there is no place for a Copernicus in judicial fact finding, but only that civil litigation is not in most circumstances the place in which to play out scientific controversies. While the experts in *A* v. *B* can continue their controversy after judgment is handed down, and eventually realize that all were wrong, *A* and *B* are bound by the finding of fact as of the day of judgment, and we should therefore perhaps be slightly conservative in our choice between E_A and E_B.

7.5 Exhortations to an overriding duty to the court

While the United States courts have tended to the view that experts are unscrupulous mercenaries, and thus have produced the *Daubert* exclusionary approach, the solution of the English courts has been to fall back on notions of decent conduct and fair play. One of the most striking features of the CPR's provisions for expert evidence is r. 35.3's imposition on experts of an overriding duty to the court:

(1) It is the duty of an expert to help the court on the matters within his expertise.
(2) This duty overrides any obligation to the person from whom he has received instructions or by whom he is paid.

This normative framework should underlie an expert's conduct, whether instructed by one party or jointly. Building on authorities beginning in the early 1980s that experts should provide objective, unbiased opinion, and should not act as advocates,[46] CPR r. 35.3 seeks to place the expert's overriding duty to the court on a statutory footing. There are definitional issues with CPR r. 35.3, since the actual content of the duty referred to in CPR r. 35.3(1) and the obligations referred to in CPR r. 35.3(2) are unclear. An initial analysis of what the nature of that content might be is undertaken here.

[45] E. Check and D. Cyranoski, 'Korean Scandal will have Global Fallout' (2005) 438 *Nature* 1056–7. See also G. Brumfiel, 'Misconduct? It's All Academic . . . ' (2007) 445 *Nature* 240–1; U. Deichmann and B. Müller-Hill, 'The Fraud of Abderhalden's Enzymes' (1998) 393 *Nature* 109–11, which considered an earlier and similar scandal.

[46] *National Justice Compania* v. *Prudential Assurance* [1993] 2 Ll Rep 68 (*The Ikarian Reefer*) (Comm. Ct), at 81; *Whitehouse* v. *Jordan* [1980] 1 All ER 650 (CA); [1981] 1 WLR 246 (HL).

7.5.1 The nature of the overriding duty

If we attempt to define 'overriding duty' then our best starting point might be to identify existing overriding duties to the court, that we might take as analogues. The leading example is that of the duty of the barrister to the court, which overrides any duty to their client: 'He will not knowingly misstate the law – he will not wilfully misstate the facts, though it be to gain the cause for his client. He will ever bear in mind that if he be... retained and remunerated... for his... services, yet he has a prior and perpetual retainer on behalf of truth and justice'.[47] Solicitors exercising rights of audience have a similar overriding duty:[48] they 'must not deceive or knowingly or recklessly mislead'.[49] Although a barrister has a duty to bring to the attention of the court legal authorities and statutes that are not favourable to her client's case, she does not have a corresponding duty to volunteer factual information detrimental to her client.[50]

If we assume that CPR r. 35.3 builds on the existing duties at common law under the RSC rather than replacing them, then the expert is precluded from interpreting her 'overriding duty' in line with the interpretation given by barristers and solicitors, since she may not act as an advocate.[51] This greater duty seems anomalous, since the justification for the barrister's overriding duty expressed in the language of commerce is that she has taken 'a permanent retainer on behalf of Justice', which is greater than that offered by her client.[52] The expert, however, has only her client's retainer. On the one hand, we might therefore say that the expert has less a duty to justice than does the barrister, but, on the other hand, we might expect that all who become involved in litigation owe an equal duty to

[47] *R.* v. *O'Connell* (1844) 7 ILR 261, at 312 (Crampton J), cited with approval in *Rondel* v. *Worsley* [1967] 1 QB 443, at 517; [1966] 3 WLR 950; [1966] 3 All ER 657 (CA) (Salmon LJ).

[48] 'Solicitor's Practice Rules' (Law Society 1990, last amended February 2005), r. 1(c).

[49] 'The Law Society's Code for Advocacy' (Law Society 1993, last amended January 2003), r. 2.2.

[50] The current balance between an advocate's duties to the court and to her client was struck in the Roman-canon courts in the 1230s: J. Brundage, 'The Ethics of the Legal Profession: Mediaeval Canonists and their Clients' (1973) 33 *The Jurist* 237; J. Brundage, 'The Calumny Oath and Ethical Ideas of Canonical Advocates', in P. Landau and J Müller (eds.), *Proceedings of the Ninth International Congress of Medieval Canon Law: Monumenta iuris canonici: Subsidia*, vol. x, (Vatican City: 1997), pp. 793–805, p. 793. Compare Helmholz, *Canon Law*, p. 44: 'In short, the canonical ideal was that the practising lawyer should always act in the interests of justice; he was an instrument in the law's search for objective fact, rather than a servant of the client's wishes.'

[51] *The Ikarian Reefer.* [52] *R.* v. *O'Connell.*

justice.[53] The resolution of this dilemma is normative. Under the CPR, the norm would appear to be that all who become involved in litigation owe an equal duty to justice, although the ways in which that duty manifests itself may vary.[54]

One solution might be to take the word 'overrides' in CPR r. 35.3 in a weaker sense than the barrister's duty, to mean that the duty to the court cannot be trumped by the duty to the party. This is closer to the duty of a non-advocate solicitor. There is no difficulty in providing the court with every assistance provided it is weighted towards one's own case. The effect of the overriding duty would therefore be to permit conscious bias to the extent that the expert gives an opinion which might reasonably be formed on the available evidence. This reins in the worst excesses of conscious expert bias, but it would mean that CPR r. 35.3 says little more than that it is possible to be both a 'servant of the court' and a 'hired gun'.[55]

The idea that an expert is a servant of the court pre-dates the CPR.[56] It may provide some assistance in defining of the expert's duty, although the exact role of the 'servant of the court' is also poorly defined. The term is also used to describe the role of fines officers, bailiffs, the Official Receiver and the Official Solicitor. In this capacity, the Official Solicitor 'may at any time be called on by a judge to carry out an investigation and to assist the court to see that justice is done between the parties'.[57] The role of 'servant of the court' is almost certainly distinct from that of 'officer of the court', the role occupied by solicitors, and possibly by barristers. Both in England and the United States, only solicitors acting in a particular capacity for the court are referred to as 'servants'. The term is to some extent rhetorical rather than being one of art. In *Rondel* v. *Worsley*,[58]

53 Although this may be a norm of English and German civil procedure (ZPO ss. 445–51, 452, 139), it is not the case in Italy, where there appears to be no duty on the parties, their advocates or their experts to be truthful (e. g. CPC art. 87). A duty to the truth was only introduced into French civil procedure in the 1970s (CC art. 10; NCPC art. 11).

54 This extends to the parties themselves, e. g. CPR r. 1.3.

55 E.g. *Marrogi* v. *Howard* 805 S 2d 1118 (2002), at [50].

56 R. Cory-Pearce, 'The Three Princes of Serendip or the Happy Avoidance of Accidents', *Society of Expert Witnesses*, March 1998, www.sew.org.uk/dispatch/three_princes.htm (east accessed 14 December 2007); A. Head, 'The Role of an Expert Defined' (1998) 9 *Dispatches* www.sew.org.uk/dispatch/role.htm (last accessed 14 December 2007).

57 *Enfield London Borough Council* v. *Mahoney* [1983] 1 WLR 749; [1983] 2 All ER 901, at 907 (May LJ) paraphrasing (without reference) *Re Harbin and Masterman* [1896] 1 Ch 351, at 368.

58 *Rondel* v. *Worsley* [1969] 1 AC 191; [1967] 1 WLR 142; [1967] 3 WLR 1666; [1967] 3 All ER 993 (HL).

barristers were variously described as 'officers of the court',[59] but possibly not in the sense that a solicitor was,[60] or an 'officer of justice'[61] or a 'minister of justice'[62] in the same sense as the judge. In practice, experts have nothing in common with bailiffs, fines officers, the Official Receiver and the Official Solicitor, in that they are not employed by the court (and hence are not contractually 'servants').

Experts would appear to have something in common with barristers and solicitors as 'officers of the court', rather than with the existing 'servants of the court', in that they are employed by the parties, but have some form of overriding duty to the court. This takes us back, then, to saying that a party expert is akin to an advocate, in that she has a duty to do work for the client instructing her, but there are overriding normative standards relating to how she is to conduct herself before the court. For example, we might say that the expert may present her client's facts in the best light, while ensuring that that light is a reasonable one, that the court's attention is drawn to all matters adverse to her client's case, and that there is overall no attempt to mislead the court. This interpretation of CPR r. 35.3 would be at odds with Lord Woolf's idea of ending expert partisanship.

Another way in which to approach the nature of the expert's duty to the court is to say that an expert has a duty to tell the truth, in the same way that an ordinary witness of fact does. The difficulty with this solution is that the expert does not function in litigation in the same way as a witness. First, expert witnesses of opinion are paid for their services, while witnesses of fact are not. Secondly, the former are selected by the parties from outside the factual matrix of the case, and are in practice volunteers, while the latter are bound up in the factual matrix, and are as such required to attend to assist the court as fact finder. Thirdly, the nature of expert opinion evidence lends itself to a wide range of choices of what material to select, what weight to give that material, and how to interpret that material, while evidence of fact is restricted to what the witness has seen and heard. Fourthly, while counsel may not speak with a witness of fact before trial, she is free to discuss a case with an expert. Although we may choose to treat witnesses of fact and experts on the same normative basis, the circumstances in which expertise comes to be presented to the court are very different from those surrounding a non-expert witness' evidence of fact.

[59] *Rondel* (HL), at 997 (Lord Reid).
[60] Ibid., at 1032 (Lord Upjohn).
[61] *Rondel* v. *Worsley* [1967] 1 QB 443 (CA), at 470.
[62] Ibid., at 517 (Salmon LJ).

7.5.2 *The nature of the overridden obligations*

CPR r. 35.3(2) obligations may be contractual or moral. We may say that the expert has a contractual duty to provide a certain type of service to the instructing party. The precise nature of that service may be defined expressly or implicitly, and it is in the possibility of implicit terms that we encounter our main difficulties. We might reasonably infer that there is an implied term that an expert undertakes to identify those facts and valid interpretations of the facts that best suit the party's case. Since the parties are contesting their case in an adversarial framework, an expert might also reasonably feel a moral obligation to assist her party in the same way that the opposing party will be assisted by her experts. If party *A* is given every valid assistance by her expert, but party *B*'s expert insists that she will remain impartial, then party *A* may be perceived as having an unfair advantage in the adversarial contest. The extent to which an expert has scope to adapt how she presents and interprets the facts depends of course on the nature of the facts and the question before the expert. In factually complex cases involving contested scientific methodologies and theoretical frameworks, there is likely to be great scope for creativity in the presentation and interpretation of facts.

In *Cala Homes*,[63] two competing theories of the expert's obligations to her party were expressed. In 1990, Mr Goodall, an eminent architect, a Fellow of the Chartered Institute of Arbitrators and a Fellow of the Academy of Experts, had written an article in which he had set out, among other things, the appropriate approach an expert should adopt when preparing a report for use in litigation.[64] He made it clear that, since the legal system 'makes no pretence of determining the truth but seeks only to weigh the persuasive effect of arguments deployed by one adversary or the other', it is 'within the rules of our particular game' to produce reports in which material is played down or omitted in order to present a particular impression. This article would appear to have passed without legal notice until *Cala Homes*, when it was raised in cross-examination, and received judicial censure.

On the one side, Goodall proposed the view that the expert is part of the litigation team, and will do what she lawfully and ethically can to ensure her party's success. To describe such conduct as 'mercenary' may be

[63] *Cala Homes (South) Ltd* v. *Alfred MacAlpine Homes East Ltd* [1995] FSR 818 (Ch.).

[64] F. Goodall, 'The Expert Witness: Partisan with a Conscience' (1990) 56 *Journal of the Chartered Institute of Arbitrators*, quoted in *Cala Homes*, at 841–4.

unfair, since such a position does not require that the expert say whatever the party wants, but only that she seeks to present the most favourable interpretation of the facts that is also a reasonable one. This may require that the expert advances an opinion in her report and under examination with which she does not herself agree. That position is not unique, and is also one in which both lawyers in litigation and experts in the workplace may find themselves.

The opposing theory is that the expert contractually undertakes to provide an opinion, but makes no assurance that the opinion will be favourable. In assessing this theory, we must distinguish between the duty to give genuinely held advice in private and the quite separate duty to do her best to achieve an agreed goal in public. This is the key from a professional ethics stance. A professional (specialist) should think very carefully in the first place about the sort of people that they wish to work for and with.[65] From the perspective of many experts, it might seem anomalous to expect their evidence to be strictly impartial, since the expert clearly has a financial interest in the case simply by virtue of being paid by one of the parties. The scientific community is acutely aware that, where there is interest, findings should be subject to particular scrutiny. As a direct result, leading scientific journals have ethics policies on competing authorial interests.[66] One form of interest may constitute a scientist's involvement in litigation as an expert, where it may be perceived that the expert may have produced scientific research in order to benefit the effectiveness of her expert evidence.[67]

7.6 The reform of litigation privilege

Direct evidence of conscious bias in order to affect the administration of justice is rarely obtained. If this conscious bias does exist, then one of the reasons for the paucity of firm evidence for it may be that instructions and

[65] For separate reasons of public policy, English barristers are prevented from declining cases. The rule operates to protect counsel from external pressure over their choice of client, while ensuring the availability of counsel to all before the courts.

[66] E.g. 'Competing Financial Interests', www.nature.com/authors/editorial_policies/competing.html (last accessed 1 August 2008); 'Conflict of Interest Disclosure', www. sciencemag.org/feature/contribinfo/prep/coi.shtml (last accessed 1 August 2008).

[67] 'MMR doctor "to face GMC charges"' BBC News, 12 June 2006, http://news.bbc.co.uk/1/hi/health/5070670.stm (last accessed 1 August 2008). 'MMR Scare Doctor "Paid Children"', BBC News, 16 July 2007, http:// news.bbc.co.uk/1/hi/health/6289166.stm (last accessed 1 August 2008).

draft reports have been protected by litigation privilege.[68] This protects from disclosure and admission as evidence 'communications between the client and the lawyer, or between them and third parties, for the purpose of preparing for pending or contemplated legal proceedings'.[69]

The effect of litigation privilege on expert evidence is to conceal from view any expert reports which the parties have obtained, but on which they do not seek to rely (CPR rr. 31.14(2), 35.10(3)).[70] Litigation privilege does not immunize the facts on which the opinion is based from disclosure, but only the communication about those facts. It also does not prevent the opposing party from instructing the same witness, since there is no property in a witness, whether expert or lay. Legal professional privilege does not prevent a party from asking an opponent's expert, who is not called by the opponent, to give evidence about what she observed and what conclusions she drew. As Pattenden rightly notes, if the law were otherwise, a party could lock out experts from the case by consulting them, contrary to at least the spirit of CPR r. 35.3.[71]

Litigation privilege therefore provides a potential shield behind which parties can make preparations that seek to thwart some of the norms within which that litigation should be conducted, such as the 'cards on the table' ethos of the CPR,[72] and the overriding duty of the expert to the court. The CPR has slightly amended this privilege, in that it now requires disclosure of those 'material' instructions on the basis of which the expert's disclosed report was written (CPR r. 35.10(3)). There remains of course some discretion on the parts of the party and of the expert as to what instructions should be considered material.[73] Although the court and other parties see the final expert report on which the party seeks to rely, they do not see the reports that were rejected because they were unfavourable, or the correspondence with experts about possible amendments to reports. If we were to attempt to address expert bias by focusing on actual rather than presumed or apparent bias, then we would

[68] R. Pattenden, 'Litigation Privilege and Expert Opinion Evidence' (2000) 4 *Evidence and Proof* 213–45

[69] Zuckerman, *Civil Procedure*, p. 612.

[70] *Alan Jackson* v. *Marley Davenport Ltd* [2004] EWCA Civ 1225; [2004] 1 WLR 2926.

[71] Pattenden, 'Litigation Privilege', 223.

[72] *Three Rivers DC* v. *Governor and Company of the Bank of England* [2004] UKHL 48; [2005] 1 AC 610; [2004] 3 WLR 1274; [2005] 4 All ER 948, at [53] (Lord Scott, Lord Rodger concurring).

[73] A party is currently only entitled to obtain full disclosure of instructions where there is reason to suppose that the expert has not accurately disclosed the nature of those instructions: *Alan Jackson* v. *Marley Davenport*.

need access to evidence that is mostly now hidden from us. The leading examples of conscious expert bias in England in recent times come from cases where there was documentary evidence either of the amendment of expert opinions to suit the party's case,[74] or of the expert's perception of his role as an advocate.[75] If we take litigation privilege to be incompatible with the basic norms of the CPR, then is there scope to amend the application of litigation privilege in relation to civil expert reports? A starting point might be to argue that litigation privilege is fundamentally tied to the adversarial nature of proceedings, and so, where proceedings are not adversarial, we might reasonably expect the privilege to cease to apply. Authority for this comes from three areas of non-adversarial proceedings: Family, asylum and Coroner's hearings.[76]

In relation to Family proceedings, the House of Lords held in *Re L (a minor)*,[77] that there is no litigation privilege for reports obtained for the purpose of wardship and care proceedings, where the reports could not have been prepared had the Family court not given leave for papers to be shown to the expert.[78] The majority of their Lordships explained this by saying that care proceedings were non-adversarial and investigative in nature, and so a rule designed to facilitate the adversarial process was out of place. Lord Nicholls, dissenting, noted that some aspects of care proceedings are adversarial, and the relevant explaining factor is instead the paramount concern of the court, as *parens patriae*, to advance the best interests of the child. Similarly, in the asylum case of *ex parte Gashi*,[79] Thorpe LJ said, *obiter*, that in a field of litigation that is not purely adversarial and in which the court has an overriding obligation to promote a welfare consideration, litigation privilege does not allow a party to the litigation to refuse the production of any expert report that has been obtained for the purposes of the case.[80] It was 'at the very least arguable' that that principle would apply in an asylum case.

[74] *Whitehouse* v. *Jordan*; *Vernon* v. *Bosley (No. 2)*, in which the evidence of bias was improperly obtained.

[75] *Cala Homes.*

[76] *R.* v. *HM Coroner for Inner North London District* ex p. *Gregory Linnane (No. 2)* (1991) 155 JP 343 (DC).

[77] *Re L (a minor)* [1996] 2 WLR 395; [1996] 2 All ER 78.

[78] Family Proceedings Rules 1991 (SI 1991/1247), r. 4.23.

[79] *R.* v. *Secretary of State for the Home Dept* ex p. *Gashi* [1999] INLR 276 (CA), at 308.

[80] As in *Re L.*

While the Crown appears able to remove its subject's litigation privilege, for example when it acts as *parens patriae* or conducts an inquest, it bars itself from relying on litigation privilege where this might result in a miscarriage of justice. In a criminal trial, the prosecution is under an obligation, at common law,[81] under statute[82] and under the European Convention[83] to disclose to the defence all unused material, including expert material, which might undermine the prosecution case or assist the defence. The primary policy justification for this absence of litigation privilege for the Crown is that the huge inequality of resources between Crown and defence requires some effort by the Crown to level the playing field, so as to reduce the risk of a miscarriage of justice. There is, however, an underlying policy consideration that the Crown's interest in criminal proceedings is that the defendant is convicted, and the innocent protected.[84] The court and the Crown have a duty to protect the innocent accused in criminal matters,[85] and counsel for the Crown must act with restraint as ministers of justice.[86] In those matters where the Crown has a direct interest in the ascertainment of truth, therefore, the courts have not provided, or have withdrawn, litigation privilege.[87]

Although the House of Lords has hinted that litigation privilege is ripe for reform in the civil litigation environment created by the CPR,[88] the recent decisions by the Court of Appeal in relation to expert bias and litigation privilege have failed to adopt a common principled approach, although the decisions are not strictly inconsistent with one

81 *R.* v. *McIlkenny* [1992] 2 All ER 417, at 426.

82 Criminal Procedure and Investigations Act 1996, s. 3(1).

83 *Edwards* v. *UK* (1992) 15 EHRR 417, at 432.

84 *R.* v. *Stinchcombe* (1991) CCC (3rd ser.) 1, at 7 (Soprinka J) approved by the House of Lords in *R.* v. *Mills* [1998] AC 382, at 403; [1997] 3 WLR 458; [1997] 3 All ER 780. Criminal Procedure Rules 2005, r. 1.1(2)(a) "Dealing with a criminal case justly includes acquitting the innocent and convicting the guilty."

85 J. Langbein, *The Origins of the Adversary Criminal Trial* (Oxford: Oxford University Press, 2003), p. 16.

86 P. Roberts and A. Zuckerman, *Criminal Evidence* (Oxford: Oxford University Press, 2004), p. 57

87 Litigation privilege also does not apply to communications between the police and the crown prosecution service ('CPS'), since the police submit material to the CPS to enable them to conduct the case, and not for legal advice. Thus the framework for litigation privilege in *Waugh v British Railways Board* [1980] AC 521, at 541–2; [1979] 3 WLR 150; [1979] 2 All ER 1169 (Lord Edmund-Davies) is not present. These communications may, however, be subject to public interest immunity, which does not provide the absolute shield that litigation privilege does.

88 *Three Rivers DC*, at [29] (Lord Scott), at [53] (Lord Rodger).

another.[89] In *Alan Jackson* v. *Marley Davenport Ltd*, the Court of Appeal held that CPR r. 35.10(3) could only properly be invoked to require full disclosure where there was reason to suppose that the expert had not reasonably complied with the requirement that all material instructions be disclosed.[90] In addition, legal professional privilege protected communications between expert and instructing solicitors. Although CPR r. 35.10(4) provided that instructions to experts are not privileged, r. 35.10 as a whole refers only to 'the expert's intended evidence, and not to earlier and privileged drafts of what may or may not in due course become the expert's evidence'.[91] Any further limitation to privilege, the Court of Appeal held, should be expressly stated by the CPR and should not be inferred by the courts.

There are at least two difficulties with this approach. The first is that it draws an artificial distinction between 'instructions' and other reports made by lawyers to experts, which may also have materially affected the substance of the expert's report. The second is that the expert not only provides advice on the construction of a case, but is involved in the construction of evidence in the form of her report. Longmore LJ recognized in his judgment that drafts of expert reports are circulated among a party's legal team, and therefore, implicitly, that lawyers are able to affect the content of a report. This may be in terms of either the substance, or the manner of presentation. This construction of evidence is very different from enabling the open exchange of information and advice between lawyer and client that litigation privilege is intended to provide, unless of course we depart from the CPR and allow that an expert acts for the client as an advocate.

While strictly consistent with *Jackson*, the Court of Appeal in *Beck* v. *Ministry of Defence*,[92] and in *Hajigeorgiou* v. *Vasiliou*,[93] took a different, and more creative, approach to restricting the parties' ability to create structurally biased evidence. In *Beck*, the defendant sought permission to appoint a second expert psychiatrist, claiming that the report of the first expert was of poor quality. The Court of Appeal upheld the decision of the district judge to grant the application without requiring disclosure

89 See also A. Zuckerman, 'Disclosure of Expert Reports' (2005) 24 *Civil Justice Quarterly* 293–7.

90 See also *Lucas* v. *Barking Havering and Redbridge Hospitals NHS Trust* [2003] EWCA Civ 1102 [34] on what materials might constitute 'instructions' to an expert.

91 *Jackson* v. *Marley Davenport*, at [14].

92 *Beck* v. *Ministry of Defence* [2003] EWCA Civ 1043; [2005] 1 WLR 2206.

93 *Hajigeorgiou* v. *Vasiliou* [2005] EWCA Civ 236; [2005] 1 WLR 2195, at [29].

of the first expert's report, saying that it would be unfair to require the defendants to disclose the first expert's report in order for the court to consider the application for a second expert, since, if the application were refused, the defendant might be forced to rely on an expert report against which it had previously made adverse submissions. It would, however, be reasonable, and in line with *Lane* v. *Willis*,[94] to require that the first expert report be disclosed as a condition of permission being granted for the second expert to be appointed. In *Lane*, Sachs LJ noted that an order for a medical examination is an invasion of personal liberty. It should therefore only be granted when it is reasonable in the interests of justice to do so. In particular, such medical evidence as the applicant party had already obtained should be produced so as to restrict expert shopping.

In *Hajigeorgiou*, the Court of Appeal held that the defendant was entitled to appoint a second expert without disclosing the first expert's report, since the order granting permission for each party to appoint one expert,[95] which had been settled by counsel,[96] had not specified a named expert, even though the defendant's solicitors had made it clear in applying for that order that they intended to appoint a Mr Watson, and had adduced evidence of his suitability. Further, CPR r. 35.4 did not restrict the right of the parties to instruct experts, but only to 'call' an expert or 'put in evidence an expert's report'. Dyson LJ, giving the judgment of the court, declined to extend the rule in *Lane*, holding that a restaurant inspection, as in *Hajigeorgiou*, could not be likened to a medical examination. To provide guidance in future similar cases, the Court of Appeal further held that, if permission to appoint a second expert were to be required, then the first expert report should be disclosed, following *Beck*.[97]

This decision is problematic, in that Dyson LJ did not consider that this approach was 'abrogating or emasculating' privilege in any way.[98] He cites the authority of *Jackson*, that all documents produced by an expert with a view to litigation are privileged unless and until they are disclosed. Her instructions, however, are not privileged (CPR r. 35.10(4)). It is misleading though to say, as Dyson LJ does, that a party is 'merely' required to waive privilege as a condition of instructing a subsequent expert.[99] The effect of this approach, also taken in *Beck*, is to restrict privilege where it might be used to shield an abuse of the litigation process, through the instruction of multiple experts until a satisfactory one is identified. Dyson LJ also

[94] *Lane* v. *Willis* [1972] 1 WLR 326; [1972] 1 All ER 430. [95] *Hajigeorgiou*, at [16].
[96] *Bristol-Myers Squibb* v. *Baker Norton Pharmaceuticals* [2001] EWCA Civ 414.
[97] *Hajigeorgiou*, at [27]. [98] Ibid., at [29]. [99] *Hajigeorgiou*, at [29].

proposes that this waiver should extend to all reports prepared by the first expert containing the substance of his or her opinion.[100] This appears to go beyond what was intended in *Jackson*: that only the final report is in issue in discussions over disclosure.

The limits on expert shopping imposed by *Hajigeorgiou* remain only partial, where the court has knowledge of previous experts through the case management process. Where an expert does not require contact with the opposing party, the instructing party remains free to instruct a number of experts prior to the case management stage, and to obtain a number of privileged reports, in order to identify the most favourable opinion. A clear policy statement is required on the extent to which expert shopping and the amendment of expert reports by legal teams is permissible, and on what steps are permissible to control or prevent such conduct. Possible steps might include requiring parties to disclose the names of all experts consulted in a case, or to give judicial discretion to order the disclosure of all correspondence between party andexpert.

7.7 Criminal, civil and professional sanctions

If there are reasonable grounds to believe that there has been actual bias on the part of an expert, then what is to be done? In relation to the instant case, the court needs to consider whether such evidence should be ruled inadmissible or else given no weight. Beyond the instant case, then there are potential remedies, criminal and civil, both against the expert herself and, potentially, against the party instructing her and the legal team.

7.7.1 Criminal sanctions

7.7.1.1 Perjury

If a witness, including an expert, lies under oath, then criminal sanctions are available for perjury.[101] The Perjury Act 1911, s. 13, sets a high evidential threshold, that perjury requires the corroboration of two witnesses. The court may be slow to prosecute witnesses for perjury,[102] preferring

[100] Ibid., at [30].

[101] Perjury Act 1911 s. 1(1). On possible reforms to the law on perjury, see Roberts and Zuckerman, *Criminal Evidence*, p. 470.

[102] *R.* v. *Davies* (1974) Cr App R 311 (CA), at 313 (Roskill LJ). There are approximately 200 cautions or convictions a year: K. Soothill, 'Perjury and False Statements: A Criminal Profile of Persons Convicted 1979–2001 '[2004] *Criminal Law Review* 926–35.

instead to ignore their testimony, but prosecutions of experts for perjury are virtually unknown. The difficulty is that it is a moot point whether the phrase 'knows to be false or does not believe to be true', used in s. 1 of the Perjury Act 1911, extends to an opinion. The second of Coke's three reasons for the inadmissibility of opinion as evidence, given in *Adams* v. *Canon* in 1621, was that a witness cannot be prosecuted for perjury for merely giving an opinion.[103] However, as Lord Mansfield was to point out a century and a half later, it was not only accepted practice that evidence of opinion on handwriting was admissible, but 'for false evidence on such questions a man may be indicted for perjury'.[104]

From a subjective angle, an expert can give an opinion that falls within the range of possible opinions that a reasonable expert might give, while not herself believing that that is the correct opinion. The expert therefore does not believe her opinion to be true, but she is also aware that it would be difficult to prove that it was actually false. Even if we could show that the content of the opinion was objectively false (for example, the expert says that an injury was caused by one scenario and CCTV footage then shows that it was a different scenario), the expert is required subjectively to believe the opinion to be false. We would therefore require proof that the expert knew that she was giving an opinion in which she did not herself believe. The most likely route by which such evidence would be obtained would be through litigation-related correspondence with the expert, which would in most circumstances only be obtainable if litigation privilege were to be removed. Under current arrangements, the prosecution of an expert for perjury is therefore very unlikely to arise.

7.7.1.2 Perverting the course of justice

Perverting the course of justice is an offence at common law, carrying a maximum penalty of life imprisonment.[105] It is now clear both that conduct in a civil trial can amount to perverting the course of justice,[106] and that witnesses as well as parties can be found guilty of the offence.[107] Such a prosecution would probably require that the expert had agreed with the party or an associated lawyer to give false evidence, or consciously to

103 *Adams* v. *Canon* (1621) Dyer 53b n 15. The other two were that the judge must give sentence on the basis of more sure ground than thinking, and judges must give judgment on what has been alleged and proven.

104 *Folkes* v. *Chadd* (1782) 3 Doug 152, at 159; 99 ER 589

105 S. Edwards, 'Perjury and Perverting the Course of Justice Considered' [2003] *Criminal Law Review* 525–40.

106 *R.* v. *Archer* [2002] EWCA Crim 1996.

107 *R.* v. *Bassi* [1985] Crim LR 671.

fabricate or destroy evidence. Perverting the course of justice is of course a charge that could be brought not only against the expert but potentially against all those, including party, solicitors and counsel, who had acted towards the perversion.

7.7.2 Civil sanctions

An alternative to criminal prosecution is for a party, on the basis of reasonable evidence, to bring an action against a biased expert, and potentially against any colluding party or member of the legal team, for wasted time and cost, for example in considering how to respond to the opinion of a biased expert, and in implementing that response.[108] The principle behind the decision in *Phillips* is surely sound, that, since a party has incurred unnecessary costs as the result of an expert's breach of her CPR r. 35.3 duty to the court, whether that breach was negligent or intentional, then the party should be entitled to recover from the expert.[109] Although the situation does not arise on the facts of this case, the party might presumably also seek to recover from the instructing party, where that party knew of the expert's bias or negligence.

However, the courts have also been keen to protect experts from civil litigation that might otherwise deter them from undertaking work as experts. Thus in *Stanton* v. *Callaghan*,[110] which concerned the immunity of an expert structural engineer who was said to have produced his report negligently, the Court of Appeal held that there were clear public policy reasons to protect experts, in both civil and criminal cases, from civil suit, in the same way that other witnesses were protected, lest witnesses be inhibited from giving frank and fearless evidence.[111] In *Meadow* v. *General Medical Council*,[112] Collins J emphasized that this immunity applies to the dishonest as much as to the honest witness. The correct response to false evidence is therefore through the criminal courts. The decision in *Meadow*

[108] *Phillips* v. *Symes (a bankrupt)* [2004] EWHC 2329 (Ch.). No such action appears to have been brought in relation to the *Phillips* litigation.

[109] See also the Civil Justice Council's *Protocol for the Instruction of Experts to Give Evidence in Civil Claims* (London: 2005), [4.7], for an expectation that the approach in *Phillips* will be taken as a standard approach to experts who breach their duty to the court.

[110] *Stanton* v. *Callaghan* [2000] QB 75; [1999] 2 WLR 745; [1998] 4 All ER 961 (CA).

[111] Ibid., at 109 (Nourse LJ).

[112] *Meadow* v. *General Medical Council* [2006] EWHC 146 (Admin.), at [14]–[16]; [2006] 1 WLR 1452; [2006] 2 All ER 329.

is likely, in effect, to prevent actions against experts for false or negligent testimony. It shows that expert immunity has survived the decision on *Arthur J. S. Hall* v. *Simons* that the immunity of advocates from suit should be abolished.[113]

7.7.3 Disciplinary sanctions

7.7.3.1 Professional misconduct

An alternative approach, adopted in *Pearce* v. *Ove Arup*,[114] is for the expert to be referred to her professional body. In *Pearce*, Jacob J dismissed an action for architectural plagiarism as being 'one of pure fantasy – preposterous fantasy at that'.[115] Particular criticism was made of the claimant's architectural expert, Mr Wilkey, who had failed in his duty to the court, since his evidence was 'so biased and irrational'.[116] In the absence of any rule dealing with breach of the CPR r. 35.3 duty, and in the absence of an official scheme of expert accreditation, Jacob J directed that a copy of his judgment should be sent to Wilkey's professional body, the Royal Institute of British Architects. This approach carried a risk, that the expert's professional body might disagree with the trial judge about the expert's conduct, and that risk materialized in Wilkey's case. In February 2003, Mr Wilkey appeared before the Professional Conduct Committee of the Architect's Registration Board.[117] He was cleared of charges of unacceptable professional conduct and of serious professional misconduct. With hindsight, the Committee held, Wilkey might have made the nature of his investigations and his instructions clearer in his written report, and might have answered some questions in cross-examination more clearly. It was agreed that 'an architect acting reasonably could have found similarities in the drawings'.

A different course of events has unfolded in relation to a complaint for professional misconduct against Professor Sir Roy Meadow by Sally Clark.[118] Following her acquittal by the Court of Appeal,[119] Clark brought

[113] *Arthur J. S. Hall* v. *Simons* [2002] 1 AC 615; [2000] 3 WLR 543; [2000] 3 All ER 673 (HL).

[114] *Pearce* v. *Ove Arup Partnership Ltd (Copying)*, Chancery Division, 2 November 2001.

[115] Ibid., at [2]. [116] Ibid., at [59].

[117] *Re Michael Wilkey*, Architects Registration Board, 5 February 2003.

[118] It is important to note that the allegation against Williams and Meadow was that they had been negligent rather than had acted with ill will.

[119] *R.* v. *Clark (Sally) (No. 2)* [2003] EWCA Crim 1020 (CA). D. Dwyer, 'The Duties of Expert Witnesses of Fact and Opinion' (2003) 7 *Evidence and Proof* 264–9.

actions for professional misconduct against both Dr Williams and Professor Meadow. On 3 June 2005, the General Medical Council ('GMC') found Dr Williams guilty of serious professional misconduct in the *Clark* case, and banned him from work as an expert for three years.[120] In July 2005, the GMC similarly found against Professor Meadow, and ordered that his name be erased from ('struck off') the register of medical practitioners. Meadow was some seventy-two years old at the time of this decision, and had retired from clinical practice. The GMC's decision would appear to have been motivated by a desire to protect the reputation of the medical profession. Meadow's conduct in the *Clark* trial had become infamous in the United Kingdom, although, on appeal to the High Court, Collins J questioned whether that infamy was justified. The decision of the GMC was reversed in the High Court on the basis that it was in the public interest that witnesses, including experts, should not be deterred from giving evidence for fear of civil litigation. At least in part, the court was motivated by concern that there was increasing difficulty in getting paediatricians to appear as experts, following the *Clark* case. Collins J did qualify this protection in two important regards. The first was that the expert 'will not expect to receive protection if he is dishonest or malicious or deliberately misleading'.[121] The second was that it should remain open to the trial judge, as in *Pearce*, to refer the matter herself to a professional body. The decision of the High Court was overturned in the Court of Appeal, however.[122] There, a distinction was drawn between civil actions, which are remedial, and professional conduct actions relating to fitness to practise, which are prospective. While the purpose of the former is to provide remedies for past wrongdoing, the purpose of the latter is solely to protect the public from inappropriate professional conduct. Professional bodies deciding on a member's fitness to practise should therefore not be bound to consider the principle of witness immunity.

7.7.3.2 Expert regulation

There is currently no official system for the registration or accreditation of experts in England and Wales. If such a system were in place, it

[120] 'Court Work Ban for Clark Doctor' BBC News 3 June 2005, http://news.bbc.co.uk/1/hi/health/4595839.stm (last accessed 1 August 2008).

[121] *Meadow* (Admin.), at [20].

[122] *Meadow* v. *General Medical Council* [2006] EWCA Civ 1390; [2007] QB 462; [2007] 2 WLR 286; [2007] 1 All ER 1. D. Dwyer, 'Legal Remedies for the Negligent Expert' (2008) 12 *Evidence and Proof* 93–115.

would be possible for judges to refer expert misconduct, including alleged bias, to this body for consideration of breach of the specific duty of an expert, rather than to the specialist's body for consideration of professional conduct. Auld LJ's *Review of the Criminal Courts*,[123] like the Runciman Commission before it, recommended that a central expert professional body be created, to oversee matters such as accreditation, performance evaluation and training. Auld proposed the merger of the existing expert bodies, i.e. the Academy of Experts, Expert Witness Institute, Society of Expert Witnesses, Forensic Science Society, and Council for the Registration of Forensic Practitioners.[124] That proposal has been resisted by the bodies themselves.[125] One advantage of a regulatory body for experts, such as the Council for the Registration of Forensic Practitioners, is that it would be more straightforward for the courts to initiate action to have an individual de-registered as an expert while retaining the right to practice professionally, than it would be for the court to refer the expert back to their professional body. In particular, such an approach would remove the complication that a perfectly competent professional can make an incompetent expert, and it would be inequitable to deprive the professional of her livelihood, and potentially society of her services, solely because she is unable to act responsibly in a secondary capacity as an expert.

7.8 Conclusion

The procedural devices that one might employ to address expert bias depend very much on two things: the role that one expects the expert to play in civil litigation, and the types of bias that one considers most

[123] R. Auld, *Review of the Criminal Courts of England and Wales* (London: Her Majesty's Stationery Office, 2001), p. 572, [11.130].

[124] These bodies do not all serve the same function, and so merger is unlikely to occur. The first three are trade protection bodies. The Forensic Science Society is a scientific body whose members practise one kind of science which brings them into contact with the courts. The Council for the Registration of Forensic Practitioners is a voluntary body, intended to accredit all those whose forensic work provides the courts with specialist expertise and opinion evidence: E. Ebsworth, 'Accreditation: A Novel Approach', in L. Blom-Cooper (ed.), *Experts in the Civil Courts* (Oxford: Oxford University Press, 2006), pp. 17–28.

[125] Comments on the Auld Report received by the Department for Constitutional Affairs from the Expert Witness Institute (www.dca.gov.uk/criminal/auldcom/op/op1.htm) and Council for the Registration of Forensic Practitioners (www.dca.gov.uk/criminal/auldcom/op/op2.htm) (last accessed 1 August 2008).

damaging to the court's ability to determine the facts accurately. The second of these may in turn depend on the type of question that the expert is addressing. This is an example of an occasion when the obvious answer is not wrong. If we expect the expert to act alone, or in a team, as a direct or indirect servant of the court, then discussion of litigation privilege is inappropriate, and inadmissibility rules are probably misplaced. Conversely, it would be difficult to justify simultaneously saying that the expert is part of the party's advocacy team, as in the United States or Italy, and then discussing the use of single experts, recusal or even, realistically, the expert's duty to the court. Courts in the United States may express the view that an expert's professional duty is not to the party that pays her, but to the court and to the truth-finding process of the trial,[126] but this norm is lost behind the much more pervasive and powerfully pursued norm of litigation pugnacity.

The significant difficulties that may be encountered in proving that expertise is biased to the point of being unreliable or even untrue impede the effectiveness of many of the approaches to bias. The evidential difficulties with *Daubert* are renowned, but there are also significant evidential difficulties with any of the penalties discussed in Section 7.7. If experts are not prosecuted for perjury, or brought before a professional conduct hearing, for example, it is because it is very difficult to prove that the opinion presented by the expert was not her genuine opinion, or else that she was reckless in forming that opinion. As the cases of *Wilkey* (following *Pearce* v. *Ove Arup*) and *Meadow* (following *R.* v. *Clark (Sally)*) have shown, the question of whether the substance of an expert's opinion was reasonable is open to wide interpretation, and may result in dispute between the courts and the relevant professional body. The removal of adversarial devices such as litigation privilege would assist in detecting such biases, since the court and opposing parties would at least in principle have access to the expert's *travaux préparatoires*, which might show how expert opinions changed to better assist the case of the instructing party. Techniques such as presumptive recusal and the overriding objective may be effective precisely because there is little or no evidential element in their operation.

The final point to draw out from this conclusion is to reiterate that expert bias is neither amorphous nor inevitable. I proposed in Section 3.6 that we can break bias down into a number of constituent elements,

[126] Bernstein, 'Expert Witnesses', fn. 13.

a taxonomy of bias, and I have similarly proposed in this chapter, building on Chapter 6, that the detail of the way in which we construct our procedural provisions for expert evidence can be effective in reducing the opportunities for certain types of bias to arise. It is unlikely that a civil procedure could be developed that would eliminate all forms of expert bias, and so it is important to prioritize the forms that most offend against one's concept of due process.

CONCLUSION

> Let there be no mistake. As science continues to change the social world, great transformations of social enquiry lie ahead for all justice systems. These transformations could turn out to be as momentous as those that occurred in the twilight of the Middle Ages, when magical forms of proof retreated before the prototypes of our present evidentiary technology.[1]

In this book I have sought to address two fundamental questions about the judicial assessment of expert evidence. First, how can a non-specialist court accurately determine facts that require specialist knowledge? This includes the subsidiary question of how, if a specialist advises the court, the non-specialist court can know whether to accept the advice? Secondly, how should we arrange our legal processes to best support our expectations of accurate fact determination, and other procedural goals, arising in whole or in part from expert evidence? Broadly, the first question has been addressed in Chapters 1 to 3, and the second question in Chapters 4 to 7. But the first question cannot be properly answered without an answer to the second, and vice versa. There are two integrating themes that have helped to define the approach taken in this book. The first has been an attempt to begin to re-integrate legal evidence theory with classical epistemology. The second has been an attempt to begin to re-integrate the study of evidence with that of procedure. Although these fundamental questions are ultimately questions of applied philosophy, it becomes apparent that they are not pure questions of epistemology. Running throughout this analysis has been a reference back to the values that are embodied in the fact-finding processes of a legal system. This is most clearly expressed in Chapter 4, but we can also see this reference to values elsewhere, beginning in Chapter 1 with how we select the basis of generalizations and meta-justification, and ending in Chapter 7 with

[1] M. Damaška, *Evidence Law Adrift* (New Haven CT: Yale University Press, 1997), p. 151.

how we ought to resolve conflicting judgments about acceptable expert conduct.

1 Specialist knowledge and non-specialist courts

Our starting question, of how a non-specialist court can accurately determine facts that require specialist knowledge, turns out, on more careful analysis, to be a misleading one, in at least four ways. First, any court that involves lawyers is in a strict sense a 'specialist' court, since lawyers are specialists in dealing with both normative and factual questions in a 'legal' fashion. So when we talk about 'specialist' in this context, what we are perhaps really intending to refer to is an understanding of our approach to factual questions that is neither legal nor one that is broadly 'common-sense' (by which I mean an approach or understanding held commonly in society). It is tempting to say that 'specialist' is a synonym for 'scientific', but this in turn of course begs the question, raised in Chapter 3, of what exactly we might mean by 'scientific'. The second way in which the question is misleading is that we are talking about 'knowledge'. There appears to be a tendency in legal, particularly socio-legal, studies of expertise to talk about 'knowledge' in very loose terms,[2] while in philosophy 'knowledge' is a term of art.[3] What our question refers to is usually not 'specialist knowledge' per se but rather the considered opinions of those with experience of and/or learning about a collection of factual propositions (including probabilistic generalizations) not commonly available, and techniques for investigating facts not commonly in use. The third way in which the question is misleading is that the facts do not require specialist knowledge, but rather we have chosen to apply certain propositions, generalizations, methods to certain types of facts. This is a meta-justificatory issue. It may be that we can resolve the factual issues using only common-sense propositions and methods, or a combination of the common-sense and the specialist. The fourth way in which the question is misleading is that it suggests that the factual issue in question can be resolved in isolation, while the approach proposed in Chapters 1

[2] E.g. D. Nelken, 'Law and Knowledge / Law as Knowledge' (2006) 15 *Social Legal Studies* 570–3; W. Twining, 'Some Scepticism About Some Scepticisms', in *Rethinking Evidence: Exploratory Essays*, 2nd edn (Cambridge: Cambridge University Press, 2006), pp. 99–164, pp. 120–2.

[3] E.g. E. Gettier, 'Is Justified True Belief Knowledge?' (1963) 23 *Analysis* 121–3; T. Williamson, *Knowledge and its Limits* (Oxford: Oxford University Press, 2000).

and 2 is for questions involving expert evidence to be resolved within the context of the evidential matrix of the case as a whole.

Socio-legal studies of the assessment of expert evidence often tend to present a dichotomy between the legal and the expert view(s) of the world (such as the reified 'science' or 'medicine'). Thus the problem readily arises of how 'law' understands the propositions of 'science', and incorporates these into its own view of the world. In the more extreme forms of this approach, law and science become incommensurable. We saw this, for example, in Section 2.5 in relation to attempts to apply autopoietic systems theory to expert evidence. But this conception of a fragmentation of knowledge, and perhaps of rationality itself, is erroneous. The functional specialization of factual beliefs and methodologies within and across disciplines need not take us away from a commonality that underlies these disciplines. So the various forms of expert evidence are merely forms of evidence that rely on specialist beliefs and methodologies, and the way in which the courts assess expert evidence is the same as the way in which they assess 'ordinary' evidence: the same, but different. Different in the sense that different generalizations and methodologies are applied. So a question such as 'Can the courts assess expert evidence?' is fundamentally just a variant of the question 'Can the courts assess evidence in general?' The answer to the latter is generally agreed to be 'yes'. If it were not, we must question why we bother with evidence at all. It is, however, an important variant, to the extent that I would suggest that the court's epistemic competence to assess expert evidence is likely to be more limited than that available to the court to assess evidence generally. Hence the concept, introduced in Chapter 2, of 'limited epistemic competence'.

The court's difficulties in assessing expert evidence are most apparent when it comes to deciding between two or more expert opinions. Whereas with a single expert the court might delegate its fact-finding responsibilities de facto to the expert, this obviously cannot happen where there is a choice of experts and opinions. We might therefore suspect that enthusiasm for a single expert report is an enthusiasm for delegation. But the analysis that was undertaken in Chapter 3, on the nature of expert disagreement, suggests that the picture is in fact more complex, for three reasons in particular. The first is that disagreement as to the correct interpretation of facts in a specific case is to be expected in a wide range of disciplines. This is particularly true where the discipline does not normally address the questions that the forensic process may ask; for example medical doctors are usually more concerned with questions of identification and treatment of a condition than with questions of causation. The second reason is that it is not agreed among philosophers, particularly philosophers of science, that there can be a uniquely epistemologically correct account of facts or events (separate from the question of whether there can be a uniquely ontologically correct account). A realist account has been adopted in the present work, which allows us to say that we can determine which account is most warranted by the available evidence. The third reason is that, even if we accept a realist account, we have to allow that, at any given point in time, our theoretical account of the world may not be complete. While the hypotheses of scientists or engineers can be revisited with the benefit of further experience, the decision of the court is final.

It might therefore be tempting to say that, if two experts can genuinely disagree about a set of facts – even without the further complicating factors relating to bias that may arise in litigation – and produce two valid opinions, then it would be simpler just to pick one expert, for example by tossing a coin. But such a solution would be reprehensible, both on moral grounds (disputes between people should be determined through the application of reason and not as a game of chance) and as epistemologically incomplete. We can go back to the idea of the evidential matrix of the case. Although it may not be possible to decide between the opinions of two experts taken in isolation, the court is actually considering the expert opinions in a much wider context, and one opinion may fit with the other available evidence better than the other opinion.

Expert bias is not solely the product of an adversarial mode of litigation. Indeed, a careful analysis of the concept of expert bias (Section 3.6) indicates that much of the bias ascribed to experts may arise directly from the conduct of the litigants, in the way that experts are chosen ('expert shopping'), rather than from the attitude of the experts themselves. But expert bias may nevertheless arise through pre-dispositions in relation to the case, or interests in the outcome of the case. This is as true for single experts as it is for party experts, and indeed the dangers may be greater where only a single expert is used because the effects of the biases may be harder to detect. Such biases are not unique to the legal process; they can be found, for example, in communities of scientific research.

2 Arranging legal processes to best support accurate fact determination

So with this understanding of the nature of the court's limited epistemic competence, and of the nature of expert disagreement and bias, what can we do with our second question? How should we arrange our legal processes to best support our expectations of accurate fact determination, and other procedural goals, arising in whole or in part from expert evidence? Unfortunately, this is not as simple as a question such as 'Should we have court experts or party experts?' This is for three reasons. The first is that we have expectations about the use of expert evidence in civil litigation that sit alongside the goal of accurate fact determination. Some of the main expectations were examined in Chapter 4. The second reason is that simple high-level concepts such as 'court expert' and 'party expert' carry with them a lot of procedural detail, which is not immediately visible. So, for example, we must consider the ways in which experts are selected and instructed, how and when their opinions are presented to opponents and to the court, and how they may be challenged. France, the United States and, until recently, England all have a concept of a 'court expert', but the title means different things in different places, and at different points in history. Taking England as a detailed case study, Chapters 5 and 6 began to unpick some of this procedural detail, and look at how procedural options can be combined together in a variety of ways. The third reason is that there may be non-epistemological advantages and disadvantages to each of the procedural options, and the choice of the procedural approach to be taken is therefore likely to depend to a large extent on these non-epistemological factors. An example of this was provided in Chapter 7, when a number of approaches to managing expert bias were examined.

3 The foundational norms of evidence law

There have been a number of points in this book where legal philosophy has come to an end, and the questions have moved towards political philosophy, which is outside the scope of the present work. For example, should we accept a rationalist meta-justificatory approach to legal fact determination? Should courts be allowed to delegate fact finding to experts? Should we use specialist or common-sense generalizations in fact finding? Should we accept the decision of a court or that of a professional body in deciding whether an expert's conduct in court has been culpable? All four of these questions are political, in the sense that they require decisions of policy rather than law. They are all of constitutional significance, because they go to the heart of the nature of the courts' role in resolving disputes in society.

Currently the first two of these questions are effectively settled. Our principles of fact determination should follow the Rationalist Tradition, and our courts should not delegate fact finding to experts. These answers generally hold for civil evidence across the western legal tradition. But the second two questions are not as satisfactorily answered. At least in the Anglo-American legal world, the choice between common-sense and specialist generalizations varies depending on the subject matter and the jurisdiction. Since the late 1970s, the main areas of contention have concerned the authority of expert evidence in relation to states of mind and behaviour, in both criminal and civil proceedings.[4] The balance of power between the courts and specialist/professional institutions remains largely unresolved, but the problem is not insoluble.

In 2001, the then Lord Chief Justice, Lord Woolf, indicated that the English courts would no longer be as deferential to medical opinion as may previously have been the case.[5] However, to show less deference is not the same as to show no deference. For example, in relation to an appeal from a decision of the Fitness to Practise Panel of the General Medical Council, Davis J held in *Williams* v. *General Medical Council* that:

> On any view, it is clear, and as is confirmed by authority, that a degree of respect should be shown to a specialist panel such as the present as being representative of the profession and as being there to uphold medical standards: particularly where an evaluative finding of serious professional misconduct is made or a particular sanction imposed.[6]

At the root of these four questions of political philosophy lie two evidential foundational norms, which exist prior to legal philosophy: first, the basis on which factual disputes will be resolved in law; secondly, whether these disputes should be resolved by a court of law or by another person or institution deemed better able to arrive at an accurate determination. In relation to the first foundational norm, we might like to think that history has brought us to a stage in which the Rationalist Tradition has, at least in general terms, prevailed. This prevalence is not, however, unassailable. There are people, openly in academia but also elsewhere in society, who believe that there is no such thing as truth, and that rhetoric prevails

[4] E.g. *R.* v. *Turner* [1975] QB 834; 60 Cr App R 80; R. Mackay and A. Colman, 'Equivocal Rulings on Expert Psychological and Psychiatric Evidence: Turning a Muddle into a Nonsense' [1996] *Criminal Law Review* 88–95; N. Vidmar and R. Schuller, 'Juries and Expert Evidence: Social Framework Testimony' (1989) 52 *Law and Contemporary Problems* 133–76.

[5] Lord Woolf, 'Are the Courts Excessively Deferential to the Medical Profession?' (2001) 9 *Medical Law Review* 1–16.

[6] *Williams* v. *General Medical Council* [2007] EWHC 2603 (Admin.), at [13].

over facts.[7] Truth and knowledge (usually in this usage appearing in scare quotes) are thus produced through some form of social negotiation, as a mere fiction.[8]

In relation to the second foundational norm, whether disputes should be resolved by a court or an expert, it might be objected that legal fact finding not only is a question of accurate fact determination, but rather incorporates a number of legal and moral judgments. But this is simply to side-step the issue, because we could reform our legal categories, so that findings of fact are more clearly separated out from legal and moral judgments on those facts. It is also not enough to say that cases rarely turn on one area of specialist knowledge, since we might introduce a system where specific specialist questions are put to the expert,whose answers the court is then bound to accept. In France, for example, the *expert* is allocated a carefully defined issue on which to conduct an *expertise*; the court is not, however, bound by the *expert*'s opinion. Let us say that we place a very high value on accurate fact determination, and would only restrain our ability to achieve this if there is some other political value that conflicts with it. For example, we might prevent civil parties from relying on evidence that they obtained unlawfully or otherwise unconscionably. So why should we not require that all engineering questions within a case should be decided by an engineer? The answer may partly be epistemological, in that, to answer the engineering question definitively, one must resolve other parts of the evidential matrix. But it is likely that the question is really about whether our disputes (and potentially our criminal charges) should be decided by the legal institution, or (or 'as well as') by some other institution that is deemed constitutionally appropriate. That may in turn go to the heart of the question of the role of specialized legal institutions in the legal process. Perhaps because of the way in which I have expressed the second foundational norm, it may be tempting to see the expert as necessarily providing the more accurate determination of fact. But this of course risks taking us back into the very territory from which Chapter 3 has already rescued us. Rather than experts providing us with finality, they may present us instead with a range of very well-defined opinions.

[7] Against this view, see, e.g., A. Goldman, *Knowledge in a Social World* (Oxford: Oxford University Press, 1999), p. 7 and ch. 3.

[8] This is a position classically expressed, for example, by Rorty: '[W]e understand knowledge when we understand the social justification of belief, and thus have no need to view it as accuracy of representation': *Philosophy and the Mirror of Nature* (Princeton: Princeton University Press, 1970), p. 170. Similarly, to say that *A* knows *P* is to say 'something about the way human beings interact': ibid., p. 175.

Selecting between those expert opinions may require a different set of skills, perhaps those of the legal tribunal of fact. This thought echoes the civilian maxim that *iudex peritus peritorum* ('the judge is the expert of the experts').

This book has sought to contribute to the development of a general theory of the judicial assessment of expert evidence, beginning with a special theory relating to civil expert evidence. In turn, it is hoped that the book further contributes to a general theory of the judicial assessment of all forms of evidence, which might be applicable in any legal system. Expert evidence was chosen as the subject for this initial work because it readily throws into relief many of the key epistemological and non-epistemological issues with which an integrated theory of evidence and procedure must engage. This extends to including questions about the relationship between a country's evidence law and its constitutional settlement.

Appendix 1

Part 35 of the Civil Procedure Rules 1998

35.1 Duty to restrict expert evidence

Expert evidence shall be restricted to that which is reasonably required to resolve the proceedings.

35.2 Interpretation

A reference to an 'expert' in this Part is a reference to an expert who has been instructed to give or prepare evidence for the purpose of court proceedings.

35.3 Experts – overriding duty to the court

(1) It is the duty of an expert to help the court on the matters within his expertise.

(2) This duty overrides any obligation to the person from whom he has received instructions or by whom he is paid.

35.4 Court's power to restrict expert evidence

(1) No party may call an expert or put in evidence an expert's report without the court's permission.

(2) When a party applies for permission under this rule he must identify –

(a) the field in which he wishes to rely on expert evidence; and

(b) where practicable the expert in that field on whose evidence he wishes to rely.

(3) If permission is granted under this rule it shall be in relation only to the expert named or the field identified under paragraph (2)

(4) The court may limit the amount of the expert's fees and expenses that the party who wishes to rely on the expert may recover from any other party.

35.5 General requirement for expert evidence to be given in a written report

(1) Expert evidence is to be given in a written report unless the court directs otherwise.

(2) If a claim is on the fast track, the court will not direct an expert to attend a hearing unless it is necessary to do so in the interests of justice.

35.6 Written questions to experts

(1) A party may put to –

(a) an expert instructed by another party; or

(b) a single joint expert appointed under rule 35.7, written questions about his report.

(2) Written questions under paragraph (1) –

(a) may be put once only;

(b) must be put within 28 days of service of the expert's report; and

(c) must be for the purpose only of clarification of the report, unless in any case –

  (i) the court gives permission; or

  (ii) the other party agrees.

(3) An expert's answers to questions put in accordance with paragraph (1) shall be treated as part of the expert's report.

(4) Where –

(a) a party has put a written question to an expert instructed by another party in accordance with this rule; and

(b) the expert does not answer that question, the court may make one or both of the following orders in relation to the party who instructed the expert –

  (i) that the party may not rely on the evidence of that expert; or

  (ii) that the party may not recover the fees and expenses of that expert from any other party.

35.7 Court's power to direct that evidence is to be given by a single joint expert

(1) Where two or more parties wish to submit expert evidence on a particular issue, the court may direct that the evidence on that issue is to given by one expert only.

(2) The parties wishing to submit the expert evidence are called 'the instructing parties'.

(3) Where the instructing parties cannot agree who should be the expert, the court may –

(a) select the expert from a list prepared or identified by the instructing parties; or
(b) direct that the expert be selected in such other manner as the court may direct.

35.8 Instructions to a single joint expert

(1) Where the court gives a direction under rule 35.7 for a single joint expert to be used, each instructing party may give instructions to the expert.
(2) When an instructing party gives instructions to the expert he must, at the same time, send a copy of the instructions to the other instructing parties.
(3) The court may give directions about –
(a) the payment of the expert's fees and expenses; and
(b) any inspection, examination or experiments which the expert wishes to carry out.
(4) The court may, before an expert is instructed –
(a) limit the amount that can be paid by way of fees and expenses to the expert; and
(b) direct that the instructing parties pay that amount into court.
(5) Unless the court otherwise directs, the instructing parties are jointly and severally liable for the payment of the expert's fees and expenses.

35.9 Power of court to direct a party to provide information

Where a party has access to information which is not reasonably available to the other party, the court may direct the party who has access to the information to –

(a) prepare and file a document recording the information; and
(b) serve a copy of that document on the other party.

35.10 Contents of report

(1) An expert's report must comply with the requirements set out in the relevant practice direction.
(2) At the end of an expert's report there must be a statement that –
(a) the expert understands his duty to the court; and
(b) he has complied with that duty.
(3) The expert's report must state the substance of all material instructions, whether written or oral, on the basis of which the report was written.

(4) The instructions referred to in paragraph (3) shall not be privileged against disclosure but the court will not, in relation to those instructions –

(a) order disclosure of any specific document; or

(b) permit any questioning in court, other than by the party who instructed the expert, unless it is satisfied that there are reasonable grounds to consider the statement of instructions given under paragraph (3) to be inaccurate or incomplete.

35.11 Use by one party of expert's report disclosed by another

Where a party has disclosed an expert's report, any party may use that expert's report as evidence at the trial.

35.12 Discussions between experts

(1) The court may, at any stage, direct a discussion between experts for the purpose of requiring the experts to –

(a) identify and discuss the expert issues in the proceedings; and

(b) where possible, reach an agreed opinion on those issues.

(2) The court may specify the issues which the experts must discuss.

(3) The court may direct that following a discussion between the experts they must prepare a statement for the court showing –

(a) those issues on which they agree; and

(b) those issues on which they disagree and a summary of their reasons for disagreeing.

(4) The content of the discussion between the experts shall not be referred to at the trial unless the parties agree.

(5) Where experts reach agreement on an issue during their discussions, the agreement shall not bind the parties unless the parties expressly agree to be bound by the agreement.

35.13 Consequence of failure to disclose expert's report

A party who fails to disclose an expert's report may not use the report at the trial or call the expert to give evidence orally unless the court gives permission.

35.14 Expert's right to ask court for directions

(1) An expert may file a written request for directions to assist him in carrying out his function as an expert.

(2) An expert must, unless the court orders otherwise, provide a copy of any proposed request for directions under paragraph (1) –

(a) to the party instructing him, at least 7 days before he files the request; and

(b) to all other parties, at least 4 days before he files it.

(3) The court, when it gives directions, may also direct that a party be served with a copy of the directions.

35.15 Assessors

(1) This rule applies where the court appoints one or more persons (an 'assessor') under section 70 of the Supreme Court Act 1981(1) or section 63 of the County Courts Act 1984(2).

(2) The assessor shall assist the court in dealing with a matter in which the assessor has skill and experience.

(3) An assessor shall take such part in the proceedings as the court may direct and in particular the court may –

(a) direct the assessor to prepare a report for the court on any matter at issue in the proceedings; and

(b) direct the assessor to attend the whole or any part of the trial to advise the court on any such matter.

(4) If the assessor prepares a report for the court before the trial has begun –

(a) the court will send a copy to each of the parties; and

(b) the parties may use it at trial.

(5) The remuneration to be paid to the assessor for his services shall be determined by the court and shall form part of the costs of the proceedings.

(6) The court may order any party to deposit in the court office a specified sum in respect of the assessor's fees and, where it does so, the assessor will not be asked to act until the sum has been deposited.

(7) Paragraphs (5) and (6) do not apply where the remuneration of the assessor is to be paid out of money provided by Parliament.

Appendix 2

Tables of pre-1800 civil cases involving expert evidence

Table A.1. Expert evidence in common law courts

Case	Year	Primary citation	Secondary citation	Expert	Purpose of using expert
Buckley v. *Rice Thomas*	1555	1 Plowd 118	75 ER 182	logician, grammarian	examples of experts in earlier cases, in case on interpretation of Latin document
Giles v. *Ferrers*	1587	Cro Eliz 59	78 ER 320	grammarian	
Hedd v. *Chalenor*	1590	Cro Eliz 176	78 ER 433	grammarian	
Sheldon's Case	1590	1 Leo 241	74 ER 220	grammarian	
Thomas Palmer Knight v. *Richard Greenwill*	1613	Bridg J 46	123 ER 1189	surveyor	
Everard v. *Hopkins*	1615	2 Bulst 332	80 ER 1164	surgeon	no expert evidence called regarding treatment by surgeon
Alsop v. *Bowtrell*	1619	Cro Jac 541	79 ER 464	physician, man-midwife	length of gestation
Alsop & Stacy pur Trespass de 40l	1619	Palm 9	81 ER 953	physician, man-midwife	length of gestation
Pickering v. *Barkley*	1658	Sty 132	82 ER 587	Trinity Master	whether pirates are considered 'perils of the sea'
Beckman v. *Maplesden*	1662	Bridg O 60	124 ER 468	physician, surgeon, curtian [*sic*], grammarian, brewer	examples of experts in earlier cases, in a case on standard measures

R. v. *Salisbury*	1723	1 Str 547	93 ER 691	physician, surgeon	examination of victim by defendant witnesses prior to *habeas corpus* hearing
R. v. *Strudwick*	1730	1 Barn KB 402	94 ER 271	apothecary	affidavit on whether defendant fit to attend *habeas corpus* hearing
Burton v. *Baynes*	1733	Bar N 153	94 ER 852	surgeon	examination of plaintiff's eye for adjustment of damages
Darlow v. *Late Duke of Wharton*	1739	Bar N 258	94 ER 904	physician	administrator a lunatic
Benson v. *Vernon*	1745	3 Bro PC 626	1 ER 1539	physician, apothecary	House of Lords. Appellant submitted certificates that he was too ill to put in an answer to Court of Exchequer.
Ekins v. *Macklish*	1753	Ambler 184	27 ER 125	merchant	sale of a navy bill
Fearon v. *Bowers*	1753	1 H Bl 365	126 ER 214	merchant	correct use of bills of lading
Maddox v. *Dr M*	1754	*British Trials*,[a] no. 303		'Several physicians and man-midwives'	medical negligence
Stretch v. *Wheeler*	1754	Bar N 497	94 ER 1021	apothecary	defendant witness too ill to attend
Cruger v *Wilcox*	1755	Dickens 269, Ambler 252	21 ER 272, 27 ER 168	merchant	consignment of goods
Grant v. *Vaughan*	1764	1 Black W 485	96 ER 281	special jury	use of bills of exchange

(*cont.*)

Table A.1. (*cont.*)

Case	Year	Primary citation	Secondary citation	Expert	Purpose of using expert
Carter v. *Boehm*	1766	3 Burr 1905	97 ER 1162	special jury	insurance
Slater v. *Baker*	1767	2 Wils KB 359	95 ER 860	apothecary, surgeon	medical negligence
Vallejo v. *Wheeler*	1774	1 Cowp 143	98 ER 1012	special jury	barratry
Wilkinson & Wilkinson Section Commissioners of the Navy	*c.* 1780	501 nb 117	Oldham, *Mansfield Manuscripts*,[b] p. 392	nautical assessors	
Folkes v. *Chadd*	1782	3 Douglas 157	99 ER 589	engineer	cause of harbour silting
Turner v. *Winter*	1787	1 Tr 602	99 ER 1274	chemist	Patent case
Nutt v. *Verney*	1790	4 Tr 121	100 ER 928	physician	discharge from custody on basis of insanity
Chaurand v. *Angerstein*	1791	Peake 61	170 ER 79	merchants, commercial men	
Scammel v. *Willett*	1799	3 Esp 29	170 ER 527	physician	effect on defendant's health of a particular location

[a] *British Trials*: *British Trials 1660–1900: The Guide to the Microfiche Edition Containing a Full Bibliographical Listing Together with Nine Indexes* (Cambridge: Chadwyck-Healey, 1990).

[b] Oldham, *Mansfield Manuscripts*: J. Oldham, *The Mansfield Manuscripts and the Growth of English Law in the Eighteenth Century* (Chapel Hill NC: North Carolina University Press, 1992).

Table A.2. Expert evidence in the court of chancery

Case	Year	Primary citation	Secondary citation	Expert Type	Purpose of using expert
Anon.		Herts. Archives and Local Studies MS. Verulam XII. A.50 fos. 59–76	Bryson,[a] vol. I, 318 no. 120–[2]	Trinity Master	issues regarding charter parties and mariners' wages.
Foubert v. *de Cresseron*	1698	Shower PC 194	1 ER 130	in previous cases (including King's Bench) courts have consulted merchants, Trinity House, grammarians, 'Criticks', chemists, and artificers, on words	interpretation of a French will
Brereton v. *Cowper*	1724	1 Bro PC 211	1 ER 521	surveyor	size and value of property
Ex p. *Ferrers*	1730	Mosely 332	25 ER 423	physician, surgeon	insanity
Graves v. *Budgel*	1737	West T. Hard. 44, 1 Atk 444	25 ER 812, 26 ER 283	physician, apothecary	poor health of defendant
Evans v. *Blood*	1746	3 Brown PC 632	1 ER 1543	physician	declaration of insanity

(*cont.*)

Table A.2. (*cont.*)

Case	Year	Primary citation	Secondary citation	Expert type	Purpose of using expert
Pike v. *Hoare*	1763	2 Eden 182	28 ER 867	physician, apothecary	whether experts in a land case can feasibly attend a hearing in Pennsylvania
Filmer v. *Gott*	1774	4 Bro PC 230	2 ER 156	surveyor	use of surveyor's 'opinion'
Sayer v. *Bennet*	1784	1 Cox 107	29 ER 1084	apothecary	
Ex p. *Bellett*	1786	1 Cox 297	29 ER 1174	midwife	would have expected affidavit from midwife in petition for writ *de ventre inspiciendo*
Fox v. *Mackreth*	1788	2 Cox 320	30 ER 148	surveyor	
Jackson v. *Lever*	1792	3 Bro CC 605	29 ER 724	physician, apothecary	poor health of defendant
In the Matter of Martha Brown, ex p. *Newton Wallop*	1792	4 Bro CC 90	29 ER 794	midwife	petition for writ *de ventre inspiciendo*
Ex p. *Gillam*	1795	2 Ves Jun 587	30 ER 790	physician	lunacy
Ex p. *Mildmay*	1795	3 Ves Jun 2	30 ER 862	apothecary, surgeon	health of a lunatic

[a] Bryson: W. Bryson, *Cases Concerning Equity and the Courts of Equity 1550–1660*, 2 vols., folios 117 and 118 (London: Selden Society, 2000 and 2001)

Table A.3. Expert evidence in the ecclesiastical courts

Case	Year	Primary citation	Secondary citation	Expert	Purpose of using expert
–	*c.* 1575	precedent book, NRO PCD/2/3, fo. 19	Helmholz,[a] 333	builders	to appraise extent of dilapidations of church property
–	*c.* 1630	formulary, DRO, Chanter MS, 724 fos. 64v–65	Helmholz,[a] 501	engineers and builders	to estimate repairs required
–	unknown	Borthwick Institute for Historical Research, York, Prec. Bk 2, pp. 127–8	Helmholz,[a] 501	two artificers	to estimate repairs required
Andrews v. *Powis*	1728	1 Lee 242	161 ER 90	apothecary	mental capacity of testator
Welde v. *Welde*	1731	2 Lee 580	161 ER 447	surgeon	impotence
Gardiner v. *Johnston*	1753	1 Lee 358	161 ER 132	physician	mental capacity of testator
Jekyll (Lady) v. *Jekyll*	1753	1 Lee 419	161 ER 155	physician	health of deceased
Lethes v. *Edsforth*	1753	1 Lee 462	161 ER 171	physician	mental capacity of testator
Lloyd v. *Nevill*	1754	1 Lee 559	161 ER 206	apothecary	not examined, but might have been

(*cont.*)

Table A.3. (*cont.*)

Case	Year	Primary citation	Secondary citation	Expert	Purpose of using expert
Stratton and Stratton v. *Ford*	1755	2 Lee 216	161 ER 318	apothecary	swore falsely to insanity
Taylor v. *Taylor*	1755	2 Lee 172	161 ER 303	surgeon	domestic abuse
Rodd v. *Lewis*	1755	2 Lee 176	161 ER 304	physician	mental capacity of testatrix
Braddyll v. *Jehen*	1755	2 Lee 193	161 ER 310	apothecary	cause of death
Bittleston v. *Clark*	1755	2 Lee 229	161 ER 323	apothecary	whether testator senseless when will said to have been made
Sheafe v. *Row*	1757	2 Lee 415	161 ER 389	physician, apothecary	mental capacity of testator
Robins v. *Wolseley*	1757	2 Lee 421	161 ER 391	physician	party's health

[a]Helmholz: R. Helmholz, *The Oxford History of the Laws of England*, vol. I: *The Canon Law and Ecclesiastical Jurisdiction from 597 to the 1640s* (Oxford: Oxford University Press, 2004).

Table A.4. Expert evidence in the Court of Admiralty

Case	Year	Primary citation	Secondary citation	Expert	Purpose of using expert
Leighton con *Moore*	1600	Libel file 68, no. 108, 1600–1	Marsden,[a] lxxv	Trinity Master	whether damage was by fault or weather
Dale v. *Hall (the Laurel and the Houghton)*	1765	Burrell 323	167 ER 592	Trinity Master	collision
The Marquis of Granby	1770	Burrell 323	167 ER 592	Elder Brethren, merchants	collision
Stoker v. *Hutton (The Friend's Goodwill* v. *The Peggy)*	1785	Burrell 328	167 ER 594	Elder Brethren	collision

[a]Marsden: G. Marsden (ed.), *Select Pleas in the Court of Admiralty*, vol. II: *The High Court of Admiralty (AD 1547–1602)* (Selden Soc. 11), London, 1897.

BIBLIOGRAPHY

Academy of Experts, *Code of Guidance for Experts and Those Instructing Them*, 2nd edn (London: Academy of Experts, 2001)

Aigler, R. and Yates, I. 'The Triangle of Culture, Inference and Litigation System' (2003) 2 *Law Probability and Risk* 137–50

Alexy, R. *A Theory of Legal Argumentation: The Theory of Rational Discourse as Theory of Legal Justification* (Oxford: Oxford University Press, 1989)

Allen, C. *The Law of Evidence in Victorian England* (Cambridge: Cambridge University Press, 1997)

Allibone, T. 'The Club of the Royal College of Physicians, the Smeatonian Society of Civil Engineers and their Relationship to the Royal Society Club' (1967) 22 *Notes and Records of the Royal Society of London* 186–92

Anderson, R. and Pichert, J. 'Recall of Previously Unrecallable Information Following a Shift in Perspective' (1978) 17 *Journal of Verbal Learning and Verbal Behavior* 1–12

Anderson, T. 'On Generalizations I: A Preliminary Exploration' (1999) 40 *South Texas Law Review* 455–81

'Wigmore Meets "The Last Wedge"', in W. Twining and I. Hampsher-Monk (eds.), *Evidence and Inference in History and Law: Interdisciplinary Dialogues* (Evanston, IL: Northwestern University Press, 2003), pp. 140–215

Anderson, T., Schum, D. and Twining, W. *Analysis of Evidence*, 2nd edn (Cambridge: Cambridge University Press, 2005)

Angell, M. *Science on Trial: the Clash of Medical Evidence and the Law in The Breast Implant Case* (New York: Norton, 1996)

Anscombe, G. 'On Brute Facts' (1958) 18 *Analysis* 69–72

Atiyah, P. and Summers, R. *Form and Substance in Anglo-American Law* (Oxford: Oxford University Press, 1987)

Aubry, C. and Rau, C. *Cours de droit civil français*, 5th edn (Paris: Billard, 1922)

Auld, R. *Review of the Criminal Courts of England and Wales* (London: Her Majesty's Stationery Office, 2001)

Bacon, F. *Advancement of Learning* (London: 1605)

Bailey, R. 'Overcoming Veriphobia – Learning to Love Truth Again' (2001) 49 *British Journal of Educational Studies* 159–72

Bainham, A. *Children: The Modern Law*, 2nd edn (Bristol: Jordan Publishing, 1998)
Baker, J. *An Introduction to English Legal History*, 4th edn (London: Butterworths, 2002)
Bardet-Giraudon, M. 'The Place of the Expert in the French Legal System', in J. Spencer, G. Nicholson, R. Flin and R. Bull (eds.), *Children's Evidence in Legal Proceedings. An International Perspective* (Cambridge: Cambridge Law Faculty, 1990), pp. 68–70
Barnes, B., Bloor, D. and Henry, J. *Scientific Knowledge: A Sociological Analysis* (Chicago: University of Chicago Press, 1996)
Basten, J. 'The Court Expert in Civil Trials – A Comparative Appraisal' (1977) 41 *Modern Law Review* 174–91
Beardsley, J. 'Proof of Fact in French Civil Procedure' (1986) 34 *American Journal of Comparative Law* 459–86
Becker, S. 'Child Sexual Abuse Allegations against a Lesbian or Gay Parent in a Custody or Visitation Dispute: Battling the Overt and Insidious Bias of Experts and Judges' (1996) 74 *Denver University Law Review* 75–158
Beecher-Monas, E. *Evaluating Scientific Evidence: An Interdisciplinary Framework for Intellectual Due Process* (Cambridge: Cambridge University Press, 2006)
Benn, A. *The History of English Rationalism in the Nineteenth Century* (London: Longmans, Green & Co., 1906)
Bentham, J. *Rationale of Judicial Evidence* (London, 1827)
Traité des preuves judiciaires (Paris: 1823)
Berger, P., and Luckmann, T. *The Social Construction of Reality* (London: Allen Lane, 1966)
Bergmann, G. *Philosophy of Science* (Madison WI: Wisconsin University Press, 1957)
Berkeley, G. *Principles of Human Knowledge* (1710), ed. R. Woolhouse (London: Penguin, 1988)
Bernstein, D. 'Expert Witnesses, Adversarial Bias, and the (Partial) Failure of the Daubert Revolution' (2007) *George Mason University Law and Economics Research Paper Series* 07–11 http://papers.ssrn.com/sol3/papers.cfm?abstract_id=963461 (last accessed 1 August 2008)
Bertelsen, K. 'From Specialized Courts to Specialized Juries: Calling For Professional Juries in Complex Civil Litigation' (1998) 3 *Suffolk Journal of Trial and Appellate Advocacy* 1
Best, W. *Principles of the Law of Evidence and Practice as to Proofs in Courts of Common Law* (London: Sweet, 1849)
Principles of the Law of Evidence and Practice as to Proofs in Courts of Common Law, 2nd edn (London: Sweet, 1854)
A Treatise on Presumptions of Law and Fact with the Theory and Rules of Presumptive or Circumstantial Proof in Criminal Cases (London: Sweet, 1844)
Beuscher, J. 'The Use of Experts by the Courts' (1941) 54 *Harvard Law Review* 1105–27

Beyleveld, D. and Brownsword, R. *Human Dignity in Bioethics and Biolaw* (Oxford: Oxford University Press, 2001)

Bex, F., Prakken, H., Reed, C. and Walton, D. 'Towards a Formal Account of Reasoning about Evidence: Argumentation Schemes and Generalizations' (2003) 11 *Artificial Intelligence and Law* 125–65

Bex, F. van den Braak, van Oostendorp, S., Prakken, H., Verheij, B. and Vreeswijk, G. 'Sense-making Software for Crime Investigation: How to Combine Stories and Arguments?' (2007) 6 *Law Probability and Risk* 145–68

Bingham, T. 'Hired Gun Takes a Bullet' (2005) 5 *Building* 50

Bishop, M. and Trout, J. *Epistemology and the Psychology of Human Judgment* (Oxford: Oxford University Press, 2004)

Blom-Cooper, L. 'Experts and Assessors: Past, Present and Future' (2002) 21 *Civil Justice Quarterly* 341–456

'Historical Background', in L. Blom-Cooper (ed.), *Experts in the Civil Courts* (Oxford: Oxford University Press, 2006), pp. 1–15.

(ed.) *Experts in the Civil Courts* (Oxford: Oxford University Press, 2006)

BonJour, L. *The Structure of Empirical Knowledge* (Cambridge MA: Harvard University Press, 1985)

Bonnier, É. *Traité théorique et pratique des preuves en droit civil et en droit criminal*, 2nd edn (Paris: Durand, 1852)

Bornstein, B. 'The Ecological Validity of Jury Simulations: Is the Jury Still Out?' (1999) 23 *Law and Human Behaviour* 75–91

Bourcier, D. and De Bonis, M. *Les paradoxes de l'expertise: savoir ou juger?* (Paris: Institut Synthélab, 1999)

Bowden, P., Croall, P. and Parker, R. *The Woolf Reforms in Practice: Freshfields Assess the Changing Landscape* (London: Butterworths, 1999)

Bower, G., Black, J. and Turner, T. 'Scripts in Memory for Texts' (1979) 11 *Cognitive Psychology* 177–220

Boyd, R. 'On the Current Status of Scientific Realism' (1983) 19 *Erkenntnis* 45–90.

Brad Wray, K. 'Science, Biases, and the Threat of Global Pessimism' (2001) 68 *Philosophy of Science* S467–S478

Brewer, S. 'Scientific Expert Testimony and Intellectual Due Process' (1998) 103 *Yale Law Journal* 1535–681

British Trials 1660–1900: The Guide to the Microfiche Edition Containing a Full Bibliographical Listing Together with Nine Indexes (Cambridge: Chadwyck-Healey, 1990)

Brophy, J., Bates, P., Brown, L., Cohen, S. and Radcliffe, P. *Expert Evidence in Child Protection Litigation – Where Do We Go From Here?* (London: The Stationery Office, 1999)

Brubaker, R. *The Limits of Rationality: An Essay on the Social and Moral Thought of Max Weber* (London: George Allen & Unwin, 1984)

Brumfiel, G. 'Misconduct? It's All Academic . . . ' (2007) 445 *Nature* 240–1

Brundage, J. 'The Calumny Oath and Ethical Ideas of Canonical Advocates', in P. Landau and J. Müller (eds.), *Proceedings of the Ninth International Congress of Medieval Canon Law: Monumenta iuris canonici: Subsidia* vol. 10 (Vatican City: 1997), pp. 793–805

'The Ethics of the Legal Profession: Mediaeval Canonists and their Clients' (1973) 33 *Jurist* 237–48

Bryson, W. *Cases Concerning Equity and the Courts of Equity 1550–1660*, 2 vols., folios 117 and 118 (London: Selden Society, 2000 and 2001)

Burn, S. *Successful Use of Expert Witnesses in Civil Disputes* (Crayford: Shaw and Sons, 2005)

Burn, S. and Thompson, B. 'Single Joint Expert', in L. Blom-Cooper (ed.), *Experts in the Civil Courts* (Oxford: Oxford University Press, 2006), pp. 57–75

Burns, R. *A Theory of the Trial* (Princeton NJ: Princeton University Press, 1999)

Cadiet, L. 'The New French Code of Civil Procedure (1975)', in C. van Rhee (ed.), *European Traditions in Civil Procedure* (Antwerp: Intersentia, 2005), pp. 49–68

(ed.) *Dictionnaire de la justice* (Paris: Presses Universitaires de France, 2004)

Cadiet, L. and Jeuland, E. *Droit judiciaire privé*, 5th edn (Paris: Litec, 2006)

Cappelletti, M. and Perillo, J. *Civil Procedure in Italy* (The Hague: Martinus Nijhoff, 1965)

Carson, D. *Professionals and the Courts – A Handbook for Expert Witnesses* (Birmingham: Venture Press, 1990)

Carter, F. 'Court Order Violations, Witness Coaching, and Obstructing Access to Witnesses: An Examination of the Unethical Attorney Conduct that Nearly Derailed the Moussaoui Trial' (2007) 20 *Georgetown Journal of Legal Ethics* 463–74

'The Case for Special Juries in Complex Civil Litigation' (1980) 89 *Yale Law Journal* 1155–76

Chase, O. 'Legal Processes and National Culture' (1997) 5 *Cardozo Journal of International and Comparative Law* 1–24

Check, E. and Cyranoski, D. 'Korean Scandal will have Global Fallout' (2005) 438 *Nature* 1056–7

Chesebro, K. 'Galileo's Retort: Peter Huber's Junk Scholarship' (1993) 42 *American University Law Review* 1637–726

Chiarloni, S. 'Civil Justice and its Paradoxes: An Italian Perspective', in A. Zuckerman, S. Chiarloni and P. Gottwald, *Civil Justice in Crisis: Comparative Perspectives of Civil Procedure* (Oxford: Oxford University Press, 1999), pp. 263–90

Chiovenda, G. *Principii di diritto processuale civile: le azioni, il processo di cognizione*, 3rd edn (Naples: Eugenio Jovene, 1965)

Civil Justice Council, *Protocol for the Instruction of Experts to Give Evidence in Civil Claims* (London: 2005)

Clendinnen, J. 'Ratifying Foundherentism', in C. de Waal (ed.), *Susan Haack: A Lady of Distinctions – The Philosopher Responds to Her Critics* (Amherst NY: Prometheus, 2007), pp. 73–87

Coady, A. *Testimony: A Philosophical Study* (Oxford: Oxford University Press, 1992)

Cohen, J. *The Probable and the Provable* (Oxford: Oxford University Press, 1977)

Coke, E. *Institutes of the Laws of England* (London: 1628, 1642, 1644)

Collingwood, R. 'On the So-Called Idea of Causation' (1937–8) 38 *Proceedings of the Aristotelian Society* 85–112

Collins, H. 'Scientific Evidence: A Common Sense Approach Is Needed' (1996) 4 *Expert Evidence* 156–58

'Competing Financial Interests', www.nature.com/authors/editorial_policies/competing.html (last accessed 1 August 2008)

'Conflict of Interest Disclosure', www.sciencemag.org/feature/contribinfo/prep/coi.shtml (last accessed 1 August 2008)

Consett, H. *Practice of the Spiritual or Ecclesiastical Courts* (London: Basset, 1685)

Cooper, J., Bennett, E. and Sukel, H. 'Complex Scientific Testimony: How Do Jurors Make Decisions?' (1996) 20 *Law and Human Behaviour* 379–94

Cooper, P. 'Training', in L. Blom-Cooper (ed.), *Experts in the Civil Courts* (Oxford: Oxford University Press, 2006), pp. 149–57

Corfield, P. *Power and the Professions in Britain 1700–1850* (London: Routledge, 1995)

Cory-Pearce, R. 'The Three Princes of Serendip or the Happy Avoidance of Accidents', *Society of Expert Witnesses*, March 1998, www.sew.org.uk/dispatch/three_princes.htm (last accessed 1 August 2008)

Cour de cassation, *Le nouveau code de procédure civile: vingt ans après* (Paris: La Documentation Française, 1998)

'Court Work Ban for Clark Doctor' BBC News, 3 June 2005 http://news.bbc.co.uk/1/hi/health/4595839.stm (last accessed 1 August 2008)

Cox, N. 'The Influence of the Common Law on the Decline of the Ecclesiastical Courts of the Church of England' (2001) 3 *Rutgers Journal of Law and Religion*, www.camlaw.rutgers.edu/publications/law-religion/articles/RJLR_3_1_3.pdf (last accessed 1 August 2008)

Craig, P. *Administrative Law*, 5th edn (London: Sweet and Maxwell, 2003)

Crawford, C. 'Legalizing Medicine: Early Modern Legal Systems and the Growth of Medico-legal Knowledge', in M. Clark and C. Crawford, *Legal Medicine in History* (Cambridge: Cambridge University Press, 1994), pp. 89–116

Cretney, S., Masson, J. and Bailey-Harris, R. *Principles of Family Law*, 7th edn (London: Sweet and Maxwell, 2003)

Cross, A. *Evidence* (London: Butterworth, 1958)

Damaška, M. 'Epistemology and Legal Regulation of Proof' (2003) 2 *Law Probability and Risk* 117–30

Evidence Law Adrift (New Haven CT: Yale University Press, 1997)

'Evidentiary Barriers to Conviction and Two Models of Criminal Procedure' (1973) 121 *University of Pennsylvania Law Review* 506–89

The Faces of Justice and State Authority: A Comparative Approach to the Legal Process (New Haven CT: Yale University Press, 1986)

'Presentation of Evidence and Factfinding Precision' (1975) 123 *University of Pennsylvania Law Review* 1083–106

'Rational and Irrational Proof Revisited' (1997) 5 *Cardozo Journal of International and Comparative Law* 25–39

'Truth in Adjudication' (1998) 49 *Hastings Law Journal* 289–308

David, M. 'The Correspondence Theory of Truth', in E. Zalta (ed.), *The Stanford Encyclopedia of Philosophy* (Fall 2005 Edition), http://plato.stanford.edu/archives/fall2005/entries/truth-correspondence/ (last accessed 14 December 2007)

Davies, G. 'Court Appointed Experts' (2004) 23 *Civil Justice Quarterly* 367–85

'Recent Australian Developments: A Response to Peter Heerey' (2004) 23 *Civil Justice Quarterly* 396–9

Day, J. and Le Gat, L. *Expert Evidence under the CPR: A Compendium of Cases from April 1999 to April 2001* (London: Sweet and Maxwell, 2001)

De La Roche-Flavin, B. *Arrests notables du parlement de Toulouse*, ed. N. Caranove (Toulouse: 1745)

Deichmann, U. and Müller-Hill, B. 'The Fraud of Abderhalden's Enzymes' (1998) 393 *Nature* 109–11

Dennis, I. *The Law of Evidence*, 2nd edn (London: Sweet and Maxwell, 2002)

Descartes, R. *Discours de la méthode* (Paris: 1637)

Devine, D., Buddenbaum, J., Houp, S., Stolle, D. and Studebaker, N. 'Deliberation Quality: A Preliminary Examination in Criminal Juries' (2007) 4 *Journal of Empirical Legal Studies* 273–303

Dickey, A. 'The Province and Function of Assessors in English Courts' (1970) 33 *Modern Law Review* 494–507

Dobbin, S., Gatowski, S., Richardson, J., Ginsburg, G., Merlino, M. and Dahir, V. 'Applying Daubert: How Well Do Judges Understand Science and Scientific Method?' (2002) 85 *Judicature* 244–7

Dror, I. and Charlton, D. 'Why Experts Make Errors' (2006) 56 *Journal of Forensic Identification* 600–16

Dror, I., Charlton, D. and Peron, A. 'Contextual Information Renders Experts Vulnerable to Making Erroneous Identifications' (2006) 156 *Forensic Science International* 74–8

Duxbury, N. 'Jerome Frank and the Legacy of Legal Realism' (1991) 18 *Journal of Law and Society* 175–205

Dworkin, R. *Justice in Robes* (Cambridge MA: Harvard University Press, 2006)

Taking Rights Seriously (Cambridge MA: Harvard University Press, 1977)

Dwyer, D. 'Beyond Autonomy: the Role of Dignity in "Biolaw"' (2003) 23 *Oxford Journal of Legal Studies* 319–31

'Changing Approaches to Expert Evidence in England and Italy' (2002) 1 *International Commentary on Evidence* iss. 2, art. 4, www.bepress.com/ice/vol1/iss2/art4 (last accessed 1 August 2008)

'Closed Evidence, Reasonable Suspicion and Torture' (2005) 9 *Evidence and Proof* 126–31

'The Duties of Expert Witnesses of Fact and Opinion' (2003) 7 *Evidence and Proof* 264–9

'Expert Evidence in the English Civil Courts, 1550–1800' (2007) 28 *Journal of Legal History* 93–118

'Is a Finding that a Person Deemed Unfit to be Tried "did the act . . . charged against him" Compatible with Article 6 ECHR?' (2003) 67 *Journal of Criminal Law* 307–10

'Is Man the Rational Animal?', BA dissertation, University of Southampton (1996)

'Knowledge, Truth and Justification in Legal Fact Finding' (2007) 1(4) *Reasoner* 5–6, www.kent.ac.uk/secl/philosophy/jw/TheReasoner/vol1/TheReasoner–1 (4).pdf (last accessed 1 August 2008)

'Legal Remedies for the Negligent Expert' (2008) 12 *Evidence and Proof* 93–115

'What Does it Mean to be Free? The Concept of Free Proof in the Western European Legal Tradition' (2005) 3 *International Commentary on Evidence* iss. 1, art. 6, www.bepress.com/ice/vol3/iss1/art6 (last accessed 1 August 2008)

Ebsworth, E. 'Accreditation: A Novel Approach', in L. Blom-Cooper (ed.), *Experts in the Civil Courts* (Oxford: Oxford University Press, 2006), pp. 17–28

Eco, U. *Il nome della rosa*, 47th edn (Milan: Tascabili Bompiani, 2001)

'Editorial' *Counsel* November/December 1994

Edmond, G. 'After Objectivity: Expert Evidence and Procedural Reform' (2003) 25 *Sydney Law Review* 131–64

'Judicial Representations of Scientific Evidence' (2000) 63 *Modern Law Review* 216–51

(ed.) *Expertise in Regulation and Law* (Aldershot: Ashgate, 2004)

Edmond, G. and Mercer, D. '*Daubert* and the Exclusionary Ethos: The Convergence of *Corporate* and *Judicial* Attitudes Towards the Admissibility of Expert Evidence in Tort Litigation' (2004) 26 *Law and Policy* 231–57

'Experts and Expertise in Legal and Regulatory Settings', in G. Edmond (ed.), *Expertise in Regulation and Law* (Aldershot: Ashgate, 2004), pp. 1–31

'The Invisible Branch: The *Authority* of Science Studies in Expert Evidence Jurisprudence', in G. Edmond (ed.), *Expertise in Regulation and Law* (Aldershot: Ashgate, 2004) pp. 197–291

Edwards, S. 'Perjury and Perverting the Course of Justice Considered' [2003] *Criminal Law Review* 525–40

Eekelaar, J. 'The Emergence of Children's Rights' (1986) 6 *Oxford Journal of Legal Studies* 161–82

Eggleston, R. *Evidence, Proof and Probability* (London: Weidenfeld and Nicolson, 1978)

Einstein, A. 'Physics and Reality', in S. Bargmann (ed.), *Ideas and Opinions of Albert Einstein* (New York: Crown Publishers, 1954), pp. 290–323

Eisen, A. 'The Meanings and Confusion of Weberian "Rationality"' (1978) 29 *British Journal of Sociology* 57–70

Encinas de Munagorri, R. 'La communauté scientifique est-elle un ordre juridique?' [1998] *Revue trimestrielle de droit civil* 247–83

Energy Research Advisory Board to the United States Department of Energy, *Cold Fusion Research* (Washington DC: Energy Research Advisory Board, 1999) DOE/S–0073 DE90 005611

Engelhardt, H. and Caplan, A. (eds.), *Scientific Controversies: Case Studies in the Resolution and Closure of Disputes in Science and Technology* (Cambridge: Cambridge University Press, 1987)

Epstein, L. and King, G. 'The Rules of Inference' (2002) 69 *University of Chicago Law Review* 1–133

Erichson, H. 'Mass Tort Litigation and Inquisitorial Justice' (1999) 87 *Georgetown Law Journal* 1983–2024

Erlanger, H. 'Jury Research in America: Its Past and Future' (1970) 4 *Law and Society Review* 345–70

Evans-Pritchard, E. *Witchcraft, Oracles and Magic among the Azande* (Oxford: Oxford University Press, 1937)

Feigenbaum, A. 'Special Juries: Deterring Spurious Medical Malpractice Litigation in State Courts' (2003) 24 *Cardozo Law Review* 1361–420

Feldman, R. 'Naturalized Epistemology', in E. Zalta (ed.), *The Stanford Encyclopedia of Philosophy* (Fall 2006 Edition), http://plato.stanford.edu/archives/fall2006/entries/epistemology-naturalized/ (last accessed 1 August 2008)

Ferrarese, M. 'An Entrepreneurial Conception of the Law? The American Model Through Italian Eyes', in D. Nelken (ed.), *Comparing Legal Cultures* (Aldershot: Ashgate, 1997), pp. 157–81

Feyerabend, P. 'Explanation, Reduction and Empiricism', in H. Feigl and G. Maxwell (eds.), *Minnesota Studies in the Philosophy of Science* vol. III (Minneapolis MN: Minnesota University Press, 1962), pp. 28–97

'On the "Meaning" of Scientific Terms' (1964) 61 *Journal of Philosophy* 497–509

Forbes, T. *Surgeons at the Bailey: English Forensic Medicine to 1878* (New Haven CT: Yale University Press, 1985)

Fordham, M. *Judicial Review Handbook*, 4th edn (Oxford: Hart, 2004)

Formulary (*c.* 1630) DRO. Chanter MS

Foucault, M. *The Order of Things: An Archaeology of the Human Sciences* (London: Routledge, 1970)

Frank J. *Courts on Trial* (Princeton NJ: Princeton University Press, 1950)

Law and the Modern Mind (New York: Tudor, 1930)

Frankel, M. 'The Search for Truth: An Umpireal View' (1975) 123 *University of Pennsylvania Law Review* 1031–59

Freckleton, I., Reddy, P. and Selby, H. *Australian Judicial Perspectives on Expert Evidence: An Empirical Study* (Melbourne: Australian Institute of Judicial Administration, 1999)

Freckleton, I. and Selby, H. *Expert Evidence* (Sydney: LBC, 1993)

Freckmann, A. and Wegerich, T. *The German Legal System* (London: Sweet and Maxwell, 1999)

Freemon, F. 'The Origin of the Medical Expert Witness: The Insanity of Edward Oxford' (2001) 22 *Journal of Legal Medicine* 349–73

Galanter, M. 'The Vanishing Trial: An Examination of Trials and Related Matters in Federal and State Courts' (2004) 1 *Journal of Empirical Legal Studies* 459–570.

Galilei, G. *Dialogo Sopra i due massimi sistemi del mondo* (Florence: Giovanni Battista Landini, 1632)

Gallanis, T. 'Legal History with 21st Century Tools: The *English Reports* on CD-ROM and *Bracton* on the Web' (1999) 20 *Journal of Legal History* 109

'The Rise of Modern Evidence Law' (1999) 84 *Iowa Law Review* 499–560

Geller, M. 'Wigmorean Analysis and the Survival of Cuneiform', in W. Twining and I. Hampsher-Monk (eds.), *Evidence and Inference in History and Law: Interdisciplinary Dialogues* (Evanston, IL: Northwestern University Press, 2003), pp. 216–30

Gettier, E. 'Is Justified True Belief Knowledge?' (1963) 23 *Analysis* 121–3

Gigerenzer, G., Todd, P. and the ABC Research Group, *Simple Heuristics That Make Us Smart* (Oxford: Oxford University Press, 1999)

Gilbert, G. *The Law of Evidence* (London: 1754)

The Law of Evidence, 4th edn, ed. C. Lofft (Dublin: 1795)

Glenn, P. *Legal Traditions of the World*, 3rd edn (Oxford: Oxford University Press, 2007)

Golan, T. 'The History of Scientific Expert Testimony in the English Courtroom' (1999) 12 *Science in Context* 7–34

Laws of Men and Laws of Nature: The History of Scientific Expert Testimony in England and America (Cambridge MA: Harvard University Press, 2004)

'Scientific Expert Testimony in Anglo-American Courts, 1782–1923', Ph.D. thesis, University of California at Berkeley, 1997

Goldman, A. *Knowledge in a Social World* (Oxford: Oxford University Press, 1999)

Pathways to Knowledge (Oxford: Oxford University Press, 2002)

'Social Epistemology', in E. Zalta (ed.), *The Stanford Encyclopedia of Philosophy* (Spring 2007 Edition), http://plato.stanford.edu/archives/spr2007/entries/epistemology-social/ (last accessed 1 August 2008)

Goodall, F. 'The Expert Witness: Partisan with a Conscience' (1990) 56 *Journal of the Chartered Institute of Arbitrators*

Gottwald, P. 'Simplified Civil Procedure in West Germany' (1983) 31 *American Journal of Comparative Law* 687–701

Graham, K. '"There'll Always be an England": The Instrumental Ideology of Evidence' (1987) 85 *Michigan Law Review* 1204–34

Grande, E. 'Italian Criminal Justice: Borrowing and Resistance' (2000) 48 *American Journal of Comparative Law* 227–59

Grevling, K. 'Restrictions on the Right to Silence – Introduction', in H. Malek (ed.), *Phipson on Evidence* (London: Sweet and Maxwell, 2005), pp. 1039–56

Gross, S. 'Expert Evidence' (1991) 6 *Wisconsin Law Review* 1113–232

Haack, S. 'The Benefit of Experience: Response to John Clendinnen', in C. de Waal (ed.), *Susan Haack: A Lady of Distinctions – The Philosopher Responds to Her Critics* (Amherst NY: Prometheus, 2007), pp. 88–91

'Crossing My i's and Dotting some t's: Response to Vern Warker', in C. de Waal (ed.), *Susan Haack: A Lady of Distinctions – The Philosopher Responds to Her Critics* (Amherst NY: Prometheus, 2007), pp. 105–8

Haack, S. *Defending Science – Within Reason: Between Scientism and Cynicism* (New York: Prometheus Books, 2003)

Evidence and Inquiry: Towards Reconstruction in Epistemology (Oxford: Blackwell, 1993)

'Innocent Realism in a Pluralistic Universe', in C. de Waal (ed.), *Susan Haack: A Lady of Distinctions – The Philosopher Responds to Her Critics* (Amherst NY: Prometheus, 2007), pp. 233–6

'Inquiry and Advocacy, Fallibilism and Finality: Culture and Inference in Science and Law' (2003) 2 *Law Probability and Risk* 205–14

'Law, Literature, and Bosh', in C. de Waal (ed.), *Susan Haack: A Lady of Distinctions – The Philosopher Responds to Her Critics* (Amherst NY: Prometheus, 2007), pp. 259–62

Manifesto of a Passionate Moderate (Chicago: University of Chicago Press, 1998)

'Of Chopin and Sycamores: Response to Ryszard Wójcicki', in C. de Waal (ed.), *Susan Haack: A Lady of Distinctions – The Philosopher Responds to Her Critics* (Amherst NY: Prometheus, 2007), pp. 69–72

'Reflections on Relativism: From Momentous Tautology to Seductive Contradiction', in S. Haack, *Manifesto of a Passionate Moderate* (Chicago: University of Chicago Press, 1998), pp. 149–66

'Trial and Error: The Supreme Court's Philosophy of Science' (2005) 95 *American Journal of Public Health* S66–S73

Habermas, J. *Between Facts and Norms* (Cambridge: Polity Press, 1997)

Hacking, I. *The Emergence of Probability: A Philosophical Study of Early Ideas About Probability, Induction and Statistical Inference* (Cambridge: Cambridge University Press, 1975)

'Experimentation and Scientific Realism' (1982) 13 *Philosophical Topics* 71–87

Hall, J. *The Practice and Jurisdiction of the Court of Admiralty* (1809) (Ann Arbor MI: Scholars' Facsimiles & Reprints, 2004)

Hammelmann, H. 'Expert Evidence' (1947) 11 *Modern Law Review* 32–9

'Rules of Evidence Under the New Italian Civil Codes' (1947) 29 *Journal of Comparative Legislation and International Law* 39–46

Hand, L. 'Historical and Practical Considerations Regarding Expert Testimony' (1901) 15 *Harvard Law Review* 40–58

Hart, H. *The Concept of Law*, 2nd edn (Oxford: Oxford University Press, 1994)

'Definition and Theory in Jurisprudence' (1954) 70 *Law Quarterly Review* 37–60

Hart, H. and Honoré, T. *Causation in the Law*, 2nd edn (Oxford: Oxford University Press, 1985)

Harvey, N. and Harries, C. 'Effects of Judges' Forecasting on their Later Combination of Forecasts for the Same Outcome' (2004) 20 *International Journal of Forecasting* 391–409

Hastie, R. *Inside the Juror: The Psychology of Juror Decision Making* (Cambridge: Cambridge University Press, 1993)

Hastie, R., Schkade, D. and Payne, J. 'A Study of Juror and Jury Judgments in Civil Cases: Deciding Liability for Punitive Damages' (1998) 22 *Law and Human Behaviour* 287–314

Head, A. 'The Role of an Expert Defined' (1998) 9 *Dispatches* www.sew.org.uk/dispatch/role.htm (last accessed 1 August 2008)

Heerey, P. 'Recent Australian Developments' (2004) 23 *Civil Justice Quarterly* 386–95

Helmholz, R. *Canon Law and the Law of England* (London: Hambledon Press, 1987)

The Ius Commune in England (Oxford: Oxford University Press, 2001)

The Oxford History of the Laws of England, vol. I: *The Canon Law and Ecclesiastical Jurisdiction from 597 to the 1640s* (Oxford: Oxford University Press, 2004)

Hempel, C. *Aspects of Scientific Explanation* (New York: Free Press, 1965)

'The Irrelevance of the Concept of Truth for the Critical Appraisal of Scientific Theories', in R. Jeffrey (ed.), *Selected Philosophical Essays [by] Carl G. Hempel* (Cambridge: Cambridge University Press, 1990), pp. 75–84

Ho, H. 'The Epistemic Basis of Legal Fact-finding' (2007) 1(2) *Reasoner* 5–6 www.kent.ac.uk/secl/philosophy/jw/TheReasoner/vol1/TheReasoner–1(2).pdf (last accessed 1 August 2008)

A Philosophy of Evidence Law: Justice in the Search for Truth (Oxford: Oxford University Press, 2008)

Hobsbawm, E. and Ranger, T. (eds.) *The Invention of Tradition* (Cambridge: Cambridge University Press, 1983)

Hodgkinson, T. and James, M. *Expert Evidence: Law and Practice* (London: Sweet and Maxwell, 2007)

Hohfeld, W. *Fundamental Legal Conceptions as Applied to Judicial Reasoning* (New Haven CT: Yale University Press, 1923)

Holmes, A. 'Moore's Appeal to Common Sense' (1961) 58 *Journal of Philosophy* 197–207

Howard, M. 'The Neutral Expert: A Plausible Threat to Justice' [1991] *Criminal Law Review* 98–105

Howlin, N. 'Special Juries: A Solution to the Expert Witness' (2004) 12 *Irish Student Law Review* 19–47

Huber, P. *Galileo's Revenge: Junk Science in the Courtroom* (New York: Basic Books, 1991)

Hume, D. *Enquiries Concerning Human Understanding* (1748), ed. P. Nidditch, 3rd edn (Oxford: Oxford University Press, 1975)

A Treatise of Human Nature (1740), ed. P. Nidditch, 2nd edn (Oxford: Oxford University Press, 1978)

Hutter, M. and Teubner, G. 'Homo juridicus and Homo oeconomicus: Communicate Fictions', in T. Baums, K. Hopt and N. Horn (eds.), *Corporations, Capital Markets and Business in the Law* (The Hague: Kluwer, 2000), p. 569

Jackson, J. 'Analysing the New Evidence Scholarship: Towards a New Conception of the Law of Evidence' (1996) 16 *Oxford Journal of Legal Studies* 309–28

'The Effect of Human Rights on Criminal Evidentiary Processes: Towards Convergence, Divergence or Realignment?' (2005) 68 *Modern Law Review* 737–64

'The Effect of Legal Culture and Proof in Decisions to Prosecute' (2004) 3 *Law Probability and Risk* 109–31

'Playing the Culture Card in Cross-Jurisdictional Transplants' (1997) 5 *Cardozo Journal of International and Comparative Law* 51–67

'The Ultimate Issue Rule: One Rule Too Many' [1984] *Criminal Law Review* 75

Jackson, J. and Doran, S. 'Judge and Jury: Towards a New Division of Labour in Criminal Trials' 60 *Modern Law Review* 759–78

Jackson, R. 'The Incidence of Jury Trial during the Past Century' (1937) 1 *Modern Law Review* 132–44

Jacob, J. *Civil Justice in the Age of Human Rights* (Aldershot: Ashgate, 2007)

The Fabric of English Civil Justice (London: Stevens, 1987)

'Meetings of Experts Without Prejudice' (1986) 5 *Civil Justice Quarterly* 279–80

Jacob, R. 'Court Appointed Experts v Party Experts: Which is Better?' (2004) 23 *Civil Justice Quarterly* 400–7

Jacquin, A. 'L'impartialité objective de l'expert judiciaire et sa récusation' 31 *Gazette du Palais* (1 February 2003) 3–8

Jasanoff, S. *Science at the Bar: Law, Science and Technology in America* (Cambridge MA: Harvard University Press, 1995)

'What Judges Should Know About the Sociology of Science' (1992) 32 *Jurimetrics* 345–59

Jeuland, E. 'Expertise', in L. Cadiet (ed.), *Dictionnaire de la justice* (Paris: Presses Universitaires de France, 2004), pp. 503–10

Johnston, P. 'Court Appointed Scientific Expert Witnesses: Unfettering Expertise' (1987) 2 *Berkeley Technology Law Journal* www.law.berkeley.edu/journals/btlj/articles/vol2/johnston.pdf (last accessed 1 August 2008)

Jolowicz, J. 'Adversarial and Inquisitorial Models of Civil Procedure' (2003) 52 *International and Comparative Law Quarterly* 281–95

On Civil Procedure (Cambridge: Cambridge University Press, 2000)

Jones, C. *Expert Witnesses: Science, Medicine, and the Practice of Law* (Oxford: Oxford University Press, 1994)

Judicature Commission, *First Report of the Commissioners* (London: Her Majesty's Stationery Office, 1869)

Kahneman, D., Slovic, P. and Tversky, A. (eds.) *Judgment under Uncertainty: Heuristics and Biases* (Cambridge: Cambridge University Press, 1982)

Kalberg, S. 'Max Weber's Types of Rationality' (1980) 85 *American Journal of Sociology* 1145

Kant, I. *Critique of Practical Reason* (1788), trans. T. Abbott (London: Longmans, Green & Co., 1898)

Kaplan, B., von Mehren, A. and Schaefer, R. 'Phases of German Civil Procedure I' (1958) 71 *Harvard Law Review* 1193–268

Keane, A. and Seabrooke, S. (eds.) *Evidence*, 6th edn (Oxford: Blackstone, 2001)

King, M. 'An Autopoietic Approach to the Problems Presented by Parental Alienation Syndrome' (2002) 13 *Journal of Forensic Psychiatry* 609–35

King, M. and Kaganas, F. 'The Risks and Dangers of Experts in Court' (1998) 1 *Current Legal Issues* 221–42

King, M. and Thornhill, C. 'Will the Real Niklas Luhmann Stand Up, Please? A Reply to John Mingers' (2003) 51 *Sociological Review* 276–85

Kitcher, P. '1953 and All That: A Tale of Two Sciences' (1984) 93 *Philosophical Review* 335–73

The Advancement of Science: Science without Legend, Objectivity without Illusions (Oxford: Oxford University Press, 1993)

'Implications of Incommensurability' (1982) 2 *Philosophy of Science Association* 689–703

'Real Realism: The Galilean Strategy' (2001) 110 *Philosophical Review* 151–97

'Theories, Theorists and Theoretical Change' (1978) 87 *Philosophical Review* 519–47

'Truth or Consequences?' (1998) 72 *Proceedings and Addresses of the American Philosophical Association* 49–63

Kötz, H. 'Civil Litigation and Public Interest' (1982) 1 *Civil Justice Quarterly* 237

Kuhn, T. *The Structure of Scientific Revolutions* (Chicago: University of Chicago Press, 1962)

The Structure of Scientific Revolutions, 2nd edn (Chicago: University of Chicago Press, 1970)

Lacey, N. *A Life of H. L. A. Hart: The Nightmare and the Noble Dream* (Oxford: Oxford University Press, 2004)

Lakatos, I. 'Science and Pseudoscience' lecture, broadcast 30 June 1973 as Programme 11 of The Open University Arts Course A303, 'Problems of Philosophy', www.lse.ac.uk/collections/lakatos/scienceAndPseudoscience.htm (last accessed 1 August 2008)

Landsman, S. 'Of Witches, Madmen, and Products Liability: An Historical Survey of the Use of Expert Testimony' (1995) 13 *Behavioral Sciences and the Law* 131–57

'One Hundred Years of Rectitude: Medical Witnesses at the Old Bailey, 1717–1817' (1998) 16 *Law and History Review* 445–94

'The Rise of the Contentious Spirit: Adversary Procedure in Eighteenth Century England' (1990) 75 *Cornell Law Review* 497–609

Langbein, J. 'Cultural Chauvinism in Comparative Law' (1997) 5 *Cardozo Journal of International and Comparative Law* 41–50.

'The German Advantage in Civil Procedure' (1985) 52 *University of Chicago Law Review* 823–66

The Origins of the Adversary Criminal Trial (Oxford: Oxford University Press, 2003)

'Shaping the Eighteenth-Century Criminal Trial: A View from the Ryder Sources' (1983) 50 *University of Chicago Law Review* 1–136

Torture and the Law of Proof: Europe and England in the Ancien Régime (Chicago: University of Chicago Press, 1977)

'Trashing the German Advantage' (1988) 82 *Northwestern University Law Review* 763–84

Laudan, L. 'A Confutation of Convergent Realism' (1981) 48 *Philosophy of Science* 19–49

Truth, Error and Criminal Law – An Essay in Legal Epistemology (Cambridge: Cambridge University Press, 2006)

Law Reform Committee England and Wales, *Evidence of Opinion and Expert Evidence*, 17th Report, Cmnd 4489 (London: Her Majesty's Stationery Office, 1970)

Leclerc, O. *Le juge et l'expert: contribution à l'étude des rapports entre le droit et la science* (Paris: LDGJ, 2005)

'Les réformes du droit de l'expertise' (2006) 71 *Experts* 12

Legrand, P. 'European Legal Systems are not Converging' (1996) 45 *International and Comparative Law Quarterly* 52–81

'The Impossibility of Legal Transplants' (1997) 4 *Maastricht Journal of European and Comparative Law* 111–24

Leibniz, G. *Monadology* (1714), trans. R. Latta (Oxford: Clarendon Press, 1898)

Lempert, R. 'Civil Juries and Complex Cases: Let's Not Rush to Judgment' (1981) 80 *Michigan Law Review* 68–132

'The New Evidence Scholarship: Analyzing the Process of Proof' (1986) 66 *Boston University Law Review* 439–77

Lennon, T. and Dea, S. 'Continental Rationalism', in E. Zalta (ed.), *The Stanford Encyclopedia of Philosophy* (Winter 2007 Edition) http://plato.stanford.edu/archives/win2007/entries/continental-rationalism/ (last accessed 14 December 2007)

Leslie, J. 'From Bear Garden to Swan Lake' *Counsel* (August 2005) 22–3

Leucari, V. 'Analysis of Complex Patterns of Evidence in Legal Cases: Wigmore Charts v Bayesian Networks' (2005), www.evidencescience.org/content/leucariA1.pdf (last accessed 14 December 2007)

Levy, M. and Salvadori, M. *Why Buildings Fall Down: How Structures Fail* (New York: Norton, 1992)

Lobban, M. 'The Strange Life of the English Civil Jury, 1837–1914', in J. Cairns and G. McLeod (eds.), *The Dearest Birthright of the People of England: The Jury in the History of the Common Law* (Oxford: Hart, 2002), pp. 173–215

Locke, J. *Essay Concerning Human Understanding* (1690), ed. J. Yolton, 3rd edn (London: Dent, 1993)

Losee, J. *Historical Introduction to the Philosophy of Science*, 3rd edn (Oxford: Oxford University Press, 1993)

Luhmann, N. *Differentiation of Society*, trans. S. Holmes and C. Larmore (New York: Columbia University Press, 1982)

'European Rationality', in G. Robinson and J. Rundell (eds.), *Rethinking Imagination: Culture and Creativity* (London: Routledge, 1994), pp. 65–83

Law as a Social System (1993), trans. K. Ziegert (Oxford: Oxford University Press, 2004)

Social Systems (1984), trans. J. Bednarz Jr (Stanford: Stanford University Press, 1995)

Lukes, S. 'Relativism in its Place', in M. Hollis and S. Lukes (eds.), *Rationality and Relativism* (Oxford: Blackwell, 1982), pp. 261–305

McAuley, F. 'Canon Law and the End of the Ordeal' (2006) 26 *Oxford Journal of Legal Studies* 473–513

McConnell, A. 'Risk and Responsibility: Dealing with Science and Uncertainty in Toxic Torts', Doctor of Laws thesis, European University Institute, 2000

McCormick, C. *Handbook on the Law of Evidence* (St Paul MN: West, 1954)

MacCormick, N. *Institutions of Law: An Essay in Legal Theory* (Oxford: Oxford University Press, 2007)

'Norms, Institutions and Institutional Facts' (1998) 17 *Law and Philosophy* 301–45

Mackay, R. and Colman, A. 'Equivocal Rulings on Expert Psychological and Psychiatric Evidence: Turning a Muddle into a Nonsense' [1996] *Criminal Law Review* 88–95

Macnair, M. *The Law of Proof in Early Modern Equity* (Berlin: Duncker and Humblot, 1999)

McPherson, K. 'One Expert's Experience', in L. Blom-Cooper (ed.), *Experts in the Civil Courts* (Oxford: Oxford University Press, 2006), pp. 159–80

Macpherson, W. *The New Procedure of the Civil Courts of British India*, 5th edn (London: Lepage & Co., 1871)

Maddox, J., Randi, J. and Stewart, W. '"High-Dilution" Experiments a Delusion' (1998) 334(6180) *Nature* 287

Magendie, J.-C., *Célérité et qualité de la justice: la gestion du temps dans le proces. Rapport au Garde des Sceaux, ministre de la Justice* (Paris: La Documentation française, 2004)

Malek, H. (ed.) *Phipson on Evidence*, 16th edn (London: Sweet and Maxwell, 2005)

Margot, P. 'The Role of the Forensic Scientist in an Inquisitorial System of Justice' (1998) 38 *Science and Justice* 71–3

Marsden, G. (ed.) *Select Pleas in the Court of Admiralty (1547–1602)*, 2 vols., folios 6 and 11 (London: Selden Society, 1892 and 1897)

Martin de Agar, J. 'Giudice e perito', paper presented at the 29th Congresso Nazionale di Diritto Canonico, Vatican City, 1998

Matson, J. *Effective Expert Witnessing*, 3rd edn (Boca Raton FL: CRC Press, 1999)

Maturana, H. and Varela, F. *Autopoiesis and Cognition: The Realization of the Living* (Dordrecht: Reidel, 1980)

Meadow, R. (ed.) *The ABC of Child Abuse*, 3rd edn (London: BMJ Publishing, 1997)

Meininger, M.-C. (ed.) 'L'administrateur et l'expert' (2002) 103 *Revue Française d'Administration Publique*, 365–527

Menashe, D. and Shamash, M. 'The Narrative Fallacy' (2005) 3 *International Commentary on Evidence* iss. 1, art. 3, www.bepress.com/ice/vol3/iss1/art3 (last accessed 1 August 2008)

Menochius, J. *Tractatus de praesumptionibus, conjecturis, signis et indiciis* (Venice: 1590)

Merton, R. *The Sociology of Science: Theoretical and Empirical Investigations* (Chicago: University of Chicago Press, 1973)

Mill, J. *System of Logic* (London: 1843)

Millar, R. (ed.), *A History of Continental Civil Procedure* (London: J. Murray, 1928)

Miner, J. 'The Jury Problem' (1946) *Journal of Criminal Law and Criminology* 1–15

Mitnick, J. 'From Neighbor-Witness to Judge of Proofs: The Transformation of the English Civil Juror' (1988) 32 *American Journal of Legal History* 201–35

'MMR Doctor "To Face GMC Charges"' BBC News, 12 June 2006 http://news.bbc.co.uk/1/hi/health/5070670.stm (last accessed 1 August 2008)

'MMR Scare Doctor "Paid Children"', BBC News, 16 July 2007, http://news.bbc.co.uk/1/hi/health/6289166.stm (last accessed 1 August 2008)

Mnookin, J. 'Scripting Expertise: The History of Handwriting Identification Evidence and the Judicial Construction of Expertise' (2001) 87 *Virginia Law Review* 1723–845

Mnookin, R. 'Child Custody Adjudication: Judicial Functions in the Face of Indeterminacy' (1975) 39 *Law and Contemporary Problems* 226–93

Mogck, D. 'Are We There Yet? Refining the Test for Expert Testimony Through *Daubert, Kumho Tire* and Proposed Federal Rule of Evidence 702' (2000) 33 *Connecticut Law Review* 303–36

Mohr, J. *Doctors and the Law: Medical Jurisprudence in Nineteenth-Century America* (Oxford: Oxford University Press, 1993)

Moore, G. 'A Defence of Common Sense', in J. Muirhead (ed.), *Contemporary British Philosophy*, 2nd series (London: Allen and Unwin, 1924), pp. 191–223

Moss, S. 'Opinion for Sale: Confessions of an Expert Witness' (2003) *Legal Affairs* March/April 2003

Murphy, P. *Evidence*, 9th edn (Oxford: Oxford University Press, 2005)

Nelken, D. 'A Just Measure of Science?' in M. Freeman and H. Reece (eds.), *Science in Court* (Aldershot: Ashgate, 1988), pp. 11–36

'Law and Disorder: A Letter from Italy' (1992) 8 *Socio-Legal Newsletter* 6

'Law and Knowledge / Law as Knowledge' (2006) 15 *Social Legal Studies* 570–3

'The Truth about Law's Truth', in A. Febbrajo and D. Nelken, *European Yearbook in the Sociology of Law 1993* (Milan: Giuffrè, 1994), pp. 87–160

Nelken, D. and Feest, J. (eds.) *Adapting Legal Cultures* (Oxford: Hart, 2001)

Ngwasiri, C. 'Some Problems of Expertise in French Civil Procedure' (1989) 8 *Civil Justice Quarterly* 168–83

Nisbett, R. and Ross, L. *Human Inference: Strategies and Shortcomings of Social Judgment* (Englewood Cliffs NJ: Prentice Hall, 1980)

Nörr, K. 'Procedure in Mercantile Matters: Some Comparative Aspects', in V. Piergiovanni (ed.), *The Courts and the Development of Commercial Law* (Berlin: Duncker and Humblot, 1987), pp. 195–201

O'Day, R. *The Professions in Early Modern England 1450–1800* (Harlow: Longman, 2000)

O'Reilly, J. and Buenger, C. *Toxic Torts Practice Guide*, 2nd edn (Eagan MN: West, 2004)

Oberhammer, P. and Domej, T. 'Germany, Switzerland and Austria (ca. 1800–2005)', in C. van Rhee (ed.), *European Traditions in Civil Procedure* (Antwerp: Intersentia, 2005), pp. 103–28

Oddie, C. *Science and the Administration of Justice* (London: Justice, 1991)

Odgers, W. 'Changes in Procedure and the Law of Evidence', in *A Century of Law Reform* (London: Macmillan, 1901), pp. 203–40

Oh, P. 'The Proper Test for Assessing the Admissibility of Nonscientific Expert Testimony Under Federal Rule of Evidence 702' (1997) 45 *Cleveland State Law Review* 437–67

Oldham, J. 'The History of the Special (Struck) Jury in the United States' (1998) 6 *William and Mary Bill of Rights Journal* 623–75

'Jury Research in the English Reports in CD-ROM', in J. Cairns and G. McLeod (eds.), *The Dearest Birthright of the People of England: The Jury in the History of the Common Law* (Oxford: Hart, 2002), pp. 131–53

The Mansfield Manuscripts and the Growth of English Law in the Eighteenth Century (Chapel Hill NC: North Carolina University Press, 1992)

'The Origins of the Special Jury' (1983) 50 *University of Chicago Law Review* 137–221

Palazzolo, G. *Prova legale e pena: la crisi del sistema tra evo medio e moderno* (Naples: Jovene, 1979)

Palmer, A. *Proof and the Preparation of Trials* (Sydney: Lawbook, 2003)

Paterson, J. 'Trans-Science, Trans-Law and Proceduralisation' (2003) 12 *Social and Legal Studies* 523–43.

Paterson, J. and Teubner, G. 'Changing Maps: Empirical Legal Autopoiesis' (1998) 7 *Social and Legal Studies* 451–86

Pattenden, R. 'Litigation Privilege and Expert Opinion Evidence' (2000) 4 *Evidence and Proof* 213–45

Peysner, J. 'Controlling Costs' (2003) 153 (7090) *New Law Journal* 1147–8

Phillips, S. *A Treatise on the Law of Evidence*, 2nd edn (London: Strahan, 1815)

Phipson, S. *The Law of Evidence*, 1st edn (London: Stevens, 1892)

Plous, S. *The Psychology of Judgment and Decision Making* (New York: McGraw Hill, 1993)

Popper, K. *The Logic of Scientific Discovery* (1934), trans. K. Popper (London: Hutchinson, 1959)

Posner, R. *Law and Legal Theory in England and America* (Oxford: Oxford University Press, 1996)

'Practice and Potential of the Advisory Jury' (1987) 100 *Harvard Law Review* 1363–81

Precedent Book (*c.* 1575) Norfolk and Norwich Record Office PCD/2/3

Prichard, J. and Yale, D. (eds.), *Hale and Fleetwood on Admiralty Jurisdiction*, folio 108 (London: Selden Society, 1992)

Porter, R. *England in the Eighteenth Century*, 2nd edn (Harmondsworth: Penguin, 1990)

Pundik, A. 'Statistical Evidence: An Investigation of its Nature and its Usage in the Criminal Context' (2006) *Social Science Research Network* http://ssrn.com/abstract=878402 (last accessed 1 August 2008)

Quine, W. 'On Empirically Equivalent Systems of the World' (1975) 9 *Erkenntnis* 313–28

Rassat, M.-L. 'Forensic Expertise and the Law of Evidence in France', in J. Nijboer, C. Callen and N. Kwak (eds.), *Forensic Expertise and the Law of Evidence* (Amsterdam: Royal Netherlands Academy of Arts and Sciences, 1993), pp. 53–62

Redmayne, M. *Expert Evidence and Criminal Justice* (Oxford: Oxford University Press, 2001)

Reed, C. and Rowe, G. 'Translating Toulmin Diagrams: Theory Neutrality in Argument Representation' (2005) 19 *Argumentation* 267–86

Resnik, J. 'Changing Practices, Changing Rules: Judicial and Congressional Rule Making on Civil Juries, Civil Justice and Civil Judging' (1997) 49 *Alabama Law Review* 133–219

'Trial as Error, Jurisdiction as Injury: Transforming the Meaning of Article III' (2000) 113 *Harvard Law Review* 924–1037

Rheinstein, M. and Shils, E. (eds.) *Max Weber on Law in Economy and Society* (Cambridge MA: Harvard University Press, 1954)

Roberts, P. 'Rethinking the Law of Evidence: A Twenty-First Century Agenda for Teaching and Research', in P. Roberts and M. Redmayne, *Innovations in Evidence and Proof: Integrating Theory, Research and Teaching* (Oxford: Hart, 2007), pp. 19–63

'Tyres with a "Y": An English Perspective on Kumho Tire and its Implications for the Admissibility of Expert Evidence' (1999) 1 *International Commentary on Evidence* iss. 2, art. 5, www.bepress.com/ice/vol1/iss2/art5 (last accessed 1 August 2008)

Roberts, P. and Zuckerman, A. *Criminal Evidence* (Oxford: Oxford University Press, 2004)

Rock, P. 'Witnesses and Space in a Crown Court' (2001) 31 *British Journal of Criminology* 266–79

Rodes, R. 'The Canon Law as a Legal System – Function, Obligation, and Sanction' (1964) 9 *Natural Law Forum* 45–94

Rorty, R. *Philosophy and the Mirror of Nature* (Princeton NJ: Princeton University Press, 1970)

Roscoe, E. *The High Court of Admiralty: The Last Phase* (London: Kelly Law Book, 1927)

Rose, N. and Valverde, M. 'Governed by Law?' (1998) 7 *Social and Legal Studies* 541–53

Rosenthal, R. 'Interpersonal Expectations: Effects of the Experimenter's Hypothesis', in R. Rosenthal and R. Rosnow (eds.), *Artifact in Behavioral Research* (New York: Academic Press, 1969), pp. 181–277

Rowe, G. and Reed, C. 'Translating Wigmore Diagrams', in *Proceedings of the First International Conference on Computational Models of Argument* (Amsterdam: IOS Press, 2006), pp. 171–82

Royal Statistical Society 'Royal Statistical Society Concerned by Issues Raised in Sally Clark Case', 23 October 2001, www.rss.org.uk/PDF/RSS%20Statement%20regarding%20statistical%20issues%20in%20the%20Sally%20Clark%20 case,%20October%2023rd%202001.pdf (last accessed 1 August 2008)

Rubin, A. 'Trial by Jury in Complex Civil Cases: Voice of Liberty or Verdict of Confusion?' (1982) 462 *Annals of the American Academy of Political and Social Science* 87–103

Ruddock, A. 'The Trinity House at Deptford in the Sixteenth Century' (1950) 65 *English Historical Review* 458–76

Russell, B. *History of Western Philosophy*, 2nd edn (London: Routledge, 1961)

Sales, B. and Shuman, D. *Experts in Court: Reconciling Law, Science, and Professional Knowledge* (Washington DC: American Psychological Association, 2005)

Samuels, A. 'A Unified Civil Court' (2006) 25 *Civil Justice Quarterly* 250–60

Schiller, F. 'Scientific Discovery and Logical Proof', in C. Singer (ed.), *Studies in the History and Method of Science*, vol. I (Oxford: Clarendon Press, 1917), pp. 235–89

Schlick, M. 'Positivismus und Realismus' (1932) 3 *Erkenntnis* 1–31

Schmitt, F. (ed.) *Socializing Epistemology: The Social Dimensions of Knowledge* (Lanham MD: Rowman and Littlefield, 1994)

Schum, D. 'Evidence and Inference About Past Events: An Overview of Six Case Studies', in W. Twining and I. Hampsher-Monk (eds.), *Evidence and Inference in History and Law: Interdisciplinary Dialogues* (Evanston, IL: Northwestern University Press, 2003), pp. 9–62

Evidential Foundations of Probabilistic Reasoning (London: John Wiley, 1994)

'A Reply to the "Schum Challenge" at UCL', 6 September 2005, www.evidence-science.org/content/D.%20Schum%20Reply.doc (last accessed 1 August 2008)

Sclater, S. and Piper, C. 'Social Exclusion and the Welfare of the Child' (2001) 28 *Journal of Law and Society* 409–29

Scott, I. 'Immunity from Suit of Expert Witnesses' (1998) 17 *Civil Justice Quarterly* 349–53

Searle, J. *Speech Acts* (Cambridge: Cambridge University Press, 1969)

Senior, W. *Doctors' Commons and the Old Court of Admiralty* (London: Longmans, Green & Co., 1922)

Sériaux, A. 'Pouvoir scientifique, savoir juridique' (1991) 13 *Droits* 61–6

Shapin, S. *A Social History of Truth: Civility and Science in Seventeenth Century England* (Chicago: University of Chicago Press, 1994)

Shapiro, B. *'Beyond Reasonable Doubt' and 'Probable Cause': Historical Perspectives on the Anglo-American Law of Evidence* (Berkeley CA: University of California Press, 1991)

A Culture of Fact: England 1550–1720 (Ithaca NY: Cornell University Press, 2000)

Simpson, J. and Weiner, E. (eds.), *The Oxford English Dictionary*, 2nd edn (Oxford: Oxford University Press, 1989)

Solomon, M. 'Scientific Rationality and Human Reasoning' (1992) 59 *Philosophy of Science* 439–55

Social Empiricism (Cambridge MA: MIT Press, 2001)

Soothill, K. 'Perjury and False Statements: A Criminal Profile of Persons Convicted 1979– 2001' [2004] *Criminal Law Review* 926–35.

Spencer, B. 'Estimating the Accuracy of Jury Verdicts' (2007) 4 *Journal of Empirical Legal Studies* 305–29

Spencer, J. 'Court Experts and Expert Witnesses: Have We a Lesson to Learn from the French?' (1992) 45 *Current Legal Problems* 213–36

'Inscrutable Verdicts, the Duty to Give Reasons and Article 6 of the European Convention on Human Rights' (2001) 1 *Archbold News* 5–8

'The Neutral Expert: An Implausible Bogey' [1991] *Criminal Law Review* 106–10

Spencer, J. and Flin, J. *The Evidence of Children – The Law and the Psychology*, 2nd edn (London: Blackstone, 1993)

Spinoza, B. *Ethics* (1677), trans. A. Boyle, ed. G. Parkinson (London: Dent, 1993)

Squibb, G. *Doctors' Commons* (Oxford: Oxford University Press, 1977)

Starkie, T. *A Practical Treatise on the Law of Evidence and Digest of Proofs in Civil and Criminal Proceedings* (London: Clarke, 1824)

Steckley, G. 'Collisions, Prohibitions, and the Admiralty Court in Seventeenth-Century London' (2003) 21 *Law and History Review* 41–67

'Merchants and the Admiralty Court During the English Revolution' (1978) 22 *American Journal of Legal History* 137–75

Stein, A. *Foundations of Evidence Law* (Oxford: Oxford University Press, 2005)

Stephen, J. *A General View of the Criminal Law of England* (London: McMillan, 1863)

The Principles of Judicial Evidence, Being an Introduction to the Indian Evidence Act (I of 1872) (Calcutta: Thacker Spink & Co., 1872)

Steup, M. 'Epistemology', in E. Zalta (ed.), *The Stanford Encyclopedia of Philosophy (*Fall *2006 Edition)*, http://plato.stanford.edu/archives/fall2006/entries/epistemology/ (last accessed 1 August 2008)

Stich, S. 'Could Man be an Irrational Animal?' (1985) 64 *Synthèse* 115–35

Strier, F. 'The Educated Jury: A Proposal for Complex Litigation' (1997) 47 *DePaul Law Review* 49–83

Sunderland, E. 'The Inefficiency of the American Jury' (1915) 13 *Michigan Law Review* 302–16

Sward, E. *The Decline of the Civil Jury* (Durham NC: Carolina Academic Press, 2001)

Taleb, N. *The Black Swan: The Impact of the Highly Improbable* (London: Penguin, 2007)

Tapper, C. *Cross and Tapper on Evidence*, 11th edn (Oxford: Oxford University Press, 2007)

Taruffo, M. *La prova dei fatti giuridici* (Milan: Giuffrè, 1992)

'Senso comune, esperienza e scienza nel ragionamento del giudice', in *Sui confini: scritti sulla giustizia civile* (Bologna: Il Mulino, 2002), pp. 121–55

Taylor, J. *A Treatise on the Law of Evidence* (London: Maxwell and Sweet, 1848)

Teubner, G. '*Altera pars audiatur*: Law in a Collision of Discourses', in R. Rawlings (ed.), *Law, Society and Economy: Centenary Essays for the London School of Economics and Political Science 1895–1995* (Oxford: Oxford University Press, 1997), pp. 149–76

'How the Law Thinks: Toward A Constructivist Epistemology of Law' (1989) 23 *Law and Society Review* 727–58

Law as an Autopoietic System (Blackwell: Oxford, 1993)

(ed) *Autopoietic Law: A New Approach to Law and Society* (Berlin: Walter de Gruyter, 1988)

Thayer, J. *A Preliminary Treatise on Evidence at Common Law* (Cambridge MA: Harvard University Press, 1898)

Select Cases on Evidence at the Common Law, 2nd edn (Cambridge MA: Charles W. Fever, 1900)

Tillers, P. 'The Authority of History for the Modern Law of Proof and Evidence' Blog Tillers on Evidence and Inference, 4 November 2003 http://tillerstillers.blogspot.com/2003/11/authority-of-history-for-modern-law-of.htm (last accessed 1 August 2008)

'Prejudice, Politics and Proof' (1988) 86 *Michigan Law Review* 768–75

Timmerbeil, S. 'The Role of Expert Witnesses in German and US Civil Litigation' (2003) 9 *Annual Survey of International and Comparative Law* 163–87

Toulmin, S. *The Uses of Argument* (Cambridge: Cambridge University Press, 1958)

Tufte, E. *Beautiful Evidence* (Cheshire CT: Graphics Press, 2006)

Turner, R. 'A New Approach to Civil Litigation', paper given at the Royal Courts of Justice, 24 June 2002

Twining, W. 'Alternative to What? Theories of Litigation, Procedure and Dispute Settlement in Anglo-American Jurisprudence: Some Neglected Classics' (1993) 56 *Modern Law Review* 380–92

'Argumentation, Stories and Generalizations: A Comment' (2007) 6 *Law Probability and Risk* 169–85

'Civilians Don't Try: A Comment on Mirjan Damaška's "Rational and Irrational Proof Revisited"' (1997) 5 *Cardozo Journal of International and Comparative Law* 69–78

'Evidence and Legal Theory' (1984) 47 *Modern Law Review* 261–83

'Freedom of Proof and the Reform of Criminal Evidence' (1997) 31 *Israel Law Review* 439–63

'Hot Air in the Redwoods, A Sequel to the Wind in the Willows' (1988) 86 *Michigan Law Review* 1523–47

Karl Llewellyn and the Realist Movement (London: Weidenfeld and Nicolson, 1973)

'Narrative and Generalizations in Argumentation about Questions of Fact' (1999) 40 *South Texas Law Review* 351–65

'The *Ratio decidendi* of the Parable of the Prodigal Son', in K. O'Donovan and G. Rubin (eds.), *Human Rights and Legal History: Essays in Honour of Brian Simpson* (Oxford: Oxford University Press, 2000), pp. 149–71

'The Rationalist Tradition of Evidence Scholarship', in *Rethinking Evidence: Exploratory Essays*, 2nd edn (Cambridge: Cambridge University Press, 2006), pp. 35–98

Rethinking Evidence: Exploratory Essays, 2nd edn (Cambridge: Cambridge University Press, 2006)

'Social Science and Diffusion of Law' (2005) 32 *Journal of Law and Society* 203–40

'Some Scepticism About Some Scepticisms', in *Rethinking Evidence: Exploratory Essays*, 2nd edn (Cambridge: Cambridge University Press, 2006), pp. 99–164

'Taking Facts Seriously', in *Rethinking Evidence: Exploratory Essays*, 2nd edn (Cambridge: Cambridge University Press, 2006), pp. 14–34

Theories of Evidence: Bentham and Wigmore (London: Weidenfeld and Nicolson, 1985)

Twining, W. and Hampsher-Monk, I. (eds.), *Evidence and Inference in History and Law: Interdisciplinary Dialogues* (Evanston, IL: Northwestern University Press, 2003)

Twining, W. and Twining, P. 'Bentham on Torture' (1973) 24 *Northern Ireland Legal Quarterly* 305–56

Ubertis, G. *Argomenti di procedura penale* (Milan: Giuffrè, 2002)

van Cleve, G. 'Somerset's Case and its Antecedents in Imperial Perspective' (2006) 24 *Law and History Review* 601–46

van Kampen, P. *Expert Evidence Compared: Rules and Practices in the Dutch and American Criminal Justice System* (Antwerp: Intersentia Rechtswetenschappen, 1998)

van Krieken, R. 'The "Best Interests of the Child" and Parental Separation: On the "Civilizing of Parents"' (2005) 68 *Modern Law Review* 25–48

Venn, J. *Principles of Inductive Logic*, 2nd edn (New York: Chelsea Publishing, 1907)

Vidmar, N. and Schuller, R. 'Juries and Expert Evidence: Social Framework Testimony' (1989) 52 *Law and Contemporary Problems* 133–76

Walker, V. 'It's Time to Cross the t's and Dot the i's', in C. de Waal (ed.), *Susan Haack: A Lady of Distinctions – The Philosopher Responds to Her Critics* (Amherst NY: Prometheus, 2007), pp. 92–104

Waller, Lord Justice (Sir Mark), Scott, I., Brooke, Sir H. *et al.* (eds.) *Civil Procedure*, 2 vols. (London: Sweet and Maxwell, 2007) (The *White Book*)

Walton, D. *Legal Argumentation and Evidence* (University Park PA: Pennsylvania State University Press, 2002)

'Rules for Reasoning from Knowledge and Lack of Knowledge' (2006) 34 *Philosophia* 355–76

Ward, T. 'Experts, Juries and Witch-Hunts: From Fitzjames Stephen to Angela Cannings' (2004) 31 *Journal of Law and Society* 369–86

'Observers, Advisers, or Authorities? Experts, Juries and Criminal Responsibility in Historical Perspective' (2001) 12 *Journal of Forensic Psychiatry* 105–22

Watson, A. *Legal Transplants*, 2nd edn (Athens GA: Georgia University Press, 1993)

'Legal Transplants and European Private Law' (2000) 4 *Electronic Journal of Comparative Law* www.ejcl.org/44/art44-2.html (last accessed 1 August 2008)

Watson, J. *The Double Helix* (New York: Norton, 1967)

Weber, M. *Gesammelte Aufsätze zur Religionssoziologie* (Tübingen: Mohr, 1922)

Weinstein, J. and Hershenov, E. 'The Effect of Equity on Mass Tort Law' [1991] *University of Illinois Law Review* 269–327

Wigmore, J. *The Science of Judicial Proof: As Given by Logic, Psychology and General Experience and Illustrated in Judicial Trials*, 3rd edn (Boston: Little, Brown, 1937)

A Treatise on the Anglo-American System of Evidence in Trials at Common Law (1923), rev. edn Chadbourn (Boston: Little, Brown, 1981)

A Treatise on the Anglo-American System of Evidence in Trials at Common Law (1923), rev. edn Tiller (Boston: Little, Brown, 1983)

Williams, B. 'Ethics', in A. Grayling (ed.), *Philosophy: A Guide Through the Subject*, 2nd edn, vol. I (Oxford: Oxford University Press, 2000), pp. 545–83

Williamson, T. *Knowledge and its Limits* (Oxford: Oxford University Press, 2000)

Wills, W. *An Essay on the Principles of Circumstantial Evidence* (London: 1838)

Winch, P. *The Idea of a Social Science* (London: Routledge and Kegan Paul, 1958).

'Understanding a Primitive Society' (1964) 1(14) *American Philosophical Quarterly* 307–24

Wittgenstein, L. *Philosophical Investigations* (Oxford: Blackwell, 1953).

Woolf, Lord *Access to Justice: Final Report* (London: Her Majesty's Stationery Office, 1996)

Access to Justice: Interim Report (London: Her Majesty's Stationery Office, 1995)

'Are the Courts Excessively Deferential to the Medical Profession?' (2001) 9 *Medical Law Review* 1–16

Woolf, Lord, Jowell, J. and Le Sueur, A. (eds.), *De Smith, Woolf and Jowell's Judicial Review of Administrative Action*, 5th edn (London: Sweet and Maxwell, 1995)

Wright, R. 'Causation, Responsibility, Risk, Probability, Naked Statistics, and Proof: Pruning the Bramble Bush by Clarifying the Concepts' (1988) 73 *Iowa Law Review* 1001–77

'Once More into the Bramble Bush: Duty, Causal Contribution and the extent of Legal Responsibility' (2001) 54 *Vanderbilt Law Review* 1071–132

Yale, D. (ed.) *Lord Nottingham's Chancery Cases*, 2 vols., folios 73 and 79 (London: Selden Society, 1954 and 1961)

Yates, C. 'Doctoring the Evidence: Medical Evidence in Child Custody Cases in Australia' (1986) 5 *Civil Justice Quarterly* 144

Zahle, H. 'William Twining and Iain Hampsher-Monk (eds.) Evidence and Inference in History and Law: Interdisciplinary Dialogues Illinois: Northwestern UP (2003)' (2004) 8 *Evidence and Proof* 211–13

Zeisel, H. and Diamond, S. '"Convincing Empirical Evidence" on the Six Member Jury' (1974) 41 *University of Chicago Law Review* 281–95

Ziegert, K. 'The Thick Description of Law: An Introduction to Niklas Luhmann's Theory of Operatively Closed Systems', in R. Banakar and M. Travers (eds.), *An Introduction to Law and Social Theory* (Oxford: Hart, 2002), pp. 55–75

Zuckerman, A. *Civil Procedure: Principles of Practice*, 2nd edn (London: Sweet and Maxwell, 2006)

'Coercion and the Judicial Ascertainment of Truth' (1989) 23 *Israel Law Review* 357–74

'Disclosure of Expert Reports' (2005) 24 *Civil Justice Quarterly* 293–7

'Miscarriage of Justice – A Root Treatment' [1992] *Criminal Law Review* 323–45

INDEX

Note. In this index: (1) entries are in **bold** denote main entries.
(2) the following abbreviations are used:

ADR	alternative dispute resolution
CFA	conditional fee agreement
CPC	Codice di procedura civile (1940)
CPR	Civil Procedure Rules (1998)
ECHR	European Convention on Human Rights
ECtHR	European Court of Human Rights
ESRC	Economic and Social Research Council
FRCP	Federal Rules of Civil Procedure (1938)
FRE	Federal Rules of Evidence (1975)
HRA	Human Rights Act (1998)
NCPC	Nouveau code de procédure civile (1975)
NIAS	Netherlands Institute for Advanced Studies
RSC	Rules of the Supreme Court
UCL	University College London
US	United States
ZPO	Zivilprozessordnung (1933)

Academy of Experts 296–7, 312–13, 319, 362–3
Access to Justice
  Final Report (1996) 4–5, 167, 208, 280–1, 284–6, 292, 307–9, 312–13, 315–16
  inquiry 296–7
  Interim Report (1995) 167, 284–6, 307–9, 315–16
actual bias, *see* bias, expert–actual
  see also sanctions
adjudication 10–11
administration of justice
  bias threat to 163
  champerty and maintenance 169
  expert discussions and conflict 297–8, 312
Admiralty, High Court of
  assessors 112, 187–8, 315–19, 332
    Access to Justice, 308, 315–16
    appointment of 320–1
    tribunal member, as 317–18
  experts, historical use of 234–6, 269–70
  pleadings, producing full 321–2
  practice 325–7
    written evidence 317
  see also assessors; ECtHR
admissibility and evaluation, rules of 24–5
ADR 47

adversarial system 33, 221–2, 227, 282–3, 294–5, 335–6
 assessors 324–7
 bias 369
 party expert witness 284
advocates *see* lawyers
American Legal Realists 10–11
Anderson, T. 102–3, 106–7
 generalizations 60–1
 graphical representations of evidential matrix 53–5
Anglo-American jurisdictions 19, 26–7, 29–30, 181–2, 370–1
 adversarial system 33, 221–2, 227
  criminal 33
 appeals 135
 atomistic reasoning *see* atomism
 audi alteram partem 294–5
 chains of inferences, use of 58
 conduct of litigation 220–32
 discovery/disclosure 200
 evidence law and Locke 81
 expertise and opinion coterminous 76–8
 fact and opinion evidence 75–6
 facts, engagement with 213–20
 generalizations 63–4
 judges 37–8
 judicial notice 74–5
 juries 38–9
 Opinion Rule 76–8
 party expert witness 284
  see also party experts
 single joint experts *see* single joint experts
  see also England; US
Anscombe, G. 92–3, 96
apparent bias 327–8, 340–1
Aristotle 117
artificial intelligence 53–5
Asian courts 47
assessors 7, 187–8, 234–6, 254, 308, 315–32
 challenging expert opinion 323–32
  assessor's opinion, challenging 324–7
  difficulties with 323–7
  retiring with court 327–32: court officials, as 330–1, expert witnesses, separate from 329–32, tribunal members, as 317–18, 329–32; delegating fact finding 332
 history of *see under* **history of expert evidence**
 nautical and ECHR 329
 pleadings, producing full 321–2
 selecting 315–21
  approaches to appointment 319–21: Admiralty Court 320–1
  roles 315–19: four distinct 317–18
 see also party experts; single joint experts
Associated Provincial Picture Houses Ltd. v Wednesbury Corp. [1948] 162
Assyriology 102–3
asylum cases 354–5
atomism and atomistic reasoning 7, 48, 51–60, 74, 100–3
 graphical representation of evidential matrix 53–5
 total inferential drag, problem of 55–60
 see also Locke
attorneys *see* lawyers
Aubry, C. 199
audi alteram partem 294–5
Auld, R. 319, 362–3
Australia 4–5
 Competition Tribunal 305–6
 federal court and assessors 330–1
 hot tubbing 305–6
 Litigation Reform Commission of Queensland 311
autopoietic social systems theory 76, 114, 122–30
 application to
  judicial assessment of expert evidence 124–6
  society and law 122
 difficulties applying to expert evidence 126–30

empirical 128–9
social phenomenon of expert evidence, understanding 129–30
theoretical 126–8
Azande 41

barristers *see* lawyers
Beardsley, J. 213–18
Beecher-Monas, E. 130–1
Bennett, E. 69–70
Bentham, J. 22–7, 42–3, 47, 301
Benveniste, J. 175–6
Bergman, G. 104
Berkeley, G. 88, 116
Bernstein, D. 344
Best, W. 11–12, 19, 24, 83–4, 271
Opinion Rule 85
best evidence rule 11–12
bias, expert 1–2, 6, 38–9, 163–78, 369
actual, manifestations of 172–6, 341, 353–4
conscious bias 172–3, 353–4
unconscious bias 173–6: cognitive heuristic biases on fact finding 173–4, interpreter effect 174–5, observer effect 175–6, verification, fallacy of 176
disagreement resulting from 163–72
financial interest 166–70: financial involvement 168–70; CFAs 169–70, unequal resources 170, *see also* equality of arms; predisposition 166–8: developing work as expert 168, employee as expert 167–8, shareholdings 166–7
intellectual interest 171–2: *see also* 'expert shopping' *under* expert predisposition 171
personal interest 164–6: personal, involvement 166, predisposition 164–6, 335–6, membership of organizations 165, moral views 164, 278–9, pre-existing personal relationships 164–5
management of *see* **management of bias**
personal and structural bias 176–8
see also 'expert shopping' *under* expert
personal bias 176
structural bias 176–7
sanctions *see* sanctions
see also **expert disagreement**
bicameral courts and tribunals 6–7, 29–30, 33–4, 223–4, 342
specialist members of tribunals 38–9
Blom-Cooper, L. 325
Bolam v. *Friern Hospital Management Committee* [1957] 111–12, 278–9
standard of care 160–2
Bonaparte, Napoleon 50
BonJour, L. 18
Bonnier, E. 83–4
Boole, J. 141
Boyd, R. 144
British Academy of Experts *see* Academy of Experts
'brute facts' 92–3, 96

Cadiet, L. 206
canon
courts, medieval 47
law 47
see also Roman-canon law
Capelletti, M. 213–14
career judiciary 37–8
Carnap, R. 142
case law 219–20
Catholic Church 47
causation
personal injury, in 150–1
toxic torts, in 151–5
certainty
legal fact finding, finality in *see under* **expert disagreement** – legal and expert factual disagreement
objective, scientific knowledge as *see under* **expert disagreement** – legal and expert factual disagreement

CFAs 169–70, 225–6
challenges, inferential *see under* **expert disagreement**
challenging expert opinion
  assessors 323–32
    challenging opinion 324–7: difficulties with 323–7
    retiring with court 327–32: court officials, as 330–1, expert witnesses, separate from 329–32, tribunal members, as 317–18, 329–32
  party experts 294–306
    before trial 296–300: exchange of written reports 296; expert discussions 296–300, 312, conflict and immunity 297–8, privilege 298–9
    trial, at 300–6: cross-examination 300–5; criticisms of 302–5: hot tubbing 305–6
  single joint experts 312–13
    cross-examination 312–13
champerty 169, 225–6
character witnesses 290–1
Charlton, D. 175
child cases 155–9, 211–12
  best interests of the child 155–9, 211–12
  court experts 190–1
    see also single experts
  distinguished from medical cases 158–9
  expert
    advice 211–12
    bias 164, 166, 171
  Official Solicitor 188, 211–12
  oral enquiry, French 212
  psychiatric evidence in 157–8
Chiovenda, G. 204–5
civil
  courts *see* courts
  litigation
    pugnacity of 224–7: *see also under* US
    social function of 198–212
  sanctions 360–1
    see also sanctions
classical epistemology *see* classical *under* **epistemology**
Clinical Disputes Forum 289–90
Coady, A. 80–1
Code de procédure civile (1806) 199–200, 215–17
  see also NCPC
Code of Guidance, Academy of Experts 312–13
codes of conduct, professional 227
cognition and cognitive psychology 7, 12–14, 58–9, 65–8, 88–9
cognitive heuristic biases 173–4
Cohen, J.
  'commonplace' generalizations 61–2
  probability 57–8
coherentism 6–7, 12–14, 16–18, 23, 51–3
Coke, Sir E. 85–7, 91
  Adam's case 85
collaborative fact finding 22–3
Collingwood, R. 88–9
common
  assumptions in rationalist theories 9, 64–5, 76–8
  investigative method 104–7
  sense 68, 75–6, 104, 106–7
    see also generalizations – common-sense
communities of practice, persistent 76, 110–13, 369
  court's decision rejected by experts 111–12
    rule in *Bolam* 111–12
  expert evidence as product of 110–11
  incorporating into tribunal of fact 112
compurgatory oaths 47
Comtean positivism 141
The Concept of Law (1961) 120–1
conduct of litigation 220–32
conflict of interest 297–8
conscious bias 172–3
constitutive facts 93–4

constructivism 76
epistemological constructivism 113–30
autopoietic social systems theory *see* autopoietic social systems theory
definition 114–15
modernity, in 116–18: specialist inferential reasoning; Kant, and 116–17, Weber, and 117–18
strong 114, 118–22: philosophy of 118–22
contingency fees *see* CFAs
contradiction 294–5
convergence and conflict 57, 59, 99
conviction intime 30–1
Cooper, J. 69–70
Copernicus 345–6
coroners' courts 329–30, 354–5
corroboration and contradiction 55–7, 59, 99
Council for the Registration of Forensic Practitioners 319, 362–3
counsel *see* lawyers
Counsel 232
courts
access to specialist knowledge *see under* **expert evidence**
assessors retiring with 327–32
Asian 47
bicameral *see* bicameral courts and tribunals
case management powers 170, 185, 189–90, 207–8
pre-trial 222–3
civil, before Judicature Acts *see under* **history of expert evidence** – civil expert evidence
common law, English 49
composition 6–7, 12–14, 29–30, 33–40
variations in arrangements 33–4: experience of court matters 21–38, expert tribunals 38–9, lawyers and non-lawyers in tribunals 36, member experience 21–38, numbers in tribunals 34–6, reasons for decisions 39
coroners' 329–330, 354–5
Crown Court 37
delegating fact finding 306–7, 313–15, 332
duty to *see* duty – to court
ecclesiastical *see* **history of expert evidence**
experts 7, 317–18, 335–8, 369–70
appointment of 189–93, 195–6
history of *see under* **history of expert evidence**
see also assessors; party experts; single experts
judges *see* judges
juries *see* juries
litigation privilege, approach to 298–9, 356–8
magistrates' courts 36–7
medieval canon 47
non-specialist and specialist knowledge 367–9
officers of 194–5, 317–18, 349–50
officials, assessors as 330–1
specialists in tribunals 38–9
Supreme *see* RSC
unicameral courts *see* unicameral
variations in arrangements 33–4
see also criminal trials; fact and opinion; legal – fact finding; tribunals
CPC 204–5, 227, 282–3
Family proceedings, special nature of 211–12
French system compared with 196–7
CPR 4–5, 8, 26–7, 184–8, 207–11, 227, 280–3
Admiralty *see* Admiralty
assessors 187–8, 315–32
case management 185, 207–8: pre-trial 222–3
duty to court 8, 187, 210–11, 360–2: overriding 347–52
code, as 282–3
equality of arms *see* equality of arms

CPR (*cont.*)
exchange of written reports 296
expert discussions 296–300, 312
extra-curial judicial guidelines 289
litigation privilege 298–9, 352–8
orality 214–15
Overriding Objective 185, 209–11, 227, 282–6, 291–3
party experts 187, 210–11, 232, 284–307
Practice Directions, and 286–7
Pre-Action Protocol for Resolution of Clinical Disputes 289–90
proportionality and costs 209–10
RSC, distinguished from 282–3
'shadow experts' 185–6, 294, 312
single joint experts *see* single joint experts
Tracks 286–7
trial 300–6
written reports 186–7
criminal justice system 319
criminal sanctions 358–60
criminal trials 1–3, 6–7
admission and weight of evidence 32
civil and criminal fact finding, differences between 30–3
complex 38–9
Crown Court 37
disclosure 355
double jeopardy rule 30–1
expert evidence provision 32
forensic science 32
historical developments in *see* **history of expert evidence**
litigation privilege 355
magistrates' courts 36–7
non-lawyers in tribunals 36
pre-trial disclosure 32
prosecuting counsel, role of 32
prosecution, advantages of, over defendant 32
reasons for decisions 39
review of conviction 30–1
standard of proof 30–1, 33
state power 31–3
Ultimate Issue Rule 277–8
see also courts; fact and opinion
Critique of Practical Reason (1788) 116
Cross, Sir R. 42–3, 79–80, 85
cross-examination 300–5, 312–13
criticisms of 302–5
Crown Court 37
see also courts

damages, quantum of *see under* personal injury
Damaska, M. 92–3, 148, 198, 211–14
Daubert v. *Merrell Dow Pharmaceuticals* (1993) 1–2, 8, 341–7
effect in England 231
'junk science' 228–30
non-scientific expert testimony, extended to 344
test for relevance/reliability 191–2
defendants favoured by 344–5
problems arising 343–6
Davies, G. 299, 306, 311
decisory oaths 47
deductive reasoning 83
deductivism 142
defendant's evidence 1–2
defendants favoured by *Daubert* test 344–5
delegating fact finding 306–7, 313–15, 332
Descartes, R. 17, 81
developing work as expert 168
dialectic fact finding 301–2
disagreement
expert *see* **expert disagreement**
legal factual *see* **expert disagreement**
disciplinary sanctions 361–3
discovery/disclosure 200, 217
criminal trials, in 355
discussions, expert 296–300, 312
double jeopardy rule 30–1
Dror, I. 175
duty
to court 8, 187, 210–11, 231, 360–1

overriding 347–52: nature of 348–50, overridden obligations 351–2
to give reasons 39

ecclesiastical courts *see* **history of expert evidence**
ECHR 358
Art. 6 right to a fair trial
assessors 317–18, 323–7, 329, 331–2
delegation prohibited 306–7
disclosure 355
duty to give reasons and fair trials 39
equality of arms 292
fair trial 323–8
tribunal, broad interpretation of 194–5, 338–9
see also HRA
ECtHR 193–4, 288, 294–5
Edmond, G. 180–1, 228–9
Effective Expert Witnessing 229–30
empirical evidence 83
empiricists, British 11–12, 17, 48–9, 88
employee as expert 167–8
England and Wales 4–6, 8
bias 164–6
concerns about 230–2
child cases 155–6
civil trials
history of expert evidence in *see* civil expert evidence *under* **history of expert evidence**
juries in 38–9
see also fair trial; juries
common law
approach 183–4
courts 49
conduct of litigation, appropriate 220–32
court composition *see* composition *under* courts
court experts 369–70
see also experts *under* courts
criminal
justice system 37: party experts, and 231, *see also* party experts
standard of proof 30–1
see also criminal trials
cross-examination in 1990s 303–4
see also cross-examination
Crown Court 37
see also courts
expert bias 164–6
expert evidence, history of *see* **history of expert evidence**
facts, engagement with *see* role of facts in civil procedure – 'fact avoidance' hypothesis *under* **role of expert**
Family proceedings, special nature of 211–12
hearsay rule 32
judges
appointment of 223–4
High Court 37–8
juries
civil trials, in 38–9
forbidden from giving reasons 39
special *see under* juries
litigation, appropriate conduct of 220–32
magistrates' courts 36–7
prosecuting counsel, role of 32
pugnacity of civil litigation 224–7
RSC *see* RSC
rules of procedure *see* CPR
single joint experts 335, 339
statistical assessment of legal proof 153–4
status of experts in society 232–3
toxic tort litigation 154
Ultimate Issue Rule *see* Ultimate Issue Rule
unified and bicameral tribunals 223–4
see also Anglo-American jurisdictions
English Reports as source analysis 240–4
epistemological constructivism *see under* constructivism
epistemology 3–7, 117–18
assessment of 70–3
atomistic reasoning *see* atomism

epistemology (*cont.*)
classical 3–7, 9–10, 12–23, 41–2
admissibility and evaluation, rules of 24
cognitive psychology 65
definition 14
effect of finding of fact 23
legal evidence theory, and 10–11
cognitive psychology, effect on 65
epistemological constructivism *see under* constructivism
generalizations *see* generalizations
individuated propositions of evidence *see* individuated propositions of evidence
legal *see* legal – epistemology
legal belief, justifying 40–64
atomistic reasoning *see* atomism
generalizations as inferential glue *see* generalizations
meta-justification *see* Rationalist Tradition of evidence scholarship
naturalized *see* naturalized epistemology
Rationalist Tradition of evidence scholarship *see* Rationalist Tradition of evidence scholarship
equality of arms 32, 170, 187, 291–3, 355
ESRC 103–4
Essay Concerning Human Understanding (1690) 81, 83–4
Europe
ADR 47
adversarial systems 221–2
appeals 135
civil procedure 183–4
court composition *see* composition *under* courts
criminal expert evidence 32
inferences as knowledge base 48
judges 37–8
liberal state, the 198–203
see also France; Germany; Italy
Evaluating Scientific Evidence (2007) 130–1
evaluation and admissibility, rules of 24–5
Evans-Pritchard, E. 41
evidence
admission and weight of 32
common assumptions in rationalist theories of 9
exclusion of 1–2, 34
expert *see* **expert evidence**
false 358–61
illegally obtained 43–4
see also exclusion of evidence
law 11–12, 19–20
foundational norms of 370–3
meaning of 51–3
prejudicial 32, 34
theory *see* legal – evidence theory
weight 1–2, 32
evidential
dissonance 55–7, 59
facts 93–4
harmony 55–7, 59
reasoning 6
substance-blind *see* substance-blind evidential reasoning
redundancy 59
Evidential Foundations of Probabilistic Reasoning (1994) 98–102
exchange of written reports 296
exclusion of evidence 1–2
experience of court matters 21–38
experiments and hypotheses 174–6
expert
assistants 330–1
bias *see* bias; **management of bias**
disagreement *see* **expert disagreement**
discussions 296–300, 312
'expert shopping' 171, 177, 284, 310, 356–8
fact finding *see under* **expert disagreement** – legal and expert factual disagreement
'facts' 90

generalizations *see under* generalizations
legal term for 242–3, 279–80
regulation 362–3
witness
changed to 'expert' 185–6
distinguished from assessors 329–32
see also experts
expert disagreement 1–2, 6, 133–79, 274
assessment of 178–9
bias, expert *see* bias
constructivism, epistemological *see* constructivism
generalizations *see* generalizations – sets, selection of
historical development *see* **history of expert evidence**
inferential challenge, types of 147–62
causation: personal injury, in 150–1, toxic torts, in 151–5
child cases: best interests of the child 155–9, distinguished from medical cases 158–9, psychiatric evidence in 157–8
property, condition of 149
quantum of damages in personal injury 149–50
standard of care in professional negligence 159–62: options to determine standard 159–160; *Bolam* case 160–2
generalizations *see* generalizations – selection of sets
legal and expert factual disagreement 135–9
expert fact finding, reasons for disagreement in 136–7
finality, need for in legal fact finding 135–6
scientific knowledge as objective certainty 138–9
personal injury *see* personal injury
professional negligence *see* negligence, professional
property, condition of *see* property, condition of
quantum of damages *see under* personal injury
see also **expert evidence**
expert evidence 6, 74–5, 90, 132
assessment 130–2
autopoietic systems, and 124–30
historical, in civil courts *see under* **history of expert evidence**
civil
approaches to *see* **role of expert**
assessment of: by non-experts 104–9, problems of 1–3, *see also* **expert disagreement**
exclusion 1–2
history *see* **history of expert evidence**
court's access to specialist knowledge 97–109
common investigative method 104–7
Hand's paradox 108–9
substance-blind evidential reasoning *see* substance-blind evidential reasoning
criminal 32
distinguished from non-expert 75–6
fact, of 76–8
litigation privilege *see* litigation – privilege
meaning 51–3
nature of 74–5, 90
distinguished from non-expert 75–6
opinion, as 75–8
product of communities of practice, as 110–13
social phenomenon of 129–30
specialist knowledge, as 75–6
strong epistemological constructivism 114, 118–22
philosophy of 118–22
unreliable, inadmissibility of 341–7

expert evidence, judicial assessment of *see* epistemology; expert disagreement; expert evidence; history of expert evidence; management of bias; role of expert
Expert Witness Institute 319, 362–3
experts
  'adversarial weapons', as 232
  assessors distinguished from 329–32
  court *see* courts – experts
  credentials 69–70
  credibility 69–70
  cross-examination 300–5, 312–13
    criticisms of 302–5
  developing work as 168
  disciplinary sanctions 361–3
  discussions 296–300, 312
  duty to court 8, 187, 210–11, 231, 360–1
    nature of overridden obligations 351–2
    overriding 347–52
  evidence *see* **expert evidence;** fact and opinion
  historical use of 234–6
  hot tubbing 305–6
  immunity 297–8, 360–2
  legal term for 242–3, 279–80
  litigation privilege *see* litigation privilege
  multiple joint experts 287–91, 311
  negligent testimony 360–1
  neutrality, increasing 170
  opinion, challenging 294–306, 312–13
    before trial 296–300: exchange of written reports 296; expert discussions 296–300, 312, conflict and immunity 297–8, privilege 298–9
    trial, at 300–6: cross-examination 300–5, 312–13; criticisms of 302–5: hot tubbing 305–6
    see also assessors
  as opposed to 'expert witnesses' 185–6
  perjury *see* perjury
  recusal *see under* recusal
  reports
    litigation privilege, and 352–8
    written, exchange of 296
  role 74, 84–5, 185–6
  'shadow' 185–6, 294, 312
  'shopping' for *see* 'expert shopping' *under* expert
  single experts *see* single experts
  status in society 232–3
  trial, in 300–6
    cross-examination 300–5, 312–13: criticisms of 302–5
    exchange of written reports before 296
    hot tubbing 305–6
  use of in society 2–3
  see also bias; **expert disagreement**
extra-curial judicial guidelines 289

fact and opinion, questions of 6, 10–12, 76–97
  distinction between fact and opinion 76–8
    contextual nature 78–80, 92–6: admissibility consequences 94–6, deciding fact or opinion 94, definition of facts 87, function of facts 93–4, usage depending on context 92–3
    operative rationales for 80–7: finality in fact finding 80–4; knowledge and judgment 81–4; safeguarding: other rules of evidence 85, perjury actions, availability of 86–7, tribunals' time 85–6; tribunal and witnesses' roles 84–5
    philosophical difficulties with 87–96: definition; fact, of 87, opinion, of 87–8: making clear the distinction 88–92; cognitive psychology 88–9, 'expert facts' 90, Lockean approach 88, 91–2, probabilistic nature of facts, essentially 91–2
    see also Opinion Rule
  expert evidence as opinion 75–8

legal epistemology, and 96–7
fact finding and determination 3–4, 9–10
delegating 306–7, 313–15, 332
dialectic 301–2
effect of 23
experience 21–38
expert *see* expert fact finding *under* **expert disagreement**
finality in 80–4
knowledge and judgment 81–4
judicial *see* judicial – fact finding
juries 37
legal *see* legal – fact finding
legal philosophy, and 10–11
legal processes supporting 369–70
Ultimate Issue Rule *see* Ultimate Issue Rule
see also common investigative method; Rationalist Tradition of evidence scholarship; substance-blind evidential reasoning
Factortame (No. 8) [2002] 225–6
facts
avoidance and aversion *see* role of facts *under* **role of expert**
constitutive 93–4
definition 87
function 93–4
role of, in civil procedure 212–20
ultimate 219–20
factual disagreement *see* 'fact avoidance' hypothesis *under* **role of expert** – role of facts in civil procedure
fair trial 39, 323–7
Family proceedings 155–9, 188, 354–5
experts, historical use of 234–6
special nature of 211–12
Fast Track 286–7
fees 207
Feyerabend, P. 143
Final Report, Lord Woolf's *see Access to Justice*
financial interest 166–70
involvement 168–70
predisposition 166–8
fingerprint evidence 175
forensic science 32, 146, 344
Forensic Science Society 319, 362–3
Foucault, M. 119–20
foundational norms of evidence law 370–3
foundationalism 6–7, 12–14, 16–17, 23, 51–3
foundherentism 6–7, 13, 16–19, 23, 51–3, 74
France 4–6, 8, 183–4, 372
adversarial system 222
appeals 135
Conseil d'état 326–7
criminal standard of proof 30–1
decisory oaths 47
experts
approved 319
court 369–70: *see also* courts – experts
preferred 319–20
experts' appointment 310
fact avoidance 213–20
Government Commissioners and fairness 327–8
oral enquiry 212
presumptions
abolished 50
recusal of experts 338–9
rules of
legal proof 49
procedure *see* NCPC
single court experts 335
recusal 338–9
status of experts in society 232–3
FRCP 188–9, 227
FRE 26–7, 188–92, 277
case management 189–90
pre-trial 222–3
court experts, appointment of 189–91, 217–18, 335
see also single experts
opinion evidence 189
panels of experts 190, 335
relevance and reliability 191–2
free proof 50
Frege, G. 141

Geller, M. 102–3
generalizations 7, 51–3, 106–7, 137
applications to base facts 6, 144–7
disagreement in interpretation accepted 145
questions not normally addressed by experts 145–6
special categories required by courts 146
specifics from generals 146–7
common-sense 106–7
expert 106–7
inferential glue, as 60–4
classification 60–1
commonplace 61–2
expert 60–1, 63–4
holistic arguments, in 62–3
non-expert, problems with 60–1, 63
presumptions, as 48
Rationalist Tradition 64–5
sets, selection of 6, 139–44
schools of philosophy: constructivism 143–4, logical positivism 141–3, scientific realism 140–1
see also **epistemology**; presumptions
Germany 4–6, 183–4
facts, and 213–14
rules of procedure *see* ZPO
status of experts in society 232–3
Gettier, E. 15–16
Gewirth, A. 117
Gilbert, G. 11–12, 42–3, 242–3
Golan, T. 251–2, 261
Goldman, A. 28, 336–7
Goodall, F. 230–1
graphical representation of evidential matrix 53–5
guidelines
judicial, extra-curial 289
practitioner 289–90

Haack, S. 6–7, 13, 16–19, 74, 173
common investigative method 104–7
foundherentism *see* foundherentism
scientific realism 140–1
Habermas, J. 128–9
Hacking, I. 48
Hammelmann, H. 228, 230–1
Hand, Learned 1–2, 97–8
paradox 108–9
Hart, H. L. A. 10–11, 120–1
hearsay
rule 11–12, 85
abolition in civil evidence 32
Hegel, G. 301–2
Hempel, C. 142–3
High Court judges 37–8
history of expert evidence, 7, 238–81
assessment
general 279–81
historical, relevance of 238–9
assessors 263–9
rise of Trinity Masters 263–6
Trinity Masters to assessors 266–9
civil expert evidence, 1500-1800 240–6
civil courts before Judicature Acts 244–6
source analysis, *English Reports* as 240–4: legal term for expert 242–3
court experts 269–74
pre-nineteenth-century 269–71
nineteenth-century 271–2
twentieth-century 272–4
party experts 246–61
criminal courts, developments in 256–8
early uses 246–9
expert disagreement, problems of 258–61
increasing reliance on 253–6: growth of specialist occupations and professions 254, need for specialist advice 255–6
inferential questions, developing complexity of 249–53
special juries 261–3
Ultimate Issue Rule 274–9
decline of in twentieth century 277–9: rationale for in criminal

cases 277–8; opinion evidence 278–9
rise of in nineteenth century 274–6: insanity cases 274–6, jury limitations 274–5
Hohfeld, W. 93–4
holistic proof *see under* proof
hot tubbing 305–6
Howard, M. 303–4, 321–2, 332
HRA 325, 363
see also ECHR
human rights *see* ECHR; HRA
Hume, D. 48–9, 57, 88, 116
hypotheses and experiments 174–6

Idea of a Social Science (1958) 120–1
identification evidence 79–80
illegally obtained evidence 43–4
immunity of experts 297–8, 360–2
inadmissibility of unreliable expert evidence 341–7
individuated propositions of evidence 51–3
atomistic reasoning about *see under* atomism
inductive reasoning 48, 59
Inductivism 142
inequality of arms *see* equality of arms
inferences and inferential reasoning 7, 48, 51–3, 66–8, 75–6, 298–9
argument, basic structures of 55–7
complex 98–100
facts observed, from 79–80
generalizations as glue 60–4
Hand's paradox 108–9
inferential
chains and Locke 91–2
challenges, types of 147–62
complexity of evidential matrices 59
drag, total 55–60, 91
philosophical basis 48–9
questions, developing complexity of 249–53
strategies 66–8
see also **expert evidence**; fact and opinion; substance-blind evidential reasoning
injury *see* personal injury
inquests 354–5
see also coroners' courts
insanity cases 274–6
institutional facts 92–3
intellectual interest 171–2, 335–6
Interim Report, Lord Woolf's *see Access to Justice*
international law, welfare of children in 155–6
interpretation, disagreements in *see* **expert disagreement, making sense of**
interpreter effect 174–5
intuitive inferential strategies 66–8
investigative method, common *see under* **expert evidence**
Italy 4–6, 183–4
adversarial elements introduced 181–2
appeals 135
decisory oaths 47
'fact avoidance' 213–20
Family proceedings, special nature of 211–12
lawyers and judges 226–7
party experts and court experts 232
rules of procedure *see* CPC
status of experts in society 232–3

Jackson, J. 80, 277–9
Jacobs, F. 299, 301
Jacquin, A. 194–5, 338–9
Jolowicz, J. 302
Jones, C. 303–4
judges 1–2, 29–30
appointment of 223–4
career judiciary 37–8
concern about party expert bias 227–32
experience of court matters 21–36, 38
recusal 166–7, 178
relationship with lawyers 226–7
see also courts; legal – fact finding
judgment and knowledge 81–4

judgmental heuristics 66–8
Judicature Acts
(1873) 184, 200–1, 266–7, 272, 282–3, 315
(1875) 184, 200–1, 235, 266–7
see also under **history of expert evidence**
judicial
assessment of expert evidence 1–2
fact finding 9–51, 74
Roman-canon courts, in 49
guidelines, extra-curial 289
justified belief 74
notice 74–5
'junk science' 8, 228–30, 342–3
juries 29–30, 36, 227, 252–3, 274–5, 277–8, 342
common law courts, English, in 49
court experts, compared to 337
experience of court matters 37
experts on 38–9
forbidden from giving reasons 39
generalizations 61–4
non-lawyer 38–9
role 74, 84–5
special 7, 38–9, 112
historical assessment 261–3
specialist information, processing 69–70
see also courts; fact and opinion; **history of expert evidence**; legal – fact finding
justice, perverting the course of 359–60
justified true belief and knowledge 15–16
see also foundationalism
justifying legal belief *see* legal belief *under* **epistemology**

Kahnemann, D. 173
Kampen, P. van 232–3
Kant, I. 76
specialist reasoning 116–17
King, M. 127–8, 130
Kitcher, P. 138–9
Klein, E. 203
knowledge
judgment, and 81–4
justified true belief, and 15–16
structures 66–8
Kuhn, T. 41–2, 121–2
scientific constructivism 143–4

Lakatos, I. 345–6
Landsman, S. 251–2, 261, 269–70
Langbein, J. 257–8
Laudan, L. 10–11, 20, 28
Law of Evidence (1754) 83, 242–3, 272
Law Reform Committee (1970) 89, 96, 187–8
lawyers
CPR, and 227
education 219–20
immunity 297–8, 360–2
judges, relationship with 226–7
litigation 221–2
roles 224–5
overriding duty to the court 348–50
tribunals, in 36, 224–5
legal
aid 169, 207
belief, justifying *see* legal belief *under* **epistemology**
early evidence theorists 11–12
education 219–20
epistemology 6–7, 12–14, 19–42
definition and meaning 9–10, 19–21
fact and opinions, and *see* fact and opinions: distinguishing 96–7
institutional variations affecting 29–40: court composition *see* composition *under* courts, criminal and civil fact finding, differences between 30–3
ontology, distinguished from 27
special, reasons why 21–9
evidence theory 10–12, 50
fact finding 12–14, 21–9
admissibility and evaluation, rules of 24–5
assumptions of rationalist fact finding, Twining's 9
collaborative fact finding 22–3

court composition *see* composition *under* courts
criminal and civil, differences between 30–3
effect of finding of fact 23
evidence, admission and weight of 32: standard of proof 30–1, state power 31–2
finality 80–4
goal 16
judicial *see* judicial – fact finding
legal process and truth, relationship between 25–9: ontology 27
practical rationality inherent in 51–3
probabilistic inferential reasoning, as 75
see also composition *under* courts; **expert disagreement**; fact finding
philosophy 10–11
process and truth, relationship between 25–9
processes supporting accurate fact determination 369–70
theory 11–12
Legrand, P. 181–2
Leverhulme Trust 103–4
liability and party experts 289
liberal state, the 198–203
linguistic philosophy 118–21
litigation
conduct of 220–32
lawyers 221–2, 224–5
overriding duty to the court 348–50
privilege 8, 358–9
effect on expert evidence 353–4
reform of 352–8
Litigation Reform Commission of Queensland 311
Locke, J. 11–12, 17, 19, 48–9, 116
distinguishing fact from opinion 88
knowledge and judgment 81–4
see also atomism
Lofft, Capel 279–80
see also Gilbert
logic of proof *see under* proof
logical positivism 141–3
Luhmann, N. 114, 123, 126–9, 131
see also autopoietic social systems theory
Lukes, S. 119
lying 218–19

Macpherson, W. 22–3
magistrates' courts 36–7
see also courts
maintenance of actions 169, 225–6
management of bias, effective 8, 334–65
assessment of 363–5
inadmissibility of unreliable expert evidence 341–7
problems with *Daubert* test 343–6
overriding duty to the court 347–52
nature of 348–50
nature of overridden obligations 351–2
presumptive recusal for bias 338–41
grounds for 339–41
reform of litigation privilege 352–8
approach of courts to 356–8
criminal proceedings, in 355
effect of privilege on expert reports 353–4
'expert shopping' 356–8
see also 'expert shopping' *under* expert
sanctions, criminal, civil and professional 358–63
civil 360–1
criminal 358–60: perjury 358–9, perverting the course of justice 359–60
disciplinary 361–3: expert regulation 362–3, professional misconduct 361–2
single experts, use of 335–8
biases and pre-disposition 335–6
comparison with single judge 336–7

managerial state, the 207–11
Mansfield, Lord 78–9, 86–7
Marx, K. 115, 301–2
Matson, J. 229–30
Maturana, H. 122–3
McAuley, F. 47
McConnell, A. 153–4
McCormick, C. 42–3, 92–3
Meadow, Professor Sir Roy 171
medical
  cases distinguished from child cases 158–9
  examinations 357
  insanity cases 274–6
  profession disagreeing 160–2
membership of organizations 165
Menashe, D. 62–3
Mercer, D. 180–1, 228–9
Merton, R. 138
meta-justification 12–14, 41–2
  see also Rationalist Tradition of evidence scholarship
Mill, J. S. 19
moral opinions 164, 278–9
multiple joint experts 287–91, 311
  see also party experts; single joint experts
Multi-Track 286–9
Munchausen's Syndrome by Proxy 171

Napoleon 50
naturalized epistemology 7, 12–14, 64–70
  cognitive psychology 65–8
  social judgment, shortcomings of 66–8
    common-sense 68
    judgmental heuristics 66–8
    knowledge structures 66–8
  specialist information, complex, processing 69–70
Nature 175–6
nautical assessors *see* assessors
NCPC 50, 51, 192–5, 205–7, 282–3
  classification by degree of inference 192
  court experts, appointment of 192–3
    see also single experts
  discovery 200
  Italian system compared with 196–7
  'mini trial' 193–4
  status of experts 194–5
  see also Code de procédure
negligence, professional
  immunity *see* immunity of experts
  misstatement 33
  negligent testimony 360–1
  party experts, and 289
  special juries 38–9
  standard of care 159–62, 289
negotiation 298–9
Netherlands, The 232–3
neutrality of experts, increasing 170
New Evidence Scholarship 10
NIAS 101–3
Nisbett, R. 66–8, 173
non-adversarial proceedings 354–5
non-expert
  assessment of expert evidence 104–9
  evidence 75–6
  opinion evidence inadmissible 76–8
non-scientific expert testimony 344
North America 198
Nottingham Trent University 294
number of party experts 290–3

oaths 47, 218–19
  and presumptions 215–17
observer effect 175–6
Odgers, W. 200–1
officers of the court 194–5, 317–18, 349–50
Official Receiver 349–50
Official Solicitor 188, 349–50
Oldham, J. 262
ontology 27
Opinion Rule 76–84, 97–8, 278–9
  exceptions 79–80
  rationale 80–7
    finality in fact finding 80–4: knowledge and judgment 81–4
    safeguarding: other rules of evidence 85, perjury actions,

availability of 86–7, tribunal and witnesses' roles 84–5, tribunals' time 85–6
opinions 278–9
challenging expert *see* challenging expert opinion
constitutive facts 93–4
definition 87–8
see also fact and opinion
optimistic rationalism 42–3
oral enquiry, French 212
orality 214–15
overriding duty to the court 347–52
nature of duty 348–50
see also duty – to court
Overriding Objective *see under* CPR

paramountcy principle 155–6
parens patriae 354–5
Parliament 268, 315
Parsons, T. 123
parties 1–2, 24–5
equality of 32–3
truth, and 26–7
party experts 7, 284–307
appropriate conduct of 227–32
bias, judicial concern about 228: England, concerns in 230–1; CPR reforms 232, *Daubert* case 231, see also *Daubert*; duty to court 231, 360–1, overriding 347–52, *see also* duty to court *under* experts; scientific evidence, importance of 231–2, terrorist convictions overturned 231; Italy, party and court experts in 232, motives for ascribing bias 228–9, US variations in practice 229–30
challenging expert opinion 294–306
before trial 296–300: exchange of written reports 296, expert discussions 296–300, 312; conflict and immunity 297–8, privilege 298–9
trial, at 300–6: cross-examination 300–5; criticisms of 302–5: hot tubbing 305–6
CPR, under 187
delegating fact finding 306–7
history of use *see under* **history of expert evidence**
liability, and 289
payment to 168–70
pleadings, producing full 294
reliance on, increasing
selecting 284–93
deciding between party and single joint experts 284–90: *Access to Justice* Reports 284–6, case law 287–9, CPR and Practice Directions 286–7, extra-curial judicial guidelines 289, practitioner guidelines 289–90
number of party experts 290–3
single joint experts *see* single joint experts
see also assessors; single joint experts
Pattenden, R. 353–4
payments to experts 168–70
case management powers 170, 185
conscious bias 172–3
Peirce, C. 104, 141
Perillo, J. 213–14
perjury 86–7, 218–19, 358–9
persistent communities of practice *see* communities
personal bias 176, 335–6
personal injury
causation 150–1
damages, quantum of 149–50
single expert 289
personal interests of experts 164–6
personal
involvement 166, 335–6
predisposition 164–6, 335–6
perverting the course of justice 359–60
philosophy, legal *see* legal – philosophy
Phipson, S. 272
pleadings, producing full 294, 312, 321–2
political criteria 370–3
criminal trials, and 30–1
expert tribunals, and 37–8
judges, selection of 37–8
meta-justification, and 41–2

Popper, K. 142, 176
Practice Directions and CPR 286–7
Practice of the Spiritual or Ecclesiastical Courts (1685) 246
practitioner guidelines 289–90
pre-action protocols *see* CPR
Pre-Action Protocol for Resolution of Clinical Disputes 289–90
predisposition, personal 164–6, 335–6
pre-existing personal relationships 164–5
prejudicial evidence 32
presumed bias 339–40
presumptions 48, 50
oaths, and 215–17
see also generalizations
presumptive recusal of experts 338–41
pre-trial disclosure 32
Principles of Judicial Proof (1913) 53
Principles of the Law of Evidence and Practice (1854) 83–4, 271
privilege *see* litigation privilege
probabilistic reasoning *see* probability
probability and probability theory 48, 51–3, 57–8, 91–2
procedural codes 227
procédure contradictoire see adversarial system
professional
codes of conduct 227
conduct actions 361–2
misconduct 361–2
negligence *see* negligence
professions and specialist occupations, growth of 254
proof
common assumptions in rationalist theories of 9
see also Rationalist Tradition
free 50
holistic 20–1
legal theory of 11–12, 50
logic of 19–21
meaning 19–20
non-rational modes 47
rules of 49
standard of *see* standard – of proof
property, condition of 149
proportionality test for expert selection 285
prosecuting counsel, role of 32
prosecution, advantages of, over defendant 32
Protocol for the Instruction of Experts 170, 184, 283
psychiatric evidence in child cases 157–8
pugnacity of civil litigation 224–7
see also US

quantum of damages *see under* personal injury
Queen's Bench Guide 289
Quine, W. 143–4

Rationale of Judicial Evidence 24
Rationalist Model of Adjudication 44–5
Rationalist Tradition of evidence scholarship 4–5, 9–10, 12–14, 41–53, 74, 119–20, 370–1
assumptions of rationalist fact finding 9
common assumptions in evidence and proof theories 9, 43–65, 76–8
Rationalist Model of Adjudication 44–5
forming justified beliefs 51–3
optimistic rationalism 42–3
see also New Evidence Scholarship
Rau, C. 199
realists 121–2, 367–9
'reasonableness' test see *Wednesbury* Unreasonableness
reasons, duty to give 39
recusal 1–2
expert 1–2, 8, 166–7, 194–5, 336–7
presumptive, for bias 338–41
judge 166–7, 178, 338–41
redundancy, evidential 59
regulation, expert 319, 362–3
Reichenbach, H. 142
relationships, pre-existing 164–5
relevance and reliability see *Daubert*

reports *see under* experts
res judicata 135–6
resources, unequal *see* equality of arms
retiring with court, assessors 327–32
review of conviction 30–1
Review of the Criminal Courts 362–3
right to reply *see* fair trial
Roberts, P. 93–4, 278–9
role of expert, non-epistemological factors, 6, 180–237
  assessment of 236–7
  assisting in determining expert roles 180–1
    effecting legal change 181–3
  civil expert evidence, approaches to 184–97
    England and Wales *see* CPR
    France *see* NCPC
    Germany *see* ZPO
    Italy *see* CPC
    United States *see* FRE
  factors in expert role definition 197–236
    conduct of litigation, appropriate 220–32: litigation lawyers 221–2; civil trial, role in 222–3, unified and bicameral tribunals 223–4: party experts, appropriate conduct of 227–32; bias, judicial concern about 228, England, concerns in 230–1; CPR reforms 232, *Daubert* case 231; see also *Daubert*; duty to court 231, 360–1; overriding 347–52, *see also* duty to court *under* experts; scientific evidence, importance of 231–2, terrorist conviction overturned 231, Italy, party and court experts in 232, motives for ascribing bias 228–9, US variations in practice 229–30; *see also* party experts: pugnacity of civil litigation 224–7; CFA and contingency fees 225–6, jury trials 227, lawyers' roles 224–5, procedural codes 227
    historical use of experts 234–6
    role of facts in civil procedure 212–20
      'fact avoidance' hypothesis 212–14: avoidance not aversion 214–18; disclosure 217, orality 214–15, presumptions and oaths 215–17, reasons for 218–20, cultural views about lying 218–19, legal education 219–20; single court experts 217–18, *see also* single experts: engagement with facts by court 213–14
      social function of civil litigation 198–212: Family proceedings, special nature of 211–12, liberal state, the 198–203; Code de procédure civile (1806) 199–200, disclosure 200; private dispute 199–200; England and Wales: RSC 200–3, parties determining procedure 202: managerial state, the 207–11; CPR *see* CPR: welfare state, the 203–7; France: NCPC 205–7, Germany: ZPO 203–4, Italy: CPC 204–5
      status of experts in society 232–3
Roman-canon law 25, 183–4, 196, 197, 199, 203
  admissibility 342
  civil courts before Judicature Acts 245
  generalizations 48
  judicial fact finding 49
  presumptions 48, 50
  recusal 338–9
  see also canon – law
Ross, L. 66–8, 173
RSC 7, 238, 282–3, 303–4
  assessors 329
  court experts 189–90, 267–8, 272–4, 280–1, 307–9
  CPR, replaced by 184
  expert discussions 296

RSC (*cont.*)
parties determining procedure 202
reform of procedures 200–3
rules
admissibility and evaluation, of 24–5
Bolam, in 111–12
evidence, of 19–20
Opinion, against *see* Opinion Rule
Runciman Commission 362–3
Russell, B. 141
Ryder, Sir Dudley 244

Sales, B. 229–30
sanctions 8, 358–63
civil 360–1
criminal 358–60
perjury 358–9
perverting the course of justice 359–60
disciplinary and professional 361–3
expert regulation 362–3
professional misconduct 361–2
Schum, D. 53–5
generalizations 60–1
graphical representations of evidential matrix 53–5
substance-blind evidential reasoning 98–102, 106–7, 109
total inferential drag 55–60
science
forensic science *see* forensic
philosophy of 121–2
see also scientific
Science of Judicial Proof 53
scientific
adviser, assessors as 317–18
constructivism 143–4
evidence
importance of recognized 231–2
reliability and *Daubert* 343–6
experts *see* experts
method not distinct 104–7
realism 121–2, 140–1
schools of philosophy
constructivism 143–4
logical positivism 141–3
scientific realism 140–1
see also specialist – knowledge
Searle, J. 92–3
Seriaux, A. 219–20
'shadow' experts 185–6, 294, 312
Shamash, M. 62–3
Shapiro, B. 255
shareholdings 166–7
shopping for experts *see* 'expert shopping' *under* expert
Shuman, D. 229–30
silicone implant cases 190
single experts 8, 335–8
child cases 211–12
court experts *see* courts – experts
CPR 187–8, 210–11, 361
expert fact, appropriate for 289
'fact avoidance', and 213–14, 217–18
Family Division, historical use in 234–6
intellectual predisposition 171
joint *see* single joint experts
payments to 170
recusal 338–41
single joint experts 187–8, 210–11, 307–15, 335, 339
challenging expert opinion 312–13
cross-examination 312–13
delegating fact finding 313–15
Fast Track 287
party, and, deciding between 284–90
no presumption in favour of single 287–9
payments to 170
pleadings, producing full 312
selecting 307–11
multiple joint experts 311
see also assessors; party experts
Slovic, P. 173
Small Claims Track 286–7
social function of civil litigation 198–212
social judgment, shortcomings of 66–8
social phenomenon of expert evidence 129–30
social systems theory, autopoietic *see* autopoietic social systems theory

Society of Expert Witnesses 319, 362–3
sociological factors in role of experts 2–3, 180–1
sociology, philosophy of 118–21
Socrates 301–2
solicitors *see* lawyers
South-East Asia 218–19
special juries *see under* juries
specialist
  advice, growth of need for 254
  information and knowledge 6, 12
    complex, processing 69–70
    expert evidence as 75–6
    knowledge, court's access to *see under* **expert evidence**
    see also fact and opinion
  knowledge and non-specialist courts 367–9
    see also scientific
  members of tribunals 38–9
    non-lawyer tribunal members 36
  occupations and professions, growth of 254
Spinoza, B. 17
standard
  of care *see* negligence
  of proof 30–1, 33
Starkie, T. 22–3, 85–6
status of experts in society 232–3
Stein, A. 3–4, 11–12, 24–5
Stephen, J. 11–12, 19
structural bias 176–7, 335–6
Structure of Scientific Revolutions, The 143
substance-blind evidential reasoning 6, 98–104
  Leverhulme/ESRC research 103–4
  NIAS Evidence Seminars 101–3
  Schum's approach 98–100
    benefits 100–1
  see also inferences
Sukel, H. 69–70
System of Logic 19

Tapper, C. 79–80, 85
Taruffo, M. 219–20
terrorist convictions overturned 231
Teubner, G. 123, 127–9
Thayer, J. 19, 42–3, 85, 89, 251–2, 262, 269
theoretical frameworks *see* generalizations
theory
  autopoietic systems, of *see* autopoietic social systems theory
  evidence, of *see* legal – evidence theory
  probability, of *see* probability
  proof, of *see* legal theory of *under* proof
toxic torts 228–9, 342–3
  causation 151–5
  Daubert test, and 344–5
Tracks 286–7
Traite de preuves judiciaires 22–3
Traite théorique et pratique des preuves (1852) 83–4
transitivity 58–9
Treatise on Presumptions of Law and Fact (1844) 83–4
trials
  exchange of written reports before 296
  experts in 300–6
    cross-examination 300–5, 312–13: criticisms of 302–5
    hot tubbing 305–6
  fair 39, 323–7
  role of, in civil litigation 222–3
tribunals
  assessors as member 317–18, 329–32
  bias 327–8, 339–41
  bicameral courts, and 6–7, 29–30, 33–4, 223–4, 342
  Commissioner as member 327–8
  delegating fact finding 306–7, 313–15, 332
  experts as members 338–41
  fact, assessing expert evidence of 104–9
  non-expert 12
  specialist 315
  see also courts

Trinity House and Masters 112, 187–8, 254, 315, 320–1
first use 269–70
history of *see under* **history of expert evidence**
see also Admiralty; assessors
truth and legal process, relationship between 25–9
Tversky, A. 173
Twining, W. 11–14, 19, 42–53, 74, 101–2, 106–7
generalizations 60–1
graphical representations of evidential matrix 53–5

UCL 103–4
ultimate fact 219–20
Ultimate Issue Rule 7, 80, 84–5, 306–7
abolition in civil evidence 32
criminal cases, in 277–8
England, abolished in 277
expert evidence on 189
history of *see under* **history of expert evidence**
US, abolished in 277
unconscious bias 173–6
unequal resources *see* equality of arms
unicameral courts 6–7, 29–30, 33–4
magistrates' courts 36–7
specialist members of tribunals 38–9
unified and bicameral tribunals 223–4
unreliable expert evidence, inadmissibility of 341–7
US 4–6, 8
bias 164
party expert 227–32: payment, historical 261
case management 189–90
pre-trial 222–3
chains of inferences, use of 58
common law approach 183–4
conduct of litigation 220–32
courts
composition of *see* composition *under* courts
experts 369–70
see also courts – experts
cross-examination in 1990s 303–4
Daubert case see *Daubert*
expert bias 164
expert tribunals 38–9
criminal expert evidence 32
'junk science' *see* 'junk science'
facts, engagement with 214–18
judges 37–8
appointment of 223–4
juries
non-lawyer 38–9
specialist information processing 69–70
liberal state, the 198–203
litigation, appropriate conduct of 220–32
panels of experts 190, 335
pugnacity of civil litigation 224–7, 342–3
rules of evidence *see* FRE
single court experts 335
statistical assessment of legal proof 153–4
status of experts in society 232–3
toxic tort litigation 154
Ultimate Issue Rule *see* Ultimate Issue Rule
unified and bicameral tribunals 223–4
see also Anglo-American jurisdictions

Varela, F. 122–3
Vaughan, C. 78–9
Venn, J. 90–1
verification, fallacy of 176

Ward, T. 337
Watson, J. 138–9
Weber, M. 76
specialist reasoning 117–18, 120–1
Wednesbury Unreasonableness 159, 162
see also *Associated Provincial Picture Houses*
welfare
of the child 155–9, 211–12
state 203–7
Wigmore, J. 11–12, 42–3, 102–3, 251–2, 277, 301, 303–4

Chart 53–5, 58–9
White Book, The 289, 292, 329
Williamson, T 15
Wills, W. 11–12
Winch, P. 118–21
witnesses 1–2
character 290–1
expert, and immunity 297–8, 360–2
fact, of 290–1
Wittgenstein, L. 118, 120–1
Woolf, Lord 4–5, 94, 232, 280–1, 290–2, 350
Access to Justice Final Report see *Access to Justice*
Access to Justice Interim Report see *Access to Justice*
medical opinion, deferring to 371
single joint experts 307–9
see also single joint experts
written reports, exchange of 296

Zahle, H. 102–4
Ziegert, K. 16, 123
ZPO 195–6, 203–4
court experts, appointment of 195
see also single experts
Zuckerman, A. 93–4, 278–9

Lightning Source UK Ltd.
Milton Keynes UK
UKHW021959210321
380757UK00003B/23